Handbook of Early Childhood Development Research and Its Impact on Global Policy

Edited by Pia Rebello Britto
Patrice L. Engle
Charles M. Super

Consulting Editors
Lonnie R. Sherrod
Nurper Ulkuer

OXFORD
UNIVERSITY PRESS

Oxford University Press is a department of the University of Oxford.
It furthers the University's objective of excellence in research, scholarship,
and education by publishing worldwide.

Oxford   New York
Auckland   Cape Town   Dar es Salaam   Hong Kong   Karachi
Kuala Lumpur   Madrid   Melbourne   Mexico City   Nairobi
New Delhi   Shanghai   Taipei   Toronto

With offices in
Argentina   Austria   Brazil   Chile   Czech   Republic   France   Greece
Guatemala   Hungary   Italy   Japan   Poland   Portugal   Singapore
South   Korea   Switzerland   Thailand   Turkey   Ukraine   Vietnam

Oxford is a registered trade mark of Oxford University Press in the UK and
certain other countries.

Published in the United States of America by
Oxford University Press
198 Madison Avenue, New York, NY 10016

Library of Congress Cataloging-in-Publication Data
Handbook of early childhood development research and its impact on global policy / edited
    by Pia Rebello Britto, Patrice L. Engle, Charles M. Super; consulting editors, Lonnie R. Sherrod,
    Nurper Ulkuer.
        p. cm.
Includes bibliographical references and index.
ISBN 978–0–19–992299–4
1. Child development—Research.   2. Child welfare — International
cooperation.   3. Children—Services for.   4. Children—Government policy.
I. Rebello Britto, Pia, 1966–   II. Engle, Patrice L.   III. Super, Charles M.
HQ767.9.H347 2013
305.231—dc23
2012024738

9 8 7 6 5 4 3
Printed in the United States of America
on acid-free paper

Patrice Lee Engle
(December 1, 1944–September 22, 2012)

It is for countless reasons that we are grateful to Pat, our extraordinary teacher and beloved friend. Pat defined a field of knowledge, policy, and practice. She has forever improved global early childhood development (ECD).

Knowledge she gave us through her own cutting-edge research across geographic boundaries, landmark publications, and motivational presentations. The global policy agenda she altered through evidence on the critical importance of ECD and tireless dialogue with policymakers. Practice she improved through innovative models of integrated service and effective evaluation of programs around the world.

All of these agenda were advanced with her brilliance and exceptional personal inspiration that moved others to action. In doing so, Pat touched the lives of millions of children who have benefited from her work, her dedication, and her steadfast belief that all children can and should reach their full potential.

Pat is a guru of ECD. We dedicate this book to Pat's spirit and our memory of her. With palms joined together, we bow in deep respect to her. –"Pranaam Guruji"

{ CONTENTS }

{ PREFACE }

This groundbreaking international volume provides a state-of-the-art summary of existing research on early childhood development (ECD) and guidelines for program development, primarily from low- and middle-income countries (LAMIC). Early childhood is a period of uncontested importance to lifelong development. The volume's goal is to present the evidence to inform effective policies and programs for advancing the positive development of young children across the globe, with a specific focus on developing countries. It attempts to combine the scientific knowledge about early child development with program experiences from the field, thereby painting a more holistic picture of how to address the developmental needs of young children in both developed and developing countries, including the most vulnerable children. The evidence is presented with a particular lens on context and attention to the conditions under which program action has been effective. Contributors to the volume include researchers, policymakers, and practitioners.

The volume is a product of a partnership between the premier organization of researchers in child development in the world, the Society for Research in Child Development (SRCD) and the largest global organization working in child development, the United Nations Children's Fund (UNICEF). SRCD has a long history of facilitating the generation and dissemination of research-based information for policy; UNICEF, representing the international child development community, is widely known and respected for addressing children's rights and well-being around the world. As a result, this is an unusual and important partnership.

In spring 2008, UNICEF and SRCD signed a Memorandum of Understanding (MoU) with the goal of bringing science to bear upon policy affecting ECD in developing countries. Given the large body of evidence supporting the importance of early childhood contexts, in part generated by SRCD membership, and the urgent call in the developing world to address the needs and rights of young children, a partnership between SRCD and UNICEF was an obvious step toward the translation of science into effective policies for early childhood. As a result, this partnership is mutually beneficial to both organizations, and we expect that the partnership will continue beyond this project.

UNICEF is the premier children's organization of the UN, working in 191 low- and middle-income countries around the world, implementing programs in partnership with governments and civil society. One of its core commitments is the survival, growth, and development of young children, and it is a respected source of technical information for the countries. SRCD has a long history within the United States of facilitating the dissemination of research-based information for policy development and revision. It has an office in Washington D.C. devoted entirely to communicating research to nonacademic audiences, with the aim of influencing policies relevant to children, youth, and families. SRCD also has a 30-year-old fellowship program that places researchers in policy settings in the United States, either with Congress or the executive branch. SRCD is also seeking to substantially expand its international presence and reach. Given SRCD's long-standing interest in promoting research–policy connections and its interest in becoming more international, collaboration with UNICEF was a logical step. It enhances the international capacity of SRCD, a priority area for the organization, and it brings the latest scientific advancements to bear upon the work of UNICEF, a desired area of growth for that agency.

Several qualities distinguish this volume. First is its content. It assembles in a comprehensive and diverse manner what is known about ECD, primarily in developing countries. Second is its focus, which aims to shed light on inequities and inequalities of early childhood in developing countries. Finally, its contributors, who represent the fields of both "research and practice" and address various aspects of ECD across the globe, distinguish the volume.

Content on Early Childhood Development

Over 200 million children under 5 years fail to achieve their full developmental potential due to challenges such as undernutrition, poor health, environmental toxins, and lack of opportunities for learning and responsive care. The discrepancy between these children's actual developmental progress and what they would have achieved with adequate care constitutes a loss of their developmental potential; it undermines these children's right to survival, development, protection, and participation. These children will benefit less from educational, cultural, and economic opportunities, and as a result, they will end up with more poorly developed cognitive skills, lowered life-time earnings, and, ultimately, they will contribute less to family, community, and society. These individual outcomes, in turn, result in increased demand for costly social services, the intergenerational transmission of poverty, and even, on occasion, political instability. The cost of such neglect is high for the individuals, their nations, and our global society.

At the same time, the science of early childhood continues to advance understanding about how to maximize the lifetime consequences of a child's early development. The period of human development from conception to 8 years of age (early childhood) is now recognized as a period essential to a healthy, happy, and productive adulthood. Across disciplines—neuroscience to economics, psychology to environmental studies, anthropology to epidemiology—a common conclusion is emerging that early childhood matters and that investment in the early years reaps especially high dividends.

Focus on the Most Vulnerable

Evidence shows that children from disadvantaged families face multiple risk factors that affect their chances to survive and thrive. Although they appear to benefit more from early childhood interventions, they also appear to have the least access to quality services. Therefore, this volume identifies pathways from poverty, and from social and economic exclusion and inequities in early childhood, and suggests strategic actions based on research and field experiences. The focus of the volume is on identifying social, economic, and cultural determinants of inequities in reference to existing conditions at home, in the community, and in society as a whole that influence the child's holistic development. By focusing on the most vulnerable, the volume places ECD at the center of emerging discussions on sustainable development with a concern for equity, social justice, and peace. The content of this volume is based on findings that the intergenerational cycle of poverty can only be stopped by focusing on the most vulnerable and on the youngest.

Diverse Contributors

It was essential that the volume include the diverse constituencies that comprise the global field of ECD: researchers, policymakers, and practitioners. A large and growing body of scientific evidence shows that good programs for ECD promote sound physical and mental growth, as well as success in school, and minimize the negative and destructive consequences of high levels of risk in the environment. We know that good ECD programs: (1) provide direct learning services to children and support to families; (2) target younger and disadvantaged children; (3) are of long duration, high quality, and sufficient intensity; and (4) are integrated with community functioning, family life, health, nutrition, and local educational systems. Although the scientific validity of this knowledge is now established, its usefulness for policy has yet to be fully exploited. That is a main goal of this volume.

An urgent need exists to create a framework for applying what has been learned across both science and program implementation. This volume is designed to bring together these two bodies of knowledge to help country governments and civil society organizations understand the full array of evidence that is needed to plan effective programs and policies in early child development.

Preparation of the Volume

This volume has been almost 5 years in preparation. The first step was appointment of a secretariat to monitor the project. Under the leadership of Pia Rebello Britto, as the senior editor of the volume, Yale University Zigler Center fulfilled this role. Planning began with meetings between small groups representing both

SRCD and UNICEF; after editors Pia Rebello Britto, Patrice Engle, and Charles Super finally emerged from these deliberations, a table of contents and list of potential contributors were generated. Once under way, a grant was obtained to hold a conference at the Rockefeller Foundation's Bellagio Center in Bellagio, Italy. This meeting was held in February 2011. Each contributor presented the first draft of his or her paper; critiques were offered, and contributors left with guidance on revision. The draft chapters of the volume were reviewed by all, and chapters were added where needed to cover gaps. The conference at the Bellagio Center provided an excellent platform for rich discussions and exchange of new knowledge among authors to further enrich existing chapters of the volume.

Lessons Learned

As the work of this partnership has progressed, we have learned some important lessons with respect to possible reasons why knowledge and evidence often do not make it into policy. The language, aims, and scientific caution of knowledge generators differ from that of knowledge consumers, who need answers to complex questions quickly. Therefore, knowledge translators are required to convert and translate the information to ensure its applicability for use. To that end, since we could not simply take the knowledge generated by members of the SRCD and share it directly with policymakers, our authors included knowledge translators—individuals who have worked in both academia and international development and who can translate research. This was a key lesson, one that is now incorporated into the workings of the partnership and its products. The result is a successful collaboration and this unique and valuable publication.

Uniqueness of the Current Volume Relative to Other Recent Publications

The number of volumes that have appeared in recent years on global ECD attest to its growing importance across the world. Four recent publications, and one to be published next year, play complementary roles. Some address the importance of ECD (dealing with so-called first-generation questions), whereas others are concerned with identifying effective strategies (second-generation questions).

The 2007 World Health Organization publication by L. G. Irwin, A. Siddiqi, and C. Hertzman, "Early Child Development: A Powerful Equalizer," was a background document for the WHO's Commission on the Social Determinants of Health and summarizes the research and arguments for focusing on early child development from an international development perspective.

A 2010 World Bank publication by S. Nadeau, N. Kataoka, A. Valerio, M. J. Neumann, and L. K. Elder provided guidance for task managers about how to approach government officials to argue for ECD. A very useful tool for World

Bank managers and for others working for government, this work summarizes investment arguments and is a guide for policy dialogue and project preparation in ECD. However, it is not intended to provide detailed research evidence.

Two other books published by the World Bank deal with specific topics in ECD, one edited by M. Garcia, A. Pence, and J. Evans on ECD in Africa (2008), and the other edited by H. Alderman (2011); they provide research and program experience, but are not comprehensive.

The forthcoming UNESCO publication "Early Childhood Care and Education: Building the Wealth of Nations," to appear in 2012/2013 is an attempt to answer questions of how to improve outcomes for children. It is similar to the current volume in addressing program issues but is more focused on education, whereas the present volume also focuses on health, nutrition, and protection. Second, it tends to examine specific program models, whereas the present volume incorporates system perspectives in improving development. For example, the current volume addresses the expansion of programs and the associated challenges of monitoring and capacity-building, which are typically systems-level considerations, whereas the UNESCO book addresses specific issues and situations that need attention (e.g., HIV, institutionalization). As a result, the points of intervention addressed by the UNESCO volume complement those of the current volume, but they are not the same. Both will be useful for practitioners and policymakers.

The present volume is the first and only to offer both an academic and policy perspective on global ECD. Other volumes are agency publications, whereas the current volume, through the collaboration of the SRCD and UNICEF, brings together both an agency and a research field perspective. As representatives of the two parenting organizations, we are very proud of this collaboration and the resulting volume and believe in its importance to early child development around the world.

Nurper Ulkuer, UNICEF
Lonnie Sherrod, SRCD
February 2012

References

Alderman, H. (Ed.). (2011). *No small matter: The impact of poverty, shocks, and human capital investments in Early Childhood Development*. Washington, D.C.: World Bank.

Garcia, M., Pence, A., & Evans, J. (Eds.). (2008). *Africa's future, Africa's challenge: Early childhood care and development in Sub-Saharan Africa*. Washington, D.C.: World Bank.

Irwin, L. G., Siddiqi, A., & Hertzman, C. (2007). *Early child development: A "powerful" equalizer*. Final Report for the World Health Organization's Commission on the Social Determinants of Health. Geneva: WHO.

Nadeau, S., Kataoka, N., Valerio, A., Neumann, M. J., & Elder, L. K. (2010). *Investing in young children: An early childhood development guide for policy dialogue and project preparation*. Washington, D.C.: World Bank.

{ ACKNOWLEDGMENTS }

We thank the leadership of the Society for Research in Child Development (SRCD), especially John Hagen and Lonnie Sherrod, and of the United Nations Children's Fund (UNICEF), especially Nurper Ulkuer, for their support. This volume would not have been possible if not for their efforts within their own organizations and between them to build the partnership.

We would like to thank also the members of the SRCD and UNICEF partnership committee for their initial guidance on establishing the relationship between the two agencies and for their recommendation for a volume to provide a framework for early childhood development (ECD) programs and policies. We thank Marc Bornstein, Merry Bullock, Cooper Dawson, Demet Gulaldi, Katherine Holland, Kathleen Letshabo, Joan Lombardi, Yuko Nonoyama, Christina Popivanova, and Jack Shonkoff. We would also like to thank the multiple individuals who were not on the SRCD-UNICEF committee, yet provided insightful and helpful input and recommendations for the outline of the volume. Scholars from the SRCD International Affairs Committee, UNICEF regional and country offices, and the Innocenti Research Center were very generous with their time and rich experiential advice. We also acknowledge the Consultative Group in ECCD, and its executive director, Louise Zimanyi, for her contribution at the Bellagio conference.

We owe a debt of gratitude to the multiple financial sponsors of this volume. A grant from Rockefeller Foundation's Bellagio Center made it possible for all the authors to review and discuss this volume at an important juncture of conceptualization and writing. Funding provided by the Mohamed S. Farsi Foundation facilitated effective management and contributed directly to the affordability of our final product, which has been a key element in our strategy for dissemination. The Edward Zigler Center in Child Development and Social Policy at Yale University and the Center for the Study of Culture, Health, and Human Development at the University of Connecticut both provided essential logistical support to this project.

This volume would have never seen the light of day, however, without the hard work of the skillful and dedicated editorial team: Anne Perdue at SRCD, and Nancy Shemrah Fallon and William Hodges at the Zigler Center.

In closing, we would like to pay tribute to Natalia Streuli (October 1976—February 2012), a scholar and author in this volume. Natalia Streuli passed away during the production of this book, after a short fight against cancer. Natalia trained as a clinical psychologist at the Pontificia Universidad Católica del Perú. She worked as a childhood specialist for the Ministry for Women and Social Development in Peru, and carried out a number of consultancy studies for Save the Children UK, Plan International, and Child Rights Information Network (CRIN), and was working with the Young Lives Study in Peru at the time of her death. Natalia will be remembered fondly as a promising scholar and wonderful colleague.

{ ABOUT THE EDITORS }

Pia Rebello Britto, Ph.D., is known internationally for her work in the area of early childhood policy and programs in low- and middle-income countries. She has been involved in policy development and analysis with a particular emphasis on understanding the translation of science for policy and programs. Dr. Britto has worked with over 40 countries to develop standards for early learning and development. Other aspects of her work include the conceptualization of a measurement model for quality early childhood services, school readiness, and parenting. Most recently, Dr. Britto has been involved in research examining the relationship between ECD and peace building. She is the recipient of several national and international grants and awards in recognition for her work and has published numerous books, articles, chapters, and reports.

Patrice L. Engle was Professor of Psychology and Child Development at Cal Poly State University, San Luis Obispo, CA. A Ph.D. from Stanford, she studied care practices and child nutrition, responsive feeding, HIV and AIDS, and women's empowerment from the perspective of early childhood development. She worked for WHO, adding care and early stimulation to IMCI, for UNICEF India as Chief of Child Development and Nutrition, and in New York as Global ECD advisor. Up until her death on September 22, 2012, she was developing assessment tools for child development for Latin America and for East Asia, and had prepared an updated review on the effectiveness of programs to improve early child development in low- and middle-income countries for the 2011 Lancet series, following on the 2007 Lancet Series on Child Development.

Charles M. Super, Ph.D., is Professor of Human Development and Pediatrics at the University of Connecticut, where he also co-directs the Center for the Study of Culture, Health, and Human Development. He is best known for his research on the way culture shapes child health and development, and the "developmental niche" framework for modeling the organization of cultural influences. He has carried out basic and applied research on six continents and published numerous articles and books. He is co-recipient (with Sara Harkness) of the inaugural award presented by the Society for Research in Child Development for "Distinguished Contributions to Cultural and Contextual Factors in Child Development."

Lonnie R. Sherrod received his Ph.D. in Psychology from Yale University in 1978, an M.A. in Biology from University of Rochester (1976), and a B.A. from Duke

University (1972). He is currently Executive Director of the Society for Research in Child Development. He was formerly Professor of Psychology in Fordham University's Applied Developmental Psychology Program (ADP) and remains Distinguished Lecturer. His area of research is Youth Political Development, and he has co-edited special issues of the *Journal of Research on Social Issues* (1998) and *Applied Developmental Science* (2002) on the topic and a recent (2010) *Handbook of Research on Youth Civic Engagement.*

Nurper Ulkuer is currently Senior Advisor for Early Childhood, and Head of Early Childhood Development Programs at UNICEF New York Headquarters. Dr. Ulkuer has worked as UNICEF Area Advisor in Central Asia covering Turkmenistan, Uzbekistan, Tajikistan, Kyrgyzstan, and Kazakhstan. She started her career with UNICEF as a National Officer in Turkey, managing programs in areas of Education, Early Childhood Development, Communication for Women, Research and Monitoring, Child Protection, Policy Planning and Advocacy. Prior to UNICEF, she was as an Associate Professor, and the Chair of Child Development at Gazi University in Ankara, Turkey. She holds B.Sc. in Child Development (Hacettepe University, Turkey), M.A. and Ph.D. in Education from the Institute of Education, University of London.

{ CONTRIBUTORS }

Lawrence Aber, Ph.D.
Willner Family Professor of
    Psychology and Public Policy
Institute of Human Development and
    Social Change
New York University,
New York, NY, USA

Adem Arkadas-Thibert, M.A.
Child Rights Policy and Advocacy
    Officer
International Children's Center (ICC)
Bilkent University
Ankara, Turkey

Oumar Barry, Ph.D.
Senior Lector
University Cheikh Anta Diop
Dakar-Fann, Senegal

Kathy Bartlett, Ph.D.
Co-Director, Education
Aga Khan Foundation
Geneva, Switzerland

Jere R. Behrman, Ph.D.
William R. Kenan, Jr. Professor of
    Economics and Sociology
University of Pennsylvania
Philadelphia, PA, USA

**Zulfiqar A. Bhutta, MBBS, FRCP,
    FRCPCH, FCPS, Ph.D.**
The Noordin Noormahomed Sheriff
    Professor & Founding Chair
Division of Women and Child
    Health
Aga Khan University
Karachi, Pakistan

Linda Biersteker, M.A.
Research Director
Early Learning Resource Unit
Newlands, South Africa

Marc H. Bornstein, Ph.D.
Head, Child and Family Research
NICHD
Bethesda, MD, USA

Pia Rebello Britto, Ph.D.
Assistant Professor
Yale University
New Haven, CT, USA

Louie Cadaing, M.Sc.
Director, Spiritual Nurture
    of Children
World Vision International
Quezon City, Philippines

Clarice da Silva e Paula, M.A.
Child Protection Specialist
UNICEF
New York, NY, USA

Andrew Dawes, M.Sc.
Professor
University of Cape Town
Cape Town, South Africa and
University of Oxford
Oxford, United Kingdom

Patrice L. Engle, Ph.D.
Professor Emeritus
California Polytechnic
    State University
San Luis Obispo, CA, USA

Marito H. Garcia, Ph.D.
Lead Economist and
Program Leader for ECD in Africa
The World Bank,
Washington, D.C., USA

Deepa Grover, D. Phil
Regional Adviser, Early Childhood
    Development
UNICEF, Regional Office for Central
    and Eastern Europe and the
    Commonwealth of Independent
    States
Geneva, Switzerland

Aster Haregot, M.Ed.
Education Advisor
UNICEF, ESARO
Nairobi, Kenya

Sara Harkness, Ph.D.
Professor of Human Development,
    Pediatrics, and Public Health, and
Director of the Center for the Study
    of Culture, Health and Human
    Development
University of Connecticut
Storrs, CT, USA

Jacqueline Hayden, Ph.D.
Professor
Macquarie University
Sydney, Australia

Clyde Hertzman, M.D., M.Sc.,
    FRCPC
Director, Human Early Learning
    Partnership
University of British Columbia
Vancouver, Canada

William P. Hodges, M.A.
Postgraduate Associate and Fellow
    at the Zigler Center in Child
    Development and Social Policy
Yale University
New Haven, CT, USA

Sara L. Hommel, M.A.
Director, HEART Program,
    Department of Education and Child
    Development, Save the Children
Washington, D.C., USA

Maha B. Homsi, M.A.
Early Childhood and Protection
    Specialist
UNICEF
Amman, Jordan

Lara A. Hussein, M.A.
Chief of Child Protection
UNICEF
Abu Dhabi, United Arab Emirates

Theresa Kilbane, M.Sc.
Senior Advisor, Child Protection
UNICEF
New York, NY, USA

Barbara Kolucki, M.A.
Consultant: Children,
    Communication and Inclusive
    Practices
UNICEF
North Abington Township, PA, USA

Cassie Landers, Ed.D., M.Ph.
Assistant Professor
Columbia University
New York, NY, USA

Jennifer E. Lansford, Ph.D.
Research Professor
Duke University
Durham, NC, USA

Dafna Lemish, Ph.D.
Professor and Chair
Southern Illinois University
Carbondale, IL, USA

Caroline Johnston Mavridis, Ph.D.
Postdoctoral Fellow
University of Connecticut
Storrs, CT, USA

Michael Frank McCarthy, B.A.
M.A. Candidate
University of Bridgeport
Bridgeport, CT, USA

Ana Maria Nieto, M.A.
Doctoral Student
Harvard Graduate School
    of Education
Cambridge, MA, USA

Chloe O'Gara, Ed.D.
Program Officer
Hewlett Foundation
Menlo Park, CA, USA

Alan Pence, Ph.D.
UNESCO Chair and Professor
University of Victoria
Victoria, Canada

Oliver Petrovic, M.Ph.
Early Childhood Development
    Programme Specialist
UNICEF
New York, NY, USA

Atif Rahman, Ph.D.
Professor
University of Liverpool
Liverpool, United Kingdom

Nirmala Rao, Ph.D.
Professor
University of Hong Kong
Hong Kong, China

Laura Rawlings, M.A.
Lead Social Protection Specialist
The World Bank
Washington, D.C., USA

Linda Richter, L.M.
Professor
Human Sciences Research Council
Durban, South Africa and
University of the Witwatersrand
Johannesburg, South Africa

Lonnie Sherrod, Ph.D.
Executive Director
Society for Research in Child
    Development
Ann Arbor, MI, USA

Jack P. Shonkoff, M.D.
Julius B. Richmond FAMRI Professor
    of Child Health and Development,
Harvard School of Public Health
    and Harvard Graduate School of
    Education ;
Professor of Pediatrics,
Harvard Medical School and
Boston Children's Hospital;
Director, Center on the Developing
    Child at Harvard University
Cambridge, MA, USA
and
Boston

Paul Stephenson, M.Sc.
Senior Director, Child Development
    and Rights Technical Cluster
World Vision International
Federal Way, WA, USA

Natalia Streuli, Ph.D.
Young Lives Qualitative Researcher
Grupo de Análisis para el Desarollo
    (GRADE)
Lima, Peru

Charles M. Super, Ph.D.
Professor of Human Development
    and Pediatrics and Co-Director of
    the Center for the Study of Culture,
    Health, and Human Development
University of Connecticut
Storrs, CT, USA

Giorgio Tamburlini, Ph.D.
Senior Scientific Advisor
Institute for Child Health Burlo
    Garofolo Trieste
Trieste, Italy

Nurper Ulkuer, Ph.D.
Senior Advisor for ECD
UNICEF
Ankara, Turkey

Sergio S. Urzúa, Ph.D.
Assistant Professor
University of Maryland
College Park, MD, USA

Ziba Vaghri, B.N., M.Sc., Ph.D.
Director of the International Research
    and Initiatives Program of HELP
University of British Columbia
Vancouver, Canada

Alexandria Valerio, Ph.D.
Senior Economist
The World Bank
Washington, D.C., USA

Emily Vargas-Barón, Ph.D.
Director
The RISE Institute
Washington, D.C., USA

Theodore D. Wachs, Ph.D.
Professor
Purdue University
West Lafayette, IN, USA

Daniel A. Wagner, Ph.D.
UNESCO Chair and Professor of
    Education
University of Pennsylvania
Philadelphia, PA, USA

Sithu Wai, MBBS, MPH, M.Sc.
Doctoral Candidate
Macquarie University
Sydney, Australia

Martin Woodhead, Ph.D.
Professor
The Open University
Milton Keynes, United Kingdom

Mohammad Y. Yakoob, MBBS, M.Sc.
Research Assistant
Aga Khan University
Karachi, Pakistan

Hirokazu Yoshikawa, Ph.D.
Walter H. Gale Professor of Education
Harvard Graduate School of Education
Cambridge, MA, USA

Mary E. Young, M.D., Dr.PH.
Pediatrician, Public Health Specialist
Center on the Developing Child at
Harvard University
Cambridge, MA, USA

Aisha K. Yousafzai, Ph.D.
Assistant Professor
Aga Khan University
Karachi, Pakistan

Marian Zeitlin, Ph.D.
Senior Visiting Fellow
Cornell University, Institute for
    African Development
Ithaca, NY, USA

Introduction and Framework for Early Childhood Development Policies

Early Childhood Development

TRANSLATING RESEARCH TO GLOBAL POLICY

Pia Rebello Britto, Patrice L. Engle, and Charles M. Super

The last decade of the 20th century spawned an unprecedented growth in the research on early childhood. Across disciplines, common conclusions began to emerge that both supported the importance of early life for the development of human potential and also provided ways to improve child outcomes and well-being. Although much of the growth in that literature emanated from high-income, Western European and North American research, the first decade of the 21st century started to see a rise in similar conclusions emerge from multidisciplinary research in low- and middle-income (LAMI) countries. This global trend is positive and promising, and we now stand at a historic moment in the growth of human understanding: We have the knowledge to dramatically improve the effectiveness of programs and policies that serve young children and families around the world. At the same time, we surely need such knowledge, as the situation for a majority of young children and families, globally, is not good.

A recent set of publications has estimated that over 200 million children under 5 years fail to achieve their developmental potential due to challenges from undernutrition, poor health; environmental toxins, and lack of stable, loving, and responsive care (Grantham-McGregor et al., 2007), and, further, that the basic rights to health, development, and protection for over one-third of the world's children under 5 are not being realized (Britto & Ulkuer, 2012). Young children around the globe bear the greatest burden of poverty; disease; war; social marginalization; and limitations in health, nutrition, and education services. These risks prevail not just for children residing in LAMIC but also for the disadvantaged children in high-income countries.

The promise of the growing literature, however, is that this negative situation for children can be altered, their outcomes can be improved, their rights can be realized, and they can achieve their developmental potential through multiple actions, programs, and services (Engle et al., 2011). We are now able to identify strategies that buffer the impact of disadvantage and mitigate the injurious effects arising from risk factors. Nevertheless, there remains a gap between that scientific knowledge and the implementation of relevant policies and programs. The result is a discrepancy between these children's actual developmental progress and what they would have achieved with adequate care. This constitutes a loss of developmental potential—they will benefit less from educational, cultural, and economic opportunities, and they will end up with poorer health; inferior cognitive skills; lowered lifetime earnings; and reduced contributions to family, community, and society (see also, for example, Heckman, 2006; Joseph, 1999). These outcomes, in turn, contribute to the intergenerational transmission of poverty, increased demand for costly social services, and, on occasion, political instability. The cost is high both for the individual and for society. Urgently required is a comprehensive, cohesive, evidence-based framework to guide investments and action for programs and policies to improve outcomes in children's earliest years.

This volume was conceived in response to the need to bring scientific evidence to guide early childhood development (ECD) policies and programs. The goal is to move beyond simple advocacy to substantial improvement in ECD. The chapters of this volume are designed to provide the evidence and information needed for understanding the variety of approaches and perspectives that represent ECD programs and services. Until now, such a comprehensive resource has not been available. The reader will find here a practical compendium of multidisciplinary and multisectoral knowledge in an evidence-based framework, organized according to implementation strategies, which should be applicable for programming and policy planning.

We begin by laying out our conceptualization of ECD, drawn from several disciplines and sectors, as a framework for the volume. We then describe the organization of the volume, and conclude with a set of guidance notes to the readers in understanding both the layout of the volume and presentation of information therein.

Defining Early Childhood Development

Early childhood development is known by a multitude of names, including "early childhood care," "early childhood care and development," "early childhood care and education," "early childhood development," "early childhood education," "early childhood intervention," and "early childhood services." The presence of these related and sometimes interchangeable terms demonstrates deliberate efforts to address the development, care, and education of young children (UNESCO, 2002). In this volume, we use the term "early childhood development" (ECD) to capture a multifaceted concept from an ecological framework that focuses on the child's outcome (development), which depends on characteristics of the child and the context, such as health, nutrition, protection, care and/or education. Given the ethos, tone, and purpose of this volume—to bridge science with policy and programs—we draw on several bodies of knowledge, including the academic, practice, and international development literatures.

THE CHILD

With respect to the child, two dimensions must be considered—age and domains of development. Our age definition of ECD covers children prenatally until 8 years of age, or until the transition to school is complete. This age specification aligns with the almost universally endorsed international declarations and conventions, such at the Convention on the Rights of the Child and the Education for All declaration (UNICEF, 2002a; UNESCO, 2005) and the developmental science of early childhood (McCartney & Phillips, 2006). The socioecological perspective adopted by this volume emphasizes that children's development is the result of good health, nutrition, early stimulation, positive social and emotional interactions with significant caregivers, play as well as learning opportunities, and protection from violence and neglect. This process starts—for better or worse—during this important period of early childhood. Although important developments lie ahead, to be sure, for the 9-year-old child, and there are always examples of plasticity, certain growth points in the child's past cannot be done over: Either social, emotional, and cognitive processes have a sound base at that point, or they do not.

With respect to domains of human development, we employ a multidimensional definition that covers several aspects of growth and learning, again emanating from the academic and "gray" literature (that is, e.g., project reports not published in scientific journals). Despite occasional detailed analysis of single domains of development, we try to maintain a holistic perspective, one that recognizes that the child is a holistic synthesis of all these domains. The fields of neuroscience, psychology, child development, health, and education all conceptualize holistic development to include, but not be limited to, physical health and motor development, cognitive and language skills, social and emotional functioning, ethical and spiritual development, and sense of national or group identity (Britto & Kagan, 2010). The gray literature, emanating from the global practice community, also employs a holistic definition of ECD. The UN's World Fit for Children (WFFC, 2002) mission statement stipulates that "a good start in life" begins "in a nurturing and safe environment that enables children to survive, be physically healthy, mentally alert, emotionally secure, socially competent, and able to learn."

It is nevertheless true that each discipline has its own lens and particular set of key outcomes of interest. Developmental psychology, for example, focuses on growth and development. Evolutionary anthropology and biology are concerned with particular vulnerabilities and strengths that mark our evolutionary adaptations to, primarily, prehistoric environments. Neuroscience focuses on brain development. Economists study ECD with respect to investment in human capital. The psychological anthropological focus concerns the acquisition of culture in all its meanings and values. Environmental science is interested in the effect of humans on the sustainability—or not—of a viable biosphere. This myriad of perspectives is evident across the chapters of the volume.

THE CONTEXT

The second element of our definition is the ecology or context of the child's development. ECD does not take place in a vacuum; the context is an important determinant of children's development and achievement of developmental potential. Theoretical models and practice frameworks posit that a host of factors influence early human development. The most prevalent and widely cited ecological model in developmental psychology was conceptualized by Bronfenbrenner (1979), with the context layered from the most proximal (closest) micro system to the most distal (distant) macro system. Other socioecological models have emphasized, for example, the cultural construction of the developmental niche (Super & Harkness, 1986), risk and protective factors as context (e.g., Sameroff, 2009), and specific stage factors in the person–environment fit (Eccles et al., 1993). International declarations and frameworks also address the ecology of early childhood by holding it responsible for child outcomes. For example, the Convention on Children's Rights, the most widely ratified human rights treaty, discusses ecological factors ranging from the most proximal (e.g., family) to the most distal (e.g., international policies), specifically with regard to their impact on child development (Hodgkin & Newell, 2007).

Global declarations and developmental science both clearly highlight the importance of a caring, safe, and stimulating environment for the holistic development of young children. Within the first few years of life, children make rapid strides in all aspects of development, in interaction with their environment (Richter, 2010; Richter, Dawes, & de Kadt, 2010). Seminal works, synthesizing research from the neurobiological, social, economic, and behavioral sciences, demonstrate that early childhood is the key period for ensuring for child well-being and social and economic development of populations, both in high-income countries (e.g., *From Neurons to Neighborhoods*, by Shonkoff & Phillips [2000], commissioned by the United States Institute of Medicine) and more globally (e.g., *Early Child Development: A Powerful Equalizer* by Irwin, Siddiqi, & Hertzman [2007], commissioned by the World Health Organization).

In the modern world, institutionally devised systems play a major role in the support and promotion of ECD, through the provision of education, health, protection, and social services (Britto, Cerezo, & Ogbunugafor, 2008). Ultimately, they operate through the family and community systems to become, from the child's point of view, a developmental niche; how well those systems are integrated with each other and with the beliefs and values of the family may be a key factor in their success (Super & Harkness, 1999).

THE DEVELOPING CHILD IN CONTEXT

It must be emphasized that the critical elements of the context vary by the child's age and by the sectors involved in implementation of programs and services.

Developmental science specifies three main age periods of ECD during which development occurs with differing risks and opportunities: Conception to 3 years, 3 to 5 years, and 6 to 9 years (McCartney & Phillips, 2006).

The First Three Years

Conception to age 3 years is the period of most rapid growth of mental and socioemotional capacities, as well as the key period for ensuring survival and adequate growth (Shonkoff & Phillips, 2000). Brain architecture is built in a "bottom-up" sequence, with each stage requiring the adequate development of earlier capacities. The development of the brain incorporates experiences—positive or negative—that shape its capacities through a complex connection of neural circuits in different parts of the functioning brain. For example, the impact of poverty on early development can be seen to occur prenatally, such that the odds of a poor infant being born of low birth weight are nearly twice that of an infant born into a family with great economic advantage (Brooks-Gunn, Britto, & Brady, 1999). With insufficient nutrition in the early years comes malnutrition, stunting, and often delayed gross and fine motor development (Cheung, Yip, & Karlberg, 2001; Kariger, Stolzfus, Olney, et al., 2005; Kuklina, Ramakrishnan, Stein, Barnhart, & Martorell, 2004). Although the brain seems to be somewhat protected from nutritional insults, it is nevertheless a bodily organ, and stunting that results from malnutrition has been linked with delayed cognitive and verbal development (Grantham-McGregor et al., 2007). Interventions during this period tend to be made through health and nutrition services and through systems of support to families and communities (WHO, 1999). It should be noted that most infant and young child deaths are preventable with adequate nutrition and protection against disease, for example exclusive breast-feeding, clean drinking water, hygienic sanitation, and oral rehydration during illness (e.g., diarrhea; Bartlett, 2005; Black, Morris, & Bryce, 2003; Lopez, 2000). In addition to the risks of poor health and nutrition, children need to be protected from the risks of exposure to violence and traumatic stress as well (Garbarino, Dubrow, Kostelny, & Padro, 1992; Osofsky, 1997). Young children benefit from positive and responsive interactions with at least one consistent caregiver, including exposure to language and opportunities for exploration and learning (Britto, Fuligni, & Brooks-Gunn, 2006; Richter, 2004). For example, verbal engagement between parents and young children is one of the strongest influences on subsequent language development (Hart & Risley, 1995). These interactions occur primarily in homes and communities (Britto, Engle, & Alderman, 2007).

Ages Three to Five Years

In the period from 3 to 5 years, the need for health and disease prevention, cognitive and learning stimulation, and emotional and social responsivity continue; but, in addition, children appear to be especially vulnerable to violence, abuse, and neglect within their homes. The issue of protection is particularly relevant as very young children who suffer violence in their homes lack the capacity to report, and many children are afraid to report incidents of violence against them for fear of the consequences (Pinheiro, 2006). Protection of children is also required to ensure their safety and security, in particular, nascent policy developments aimed at reducing the risk of disaster note an increase in childhood deaths at this age due to accidents and lack of safety. Beyond protection and safety, children also need exposure to educational opportunities in formal and nonformal group settings, preprimary and preschool, family- and community-based programs (Bowman, Donovan, & Burns, 2001; Zigler, Gilliam, & Jones, 2006), as increased participation of the family and wider community facilitates ECD. Participation in such quality early learning and development programs has been linked with improved child development outcomes (Murphy & Burns, 2002).

The End of Early Childhood

The period from 6 to 8–9 years often encompasses the transition to school, a time when group learning and socialization opportunities are likely to be highly effective (Montie, Xiang, & Schweinhart, 2006; Vogler, Crivello, & Woodhead, 2008); this apparently reflects a fundamental shift in children's learning and interaction with the environment (Super, 2005). Research has indicated that development during this phase, sometimes termed "school readiness," is linked to learning, school completion, later skill development, and acquisition of academic competencies and nonacademic success (Arnold, 2004; Coordinators' Notebook, 2008; Jaramillo & Tietjen 2001; Kagitcibasi, Sunar, & Bekman, 2001; Pianta & McCoy, 1997; Reynolds, 2000; Rouse, Brooks-Gunn, & McLanahan, 2005). Children who enter school "ready to learn" are more likely to succeed at school, stay in school, and achieve lifelong learning and productivity in later adulthood; this is human capital created through a strong foundational start. In addition to families and communities, schools play a major role (Connell & Prinz, 2002), as the three pillars of school readiness are "ready children, ready families and communities, and ready schools" (Britto, 2010). The role of schools as the fundamental context for learning in today's world is widely recognized. However, development remains vulnerable to adversity and risk, including exposure to disease and toxins in the environment, and accidents and injuries (Morgan et al., 2001; Rodier, 2004).

From a developmental science perspective, not only can environments pervert a child's development—often inalterably, from a practice perspective—but they can, of course, also protect and promote. Each sector of practice and policy has its own approaches, sometimes implicitly aligned with developmental ages. The health and nutrition sector focuses on survival, disease prevention, and growth, with maternal and child health usually highlighted for special attention. The education sector is interested in learning and primary school preparation. The protection sector focuses its efforts toward vulnerable populations. Early child development engages all these sectors, across the full stage of life.

Description of the Volume

This volume brings together the latest multidisciplinary and multisectoral evidence to inform ECD programs and practice, with a particular focus on LAMI countries. We describe the six sections of the volume, the range in the types of evidence presented, and a guide to using this volume.

The multifaceted nature of ECD, in particular with respect to understanding the context, is reflected in the organization of this volume, albeit with an emphasis on policy and practice. The diversity in ECD programs varies across several dimensions—the target age of children served (e.g., infants, preschoolers); method of service delivery (e.g., home-based, center-based), focus of the program (e.g., health, education); and actors sponsoring and implementing the programs (e.g., state, private sector) (Britto, Yoshikawa, & Boller, 2011; UNESCO, 2007). It should be noted that these dimensions are not always discrete; for example, home-based services could include home-visiting programs for mothers and nonformal child care operated from a home. Furthermore, as stated earlier, each sector involved in ECD has a slightly different focus. For example, health sector programs might focus on basic survival outcomes, and education sector programs on early learning. Although this is not always the case, it is a traditional categorization. Therefore, if this volume is going to promote improvement in programs, services, and policies, the organization of this volume should resonate with the readers, such that they are able to discern the relevance of the knowledge and its application for their research, programmatic, and policy needs and initiatives. However, each sector-based chapter stresses the importance of integrating programs to maximize early child development and provides guidelines for this integration.

SECTION 1: INTRODUCTION AND FRAMEWORK FOR EARLY CHILDHOOD DEVELOPMENT POLICIES

The first section of this volume sets the foundation on which this volume is built, through a series of chapters and an introductory commentary. The purpose is to provide a basic understanding of ECD globally.

The section opens with a commentary by Shonkoff and Richter (2013, Chapter 2, this volume) on the rationale for investing in ECD. The authors bring to this commentary not only the key arguments for why ECD is invaluable for any aspect of human, national, societal, and economic development but also a translation of the evidence for policymakers and practitioners. The commentary, a succinct synthesis of the literature, provides new evidence for those familiar with ECD and a cogent understanding of the field for those who are new to it. The chapter by Engle, Rao, and Petrovic (2013, Chapter 3, this volume) highlights the situation of young children across the world, especially in LAMI countries. Using data from the Multiple Indicator Cluster Survey (MICS), this chapter presents a global snapshot of the situation of child outcomes and contexts within which children reside.

This comprehensive image is very useful for setting the context against which the evidence on programs is presented in the subsequent sections.

The final chapter in this section, by Britto, Ulkuer, Hodges, and McCarthy (2013, Chapter 4, this volume), examines the position ECD occupies in the current global policy landscape. International declarations, such as the Millennium Development Goals (MDG) and Conventions, such as the Convention on the Rights of the Child (CRC), are some of the main policies that guide not only international action but also national-level policies that address ECD. This chapter provides a detailed understanding of the instrumental and intrinsic value accorded to ECD in the global policy landscape, thereby setting the stage for understanding how ECD can feature in the next generation of global declarations and conventions.

In summary, this opening section provides a broad overview of the situation of children, their role in global policies, and an analytical summary of the evidence behind this volume.

SECTION 2: ANALYTIC AND DISCIPLINARY PERSPECTIVES

Early childhood development is the domain of several disciplines and sectors. Therefore, any volume on the evidence has to address these disciplinary perspectives in order to provide a comprehensive understanding of programmatic impact. The focus of this second section is to provide a broad understanding of young children, families, and communities from social ecological, cultural, developmental, and economic perspectives.

In the opening chapter, Wachs and Rahman (2013, Chapter 5, this volume) provide a practical understanding of how the ideas of developmental risk and resilience can be incorporated into program design. The chapter underscores that the impact of developmental risks will vary, depending upon individual child characteristics, child age, the extent of risk exposure over time, the overall context within which risk exposure occurs, and the extent and type of protective influences children encounter. Further, because risk factors often cluster together, children living in poverty in LAMI countries have particularly high exposure to cumulative bio-ecological and psychosocial developmental risks.

The second chapter in this section, by Behrman and Urzúa (2013, Chapter 6, this volume), presents the disciplinary perspective of economics on ECD. The focus of this chapter is on the economic justification for ECD programs in general, and in LAMI countries in particular, which depends on the comparison of benefits and costs of each ECD program. The authors review the evidence of what is known. They suggest that the value of their chapter is in highlighting what is not known about economic consequences of ECD programs, and they call for more research and analyses.

The third chapter, by Harkness, Super, Mavridis, Barry, and Zeitlin (2013, Chapter 7, this volume), highlights how cultural expectations of children's competence vary widely across domains (such as literacy) that could be considered universal. They provide a brief review of concepts of culture as it applies to children and families, and provide a description of the "developmental niche" as a theoretical framework for informing policy and improving program effectiveness.

The concluding chapter, by Pence (2013, Chapter 8, this volume), presents a perspective on ECD from indigenous and minority population groups, often unheard in the current literature. This chapter is based largely on the author's work in Africa and with the indigenous groups in Canada and New Zealand. Pence demonstrates that the impressive growth in ECD evidence is lacking literatures from LAMI countries, and that this limited lens restricts the generalizability of findings. To develop a literature that is more relevant and useful for populations globally, Pence concludes, other voices and perspectives must be supported and heard. By drawing on multiple disciplines linked to ECD, this section provides a broad conceptual framing and an intellectual context within which the evidence presented in the subsequent sections can be understood.

SECTION 3: PROGRAMMATIC APPROACHES TO EARLY CHILDHOOD DEVELOPMENT

The third section of the volume provides evidence for what types of programs, strategies, and tools work best under what circumstances to produce positive developmental outcomes. In so doing, this section generates recommendations for action. Improving the well-being of the world's young children involves many actors and stakeholders, such government, civil society, communities, the private sector, and, of course, families. However, in reality, usually one sector, group, or type of organization tends to take the lead in creating a comprehensive model for children. For example, in some countries, younger children are served by health ministries and preschool-aged children by education, welfare, and protection ministries. Therefore, this section is organized in two subsections: state actors in ECD, who typically operate within sectoral divisions, and non-state actors in ECD, who typically operate from an organizational perspective.

Historically, the three dominant sectors in ECD from a state perspective are health, nutrition, and education. The health chapter is written by Engle, Young, and Tamburlini (2013, Chapter 9, this volume), the nutrition-based approaches chapter by Yousafzai, Yakoob, and Bhutta (2013, Chapter 10, this volume), and the education chapter by O'Gara (2013, Chapter 11, this volume). Each of these chapters covers the evidence on the types of programs that have been effective in improving outcomes.

Engle, Young, and Tamburlini (2013) indicate the important role the health sector has to play in supporting the goal of child well-being in ECD. They review the evidence for actions that should be taken by the health sector for all children (promotive care), children at risk (preventative care), and children with special needs (curative care), both overall and by child age, and use evidence from countries to suggest implementation strategies.

In the chapter on nutrition-based approaches to ECD by Yousafzai, Yakoob, and Bhutta (2013), a broad review of the risks of maternal and child undernutrition is provided. The authors present a set of effective programmatic strategies the combat undernutrition through iron and folate supplementation for pregnant women, exclusive breast-feeding promotion, and appropriate complimentary feeding strategies. This chapter makes an important contribution with its conclusion that nutritional adequacy alone is insufficient to promote healthy child development, as early opportunities for stimulation are critical for improving long-term outcomes.

O'Gara (2013) reviews evidence for the importance of education for national development, the nearly universal enrollment in Grade 1, and very high rate of drop-out and school failure in many LAMI countries' education systems. For an explanation of this situation, the author looks to low-quality preprimary (or pre-school) classes, a significant feature of many early childhood efforts, and, on the other side, the very low and inequitable per capita investment in the primary school years. A number of policy options are considered for their weaknesses and potentials.

Beyond this traditional triad of state sectors, two newer actors are involved in ECD: Namely, child protection and social protection; these approaches are also included in this volume. The child protection chapter, authored by Landers, Da Silva, and Kilbane (2013, Chapter 12, this volume), is one of the first reviews of programmatic initiatives in this area. Their chapter demonstrates that violence toward children is not limited by geography, ethnicity, or status. They also note that data on violence against children are difficult to assess and hence underreporting is one of the biggest challenges in understanding this issue. The authors present examples from UNICEF-supported programs that address violence reduction through linking it with existing services, enhancing program quality, increasing the reliability of program monitoring, and developing supporting legal and policy frameworks.

The chapter on social protection, by Aber, Biersteker, Dawes, and Rawlings (2013; Chapter 13, this volume), considers the gap between traditional policies on social protection and specific provisions for ECD. The chapter describes the recent history and the multiple functions of social protection with respect to ECD, with a particular emphasis placed on promising practices in closing the gap between social protection and ECD. Through an analysis of the key issues and results, the authors recommend a set of new research initiatives that are required in order to improve the capacity of social protection systems to protect and promote ECD.

These five chapters—health, nutrition, education, child protection, and social protection—although presented in sectors, cumulatively provide a comprehensive picture of government and sectoral approaches to ECD. Furthermore, they provide recommendations for intersectorality across these approaches.

The next subsection considers non-state actors. These entities tend to act more within organizational foci and less as sectors. Therefore, the chapters here address the key non-state stakeholders in ECD by organization. Community-based organizations often have the longest history in addressing ECD, and the chapter by Hayden and Wai (2013, Chapter 14, this volume) describes how programs that operate under the auspices of nongovernmental organizations (NGOs), such as philanthropic or religious organizations, are referred to as *community-based programs* (CBPs) and that the service delivery of CBPs is often provided through *community-based organizations* (CBOs). The authors explain that CBOs consist of a myriad of programs and group mixes that need to be recognized in order to understand programmatic action. The chapter discusses the issues related to community-based services and describes the interconnection between CBPs and effective ECD service delivery.

Also active in ECD in LAMI countries are faith-based organizations. Their approaches to ECD are covered in the chapter by Bartlett, Stephenson, and Cadaing (2013, Chapter 15, this volume). One of the main contributions of this chapter is a framework for understanding the types of programs that fall under this category and a discussion of the complexities behind research on faith-based provision of ECD services, including the limited relevant literature. This chapter relies on two distinct case studies of faith-based ECD efforts to explain this approach and the demand for it, including a consideration of how faith-based services can help reach marginalized populations.

Private sector approaches to ECD are reviewed by Woodhead and Streuli (2013, Chapter 16, this volume). The authors highlight that the growth of this sector has been strongly propelled by demand. Using data from the Young Lives study, the authors are able to demonstrate that the private sector plays different roles and fills different gaps in early education service provision, depending on the existing availability of services. Their observations are crucial if we are to understand how to include the private for-profit fee sector as a part of ECD programs.

The final chapter in this section addresses the newest approach to ECD programming—that of media, including television, and children's books and literature. This chapter, authored by Lemish and Kolucki (2013, Chapter 17, this volume), highlights the importance of the process of developing media-based programs and the role of media-based programs in improving child outcomes. The authors argue that, for media-based ECD programs to be effective, the process used for their development must be strong and robust. Therefore, in their chapter, they emphasize how to design developmentally appropriate communication with and for young children that is inclusive and culturally sensitive. The chapter provides several examples of such initiatives and generates a set of recommendations from that experience.

In short, these last chapters review the evidence for the several different programmatic approaches for ECD. Each has a potential role to play in building a more comprehensive and effective approach for all young children and families.

SECTION 4: MEASUREMENT AND MONITORING
OF PROGRAMS AND POLICIES

Governments and non-state entities around the world are often challenged to document the evidence from their efforts with respect to young children, families, and the context of ECD. Section 4 responds to the need for evidence with a particular focus on monitoring and measurement of ECD. One of the largest drawbacks in the global ECD literature is the minimal inclusion of evidence from LAMI countries, largely due to limited efforts for program evaluation and monitoring. This section focuses on strategies for measuring and monitoring aspects of ECD—namely, both child outcomes and the associated programs and policies—in keeping with the ecological model of this volume.

The opening chapter, by Bornstein and Lansford (2013, Chapter 18, this volume), provides guidance on the assessment of child outcomes and programs. This chapter addresses issues related to ethics, research design, psychometrics, comparison across countries or cultures, measurement equivalence, and other technical points germane to ECD assessment. The issues are addressed through illustrative examples and a series of recommendations on appropriate assessment practices, with relevance for low-resource countries.

The chapter by Hertzman, Vaghri, and Arkadas-Thibert (2013, Chapter 19, this volume) provides similar information on monitoring of policies. Their chapter suggests that improving ECD requires an understanding of how social determinants and child rights approaches can complement each other through national policies and programs. Their chapter uses General Comment 7: Implementing Rights in Early Childhood (GC7) of the CRC as an example of that complementary approach. They provide guidance on how countries' reporting of progress toward implementing the UN-CRC can improve their reporting of ECD indicators, and how such efforts can lead to equity in developmental health from the start of life.

The final chapter, by Wagner (2013, Chapter 20, this volume) provides evidence on how these monitoring data can loop back and be used to improve policies and programs. The chapter uses learning (and reading) assessments as an example to demonstrate how assessments can inform national and global policies. Of note in this chapter is the emphasis on culture and context in such an approach because, for example, the vast majority of reading research is based on a small number of international languages, with a tiny fraction devoted to other languages in the world. Wagner concludes that conducting context- and intervention-relevant research on learning quality is important for policy planning.

The chapters in this section complement each other in that they provided detailed guidance on measuring outcomes, monitoring policies, and completing the data-to-program-to-policy-loop. Only through this kind of process can data from today's interventions be used to improve the next generation of policies and programs.

SECTION 5: BUILDING AND STRENGTHENING THE EARLY CHILDHOOD DEVELOPMENT PROGRAMS

Because children are an integration of the environment around them, so are ECD programs an integration of the systems that support them. No single agency, program, or advocacy group has the knowledge, experience, and resources to understand and support all aspects of a fully functioning network of ECD. In this section, four chapters address the key issues—often overlooked until too late—of implementation, coordination, capacity building, and financing that are required for the scaling up and sustainability of programs.

The first chapter, by Homsi and Hussein (2013, Chapter 21, this volume), addresses coordination of sectors and agencies, which is vital for the effectiveness of ECD programs. This chapter draws on the dynamic ECD-focused agency in Jordan, the National Council for Families Affairs (NCFA), as an exemplar of coordination. The strength of this chapter is that it both compares the NCFA model for coordination with other similar models and also outlines a set of recommendations based on the lessons learned. The practical guidance of this chapter is very useful for understanding mechanisms of intersectorality.

The second chapter, by Hommel (2013, Chapter 22, this volume), focuses on building capacity, which is vital for scaling up ECD programs. Hommel presents a useful typology for understanding capacity—one that differentiates capacity of practice from capacity of knowledge. This differentiation then has implications for the abilities and skills that are required by ECD professionals who work in the contexts with young children (e.g., schools, clinics, child care centers) and for those who work in the systems that support those contexts (e.g., health sector, NGO technical officers). By providing such a differentiation, this chapter makes a strong contribution to efforts that seek to scale up and expand ECD programs.

In the third chapter, author Young (2013, Chapter 23, this volume) provides an examination of the barriers to service provision from the perspective of donors, currently the major players in ECD programs in LAMI countries. The chapter reviews lessons learned from external donor-supported ECD projects in LAMI countries to identify key factors causing delays in implementation. The issues relate to the preparation, management and implementation, and monitoring and evaluation of projects. Young concludes that two sets of actions can improve program implementation. These are greater attention to capacity building and a better understanding of monitoring and evaluation. These conclusions are important and dovetail nicely both with the section on monitoring and the previous chapter by Hommel on capacity building.

The next chapter takes a look at ways to improve policy planning, implementation, and advocacy and is authored by Vargas-Barón (2013, Chapter 24, this volume). The thrust of this chapter is on the identification of the complexity and diversity of national ECD systems that then require contextually embedded multisectoral and integrated approaches for policy implementation. In presenting this model, Vargas-Barón identifies the systemic differences often found between centralized and decentralized leadership, and considers the coordination and management challenges to the implementation of policies. The chapter provides eight essential elements for building and strengthening national ECD systems, including equity and rights; multisectorality, integration, and coordination; governance through participatory ECD policy development and structures; legislation, standards, regulations, and agreements; quality improvement and resource development; accountability through ECD management information systems; investment and systemic issues for going to scale; and policy advocacy and social communications.

The last chapter in this section, by Valerio and Garcia (2013, Chapter 25, this volume), examines sustainable and effective finance mechanisms for ECD. The authors begin their chapter with the oft-cited arguments of the benefits of investing in ECD, and very quickly demonstrate how competing demands for funding have often prevented such evidence from being converted into social and economic priorities. As a result, countries face critical ECD finance shortfalls, which impact the quality, comprehensiveness, and coverage of ECD services. The authors provide a conceptual framework based on a set of normative elements of effective ECD finance: Namely, sustainability, equity, and administrative simplicity. The chapter does not provide specific guidelines for implementing this framework; rather, it provides a set of principles that policymakers can use to effectively balance these three interrelated elements within their unique contexts in order to adequately support their ECD objectives.

This section of chapters is focused on providing strategies to implement the evidence on effective ECD approaches found in the previous section. Because evidence often is presented without attention to the implementation mechanisms, and this contributes to the limited applicability of knowledge for policies and programs, the chapters in this section provide ideas to overcome that challenge.

SECTION 6: CONCLUSIONS

The compilation and integration of knowledge in the previous chapters brings to light a number of important implications for shaping the research and policy agendas of the immediate future. These, in turn, suggest a perspective on how the future of ECD might be most successfully constructed.

The implications for research are addressed in the chapter by Yoshikawa and Nieto (2013, Chapter 26, this volume). In this chapter, the authors review the evidence from this volume to identify emerging paradigm shifts for research that can address the next generation of practice and policy questions for ECD in LAMI countries. The authors contend that a paradigm shift is required for examining patterns of inclusion and exclusion, cultural specificity, and the emerging partnerships among researchers, practitioners, caregivers, community members, and policymakers.

The chapter is followed by two commentaries, one by Grover (2013, Chapter 27, this volume) on the implication of this volume for development agencies and NGOs, and one by Haregot (2013, Chapter 28, this volume) on the implications for building capacity of higher education in LAMI countries. Both authors are experienced professionals with a global ECD repertoire, and they present important insights into the ways the knowledge and information presented in this volume can be used by multiple audiences. The final chapter in this volume, by the editors (Super, Britto, & Engle, 2013, Chapter 29), surveys the conclusions that emerge from the evidence with an eye to implications for moving forward a global agenda for ECD.

GUIDE TO READING THIS VOLUME

As noted in the Preface, this volume is the product of two very different organizations that nevertheless share aims and interests. The information and evidence presented in this volume share some characteristics, depending on authorship and approach. The types of evidence presented across the chapters range from scientific to experiential. Some of the chapters have drawn on experimental and evaluation results to draw conclusions for effective programs, whereas others rely on experiential results to make similar recommendations. The variation in evidence is attributable not only to the diversity of authors' backgrounds, roles, and experience, but also to the complexity of the field of ECD. Some approaches, coming from health, nutrition, and education, have been working in the field of ECD far longer than, for example, child protection and social protection approaches. Therefore, for health, nutrition, and education, there is a longer history of evidence and a larger body of knowledge to be drawn upon. Similarly, there is limited evidence on more recently recognized faith- and media-based models in LAMI countries. Despite the variety of evidence and presentation, however, we have tried to uphold two principles in the selection of information: utility and validity. It has been demonstrated that researchers accord greater attention to the validity of evidence, and policymakers accord greater attention to its utility (Huston, 2008). The audience for this volume spans scholars, practitioners, and policymakers, and it is appropriate that the evidence cited draws on both criteria.

As you read this volume, keep in mind the context as you consider the results. "Low- and Middle-Income countries" is a useful category for many purposes, but any such typology hides vast differences in political, social, and cultural ideologies and the contexts within which programs operate. Economically, the countries have a core similarity—they are all LAMI countries—and therefore one might assume that the resource allocation to ECD might also be similar; but, in reality, the policies, constraints, social decisions, politics, and cultural values vary greatly. These differences influence not only resource distribution to programs but also the emphasis on child outcomes and program modalities to be valued. Examples or results from one place may not hold true in another, so we urge you to take into consideration the contexts of the evidence presented.

Finally, we would point out that underlying the formal organization of this book are cross-cutting and reoccurring themes, not always identified as such. Beyond the ages-old and pan-human concern for the welfare of children, new, 21st-century issues challenge ECD. Regardless of discipline or sector, institutional base or place in the global ECD system, all the authors recognize that families need to be involved in ECD interventions—some of the chapters have more to say about that than others, but you will find it almost everywhere. Similarly, where evidence is available, authors address the inclusion of young children with disabilities. Lurking on the edge of many chapters, sometimes entering within, are the very current issues of climate change and natural disasters, war and other emergencies, migration and urbanization.

This is a big book, but still it leaves things out. For all our 21st-century knowledge, there are still so many things we do not understand, and so many ways our policies and programs do not live up to even what we do know. Nevertheless, if we can translate our current knowledge into locally relevant global policy, we can lessen the loss of developmental potential in the next generation.

References

Aber, L., Biersteker, L., Dawes, A., & Rawlings, L. (2013). Social protection and welfare systems: Implications for early childhood development. In P. R. Britto, P. L. Engle, & C. M. Super (Eds.), *Handbook of early childhood development research and its impact on global policy* (Chapter 13). New York: Oxford University Press.

Arnold, C. (2004). *Positioning ECCD in the 21st century.* Coordinators Notebook: An International Resource for Early Childhood Development, 28. Toronto, ON: Consultative Group on Early Childhood Development.

Bartlett, S. (2005). Water, sanitation and urban children: The need to go beyond "improved" provision. *Children, Youth & Environments, 15,* 115–137.

Bartlett, K., Stephenson, P., & Cadaing, L. (2013). *Parents and communities: The key to understanding "faith-based" early childhood services and programs.* In P. R. Britto, P. L. Engle, & C. M. Super (Eds.), *Handbook of early childhood development research and its impact on global policy* (Chapter 15). New York: Oxford University Press.

Behrman, J. R., & Urzúa, S. S. (2013). Economic perspectives on some important dimensions of early childhood development in developing countries. In P. R. Britto, P. L. Engle, & C. M. Super (Eds.), *Handbook of early childhood development research and its impact on global policy* (Chapter 6). New York: Oxford University Press.

Black, R. E., Morris, S. S., & Bryce, J. (2003). Where and why are 10 million children dying every year? *The Lancet, 361,* 2226–2234.

Bornstein, M. H., & Lansford, J. E. (2013). Assessing early child development. In P. R. Britto, P. L. Engle, & C. M. Super (Eds.), *Handbook of early childhood development research and its impact on global policy* (Chapter 18). New York: Oxford University Press.

Bowman, B., Donovan, M. S., & Burns, M. S. (2001). *Eager to learn: Educating our preschoolers.* Washington, DC: National Research Council.

Britto, P. R. (2010). *School Readiness and Child National and International Development.* New York: UNICEF.

Britto, P. R., Cerezo, A., & Ogbunugafor, B. (2008). How evidence can be used to inform policy: A case study of early childhood evidence-based policy development. *International Journal of Early Childhood, 40*(2), 101–118.

Britto, P. R., Engle, P., & Alderman, H. (2007). Early intervention and care giving: Evidence from the Uganda Nutrition and Child Development Program. *Child Health and Education, 1,* 112–133.

Britto, P. R., Engle, P. L., & Super, C. M. (2013). Introduction to volume. Early child development: Translating research to global policy. In P. R. Britto, P. L. Engle, & C. M. Super (Eds.), *Handbook of early childhood development research and its impact on global policy* (Chapter 1). New York: Oxford University Press.

Britto, P. R., Fuligni, A. S., Brooks-Gunn, J. (2006). Reading ahead? A review of early literacy intervention programs for young children from low socioeconomic families. In D. Dickinson & S. Neuman (Eds.), *Handbook of early literacy* (pp. 311–332). New York: Guilford Press.

Britto, P. R., & Kagan, S. L. (2010). Global status of early learning and development standards. In P. Peterson, E. Baker, & B. McGaw (Eds.), *International Encyclopedia of Education* (Vol. 2, pp. 138–143), Oxford: Elsevier.

Britto, P. R., & Ulkuer, N. (2012). Child development in developing countries: Child rights and policy implications. *Child Development, 83,* 92–103. doi: 10.1111/j.1467-8624.2011.01672.x

Britto, P. R., Ulkuer, N., Hodges, W., & McCarthy, M. F. (2013). Global policy landscape and early child development. In P. R. Britto, P. L. Engle, & C. M. Super (Eds.), *Handbook of early childhood development research and its impact on global policy* (Chapter 4). New York: Oxford University Press.

Britto, P. R., Yoshikawa, H., & Boller, K. (2011). Quality of early childhood development programs in global contexts: Rationale for investment, conceptual framework and implications for equity. *Social Policy Report, 25,* 2.

Bronfenbrenner, U. (1979). *The ecology of human development: Experiments by nature and design.* Cambridge, MA: Harvard University Press.

Brooks-Gunn, J., Britto, P. R., & Brady, C. (1999). Struggling to make ends meet: Poverty and child development. In M. E. Lam (Ed.), *Parenting and child development in "non-traditions" families* (Chapter 14, pp. 279–304). Mahwah, NJ: Laurence Erlbaum Associates.

Cheung, Y. B., Yip, P. S. F., & Karlberg, J. (2001). Fetal growth, early postnatal growth, and motor development in Pakistani infants. *International Journal of Epidemiology, 30,* 66–72.

Connell, C. M., & Prinz, R. J. (2002). Impact of childcare and parent-child interaction on school readiness and social skills development for low-income African-American children. *Journal of School Psychology, 40,* 177–193.

Coordinators' Notebook. (2008). *Funding the future: Strategies for early childhood investing, costing and finance.* In L. Prpich, L. Curtis, & L. Zimanyi (Eds.), *Coordinators' Notebook (No. 30), Consultative Group on Early Childhood Care and Development,* Toronto, ON: Thistle Printing, 66–71.

Eccles, J., Midgley, C., Buchanan, C., Wig field, A., Reuman, D., & MacIver, D. (1993). Developmental during adolescence: The impact of stage/environment fit. *American Psychologist, 48*, 90–101.

Engle, P. L., Fernald, L. C., Alderman, H., Behrman, J., O'Gara, C., Yousafzai, A., et al., and the Global Child Development Steering Group. (2011). Strategies for reducing inequalities and improving developmental outcomes for young children in low-income and middle-income countries. *The Lancet, 378*(9799), 1339–1353.

Engle, P. L., Rao, N., & Petrovic, O. (2013). Situational analysis of young children in a changing world. In P. R. Britto, P. L. Engle, & C. M. Super (Eds.), *Handbook of early childhood development research and its impact on global policy* (Chapter 3). New York: Oxford University Press.

Engle, P. L., Young, M. E., & Tamburlini, G. (2013). The role of the health sector in early childhood development. In P. R. Britto, P. L. Engle, & C. M. Super (Eds.), *Handbook of early childhood development research and its impact on global policy* (Chapter 9). New York: Oxford University Press.

Garbarino, J., Dubrow, N., Kostelny, K., & Padro, C. (Eds.) (1992). *Children in danger: Coping with the consequences of community violence.* San Francisco: Jossey-Bass.

Grantham-McGregor S, Cheung, Y.B., Cueto, S., and the International Child Development Steering Group Developmental. (2007). Potential in the first 5 years for children in developing countries. *The Lancet, 369*, 60–70.

Grover, D. (2013). Closing commentary: Implications for development. In P. R. Britto, P. L. Engle, & C. M. Super (Eds.), *Handbook of early childhood development research and its impact on global policy* (Chapter 27). New York: Oxford University Press.

Haregot, A. (2013). Closing commentary: Implications for capacity. In P. R. Britto, P. L. Engle, & C. M. Super (Eds.), *Handbook of early childhood development research and its impact on global policy* (Chapter 28). New York: Oxford University Press.

Harkness, S., Super, C. M., Johnston Mavridis, C., Barry, O., & Zeitlin, M. (2013). Culture and early childhood development: Implications for policy and programs. In P. R. Britto, P. L. Engle, & C. M. Super (Eds.), *Handbook of early childhood development research and its impact on global policy* (Chapter 7). New York: Oxford University Press.

Hart, B., & Risley, T. R. (1995). *Meaningful differences in the everyday experience of young American children.* Baltimore: Brookes.

Hayden, J., & Wai, S. (2013). Community-based approaches to early childhood development: A matter of degree. In P. R. Britto, P. L. Engle, & C. M. Super (Eds.), *Handbook of early childhood development research and its impact on global policy* (Chapter 14). New York: Oxford University Press.

Heckman, J. J. (2006). Skill formation and the economics of investing in disadvantaged children. *Science, 312*, 1900–1902.

Hertzman, C., Vaghri, Z., & Arkadas-Thibert, A. (2013). *Monitoring progress toward fulfilling rights in early childhood under the convention on the rights of the child to improve outcomes for children and families.* In P. R. Britto, P. L. Engle, & C. M. Super (Eds.), *Handbook of early childhood development research and its impact on global policy* (Chapter 19). New York: Oxford University Press.

Hodgkin, R., & Newell, P. (2007). *Implementation handbook for the Convention on the Rights of the Child.* Geneva: United Nations Children's Fund.

Hommel, S. L. (2013). Capacity building for early childhood development. In P. R. Britto, P. L. Engle, & C. M. Super (Eds.), *Handbook of early childhood development research and its impact on global policy* (Chapter 22). New York: Oxford University Press.

Homsi, M. B., & Hussein, L. A. (2013). National agency systems. In P. R. Britto, P. L. Engle, & C. M. Super (Eds.), *Handbook of early childhood development research and its impact on global policy* (Chapter 21). New York: Oxford University Press.

Huston, A. C. (2008). From research to policy and back. *Child Development, 79,* 1–12.

Irwin, L. G., Siddiqi, A., & Hertzman, C. (2007). *Early child development: A "powerful" equalizer.* Final Report for the World Health Organization's Commission on the Social Determinants of Health. Geneva: WHO.

Jaramillo, A., & Tietjen, K. (2001). *Early childhood development in Africa: Can we do more or less? A look at the impact and implications of preschools in Cape Verde and Guinea.* Washington, DC: World Bank.

Joseph, R. (1999). Environmental influences on neural plasticity, the limbic system, emotional development and attachment: A review. *Child Psychiatry and Human Development, 29*(3), 189–208.

Kagitcibasi, C., Sunar, D., & Bekman, S. (2001). Long term effects of early intervention: Turkish low-income mothers and children. *Journal of Applied Developmental Psychology, 22,* 333–361.

Kariger, P. K., Stolzfus, R. J., Olney, D., et al. (2005). Iron deficiency and physical growth predict attainment of walking but not crawling in poorly nourished Zanzibari infants. *Journal of Nutrition, 135,* 814–819.

Kuklina, E. V., Ramakrishnan, U., Stein, A. D., Barnhart, H. H., & Martorell, R. (2004). Growth and diet quality are associated with the attainment of walking in rural Guatemalan infants. *Journal of Nutrition, 134*(12), 3296–3300.

Landers, C., Da Silva E. Paula, C., & Kilbane, T. (2013). Preventing violence against young children. In P. R. Britto, P. L. Engle, & C. M. Super (Eds.), *Handbook of early childhood development research and its impact on global policy* (Chapter 12). New York: Oxford University Press.

Lemish, D., & Kolucki, B. (2013). Media and early childhood development. In P. R. Britto, P. L. Engle, & C. M. Super (Eds.), *Handbook of early childhood development research and its impact on global policy* (Chapter 17). New York: Oxford University Press.

Lopez, A. D. (2000). *Reducing child mortality.* Bulletin of the World Health Organization, 78, 1173.

McCartney, K., & Phillips, D. A. (Eds.). (2006). *Handbook of early childhood development.* Oxford: Blackwell Publishing.

Montie, J. E., Xiang, Z., & Schweinhart, L. J. (2006). Preschool experience in 10 countries: Cognitive and language performance at age 7. *Early Childhood Research Quarterly, 21,* 313–331.

Morgan, R. E., Garavan, H., Smith, E. G., Driscoll, L. L., Levitsky, D. A., & Strupp, B. J. (2001). Early lead exposure produces lasting changes in sustained attention, response initiation, and reactivity to errors. *Neurotoxicology and Teratology, 23*(6), 519–531.

Murphy, D. A., & Burns, C. E. (2002). Development of a comprehensive community assessment of school readiness. *Early Childhood Research and Practice, 4,* 1–15.

O'Gara, C. (2013). Education-based approaches to early childhood development. In P. R. Britto, P. L. Engle, & C. M. Super (Eds.), *Handbook of early childhood development research and its impact on global policy* (Chapter 11). New York: Oxford University Press.

Osofsky, J. D. (Ed.). (1997). *Children in a violent society*. New York: Guilford Press.

Pence, A. (2013). Voices less heard: The importance of critical and "indigenous" perspectives. In P. R. Britto, P. L. Engle, & C. M. Super (Eds.), *Handbook of early childhood development research and its impact on global policy* (Chapter 8). New York: Oxford University Press.

Pianta, R. C., & McCoy, S. J. (1997). The first day of school: The predictive validity of early school screening. *Journal of Applied Development Psychology, 18*, 1–22.

Pinheiro, P. S. (2006). *World report on violence against children* (Secretary-General's Study on Violence Against Children). Retrieved from http://www.unviolencestudy.org/

Reynolds, A. J. (2000). *Success in early intervention: The Chicago Child-Parent Centers*. Lincoln: University of Nebraska Press. (VioLit Record Number 16237)

Richter, L. (2004). *The importance of caregiver-child interactions for the survival and healthy development of young children: A review*. Geneva: World Health Organization.

Richter, L. (2010). An introduction to family-centred services for children affected by HIV and AIDS. *Journal of the International AIDS Society, 13*(Suppl 2), S1.

Richter, L., Dawes, A., & de Kadt, J. (2010). Early childhood. In Petersen, I., Bhana, A., Swartz, L., Flisher, A. and Richter, L. (Eds.), *Mental health promotion and prevention for poorly resourced contexts: Emerging evidence and practice* (pp. 91–123). Pretoria: HSRC Press.

Rodier, P. M. (2004). Environmental causes of central nervous system maldevelopment. *Pediatrics, 113*(Suppl 4), 1076–1083.

Rouse, C., Brooks-Gunn, J., & McLanahan, S. (2005). Introducing the issue, "School readiness: Closing racial and ethnic gaps." *The Future of Children, 15*(1), 5–14.

Sameroff, A. (Ed.). (2009). *The transactional model of development: How children and contexts shape each other*. Washington, DC: American Psychological Association.

Shonkoff, J. P., & Phillips, D. A. (2000). *From neurons to neighborhoods: The science of early childhood development*. Washington, DC: National Academy Press.

Shonkoff, J. P., & Richter, L. (2013). *The powerful reach of early childhood development: A science-based foundation for sound investment*. In P. R. Britto, P. L. Engle, & C. M. Super (Eds.), *Handbook of early childhood development research and its impact on global policy* (Chapter 2). New York: Oxford University Press.

Super, C. M. (2005). The globalization of developmental psychology. In D. Pillemer & S. H. White (Eds.), *Developmental psychology and social change: Research, history, and policy* (pp. 11–33). Cambridge: Cambridge University Press.

Super, C. M., Britto, P. R., & Engle, P. L. (2013). Closing commentary: The future of early childhood development in the global development agenda. In P. R. Britto, P. L. Engle, & C. M. Super (Eds.), *Handbook of early childhood development research and its impact on global policy* (Chapter 29). New York: Oxford University Press.

Super, C. M., & Harkness, S. (1986). The developmental niche: A conceptualization at the interface of child and culture. *International Journal of Behavioral Development, 9*, 545–569.

Super, C. M., & Harkness, S. (1999). The environment as culture in developmental research. In T. Wachs & S. Friedman (Eds.), *Measurement of the environment in developmental research* (pp. 279–323). Washington, DC: American Psychological Association.

UNESCO. (2002). *Is the world on track?* EFA global monitoring report. Retrieved from http://www.unesco.org/education/efa/monitoring/monitoring_2002.shtml

UNESCO. (2005). *EFA Global Monitoring Report 2006. Education for All: Literacy for Life.* Paris: UNESCO Publishing.

UNESCO. (2007). *Strong foundations: Early childhood care and education.* EFA Global Monitoring Report. Paris: UNESCO Publishing.

UNICEF (2002). *Facts for life.* New York: UNICEF, WHO, UNESCO, UNFPA, UNDP, UNAIDS, WFP, and the World Bank.

Valerio, A., & Garcia, M. H. (2013). Effective financing. In P. R. Britto, P. L. Engle, & C. M. Super (Eds.), *Handbook of early childhood development research and its impact on global policy* (Chapter 25). New York: Oxford University Press.

Vargas-Barón, E. (2013). Building and strengthening national systems for early childhood development. In P. R. Britto, P. L. Engle, & C. M. Super (Eds.), *Handbook of early childhood development research and its impact on global policy* (Chapter 24). New York: Oxford University Press.

Vogler, P., Crivello, G., & Woodhead, M. (2008). *Early childhood transitions research: A review of concepts, theory, and practice.* Working Paper 48. The Hague: Bernard van Leer Foundation.

Wachs, T. D., & Rahman, A. (2013). The nature and impact of risk and protective influences on children's development in low-income countries. In P. R. Britto, P. L. Engle, & C. M. Super (Eds.), *Handbook of early childhood development research and its impact on global policy* (Chapter 5). New York: Oxford University Press.

Wagner, D. (2013). Improving policies and programs for educational quality: An example from the use of learning assessments. In P. R. Britto, P. L. Engle, & C. M. Super (Eds.), *Handbook of early childhood development research and its impact on global policy* (Chapter 20). New York: Oxford University Press.

WHO (1999). *The critical link: Interventions for physical growth and psychological development.* Geneva: WHO.

Woodhead, M., & Streuli, N. (2013). Early education for all: Is there a role for the private sector? In P. R. Britto, P. L. Engle, & C. M. Super (Eds.), *Handbook of early childhood development research and its impact on global policy* (Chapter 16). New York: Oxford University Press.

World Fit for Children (WFFC). (2002). *Special session on children.* New York: United Nations Children's Fund.

Yoshikawa, H., & Nieto, A. M. (2013). Paradigm shifts and new directions in research on early childhood development programs in low- and middle-income countries. In P. R. Britto, P. L. Engle, & C. M. Super (Eds.), *Handbook of early childhood development research and its impact on global policy* (Chapter 26). New York: Oxford University Press.

Young, M. E. (2013). Barriers to service provision: Lessons learned from donor-supported early childhood development projects. In P. R. Britto, P. L. Engle, & C. M. Super (Eds.), *Handbook of early childhood development research and its impact on global policy* (Chapter 23). New York: Oxford University Press.

Yousafzai, A. K., Yakoob, M. Y., & Bhutta, Z. A. (2013). Nutrition-based approaches to early childhood development. In P. R. Britto, P. L. Engle, & C. M. Super (Eds.), *Handbook of early childhood development research and its impact on global policy* (Chapter 10). New York: Oxford University Press.

Zigler, E. F., Gilliam, W. S., & Jones, S. M. (2006). *A vision for universal preschool education.* New York: Cambridge University Press.

The Powerful Reach of Early Childhood Development

A SCIENCE-BASED FOUNDATION FOR SOUND INVESTMENT

Jack P. Shonkoff and Linda Richter

The vitality, sustainability, and moral standing of a society depend on the extent to which it provides opportunities for all its children to achieve their full potential, to grow up to be responsible and productive adults, and to become successful parents of the next generation. In this context, multiple aspects of adult development build on capacities that are influenced by the prenatal environment and developed during early childhood. The foundations of cognitive skills, emotional well-being, social competence, and sound health, for example, all serve as building blocks for successful adaptation later in school, in the workplace, and in the society at large. Thus, the development of capable, healthy children has implications far beyond the individual or family, and extends to the well-being of communities and nations.

This commentary is designed to inform a broad understanding of the basic science of early childhood development (ECD) and its long-term influences, in order to guide productive public and private sector investment in young children and their families. In the service of this goal, the chapter presents a set of core developmental concepts that have emerged from decades of research in neuroscience, developmental psychology, and the economics of human capital formation. These concepts have survived both rigorous peer review and lively public discussion about what science tells us about the foundations of learning, behavior, social relationships, and health. The commentary also offers implications for policy and practice within the context of a biodevelopmental framework that can be employed to catalyze fresh thinking about why a good start in life is critically important and how it can be achieved. The overarching goal is to encourage a life course approach to maximizing human potential by reducing the intergenerational transmission of limited educational attainment, poor personal and social adjustment, unemployment or low paid work, impaired health, and decreased longevity, which together impose an extraordinary burden on the world's poorest populations.

Extensive scientific evidence indicates that early life experiences shape maturing biological systems in ways that affect physical and mental health, as well as cognitive abilities and work productivity, throughout life, all of which become increasingly more difficult to "fix" beyond the early childhood years (Shonkoff & Phillips, 2000). Research also shows that an estimated 200 million young children in low- and middle-income (LAMI) countries currently fail to meet their developmental potential as a result of the burdens of environmental scarcity, stress, and instability (Grantham-McGregor et al., 2007). This number is 20-fold higher than the number of children who die before their fifth birthday and represents roughly one-third of all children under age 5 in the world.

Without assistance, children who have been deprived of the early nutrition and stimulation that their highly evolved brain systems expect, and who continue to live under poor and hazardous conditions, face extraordinarily long odds for the future. The downward spiral of increased stress and diminished capacity, confidence, motivation, and opportunity that they experience perpetuates a vicious cycle of entrenched failure and exclusion that further damages their health and shortens their lives. The moral implications of these data are self-evident. The social and economic consequences are underscored by a series of longitudinal analyses that document the increased risk of illness, loss of education, and limited adult earnings attributable to early undernutrition in LAMI countries (Victora et al., 2008).

Notwithstanding these sobering findings, there is ample evidence from studies of young children from low-income families in the United States that early educational intervention can promote a more hopeful future for the children, as well as avert the societal costs of diminished human capital (Heckman & Masterov, 2006). Evidence from studies in LAMI countries also indicates that model programs that combine nutrition and psychosocial stimulation can have positive cognitive impacts on disadvantaged children, with effect size estimates ranging from 0.3 to 1.8 (Engle et al., 2007). Interventions to reduce family poverty and remove household-based economic barriers to health care and education for children also show substantial benefits, especially for girls in societies where gender discrimination exists (Devereux, Webb, & Handa, 2010; Fiszbein, Schady, & Ferreira, 2009).

This commentary is intended to help bridge the divide that frequently exists between investments focused on child survival and investments focused on early childhood development. The aim is to illustrate the complementary nature of these two imperatives—survival *and* development—and to explain how both can be advanced through an integrated strategy driven by a common science. Our objective is to demonstrate the overlapping features of effective interventions that save children's lives and those that maximize their developmental potential, and to underscore the extent to which this artificial division is transcended by advances in developmental knowledge (Shonkoff, Richter, Van der Gaag, & Bhutta, 2012).

To fully understand the ways in which survival, growth, learning, behavior, and health are highly interrelated—and the extent to which adversities associated with deprivation, violence, and disease undermine positive outcomes in all of these domains—it is essential to understand the central role of the brain in interpreting and driving genetically endowed responses to environmental conditions, and to recognize its sensitivity to stressful exposures and events. In simple terms, the brain is the body's control center, and it regulates both physiological and behavioral responses to threat. Moreover, the brain not only controls biological effects on other organ systems and influences the development of coping and adaptive skills (McEwen, 1998), but it also changes both structurally and functionally in response to stress (McEwen, 2007). The National Scientific Council on the Developing Child (2007) has posited a conceptual framework that describes this process, and its formulation guides the discussion that follows.

Core Scientific Concepts

BRAINS ARE BUILT OVER TIME

Brains are built over time, and a substantial proportion of their circuitry is assembled during the early years of life. The basic architecture of the brain is constructed through an ongoing process that begins before birth and continues into early adulthood. This architecture and its developing capacities are built "from the bottom up," with simple circuits and skills providing the scaffolding for more increasingly complex connections and capabilities over time. This process unfolds through a succession of "sensitive periods," each of which is associated with the formation of specific neural circuits that are associated with specific abilities. As the brain matures, higher level circuits build on lower level circuits. Thus, higher levels of adaptation are more difficult to achieve if lower level circuits were not wired appropriately (Cunha, Heckman, Lochner, & Masterov, 2005; Knudsen, Heckman, Cameron, & Shonkoff, 2006).

GENES AND EXPERIENCES INTERACT

Genes and experiences interact in a mutually reciprocal fashion to shape the architecture of the developing brain. Genetics determines when specific brain circuits are laid down, and experiences shape their formation. This process is influenced by the concept of *contingent reciprocity*, which refers to the "serve and return" nature of children's relationships with the important people in their lives (i.e., family members, neighbors, and, in some cases, providers of services). This "interactive dance" between infants and their caregivers is fueled by a self-initiated, inborn drive toward competence that depends on appropriate sensory input and developmentally appropriate responsiveness from the social environment. The cumulative impact of these gene–experience interactions literally sculpts the circuitry of the developing brain (Champagne, Francis, Mar, & Meaney, 2003; Liu, Diorio, Day, Francis, & Meaney, 2000; Meaney, 2001; Reis, Collins, & Berscheid, 2000).

Experience-expectant brain development (e.g., the maturation of the visual system) illustrates universal competencies that emerge in all socioeconomic and cultural contexts. In contrast, experience-dependent development (e.g., the ability to read) does not happen unless the requisite environmental conditions are provided (Greenough & Black, 1992). Through these diverse and interrelated processes, the early experiences of young children create a foundation for lifelong learning, behavior, and health. A strong foundation formed by positive influences increases the probability of healthy physiological systems and positive life outcomes. A weak foundation replete with negative influences increases the odds of dysfunction and later impairments (Dawson & Fischer, 1994; Nelson, 2000; Nelson & Bloom, 1997; Shonkoff & Phillips, 2000).

COGNITIVE, EMOTIONAL, AND SOCIAL CAPABILITIES ARE INEXTRICABLY INTERTWINED

Cognitive, emotional, and social capabilities are inextricably intertwined throughout the life course—and learning, behavior, and both physical and mental health are deeply interconnected.

The brain is a highly integrated organ, and its multiple functions operate in a richly coordinated fashion. Thus, emotional well-being, social competence, cognitive abilities, and physiological integrity are deeply interrelated, and together they are the bricks and mortar that make up the foundation for human development (Emde & Robinson, 2000; McCartney & Phillips, 2006). Oral language acquisition, for example, depends not only on adequate hearing, the ability to differentiate sounds, and the capacity to link meaning to specific words, but also on the ability to concentrate, pay attention, engage in meaningful social interaction, and regulate one's physiological responsiveness. Most important, these domains of competence cannot be achieved passively or in isolation from human connection. They require active and mutually responsive interaction.

EXCESSIVE ADVERSITY EARLY IN LIFE CAUSES PHYSIOLOGICAL DISRUPTIONS

Excessive adversity early in life causes physiological disruptions that affect the developing brain (as well as other biological systems) in ways that can lead to long-term impairments in learning, behavior, emotional reactivity, and health. Manageable levels of stress during the prenatal and early childhood periods are essential to healthy development, but excessive or prolonged activation of stress response systems can produce physiological changes in neurohormonal, immune, and metabolic regulatory functions that adversely affect a child's reactions to the environment for the rest of his or her life (National Scientific Council on the Developing Child, 2005). Healthy adaptation depends on the capacity of stress response systems to react rapidly in the face of adversity and return to baseline when their job is done. However, when physiological responses to threat remain activated at high levels over prolonged periods, the resulting "toxic stress" can have adverse effects on developing brain architecture, as well as on other maturing organ systems (Caldji et al., 1998; Gunnar & Donzella, 2002; McEwen & Sapolsky, 1995). Beyond the risk of long-term, physiological consequences, some investigators have speculated that the comparable persistence of maladaptive psychological adaptations (e.g., excessive threat vigilance, mistrust of others, poor social relationships, impaired self-regulation, and unhealthy, risk-taking behaviors) can compound the resulting vulnerability to lifelong impairments (Miller, Chen, & Parker, 2011).

Major risk factors for toxic stress include extreme poverty, significant undernutrition, recurrent physical and/or emotional abuse, chronic neglect, severe maternal depression, parental substance abuse, exposure to violent conflict, and other crisis situations. Under such circumstances, persistent activation of the stress response can produce an internal physiological state that disrupts the architecture and chemistry of the developing brain and can lead to difficulties in learning and health-damaging behaviors that undermine well-being over time (Carrion et al., 2002; De Bellis et al., 1999a,b; Farah et al., 2006; Gunnar, 2003; Gunnar, Morrison, Chisholm, & Schuder, 2001). Although differences in outcomes may depend on constitutional variations in children's sensitivity to context (Obradovic, Bush, Stamperdahl, Adler, & Boyce, 2010), the most important predictor is the extent to which threats to well-being can be prevented or reduced and a supportive adult is available to help the child cope with adversity and thereby restore physiological homeostasis.

Inadequately buffered toxic stress in early childhood—whether precipitated by scarcity, conflict, or instability—is associated with a lifetime of greater susceptibility to physical illnesses, such as cardiovascular disease, hypertension, obesity, diabetes, and stroke (Shonkoff, Boyce, & McEwen, 2009); mental health problems such as depression, anxiety disorders, and substance abuse (Anda et al., 2006; McEwen & Seeman, 1999); and unstable or conflict-ridden relationships that lead to less social support and diminished productivity (Miller et al., 2011). When early experiences signal conditions involving a high level of stress or instability from which the child is not buffered, the biological regulatory systems retain that initial programming and put the stress response systems on a "short fuse" or "high-alert" status. For many young children facing such circumstances, the benefits of short-term survival therefore come at a significant cost to longer term health (Shonkoff et al., 2009). In simple terms, when individuals are exposed to "chains of risk" (Kuh & Ben-Schlomo, 2004), adversity begets adversity (Miller et al., 2011).

NEUROPLASTICITY AND THE ABILITY TO CHANGE
BEHAVIOR DECREASE OVER TIME

As the maturing brain becomes more specialized to execute increasingly complex functions in an effective manner, it becomes less flexible in its capacity to reorganize and adapt to new or unexpected challenges. Stated simply, once a circuit is "wired," it stabilizes with age, making it increasingly difficult to alter over time. Although "windows of opportunity" for skill development and behavioral adaptation remain open for many years, trying to change behavior or build new skills on a foundation of brain circuits that were wired initially in anticipation of different environmental conditions or expectations requires more work and is more "expensive." From a biological perspective, greater expense refers to the elevated levels of metabolic energy required to compensate for circuits that do not perform in an expected fashion (Hensch, 2005; Knudsen, 2004; Knudsen et al., 2006; Lüscher, Nicoll, Malenka, & Muller, 2000; Malenka & Nicoll, 1999; Martin, Grimwood, & Morris, 2000). From a societal perspective, higher expenses refer to a range of preventable costs, from special education and grade retention to public assistance and incarceration. In short, providing the right conditions for healthy development in early childhood is likely to be more effective and less expensive than treating problems at a later age.

Implications for Research, Policy, and Practice

Rapidly advancing frontiers in the biological and social sciences, and their converging elucidation of the foundations of lifelong learning, behavior, and health, offer an unprecedented opportunity for a new era in knowledge-driven policies and practices focused on the early childhood period (Shonkoff, 2010). This concept of common origins and diverging pathways for impairments in health and development can help guide both creative investigation through interdisciplinary research and coordinated innovation across service sectors (Shonkoff, Garner, & The Committee on Psychosocial Aspects of Child and Family Health, Committee on Early Childhood, Adoption, and Dependent Care, Section on Developmental and Behavioral Pediatrics, 2012). Although specific policy and programmatic considerations will vary widely by the needs and goals of communities, regions, and nations, science offers the following two broad principles to guide decisions about the allocation of resources and further research to catalyze new strategies for intervention.

THE CRITICAL IMPORTANCE OF REDUCING STRESS

First, the best way to build the strongest possible foundation for physical survival and healthy development is to prevent or reduce sources of toxic stress in the lives of pregnant women and young children, and to strengthen the capacities of families and communities to mitigate the negative consequences of significant adversity on children's developing brains, beginning as early as possible.

Basic concepts of neuroscience suggest that protective influences that are provided earlier rather than later in the developmental course will have the greatest positive impact, as they help establish healthy brain architecture during the sensitive periods when its foundational circuitry is being created (Shonkoff, 2011). When systems are put in place to monitor the development of all children continuously over time, problems that require attention can be identified early, and appropriate responses can be made. Such identification can be accomplished within the context of regular health care and the provision of community-based social services, as well as through the ongoing observations of skilled providers of early care and education. Fully meeting this goal requires prenatal care for all pregnant women, sustained access to a consistent source of primary health care for all children and their families, good quality child care for working parents, supplementary education for children who are at risk for developmental problems, social protection for the poorest and most vulnerable families, and new ideas about how to augment the stress-buffering capacity of each of these domains.

LEVERAGING KNOWLEDGE TO INCREASE INTERVENTION IMPACTS

Second, enhanced life prospects and greater financial returns will come from investments in early childhood policies and programs that are driven by science-based theories of change, grounded in credible evidence, and faithful to high-quality standards of implementation.

Although all young children and their families can benefit from supportive services, policies that focus on the delivery of effective interventions for those who are vulnerable will generally achieve the largest financial returns. To this end, issues of quality and cost must be viewed in the context of what a program is expected to do and the resources it has to draw on (Britto, Yoshikawa, & Boller, 2011). Programs for inexperienced parents with young children who need basic information about child development and support to cope with the added challenges of child care can be highly effective at relatively low cost. Services for families coping with significant financial hardship, violence, depression, or substance abuse require more sophisticated, well-trained staff with specific expertise that costs more money. When program resources match the needs of the children and families they are designed to serve, they can be cost-effective and produce strong impacts. When service providers are asked to address needs that are beyond their capacity, they are likely to have relatively little effect. Sound policies seek maximum impact and high value rather than minimal cost—and the strongest returns will be achieved by a more segmented approach to intervention that differentiates the generic needs of all from the highly specialized needs of the most vulnerable, within the cultural context of those who are being served.

Conclusion

The scientific foundations of physical survival and healthy development, beginning with the preconception health of the future mother and extending into the prenatal period and early childhood years, provide a framework for informing broad national and global policies focused on the building blocks for successful societies. In the highest income countries, new scientific breakthroughs are beginning to transform the treatment of disease, yet much work remains to be done to stimulate innovative thinking about the promotion of health and the facilitation of early learning. In middle-income and emerging-market nations, which have made significant progress in reducing undernutrition and child mortality but continue to face substantial socioeconomic disparities and other challenges related to social transitions, developmental science can inform the design and implementation of early childhood investments that can mitigate the impacts of significant adversity on young children. In the lowest income countries, which continue to struggle with severe malnutrition, debilitating infection, high mortality rates, and widespread illiteracy, this knowledge offers a promising framework for developing innovative interventions through an integrated approach to both child survival and early childhood development, embedded in a broader social and economic development agenda.

The time has come to close the gap between what we know (from systematic scientific inquiry across a broad range of disciplines) and what we do (through both public- and private-sector policies and practices) to strengthen the foundations of healthy development. This call to action constitutes a fundamental moral responsibility, as well as a critical investment in the social and economic future of all societies. To this end, the science of early childhood development can provide a framework for informing choices among alternative priorities and for building consensus around a shared plan of action. An integrated science of health, learning, and behavior, grounded in a growing understanding of the biology of adversity, offers tremendous promise for a brighter future for all young children and families, and especially for those who are most vulnerable.

References

Anda, R., Felitti, V., Bremner, J. D., Walker, J., Whitfield, C., Perry, B., et al. (2006). The enduring effects of abuse and related adverse experiences in childhood. *European Archives of Psychiatry and Clinical Neuroscience, 256*, 174–186.

Britto, P., Yoshikawa, H., & Boller, K. (2011). Quality of early childhood development programs in global contexts: Rationale for investment, conceptual framework and implications for equity. *Social Policy Report, 25*(2), 1–23.

Caldji, C., Tannenbaum, B., Sharma, S., Francis, D., Plotsky, P., & Meaney, M. (1998). Maternal care during infancy regulates the development of neural systems mediating the expression of fearfulness in the rat. *Proceedings of the National Academy of Sciences, 95*(9), 5335–5340.

Carrion, V., Weems, C., Ray, R., Glaser, B., Hessl, D., & Reiss, A. (2002). Diurnal salivary cortisol in pediatric post-traumatic stress disorder. *Biological Psychiatry, 51*, 575–582.

Champagne, F., Francis, D., Mar, A., & Meaney, M. (2003). Variations in maternal care in the rat as a mediating influence for the effects of environment on development. *Physiology and Behavior, 79,* 359–371.

Cunha, F., Heckman, J., Lochner, L., & Masterov, D. (2005). *Interpreting the evidence on life cycle skill formation.* Working Paper No. 11331. Cambridge, MA: National Bureau of Economic Research.

Dawson, G., & Fischer, K. (Eds.). (1994). *Human behavior and the developing brain.* New York: Guilford.

De Bellis, M., Baum, A., Birmaher, B., Keshavan, M., Eccard, C., Boring, A., et al. (1999a). A. E. Bennett Research Award: Developmental traumatology, part I: Biological stress systems. *Biological Psychiatry, 45,* 1259–1270.

De Bellis, M., Keshavan, M., Clark, D., Casey, B. J., Giedd, J., Boring, A., et al. (1999b). A. E. Bennett Research Award: Developmental traumatology, part II: Brain development. *Biological Psychiatry, 45,* 1271–1284.

Devereux, S., Webb, D., & Handa, S. (2010). *Social protection for Africa's children.* London: Routledge.

Emde, R., & Robinson, J. (2000). Guiding principles for a theory of early intervention: A developmental-psychoanalytic perspective. In J. Shonkoff & S. Meisels (Eds.), *Handbook of early childhood intervention* (2nd ed., pp. 160–178). New York: Cambridge University Press.

Engle, P., Black, M., Behrman, J., Cabral de Mello, M., Gertler, P., Kapiriri, L., et al. (2007). Strategies to avoid the loss of developmental potential among over 200 million children in the developing world. *The Lancet, 369,* 229–242.

Farah, M., Shera, D., Savage, J., Betancourt, L., Giannetta, J., Brodsky, N., et al. (2006). Childhood poverty: Specific associations with neurocognitive development. *Brain Research, 1110,* 166–174.

Fiszbein, A., Schady, N., & Ferreira, F. (2009). *Conditional cash transfers: Reducing present and future poverty.* Washington, DC: World Bank.

Grantham-McGregor, S., Cheung, Y., Cueto, S., Glewwe, P., Richter, L., & Strupp, L. (2007). Developmental potential in the first 5 years for children in developing countries. *The Lancet, 369,* 60–70.

Greenough, W., & Black, J. (1992). Induction of brain structure by experience: Substrates for cognitive development. In M. Gunnar & C. Nelson (Eds.), *Developmental behavioral neuroscience* (Vol. 24, pp. 155–200). Hillsdale, NJ: Lawrence Erlbaum Associates.

Gunnar, M. (2003). Integrating neuroscience and psychosocial approaches in the study of early experiences. In J. King, C. Ferris, & I. Lederhendler (Eds.), *Roots of mental illness in children,* **1008** (pp. 238–247). New York: New York Academy of Sciences.

Gunnar, M., & Donzella, B. (2002). Social regulation of the cortisol levels in early human development. *Psychoneuroendocrinology, 27,* 199–220.

Gunnar, M., Morrison, S., Chisholm, K., & Schuder, M. (2001). Salivary cortisol levels in children adopted from Romanian orphanages. *Development and Psychopathology, 13,* 611–628.

Heckman, J., & Masterov, D. (2006). *The productivity argument for investing in young children. Early childhood research collaborative discussion paper 104.* Retrieved from http://www.earlychildhoodrc.org/papers/catalog.cfm

Hensch, T. (2005). Critical period plasticity in local cortical circuits. *Nature Reviews Neuroscience, 6*, 877–888.

Knudsen, E. (2004). Sensitive periods in the development of the brain and behavior. *Journal of Cognitive Neuroscience, 16*, 1412–1425.

Knudsen, E., Heckman, J., Cameron, J., & Shonkoff, J. (2006). Economic, neurobiological and behavioral perspectives on building America's future workforce. *Proceedings of the National Academy of Sciences, 103*, 10155–10162.

Kuh, D., & Ben-Shlomo. (Eds.). (2004). *A life course approach to chronic disease epidemiology.* New York: Oxford University Press.

Liu, D., Diorio, J., Day, J., Francis, D., & Meaney, M. (2000). Maternal care, hippocampal synaptogenesis and cognitive development in rats. *Nature Neuroscience, 3*(8), 799–806.

Lüscher, C., Nicoll, R., Malenka, R., & Muller, D. (2000). Synaptic plasticity and dynamic modulation of the postsynaptic membrane. *Nature Neuroscience, 3*, 545–550.

Malenka, R., & Nicoll, R. (1999). Long-term potentiation: A decade of progress. *Science, 285*, 1870–1874.

Martin, S., Grimwood, P., & Morris, R. (2000). Synaptic plasticity and memory: An evaluation of the hypothesis. *Annual Review of Neuroscience, 23*, 649–711.

McCartney, K., & Phillips, D. (Eds.). (2006). *The handbook of early childhood development.* Oxford, UK: Blackwell.

McEwen, B. (1998). Protective and damaging effects of stress mediators. *New England Journal of Medicine, 338*(3), 171–179.

McEwen, B. (2007). Physiology and neurobiology of stress and adaptation: Central role of the brain. *Physiological Reviews, 87*(3), 873–904.

McEwen, B., & Sapolsky, R. (1995). Stress and cognitive function. *Current Opinion in Neurobiology, 5*(2), 205–216.

McEwen, B., & Seeman, T. (1999). Protective and damaging effects of mediators of stress: Elaborating and testing the concepts of allostasis and allostatic load. *Annals of the New York Academy of Sciences, 896*, 30–47.

Meaney, M. (2001). Maternal care, gene expression, and the transmission of individual differences in stress reactivity across generations. *Annual Review of Neuroscience, 24*, 1161–1192.

Miller, E., Chen, E., & Parker, K. (2011). Psychological stress in childhood and susceptibility to the chronic diseases of aging: Moving toward a model of behavioral and biological mechanisms. *Psychological Bulletin.* doi:10.1037/a0024768.

National Scientific Council on the Developing Child. (2005). *Excessive stress disrupts the architecture of the developing brain.* Working Paper No. 3. Cambridge, MA: Author. Retrieved from http://developingchild.harvard.edu

National Scientific Council on the Developing Child. (2007). *The science of early childhood development: Closing the gap between what we know and what we do.* Cambridge, MA: Author. Retrieved from http://developingchild.harvard.edu

Nelson, C. (2000). The neurobiological bases of early intervention. In J. Shonkoff & S. Meisels (Eds.), *Handbook of early childhood intervention* (2nd ed., pp. 204–227). New York: Cambridge University Press.

Nelson, C., & Bloom, F. (1997). Child development and neuroscience. *Child Development, 68*, 970–987.

Obradovic, J., Bush, N. R., Stamperdahl, J., Adler, N. E., & Boyce, W. T. (2010). Biological sensitivity to context: The interactive effects of stress reactivity and adversity on socio-emotional behavior and school readiness. *Child Development, 81,* 270–289.

Reis, H., Collins, W., & Berscheid, E. (2000). Relationships in human behavior and development. *Psychological Bulletin, 126,* 844–872.

Shonkoff, J. (2010). Building a new biodevelopmental framework to guide the future of early childhood policy. *Child Development, 81,* 357–367.

Shonkoff, J. (2011). Protecting brains, not simply stimulating minds. *Science, 333,* 982–983.

Shonkoff, J., Boyce, W. T. & McEwen, B. (2009). Neuroscience, molecular biology, and the childhood roots of health disparities: Building a new framework for health promotion and disease prevention. *Journal of the American Medical Association, 301,* 2242–2259.

Shonkoff, J., Garner, A., & The Committee on Psychosocial Aspects of Child and Family Health, Committee on Early Childhood, Adoption, and Dependent Care, Section on Developmental and Behavioral Pediatrics. (2012). The lifelong effects of early childhood adversity and toxic stress. *Pediatrics, 129,* e232–e246.

Shonkoff, J., & Phillips, D. (Eds.). (2000). *From neurons to neighborhoods: The science of early childhood development.* Committee on Integrating the Science of Early Childhood Development, National Research Council and Institute of Medicine. Washington, DC: National Academy Press.

Shonkoff, J., Richter L, Van der Gaag J, & Bhutta Z. (2012). An integrated scientific framework for child survival and early childhood development. *Pediatrics, 129,* e460–e472.

Victora, C., Adair, L., Fall, C., Hallal, P., Martorell, R., Richter, L., et al. (2008). Maternal and child undernutrition: Consequences for adult health and human capital. *The Lancet, 17,* 23–40.

{ 3 }

Situational Analysis of Young Children
in a Changing World
Patrice L. Engle, Nirmala Rao, and Oliver Petrovic

Statement of the Problem

Out of all the world's children, only about 8% are born in a high-income country. The other 92% of children live in low- and middle-income (LAMI) countries, where out of 100, 7 will not survive beyond the age of 5, 50 will not have their births registered, 68 will not receive early childhood education, 17 will never enroll in primary school, 30 will be stunted, and 25 will live in poverty (UNICEF, 2009). On the other hand, for the 8% born in high-income countries, the prospects are much better. Of 100 such children, fewer than 1 will die before age 5, almost all will have their births registered, very few will not attend secondary school, 20 will not attend preschool, and not more than 1 will be stunted. These figures indicate stark contrasts between high-income and developing countries, but, in addition, they also cloak large discrepancies by region, by country, and within countries. Both within and between countries, a grossly unacceptable discrepancy in the state of the world's children is evident.

This chapter defines major risk factors for early childhood development (ECD; see Wachs & Rahman [2013], Chapter 5, this volume, for a more detailed analysis of risk factors) and provides key indicators of the situation of young children (birth to 5 years). Trends over time, across regions, and between and within countries are examined for these indicators. Finally, we speculate on some of the most critical factors that may emerge as risk factors for young children in the future. These risk factors are divided into those that immediately and directly affect the child, such as malnutrition or parent stimulation; and those at the community or broader social and environmental level, such as poverty or environmental toxicities, which affect the child through a variety of other pathways, such as the amount of food available or the access to high-quality services. These factors may not always have the same effect on children and vary depending on their context and other factors. As with any assessment across countries, we are dependent on those indicators that are available for young children, and here we attempt to identify the most important ones to assess regularly for understanding the large-scale effects of policy and intervention programs.

Key Indicators Analysis of Child and Family Risk Factors

The risk factors described in this chapter are those that have impacts on a child's cognitive, social, emotional, or motor development, often in addition to the child's physical development, health, and even survival. Many of the risk factors for poor development, or opportunities for improved development, are the same as those for survival and growth development. Table 3.1 presents a summary of all of these risk factors, and the approximate number of children affected.

Health Risks

KEY INDICATOR: UNDER-5 MORTALITY RATE

Survival

The greatest risk for child development is death. The infant and under-5 mortality rates (U5MR) indicate the probability of dying between birth and 12 months, or between birth and 5 years of age respectively, per 1,000 live births. Child mortality is often used as a barometer of child well-being in general, and child health in particular, because it is the result of a variety of factors in child life and family functioning, such as the nutritional status of children and mothers, the availability and use of maternal and child health services, income and food availability of the family, the availability of safe drinking water and sanitation, and the overall safety of environment.

Illnesses and Health: Malaria, HIV, Diarrhea

Most normal and even severe illnesses of childhood have not been linked specifically to developmental delays or poor cognitive development. However, there are some exceptions: malaria—in particular, cerebral malaria—has been associated with poorer levels of development, as has infection with HIV. Children who are HIV positive from birth are much more likely to show developmental impairment than are other children. In a recent review, Sherr et al. (2009) observed that in 36 out of 43 studies from both high-income and LAMI countries, detrimental effects of HIV infection on neurocognitive development were found. Evidence for the effects of diarrhea on a child's development has also been reported, but it appears to be mediated by the effects of diarrhea on stunting, which affects cognitive and social-emotional development (Walker et al., 2011).

TABLE 3.1 Prevalence of major risk factors for child development, effects on children, and the strength of the evidence that it is a risk factor by type of risk

Risk	Prevalence	Effects on Children	Strength of Evidence
NUTRITIONAL RISKS (CHILD AND FAMILY LEVEL)			
Stunting	25%–30%	6–13 DQ points (0.4–0.8 SD), social and emotional effects	Strong
Iodine deficiency	35%	9–13 IQ points (1 SD)	Strong
Iron deficiency anemia	20%–30%	1.73 IQ/10 g/L Hb; Some supplementation trials show benefits to motor, social-emotional, and cognitive development of 0.3–0.4 SD	Strong
Intrauterine growth retardation	11%	0.25 to 0.5 SD compared to non-LBW	Associated with developmental deficits to age 3 years; need for longitudinal studies
Lack of breast-feeding	40%–50%	Small effects on cognition (2–5 IQ points), may affect bonding	Consistent but small to moderate effects; hard to design good studies
Zinc deficiency	33%	Cognitive development and activity	Mixed results
PSYCHOSOCIAL RISKS (CHILD AND FAMILY LEVEL)			
Lack of child stimulation and learning opportunities	60%–90% of parents do not stimulate	Provision of stimulation/learning opportunities has benefits of 0.5–1.0 SD in IQ	Strong
Lack of preschool and alternate child care (day care, nonformal care)	Preschool attendance rates vary from 1% to 94% by country; with mean for 3- to 5-year-olds of 35%; Percent of mothers of young children working for earnings and using day care or informal systems not available	High quality care and preschool associated with cognitive benefits; less is known about effects of day care and day care quality in developing countries	Preschools: strong evidence of impact if quality is acceptable; little information about day care or alternative nonformal care
Maternal depression	17%, rates may be higher	0.5–1.0 SD in cognitive development scores	Correlations clear; need for treatment approaches
Child exposure to societal violence	Major armed conflict in 27%–38% countries from 1990–2003, affects 20 million children	Behavior problems, PTSD	Urgent need for research, particularly on interventions

(continued)

TABLE 3.1 (Continued)

Risk	Prevalence	Effects on Children	Strength of Evidence
Parental loss or parental illness; community affected by HIV	Over 43 m orphans in Sub-Saharan Africa, 16% below age 6 (7 million) in 2003	Descriptive studies show higher rates of mortality, some behavior problems, sense of vulnerability, depression, improves over time	Need for interventions and intervention research
Lack of maternal responsivity	Unknown	Associated with less secure attachment, lower cognitive ability, and more behavior problems	Need for more intervention studies
Abuse and neglect	Data for young children not readily available	Multiple; increase in aggression, long-term deficit in productivity	Strong in industrialized countries; not much data in developing countries
HEALTH-RELATED RISK FACTORS (CHILD AND FAMILY LEVEL)			
Malaria	40% of population in 90 countries: 300–600 million	Significant cognitive impairments associated with severe malaria or cerebral malaria, or number of episodes of malaria	Negative associations clear; needs further study
Intestinal helminths	33%	Cognitive development	Inconsistent results
HIV infection	2%	Can be severe; developmental delays, language delays, mortality in first 5 years if untreated	Evidence for risk is strong; little data on interventions
Diarrhea	Common	Some associations with cognitive development found	Suggestive; needs further study
ENVIRONMENTAL TOXICITIES (COMMUNITY AND ENVIRONMENTAL LEVEL)			
High lead levels	40%	2–5 IQ points	Correlational studies in developed and developing countries
Arsenic	High in areas such as Bangladesh	Lowered IQ	Correlational data; only investigated in older children
Manganese, pesticides	Depends on area	Lowered IQ	Some data available, but need for more

Sources: Grantham-McGregor, S., Cheung, Y. B., Cueto, S., Glewwe, P., Richter, L., Strupp, B., et al. (2007). Developmental potential in the first 5 years for children in developing countries. *The Lancet*, 369, 60–70; Walker, S. P., Wachs, T. D., Gardner, J. M., Lozoff, B., Wasserman, G. A., Pollitt, E., et al. (2007). Child development: Risk factors for adverse outcomes in developing countries. *The Lancet*, 369, 145–157.

NUTRITION RISKS

KEY INDICATOR: STUNTING

Walker et al. (2007) reviewed the evidence for the effects of nutritional conditions on ECD, and concluded that the three risks with the strongest evidence were stunting, iron deficiency, and iodine deficiency. Low birth weight and intrauterine growth retardation have also been linked with negative outcomes (Walker et al., 2011). Breast-feeding has been shown to be associated with improved cognitive development (Walker et al., 2011). These issues are discussed more fully in Chapter 10 (Yousafzai, Yakoob, & Bhutta, 2013).

Although a number of nutrition measures are reported (e.g., iodine deficiency, measured through surveys of the urine level of iodine in school-aged children; iron deficiency anemia, measured through blood samples; low birthweight), the most commonly available and easiest to collect measures are child height and weight. Child height for age is used to measure stunting. Stunting is defined as a height for age of less than 2 standard deviations below the norms developed by the World Health Organization (WHO) on a global sample of well-nourished, breast-fed children. Stunting has consistently been associated with poorer cognitive development and alterations in social development, and it is the best indicator of nutritional risk for impaired child development.

PSYCHOSOCIAL RISKS

KEY INDICATORS (PROXIES): LEARNING MATERIALS OR PARENTAL ACTIVITIES, QUALITY CHILD CARE, PRESCHOOL ATTENDANCE

Ideally, one would have a measurement of early child development, but a globally accepted indicator of children's capacities has not yet been developed. Hence, we rely on several proxy indicators of risk for poor development.

Quality of Home Stimulation

Two common proxies are the level of stimulation in the home, reflected here in (a) the number of activities with each child under 5 years in the last 3 days as reported by the mother, father, and all household members and (b) the presence of children's books and toys in the household. There is extensive evidence that reading books and home stimulation are positively associated with children's cognitive development (as measured by school-related, more Western tests) and with their school performance in early grades (Bradley & Corwyn, 2005; Hamadani, Tofail, Yesmin, Hud, Engle, & Grantham-McGregor, 2010; Maulik & Darmstadt, 2009) in low-, middle-, and high-income countries. Most of the common measures of quality of home stimulation focus on the mother's participation; far less is known about fathers' involvement with young children, but the

evidence does suggest that father involvement is an important contributing factor
to eventual achievement (Engle & Breaux, 1998) and should be tracked separately
if possible.

Preschool Participation

Another proxy for psychosocial risk to child development is lack of preschool participation. In a number of experiments with strong designs, a causal relationship
has been found between attendance at a high-quality preschool and later school
achievement and social development, particularly among the lowest income
segment of a population. As with parental activities, quality preschool participation has been shown to influence children's development, so it is a rough indicator
of a child's eventual development. However, as with measures of home stimulation, the characteristics of the family and the child will influence these behaviors
(stimulating child, sending child to preschool), so that they reflect a broader set of
parenting values, decisions, and investment strategies.

Quality of Alternate Child Care

Women's work increases the resources available in the household, which can be
used to promote child development—but it also decreases the mother's availability
to care for her children. Further, as noted in the United Nations (UN) Millennium
Development Goal (MDG) Report, "Women's access to paid employment is lower
than men's in most of the developing world...Women are less likely than men
to hold paid and regular jobs and more often work in the informal economy,
which provides little financial security" (UN, 2005). When women are engaged
in low-wage work and/or have unstable jobs, they cannot afford to pay for high-
quality child care, possibly resulting in impaired child development. Many women
in this situation rely on informal care systems or family members, who may or
may not provide high-quality care. For the purposes of monitoring this indicator,
measures of women's work are usually available, but types of alternate care are not
systematically tracked (Heymann, 2006).

CHILD PROTECTION RISKS

KEY INDICATORS: BIRTH REGISTRATION
AND VIOLENT PARENTAL DISCIPLINE

Child protection measures applicable to early childhood include registration of
births, percent of children with disabilities, percent of children without parental
care (including children in institutions and those in foster care), and percent of
children experiencing violent discipline.

Birth registration is considered protective (and the lack of it is a risk), not
only because it is every child's right, but also because many services, rights, and

privileges of a society depend on being a registered member of that society. School attendance, residence, even mobility may be linked to birth registration. Some cultural and ethnic groups are at much greater risk of not being registered than are others, thereby exacerbating the risk from social difference. The key indicator used here is birth registration, although at some point enough data on the others measures may become available. Data on the percent of children in non-parental care is not widely available, and percent in preschool is an underestimate.

Frequency of disability, defined as long-term physical, mental, intellectual or sensory impairments which in interaction with various barriers may hinder a person's full and effective participation in society on an equal basis with others. (Gottlieb, Maenner, Cappa, & Durkin, 2009), has been difficult to obtain, but UNICEF's 2005–2006 MICS survey of parents in 18 low- and middle-income countries (191, 199 children aged 2–9) reported a median of 23% with any kind of disability (ranging from 3% to 48%), and for children 2–4, 26% (range 4–51%) (Gottlieb et al., 2009). These frequencies are similar to a recent survey in Mexico and Cuba using a screening test rather than parent report, showing 22% of children with global delay (Guadarrama-Celaya et al., 2012).

"Violent" discipline, defined by the United Nations Children's Fund (UNICEF) as either physical punishment or verbal aggression, such as threatening or shouting (UNICEF, 2010), is considered to be damaging to the growing child's mind and social orientation. Several studies have tried to document the extent of corporal punishment for children of varying ages. Three different global surveys reviewed below all came to two conclusions.: over half of children aged 2–14 are reported to experience corporal punishment and about 15% experience severe physical punishment. Second, there is huge variability among countries.

In a study of 1417 families with children aged 7–10 in nine countries, Lansford et al. (2010) found that 54% of girls and 58% of boys had experienced mild physical punishment, and 13% of girls, and 14% of boys had experienced severe punishment. Among the six LAMI countries in their study, rates ranged from a low of 4% in Thailand to a high of 62% in Kenya. Runyan et al. (2010) examined parent reports of punishment of children aged 0–18 years using the Conflict Tactics scale in five LAMI countries and the United States, and found that 55% had used some kind of physical punishment, including 16% who used harsh punishment. Rates of physical punishment varied from a low of 15% among educated families in India to a high of 76% in rural Philippines. UNICEF (2010) reported data from the 2005–2006 MICS national surveys for 33 countries, and again found that about 50% of children aged 2–14 years had experienced physical punishment in the past month, and 17% had experienced severe physical punishment (e.g., being hit with an object). Over 75% of children had experienced either or both physical and psychological aggression (labeled violent punishment). As in the other studies, rates of violent punishment varied considerably by country from a low of 38% in Bosnia to a high of 95% in Yemen.

Summary of Evidence to Guide Programs and Policies

To evaluate the situation of children between and within countries and over time, we must have sufficient indicators. Some of the recommended indicators have not been assessed with a sufficiently representative sample to be useful in drawing valid conclusions. Therefore, in order to have the best information available to examine changes over time and between and within countries, we have selected one or two indicators from each of the four areas: U5MR, stunting, parent stimulation, preschool participation, birth registration, and parent discipline.

SURVIVAL: UNDER-5 MORTALITY RATE

The UN MDG4 calls for a two-thirds reduction in the mortality rate of children under 5 years of age between 1990 and 2015. Since 1990, the overall number of deaths of children under 5 has declined from 12.5 million annually to 8.8 million in 2008 (Figure 3.1), and the rate of deaths per 1,000 has declined from 90 to 65 from 1990 to 2008.

The rate of decline in under-5 mortality increased to an average annual rate of 2.2% in 2000–2006, compared with 1.4% for 1990–2000. However, progress is still insufficient to reach MDG4 by 2015—it needs to be accelerated to over 5% per year to meet this goal. Globally, of the 191 countries with adequate data, UNICEF estimates that 129 are on track to meet the MDG goal having reduced the U5MR to below 40 per 1,000 live births. An additional 35 countries are making progress, but at an insufficient rate to meet MDG4. Finally, the real concern is with 27 countries that have registered scant progress or have U5MRs that are stagnant or

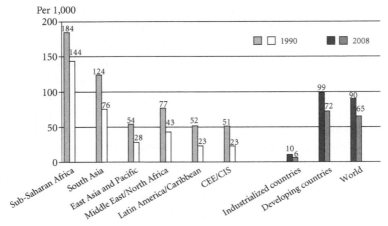

FIGURE 3.1 *Significant declines in under-5 mortality rates between 1990 and 2008 in all regions*

Source: UNICEF. (2009). *Tracking progress on child and maternal nutrition.* New York: Author.

even higher than in 1990. Although there have been significant declines in U5MRs in all regions of the world, Sub-Saharan Africa accounted for half of child death worldwide in 2008, and South Asia accounted for one-third of child deaths in 2008. These regions still lag behind others.

There is a growing concern as well that the progress that has been made, based on national averages, conceals within-country disparities. Across all regions, on average, the U5MR is more than twice as high for the poorest fifth of the households as for the richest fifth. It is also higher in rural populations, among less educated mothers, for boys rather than girls, and among minority population groups. Most troubling, in some countries, a mean reduction of under-5 mortality has been accompanied by increasing inequity between rich and poor (Figure 3.2). For example, in 18 of 26 countries with a decline in U5MR of 10% or more, inequality between the poorest fifth and richest fifth of households either increased or stayed the same, as shown by the cases in the upper left quadrant of Figure 3.2. Only those countries in the bottom left quadrant are both reducing mortality and reducing inequality. Thus, progress overall in some countries is resulting in increased disparities.

Many causes or factors are related to child deaths. Primary among these is insufficient knowledge of how to care for young children, which may lead to poor caregiving practices, such as lack of breastfeeding. Second is limited access to and utilization of health, nutrition, and other basic social services for young children and their mothers, and for pregnant and lactating women. A third factor is the absence of policies that have a special focus on the most marginalized and deprived children. Relatedly, a fourth factor is the insufficient allocation of

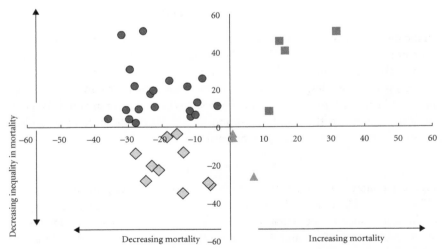

FIGURE 3.2 *Increasing inequity in reducing under-5 mortality (circles: decreasing mortality but increasing inequality)*

Source: UNICEF. (2010). *Progress for Children: Achieving the MDGs with Equity.* New York: Author.

human and financial resources to maternal, newborn, and child health. Most of these causes or factors related to child death are rooted in poverty, discrimination, and social exclusion.

The Countdown Initiative (UNICEF 2008b), established in 2005 to reduce U5MR, promotes the following immediate actions by governments:

- Sustain and expand equitable coverage for priority interventions. Barriers to universal coverage of health services can be overcome by prioritizing diseases of the poor, deploying services where the poor live, removing financial barriers, and monitoring coverage and impact with an "equity lens." In other words, not only the mean levels of indicators, but also inequities in these indicators should be tracked.
- Ensure a "continuum of care" for mother and baby, linking the places of caregiving (households, communities, and health facilities) and linking across the times of caregiving (adolescence, pregnancy, birth, postpartum, neonatal, infancy, childhood). As child mortality rates fall, neonatal deaths (in the first month of life) are becoming the most frequent type of mortality. Therefore, within the concept of continuum of care, special focus should be given during the pre-, peri-, and immediate postnatal period (Figure 3.3).
- Prioritize improvement of the nutritional status of mothers and young children.
- Strengthen the health system.
- Set geographic and population priorities for the reduction of mortality rates.

NUTRITION: STUNTING

In the developing world, malnutrition and stunting continue to be one of the largest contributors to child mortality and to reducing a child's potential for development. In the developing world, stunting affects approximately 195 million children under 5 years of age, despite a reduction from 40% in 1990 to 29% in 2008. Changes have not been the same in all regions; change has been greater in South Asia than in other regions. In the Middle East and North Africa, the percent of under-5 children suffering from stunting is increasing.

Variation by Region

Figure 3.4 shows, by region, the percent of children whose growth was stunted (UNICEF, 2009). Almost all stunted children live in the least developed regions of the world, such as Sub-Saharan Africa and South Asia. The highest rates are in West and Central Africa and East and Southern Africa, with South Asia not far behind. On the other hand, in three regions (Central and Eastern Europe and the Commonwealth of Independent States; CEE/CIS. East Asia and the Pacific, and Latin America and the Caribbean), the rates are less than 15%.

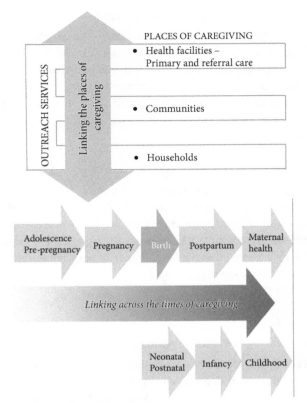

FIGURE 3.3 *Continuum of care in time and place*
Source: UNICEF. (2010). Presentation at the Executive Board. Unpublished.

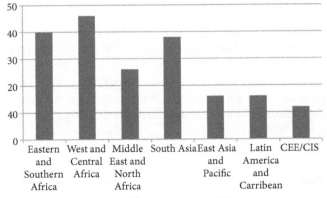

FIGURE 3.4 *Percent of children stunted, by region, 2003–2008*
Source: UNICEF. (2009). *Tracking progress on child and maternal nutrition.* New York: Author.

Variation by Country

The prevalence of stunting in developing countries varies from 1% to 60%. The highest rates are 59% and 58% in children under 5 in Afghanistan and Yemen, respectively, whereas the lowest rates are in Chile and Croatia, with only 1% of children stunted. With a high prevalence of stunting (48%) and a large population, India alone has an estimated 61 million stunted children who are under 5 years, accounting for more than 3 out of every 10 stunted children in the developing world.

Variation Within Countries

Rates of stunting are much higher in rural than in urban areas, although the differences are less marked in European countries, which have lower levels of stunting. In all countries, over twice as many children from the poorest quintile are stunted compared to the highest quintile. The rates of stunting in the richest quintile range from almost none to 25% in Sierra Leone, whereas for the poorest quintile, they range from 6% in Belarus to over 50% in Laos.

PSYCHOSOCIAL DEVELOPMENT

Child Development Levels

As noted earlier, no globally accepted child development tests are available presently, although several efforts are being made to develop an assessment tool that can be used across countries in East Asia (Asia Pacific Regional Network for Early Childhood [ARNEC]), Latin America (Inter-American Development Bank), and globally (UNICEF Multiple Indicator Cluster Survey, MICS4 ECD module). These efforts will provide a stronger base for programming and policies in ECD.

Perhaps the most extensive effort to measure child development in LAMI countries has been initiated by the World Bank (Fernald, Weber, Galasso, & Ratsifandrihamanana, 2010, Nadeau, Martinez, Premand, & Filmer, 2011). Using data from Ecuador, Nicaragua, Madagascar, Mozambique, and Cambodia, comparisons by age and socioeconomic status (SES) were possible. In all five countries, the Peabody Picture Vocabulary Test, a measure of receptive language for children ranging in age from 2.5 to 18 years, was used. To respond to test items, the child must select the correct picture representing a vocabulary word (noun or verb) from four pictures. Although the test has many limitations, such as being subject to cultural differences and therefore underestimating ability in some cultures, the associations with SES and age are strikingly similar across the five countries. In each case, differences by SES were small at age 3, the youngest age at which the test can be administered, and the differences by SES widen as children approach school age. These findings are consistent with a number of studies that have described a cumulative deficit or increasingly wide differences between rich and poor as children grow and as language becomes a larger portion of the test battery. These results illustrate the benefits of having a measure, even if imperfect, to provide an impetus for actions to confront the major inequalities in early child development in LAMI countries.

Nadeau et al. (2011) and Fernald et al. (2010) found that even though SES appears to be strongly associated with the child's cognitive development, home stimulation and nutrition play major independent roles in child development; they continue to be significant predictors of cognitive development even when controlling for SES. Many studies in the past have found that home stimulation is a mediating factor between SES and children's cognitive development (e.g., Bradley & Corwyn, 2005).

Learning Materials: Books and Toys for Young Children

The number of children's books in the home varied markedly across regions and family wealth (Figure 3.5). Children from Sub-Saharan Africa and the Middle East had fewer books than those from other regions.

The availability of toys at home is very low in most settings, according to our analysis of the MICS3 data. The percent of families that have two or more sources

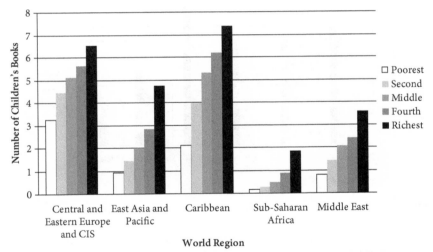

FIGURE 3.5 *Mean number of children's books in household by a sample of countries within each region and within-country wealth quintile. Thirty-three countries are surveyed. MICS3. Central and Eastern Europe, Commonwealth of Independent States: Eleven countries (Albania, Bosnia, Georgia, Kazakhstan, Kyrgyzstan, Macedonia, Montenegro, Serbia, Tajikistan, Uzbekistan, Ukraine); East Asia and Pacific: Five countries (Laos, Mongolia, Thailand, Vanuatu, Vietnam); Caribbean: Five countries (Belize, Guyana, Jamaica, Surinam, Trinidad and Tobago); Sub-Saharan Africa: Eight countries (Cameroon, Central African Republic, Djibouti, Ghana, Ivory Coast, Nigeria, Sierra Leone, Togo); Middle East: Three countries (Lebanon, Syria, Yemen). Source: MICS3 data from Childinfo.org; analyses by author.*

of toys for children (purchased, homemade, found in the home, or natural objects) varies across countries. The country in which the highest percent of families has access to two or more types of toys is Sierra Leone, at 52%, and the lowest are Mongolia (6%), Georgia (6%), Vietnam (4%), Djibouti (4%), and Macedonia (2%). In these five countries, however, almost all children have access to purchased toys, and tend not to use other of types of toys.

Family Activities

Family activities were measured by asking the caregiver to report whether she, the child's father, or any other member of the family over the age of 15 had done any activities with children in the last 3 days. The questions were asked for each specific activity: telling stories, singing songs, playing, taking the child outside to a market, reading books, or counting, drawing, and naming. A sum was constructed for mother activities, father activities, and total household members' activities (Figures 3.6 and 3.7).

Mean number of mothers' activities out of six is shown for sampled countries within regions and by within-country measures of family wealth in Figure 3.6.

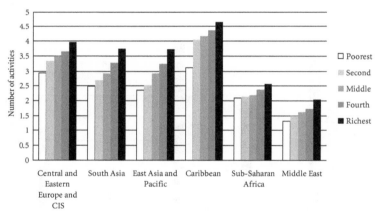

FIGURE 3.6 *Mean number of mothers' activities for sampled countries within regions and within-country wealth quintile. Thirty-eight countries surveyed (MICS3).Central and Eastern Europe, Commonwealth of Independent States: Eleven countries (Albania, Belarus, Bosnia, Georgia, Kazakhstan, Kyrgyzstan, Macedonia, Montenegro, Serbia, Tajikistan, Uzbekistan); South Asia: One country (Bangladesh); East Asia and Pacific: Five countries (Laos, Mongolia, Thailand, Vanuatu, Vietnam); Caribbean: Five countries (Belize, Guyana, Jamaica, Surinam, Trinidad and Tobago); Sub-Saharan Africa: Fourteen countries (Burkina Faso, Burundi, Cameroon, Central African Republic, Djibouti, Gambia, Ghana, Guinea-Bissau, Ivory Coast, Mauritania, Nigeria, Sierra Leone, Somalia, Togo); Middle East: Two countries (Iraq, Yemen).*

Source: MICS3 data from Childinfo.org; analyses by author.

Reprinted from Engle, P. L., Lia C.H. Fernald, L. C. H., Alderman, H., et al. (2011). Strategies for reducing inequalities and improving developmental outcomes for young children in low-income and middle-income countries. *Lancet*, 378(9799), 1339–1353, with permission from Elsevier.

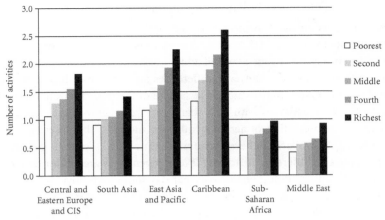

FIGURE 3.7 *Mean number of fathers' activities by sampled countries within regions and within-country wealth quintile. Thirty-eight countries surveyed (MICS3). Central and Eastern Europe, Commonwealth of Independent States: Eleven countries (Albania, Belarus, Bosnia, Georgia, Kazakhstan, Kyrgyzstan, Macedonia, Montenegro, Serbia, Tajikistan, Uzbekistan); South Asia: One country (Bangladesh); East Asia and Pacific: Five countries (Laos, Mongolia, Thailand, Vanuatu, Vietnam); Caribbean: Five countries (Belize, Guyana, Jamaica, Surinam, Trinidad and Tobago); Sub-Saharan Africa: Fourteen countries (Burkina Faso, Burundi, Cameroon, Central African Republic, Djibouti, Gambia, Ghana, Guinea-Bissau, Ivory Coast, Mauritania, Nigeria, Sierra Leone, Somalia, Togo); Middle East: Two countries (Iraq, Yemen).*

Reprinted from Engle, P. L., Lia C.H. Fernald, L. C. H., Alderman, H., et al. (2011). Strategies for reducing inequalities and improving developmental outcomes for young children in low-income and middle-income countries. Lancet, 378(9799), 1339–1353, with permission from Elsevier. *Source:* MICS3 data from Childinfo.org; analyses by author.

Mothers' activities are most frequent in the Caribbean and lowest in the Middle East.

Maternal support for learning or doing activities with children varied by income level within country, although only one of the six activities requires additional funds (reading a book). These differences were seen in all areas except sub-Saharan Africa, where maternal activities were less common in general.

Fathers' Involvement in the Child's Activities

Fathers' direct involvement in child activities remains low in many countries, as seen in Figure 3.7. These figures, shown for sampled countries within regions and by family wealth within region, show the number of activities mothers report fathers doing with their children in the past 3 days. Fathers are doing less than a third of the number of activities that mothers are reporting across countries and income levels.

Differences in Parenting Interactions by Gender

Whether parents engaged in more activities with the same-sex or opposite-sex child was tested with the MICS3 data. The analysis did not show significant differences in household engagement (all adults) based on a child's gender for most of the countries surveyed. However, differences are found as a function of child age and parent gender. Across the entire sample of 170,000 children, mothers do significantly more activities with girls than boys from age 2–3 through age 4–5, but there is no interaction of age by gender for mothers; the difference is constant across age. Similarly, fathers spend more time with boys than girls at every age. However, this difference in activity levels by gender is greater for fathers than mothers, with fathers doing one activity per day more with boys than with girls beginning at age 2–3 years. The interaction of age and gender is also significant for boys—the older the child (up to age 5), the more activities fathers do with boys over girls. Thus, although boys receive slightly less attention from mothers than do girls, girls receive much less attention from fathers than do boys, and the difference increases with age (Sun, Rao, Zhang, & Engle, 2011).

Women's Work and Low-Quality Child Care

Paid employment for women is considered good for women, good for children (as women are more likely than fathers to invest their extra income to promote child well-being), and therefore good for the nation. It is estimated that women perform 66% of the world's work, produce 50% of the food, but earn 10% of the income (UNICEF, 2007b). Within the developing world, in some regions, women provide 70% of agricultural labor (World Economic Forum, 2005) and form about 60%–80% of the export manufacturing workforce (World Bank, 2009a). However, despite differences in size, geographic location, and income level, data from a variety of developing countries suggest that about 50%–80% of nonagricultural employment is informal (UNIFEM, 2005). Hence, in developing country contexts, women have less job security and fewer benefits than do men because they make up the majority of the part-time and temporary workforce.

The dearth of adequate child care is considered a barrier to poor women engaging in paid employment, and the lack of income negatively impacts child development. As noted above, in the developing world, many women with low levels of education work in the informal economy for very low wages and cannot afford to pay for child care (World Bank, 2009b); their older children thus may not attend school and instead stay home to look after their younger siblings. Women who engage in low-wage, insecure, and physically demanding work may have little time and energy to interact with their young children when they return home. Hence, this type of work may contribute to (lack of) parental activities with children and is considered a risk factor for poor child development.

Who looks after these children when the mother is at work? The best case is that the child is in high-quality child care or looked after by female relatives in an extended family situation. When there is neither family support nor high-quality and affordable day care centers, families may have to resort to poor-quality child care, leading to poorer outcomes for children. If working families have less time for stimulating young children, the children may be doubly disadvantaged.

Preschool Participation

Preschool participation rates have also changed over time, with the fastest increase in Latin America and the Caribbean; some areas, however, actually show decreasing rates of preschool attendance (Figure 3.8). Although preprimary education appears to be expanding in much of the world, there is a notable difference between developing regions. Latin America and the Caribbean have been experiencing rapid advancements since the 1980s, whereas Sub-Saharan Africa and the Arab States still show gross enrollment ratios below 20.

Figure 3.9 shows preschool attendance rates of 3- to 4-year-olds from UNICEF's MICS3 data, according to income levels for sampled countries by region. This figure illustrates, as one might expect, that preschool attendance varies more by income level than do mother and father play activities. Differences are marked in the CEE/CIS as well as in some of the West African countries.

CHILD PROTECTION

Birth Registration

The lack of a birth certificate may prevent a child from receiving most forms of child protection, such as health care. In 2007, about 51 million children's births were not registered, about half of them in South Asia. The other regions are doing well with respect to birth registration rates (see Figure 3.10).

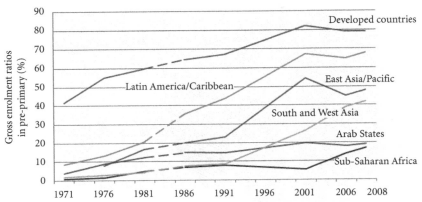

FIGURE *3.8 Regional trends in preprimary gross enrolment ratios of children aged 3–6 (1970–2008)*

Sources: EFA Global Monitoring Reports 2007, 2010, and 2011.

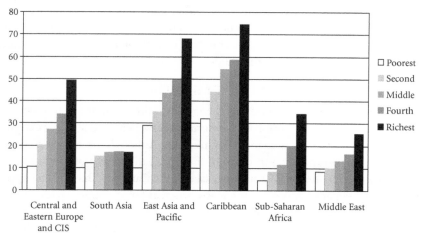

FIGURE 3.9 *Proportion of young children attending preschool in 58 low- and middle-income countries by income quintile within country, summed across sampled countries within region. Countries sampled in each region are Burkina Faso, Burundi, Cameroon, Central African Republic, Djibouti, Gambia, Ghana, Guinea-Bissau, Ivory Coast, Malawi, Mauritania, Nigeria, Sierra Leone, Somalia, Togo (Sub-Saharan Africa); Bangladesh (South Asia); Laos, Mongolia, Thailand, Vanuatu, Vietnam (East Asia and Pacific); Belize, Guyana, Jamaica, Suriname, Trinidad and Tobago (Caribbean); Albania, Belarus, Bosnia and Herzegovina, Georgia, Kazakhstan, Kyrgyzstan, Macedonia, Serbia, Tajikistan, Ukraine, Uzbekistan (Central and Eastern Europe, Commonwealth of Independent States and Baltic states); Iraq, Lebanon, Syria, Yemen (Middle East). Percent of 3- and 4-year-olds whose caregivers reported that they attended an organized early learning center by income quintile.*

Source: MICS3 – Childinfo.org. Data are from the UNICEF's 2005 Multiple Indicator Cluster Survey 3 for children aged 3 and 4.

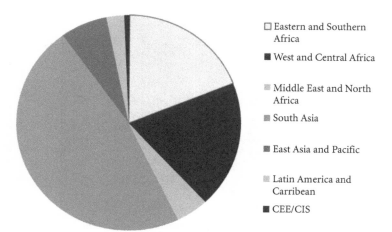

FIGURE 3.10 *Birth registration by region (% of children not registered in region)*
Source: Childinfo.org and MICS3 data (2005).

Violent Punishment

Although the highest rates of punishment appear to be directed to children aged 5–9 years, according to parental report, recent MICS3 data (see Figure 3.11) suggest that children ranging in age from 2 to 4 years in most countries experience relatively high rates of violent discipline, defined as either use of physical punishment or verbal aggression (yell, threaten) (UNICEF, 2010).

Critical Community and Environmental Risk Factors

The most critical risk factors include the interrelated issues of poverty, social exclusion, and gender. Poverty is a proxy for factors such as low social class, lack of food security, poor access and quality of services, economic shocks, and low levels of choice. All of these factors are made more challenging by economic crises and emergencies.

POVERTY

Children growing up in poverty are frequently exposed to multiple and cumulative risks. These include the biological risks described above, such as nutritional deficiencies, low birth weight, and exposure to environmental toxins. The greater the number of risks to which a child is exposed, the more a child's development is compromised (Wachs, 2000; Walker et al., 2007), and the impact of exposure to these biological risk factors can be exacerbated by poverty. Similarly, whereas known psychological risk factors such as of lack of stimulation, low maternal responsivity, parental loss, abuse and neglect, and maternal depression may occur across a wide variety of economic levels, the combined effect of these problems

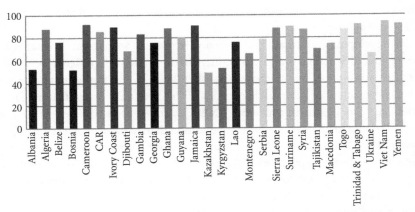

FIGURE 3.11 *Percentage of children aged 2–4 years experiencing violent punishment (physical punishment or psychological aggression) in the past month by parent report*

Source: UNICEF. (2010). *Progress for children: Achieving the MDGs with equity.* New York: Author.

with poverty exacerbates the problems. Poverty is one of the most pervasive sources of disadvantage in education because the cost of schooling competes with other basic needs, such as health care and food.

How should poverty be defined? Should it be considered solely in economic terms, or as part of a broader social disadvantage? The economic definition of poverty is typically based on income measures, with the absolute poverty line calculated as the food expenditure necessary to meet dietary recommendations, supplemented by a small allowance for nonfood goods (Ravallion, 1992). However, many poverty researchers use a broader definition for "poor," including not only lack of material assets and health, but also lack of social capital, including social belonging, cultural identity, respect and dignity, and information and education (Sen, 1995). Tilly (2007) adds social exclusion, which prevents groups or categories of peoples from moving out of poverty The complex and multifaceted conditions that prevent people from moving out of poverty in developing countries are illustrated in 60,000 interviews from 60 countries in *Voices of the Poor* (Narayan, & Petesch, 2002),

Poverty is a dynamic process, with some families cycling in and out of poverty in a relatively short time, resulting in intermittent rather than persistent poverty. In a study of 30,000 households in India, Peru, and Uganda, Krishna (2007) reported that nearly one-third of individuals currently living in poverty were not born poor. Mobility out of poverty has been described as the interaction of (a) changes in the *opportunity structure,* consisting of the dominant institutional climate and social structures within which disadvantaged actors must work to advance their interests; and (b) changes in the capabilities of poor individuals or groups to take purposeful actions—that is, to exercise *agency* (Narayan & Petesch, 2007). An individual's agency depends on individual assets, such as education and self-confidence, and collective and family assets, such as organization, identity, and having a voice. Much of the risks described in this chapter relate to lack of agency, but the social structures noted above may limit a sense of agency.

In developing countries, children living in poverty are at much greater risk of never attending school than are wealthier children, and these differences are wide (e.g., in a sample of 80 countries, 12% of children in the top quintile of households never attended school, whereas 38% of children in the poorest quintile never attended school (Bruneforth, 2006; UNESCO, 2006). These differences are more highly related to wealth and mothers' education than to urban/rural residence and gender (UNESCO, 2006). Children raised in poverty also achieve less in school. Analyses show strong positive relationships between SES and student achievement across countries, across age levels, and across academic areas of study (UNESCO, 2006). Further, SES differences in achievement scores (often called *socioeconomic gradients*) exist within most countries, reflecting SES-related inequality in educational outcomes (Ross, Zuze, & Ratsatsi, 2005).

SOCIAL EXCLUSION

As noted earlier, social exclusion can be considered one indicator of poverty. Social barriers are risk factors for a child's development because they may result in exclusion from education. Other social factors associated with exclusion from education include speaking a minority language, remote residence, and physical or intellectual disabilities.

GENDER

Being a girl is a risk factor for development and survival. A most worrying trend is the "missing girl" phenomenon in the under-6 population in countries in the developing world, where son preference is prevalent. In the absence of sex selection practices, the usual sex ratio at birth is 105 males to 100 females (Guilmoto, 2009). The imbalance in sex ratios during the early childhood period in China and India is marked. In India, sex ratios are reported based on 100 for males: In 2000, the male-to-female ratio was 100 to 92.7 for the birth to 6 years age group (Government of India, 2001), but the sex ratio at birth has begun to improve since 2001 (Sharma & Haub, 2008). The skewed sex ratios reflect discrimination against females in Indian society, especially since these low ratios are evident in all age groups. As a composite indicator, it captures unfavorable practices including female infanticide and feticide and the neglect of girls through inadequate nutrition and health care, little or no education, early marriage, premature child bearing, and poor maternal nutrition. Son preference is the outcome of cultural, social, and religious beliefs and social norms, and cuts across all strata of society.

China also has a serious gender imbalance. In 2005, the sex ratio at birth in China was 114 boys to 100 girls. Again, caution must be exercised in interpreting national figures because they conceal disparities within countries. This difference was greatest in provinces with strong traditional cultures (Li, 2007). For example, Jiangxi and Henan provinces had ratios of over 140 boys to 100 girls in the 1 to 4 age group (Zhu & Lu, 2009). Some areas within China (as well as in India and other affected countries) show relatively little son preference.

On other indicators, gender differences are more mixed. In an analysis of MICS3 data on preschool attendance, gender did not seem to affect preprimary participation rates (Nonoyama-Tarumi, Loaza, & Engle, 2009). However, in some areas, gender affects the quality of preschool that a child attends, with boys being sent to higher quality preschools in India. Gender differences in stunting have not been consistently found, although gender differences in mortality may mask these differences. In some areas, boys are more likely to be malnourished than girls (Kabubo-Mariara, Ndenge, & Mwabu, 2006). Gender differences in school attendance were very high in some areas, but have declined recently.

Emerging Issues

THE GLOBAL ECONOMIC CRISIS

The *Global Monitoring Report 2010: The MDGs After the Crisis* (World Bank, 2009) has suggested a number of possible consequences of an economic crisis such as the one that occurred in 2008. Whereas there has been a tendency for indicators of human development to decline more in bad times than they improve in good times, it remains to be seen if the recent economic crisis will have a similar result. The global poverty rate is expected to increase after a crisis; current projections are 15% in 2015 instead of the 14.1% projected before the crisis, thus improvements made in decreasing poverty may be nullified in the aftermath of the recent crisis. Poverty adversely affects access to education as the cost of schooling competes with other basic needs, and food and health care expenditures may exhaust limited resources. It is noteworthy that young children are those most vulnerable to the effects of poverty (World Bank, 2009). Slower economic growth has a negative effect on access to early childhood education programs. Further, trend analyses of child mortality under 5, access to safe drinking water, and gender parity in primary and secondary education indicate that all are negatively impacted by lower economic growth rates. These factors could be more severe and have harmful consequences should a deteriorating economy cause reforms to be abandoned or policies to be reversed.

In addition to the global economic crisis, other global crises can have very harmful effects on humanity. According to UNESCO, "Four interrelated global crises are mutually reinforcing each other: climate change, the energy crisis, the food crisis and the financial and economic crisis. The consequences of these crises for development are likely to be devastating, hence the urgent need to develop effective counterstrategies" (UNESCO, 2009b).

SOCIAL CHANGE, URBANIZATION, AND MIGRATION

The world is rapidly becoming urban. Over 70% of the population in industrialized countries and Latin America are urban, with the CEE/CIS and the Middle East and North Africa not far behind (63% and 58%, respectively). At the lower end, East Asia is rapidly urbanizing (42%), as is Sub-Saharan Africa (36%); the least urbanized area to date is South Asia (28%) (UNICEF, 2006b). Large-scale migration to urban areas can be a risk factor for ECD, whether or not parents leave their children behind in rural areas. For example, China's urban population has been increasing at a rate of 1% per annum in recent years. In 2005, the migrant population living in cities was about 147 million. It is expected that another 300 million people will move from rural areas to cities within the next decade. This migration has clearly strained public services in the cities, and the state still faces challenges to ensure that these migrants enjoy rights related to medical service, health care, social security, and children's education (Chinese National Centre for Education Development Research & Chinese National Commission for UNESCO, 2008). At the same time, there are concerns that the learning needs of children "left behind" with grandparents or other relatives in rural areas may be neglected. In some countries, high rates of migration have left many women to manage large families and farming on their own. Many mothers worry that they have neither the time nor the knowledge to help their children learn, grow, and develop. In other parts of the world, both internal and international migration are associated with emergencies and conflict. Countries that have received the largest percentage of migrants are often those least able to handle them. This migration is often due to conflict and natural or man-made disasters.

In simple comparisons of urban and rural children, urban children almost always have better outcomes, possibly due to greater wealth in urban families. However, there are other differences between rural and urban families besides wealth. Urban families tend to be smaller, more educated, and have more access to services; in addition, there are rural–urban differences in caregiver beliefs and rearing practices (Bornstein & Lamb, 2008). Sachs (2005) has proposed that remoteness in itself is a risk factor, with greater poverty associated with more remote location, even in rural areas.

EMERGENCIES AND CONFLICT

Emergencies, both natural disasters and human conflict, have a huge cost for infants and young children. These costs are normally considered to be health and nutrition risks, but there is increasing awareness of the psychosocial impacts of emergencies on caregivers and young children. Not only do risk factors include depression, but also exposure to violence may be more common in these situations. Lustig (2009) outlines the effects of the separations and chaotic experiences of refugee children and interventions that have been shown to make a difference.

EXPOSURE TO TOXINS

Infants are more likely to be exposed to toxins in the developing world than in the industrialized world—but much exposure is unknown and unreported (Engle, 2010). Stein et al. (2002) point out that although there are 80,000 chemicals in regular use, with about 3,000 new ones added each year, only 12 have been studied for their effects on child development. Although some think of pollution as being greater in industrialized countries, a recent summary of the top 10 most polluted cities in the world found that all were in developing countries— two in China, two in India, one in Peru, four in Russia and the former Soviet republics, and one in Zambia (http://www.time.com/time/specials/packages/completelist/0,29569,1661031,00.html). These are often cities with unregulated manufacturing and mining plants producing coal gas and particulates pollution, or are cities with mines and industries spewing out lead, heavy metals, chromium, or cadmium. Too often, toxin safeguards are either not present or remain unrecognized as important, as in the former Soviet Union. As a result, people live in desperate circumstances that include toxic exposures far beyond what is acceptable.

Mercury was one of the first substances to have its toxicity identified (Stein et al., 2002). More recently, Walker et al. (2007), documented negative effects of manganese, arsenic, lead, and pesticides on cognitive development in developing countries. In a study in Tongling, China, Tang et al. (2008) found that 2-year-olds who had higher levels of polycyclic aromatic hydrocarbons (PAH) from coal-burning plants and lead in their umbilical cord blood scored significantly lower on a test of developmental functioning than those who had had no signs of either lead or PAH.

One of the most tragic cases of toxin exposure resulted from thousands of wells dug in Bangladesh and eastern India to help the region deal with water shortages. Later, it was learned that these wells were contaminated with arsenic. Studies on the long-term effects of arsenic suggest that there will probably be impacts of various kinds on exposed children (Calderon et al., 2001; Tsai, Chou, The, Chen, & Chen, 2003; Wasserman et al., 2004). These children are particularly at risk of suffering from the adverse effects of high exposures to arsenic (at concentrations of 100 μg/L and more), which is widespread in well water, since no alternative drinking water sources are accessible to them.

The effects of alcohol and nicotine on the developing fetus are now well recognized; not only do they cause low birth weight, but there is evidence of short- and long-term effects on mental functioning (Stein et al., 2002; WHO, 2003). In the United States, the rate of women's smoking dropped from 34% in 1965 to 22% in 1999, but the rate continues to be high in many developing countries and is likely to increase (WHO, 2003). Further, rates of smoking by men are extremely high in many developing countries, with more than 60% of men smoking in western Asia, Russia, Mongolia, Yemen, and Kenya (WHO, 2003). Thus, in these countries, even though women on the whole are smoking relatively little, they are exposed to a tremendous amount of passive smoke. The losses due to cigarette smoking include not only health risks to parents and risks to children's health and development, but also a loss of income for the family, deforestation for growing tobacco, and misuse of agricultural land.

Similarly, although in industrialized countries there is increasing awareness of the negative effects of alcohol on fetal development, alcohol use is on the rise in some developing regions. In its global status report in 2004, the WHO reported that the highest rates of alcohol dependence among women were in South Africa (9.9%) and Brazil (5.9%), only slightly higher than in the United States (4.8%) (WHO, 2004). Heavy drinking among women was highest in Nigeria (36%), the United Kingdom (42%), Columbia (21%), and Uganda (20%) (WHO, 2004). These rates refer to all women, and do not distinguish pregnant from nonpregnant women. Current figures suggest that overall rates are decreasing in the European and American regions, but increasing slightly in the East Asia and West Asia regions, although from an already low level (WHO, 2004).

Maternal alcohol consumption during pregnancy can result in fetal alcohol syndrome in children, and parental drinking is correlated with child abuse. Drinking impacts a child's environment in many social, psychological, and economic ways. Parents' alcohol intake can impair performance as a parent, as a spouse or partner, and as a contributor to household functioning. Excessive alcohol intake may reduce time with families, increase expenditures outside the home, result in fewer resources for families, and increase chances of child neglect and abuse (WHO, 2004). The neglect of young children due to alcohol abuse means that these children often are undersocialized, which leads to reduced school attendance, and they may be driven to begging for or stealing food to survive (Molamu & MacDonald, 1996 cited in WHO, 2004).

Conclusion

It has been estimated that over 200 million under-5 children around the world do not develop adequately because they live in poverty and have poor health services, nutrition, and care (Grantham-McGregor et al., 2007). These children are at risk for delayed development and for underachievement at school, and poor child development has costs in terms of both psychological well-being and economic development (Grantham-McGregor et al., 2007). The countries with the highest percent of children not achieving their potential tend to be in South and West Asia and Sub-Saharan Africa.

Yet, integrated, intensive, long-lasting, high-quality early childhood interventions are effective in promoting child development and can reduce the loss of young children's development potential (Engle et al., 2007). The need for these programs will increase as the challenges of the next decade increase pressure on the poorest.

The sharp distinction between the old "First World" and "Third World" countries is disappearing, replaced by the emergence of a continuum of child well-being around the world. Overall, the situation of young children globally is improving in the areas of health, nutrition, and preschool participation, but disparities within countries are still large and, in many cases, increasing. In addition, national-level statistics mask increasing unevenness in the level of improvement (or in some cases, decay). Not all children are benefitting equally from improvements.

As the global stresses of climate change, the energy crisis, the food crisis, and the financial and economic crisis come together, the consequences will be felt unequally. They will be greatest for young children because they are the most vulnerable. Ironically, the children—and, in many cases, their impoverished countries—have played no part in creating these problems. If we are concerned about each child's rights, we must track these changes and urgently work toward protecting our most vulnerable citizens from our own ignorance and folly.

RECOMMENDATIONS

- *Reduce disparities within and across countries.* Although the conditions of young children in LAMI countries are generally improving, disparities are increasing in most countries.
- *Increase access to early child development programs and services,* and provide more learning materials for children, particularly for the most disadvantaged, to prevent multiple disadvantages. Families with less access to services also tend to provide fewer books and toys, and somewhat lower levels of parental stimulation.
- *Collect accurate data.* Governments should exert efforts to collect accurate data on mortality, stunting, and access to preschool programs. Data should be disaggregated by age, gender, and area or residence, and, in the case of preschool attendance, by the type of program attended.
- *Document changes.* Document changes in social, demographic, and climate change factors that may put the development of young children at even greater risk.
- *Continue to exert efforts to develop a global tool to assess early child development.* A tool that can be used to document and track progress on child development indicators is urgently needed.

References

Bornstein, M., & Lamb, M. E. (2008). *Development in infancy: An introduction (5e).* Mahwah, NJ: Erlbaum.

Bradley, R. H., & Corwyn, R. F. (2005). Caring for children around the world: A view from HOME. *International Journal of Behavioral Development, 29,* 468–478.

Bruneforth, M. (2006). *Characteristics of children who drop out of school and comments on the drop-out population compared to the population of out-of-school population.* EFA Global Monitoring Report 2006. Paris: UNESCO.

Calderon, J., Navarro, M. E., Jimenez-Capdeville, M. E., Santos-Diaz, M. A., Golden, A., Rodriguez-Leyva, I., et al. (2001). Exposure to arsenic and lead and neuropsychological development in Mexican children. *Environment Research Journal, 8,* 69–76.

Chinese National Centre for Education Development Research & Chinese National Commission for UNESCO. (2008). *National report on mid-term assessment of Education for All in China.* Retrieved from http://www.un.org.cn/public/resource/f159de42fcf9d 1559de2b7f47f0ad3a6.pdf

Engle, P. L. (2010). Infant development in the developing world. In J. Gavin Bremner & T. D. Wachs (Eds.), *The Wiley-Blackwell handbook of infant development* (2nd ed., Vol. 2, pp. 140–164). Applied and policy issues. London: Wiley-Blackwell.

Engle, P. L., Black, M. M., Behrman, J. R., de Mello, M. C., Gertler P. J., Kapiriri, L., et al. (2007). Child development in developing countries 3: Strategies to avoid the loss of developmental potential in more than 200 million children in the developing world. *The Lancet, 369,* 229–242.

Engle, P. L., & Breaux, C. (1998). Fathers' responsibility for children: A cross-cultural perspective. *Social Policy Report of the Society for Research in Child Development, 12*(1), 1–23.

Fernald, L., Weber, A., Galasso, E., & Ratsifandrihamanana, L. (2010). Socio-economic gradients and child development in a very low income population: Evidence from Madagascar. *Developmental Science, 11,* 1–16. doi: 10.1111/j.1467-7687.2010.01032.x

Gottlieb, C. A., Maenner, M. J., Cappa, C., & Durkin, M. S. (2009). Child disability screening, nutrition, and early learning in 18 countries with low and middle incomes: Data from the third round of UNICEF's Multiple Indicator Cluster Survey (2005–6). [Research Support, Non-U.S. Gov't]. *Lancet, 374*(9704), 1831–1839.

Government of India. (2001). *Census of India 2001.*Retrieved from http://www.censusindia.net/results/resultsmain.html

Grantham-McGregor, S., Cheung, Y. B., Cueto, S., Glewwe, P., Richter, L., Strupp, B., et al. (2007). Developmental potential in the first 5 years for children in developing countries. *The Lancet, 369,* 60–70.

Guadarrama-Celaya, F., Otero-Ojeda, G. A., Bernardo Pliego-Rivero, F., Del Rosario Porcayo-Mercado, M., Ricardo-Garcell, J., & Cecilia Perez-Abalo, M. (2012). Screening of neurodevelopmental delays in four communities of Mexico and Cuba. [Comparative Study; Multicenter Study]. *Public health nursing (Boston, Mass.), 29*(2), 105–115.

Guilmoto, C. Z. (2009). The sex ratio transition in Asia. *Population and Development Review, 35,* 519–549.

Hamadani, J. D., Tofail, F., Yesmin, S., Hud, S. N., Engle, P., & Grantham-McGregor, S. M. (2010). Validating family care indicators in Bangladesh. *Journal of Health Population and Nutrition, 28*(1), 23–33.

Heymann, S. J. (2006). *Forgotten families: Ending the growing crisis confronting children and working parents in the global economy.* New York: Oxford University Press.

Kabubo-Mariara, J., Ndenge, G. K., & Mwabu, D. K. (2006). *Evolution and determinants of non-monetary indicators of poverty in Kenya: Children's nutritional status, 1998–2003.* Paper presented at Conference on Advancing Health Equity. Retrieved from http://www.bvsde.paho.org/bvsacd/cd56/kabubomariara-180906.pdf

Krishna, A. (2007). *Escaping poverty and becoming poor in three states of India, with additional evidence from Kenya, Uganda, and Peru.* Washington, DC: Palgrave and the World Bank.

Lansford, J. E., Alampay, L. P., Al-Hassan, S., Bacchini, D., Bombi, A. S., Bornstein, M. H., Chang, L., Deater-Deckard, K., Di Giunta, L., Dodge, K. A., Oburu, P., Pastorelli, C., Runyan, D. K., Skinner, A. T., Sorbring, E., Tapanya, S., Tirado, L. M., & Zelli, A. (2010). Corporal punishment of children in nine countries as a function of child gender and parent gender. *Int J Pediatr, 2010*(672780), 1–12.

Li, S. (2007, October 29–31). *Imbalanced sex ratio at birth and comprehensive intervention in China.* Paper presented at the 4th Asia Pacific Conference on Reproductive and Sexual Health and Rights, Hyderabad, India.

Lustig, S. (2009). An ecological framework for the refugee experience: What is the impact on child development. In G.W. Evans & T. D. Wachs (Eds.), *Chaos and children's development: Levels of analysis and mechanisms.* Washington, DC: American Psychological Association.

Maulik, P. K., & Darmstadt, G. L. (2009). Community-based interventions to optimize early childhood development in low resource settings. *Journal of Perinatology, 29*(8), 531–542.

Molamu L., & MacDonald, D. (1996). Alcohol abuse among the Basarwa of the Kgalagadi and Ghanzi districts in Botswana. *Drugs: Education, Prevention and Policy, 3*(2), 145–152.

Narayan, D., & Petesch, P. (2002). *Voices of the poor: From many lands.* Washington, DC: World Bank.

Narayan, D., & Petesch, P. (2007). Agency, opportunity structure, and poverty escapes. In D. Narayan & P. Petesch (Eds.), *Moving out of poverty: Cross-disciplinary perspectives on mobility* (pp. 13–45). Washington, DC: Palgrave MacMillian and the World Bank.

Nadeau, S., Martinez, S., Premand, P., & Filmer, D. (2011). Cognitive development among young children in low-income countries. In H. Alderman (Ed.), *Early childhood development* (pp. 9–50). Washington, DC: World Bank.

Nonoyama-Tarumi, Y., Loaiza, E., & Engle, P. L. (2009). Inequalities in attendance in organized early learning programmes in developing societies: Findings from household surveys. *Compare: A Journal of Comparative and International Education, 39*, 385–409.

Ravallion, M. (1992). *Poverty comparisons: A guide to concepts and methods.* Washington, DC: World Bank.

Ross, K., Zuze, L, & Ratsatsi, D. (2005, September 28–October 2). *The use of socioeconomic gradient lines to judge the performance of school systems.* Presented at SACMEQ Research Conference, Paris.

Runyan, D. K., Shankar, V., Hassan, F., Hunter, W. M., Jain, D., Paula, C. S., Bangdiwala, S. I., Ramiro, L. S., Muñoz, S. R., Vizcarra, B., & Bordin, I. A. (2010). International variations in harsh child discipline. *Pediatrics, 126*, e701–711.

Sachs, J. (2005). *The end to poverty.* New York: Penguin Group.

Sen, A. (1995). The political economy of targeting. In D. van de Walle & K. Nead (Eds.), *Public spending and the poor: Theory and evidence* (pp. 11–24). Baltimore/London: John Hopkins University Press.

Sharma, O. P., & Haub, C. (2008). *Sex ratio at birth begins to improve in India.* Retrieved from http://www.prb.org/Articles/2008/indiasexratio.aspx

Sherr L., Mueller J., & Varrall R. (2009). A systematic review of cognitive development and child human immunodeficiency virus infection. *Psychology, Health and Medicine, 14*, 387–404.

Stein, J., Schettler, T., Wallinga, D., & Valenti, M. (2002). In harm's way: Toxic threats to child development. *Developmental and Behavioral Pediatrics, 23*(18), s13–s20.

Sun, J., Rao, N., Zhang, X., & Engle, P. L. (2011, March). *Mothers' and fathers' language related activities with children in 22 less-developed countries.* Poster presented at the Society for Research in Child Development 2011 Biennial Meeting, Montreal, Canada.

Tang, D., Li, T. Y., Liu, J. J., Zhou, Z. J., Yuan, T., Chen, Y. -H., et al. (2008). Effects of prenatal exposure to coal-burning pollutants on children's development in China (Children's Health). *Environmental Health Perspective, 116*(5), 674–679.

Tilly, C. (2007). *Poverty and the politics of exclusion.* Washington, DC: World Bank.

Tsai S. Y., Chou H. Y., The, H.W., Chen, C. M., & Chen, C. J. (2003). The effects of chronic arsenic exposure from drinking water on the neurobehavioral development in adolescence. *Neurotoxicology, 24*, 747–753.

UN. (2005). *The millennium development goals report*. New York. Author.

UNESCO. (2007). *EFA Global Monitoring report: Strong foundations: Early childhood care and education*. Paris: Author.

UNESCO. (2010). *EFA Global Monitoring Report: Reaching the marginalized*. Paris: Author.

UNESCO. (2009). *The impact of the global economic crisis*. Retrieved from http://unesdoc. unesco.org/images/0017/001796/179657e.pdf

UNESCO (2011). *EFA Global Monitoring Report: The Hidden Crises: Armed Conflict and Education*. Paris: Author.

UNICEF. (2006a). *Africa's orphaned and vulnerable generations: Children affected by AIDS*. New York: Author.

UNICEF. (2006b). *The state of the world's children: Excluded and invisible*. New York: Author.

UNICEF. (2007a). *The state of the world's children 2006*. New York: Author.

UNICEF. (2007b). *Gender equality: The big picture*. New York: Author.

UNICEF. (2008a). *The state of the world's children. Child survival*. New York: Author.

UNICEF. (2008b). *Countdown to 2015 Report: Tracking progress in maternal, newborn and child survival*. New York: Author.

UNICEF. (2009). *Tracking progress on child and maternal nutrition*. New York: Author.

UNICEF. (2010). *Presentation at the Executive Board*. Unpublished.

UNICEF. (2010a). *Progress for children: Achieving the MDGs with equity*. New York: Author.

UNICEF. (2010b). *Child disciplinary practices at home: Evidence from a range of low- and middle-income countries*. New York: UNICEF.

UNIFEM. (2005). *Progress of the world's women 2005. Women, work and poverty*. New York: United Nations Development Fund for Women (UNIFEM).

Wachs, T. D. (2000). *Necessary but not sufficient: The role of individual and multiple influences on human development*. Washington, DC: American Psychological Association Press.

Wachs, T. D., & Rahman, A. (2013). The nature and impact of risk and protective influences on children's development in low-income countries. In P. R. Britto, P. L. Engle, & C. M. Super (Eds.), *Handbook of early childhood development research and its impact on global policy* (Chapter 5). New York: Oxford University Press.

Walker, S. P., Wachs, T. D., Gardner, J. M., Lozoff, B., Wasserman, G. A., Pollitt, E., et al. (2007). Child development: Risk factors for adverse outcomes in developing countries. *The Lancet, 369*, 145–157.

Walker, S. P., Wachs, T. D., Grantham-McGregor, S., Black, M. M., Nelson, C. A., Huffman,S. I., et al. (2011). Inequality in early childhood: Risk and protective factors for early child development. *Lancet, 378*(9799), 1325–1338.

Wasserman, G. A., Liu X., Parvez F., Ahsan, H., Factor-Litvak, P., van Geen, A., et al. (2004.) Water arsenic exposure and children's intellectual function in Araihazar, Bangladesh. *Environmental Health Perspective, 112*, 1329–1333.

WHO. (2003). *Gender, tobacco and health*. Geneva: Author.

WHO. (2004a). *Global database on iodine deficiency. Iodine status worldwide*. Geneva: Author.

WHO. (2004b). *Global status report on alcohol*. Department of Mental Health and Substance Abuse WHO Geneva: Author.

World Bank. (2009a). *World Bank calls for expanding economic opportunities for women as global economic crisis continues* [Press release]. Retrieved from http://web.worldbank.

org/WBSITE/EXTERNAL/NEWS/o,,contentMDK:22048737~pagePK:64257043~piPK:437376~theSitePK:4607,00.html

World Bank. (2009b). *Women in 33 countries highly vulnerable to financial crisis effects—World Bank estimates increase in infant mortality, less girl education and reduced earnings.* Retrieved from http://web.worldbank.org/WBSITE/EXTERNAL/TOPICS/EXTGENDER/o,,contentMDK:22445436~pagePK:148956~piPK:149081~theSitePK:336868,00.html

World Bank. (2009). *Global monitoring report 2010: The MDGs after the crisis.* Washington, DC: Author.

World Economic Forum. (2005). *Women's empowerment: Measuring the global gender gap.* Retrieved from https://members.weforum.org/pdf/Global_Competitiveness_Reports/Reports/gender_gap.pdf

Yousafzai, A. K., Yakoob, M. Y., & Bhutta, Z. A. (2013). Nutrition-based approaches to early childhood development. In P. R. Britto, P. L. Engle, & C. M. Super (Eds.), *Handbook of early childhood development research and its impact on global policy* (Chapter 10). New York: Oxford University Press.

Zhu, W. X., & Lu, L. (2009). China's excess males, sex selective abortion, and one child policy: Analysis of data from 2005 national inter-census survey. *British Medical Journal, 338,* 1136–1141.

4

Global Policy Landscape and Early Childhood Development

Pia Rebello Britto, Nurper Ulkuer, William P. Hodges,
and Michael F. McCarthy

International social, economic, and human rights declarations and conventions are powerful guiding forces on the global policy stage. They have been effective in mobilizing the world community on several vital issues. For example, the Universal Declaration of Human Rights, adopted by United Nations (UN) General Assembly, moved the world community in unanimous support to uphold human dignity and observe fundamental freedoms (UN General Assembly, 1948). Additionally, over time, this declaration has been instrumental in spawning a series of conventions across a range of social, economic, political, and civil rights. In general, international declarations and conventions play a unique role in global development by protecting human rights through principles of equality and nondiscrimination and establishing standards and expectations for development for the world community (UN Human Rights Committee, 1989).

International declarations and conventions define the global vision for universally accepted goals, which often are the benchmarks against which country-level progress is charted and compared. Furthermore, these international policy frameworks are often accompanied by very large funding and aid initiatives. For example, international development declarations define what priorities a government must adopt if it wishes to gain access to international aid (Fowler, 2003). In other words, behind these global declarations and conventions is an ethical and financial authority that often profoundly influences national-level policies, budgets, and priorities. Simply put, the importance of international declarations and conventions cannot be underestimated. Given this, it is important to know how early childhood development (ECD) is represented in these international conventions and declarations, and what impact they might have on aspects of ECD that are deemed important on the international development agenda: namely, equity, access, and quality of ECD services.

It is commonly assumed—correctly—that young children are mentioned in these global documents, but curiously, there has never been a systematic examination of how they are presented. What is it about children that warrants their special mention? In considering this question, it is important to distinguish between statements concerning children as intrinsically valuable humans, important in their own right and deserving of services, and children as instrumentally valuable, an important locus of investment due to their future contribution to society.

The science of ECD is rapidly emerging as a focus of international attention (UNESCO, 2007). The rise in importance of ECD can be attributed to several factors, including evidence indicating high dividends on investment in the early years (Heckman & Krueger, 2003) and early childhood as a means to equity and equality in society (Irwin, Siddiqi, & Hertzman, 2007). Governments around the world are concerned with the economic advancement of their countries and in establishing equity. The scientific evidence of ECD provides support for reaching these national development goals.

The main thrust of this chapter is to provide a clear understanding of how ECD is reflected in international declarations and conventions. The first section presents an overview of the international declarations and conventions landscape. The second section presents the results of a policy analysis study examining the intrinsic and instrumental value of ECD accorded in these international conventions and declarations. The third section of this chapter discusses these results and their implications for the next generation of global policies and ECD.

International Policy Landscape

In this chapter, we consider the primary international statements of social, economic, and human rights concerns for children in two categories: declarations and conventions. *Declarations* are the guiding documents for international development and human rights agencies, such as the UN. A declaration is an instrument that can be used to guide and inform international and national efforts, but it is not legally binding. Adopting a declaration is not linked with binding obligations; rather, it is considered a statement of specific aspirations. Because of their nonbinding nature, declarations are often universally endorsed. A *convention*, on the other hand, is a legally binding treaty that comes into force when a country ratifies it (UN Department of Public Information, 1997). Ratification indicates that a country has agreed for its national laws to be aligned with those of the convention.

There is a host of declaration frameworks on the global development landscape. We focus here on the Millennium Development Goals (MDGs), the Education for All (EFA) Declaration, and the Health for All (HFA) Declaration because of their relevance to children.

TABLE 4.1 Typology of international declarations and conventions associated with early childhood development (ECD)

	1970	1980	1990	2000
Declarations	*Health for All (HFA) (WHO, 1978)* Focus: Protection and promotion of health		*Education for All (EFA) (UNESCO, 1990)* Focus: Education as a tool for development	*UN Millennium Declaration (MDG) (UN General Assembly, 2000)* Focus: Investment in economic and social development
Conventions			*Convention on the Rights of the Child (CRC) (UN General Assembly, 1989)* Focus: Survival, development, protection, and participation rights for all children	

With regard to the more binding conventions, there are seven core human rights treaties to consider: the International Covenant on Civil and Political Rights (ICCPR); the International Covenant on Economic, Social, and Cultural Rights (ICESCR); the Convention on the Elimination of All Forms of Racial Discrimination (ICERD); the Convention on the Elimination of All Forms of Discrimination Against Women (CEDAW); the Convention Against Torture and Other Cruel, Inhuman, or Degrading Punishment (CAT); the Convention on the Rights of the Child (CRC); and the International Convention on the Protection of the Rights of All Migrant Workers and Members of Their Families (MWC) (Bernard van Leer Foundation, 2006). Although each of these is relevant to children, in this chapter, we review primarily the CRC because of its direct relevance to children and its status as the benchmark international convention on child rights (see Table 4.1). We now provide a brief overview of these declarations and the CRC.

INTERNATIONAL DECLARATIONS

Education for All

In Jomtien, Thailand, at the World Conference on Education, the EFA Declaration (UNESCO, 1990) was sponsored by the UN Educational, Scientific, and Cultural Organization (UNESCO), the UN Development Programme (UNDP), the UN Population Fund (UNFPA), the UN Children's Fund (UNICEF), the World Bank, and nongovernmental organizations (NGOs), and was and signed by delegates of 155 countries, thereby signifying a global movement in recognition of education. The declaration signified a "global commitment to provide quality basic education for all children, youth and adults," and the participants "pledged to universalize primary education and massively reduce illiteracy by the end of the decade" (UNESCO, n.d.). By 2000, however, because these goals were far from having been reached, 164 governments met at the World Education Forum in Dakar, Senegal, and identified six goals to be achieved by 2015 (UNESCO, 2000b):

- *Goal 1.* Expanding and improving *comprehensive early childhood care and education,* especially for the most vulnerable and disadvantaged children
- *Goal 2.* Ensuring that, by 2015, all children, particularly girls, children in difficult circumstances, and those belonging to ethnic minorities have access to *complete, free, and compulsory primary education* of good quality
- *Goal 3.* Ensuring that the learning needs of all young people and adults are met through *equitable access to appropriate learning and life skills*
- *Goal 4.* Achieving a 50% *improvement in levels of adult literacy* by 2015, especially for women, and equitable access to basic and continuing education for all adults
- *Goal 5.* Eliminating *gender disparities* in primary and secondary education by 2005, and achieving gender equality in education by 2015, with a focus on ensuring girls' full and equal access to and achievement in basic education of good quality
- *Goal 6. Improving all aspects of the quality of education* and ensuring excellence of all, so that recognized and measurable learning outcomes are achieved by all, especially in literacy, numeracy, and essential life skills

Health for All

Access to basic health care was unanimously endorsed as a fundamental human right by all countries that are members of the World Health Organization (WHO) in the Alma-Ata Declaration (WHO, 1978) in Kazakhstan. Health is defined as a state of complete physical, mental, and social well-being and not merely the absence of disease or infirmity (WHO, 1978). This declaration formally adopted primary health care (PHC) as the means for providing comprehensive, universal, equitable, and affordable health care for all countries (Hall & Taylor, 2003). The emphasis on PHC is rooted in the scientific evidence that "it is an integral part both of the country's health system, of which it is the central function and main focus, and of the overall social and economic development of the community." The goals of PHC were expected to be achieved by 2000; however, several of the targets were not met.

In the wake of unmet goals, the HFA spawned several health-related resolutions. The resolution, "Health-for-all in the twenty-first century" was adopted by the 51st World Health Assembly in 1998 to accelerate achievement of HFA goals by addressing the challenges that blocked progress, the most vulnerable populations, and governance of the declaration. Most recently, in 2010, the UN General Assembly, through a resolution, recognized that mental health problems are of major importance to all societies, are significant contributors to the burden of disease and the loss of quality of life, and have huge economic and social costs. This resolution signals a new direction for global health and one that is very important for ECD, given the association between maternal depression and child outcomes (Fernald, Jones-Smith, Ozer, Neufield, & DiGirolamo, 2008).

United Nations Millennium Declaration

In its 55th session, the UN General Assembly adopted the UN Millennium Declaration (UN General Assembly, 2000)—a vision for the 21st century based on the principles of the Charter of the UN. This declaration was signed by 191 countries in 2000 as a commitment to social and economic development to be achieved by 2015. The implementation of the declaration was proposed through a series of eight goals, the MDGs, that address common conditions that prevent countries from making economic and social progress. The eight goals are eradicating extreme poverty and hunger; achieving universal primary education; promoting gender equality and empowerment of women; reducing child mortality; improving maternal health; combating HIV/AIDS, malaria, and other diseases; ensuring environmental sustainability; and developing a global partnership for development. The Millennium Declaration could be considered to set the global standards for economic development and social equity.

INTERNATIONAL CONVENTIONS

The second type of international policy statement that drives the global and national policy agenda is human rights conventions. These instruments recognize the inherent dignity and inalienable rights of human beings, and obligate the state governments that ratify them to adhere to provisions within the conventions.

Convention on the Rights of the Child

This convention is not only the clearest and most comprehensive expression of what the world community wants for its children but also the most widely ratified human rights treaty. Leaders around the world realized that all persons under 18 years of age, irrespective of race, color, gender, language, religion, opinions, origins, wealth, birth status, or ability need special care and protection of their human rights. This formed the rationale for the CRC in 1989, three decades after the Declaration of the Rights of the Child. The CRC, through a set of 54 articles, is the only treaty that puts into legally binding form the entire range of child rights: civil, political, economic, social, and cultural (UN General Assembly, 1989). The four core principles of the CRC include (1) nondiscrimination; (2) the right to life, survival, and development; (3) emphasis on what is in the best interest of the child; and (4) respect for the viewpoint of the child. It spells out basic human rights that children everywhere in the world have with respect to survival and development to the fullest and protection from harmful influences, abuse, and exploitation, as well as participation in family, cultural, and social life.

The CRC has also made a vital contribution to recognizing the importance of the family and establishing clear responsibilities for the larger community (e.g., country) to uphold standards for all children everywhere (Britto, 2005). The CRC provides an implementation framework of roles and responsibilities of all duty bearers, beginning with the family and extending to national governments, to meet children's rights (Britto & Ulkuer, 2012). The stated responsibilities, if adhered to at the multiple levels and contexts surrounding the child, can facilitate achievement of meeting all child rights for survival, development, protection, and participation (Hodgkin & Newell, 2007). The CRC is monitored by the UN Committee on the Rights of the Child, which is comprised of elected States Parties of the CRC. The main aim of the committee is to make sure the CRC is properly implemented in member countries and to examine progress periodically. The member countries include nations that have ratified the convention by agreeing to its non-negotiable standards and obligations.

Yet, although articles regarding the right to nutrition and health, education, leisure, and play exist in the CRC, they are not integrated sufficiently to advance ECD. In the first place, the interpretation of rights for ECD has been narrowly confined to areas such as child survival, birth registration, right to a name, and nationality. Second, reporting on the implementation of rights for early childhood has yielded mixed results, as countries appeared unsure of how to interpret the rights of young children. Due to these reasons, a General Comment was added to the CRC, namely General Comment 7 (GC7), which refers to the implementation of all rights for ECD (UN Committee on the Rights of the Child, 2006).

General Comment 7 represents authoritative guidance to countries in fulfilling their CRC obligations to young children. For example, Article 5 of the CRC obligates States Parties to "respect the responsibilities, rights and duties of parents or, where applicable, the members of the extended family or community as provided for by local custom, legal guardians or other persons legally responsible for the child, to provide, in a manner consistent with the *evolving capacities of the child*, appropriate direction and guidance in the exercise by the child of the rights recognized in the present Convention" (UN General Assembly, 1989). The emphasis here is on understanding that in the early years children make rapid advances in development and that these advances differ across the age groups defining early childhood (commonly understood to be birth to 8 years). The Early Childhood Rights Indicators Group has developed a Child Rights Indicators Manual for Early Childhood using the GC7 as a conceptual framework to guide countries in the implementation of their CRC obligations during the period of early childhood and in reporting to the monitoring committee.

October 2010 stands as a historical landmark for international early childhood advocates, for the UN General Assembly passed a resolution on implementing

child rights in early childhood (UN General Assembly, 2011). This milestone especially an opportunity to examine the impact of legally binding conventions and
development frameworks on early childhood.

This brief overview of the international declarations and conventions landscape
indicates that several vital global statements and frameworks could potentially
address ECD. Therefore, we now turn our attention to understanding how exactly
ECD is represented in them.

Early Childhood and International Declarations and Conventions

Given that international declarations and conventions can drive national legislation, policy, and international aid and funding, we conducted a content analysis
study to examine how ECD is valued in these documents. In particular, we examined three questions: (1) Is the intrinsic value of early childhood expressed in these
documents? (2) Is the instrumental value of early childhood expressed in these
documents? And (3), are there directives in these documents that accord importance to principles of access, equity, and quality of programs and services?

The conceptualization of "intrinsic value" stems from the human rights theory
that argues that the duty-bearers of human rights (e.g., governments) are obligated to respect, protect, and fulfill the rights of the rights-holders, which, in
this case, would focus on the inherent value of early childhood (Donnelly, 2003;
Shue, 1996). Furthermore, this conceptualization stems from the normative landscape of human rights that has been fostered for decades, following the Universal
Declaration of Human Rights in 1948, which recognizes the "inherent dignity" and
"equal and inalienable rights of all members of the human family" (UN General
Assembly, 1948). The conceptualization of the instrumental value of children stems
from the evidence-based arguments that have been made to advocate for ECD
as a conscious investment by governments for national sustainable development.
The economic evidence indicates that returns on investment in early childhood
may include reduced school drop-out and higher retention rates, higher skilled
human capital, reduced crime rates, and more responsible citizenship (Heckman
& Krueger, 2003). The conceptualization of the interlinked dimensions of access,
equity, and quality as necessary components of early childhood programs and
services stems from the international development and program evaluation literature, where these dimensions are most closely linked with positive child outcomes
(Irwin et al., 2007). The goal of equity is defined as the greatest possible opportunity to access and participate in quality programs and services that are made
available to *all* children and families, especially the most vulnerable populations.
Lacking quality, programs and services are unlikely to generate the intended child
and family outcomes (Britto, Yoshikawa, & Boller, 2011).

Our rationales for ECD in international declarations and conventions thus
required an examination of the CRC, MDGs, EFA, and HFA. These instruments are

TABLE 4.2 Sample of international policy documents

Document Family	Document
CRC	The Convention on the Rights of the Child (1989)
	General Comment no. 7: Implementing Child Rights in Early Childhood (2005)
	Optional Protocol on the Sale of Children, Child Prostitution and Child Pornography (2000)
	Optional Protocol on the Involvement of Children in Armed Conflict (2000)
MDG	UN Millennium Declaration (2000)
	Millennium Development Goals (2000)
EFA	World Declaration on Education for All (1990)
	Framework for Action to Meet Basic Learning Needs (1990)
	Education for All: Achieving the Goal—The Amman Affirmation (1996)
	The Dakar Framework for Action—Education for All: Meeting Our Collective Commitments (2000)
	Expanded Commentary on the Dakar Framework for Action (2000)
	NGO Declaration on Education for All (2000)
	Regional Frameworks for Action (2000):
	• Education for All—A Framework for Action in Sub-Saharan Africa: Education for African Renaissance in the Twenty-first Century
	• Education for All in the Americas: Regional Framework of Action
	• Education for All in the Arab States: Renewing the Commitment—The Arab Framework for Action to Ensure Basic Learning Needs in the Arab States in the Years 2000–2010
	• Asia and the Pacific Regional Framework for Action: Education for All – Guiding Principles, Specific Goals and Targets for 2015
	• Regional Framework for Action – Europe and North America
	• Recife Declaration of the E-9 Countries
HFA	Declaration of Alma-Ata (Health for All Declaration) (1978)
	Ottawa Charter for Health Promotion (1986)
	Jakarta Declaration on Leading Health Promotion into the 21st Century (1997)
	Rio Political Declaration on Social Determinants of Health (2011)

Note: E-9 countries are Bangladesh, Brazil, China, Egypt, India, Indonesia, Mexico, Nigeria, Pakistan

often accompanied by a set of documents that provide technical background. We term this set of documents, for a declaration or convention, as a "family" of documents, and, all together, they constitute 22 objects for coding (see Table 4.2). The CRC, optional protocols, GC7, and UN Millennium Declaration were all retrieved from the website of the Office of the High Commissioner for Human Rights. The EFA and HFA documents were retrieved from the UNESCO and WHO websites, respectively.

To properly understand the relative emphasis on the intrinsic and instrumental values of children, we needed to make one more distinction, regarding specificity of an early childhood reference. Specific reference to early childhood (EC) includes the following particular early childhood terminology, which we define as "EC Specific" codes; "early childhood care," "early childhood care and development," "early childhood care and education," "early childhood development," "early childhood education," and "early childhood intervention," as well as basic references to the phrase "early childhood," which signifies an unequivocal reference to that age period (UNESCO, 2002). Other more colloquial or descriptive terms also meet this requirement, such as "young children," "babies," "preschool," and the like. All

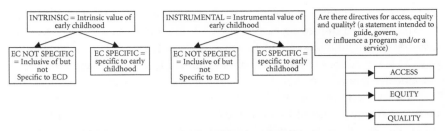

FIGURE 4.1 *Coding system for early childhood development (ECD) intrinsic and instrumental reference in international declarations and conventions*

other references that imply the inclusion of the early years, but do not specifically address them, we define as "EC Not-Specific" codes. For example, the CRC, taken as a whole, sets forth human rights for all children, 0–18 years of age, which is certainly inclusive of early childhood, but not specific to it. We found in an earlier analysis that among the declarations (EFA, HFA, and MDG), only the EFA family of documents featured ECD specifically (Hodges, Hilibrand, & Britto, 2011).

Thus, the coding of the 22 documents (Table 4.2) focused on three distinctions: (1) the instrumental and/or intrinsic value accorded to children in arguing for ECD; (2) the specificity (or lack thereof) in referring to early childhood; and (3) attention to principles of access, equity, and quality. Figure 4.1 illustrates the coding system used by two independent coders, using ATLAS.ti, a qualitative data analysis software tool. We did not include the codes identified in an analysis of GC7 in the results presented below because the entire focus of the GC7 is already known to be on ECD.

The results of this coding are presented in Table 4.3. Several findings are of interest. First, it can be seen that there is considerable variation in whether these international documents recognize the intrinsic value of early childhood development (first column of numbers). The EFA family of documents contains the highest number of instances of such recognition, and the HFA the least. Because the page lengths of these families of documents also vary, the density of references to ECD within each document cannot be compared to an equal standard, but it does provide an indication of the attention to the intrinsic value of ECD and where it lies. Further, in almost a quarter of the EFA's references to the intrinsic value of ECD, it was specific to early childhood, not generic—that is, 22 of the 86 intrinsic codes identified in the EFA family of documents co-occurred with the EC-Specific code. Unsurprisingly, the majority of the co-occurrences were noted around the framing

TABLE 4.3 Frequency of intrinsic and instrumental value of early childhood and specificity of reference in international conventions and declarations

Document Family	Intrinsic	EC Specific	Both	Instrumental	EC Specific	Both
CRC (not including GC7)	63	6	6	3	6	0
MDG	22	14	4	6	14	0
EFA	86	43	22	37	43	0
HFA	17	3	0	10	3	0

and articulation of the first goal of the declaration, specifically according attention to expanding and improving early childhood care and development (UNESCO, 2000b). This attention has an intrinsic tone to it, in that the early learning aspect of ECD is valued for the inherent right of children to education and their social, emotional, cognitive, psychological, and physical development.

With respect to the health-related family of documents (HFA), no co-occurrenceswere noted between the intrinsic value accorded to early childhood and a specific focus on it. References to early childhood were mainly limited to examples of maternal and child health in primary health care systems; given the recent Rio Political Declaration (WHO, 2011), however, and the voluminous research in the past decade on early childhood health and development, we had anticipated a greater early childhood-specific focus. The CRC specifically accorded attention to the intrinsic value of early childhood, as opposed to just including it in the document, which was expected, given that the articles of the CRC are focused on the inherent dignity and rights of all children, although only a small proportion of the total intrinsic codes are specific to early childhood (see Table 4.3).

Finally, with respect to the MDG family of documents, where ECD was specifically addressed, the limited number of co-occurrences was due to the single topic of health and survival in early childhood. Overall, these results provide a clear understanding of the importance accorded to the inherent value of ECD in the international guiding statements and have implications for the next generation of these policies, topics that are discussed in the final section of the chapter.

We now turn our attention to understanding how the instrumental value of ECD is reflected in key international declarations and conventions. As indicated earlier, the impetus for understanding the instrumental value emanates from the evidence of ECD indicating that is a period of human development with strong results on investment. The results indicate a similar pattern to the "intrinsic" results: the EFA documents contain the highest number of instances coded, whereas the least number of codes was found in the CRC—unsurprising, given that convention's focus on inherent human rights. However, unlike the intrinsic value, we found no instances of the instrumental value of early childhood and EC-Specific codes co-occurring. In other words, although both the instrumental and EC-Specific codes were identified (separately) in all four sets of document families, they never occurred together. The instrumental value of ECD, then, was implied in a general way, but was not specifically highlighted. For example, the MDG targets include goals for achieving universal primary education, reducing child mortality, and improving maternal health. Each goal is directly relevant to early childhood. However, none of the language or perspective around these goals specifically addresses ECD, which is understandable, considering the MDGs are broad international benchmarks to meet, as opposed to specific goals for the development of young children. We take particular note of this result and, later in this chapter, present implications for how the instrumental value of ECD could be included in future generations of declarations and conventions.

In the final set of analyses, we examined how access, equity, and quality in early childhood were reflected in these key international policy statements

TABLE 4.4 Frequency of access, equity, and quality
in international conventions and declarations

Document Family	Access	Equity	Quality
CRC (not including GC7)	11	11	8
MDG	8	17	0
EFA	72	96	95
HFA	15	48	9

(Table 4.4). Because international conventions and declarations are such over-arching policy statements, access, equity, and quality appear as general principles, necessary components that apply across all human rights and development goals; therefore, we did not code for EC specificity in this analysis.

The CRC documents made roughly equal mention of access, equity, and quality. Of particular importance to understanding the reasoning about ECD programs is the attention given to certain services as a human right. For example, access to child care services and facilities for working parents, and special care of disabled children are noted as essential for the realization of children's right. The principle of equity was coded particularly through the emphasis on nondiscrimination and service to vulnerable populations. The CRC states that children living in exceptionally difficult conditions need "special consideration," which should include equitable and accessible early childhood programs and services for those who need them most—indeed, the most vulnerable children. The principle of quality was found in discussions of standards and training of those responsible for providing services that ensure children's rights. For example, the CRC requires governments to ensure that "the institutions, services and facilities responsible for the care or protection of children...conform with the standards established by competent authorities, particularly in the areas of safety, health, in the number and suitability of their staff, as well as competent supervision" (UN General Assembly, 1989). In summary, the CRC attends to the principles of equity, access, and quality from a perspective of intrinsic value for all children, without a special focus on ECD.

The EFA documents cited the general principle of quality 95 times, most commonly in phrases such as "quality education," "basic education services of quality," "quality basic education," and "basic education of high quality." The term "quality" in this context is used to accentuate the idea that, to successfully ensure the right to education, educational services must be of good quality. However, there is no detailed explanation or description of what "quality" entails. The concepts of equity and access also appear frequently throughout the EFA documents (see Table 4.4). Although the EFA initiative is concerned with education broadly, across the lifespan, it is noteworthy here that the initiative particularly emphasizes equity by urging states to ensure that children in difficult or disadvantaged circumstances (such as girls and children belonging to ethnic minorities) receive free and compulsory primary education. The principle of access is also referenced frequently and appears explicitly in the first EFA goal, which is to expand early childhood care and education services. The principle of access also appears frequently in the context of expanding primary education (the first part of which often covers the end of early childhood) to the 113 million children without access to it (UNESCO, 2000b). It should be noted that the EFA family of documents was the only one in which these three principles—access, equity, and quality—converged into a single formulation: To ensure the fundamental human right to education, education must be of good quality and accessible to all people, regardless of their race, religion, origin, and/or status.

Access, equity, and quality are all stated as important principles in the UN Millennium Declaration and the MDGs, although, again, as broad concepts and not specific to early childhood. The later evolution of the HFA into declarations concerning health promotion (Ottawa Charter and Jakarta Declaration) and the social determinants of health (Rio Political Declaration) continue to uphold the three principles. In particular, of the 72 applications of the three codes in the HFA documents, 51 were in applied in the Rio Political Declaration alone; these were mostly focused on equity, which follows naturally from this declaration's commitment to social and health equity within and between countries, "both for vulnerable groups and the entire population" (WHO, 2011). However, other than general references to child mortality and maternal and child health, only one explicit reference was made to ECD in the Rio Political Declaration.

In summary, this content analysis of the key international declarations and conventions suggests that, overall, ECD gets little specific attention. When it is singled out for mention, it is primarily from an education perspective, with EFA featuring ECD most specifically. We now turn our attention to the implications of these results for the next generation of global policies that will be declared in 2015 and beyond.

Conclusion

The global policy arena will soon be drafting the next generation of declarations, in particular the MDGs and the EFA. The analysis of the current generation of documents with respect to ECD has several sets of results that could be useful and important to consider during this stage of conceptualization. We begin this section by reflecting on these results with their implications for these forthcoming global policy statements. The second part of this section addresses the potential implications of these results for national level policies that address ECD.

If we use a historical lens to examine the association between these key declarations and conventions in connection with key scientific publications, we find a limited although effective pattern of influence. The limited nature of the influence could be attributed to the fact that information is only one of the many factors that influences policy (Weiss, 1995). We begin by noting Robert Myers' (1992) foundational work,

The Twelve Who Survive and the events that led up to it. That publication drew on data from low- and middle-income (LAMI) countries to make a case that focusing solely on child survival was an inadequate way to address child well-being because those who survived often did not receive adequate services and programs. Taking this position, the Consultative Group (which Meyers headed at the time), along with others, pressed successfully to include in the World Declaration on Education for All a perspective highlighting that "learning begins at birth" (UNESCO, 1990). In our review, we found that, of all the declarations, the EFA had the highest frequency of ECD-specific inclusions, thus testifying to the potential effectiveness of factual presentations in influencing global institutional policy.

Although the scientific study of early childhood began in the 18th century with the writings of Locke, Kant, Rousseau, Pestalozzi, and Froebel (Wolfe, 2002), it is only in the 20th century that the science of ECD has come of age. At the turn of the century, high-income countries saw a surge in publications on ECD and the appearance of the landmark volume *From Neurons to Neighborhoods* (Shonkoff & Phillips, 2000). The decade following saw a similar spike in ECD publications from LAMI countries. More recently, we note an association between a publication and a declaration: The 2007 Irwin, Siddiqi, and Hertzman report, *Early Child Development: A Powerful Equalizer,* sponsored by WHO's commission on the Social Determinants of Health, was one of the key reports to inform the Rio Declaration, which is the only document from the family of health documents that calls for "early childhood development in public policies and social health services" (WHO, 2011). However, it should be underscored that these individual publications do not stand alone; rather, they are supported by a more detailed, scientific foundation of articles, documents, and reports (such as the *Lancet* series of 2007 and 2011; Engle et al., 2007, 2011) that are used to advocate for ECD.

The results clearly indicated that the instrumental value of ECD is missing from the declarations although the science on the instrumental value is strong and burgeoning. This science, particularly for LAMI countries, has come of age in the past decade. Therefore, it is not surprising that we do not find it mentioned in declarations that were drafted at the turn of the century, approximately one decade ago. For the post-2015 MDG goals, such an omission will be unacceptable. The science of ECD, particularly with its emphasis on the instrumental value of early childhood, needs to be incorporated into the next generation of declarations. One purpose of the present volume is to translate the evidence concerning ECD to serve as a reference point for these upcoming global declarations and conventions.

With respect to the achievement of the MDG goals by 2015, it is currently speculated that many of these goals will not be met and new strategies will be required. Based on the science of ECD, we propose the following recommendations for the new generation of goals, should they follow the same emphasis. For example, MDG2, which currently addresses universal primary education, should move beyond schooling to include targets for learning. The data indicate that although children are being enrolled in school, they are not learning. Furthermore, drop-out rates globally are staggering. The evidence from ECD is clear on this phase being foundational for later learning and school achievement. Similarly, MDG3 should include affordable and quality child care to become part of decent work for women, including shared child care. The rationale for this recommendation stems not only from recent economic evidence from several countries, but also from the rights upheld in the CRC.

We also propose that the implications of this volume go beyond global declarations to influence national-level policies focused on ECD. Our definition of ECD policies is adapted from the Zigler and Hall (2000) definition of a child policy. We define social policies that address ECD as a plan or course of action, supported by a publicly funded institution (e.g., government) that has an impact on the lives of young children, from the prenatal stage to 8 years of age. The plan or course of action is a deliberate strategy, with actionable activities that key stakeholders and sectors should undertake to most effectively use resources to achieve the desired ECD policy goals. The policy provides an umbrella to ensure that all program activities and projects are supported by the highest national legislative, policy, and decision-making bodies, and at more decentralized levels of government, if relevant to the governance structures in the country (Britto, Cerezo, & Ogbunugafor, 2008).

An informal analysis of a UNICEF Headquarters' survey indicated that, in 2002, only 17 out of 150 countries stated that they had at least some kind of ECD policy (Ulkuer, personal communication). The following year, 2003, the number rose to 40; in subsequent years (2004 and 2005), the figure remained essentially the same (Babajanova, 2006). Although these are self-reported data and not actual submission of the policy—and the type of policy is often not clearly specified— these results suggest that the number of countries articulating a national statement dedicated to young children is increasing. This increase in the number of country policies suggests that this would be a good time to consider carefully how best to use evidence to influence them.

As stated in the introduction, international declarations and conventions are assumed to influence national polices due to their financial and ethical strength. Although such a causal relationship cannot be established, a small body of work suggests the influence of international policies on national policies for ECD. For example, with respect to ECD policy development and implementation in Africa, Pence (2004) notes that, prior to 1990, issues of young children were generally diffused throughout broader social policies. However, 1990 was a historical year for ECD (as the EFA declaration emphasized that learning begins at birth) and children in general, as the CRC became international law. The analyses suggest that, post-1990, the importance of ECD in national policies in several countries (e.g., Ghana, Senegal, and Namibia) can be attributed to greater governmental engagement with the CRC and the EFA Jomtien and Dakar meetings. Thus, the ability to date the change in emphasis on ECD in national documents is closely linked with the international declarations. Another example of this suggested influence is presented from Jordan. In 2009, Jordan published its comprehensive national ECD strategy, *Jordan's Early Childhood Development Initiative: Making Jordan Fit for Children*. Of the three motivating factors that led to the development of this policy, building human capital and human rights are cited as two reasons, with Jordan's demography listed as the third (Sultana, 2009). In other words, the UN General Assembly Resolution *A World Fit for Children* (UN General Assembly, 2002), the UN Millennium Declaration, and the CRC were influential in the development and design of the Jordanian national policy for ECD. This literature suggests that research is required to understand the exact association between international- and national-level policies so that evidence can be used to inform national-level policies.

The literature on ECD in LAMI countries is coming of age, a new generation of international declarations is being conceived, and we are noting a great rise in national-level ECD policies. The confluence of timing for these three aspects is a clear indication that the evidence of ECD, intrinsically and instrumentally, needs to be translated and effectively communicated to inform global and national policies. The further development of global and national ECD policies, in turn, provides greater impetus for the next generation of ECD research.

Acknowledgments

We thank the Bernard van Leer Foundation for its generous support of the study on child rights in ECD. We also acknowledge the guidance of Liliana Angelica Ponguta and Adrian Cerezo in establishing the coding system.

References

Babajanova, S. (2006). *Report on UNICEF Organizational priority in 2002–2005: Integrated early childhood development*. New York: UNICEF Report.

Bernard van Leer Foundation. (2006). *A guide to general comment 7: Implementing child rights in early childhood*. The Hague: Bernard van Leer Foundation.

Britto, P. R. (2005). The United Nations Convention on the Rights of the Child: Relationship of children's rights to the family, schools, and communities. In N. Salkind (Ed.), *Encyclopedia of human development* (Vol. 1, pp. 259–260). Thousand Oaks, CA: Sage Publications.

Britto, P. R., Cerezo, A., & Ogbunugafor, B. (2008). National ECD policy development: Case study from the People's Democratic Republic of Lao. *International Journal of Early Childhood, 40*, 101–118.

Britto, P. R., & Ulkuer, N. (2012). Child development in developing countries: Child rights and policy implications. *Child Development, 83*(1), 92–103.

Britto, P. R., Yoshikawa, H., & Boller, K. (2011). Quality of early childhood development programs in global contexts: Rationale for investment, conceptual framework and implications for equity. *Social Policy Report, 25*(2).

Donnelly, J. (2003). *Universal human rights in theory and practice* (2nd ed.). Ithaca, NY: Cornell University Press.

Engle, P. L., Black, M. M., Behrman, J. R., Cabral de Mello, M., Gertler, P., Kapiriri, L., et al. (2007). Strategies to avoid the loss of developmental potential in more than 200 million children in the developing world. *Lancet, 369,* 229–242.

Engle, P. L., Fernald, L. C. H., Alderman, H., Behrman, J., O'Gara, C., Yousafzai, A., et al. (2011). Strategies for reducing inequalities and improving developmental outcomes for young children in low-income and middle-income countries. *Lancet, 378,* 1339–1353.

Fernald, L. C., Jones-Smith, J. C., Ozer, E. J., Neufield, L. M., & DiGirolamo, A. M. (2008). Maternal depressive symptoms and physical activity in very low-income children. *Journal of Developmental and Behavioral Pediatrics, 29*(5), 385–393.

Fowler, A. (2003). *International development frameworks, policies, priorities and implications: A basic guide for NGOs.* Ottawa, ON: Oxfam. Retrieved from http://www.oxfam.ca/sites/default/files/international-development-frameworks-policies-priorities-and-implications-a-basic-guide-for-ngos.pdf

Hall, J. J., & Taylor, R. (2003). Health for all beyond 2000: The demise of the Alma-Ata Declaration and primary health care in developing countries. *The Medical Journal of Australia, 178*(1), 17–20.

Heckman, J. J., & Krueger, A. B. (2003). *Inequality in America: What role for human capital policies?* London: MIT Press.

Hodges, W., Hilibrand, J., & Britto, P. (2011). *Early childhood and international frameworks. Asia-Pacific Regional Network for Early Childhood (ARNEC) e-News Flash August 2011.* Retrieved from http://www.arnec.net/cos/o.x?ptid=1036089&c=/swt_arnec/articles&func=view&rid=317

Hodgkin, R., & Newell, P. (2007). *Implementation handbook for the Convention on the Rights of the Child.* Geneva: UNICEF.

Irwin, L. G., Siddiqi, A., & Hertzman, C. (2007). *Early childhood development: A powerful equalizer.* WHO Commission on the Social Determinants of Health.

Myers, R. G. (1992). *The twelve who survive: Strengthening programmes of early childhood development in the third world.* London: Routledge.

Pence, A. (2004). *ECD Policy development and implementation in Africa. UNESCO Early Childhood and Family Policy Series, 9.* Paris: UNESCO.

Shonkoff, J. P., & Phillips, D. A. (Eds.). (2000). *From neurons to neighborhoods: The science of early childhood development.* Washington, DC: National Academy Press.

Shue, H. (1996). *Basic rights: Subsistence, affluence, and US foreign policy (2nd ed.).* Princeton, NJ: Princeton University Press.

Sultana, R. (2009). *Jordan's early childhood development initiative: Making Jordan fit for children.* UNICEF-MENA Regional Office Learning Series, 2.

UN Committee on the Rights of the Child (UNCRC). (2006). *General Comment no. 7 (2005): Implementing child rights in early childhood* (CRC/C/GC/7/Rev.1.). Retrieved from http://www.unhcr.org/refworld/docid/460bc5a62.html

UN Department of Public Information. (1997). *Human rights at your fingertips: Questions.* Retrieved from http://www.un.org/rights/50/game.htm28

UN General Assembly. (1948). *Universal declaration of human rights.* Retrieved from http://www.unhcr.org/refworld/docid/3ae6b3712c.html

UN General Assembly. (1989). *Convention on the rights of the child.* Retrieved from http://www2.ohchr.org/english/law/crc.htm

UN General Assembly. (2000). *United Nations millennium declaration.* Retrieved from http://www.un.org/millennium/declaration/ares552e.pdf

UN General Assembly. (2002). *A world fit for children.* Resolution adopted by the General Assembly (A/RES/S-27/2). Retrieved from http://www.unicef.org/worldfitforchildren/files/A-RES-S27-2E.pdf

UN General Assembly. (2011). *Resolution adopted by the General Assembly [on the report of the Third Committee] 65/197. Rights of the child.* A/RES/65/197. New York: United Nations.

UN Human Rights Committee (HRC). (1989). *CCPR general comment No. 18: Non-discrimination.* Retrieved from http://www.unhchr.ch/tbs/doc.nsf/0/3888b0541f85 01c9c12563ed004b8doe?Opendocument

UNESCO. (n.d.). *Education for all: History.* Retrieved from http://www.unesco.org/new/en/education/themes/leading-the-international-agenda/education-for-all/the-efa-movement/

UNESCO. (1990). *World declaration on education for all and framework for action to meet basic learning needs.* Retrieved from http://www.unesco.org/education/pdf/JOMTIE_E.PDF

UNESCO. (1996). *Education for all: Achieving the goal. Amman affirmation.* Retrieved from http://www.unesco.org/education/information/nfsunesco/pdf/AMMAN_E.PDF

UNESCO. (2000a). *NGO declaration on education for all: International consultation of Non- Governmental Organizations.* Retrieved from http://www.unesco.org/education/efa/wef_2000/cov_ngo_declaration.shtml

UNESCO. (2000b). *The Dakar framework for action.* Retrieved from http://unesdoc.unesco.org/images/0012/001211/121147e.pdf

UNESCO. (2002). *Early childhood care? Development? Education?* UNESCO Policy Briefs on Early Childhood No. 1.

UNESCO. (2007). *Strong foundations: Early childhood care and education. EFA global monitoring report.* Paris: UNESCO Publishing.

Weiss, C. (1995). The four 'I's' of school reform: how interests, ideology, information and institution affect teachers and principals. *Harvard Educational Review, 65*(4), 571–592.

Wolfe, J. (2002). *Learning from the past: Historical voices in early childhood education.* Alberta, Canada: Piney Branch Press.

World Health Organization (WHO). (1978). *Primary health care: Report of the International Conference on Primary Health Care.* Retrieved from http://www.searo.who.int/LinkFiles/Primary_and_Community_Health_Care_HFA_S1.pdf

World Health Organization (WHO). (1986). *Ottawa charter for health promotion.* Retrieved from http://www.who.int/hpr/NPH/docs/ottawa_charter_hp.pdf

World Health Organization (WHO). (1997). *Jakarta declaration on leading health promotion into the 21st century.* Retrieved from http://www.who.int/healthpromotion/conferences/previous/jakarta/declaration/en/

World Health Organization (WHO). (2011). *Rio political declaration on social determinants of health.* Retrieved from http://www.who.int/sdhconference/declaration/Rio_political_declaration.pdf

Zigler, E. F., & Hall, N. W. (2000). *Child development and social policy.* Boston, MA: McGraw-Hill Higher Education.

Analytic and Disciplinary Perspectives

5

The Nature and Impact of Risk and Protective Influences on Children's Development in Low-Income Countries

Theodore D. Wachs and Atif Rahman

The aim of this chapter is three-fold: (1) to summarize what is known about the types of developmental risk and protective influences commonly encountered by infants and children from low- and middle-income (LAMI) countries growing up in poor families; (2) to document the principles underlying the translation of risk and protective influences into cognitive or social-emotional developmental deficits or children's developmental resilience in the face of adversity; and (3) to illustrate how knowledge about underlying principles can be used to formulate more effective intervention strategies and policy decisions to promote cognitive and social-emotional competence for children growing up in LAMI countries. The potential importance of this knowledge is seen in evidence showing significantly lower cognitive and social-emotional competence for over 200 million young children from LAMI countries (Grantham-McGregor et al., 2007). Reduced early cognitive and social-emotional competence undermines young children's school readiness, subsequent school performance and, ultimately, contributes to the intergenerational transmission of poverty (Engle et al., 2007).

Although we will be emphasizing the nature and impact of risk and protective influences, in the early years of life, it is essential to avoid the assumption that only early risks are critical or that early interventions can act as an inoculation against all later risks. Exposure to risks occurring in middle childhood or adolescence, such as societal violence (Qouta, Punamäki & Sarraj, 2008; Williams, 2007) or low-quality school systems (Reimers, 2000) can have adverse long-term consequences. Similarly, exposure to protective factors in childhood or adolescence, such as social support (Hestyanti, 2006), community acceptance (Betancourt et al., 2010), or school-based feeding (Jomaa, McDonnell, & Probart, 2011) and intervention programs (Slone & Shoshani, 2008), can promote development or recovery in the face of severe stress. Given this, we include information on older children when results seem applicable to the early years.

Our review will focus on research done in LAMI countries, but we will utilize information from high-income countries when it involves conceptual issues or fundamental knowledge (e.g., neuroscience). In addition, our emphasis will be on potentially *preventable* risks that are common in LAMI countries. There is evidence that certain alleles predispose to antisocial behavior (Dick et al., 2009) or depression (Kaufman et al., 2004) in childhood and adolescence. Similarly, exposure to natural disasters such as earthquakes (Kiliç, Özgüven, & Sayil, 2003) or tsunamis (Neuner, Schauer, Catani, Ruf, & Ebert, 2006) has been linked to increased levels of child behavioral problems. However, the occurrence of natural disasters or the inheritance of risk alleles is not presently amenable to intervention or changes in public policy. In addition, larger ecological or social forces also can impact upon children but may be extremely difficult to modify, such as climate change (Sheffield & Landrigan, 2011), mass migration linked to societal violence (Lustig, 2010), and increasing urbanization (Sheuya, 2008). Our focus will be on risk and protective influences where intervention is currently possible.

Developmental Risk and Protective Influences

THE NATURE OF RISK AND PROTECTIVE INFLUENCES

Developmental risks refer to bioecological and/or psychosocial influences that are known to compromise children's cognitive, social-emotional, or physical-neural development (Krishnakumar & Black, 2002; Sameroff, Gutman, & Peck, 2003). Although such a definition may seem circular in nature (defining a factor as a risk by its outcome), the risks that will be discussed are those that have been repeatedly found to be linked to adverse developmental consequences and are therefore empirically defined. Because of its very nature, risk functions in a probabilistic manner when impacting upon development.[1] Exposure to a developmental risk increases the likelihood of compromised development but does not guarantee that development will be compromised. Thus, although iron deficiency anemia is a known risk factor for developmental delay, it would be incorrect to conclude that an anemic child will inevitably be developmentally delayed. What can be concluded is that an anemic child is significantly more likely to be developmentally delayed than a nonanemic child.

Protective influences refer to biological, individual, or contextual characteristics that can enhance children's competence and can reduce the likelihood of adverse consequences when children are exposed to risks (Masten, 2001; Masten & Powell, 2003).[2] As with risk, protective influences also operate in a probabilistic fashion. Exposure to protective factors increases the likelihood of more optimal development, but does not guarantee optimal development.

Although it is common to treat risk and protective factors as distinct concepts, in many cases, protective factors are the mirror image of risk factors. For example, low levels of maternal education can act as a risk factor inhibiting offspring cognitive development, whereas higher levels of maternal education can act as a protective factor facilitating offspring cognitive development (Emond, Lira, Lima, Grantham-McGregor, & Ashworth, 2006; Stith, Gorman, & Choudhury, 2003). In other cases, risk and protective factors are distinctly different. For example, adequate iron or zinc status can attenuate the detrimental effects of lead exposure upon child cognitive functioning (Hubbs-Tait, Nation, Krebs, & Bellinger, 2005; Solon et al., 2008).

WHY DO DEVELOPMENTAL RISKS AND PROTECTIVE INFLUENCES OPERATE IN A PROBABILISTIC FASHION?

The Role of Individual Differences

Whether exposure to a known risk factor results in compromised development will partly depend on individual biological or psychosocial characteristics. Illustrating the influence of individual biological characteristics, research carried out in Brazil has identified specific alleles that act to protect against both susceptibility to and the later cognitive consequences of early diarrhea burden (Oria et al., 2005). Illustrating the influence of individual psychosocial characteristics, evidence has shown that, under stressful conditions, children who are high in negative emotionality are more likely to use ineffective or rigid coping strategies, compared to children who are low in this trait (Lengua & Long, 2002). As will be noted later, the influence of individual characteristics has important implications for the design and evaluation of intervention programs for at-risk children.

The Role of Context

The impact of exposure to risk factors can also vary depending on the context within which the exposure occurs. For example, depending on culture, the use of multiple caregivers (Weisner, 2010) or child gender (Patel, Rahman, Jacob, & Hughes, 2004) may or may not serve as a developmental risk. In some cases, depending on context, the same influence may contain both risk and protective influences. Maternal seasonal migration to earn income may be a risk factor in terms of reducing caregiving and stimulation to the child. However, if the extra income results in better child nutrition, then health development may be facilitated (Macours & Vakis, 2007). Similarly, mothers who work in commercial farming industries may increase the likelihood of their children being exposed to pesticides, but the income mothers earn may also provide better access to health care for their children (Handal, Lozoff, Breilh, & Harlow, 2007).

Contextual characteristics also operate upon protective influences. Harkness (2013, Chapter 7, this volume) provides a detailed description of how the success or failure of early childhood development (ECD) interventions partly depends on whether the intervention is consistent with local developmental "agendas." Evidence from LAMI countries has also shown that the degree of benefit at-risk children get from participating in ECD intervention programs will partly depend on larger contextual characteristics, such as the level of family economic disadvantage (Nores & di Gropello, 2009), the level of maternal education (Umek, Marjonovic, Fekonja, & Bajc, 2008), or whether there is ongoing societal violence during the intervention period (Thabet, Vostanis, & Karim, 2005).

The Role of Timing

Whether a given bioecological or psychosocial factor serves as a risk or protective influence will partly depend on the age of the child. During certain age periods, specific risk or protective influences may be particularly salient (sensitive periods; see Knudsen, 2004; Shonkoff, Boyce, & McEwen, 2009). For example, long-term adverse cognitive and social-emotional consequences can occur as a result of iron deficiency anemia in the first year of life (Lozoff, Beard, Connor, Felt, Georgieff, & Schallert, 2006). Similarly, the positive impact of early adoption of institutionalized infants (Rutter et al., 2010) may reflect the first year of life as a sensitive period for certain aspects of brain development and the development of basic trust (van IJzendoorn & Juffer, 2006).

The Role of Dosage

Whether a given bioecological or psychosocial influence acts to impair or promote child competence also will depend upon "dosage." Dosage refers to the number and intensity of risk or protective influences the child encounters and the length of time the child is exposed to these influences. Time-limited exposure to stressful experiences or exposure to mild levels of risk are not likely to be harmful and, in some cases, may even facilitate development (Shonkoff et al., 2009; Tronick, 2006). In contrast, exposure to highly intense or repeated risks (toxic stress) is likely to result in developmental impairments (Shonkoff et al., 2009).

The Interplay of Risk and Protective Influences

The developmental literature has documented that significant numbers of children are doing substantially better than would be expected, given their level of risk exposure (Kreppner et al., 2007; Rutter, 2006; Werner & Smith, 1982, 1992). These children are referred to as "resilient" (Luthar, Cicchetti, & Becker, 2000).[3] The phenomenon of resilience illustrates that a child's level of competence does not depend simply on the number of risks the child encounters. Rather, it is the interplay among and between risk and protective influences that promotes developmental competence or vulnerability in children (Luthar et al., 2000; Wachs, 2000). Children who are exposed to multiple developmental risks are less likely to have adverse developmental outcomes if these children also encounter multiple protective influences (Rutter, 2006; Sameroff et al., 2003).

Common Risk and Protective Factors in Low- and Middle-Income Countries

RISK FACTORS

Risk factors that can compromise the cognitive or social-emotional development of children fall into three categories: bioecological risks, contextual risks, and risks deriving from individual characteristics. At present, very little evidence links individual risk factors identified in high-income countries (e.g., insecure attachment, low self-regulation capacities) to ECD outcomes in children from LAMI countries. This lack of evidence does not mean that individual characteristic risk factors are unimportant influences on developmental outcomes in these countries. Children with preexisting individual vulnerabilities, such as mental health problems or physical or sensorimotor disabilities, may be particularly vulnerable when exposed to societal violence, natural disasters, or trauma (Peek & Stough, 2010; Pine, Costello, & Masten, 2005). However, with a few exceptions to be noted later, the general paucity of evidence makes it difficult to come to any firm conclusions about the developmental consequences of individual characteristic risk factors for children from LAMI countries.

Many of the same bioecological and contextual risks that are commonly encountered by children growing up in poverty in LAMI countries are also encountered by poor children growing up in high-income countries (e.g., increased exposure to environmental toxins, reduced exposure to cognitively stimulating activities in the home; Evans, 2004). However, in LAMI countries, poor children are exposed to a greater number of risks (Richter, 2003; UNICEF, 2004; Walker et al., 2007), and certain types of bioecological or contextual risks are primarily seen in LAMI countries (e.g., malaria, refugee status as a result of societal violence). Common childhood risks in LAMI countries that predict compromised ECD have been identified in a number of detailed reviews (Engle & Black, 2008; Irwin, Siddiqi, & Hertzman, 2007; Wachs, 2003; Walker et al., 2007). A summary of identified developmental risks in LAMI countries is shown in Table 5.1.

Some readers may be surprised by the notable omission of poverty from Table 5.1. Although poverty has been consistently associated with ECD deficits in both high-income (Chen, Hetzner, & Brooks-Gunn, 2010) and LAMI countries (Fernald, Burke, & Gunnar, 2008; Grantham-McGregor et al., 2007), the developmental impact of growing up in poverty appears to be indirect rather than direct in nature. That is, poverty may serve as a marker for multiple developmental risks, which are the primary influence on child cognitive or social-emotional competence (Bradley, Corwyn, McAdoo, & Coll, 2001; Marais, Esser, Godwin, Rabie, &

TABLE 5.1 Known developmental risks compromising early childhood development in
low- and middle-income (LAMI) countries

Identified Risk:	Supportive Evidence:
BIOECOLOGICAL RISKS	
Intrauterine growth retardation/low birth weight	Rahi, Kumavat, Garg, & Singh, 2005 St. Clair et al., 2005
Malaria	Jukes et al., 2006
Protein calorie malnutrition	Tomlinson & Landman, 2007 Victora et al., 2008
Iodine deficiency	Field, Robles & Torero, 2009
Iron deficiency	Corapci, Radan, & Lozoff, 2006 Lozoff et al., 2006 Wachs, Posada, Carbonell, Creed-Kanashiro, & Gurkas, 2011
Child exposure to environmental lead	Solon et al., 2008
Child exposure to other environmental toxins (e.g., arsenic, mercury, pesticides)	Handal et al., 2007 Jedrychowski et al., 2006
Parasitic infections	Berkman, Lescano, Gilman, Lopez, & Black, 2002
Chronic diarrhea	Patrick et al., 2005
Childhood HIV infection	Abubakar, Van Baar, Van de Vijver, Holding, & Newton, 2008 Dobrovka-Krol, van IJzendoorn, Bakermans-Kranenburg, & Juffer, 2010 Sherr, Mueller, & Varral, 2009
CONTEXTUAL RISKS	
Inadequate opportunities for cognitive stimulation in the home	Paxon & Schady, 2007 Santos et al., 2008
Maternal depression	Adewuya & Ologun, 2006 Fernald, Burke, & Gunnar, 2008 Ozer et al., 2008
Exposure to domestic or societal violence	Catani, Schauer, & Neuner, 2008 Gewirtz, Forgatch, & Weiling, 2008 Kithakye, Morris, Terranova, & Myers, 2010 Kohrt al., 2008 Reichenheim, de Souza, Moraes, Jorge, da Silva, & Minayo, 2011 Williams, 2007
Insensitive or nonresponsive parenting	Paxon & Schady, 2007
Parental use of harsh physical punishment	Alyahri & Goodman, 2008 Fleitlich & Goodman, 2001 Goodman, Fleitlich-Bilyk, Patel, & Goodman, 2007
Institutional rearing that continues past the first year of life	Kreppner et al., 2007 van IJzendoorn, Luijk, & Juffer, 2008
Being orphaned	Cluver & Gardner, 2007 UNAIDS, 2008
Refugee status as a consequence of societal violence	Lustig, 2010 Murthy & Lakshminarayana, 2006 Schmidt, Kravic, & Ehlert, 2008

(continued)

TABLE 5.1 (Continued)

Identified Risk:	Supportive Evidence:
High levels of parental stress	Goodman et al., 2007 Grover, Pensi, & Banerjee, 2007
Crowded or highly chaotic home environments	Adewuya & Ologun, 2006 Ozer et al., 2008 Paxon & Schady, 2007 Rahi et al., 2005
Lack of services or societal stigmatization of children with developmental disabilities	Mirza, Tareen, Davidson, & Rahman, 2009

Note: A very detailed recent review with additional supportive evidence relating risks listed above to adverse child outcomes in LAMI countries is found in Walker, Wachs, Grantham-McGregor, Black, Nelson, Huffman, et al. (2011).

Cotton, 2008). Supporting this assertion is evidence from a large body of studies showing a significant developmental impact of specific risk factors such as malnutrition, environmental toxins, low maternal education level, family conflict, and crowding, even after controlling for family economic status (Barros, Matijasevich, Santos, & Halpern, 2010; Goodburn, Ebrahim, & Sanapti, 1990; Okiro et al., 2008; Ozer, Fernald, & Roberts, 2008; Partnership for Child Development, 1999; Robila & Krishnakumar, 2005; Wasserman et al., 2007). Implications of this assertion will be considered later in this chapter.

In addition to the information contained in Table 5.1, there is recent evidence showing that the consequences of exposure to developmental risk operate at both a behavioral and a neural level (Hackman & Farah, 2009). Exposure to developmental risks involving increased stress or reduced exposure to cognitive stimulation can result in alterations in the efficiency of brain areas involved in information processing, such as the prefrontal cortex, or in altered regulation of brain functions involved in stress reactivity, such as the hypothalamic-pituitary-adrenal (HPA) axis (Fernald & Gunnar, 2009; Hertzman & Boyce, 2010; Kishiyama, Boyce, Jimenez, Perry, & Knight, 2008).

PROTECTIVE FACTORS OPERATING IN LOW- AND MIDDLE-INCOME COUNTRIES

A large and growing body of evidence from high-income countries identifies biological and psychosocial influences that act either to promote ECD or to protect against the impact of developmental risks (Lester, Masten, & McEwen, 2006; Luthar, 2003). Presently, far less is known about the nature of protective influences in LAMI countries. Protective influences also fall into three categories: bioecological, contextual, and individual characteristics. Currently, there is very little evidence from LAMI countries identifying individual protective characteristics, again making it difficult to come to any firm conclusions in this area. However, this lack of evidence does not necessarily mean that individual characteristics do

TABLE 5.2 Known developmental protective influences in low- and middle-income (LAMI) countries

Protective Characteristic:	Supportive Evidence:
BIOECOLOGICAL PROTECTIVE INFLUENCES	
Sufficient intake of macronutrients	Macours & Vakis, 2007
Sufficient intake of folate	Solon et al., 2008
Breast-feeding	Kramer et al., 2008
Iron supplementation	Lozoff et al., 2006 Murray-Kolb & Beard, 2009
Prenatal iodine supplementation	Zimmermann, 2009
Multiple micronutrient supplementation	Allen, Peerson & Olney, 2009
CONTEXTUAL PROTECTIVE INFLUENCES	
Higher educational or language stimulation in the home	Barros et al., 2010 Dobrova-Krol et al., 2010
Programs promoting stimulating, responsive parenting	Cooper et al., 2009 Engle et al., 2007 Leung, Sanders, Leung, Mak, & Lau, 2003 Maulik & Darmstadt, 2009 Walker, Chang, Powell, Simonoff, & Grantham-McGregor, 2006
Preschool attendance, particularly in higher quality preschools	Engle & Black, 2008 Umek et al., 2008 Raine, Mellingen, Liu, Venables, & Mednick, 2003 Engle et al., 2007 Mwaura, Sylva, & Malmberg, 2008
Higher social support to parents and/or children	Cluver, Fincham, & Seedat, 2009 Williams, 2007
Maternal ability to cope with stress	DeZulueta, 2007 Williams, 2007
Higher maternal education level, which can either directly promote early childhood development or reduce the incidence or detrimental impact of risk factors	Austin et al., 2006 Santos et al., 2008 Hunter, Jain, Sadowski, & Sanhueza, 2000 Li, Zhang, & Zhu, 2008 Lovisi, López, Coutinho, & Patel, 2005
Early adoption of institutionalized children	Kreppner et al., 2007 van IJzendoorn & Juffer, 2006

not act to protect against developmental risks in LAMI countries. As will be noted later in this chapter, individual differences in both intelligence and temperament can influence the degree to which children react to stressors. Known bioecological or contextual influences that act to protect or promote the development of children from LAMI countries are shown in Table 5.2.

In contrast to developmental risks, there are far fewer bioecological protective factors that have been identified in LAMI countries. This discrepancy may be due to the fact that much of the research on potential bioecological protective factors done in these countries uses medical rather than ECD outcomes. Examples of these types of findings will be noted later in this chapter. What is shown in Table 5.2 is that identified contextual protective influences typically involve either direct parent–child interactions or influences that promote more stimulating or supportive parent–child interactions.

Mechanisms Underlying the Interplay of Risk and Protective Influences

From the standpoint of developing interventions, the sheer number of identified risks commonly encountered by children in LAMI countries seems daunting. However, rather than focusing on individual risk or protective influences, a fundamental thesis of this chapter is that risk and protective influences are linked. Because of such linkages, the developmental consequences of exposure to risk and protective influences are better understood in systems terms rather than individually (Wachs, 2000). Examples of what is meant by a linked system of risk and protective influences are provided below.

COVARIANCE AMONG RISK AND PROTECTIVE FACTORS

A substantial body of evidence from high-income countries shows that bioecological and contextual risk factors often cluster together (covary). As a result, children are more likely to encounter clusters of risks, rather than single isolated risks (Appleyard, Egeland, van Dulmen, & Sroufe, 2005; Bradley & Corwyn, 2002; Evans, 2004; Frank, Augustyn, Knight, Pell, & Zuckerman, 2001; Hetherington & Elmore, 2003; Wachs, 2000). Covariance among bioecological and contextual risk factors is especially critical for children growing up in poverty in LAMI countries. Examples of covariance between and among bioecological and contextual risks are illustrated in Table 5.3. As will be discussed below, one of the important consequences of covariance among risk factors is an increased likelihood of the child being exposed over time to accumulating numbers of risks (cumulative risk).

At present, there is far less evidence from LAMI countries documenting covariance among protective factors. However, some studies have shown that protective factors are associated with reduced exposure to known risk factors. For example, higher levels of social support to mothers are linked to a reduced risk of both infant malnutrition (Surkan, Ryan, Viera, Berkman, & Peterson, 2007) and maternal depression (Kuscu et al., 2008). In addition, breast-feeding has been shown to be associated with a reduced risk of infant and childhood morbidity (Bhutta et al., 2008; Tomlinson & Landman, 2007). Covariance among developmental risk factors or between risk and protective factors occurs even after taking account of the contributions of family economic status (Alyahri & Goodman, 2008; Armar-Klemusu, Ruel, Maxwell, Levin, & Morris, 2000; Baig-Ansari, Rahbar, Bhutta, & Badruddin, 2006; Desai & Alva, 1998; Ozer et al., 2008; Sinha, Deshmukh, & Garg, 2008).

TABLE 5.3 Covariances among bioecological and/or contextual risks in low- and middle-income (LAMI) countries

Risk:	Covaries with an Increased Risk of:
Nutritional deficiencies in infancy and early childhood	Infectious disease in infancy and childhood (Bhutta et al., 2008; Black et al., 2008; Guerrant, Oriá, Moore, Oriá, & Lima, 2008; Mussi-Pinhata, et al., 2007)
	Growing up in home environments characterized as less stimulating with parents who are less involved, responsive, or sensitive (Grantham-McGregor, 1984; Tomlinson & Landman, 2007)
Growing up in an overcrowded home	Infection in infancy or childhood (Abe et al., 2009; Hasan et al., 2006; Kristensen & Olsen, 2006; Mussi-Pinhata et al., 2007; Okiro, Ngama, Bett, Cane, Medley, & Nokes, 2008)
	Child ingestion of toxic substances (Siddiqui, Ruzzak, Naz, & Khan, 2008),
	Child not getting full course of immunization (Ndiritu et al., 2006)
	Infant or child malnutrition (Baig-Ansari et al., 2006; Gupta, Gehri, & Stettler, 2007; Hien & Kam, 2008)
	Spousal violence (Jeyaseelan et al., 2007).
	Parental use of harsh physical punishment with children (Alyahri & Goodman, 2008; Hunter et al., 2000)
	Maternal depression (Wachs et al., 2009)
Exposure to societal violence	Child abuse (Catani et al., 2008)
	Disruption of family or community support systems (DeZulueta, 2007; Lustig, 2010)
	Rejecting or neglecting parenting and/or maternal depression (Qouta et al., 2008)
	Child nutritional deficiency (Abdeen, Greenough, Chandran, & Qasrawi, 2007; Guha-Sapir, van Panhuis, Degomme, & Teran, 2005) Child not immunized (Agadjanian & Prata, 2003)
Infant or child HIV infected	Living in home environments characterized by a less adequate physical environment, a lower variety of stimulation, and lower caregiver acceptance of the child (Dobrova-Krol et al., 2010)
	Loss of parents/orphan status (Shah, 2008)

GOING BEYOND COVARIANCE: THE STRUCTURE OF RISK AND PROTECTIVE INFLUENCES

Developmental theorists have proposed that the bioecological and psychosocial environments of the child are organized hierarchically, going from distal macro-contextual influences like culture or economic status to specific proximal family-level characteristics, such as cognitive stimulation or food insecurity (Bronfenbrenner & Crouter, 1983; Wachs, 2003). A schematic diagram illustrating this hierarchical organization is shown in Figure 5.1. This figure illustrates not only that risk and protective factors covary, but that they are also organized in hierarchical linked chains going from distal to proximal influences.

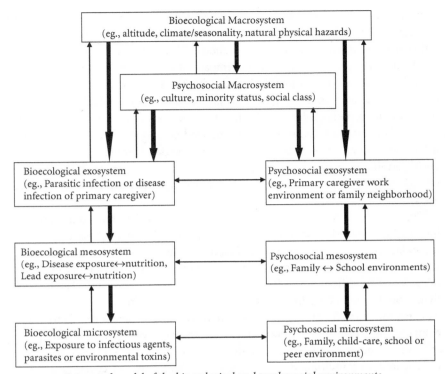

FIGURE 5.1 *Integrated model of the bioecological and psychosocial environments*

Source: Wachs, T. D. (2003). Expanding our view of context: The bio-ecological environment and development. In R. Kail (Ed.), *Advances in child development and behavior* (Vol. 31, pp. 365–411). New York: Academic Press. Reprinted with permission from Elsevier.

Three implications are inherent in this figure. First, consistent with what was discussed previously, links between proximal and distal portions of the chain are probabilistic. Living in poverty increases the probability of increased child exposure to developmental risk and reduces the probability of child exposure to protective factors (Alyahri & Goodman, 2008; Engle & Black, 2008; Richter, 2003), but this does not mean that all children from poor families have high exposure to risk influences and low exposure to protective influences. Support for this assertion is seen in evidence indicating that, even with significant increases in economic circumstances, the incidence of risk factors such as child nutritional deficits can remain stable, decrease slightly, or even increase (Alderman & Garcia, 1992; Alderman & Linnemayr, 2009; Aromolaran, 2004; Pongou, Ezzati, & Salomon, 2006; Sakisaka et al., 2006).

A second implication is that the strongest impact upon ECD will come from influences in the chain that are most proximal to the child (Bronfenbrenner, 1999; Grantham-McGregor et al., 2007; Walker et al., 2007). For example, evidence from LAMI countries has shown that the relation of family economic level to child cognitive performance depends, in part, on the level of cognitive stimulation in the home (Santos et al., 2008). Similarly, the detrimental impact of exposure to large-scale disruptions, such as societal violence or natural disasters, is more strongly associated with daily living stresses that result from the disruptions, rather than the disruptions per se (Fernando, Miller, & Berger, 2010).

Third, although the developmental impact of distal aspects of the chain may be indirect, distal aspects may influence whether and how proximal aspects of the chain translate into development deficits or resilience (Bronfenbrenner, 1999). For example, there is evidence indicating that the association between family size and child educational attainment differs, depending upon whether children live in urban versus rural areas (Eloundou-Enyegue & Williams, 2006; Li, Zhang, & Zhu, 2008). Similarly, in patriarchical cultures, paternal posttraumatic stress disorder (PTSD) may be more critical for child outcomes than maternal PTSD (Kiliç et al., 2003).

Figure 5.2 illustrates a chain of linked developmental risks known to be operating in LAMI countries. As seen in Figure 5.2, poverty increases the likelihood that urban families will live in slum areas. Families living in slum areas are more likely to encounter unsafe water, inadequate sanitation facilities, substandard housing, dense living conditions, hazardous locations, and insecure residential status. These living conditions, in turn, increase the likelihood that children growing up in slums will encounter a wide variety of known proximal developmental risk factors, such as an increased exposure to infectious disease agents, environmental toxins, physical injury, maternal depression, and domestic violence. The increased likelihood for encountering multiple developmental risks, as a result of covariance among individual risks and hierarchically organized multilevel risks, results in another underlying mechanism (cumulative risk) that has especially critical implications for children in LAMI countries.

DOSAGE AND CUMULATIVE RISK

Dosage can refer either to the intensity of the risk or protective factors the child encounters at a given point of time, or to the amount or number of exposures the child has to risk or protective factors over time (cumulative risk). Evidence from high-income countries has shown that exposure to high-intensity (toxic) stressors is more likely to disrupt neural, physical, and behavioral development than is exposure to less intense stressors (Shonkoff et al., 2009). Illustrating this point is evidence showing dose–response relations between exposure to certain environmental toxins during pregnancy to child health outcomes (Wigle et al., 2008). Similarly, in LAMI countries, children's exposure to highly intense stressors such as intrasocietal warfare or natural disasters can also result in increasingly compromised development (Catani et al., 2010; Murthy & Lakshminarayana, 2006). For example, the level of child PTSD is linearly related to the number of family members killed during a tsunami (Neuner et al., 2006).

Although developmental risks are all too frequent in LAMI countries, many do not reach the level required to produce toxic stress. Rather, because individual

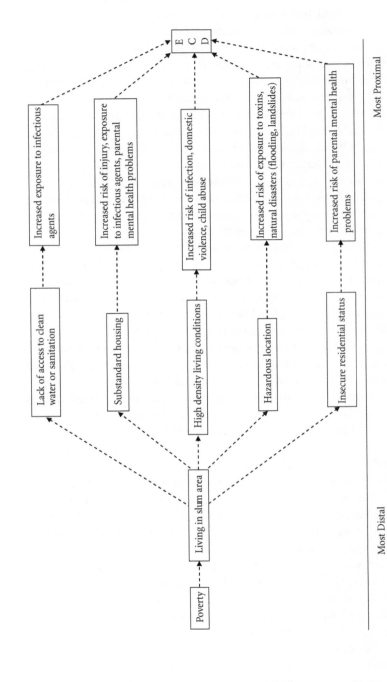

FIGURE 5.2 *Risk chain going from distal to proximal risks*

Note: Dotted lines denote that connections among risks are probabilistic. Links among risks adapted from, Sheuya. (2008). Improving the health and lives of people living in slums. *Annals of the New York Academy of Sciences, 136,* 298–306.

risk factors covary and are organized into hierarchical chains, what is more likely to occur in LAMI countries is an increased probability of children being exposed to less intense, cumulative multiple risks.[4] Evidence from both high-income (Appleyard et al., 2005; Evans, 2004; Masten & Obradovic, 2006; Sameroff, et al., 2003) and LAMI countries (Allwood, Bell-Dolan, & Husain, 2002; Gorman & Pollitt, 1996; Suliman et al., 2009; Walker et al., 2007, 2111) has consistently shown that the higher the number of cumulative risks the child encounters, the more development is compromised. For example, studies done in Central America have shown that the more chronic or the higher the number of risk factors a child encounters in early childhood, the lower the child's level of later school attainment (Gorman & Pollitt, 1996) and the higher the level of adolescent externalizing behavior problems (Corapci, Calatroni, Kaciroti, Jimenez, & Lozoff, 2010). Even when children are exposed to high-intensity risks, as in the case of child soldiers, it is the aggregated number of war trauma incidents children were exposed to, rather than any single aspect of war trauma, that was the strongest predictor of child mental health problems (Kohrt et al., 2008).

One major reason why cumulative risks may be particularly detrimental is illustrated by evidence on the physiological impact of risks that lead to increased individual stress levels. Physiological reactions to stress involve the activation of hormonal systems, such as the hypothalamic-pituitary-adrenal (HPA) axis, which functions to promote biological and behavioral adaptation to acute, time-limited stress. If stress is cumulative, continued secretion of HPA stress hormones leads to physiological damage, with a substantially increased risk of long-term adverse consequences on health, development, and well-being (i.e., *allostatic load*; Boyce & Ellis, 2005; Shonkoff et al., 2009). Evidence from both high-income (Hertzman & Boyce, 2010) and LAMI countries (Fernald & Gunnar, 2009) has indicated that the increased levels of cumulative stress associated with growing up in poverty can result in potential long-term dysregulation of the HPA system.

Exposure to cumulative risks may also be particularly detrimental for children's cognitive and social-emotional competence because cumulative risks can operate over time. Evidence from high-income countries has shown that early exposure to cumulative risks can increase the likelihood of exposure to later-occurring risks (Hertzman & Boyce, 2010). An example of this phenomena seen in LAMI countries occurs when poverty related chronic parental health problems requires children to care for ailing parents or to go to work to provide the family with money, which in turn forces children to drop out of school or delay schooling (Boyden, 2009; Nugent, 2008). There are long-term adverse human capital consequences associated with less schooling (Engle et al., 2007), as well as an increased risk of mental health problems among child laborers (Fekadu, Alem, & Hägglöf, 2006).

Evidence from high-income countries also has illustrated how exposure to cumulative risks can increase the child's sensitivity to later risks (*sensitization*; Hill-Soderlund et al., 2008). A similar sensitization phenomenon has been shown in LAMI countries, where studies have reported that previously malnourished children are more sensitive to later short-term nutritional deprivation than are adequately nourished children (Grantham-McGregor, Chang, & Walker, 1998; Pollitt, Cueto, & Jacoby, 1998), and that the risk of PTSD (Neuner et al., 2006) or poor adaptation (Catani et al., 2010) following a major tsunami was greatest for those children who had previous exposure to societal violence. In addition, results from a study by Macours and Vakis (2007) showed that better child nutritional status results in an increased likelihood that the child will benefit from participating in early intervention programs. This latter finding suggests that protective sensitization can also occur with exposure to one protective factor (better nutrition), thus increasing the positive impact of exposure to other protective factors (early schooling).

A related phenomenon is *blunting*, which occurs when previous risk exposure makes a child less able to make use of later protective experiences (Wachs, 2000). A substantial body of evidence from research done in both high-income (Masten & Obradovic, 2006; Sameroff & Rosenblum, 2006; Vanderbilt-Adriance & Shaw, 2006) and LAMI countries (Armar-Klemesu et al., 2000; Thabet et al., 2005) documents that high cumulative levels of exposure to developmental risks can compromise the positive influence of protective factors. For example, children with poor early nutritional status benefit less from later rearing in advantaged circumstances than do children with better early nutrition (Winick, Meyer, & Harris, 1975), and children with extended rearing in highly depriving orphanages are less likely to benefit from subsequent rearing in high-quality adoptive homes than are children with shorter durations of institutionalization (Beckett et al., 2006).

A CAUTIONARY NOTE: THE INTERPLAY OF RISK AND PROTECTIVE INFLUENCES MAY NOT BE LINEAR

Up to now, what we have presented is an additive model, wherein individual differences in child competence fundamentally reflect the difference between the number of risks and protective influences the child encounters. However, there is increasing evidence that the interplay of risk and protective factors can also be nonadditive (interactive). In an interactive model, the impact of a specific risk factor will depend on the nature and timing of other risk or protective factors (Rutter, 2006). For example, high individual reactivity to the environment may act to promote development when the environment is supportive or nurturing, but may act as a risk factor when the environment is stressful or neglectful (Boyce & Ellis, 2005). One important consequence of a nonlinear influence of risk and protective factors upon ECD is marked outcome differences in children exposed to similar types and levels of risk. For example, AIDS orphans in South Africa have the same level of exposure to community and household violence as non-AIDS orphans (Cluver, Fincham, & Seedat, 2009), but AIDS orphans have significantly higher levels of PTSD (Cluver, Gardner, & Operario, 2007).

Individual outcome differences in children exposed to similar levels of risk and protective influences are the likely result of the nonlinear interplay among multiple individual biological characteristics (e.g., genes: Caspi et al., 2002); behavioral characteristics (e.g., temperament: Wachs, 2006); the larger context (e.g., culture: Super & Harkness, 2010); and the timing of events (e.g., van IJzendoorn & Juffer, 2006). Illustrating the contribution of *individual biological characteristics*, research carried out in the Philippines showed that the negative relation between child blood lead level and cognitive performance was attenuated for children with higher levels of serum folate (Solon et al., 2008). Illustrating the contribution of *individual behavioral characteristics*, research done with a sample of Brazilian children living in a high-risk context has shown reduced mental health problems for children with higher levels of intelligence (Goodman Fleitlich-Bilyk, Patel, & Goodman, 2007). Similarly, the detrimental impact of societal violence upon the adjustment of young Kenyan children was significantly greater for children with a lower capacity for emotional self-regulation than for those with better self-regulation (Kithakye, Morris, Terranova, & Myers, 2010). Illustrating the contribution of *context,* there is evidence showing that the contributions of maternal sensitivity, depression, and level of social support to child cognitive and social-emotional development varies, depending on whether the children were Israeli or Palestinian (Feldman & Masalha, 2007). Illustrating the contributions of *timing,* Williams (2007) has documented how the nature and degree of impact of exposure to societal violence varies depending on the age of the child.

The operation of nonlinear processes does not mean that we need not be concerned with the impact of additive combinations of risk or protective factors. What it does mean is that we should not be surprised when we find marked individual differences in outcomes, even after taking into account the level of exposure to risk and protective influences. This caution may seem to add an additional level of complexity to an already complex set of processes, but it reflects the nature of reality and has implications when attempting to design or evaluate interventions to promote ECD.

Implications for Early Childhood Development Intervention and Policy

Much of what has been presented so far will be quite familiar to practitioners working in the field of ECD. However, it is critical to reinforce certain messages to emphasize their importance for both the design of interventions and policy decisions involving ECD.

TIMING OF INTERVENTIONS

The early years of life appear to be a particularly sensitive period for both brain and behavioral development (Shonkoff et al., 2009). An emphasis on interventions targeted at the early years is strongly supported by biological evidence on the effects of maternal prenatal iodine supplementation (Zimmermann, 2009) and the long-term neural consequences of infant iron deficiency anemia (Lozoff et al., 2006). Also supportive of the importance of early intervention is evidence involving psychosocial influences, such as the long-term detrimental consequences if infants are institutionalized past the first year of life (Rutter et al., 2010), and the consequences of postpartum maternal depression for both mother and infant (Wachs, Black, & Engle, 2009). Even without invoking the concept of sensitive periods, this conclusion is further validated by previously cited evidence, which has shown that exposure to cumulative early risks may sensitize the child to later risk, increase the likelihood of the child's encountering later risk conditions, and reduce the impact of the child's exposure to protective factors or interventions designed to promote ECD.

A Second Cautionary Note

As noted earlier, although we emphasize the importance of early intervention as a necessary means to promote ECD, we must not fall into the trap of assuming that early intervention per se is sufficient. Early intervention to promote developmental competence is an essential first step in a long-term continuing process, and not an end in itself (Wachs, 2000).

DETERMINING EFFECTIVE INTERVENTIONS

Interventions designed to remediate or reduce just one risk are less likely to have a strong or long-term impact, particularly for young children growing up in poverty in LAMI countries, where there is a substantially greater probability of the child encountering multiple bioecological and contextual risks (Irwin et al., 2007; Walker et al., 2007). Evidence supporting the use of *multidimensional interventions* comes from studies showing significantly stronger benefits when combining nutritional supplementation and cognitive stimulation, as compared to unidimensional interventions that utilize only supplementation or stimulation (Engle et al., 2007; Gardner et al., 2005; Lozoff et al., 2010; Nores & Barnett, 2009; Tomlinson & Landman, 2007). At a policy level, multidimensional interventions are more likely to occur when collaboration is promoted between governmental or nongovernmental institutions focusing on different child-related domains (e.g., medical, nutrition, ECD) for the purpose of delivering cross-domain intervention packages. Real-world examples of such collaboration are presented in Box 5.1.

PROMOTING EFFECTIVE INTERVENTION STRATEGIES
WITHIN THE CONSTRAINTS OF POLICY

When developmental scientists make policy-related recommendations, such as multidimensional interventions, or interventions starting early and carried out across time, an issue that is often raised is too few resources in LAMI countries

BOX 5.1. Intersectoral Collaboration to Address Child Development

The risk and resiliency literature shows that a number of sectors have key roles
to play in ameliorating risk and promoting positive practices for early childhood
development (ECD). These include health, education, women's development, and
social welfare, to name a few. In low- and middle-income (LAMI) countries, a
number of programs can be potential vehicles for ECD (Irwin et al., 2007). In the
health sector, the World Health Organizations (WHO) Integrated Management of
Childhood Illnesses (IMCI) program seeks to reduce childhood mortality, illness,
and disability, as well as promote health and development among children aged
0–5 years. The IMCI has both preventive and curative aspects, which are designed
to be implemented at the level of the family, the community, and through health
centers. In partnership with the United Nations Children's Fund (UNICEF), the
WHO has developed a special ECD component, called the Care for Development,
intended to be incorporated into existing IMCI programs. Health care professionals
are encouraged to view children's visits for acute minor illnesses as opportunities to
spread the messages of Care for Development, such as the importance of active and
responsive feeding to improve children's nutrition and growth and the importance
of play and communication activities to help children move to the next stages in
their development.

to simultaneously address all existing risk conditions (Bryce et al., 2008). One
approach to dealing with this issue is to place a greater emphasis on supporting interventions that utilize existing community resources (e.g., use of traditional healers to meet the mental health needs of orphaned children; Kayombo,
Mbwambo, & Massila, 2005) or supporting the use of empirically validated
traditional rearing practices that promote positive parent–infant interactions (e.g.,
skin-to-skin "kangaroo mother care"; Maulik & Darmstadt, 2009). Such interventions are more cost-effective and may be more sustainable.

In addition to emphasizing greater utilization of existing community resources,
the question of how to develop optimal ECD interventions, given policy realities,
can also be addressed by considering three critical issues. In addressing each issue,
we will propose specific recommendations. The recommendations proposed are
consistent with existing scientific knowledge on the nature and impact of risk and
protective factors, can be implemented with existing resources, and lend themselves to specific policy recommendations.

PRIORITIZING RISK OR PROTECTIVE FACTORS
IN INTERVENTION DESIGN

Risk Factors

The evidence cited earlier establishes that, unless we are dealing with a high-intensity
risk factor, developmental deficits will most likely result from the combined impact
of covarying multiple cumulative risks. This clearly implies the need to intervene

to reduce cumulative risk exposure. How can this be done with limited resources or without proposing highly complex intervention strategies? One way is to build upon existing covariances and target those risks that have the densest covariance networks with other risks. One example of a known developmental risk factor with a dense covariance network is maternal depression. As shown in Figure 5.3, maternal depression covaries with a number of other known developmental risks. Importantly, there is increasing evidence that maternal depression can be successfully treated in LAMI countries using existing resources or low-cost interventions (Baker-Henningham, Powell, Walker, & Grantham-McGregor, 2005; Rahman, Malik, Sikander, Roberts, & Creed, 2008; Rojas et al., 2007).

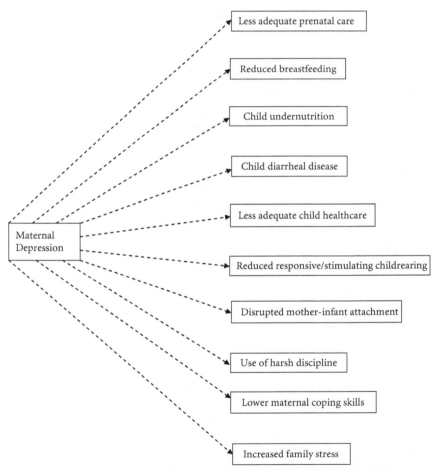

FIGURE 5.3 *Covariates of maternal postpartum depression with other developmental risks*

Note: Depression covariates adapted from Field, T. (2010). Postpartum depression effects on early interactions, parenting, and safety practices: A review. In*fant Behavior & Development, 33*, 1–6; and Wachs, T. D., Black, M., & Engle, P. (2009). Maternal depression: A global threat to children's health, development and behavior and to human rights. *Child Development Perspectives, 3*, 51–59.

Given the probabilistic nature of development, and the associational nature of much of this evidence, there is no guarantee that treating maternal depression will necessarily reduce the incidence of the multiple risks that covary with maternal depression. However, evidence from LAMI countries indicates that when low-cost interventions are used to treat maternal depression, an additional benefit is a reduction in infant risk factors, such as gastrointestinal illness or insecure attachment, and an increase in protective factors such as infant immunization, mother–infant play, maternal sensitivity, and maternal perception of social support (Cooper et al., 2009; Rahman et al., 2008). Box 5.2 provides a real-world example of this process.

BOX 5.2. An Example of an Early Multidimensional Program: Targeting a Key Risk Factor with Dense Covariance

Mothers provide the prenatal and postnatal environment to their infants, and they are key to the delivery of a wide range of early interventions impacting development, such as optimal nutrition, stimulation, and immunization. It is clear from the risk and resiliency literature that maternal depression is both a *risk factor* for impaired child development and a *marker* for covariate risks such as poor parental education, lack of support, and low economic status.

The Thinking Healthy Program developed in rural Pakistan addressed this key risk factor with a home-based intervention delivered by community health workers to pregnant and postnatal mothers (Rahman, 2007; Rahman et al., 2008). It consisted of mobilizing family support around the agenda of the child (rather than addressing maternal depression directly, as this often met with resistance) and individual counseling for mothers using cognitive behavioral techniques that addressed not only the mother's mood state but also her interactions with her infant. The mothers were provided health education in a manner that built up their self-confidence and belief in their parenting abilities. The community health workers were encouraged to assist the mother in problem solving (e.g., helping nonliterate mothers negotiate the health care system). The workers were able to titrate and tailor the intervention according to the individual needs of each family and, in the process, target those with the greatest needs.

The program had a significantly positive impact on maternal depression and associated disability. The mothers' functioning and social/partner support improved. Both parents spent more time playing with their infant, and their infant had fewer diarrheal episodes and increased rates of immunization.

The program had some important "selling-points" for policymakers in LAMI countries, who often do not see child development or maternal mental health as a priority. First, the intervention was integrated into the routine work of community health workers and was therefore not seen as a "vertical" program with large cost implications. Second, it addressed infant development in a holistic manner, incorporating nutrition, immunization, and protection from infectious disease— priorities for policymakers. These features facilitate the scaling-up of such programs.

Protective Factors

Previously cited evidence has shown that the impact of protective influences can be significantly attenuated when risk conditions are very high. Such evidence would seem to emphasize the necessity for initially attempting to reduce the level of cumulative risks encountered by infants and young children from LAMI countries, rather than a strategy involving increasing exposure to protective factors. However, promoting exposure to protective factors may be a viable intervention strategy if we can identify protective factors that also have dense covariance networks. At least one such protective influence does exist. As shown in Figure 5.4, higher maternal education is a protective factor with a documented dense covariance to both reduced risk and increased protective influences. Interventions targeted to promote maternal education have the potential to increase the child's exposure to multiple covarying protective influences. This is particularly true given evidence that more educated women are at lower risk for depression.

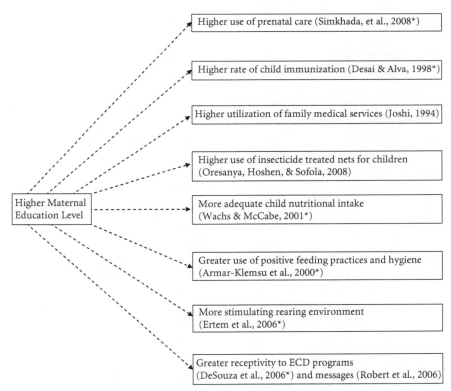

FIGURE 5.4 *Covariates of higher maternal education level with other protective influences.*

*Education level results are significant after accounting for family income or independent of family income.

Note: Additional supportive evidence found in Walker, S., Wachs, T. D., Grantham-McGregor, S., Black, M., Nelson, C., Huffman, S., et al. (2011). Inequality begins by early childhood: Risk and protective factors for early child development. *The Lancet, 378,* 1325–1338.

Emphasizing interventions that target risk and protective factors with the densest covariance networks is both cost-effective and consistent with current scientific knowledge about the relation of risk and protective influences upon ECD. These are not either/or strategies. Simultaneously investing in programs designed to reduce maternal depression and to promote maternal education are complementary, given the time span over which such programs would operate. Investment in programs to reduce the level of maternal depression is a strategy whose effects may be both immediate and broad in scope. Although potential gains in ECD associated with investing in increased maternal education may not be seen immediately, this is an important intervention that has long-term positive effects for the offspring of more educated women.

TARGETING THE LEVEL OF INTERVENTION

As discussed earlier, risk and protective influences are organized structurally in a chain of influences going from distal to proximal. In most cases, interventions that target proximal influences that directly impact upon the child should be favored. This conclusion is based on the probabilistic nature of the hierarchical chain. Intervening at higher levels of the chain may increase the chances that benefits of the intervention will directly impact upon the child, but there is no guarantee that this will actually occur. For example, evidence shows that mothers are more likely than their male partners to use family economic resources in ways that will promote offspring nutrition and health (Hindin, 2000; Kusago & Barham, 2001; Pfeiffer, Gloyd, & Li, 2001). Hence, providing extra income to families living in poverty is less likely to directly benefit the child if the income goes to the father rather than the mother.

However, there are situations in which intervening at more distal levels of the influence chain may be necessary. One such situation is when distal interventions are effective, low in cost, and relatively easy to supply, as in the case of providing micronutrient supplementation (Allen, Peerson, & Olney, 2009). A second situation occurs when distal contextual characteristics adversely impact on the efficacy of more proximal interventions. For example, the normally protective influence of maternal education or of training mothers in better infant feeding practices may not be effective in contexts that are severely resource depleted. In resource-depleted contexts, there is little that even the most educated or well-trained mother can do to help her child thrive (Armar-Klemusu et al., 2000; Reed, Habicht, & Niameogo, 1996; Tomlinson & Landman, 2007). In these situations, focusing on more distal interventions—such as increased access to nutritional or health resources—would be a necessary starting point before moving to more proximal interventions (Baig-Ansari et al., 2006). Similarly, promoting in-country adoption or foster parenting can be an important way of keeping orphaned children out of institutions. However, the benefits of such interventions may be significantly attenuated if adequate levels of resources, support, or monitoring of child progress are not provided to adoptive or foster parents (Miller, Gruskin, Subramanian, Rajaraman, & Heymann, 2006; Wolff & Fesseha, 2005). Under these conditions, more distal interventions, such as developing infrastructure capabilities to provide support and resources to foster or adoptive families, may be necessary if the potential benefits of fostering or adoptions are to be realized.

Findings such as these emphasize the need for policymakers to understand the chain of risk and protective influences as an initial starting point when considering interventions. As a general rule, proximal interventions are more likely to have a more immediate impact on ECD. However, knowing when more distal influences are acting to attenuate the impact of proximal influences is a necessary step in developing more cost-effective interventions, and one that is consistent with available knowledge on the nature of risk and protective influences. One way to integrate the proximal and distal are through community-based interventions involving local personnel who have knowledge of community contextual conditions that may influence the success or failure of interventions (Rahman, 2007).

UNIVERSAL VERSUS TARGETED INTERVENTIONS

As discussed earlier, the impact of risk and protective influences on ECD may vary depending upon individual characteristics. For example, some studies from high-income countries have indicated that children with a high reactive temperament appear to be more sensitive to both developmental risks and developmental protective factors than are children with a low reactive temperament (Boyce & Ellis, 2005). Studies carried out in LAMI countries have reported that females are significantly more likely than males to respond to interventions designed to reduce depression (Bolton et al., 2007) or PTSD (Tol et al., 2008). Studies from LAMI countries have also shown that women with lower levels of education (Ertem et al., 2006; Goodburn et al., 1990; Robert et al., 2006) or illiterate mothers (Roberfroid, Pelto, & Kolsteren, 2007) are less likely to benefit from interventions designed to promote child health or nutrition than are more educated or more literate mothers.[5]

Research-based evidence identifying specific individual characteristics that moderate the impact of known interventions emphasizes the importance of targeting existing interventions to those who are most likely to benefit, and for designing alternative or more intense interventions for those who are less likely to benefit. Targeting groups of individuals rather than total populations may seem to policymakers as yet one more example of an impractical "ivory tower" recommendation. Certainly, this would be so in a context where a very high proportion of children are being impacted by a high-dosage risk factor that can be eliminated through a low-cost intervention (e.g., providing iodized salt in populations with a known risk for severe iodine deficiency). However, in situations where these conditions do not occur, and where intervention resources are scarce, using existing evidence to identify and target subpopulations that are more likely to respond to a specific intervention may be a significantly more cost-effective measure than basing interventions on the poorly validated assumption that one size fits all.[6] Acting on the assumption that a one-size-fits-all intervention strategy will benefit everyone is likely to result in considerable waste of scarce resources and a less cost-effective intervention, as compared to a more targeted intervention strategy.

Conclusion

This chapter has summarized risk and protective factors that can act to compromise or promote ECD in children from LAMI countries. We have also presented evidence illustrating mechanisms such as covariance among risk and protective influences, the underlying structure of risk and protective influences, and the role of timing and cumulative risk, which influence how risk and protective influences result in developmental deficits or resilience. A fundamental thesis of this chapter is that an understanding of these underlying mechanisms is essential for the formulation of cost-effective intervention strategies to promote ECD, particularly for children growing up in LAMI countries. An important recommendation that follows from knowledge on the nature and role of risk and protective factors is the need to convince policymakers and elected officials to take such factors into account when formulating interventions that impact upon parents and children. One means to this end involves finding ways to promote meaningful dialogue between those working in the fields of developmental science and public policy, so as to avoid the all-too-common practice of oversimplified solutions to complex problems, or the all-too-common recommendation of overly complex programs that do not fit existing realities on the ground (McCall, 2009). Hopefully, this chapter is a small step in promoting such a dialogue.

Notes

1. Like risk, related concepts such as trauma or stressors are also often identified by their outcomes (harm, stress). Although there are certain differences among these concepts, for simplicity's sake, we will use terms such as stress and risk interchangeably in this chapter.
2. Developmental scientists often make a conceptual distinction between *protective* and *promotive* influences (Sameroff, Bartko, Baldwin, Baldwin, & Seifer, 1998). Protective influences operate primarily when the child is exposed to developmental risks and act to attenuate the detrimental impact of risk exposure. Promotive influences enhance development regardless of the child's risk status. Whereas the distinction between protective and promotive factors is important conceptually, this distinction may be less

critical in the real world. A quality bioecological and psychosocial environment will likely both promote development and protect against developmental risks (Sameroff et al., 1998). In this chapter, we will use the term "protective" to refer to both protective and promotive influences.

3. Child resilience is not an all-or-none phenomenon. Children can show resilience in one outcome domain while doing poorly in other outcome domains (Cicchetti & Blender, 2006; Rutter, 2006). In addition, children who display resilience at one time point can show developmental impairments at later time points (Luthar et al., 2000), especially when these later time points are more stressful.

4. Although covariance and hierarchical chaining processes are also likely occurring for protective factors, there is little direct evidence for the validity of this assumption. Hence, this chapter focuses primarily on covariance and chaining of risk influences.

5. Whereas poorly educated mothers may benefit less from ECD interventions, the children of less well-educated mothers are at greater risk for compromised ECD and may benefit more from receiving interventions that promote ECD. Low maternal education level may be a critical and low-cost indicator for identifying at-risk children (Barros et al., 2010).

6. The potential impact of individual difference characteristics upon reactivity to interventions also emphasizes the need to look for significant outcome differences within groups of children receiving intervention. Even when there are overall gains in development for children receiving intervention, there also may be significant numbers of children in the intervention condition who show little or no gain (Wachs, 2000).

References

Abdeen, Z., Greenough, P. G., Chandran, A., & Qasrawi, R. (2007). Assessment of the nutritional status of preschool-age children during the second Intifada in Palestine. *Food and Nutrition Bulletin, 28,* 274–282.

Abe, T., Honda, S., Nakazawa, S., Tuong, T., Thieu, N., Hung, L., et al. (2009). Risk factors for malaria infection among ethnic minorities in Binh Phuoc, Vietnam. *Southeast Journal of Tropical Medicine and Public Health, 40,* 18–29.

Abubakar, A., Van Baar, A., Van de Vijver, F. J. R., Holding, P., & Newton, C. R. J. C. (2008). Paediatric HIV and neurodevelopment in sub-Saharan Africa: A systematic review. *Tropical Medicine and International Health, 13,* 880–887.

Adewuya, A., & Ologun, Y. (2006). Factors associated with depressive symptoms in Nigerian adolescents. *Journal of Adolescent Health, 39,* 105–110.

Agadjanian, V., & Prata, N. (2003). Civil war and child health: Regional and ethnic dimensions of child immunization and malnutrition in Angola. *Social Science & Medicine, 56,* 2515–2527.

Alderman, H., & Garcia, M. (1992). Food security and health security: Explaining the levels of nutritional status in Pakistan. *Economic Development and Cultural Change, 42,* 485–507.

Alderman, H., & Linnemayr, S. (2009). Anemia in low-income countries is unlikely to be addressed by economic development without additional programs. *Food and Nutrition Bulletin, 30,* 265–269.

Allen, L. H., Peerson, J. M., & Olney, D. K. (2009). Provision of multiple rather than two or fewer micronutrients more effectively improves growth and other outcomes in micronutrient-deficient children and adults. *The Journal of Nutrition, 139*, 1022–1030.

Allwood, M. A., Bell-Dolan, D., & Husain, S. A. (2002). Children's trauma and adjustment reactions to violent and nonviolent war experiences. *Journal of the American Academy of Child and Adolescent Psychiatry, 41*, 450–457.

Alyahri, A., & Goodman, R. (2008). Harsh corporal punishment of Yemeni children: Occurrence, type and associations. *Child Abuse and Neglect, 32*, 766–773.

Appleyard, K., Egeland, B., van Dulmen, M. H. M., & Sroufe, L. A. (2005). When more is not better: The role of cumulative risk in child behavior outcomes. *Journal of Child Psychology and Psychiatry, 46*, 235–245.

Armar-Klemesu, M., Ruel, M. T., Maxwell, D. G., Levin, C. E., & Morris, S. S. (2000). Poor maternal schooling is the main constraint to good child care practices in Accra. *The Journal of Nutrition, 130*, 1597–1607.

Aromolaran, A. (2004). Household income, women's income share and food calorie intake in South Western Nigeria. *Food Policy, 29*, 507–530.

Austin, A., Blevins-Knabe, B., de Aquino, C., Burro, E., Kyung-Eun, P., Bayley, B., et al. (2006). Parent socialization, family economic well-being and toddlers' cognitive development in rural Paraguay. *Journal of Research in Childhood Education, 20*, 255–273.

Baig-Ansari, N., Rahbar, M. H., Bhutta, Z. A., & Badruddin, S. H. (2006). Child's gender and household food insecurity are associated with stunting among young Pakistani children residing in urban squatter settlements. *Food and Nutrition Bulletin, 27*, 114–127.

Baker-Henningham, H., Powell, C., Walker, S., & Grantham-McGregor, S. (2005). The effect of early stimulation on maternal depression: A cluster randomized controlled trial. *Archives of Disease in Childhood, 90*, 1230–1234.

Barros, A. J. D., Matijasevich, A., Santos, I. S., & Halpern, R. (2010). Child development in a birth cohort: Effect of child stimulation is stronger in less educated mothers. *International Journal of Epidemiology, 29*, 285–294.

Beck, S., Wojdyla, D., Say, L., Betran, A. P., Merialdi, M., Harris Requejo, J., et al. (2010). The worldwide incidence of preterm birth: A systematic review of maternal mortality and morbidity. *Bulletin of the World Health Organization, 88*, 31–38.

Beckett, C., Maughan, B., Rutter, M., Castle, J., Colvert, E., Groothues, C., et al. (2006). Do the effects of early severe deprivation on cognition persist into early adolescence? Findings from the English and Romanian adoptees study. *Child Development, 77*, 696–711.

Berkman, D., Lescano, A., Gilman, R., Lopez, S., & Black, M. (2002). Effects of stunting, diarrhoeal disease and parasitic infection during infancy on cognition in late childhood: A follow-up study. *The Lancet, 359*, 564–571.

Betancourt, T., Borisova, I., Williams, T., Brennan, R., Whitfield, T., de la Soudiere, M., et al. (2010). Sierra Leone's former child soldiers: A follow-up study of psychosocial adjustment and community reintegration. *Child Development, 81*, 1077–1097.

Bhutta, Z. A., Ahmed, T., Black, R. E., Cousens, S., Dewey, K., Giugliani, E., et al. (2008). What works? Interventions for maternal and child undernutrition and survival. *The Lancet, 371*, 417–440.

Black, R. E., Allen, L. H., Bhutta, Z. A., Caulfield, L. E., de Onis, M., Ezzati, M., et al. (2008). Maternal and child undernutrition: Global and regional exposures and health consequences. *The Lancet, 371*, 243–260.

Bolton, P., Bass, J., Betancourt, T., Speelman, L., Onyango, G., Clougherty, K. F., et al. (2007). Interventions for depression symptoms among adolescent survivors of war and displacement in northern Uganda: A randomized controlled trial. *Journal of the American Medical Association, 298*, 519–527.

Boyce, W. T., & Ellis, B. (2005). Biological sensitivity to context: I. An evolutionary-developmental theory of the origins and functions of stress reactivity. *Development and Psychopathology, 17*, 271–301.

Boyden, J. (2009). Risk and capability in the context of adversity: Children's contributions to household livelihoods in Ethiopia. *Children, Youth and Environments, 19*, 111–137.

Bradley, R. H., & Corwyn, R. (2002). Socioeconomic status and child development. *Annual Review of Psychology, 53*, 371–399.

Bradley, R. H., Corwyn, R. F., McAdoo, H., & García Coll, C. (2001). The home environments of children in the United States Part I: Variations by age, ethnicity, and poverty status. *Child Development, 72*, 1844–1867.

Bronfenbrenner, U. (1999). Environments in developmental perspective: Theoretical and operational models. In S. Friedman & T. D. Wachs (Eds.), *Measuring environment across the life span: Emerging methods and concepts* (pp. 3–30).Washington, DC: American Psychological Association.

Bronfenbrenner, U., & Crouter, A. (1983). The evolution of environmental models in developmental research. In P. Mussen & W. Kessen (Eds.), *Handbook of child psychology, Vol. 1: History, theory and methods* (4th ed., pp. 357–414). New York: Wiley.

Bryce, J., Coitinho, D., Darnton-Hill, I., Pelletier, D., Pinstrup, P., & Andersen, P. (2008). Maternal and child undernutrition: Effective action at national level. *The Lancet, 371*, 510–526.

Caspi, A., McClay, J., Moffitt, T., Mill, J., Martin, J., Craig, I., et al. (2002). Role of genotype in the cycle of violence in maltreated children. *Science, 297*, 851–854.

Catani, C., Gewirtz, A., Wieling, E., Schauer, E., Elbert, T., & Neuner, F. (2010). Tsunami, war and cumulative risk in the lives of Sri Lankan schoolchildren. *Child Development, 81*, 1176–1191.

Catani, C., Schauer, E., & Neuner, F. (2008). Beyond individual war trauma: Domestic violence against children in Afghanistan and Sri Lanka. *Journal of Marital and Family Therapy, 34*, 165–176.

Chen, J., Hetzner, N., & Brooks-Gunn, J. (2010). Growing up in poverty in developed countries. In G. Bremner & T. D. Wachs (Eds.), *Wiley-Blackwell handbook of infant development Vol. 2* (2nd ed., pp. 115–139). Boston: Wiley-Blackwell.

Cicchetti, D., & Blender, J. (2006). A multiple-levels-of-analysis perspective on resilience. *Annals of the New York Academy of Sciences, 1094*, 248–258.

Cluver, L., Fincham, D., & Seedat, S. (2009). Posttraumatic stress in AIDS-orphaned children exposed to high levels of trauma: The protective role of perceived social support. *Journal of Traumatic Stress, 22*, 106–112.

Cluver, L., & Gardner, F. (2007). The mental health of children orphaned by AIDS: A review of international and southern African research. *Journal of Child and Adolescent Psychiatry, 19*, 1–17.

Cluver, L., Gardner, F., & Operario, D. (2007). Psychological distress amongst Aids-orphaned children in Urban South Africa. *Journal of Child Psychology and Psychiatry, 48*, 755–763.

Cooper, P., Tomlinson, M., Swartz, L., Landman, M., Molteno, C., Stein, A., et al. (2009). Improving quality of mother-infant relationship and infant attachment in socioeconomically deprived community in South Africa: Randomized controlled trial. *British Medical Journal, 338,* 997–1002.

Corapci, F., Calatroni, A., Kaciroti, N., Jimenez, E., & Lozoff, B. (2010). Longitudinal evaluation of externalizing and internalizing behavior problems following iron deficiency in infancy. *Journal of Pediatric Psychology, 35,* 296–305.

Corapci, F., Radan, A. E., & Lozoff, B. (2006). Iron deficiency in infancy and mother-child interaction at 5 years. *Developmental and Behavioral Pediatrics, 27,* 371–378.

Desai, S., & Alva, S. (1998). Maternal education and child health: Is there a strong causal relationship? *Demography, 35,* 71–81.

DeSouza, N., Sardessai, V., Joshi, K., Joshi., V., & Hughes, M. (2006). The determinants of compliance with an early intervention programme for high-risk babies in India. *Child: Care, Health and Development, 32,* 63–72.

DeZulueta, F. (2007). Mass violence and mental health: Attachment and trauma. *International Review of Psychiatry, 19,* 221–233.

Dick, D. M., Latendresse, S. J., Lansford, J. E., Budde, J. P., Goate, A., Dodge, K. A., et al. (2009). Role of GABRA2 in trajectories of externalizing behavior across development and evidence of moderation by parental monitoring. *Archives of General Psychiatry, 66,* 649–657.

Dobrova-Krol, N. A., van IJzendoorn, M. H., Bakermans-Kranenburg, M. J., & Juffer, F. (2010). Effects of perinatal HIV infection and early institutional rearing on physical and cognitive development of children in Ukraine. *Child Development, 81,* 237–251.

Eloundou-Enyegue, P. M., & Williams, L. B. (2006). Family size and schooling in sub-Saharan African settings: A reexamination. *Demography, 43,* 25–52.

Emond, A., Lira, P., Lima, M., Grantham-McGregor, S., & Ashworth, A. (2006). Development and behaviour of low-birthweight term infants at 8 years in northeast Brazil: A longitudinal study. *Acta Paediatrica, 95,* 1249–1257.

Engle, P. L., & Black, M. M. (2008). The effect of poverty on child development and educational outcomes. *Annals of the New York Academy of Sciences, 1136,* 234–256.

Engle, P. L., Black, M. M., Behrman, J., Cabral de Mello, M., Gertler, P., Kapirri, L., et al. (2007). Child development in developing countries 3: Strategies to avoid the loss of developmental potential in more than 200 million children in the developing world. *The Lancet, 369,* 229–242.

Ertem I., Atay, G., Bingoler, B. E., Dogan, D. G., Bayhan, A., & Sarica, D. (2006). Promoting child development at sick-child visits: A controlled trial. *Pediatrics, 118,* e124–e131.

Evans, G. (2004). The environment of childhood poverty. *American Psychologist, 59,* 77–92.

Fekadu, D., Alem, A., & Hägglöf, B. (2006). The prevalence of mental health problems in Ethiopian child laborers. *Journal of Child Psychology and Psychiatry, 47,* 954–959.

Feldman, R., & Masalha, S. (2007). The role of culture in moderating the links between early ecological risk and young children's adaptation. *Development and Psychopathology, 19,* 1–21.

Fernald, L. C. H., Burke, H. M., & Gunnar, M. R. (2008). Salivary cortisol levels in children of low-income women with high depressive symptomatology. *Development and Psychopathology, 20,* 423–436.

Fernald, L. C. H., & Gunnar, M. (2009). Poverty-alleviation program participation and salivary cortisol in very low-income children. *Social Science and Medicine, 68,* 2180–2189.

Fernando, G., Miller, K., & Berger, D. (2010). Growing pains: The impact of disaster-related and daily stressors on the psychological and psychosocial functioning of youth in Sri-Lanka. *Child Development, 81,* 1192–1210.

Field, E., Robles, O., & Torero, M. (2009). Iodine deficiency and schooling attainment in Tanzania. *American Economic Journal: Applied Economics, 1,* 140–169.

Field, T. (2010). Postpartum depression effects on early interactions, parenting, and safety practices: A review. *Infant Behavior and Development, 33,* 1–6.

Fleitlich, B., & Goodman, R. (2001). Social factors associated with child mental health problems in Brazil: Cross sectional survey. *British Medical Journal, 323,* 599–600.

Frank, D., Augustyn, M., Knight, W., Pell, T., & Zuckerman, B. (2001). Growth, development and behavior in early childhood following prenatal cocaine exposure: A systematic review. *Journal of the American Medical Association, 285,* 1613–1625.

Gardner, J., Powell, C., Baker-Henningham, H., Walker, S., Cole, T., & Grantham-McGregor, S. (2005). Zinc supplementation and psychosocial stimulation: Effects on the development of undernourished Jamaican children. *American Journal of Clinical Nutrition, 82,* 399–405.

Gewirtz, A., Forgatch, M., & Weiling, E. (2008). Parenting practices as potential mechanisms for child adjustment following mass trauma. *Journal of Marital and Family Therapy, 34,* 177–192.

Goodburn, E., Ebrahim, G. J., & Senapati, S. (1990). Strategies educated mothers use to ensure the health of their children. *Journal of Tropical Pediatrics, 36,* 235–239.

Goodman, A., Fleitlich-Bilyk, B., Patel, V., & Goodman, R. (2007). Child, family, school and community risk factors for poor mental health in Brazilian schoolchildren. *Journal of the American Academy of Child and Adolescent Psychiatry, 46,* 448–456.

Gorman, K., & Pollitt, E. (1996). Does schooling buffer the effects of early risk. *Child Development, 67,* 314–326.

Grantham-McGregor, S. (1984). The social background of childhood malnutrition. In B. Schurch & J. Brozek (Eds.), *Malnutrition and behavior* (pp. 358–374). Lausanne, CH: IDECG.

Grantham-McGregor, S., Chang, S., & Walker, S. (1998). Evaluation of school feeding programs: Some Jamaican examples. *American Journal of Clinical Nutrition. Supplement, 67,* 785s–789s.

Grantham-McGregor, S., Cheung, Y., Cueto, S., Glewwe, P., Richter, L., Strupp, B., et al. (2007). Child development in developing countries 1: Developmental potential in the first five years for children in developing countries. *The Lancet, 369,* 60–70.

Grover, G., Pensi, T., & Banerjee, T. (2007). Behavioural disorders in 6–11-year-old, HIV-infected Indian children. *Annals of Tropical Paediatrics, 27,* 215–224.

Guerrant, R., Oriá, R., Moore, S., Oriá, M., & Lima., A. (2008). Malnutrition as an enteric infectious disease with long-term effects on child development. *Nutrition Reviews, 66,* 487–505.

Guha-Sapir, D., van Panhuis, W. G., Degomme, O., & Teran, V. (2005). Civil conflicts in four African countries: A five-year review of trends in nutrition and mortality. *Epidemiologic Reviews, 27,* 67–77.

Gupta, N., Gehri, M., & Stettler, N. (2007). Early introduction of water and complementary feeding and nutritional status of children in Northern Senegal. *Public Health Nutrition, 10,* 1299–1304.

Hackman, D., & Farah, M. (2009). Socioeconomic status and the developing brain. *Trends in Cognitive Sciences, 13*, 65–73.

Handal, A. J., Lozoff, B., Breilh, J., & Harlow, S. D. (2007). Neurobehavioral development in children with potential exposure to pesticides. *Epidemiology, 18*, 312–320.

Harkness, S., Super, C. M., Johnston Mavridis, C., Barry, O., & Zeitlin, M. (2013. Culture and early childhood development: Implications for policy and programs. In P. R. Britto, P. L. Engle, & C. M. Super (Eds.), *Handbook of early childhood development research and its impact on global policy* (Chapter 7). New York: Oxford University Press.

Hasan, K., Jolly, P., Marquis, G., Roy, E., Podder, G., Alam, K., et al. (2006). Viral etiology of pneumonia in a cohort of newborns till 24 months of age in rural Mirzapur, Bangladesh. *Scandinavian Journal of Infectious Diseases, 38*, 690–695.

Hertzman, C., & Boyce, T. (2010). How experience gets under the skin to create gradients in developmental health. *Annual Review of Public Health, 31*, 329–347.

Hestyanti, Y. (2006). Children survivors of the 2004 tsunami in Aceh, Indonesia: A study of resilience. *Annals of the New York Academy of Sciences, 1094*, 303–307.

Hetherington, E., & Elmore, A. (2003). Risk and resilience in children coping with their parents' divorce and remarriage. In S. Luthar (Ed.). *Resilience and vulnerability: Adaptation in the context of childhood adversities* (pp. 182–212). New York: Cambridge University Press.

Hien, N., & Kam, S. (2008). Nutritional status and the characteristics related to malnutrition in children under five years of age in Nghean, Vietnam. *Journal of Preventative Medicine and Public Health, 41*, 232–240.

Hill-Soderlund, A., Mills-Koonce, W. R., Propper, C., Calkins, S., Granger, D., Moore, G., et al. (2008). Parasympathetic and sympathetic responses to the strange situation in infants and mothers from avoidant and securely attached dyads. *Developmental Psychopathology, 50*, 361–376.

Hindin, M. (2000). Women's power and anthropometric status in Zimbabwe. *Social Science and Medicine, 51*, 1517–1528.

Hubbs-Tait, L., Nation, J., Krebs, N., & Bellinger, D. (2005). Neurotoxicants, micronutrients, and social environments. *Psychological Science in the Public Interest, 6*, 57–121.

Hunter, W. M., Jain, D., Sadowski, L. S., & Sanhueza, A. I. (2000). Risk factors for severe child discipline practices in rural India. *Journal of Pediatric Psychology, 25*, 435–447.

Irwin, L., Siddiqi, A., & Hertzman, C. (2007). *Early child development: A powerful equalizer.* Final report for the WHO Commission on the Social Determinants of Health. Geneva: WHO.

Jedrychowski, W., Jamowski, J., Flak, E., Skarupa, A., Mroz, E., Sochacka-Tatara, E., et al. (2006). Effects of prenatal exposure to mercury on cognitive and psychomotor function in one year-old infants. *Annals of Epidemiology, 16*, 439–447.

Jeyaseelan, L., Kumar, S., Neelakantan, N., Peedicayil, A., Pillai, R., & Duvvury, N. (2007). Physical spousal violence against women in India: Some risk factors. *Journal of Biosocial Science, 39*, 657–670.

Jomaa, L., McDonnell, E., & Probart, C. (2011). School feeding programs in developing countries: Impacts on children's health and educational outcomes. *Nutrition Reviews, 69*, 76–82.

Joshi, A. (1994). Maternal schooling and child health: Preliminary analysis of the intervening mechanisms in rural Nepal. *Health Transitions Review, 4*, 1–28.

Jukes, M. C. H., Pinder, M., Grigorenko, E., Smith, H. B., Walraven, G., Bariau, E. M., et al. (2006). Long-term impact of malaria chemoprophylaxis on cognitive abilities and educational attainment: Follow-up of a controlled trial. *PLoS Clinical Trials, 1*, e19.

Kaufman, J., Yang, B. Z., Douglas-Palumberi, H., Houshyar, S., Lipschitz, D., Krystal, J. H., et al. (2004). Social supports and serotonin transporter gene moderate depression in maltreated children. *Proceedings of the National Academy of Sciences of the USA, 101*, 17316–17321.

Kayombo, E., Mbwambo, Z., & Massila, M. (2005). Role of traditional healers in psychosocial support in caring for the orphans: A case of Dar-es Salaam City, Tanzania. *Journal of Ethnobiology and Ethnomedicine, 1*, 3–16.

Kiliç, E. Z., Özgüven, H. D., & Sayil, I. (2003). The psychological effects of parental mental health on children experiencing disaster: The experience of Bolu earthquake in Turkey. *Family Process, 42*, 485–495.

Kishiyama, M., Boyce, W., Jimenez, A., Perry, L., & Knight, R. (2008). Socioeconomic disparities affect prefrontal function in children. *Journal of Cognitive Neuroscience, 21*, 1106–1115.

Kithakye, M., Morris, A., Terranova, A., & Myers, S. (2010). The Kenyan political conflict and children's adjustment. *Child Development, 81*, 1114–1128.

Knudsen, E. I. (2004). Sensitive periods in the development of the brain and behavior. *Journal of Cognitive Neuroscience, 16*, 1412–1425.

Kohrt, B. A., Jordans, M. J. D., Tol, W. A., Speckman, R. A., Maharjan, S. M., Worthman, C. M., et al. (2008). Comparison of mental health between former child soldiers and children never conscripted by armed groups in Nepal. *Journal of the American Medical Association, 300*, 691–702.

Kramer, M. S., Aboud, F., Mironova, E., Vanilovich, I., Platt, R. W., Matush, L., et al. (2008). Breastfeeding and child cognitive development. *Archives of General Psychiatry, 65*, 578–584.

Kreppner, J., Rutter, M., Beckett, C., Castle, J., Colvert, E., Groothues, C., et al. (2007). Normality and impairment following profound early institutional deprivation: A longitudinal follow-up into early adolescence. *Developmental Psychology, 43*, 931–946.

Krishnakumar, A., & Black, M. (2002). Longitudinal predictors of competence among African-American children. The role of distal and proximal risk factors. *Journal of Applied Developmental Psychology, 23*, 237–266.

Kristensen, I., & Olsen, J. (2006). Determinants of acute respiratory infections in Soweto-a population-based birth cohort. *South African Medical Journal, 96*, 633–640.

Kusago, T., & Barham, B. (2001). Preference heterogeneity, power, and intrahousehold decision-making in rural Malaysia. *World Development, 29*, 1237–1256.

Kuscu, M., Akman, J., Karabekrioglu, A., Yardakul, Z., Orhan, L., Ozdemir, N., et al. (2008). Early adverse emotional response to childbirth in Turkey: The impact of maternal attachment styles and family support. *Journal of Psychosomatic Obstetrics and Gynecology, 29*, 33–38.

Lengua, L., & Long, A. (2002). The role of emotionality and self-regulation in the appraisal coping process: Tests of direct and moderating effects. *Journal of Applied Developmental Psychology, 23*, 471–493.

Lester, B., Masten, A., & McEwen, B. (2006). Resilience in children. *Annals of the New York Academy of Sciences, 1094*.

Leung, C., Sanders, M., Leung, S., Mak, R., & Lau, J. (2003). An outcome evaluation of the implementation of the triple P-positive parenting program in Hong Kong. *Family Process*, *42*, 531–544.

Li, H., Zhang, J., & Zhu, Y. (2008). The quantity-quality trade-off of children in a developing country: Identification using Chinese twins. *Demography*, *45*, 223–243.

Lovisi, G. M., López, J. R. R. A., Coutinho, E. S. F., & Patel, V. (2005). Poverty, violence and depression during pregnancy: A survey of mothers attending a public hospital in Brazil. *Psychological Medicine*, *35*, 185–1492.

Lozoff, B., Beard, J., Connor, J., Felt, B., Georgieff, M., & Schallert, T. (2006). Long-lasting neural and behavioral effects of iron deficiency in infancy. *Nutrition Review*, *64*, s34–s43.

Lozoff, B., Smith, J., Clark, K., Perales, C., Rivera, F., & Castillo, M. (2010). Home intervention improves cognitive and social-emotional scores in iron-deficient anemic infants. *Pediatrics*, *126*, e884–e894.

Lustig, S. (2010). An ecological framework for the refugee experience: What is the impact on child development? In G. W. Evans & T. D. Wachs (Eds.), *Chaos and its influence on children's development: An ecological perspective* (pp. 239–252). Washington, DC: American Psychological Association.

Luthar, S. (2003). *Resilience and vulnerability: Adaptation in the context of childhood adversities*. Cambridge, UK: Cambridge University Press.

Luthar. S., Cicchetti, D., & Becker, B. (2000). The construct of resilience: A critical evaluation and guidelines for future work. *Child Development*, *71*, 543–562.

Macours, K., & Vakis, R. (2007). *Seasonal migration and early childhood development*. World Bank Social Protection Discussion Paper 0702. Washington DC: The World Bank.

Marais, B., Esser, M., Godwin, S., Rabie, H., & Cotton, M. (2008). Poverty and human immunodeficiency virus in children: A view from the Western Cape, South Africa. *Annals of the New York Academy of Sciences*, *1136*, 21–27.

Masten, A. (2001). Ordinary magic: Resilience processes in development. *American Psychologist*, *56*, 227–238.

Masten, A., & Obradovic, J. (2006). Competence and resilience in development.. *Annals of the New York Academy of Sciences*, *1094*, 13–27.

Masten, A., & Powell, J. (2003). A resilience framework for research, policy, and practice. In S. Luthar (Ed.), *Resilience and vulnerability: Adaptation in the context of childhood adversities* (pp. 1–28). New York: Cambridge University Press.

Maulik, P., & Darmstadt, G. (2009). Community-based interventions to optimize early childhood development in low resource settings. *Journal of Perinatology*, *29*, 531–542.

McCall, R. B. (2009). Evidence-based programming in the context of practice and policy. *Social Policy Report*, *23*, 3–18.

Miller, C. M., Gruskin, S., Subramanian, S. V., Rajaraman, D., & Heymann, S. J. (2006). Orphan care in Botswana's working households: Growing responsibilities in the absence of adequate support. *American Journal of Public Health*, *96*, 1429–1435.

Mirza, I., Tareen, A., Davidson, L., & Rahman, A. (2009). Community management of intellectual disabilities in Pakistan: A mixed methods study. *Journal of Intellectual Disabilities Research*, *53*, 559–570.

Murray-Kolb, L. E., & Beard, J. L. (2009). Iron deficiency and child and maternal health. *American Journal of Clinical Nutrition*, *89*, 946S–950S.

Murthy, R. S., & Lakshminarayana, R. (2006). Mental health consequences of war: A brief review of research findings. *World Psychiatry, 5*, 25–30.

Mussi-Pinhata, M., Freimanis, L., Yamamoto, A., Koerelitz, J., Pinto, J., Cruz, M., et al. (2007). Infectious disease morbidity among young HIV-1- exposed but uninfected infants in Latin America and Caribbean Countries. *Pediatrics, 119*, e694–e704.

Mwaura, P., Sylva, K., & Malmberg, L. (2008). Evaluating the madrasa preschool programme in East Africa: A quasi-experimental study. *International Journal of Early Years Education, 16*, 237–255.

Ndiritu, M., Cowgill, K. D., Ismail, A., Chiphatsi, S., Kamau, T., Fegan, G., et al. (2006). Immunization coverage and risk factors for failure to immunize within the expanded programme on immunization in Kenya after introduction of new Haemophilus influenzae type b and hepatitis b virus antigens. *BMC Public Health, 6*, 132.

Neuner, F., Schauer, E., Catani, C., Ruf, M., & Elbert, T. (2006). Post-tsunami stress: A study of posttraumatic stress disorder in children living in three severely affected regions in Sri Lanka. *Journal of Traumatic Stress, 19*, 339–347.

Nores M., & Barnett, W. (2009). Benefits of early childhood interventions across the world: (Under) Investing in the very young. *Economics of Education Review, 29*, 271–282.

Nores, M., & di Gropello, E. (2009, April). Pre-K availability in Vietnam: Determinants of early attainment and progress. Symposium Presentation, Society for Research in Child Development, Denver.

Nugent, R. (2008). Chronic diseases in developing countries: Health and economic burdens. *Annals of the New York Academy of Sciences, 1136*, 70–79.

Okiro, E. A., Ngama, M., Bett, A., Cane, P.A., Medley, G. F., & Nokes, D. J. (2008). Factors associated with increased risk of progression to respiratory syncytial virus-associated pneumonia in young Kenyan children. *Tropical Medicine and International Health, 13*, 914–926.

Oresanya, O. B., Hoshen, M., & Sofola, O. (2008). Utilization of insecticide-treated nets by under-five children in Nigeria: Assessing progress towards the Abuja targets. *Malaria Journal, 7*, 145.

Oria, R., Patrick, P., Zhang, H., Lorntz, B., de Castro, C., Brito, G., et al. (2005). APOE4 protects the cognitive development in children with heavy diarrhea burdens in Northeast Brazil. *Pediatric Research, 57*, 310–316.

Ozer, E. J., Fernald, L. C. H., & Roberts, S. C. (2008). Anxiety symptoms in rural Mexican adolescents. *Social Psychiatry and Psychiatric Epidemiology, 43*, 1014–1023.

Partnership for Child Development. (1999). Short stature and the age of enrolment in primary school: Studies in two African countries. *Social Science and Medicine, 48*, 675–682.

Patel, V., Rahman, A., Jacob, K. S., & Hughes, M. (2004). Effect of maternal mental health on infant growth in low income countries: New evidence from South Asia. *British Medical Journal, 328*, 820–823.

Patrick, P., Oria, R., Madhaven, V., Pinkerton, R., Lorntz, B., Lima, A., & Guerrant, R. (2005). Limitations in verbal fluency following heavy burdens of early childhood diarrhea in Brazilian shantytown children. *Child Neuropsychology, 11*, 233–244.

Paxon, C., & Schady, N. (2007). Cognitive development among young children in Ecuador: The roles of wealth, health and parenting. *Journal of Human Resources, 42*, 49–84.

Peek, L., & Stough, L. (2010). Children with disabilities in the context of disaster: A social vulnerability perspective. *Child Development, 81*, 1260–1270.

Pfeiffer, J., Gloyd, S., & Li, L. (2001). Intrahousehold resource allocation and child growth in Mozambique: An ethnographic case-control study. *Social Science and Medicine, 53*, 83–97.

Pine, D., Costello, J., & Masten, A. (2005). Trauma, proximity, and developmental psychopathology: The effects of war and terrorism on children. *Neuropsychopharmacology, 30*, 1781–1792.

Pollitt, E., Cueto, S., & Jacoby, E. (1998). Fasting and cognition in well and undernourished school children. *American Journal of Clinical Nutrition. Supplement, 67*, 779s–785s.

Pongou, R., Ezzati, M., & Salomon, J. (2006). Household and community socioeconomic and environmental determinants of child nutritional status in Cameroon. *BMC Public Health, 6*, 98.

Qouta, S., Punamäki, R. L., & Sarraj, E. E. (2008). Child development and family mental health in war and military violence: The Palestinian experience. *International Journal of Behavioral Development, 32*, 310–321.

Rahi, M., Kumavat, A., Garg, S., & Singh, M. (2005). Socio-demographic co-relates of psychiatric disorders. *Indian Journal of Pediatrics, 72*, 395–398.

Rahman, A. (2007). Challenges and opportunities in developing a psychological intervention for perinatal depression in rural Pakistan-a multi-method study. *Archives of Women's Mental Health, 10*, 211–219.

Rahman, A., Malik, A., Sikander, S., Roberts, C., & Creed, F. (2008). Cognitive behavior therapy-based intervention by community health workers for mothers with depression and their infants in rural Pakistan: A cluster-randomized controlled trial. *The Lancet, 372*, 902–909.

Raine, A., Mellingen, K., Liu, J., Vebables, P., & Mednick, S. (2003). Effects of environmental enrichment at ages 3–5 years on schizotypal personality and antisocial behavior at ages 17 and 23 years. *American Journal of Psychiatry, 160*, 1627–1635.

Reed, B. A., Habicht, J. P., & Niameogo, C. (1996). The effects of maternal education on child nutritional status depend on socio-environmental conditions. *International Journal of Epidemiology, 25*, 585–592.

Reichenheim, M., de Souza, E., Moraes, C., Jorge, M., da Silva, C., & Minayo, M. (2011). Violence and injuries in Brazil: The effect, progress made, and challenges ahead. *The Lancet, 377*, 1962–1975.

Reimers, F. (2000). Unequal schools, unequal chances: The challenges to equal opportunity in the Americas. In F. Reimers (Ed.), *David Rockefeller Center series on Latin American studies*. Cambridge, MA: Harvard University Press.

Richter, L. M. (2003). Poverty, underdevelopment, and infant mental health. *Journal of Paediatrics and Child Health, 39*, 243–248.

Roberfroid, D., Pelto, G., & Kolsteren, P. (2007). Plot and see! Maternal comprehension of growth charts worldwide. *Tropical Medicine and International Health, 12*, 1074–1086.

Robert, R., Gittelsohn, J., Creed-Kanashiro, H., Penny, M., Caulfield, L., Narro, M., et al. (2006). Process evaluation determines the pathway of success for a health center-delivered nutrition education intervention for infants in Trujillo, Peru. *Journal of Nutrition, 136*, 634–641.

Robila, M., & Krishnakumar, A. (2005). Effects of economic pressure on marital conflict in Romania. *Journal of Family Psychology, 19*, 246–251.

Rojas, G., Fritsch, R., Solis, J., Jadresic, E., Castillo, C., Gonzalez, M., et al. (2007). Treatment of postnatal depression in low-income mothers in primary-care clinics in Santiago, Chile: A randomised controlled trial. *The Lancet, 370*, 1629–1637.

Rutter, M. (2006). Implications of resilience concepts for scientific understanding.. *Annals of the New York Academy of Sciences, 1094*, 1–12.

Rutter, M., Sonuga-Barke, E., Beckett, C., Castle, J., Kreppner, J., Kumsta, R., et al. (2010). Deprivation-specific psychological patterns: Effects of institutional deprivation. *Monographs of the Society for Research in Child Development, 75*, 295.

Sakisaka, K., Wakai, S., Kuroiwa, C., Flores, L., Kai, I., Aragón, M., et al. (2006). Nutritional status and associated factors in children aged 0–23 months in Granada, Nicaragua. *Public Health, 120*, 400–411.

Sameroff, A., Bartko., W., Baldwin, A., Baldwin, C., & Seifer, R. (1998). Family and social influences on the development of competence. In M. Lewis & C. Feiring (Eds.), *Families, risk and competence* (pp. 161–186). Mahwah, NJ: Erlbaum.

Sameroff, A., Gutman, L., & Peck, S. (2003). Adaptation among youths facing multiple risks: Prospective research findings. In S. Luthar (Ed.). *Resilience and vulnerability: Adaptation in the context of childhood adversities* (pp. 364–391). New York: Cambridge University Press.

Sameroff, A., & Rosenblum, K. (2006). Psychosocial constraints on the development of resilience. *Annals of the New York Academy of Sciences, 1094*, 116–124.

Santos, D., Assis, A., Bastos, A., Santos, L., Santos, C., Strina, A., et al. (2008). Determinants of cognitive function in childhood: A cohort study in a middle income context. *BMC Public Health, 8*, 202–217.

Schmidt, N., Kravic, N., & Ehlert, U. (2008). Adjustment to trauma exposure in refugee, displaced, and non-displaced Bosnian women. *Archives of Women's Mental Health, 11*, 269–276.

Shah, I. (2008). Prevalence of orphans among HIV infected children-A preliminary study from a pediatric HIV centre in Western India. *Journal of Tropical Pediatrics, 54*, 258–260.

Sheffield, P., & Landrigan, P. (2011). Global climate change and children's health: Threats and strategies for prevention. *Environmental Health Perspectives, 119*, 291–298.

Sherr, L., Mueller, J., & Varrall, R. (2009). A systematic review of cognitive development and child human immunodeficiency virus infection. *Psychology, Health & Medicine, 14*, 387–404.

Sheuya, S. (2008). Improving the health and lives of people living in slums. *Annals of the New York Academy of Sciences, 1136*, 298–306.

Shonkoff, J., Boyce, W. T., & McEwen B. (2009). Neuroscience, molecular biology and the childhood roots of health disparities: Building a new framework for health promotion and disease prevention. *Journal of the American Medical Association, 301*, 2252–2259.

Siddiqui, E., Razzak, J., Naz, F., & Khan, S. (2008). Factors associated with hydrocarbon ingestion in children. *Journal of the Pakistan Medical Association, 58*, 608–612.

Simkhada, B., Teijlingen, E., Porter, M., & Simkhada, P. (2008). Factors affecting the utilization of antenatal care in developing countries: Systematic review of the literature. *Journal of Advanced Nursing, 61*, 244–60.

Sinha, N., Deshmukh, P. R., & Garg, B. S. (2008). Epidemiological correlates of nutritional anemia among children (6–35 months) in rural Wardha, Central India. *Indian Journal of Medical Science, 62,* 45–54.

Slone, M., & Shoshani, A. (2008). Efficacy of a school-based primary prevention program for coping with exposure to political violence. *International Journal of Behavioral Development, 32,* 348–358.

Solon, O., Riddell, T. J., Quimbo, S. A., Butrick, E., Aylward, G. P., Bacate, M. L., et al. (2008). Associations between cognitive function, blood lead concentration, and nutrition among children in the central Philippines. *Journal of Pediatrics, 152,* 237–243.

St. Clair, D., Xu, M., Wang, P., Yu, Y., Fang, Y., Zhang, F., et al. (2005). Rates of adult schizophrenia following prenatal exposure to the Chinese famine of 1959–1961. *Journal of the American Medical Association, 294,* 557–562.

Stith, A., Gorman, K., & Choudhury, N. (2003). The effects of psychosocial risk and gender on school attainment in Guatemala. *Applied Psychology: An International Review, 52,* 614–629.

Suliman, S., Mkabile, S. G., Fincham, D. S., Ahmen, R., Stein, D. J., & Seedat, S. (2009). Cumulative effect of multiple trauma on symptoms of posttraumatic stress disorder, anxiety, and depression in adolescents. *Comprehensive Psychiatry, 50,* 121–127.

Super, C., & Harkness, S. (2010). Culture and Infancy. In G. Bremner & T. D. Wachs (Eds.), *Wiley-Blackwell handbook of infant development* (Vol. 1, 2nd ed., pp. 623–649). Boston: Wiley-Blackwell.

Surkan, P., Ryan, L., Viera, L., Berkman, L., & Peterson, K. (2007). Maternal social and psychological conditions and physical growth in low-income children in Piaui, Northeast Brazil. *Social Science and Medicine, 64,* 375–388.

Thabet, A. A., Vostanis, P., & Karim, K. (2005). Group crisis intervention for children during ongoing war conflict. *European Child & Adolescent Psychiatry, 14,* 262–269.

Tol, W. A., Komproe, I. H., Susanty, D., Jordans, M. J. D., Macy, R. D., & De Jong, J. (2008). School-based mental health intervention for children affected by political violence in Indonesia: A cluster randomized trial. *Journal of the American Medical Association, 300,* 655–662.

Tomlinson, M., & Landman, M. (2007). "It's not just about food": Mother-infant interaction and the wider context of nutrition. *Maternal and Child Nutrition, 3,* 292–302.

Tronick, E. (2006). The inherent stress of normal daily life and social interaction leads to the development of coping and resilience and variation in resilience in infants and young children. *Annals of the New York Academy of Sciences, 1094,* 83–104.

Umek, L., Marjanovic K., Fekonja, U., & Bajc, K. (2008). The effect of preschool on children's school readiness. *Early Child Development and Care, 178,* 569–588.

UNAIDS. (2008). *2008 report on the global AIDS epidemic.* Geneva: Joint United Nations Programme on HIV/AIDS.

UNICEF. (2004). *The state of the world's children 2005: Childhood under threat.* New York: UNICEF.

van IJzendoorn, M. H., & Juffer, F. (2006). The Emanuel Miller Memorial Lecture 2006: Adoption as intervention. Meta-analytic evidence for massive catch-up and plasticity in physical, socio-emotional, and cognitive development. *Journal of Child Psychology and Psychiatry, 47,* 1228–1245.

van IJzendoorn, M. H., Luijk, M. P. C. M., & Juffer, F. (2008). IQ of children growing up in children's homes. *Merrill-Palmer Quarterly, 54*, 341–366.

Vanderbilt-Adriance, E., & Shaw, D. (2006). Neighborhood risk and the development of resilience. *Annals of the New York Academy of Sciences, 1094*, 359–362.

Victora, C. G., Adair, L., Fall, C., Hallal, P. C., Martorell, R., Richter, L., et al. (2008). Maternal and child undernutrition: Consequences for adult health and human capital. *The Lancet, 371*, 340–357.

Wachs, T. D. (2000). *Necessary but not sufficient: The role of individual and multiple influences on human development*. Washington, DC: American Psychological Association Press.

Wachs, T. D. (2003). Expanding our view of context: The bio-ecological environment and development. In R. Kail (Ed.), *Advances in child development and behavior: Vol. 31* (pp. 365–411). New York: Academic Press.

Wachs, T. D. (2006). Contributions of temperament to buffering and sensitization processes in children's development.. *Annals of the New York Academy of Sciences, 1094*, 28–39.

Wachs, T. D., Black, M., & Engle, P. (2009). Maternal depression: A global threat to children's health, development and behavior and to human rights. *Child Development Perspectives, 3*, 51–59.

Wachs, T. D., & McCabe, G. (2001). Relation of maternal intelligence and schooling to offspring nutritional intake. *International Journal of Behavioral Development, 25*, 444–449.

Wachs, T. D., Posada, G., Carbonell, O., Creed-Kanashiro, H., & Gurkas, P. (2011). Infant nutrition and 12 and 18 months secure base behavior: An exploratory study. *Infancy, 16*, 91–111.

Walker, S., Chang, S., Powell, C., Simonoff, E., & Grantham-McGregor, S. (2006). Effects of psychosocial stimulation and dietary supplementation in early childhood on psychosocial functioning in late adolescence: Follow-up of randomized controlled trial. *British Medical Journal, 333*, 472.

Walker, S., Wachs, T. D., Grantham-McGregor, S., Black, M., Nelson, C., Huffman, S., et al. (2011). Inequality begins by early childhood: Risk and protective factors for early child development. *The Lancet, 378*, 1325–1338.

Walker, S., Wachs, T. D., Meeks-Gardner, J., Lozoff, B., Wasserman, G., Pollitt, E., et al. (2007). Child development in developing countries 2: Risk factors for adverse outcomes in developing countries. *The Lancet, 369*, 145–157.

Wasserman, G. A., Liu, X., Parvez, F., Ahsan, H., Factor-Litvak, P., Kline, J., et al. (2007). Water arsenic exposure and intellectual function in 6-year-old children in Araihazar, Bangladesh. *Environmental Health Perspectives, 115*, 285–289.

Weisner, T. (2010). Well-being, chaos and culture: Sustaining a meaningful daily routine. In G. W. Evans & T. D. Wachs (Eds.), *Chaos and its influence on children's development: An ecological perspective* (pp. 211–224). Washington, DC: American Psychological Association.

Werner, E., & Smith, R. (1982). *Vulnerable but invincible: A longitudinal study of resilient children and youth*. New York: McGraw-Hill.

Werner, E., & Smith, R. (1992). *Overcoming the odds: High risk children from birth to adulthood*. Ithaca, NY: Cornell University Press.

Wigle, D. T., Arbuckle, T. E., Turner, M. C., Berube, A., Yang, Q., Liu, S., et al. (2008). Epidemiologic evidence of relationships between reproductive and child health outcomes and environmental chemical contaminants. *Journal of Toxicology and Environmental Health Part B: Critical Reviews, 11,* 373–517.

Williams, R. (2007). The psychosocial consequences for children of mass violence, terrorism and disasters. *International Review of Psychiatry, 19*(3), 263–277.

Winick, M., Meyer, K., & Harris, R. (1975). Malnutrition and environmental enrichment by early adoption. *Science, 190,* 1173–1175.

Wolff, P. H., & Fesseha, G. (2005). The orphans of Eritrea: What are the choices? *American Journal of Orthopsychiatry, 75,* 475–484.

Zimmermann, M. B. (2009). Iodine deficiency in pregnancy and the effects of maternal iodine supplementation on the offspring: A review. *American Journal of Clinical Nutrition, 89,* 668S–672S.

6

Economic Perspectives on Some Important Dimensions of Early Childhood Development in Developing Countries

Jere R. Behrman and Sergio S. Urzúa

Early childhood development (ECD) has been widely recognized as possibly having high returns over the life cycle in both developing and developed countries. The cognitive, socioemotional, and physical health developments of preschool-aged children are increasingly seen as critical factors in schooling attainment, skill acquisition, and health and socioeconomic well-being later in life. In a recent *Lancet* paper on ECD, Grantham-McGregor et al. (2007) estimate that more than 200 million children under 5 years of age in developing countries do not reach their developmental potential, which likely means that they are substantially less able to take advantage of educational opportunities later in life and are less healthy, less productive, and of lower socioeconomic status as adults. Delayed child development is a cumulative process that starts as early as in the womb and, once begun, may be difficult (or very costly) to reverse during school years and adulthood. Thus, Heckman (2006) and others have argued that policies to improve human development are most cost effective if they begin as early as possible and are targeted to the most disadvantaged groups.[1]

Advocacy for and resources devoted to ECD have increased rapidly, particularly in developing countries. Figure 6.1 gives gross preschool enrollment rates for children of 0–5 years (the age range of interest for this chapter) for selected years starting in 1999 for major world regions. As the figure indicates, enrollment rates for preschool children have increased monotonically in all of the regions, although there is a fair amount of variance across regions.

Yet, very little is known with confidence about the economic justification for ECD programs in general and in developing countries in particular. The economic justification must depend on the comparison of benefits and costs of each ECD program. Recent surveys in *Lancet* point to considerable potential for ECD programs in developing countries (Engle et al., 2007, 2011), but what is known is based

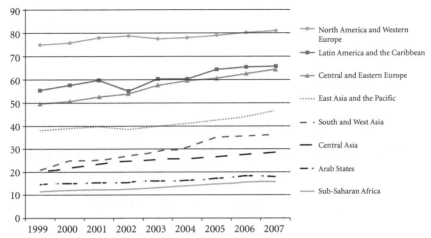

FIGURE *6.1 Trends in preschool gross enrollment rates, 1999–2007*
Source: Authors' calculations based on data from UNESCO (2010).

on relatively few studies, usually with small samples, limited outcome indicators, limited program information, and a small scale of operation. Furthermore, there is little or no effort in the literature to combine multiple impacts into an overall benefit. Evidence on costs is even scarcer, particularly for developing countries, with a lot of what is available referring not to the total resource costs of interest but to governmental expenditures that do not include private resource costs but may include pure transfers that are not resource costs.[2]

In this chapter, we review what is known and, perhaps more importantly, what is not known about components of economic analysis of ECD programs. The section "Framework for Analysis of Benefits and Costs" presents a framework for analyzing the impacts and costs of ECD investments over the life cycle and then considers benefits and costs. The next section turns to financing and management considerations. The final section summarizes the gaps in our knowledge and how we should move forward with regard to integrated data collection and analysis in order to better evaluate what works best regarding ECD.

Framework for Analysis of Benefits and Costs

To consider the economic benefits and costs from investments in ECD, we consider a life-cycle framework, with multiple life-cycle stages (Figure 6.2): prenatal, childhood, adolescence, adulthood, and old age. Early childhood development focuses on early childhood, typically preschool ages from 0 to 5 years, although for some purposes a somewhat longer age span is considered. As indicated in the figure, we conceptualize children as starting early childhood with genetic and environmental

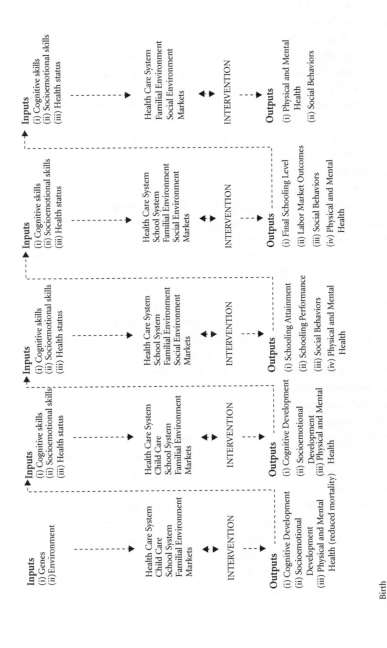

Inputs
(i) Genes
(ii) Environment

Health Care System
Child Care
School System
Familial Environment
Markets

INTERVENTION

Outputs
(i) Cognitive Development
(ii) Socioemotional
      Development
(iii) Physical and Mental
       Health (reduced mortality)

Inputs
(i) Cognitive skills
(ii) Socioemotional skills
(iii) Health status

Health Care System
Child Care
School System
Familial Environment
Markets

INTERVENTION

Outputs
(i) Cognitive Development
(ii) Socioemotional
      Development
(iii) Physical and Mental
       Health

Inputs
(i) Cognitive skills
(ii) Socioemotional skills
(iii) Health status

Health Care System
School System
Familial Environment
Social Environment
Markets

INTERVENTION

Outputs
(i) Schooling Attainment
(ii) Schooling Performance
(iii) Social Behaviors
(iv) Physical and Mental
       Health

Inputs
(i) Cognitive skills
(ii) Socioemotional skills
(iii) Health status

Health Care System
School System
Familial Environment
Social Environment
Markets

INTERVENTION

Outputs
(i) Final Schooling Level
(ii) Labor Market Outcomes
(iii) Social Behaviors
(iv) Physical and Mental
       Health

Inputs
(i) Cognitive skills
(ii) Socioemotional skills
(iii) Health status

Health Care System
Familial Environment
Social Environment
Markets

INTERVENTION

Outputs
(i) Physical and Mental
      Health
(ii) Social Behaviors

Conception — Birth — Early Childhood — Late Childhood — Adolescence — Prime-age Adulthood — Old Age

FIGURE 6.2 *Human development at each stage (inputs/outputs)*

endowments or "inputs."[3] Conditional on these endowments, ECD is directly affected by factors such as the health care system, child care options, the school system, markets, and the familial environment. Some of these factors reflect public policy decisions, such as the accessibility and quality of preschool ECD programs. Others reflect familial decisions, such as the nature and extent of stimulation and nutrition in the home environment and to what extent the child is exposed to the health care system and preschool ECD programs. Economic modeling suggests that parents (or other caregivers) will make these decisions in part based on the resources that they have, the prices and policies that they face, and the motives that they have for investing in their children (including altruism and expected possible future benefits, such as old-age support from the children). Examples of these decisions are parental decisions to enroll children in formal center-based versus informal care (i.e., non–center-based care by grandparents, siblings, other relatives, or nonrelatives); to enroll children in preschool, taking into account the effect of this on parental labor market participation (an issue particularly important for mothers); and whether to enroll children in private versus public child care centers (Bernal & Keane, 2010, 2011; Noboa-Hidalgo & Urzúa, 2012; also see Woodhead (2013), Chapter 16, this volume). Because these motives are likely to be forward-looking, the expected impacts of these decisions on outcomes over the child's life and the expected future school, work, and other conditions that may affect the value of these impacts all enter into the parental decisions about investment in ECD. Of course, these parental decisions affect many dimensions of ECD, but, for simplicity, we aggregate these dimensions of interest into three outcomes at the end of the early childhood life-cycle stage: cognitive skills, socioemotional skills, and health and nutritional status. And, at least for some purposes, we assume that these three composite outcomes propagate all the impacts of early childhood over all stages of later life.

The next column in Figure 6.2, therefore, starts with the "inputs" of cognitive skills, socioemotional skills, and health and nutritional status at the end of the early childhood. As during early childhood, there are a number of policy-related, market, and familial factors that, conditional on these inputs, affect the "outcomes" of this stage. For example, the form of child care (private or public, formal or informal) might determine the socioemotional and cognitive development of the children. Likewise, the type of health care provider (public or private) can affect the chances of preventing the development of illness among children. Thus, child and health care, as well as other factors, may interact with the "inputs" of this stage (the "outcomes" of the previous stage), so that dynamic complementarities of the types are emphasized, as, for example, by Cunha et al. (2006) and Cunha and Heckman (2007). Because of such complementarities, for instance, there may be higher returns to schooling investments for children with greater cognitive and socioemotional development when they enter school. The outcomes of this stage, in turn, are the inputs into the next stage, and so on through the life course.

BENEFITS OF EARLY CHILDHOOD DEVELOPMENT INVESTMENTS

We define the benefits of ECD investments to include appropriately weighted sums of all the impacts of these investments where, in Figure 6.2, by "impacts" we mean changes in outcomes, such as in labor market outcomes or physical and mental health. Given this framework, to access the benefits of ECD or of interventions to enhance ECD (such as preschool programs) is quite challenging for several reasons. First, decisions to invest in ECD are behavioral decisions that parents or other caregivers make in response to a number of factors, some important ones of which are likely to be unobserved by analysts, such as genetically influenced abilities, health, and some prices. If these unobserved factors have direct impact on outcomes later in the life cycle, in addition to any impact through the observed outcomes at the end of the early childhood life-cycle stage, it may be difficult to identify confidently the impacts of the investments in components of ECD versus the impacts of these unobserved factors. For this reason, randomized controlled trials or econometric methods[4] identifying causal impacts of investments in ECD are likely to be informative, as are structural models of the underlying behaviors that permit the investigation of counterfactual policies.[5] To understand the importance of this, consider, for example, the evaluation of a program aimed at boosting self-control among children. Suppose that "good" parents are aware of the benefits associated with such programs, and, consequently, they are more likely to send their children to such programs, and, consequently, children with worse parents are less likely to participate in such programs. Omitting the fact that parents self-selected their children into those programs ("treatment") would lead to a comparison of "apples" with "oranges." Participant children would be fundamentally different from nonparticipant children, for reasons beyond the programs themselves. Without understanding what motivated parents to enroll children in the programs, one cannot infer their causal impact, nor can one understand how parents would react to changes in the policy. Therefore, the combination of formal statistical and economic models can inform about the impact of these programs.

Second, to evaluate the total benefits, decisions have to be made regarding the outcomes of interest and the intermediate or mediating channels. For example, to researchers and policymakers should evaluate if cognitive skills.... cognitive skills at the end of the early childhood stage an outcome of interest in themselves versus a channel through which ECD investments affect schooling success and adult productivities in labor markets and home activities. To the extent that these cognitive skills at the end of the early childhood stage are mediating channels, it would be double-counting to include among the benefits of ECD both the impact on cognitive skills at the end of the early life stage *and* changes in adult productivities.

Third, as illustrated in Figure 6.2, the outcomes of interest vary considerable in kind, from labor market outcomes to better social behaviors to better health and reduced mortality. But to estimate the overall benefits or to be able to compare benefits with costs requires some weights or "prices" to combine the various impacts. For some possible impacts, such as increased wages in labor markets, valuing the impacts in monetary terms is relatively easy. But for other impacts, such as averting mortality and improving social relations, valuations are difficult and controversial. For instance, the value of averted mortality at times is empirically measured by the cheapest alternative means of averting mortality and at times by the income-mortality risks adults accept in their occupational choices. The resulting range in the values of averted mortality is enormous. Summers (1992), for example, uses the cheapest alternative way to avert mortality for estimates from Pakistan (vaccinations), which translates into $1,250 (2005 US$). Perhaps at the other extreme is the "revealed-preference" model based on labor market choices and mortality risk-wage choices, probably the leading approach for estimates of the value of averting mortality in the United States. This approach has been developed and promoted most visibly by Viscusi (1993, 2008) and has been adopted for use by various U.S. governmental agencies (Robinson, 2007; Viscusi & Aldy, 2003). This approach, as applied by Bartick and Reinhold (2010), for example, values the cost of a death of an infant in the United States at $10.56 million (2007 dollars), which, with the expected life at birth in 2007 of 77.7 years in the United States and with a 3% annual rate of return, would yield a constant annuity stream of $342,000 per year or 7.9 times the mean real U.S. gross domestic product (GDP) per capita in 2007.[6]

Fourth, impacts of ECD investments are posited to occur over many years in subsequent life-cycle stages, as shown in Figure 6.2. This adds two additional dimensions, beyond valuing the impacts when they occur and aggregating the impacts to obtain total benefits. The first additional dimension is that if there is a return to using resources for other investments, then $1,000 received now is more valuable than $1,000 received, say, in 40 years, when the child becomes a prime-age adult. This is because, in the intervening decades, the dollars received can now be reinvested. Therefore, it is desirable to calculate the present discounted value (PDV) of impacts of investments that occur with some lags into the future. This may affect the value of these investments considerably. For instance, the PDV of receiving $1,000 in 40 years is $307 today, if the discount rate is 3%, $97 if it is 6%, and only $22 if it is 10% (Table 6.1).

TABLE 6.1 Present discounted value (PDV) of $1,000 received, with various lags at alternative discount rates

Discount Rate	3.00%	6.00%	10.00%
LAG IN YEARS			
10	$744	$558	$386
40	$307	$97	$22
60	$170	$30	$3

TABLE 6.2 Present discounted value (PDV) of $1,000 received, with various lags at alternative discount rates, adjusted for survival probabilities

Discount Rate	3.00%	6.00%	10.00%	Survival Probability
LAG IN YEARS				
10	$675	$506	$350	0.9067
40	$252	$80	$18	0.8232
60	$112	$20	$2	0.6615

Survival probabilities based on life tables for India.

The second additional dimension is that obtaining these returns depends on survival, adjusting for which further reduces their PDVs (Table 6.2).

Fifth, for the purpose of guiding policies, it would be desirable to have estimates of the social benefits of ECD investments that include, for example, spillover effects (whether negative or positive) on others (Knowles & Behrman, 2004, 2005). This is the case because one major motive for policy interventions—the *efficiency motive*—is to improve efficiency if there is a differential between the private and the social rates of return, a difference that may arise because of the difference between the private and the social benefits.[7] This is a major motive for policy because if differentials exist between the private and the social rates of return to an action, then, through reallocations, it would be possible to make everyone better off with the same resources and the same technology. Or, to make the same point in a different way, if the private incentives are identical to the social incentives, there is no efficiency motive for changing policies to try to change private behaviors (although there may be distributional motives, such as reducing poverty).

Sixth, society may have concerns about income distribution, and thus weigh the benefits from ECD programs differentially depending on who receives the benefits. There may be more concern, for example, in the ECD of children from poor families because of interests in breaking the intergenerational transmission of poverty. If so, then, in evaluating ECD programs, differential welfare weights might be placed on the outcomes depending on the family backgrounds of the children affected. Recent evidence suggests, for example, that in developing countries preschool attendance is often higher for children from better-off families than for children from poorer families and that cognitive skills differentials favor children from better-off families very early in life and are maintained or increased as the children age into the school years (Behrman, Engle, & Fernald, in press; Engle et al., 2011; Paxson & Schady, 2007; Schady et al., 2011). The literature reflects this concern crudely by often focusing on children from poor households, but does not tend to have a more nuanced characterization of variations in family background that captures the existing substantial variance among the poor and among the near-poor and better-off.

The available empirical estimates of the impacts of investments in ECD generally do not deal well with these six issues related to calculating the benefits of such
investments. Instead, they tend to focus on one or a few impacts, usually for some
relatively small age range, generally early in the life cycle. Nevertheless, these estimates may be informative about some possibly key building blocks for obtaining
estimates of benefits of investing in ECD.

Engle et al. (2007, 2011) provide two recent reviews of ECD program impacts
in developing countries. The studies included in these reviews (a) had to deal with
programs that promote child development through components of psychosocial
support such as stimulation, responsive interaction, early education, or other
social investments, often in combination with health, nutritional, social safety
net, or educational interventions (thus, programs that have significant impacts on
children in developing countries, such as salt iodization, but do not have a psychosocial program component are not included);[8] (b) had to be completed since
1990; (c) had to have what Engle et al. (2007, 2011) judged as adequate comparison
groups to permit causal inferences; and (d) had to focus on children 0–6 years old
and to report cognitive, language, social-emotional, or mental health outcomes
(although analyses examining related outcomes, such as parent caregiving or preschool attendance, are also considered). Engle et al. (2007) identified 20 studies
that met these criteria; Engle et al. (2011) identified 42 additional studies that met
these criteria. Most of these studies deal with programs that are directed considerably or even exclusively to children from disadvantaged backgrounds, particularly
with regard to poverty. Despite the thorough search underlying these reviews,
fairly few studies permit even relatively crude comparisons because of the range
of instruments used and varying approaches to estimation (e.g., what controls are
included). If all the studies using different measures for cognitive skills are considered together, there are eight studies for parenting/family strengthening programs (often part of primary health care or other programs) and 14 studies for
organized early childhood learning centers (e.g., preschools) for which effect sizes
(calculated using standard techniques) are presented.[9] Table 6.3 gives the medians
and the ranges for the effect sizes on cognitive skills from these studies. For both
parenting and center programs, the ranges of estimated effect sizes are fairly large,
but for both type of programs, the median estimates are about 0.30, which is a
considerable effect size.[10]

These estimates are promising, but—situated within the frameworks above—
have a number of definite limitations. First, these estimates refer to but one of the
major aggregate outcomes of the early childhood stage in Figure 6.2. Second, they
are mostly for outcomes for children still in that life-cycle stage or not far beyond
that stage. Therefore they provide very little direct information about the effects
on longer-run subsequent outcomes of interest—schooling success, labor market
outcomes, adult social behaviors, and the like—Third, they are conditional on
the few particular market and policy contexts considered and may not generalize to other contexts. Fourth, the estimates summarized in Table 6.3 provide

TABLE 6.3 Impacts of early childhood development (ECD) programs in developing countries

	Cognitive Skills Effect Sizes		
	Median	Range	No. Studies
Center-based preschool and day care	0.33	−0.14 to 1.15	14
Parent and parent–child interactions	0.28	−0.05 to 0.80	8

Source: Compiled from Engle et al. (2007, 2010).

no information about the impact of supply-side variations in the quality of such programs or what policies most effectively could cause improved ECD (although Engle et al. [2011] do provide some information about effects of program characteristics for some programs; also see Behrman, Engle, & Fernald, in press). Fifth, they generally do not provide much information about the dependence of the program impacts on the ages when children enroll, the duration of exposure, or interactions between program characteristics and family background, although a few studies in which they are included find these to be important factors (e.g., Armecin et al., 2006; Behrman, Cheng, & Todd, 2004; Ghuman, Behrman, Borja, Gultiano, & King, 2005; Noboa-Hidalgo & Urzúa, 2012; Urzúa & Veramendi, 2010). Sixth, information on impacts alone does not provide enough information to judge whether programs are desirable or not. Quite aside from the challenges of going from multiple impacts to obtain overall benefits, there is the separate challenge of measuring the resource costs of the programs, which the next subsection discusses.

More information exists about the impacts of ECD interventions in developed economies, particularly the United States. This evidence suggests that human development can be altered in early childhood by effective interventions that change the balance between risk and protection, thereby shifting the odds in favor of more adaptive outcomes. Early childhood development programs that deliver carefully designed interventions with well-defined objectives and that include well-designed evaluations have been shown to influence the developmental trajectories of children whose well-being is threatened by socioeconomic disadvantages, family disruptions, and disabilities. Programs that combine child-focused educational activities with explicit attention to parent–child interactions and relationship-building appear to have the greatest impact (Heckman, 2006; Shonkoff & Phillips, 2000). However, the effects of ECD programs depend on their specific designs and on the characteristics of the affected population (Blau & Currie, 2006; Haveman & Wolfe, 1994; Lamb, 1996). Out-of-home ECD services might have positive or negative effects depending on ECD center quality (Baydar & Brooks-Gunn, 1991; Blau, 1999; Currie & Thomas, 1995; Duncan, 2003; Love, 2003; Network, 2003), time spent in child care (Fabes, Hanish, & Martin, 2003; Maccoby & Lewis, 2003), parental characteristics (Ahnert & Lamb, 2003; Baydar & Brooks-Gunn, 1991; Currie & Thomas, 1995), and the child (Crockenberg, 2003; Currie & Thomas, 1995; Fabes et al., 2003; Greenspan, 2003). The effects of ECD programs are more consistently positive for cognitive outcomes than for noncognitive or social-emotional outcomes (Dmitrieva, Steinberg, & Belsky, 2007), except among high-quality child care centers (Sammons et al., 2007). But these results from developed countries cannot safely be transplanted directly to developing countries as they depend on different market, policy, resource, and cultural contexts. These studies also, in many cases, have the same limitations as noted in the previous paragraph for studies on developing countries. Thus, the literature on ECD interventions in developed economies poses some important questions to be investigated for developing countries, more than it provides answers to such questions.

EARLY CHILDHOOD DEVELOPMENT RESOURCE COSTS AND BENEFIT-TO-COST RATIOS

To fully evaluate ECD interventions and to compare them with alternative uses of public resources, it is necessary to also have estimates of resource costs in order to be able to calculate benefit–cost ratios or internal rates of return. We empha-size that the correct cost concept refers to the real resources that society uses for an intervention, whether public or private resources or distortions introduced by taxes and other means of financing public expenditures. The public real resource costs include the time of public employees and goods and services that have alter-native uses, but *not* pure transfers that only redistribute purchasing power among members of society. It is impossible to track how people use those transfers. For this reason, the public budgetary costs do not necessarily represent the public real resource costs (to say nothing of the total real resource costs) because transfers may be important components of public expenditures—with many conditional cash transfer programs providing important examples. In addition to the pub-lic resource costs, the private resource costs may be considerable if, for example, mothers have to spend considerable time to assure that their children attend pre-school centers or to participate in such programs. The distortion costs reflect the impacts of changed incentives due, for example, to taxes on labor efforts. These may be considerable—for example, some estimates suggest a quarter of public sec-tor expenditures or more (Harberger, 1997). For all of these reasons, studies that compare governmental budgetary costs across interventions are not comparing real resource costs and may be fundamentally misleading about the relative real resource costs across interventions.

We also note that, within the framework presented in Figure 6.2, most of the real resource costs of ECD interventions occur in early childhood, not with lags of many years, as occurs for many of the impacts of interest for such interven-tions. Therefore, the importance of discounting and adjusting for child survival is likely to be much less on the cost side than on the benefit side for ECD interven-tions. But these costs are not likely to be entirely absent. If ECD interventions result in subsequent increased schooling or training, for example, there are likely to be associated increased real resource costs in adolescence or adulthood for those activities. And, again, these are likely to include public sector (in the form of teacher time and other school inputs), private (in the form of the opportunity costs of delayed labor force entry due to more schooling), and distortion costs (to raise the public funds for the additional public schooling expenditures).

Given that, to calculate benefit-cost ratios or internal rates of return, the real resource costs are equally important as the benefits, it might seem that there would be more or less equal efforts made to assemble information on real resource costs for ECD interventions throughout the developing world as for ECD impacts. But that is not the case. In sharp contrast to the reviews of impacts in Engle et al. (2007, 2011) and elsewhere, we are unaware of any such surveys of real resource costs of individual ECD interventions in developing countries. Engle et al. (2011), however, provide some suggestive estimates based on aggregate data of the potential gains to be obtained from partially closing the gap between preschool participation rates for children from families in the top quintile of the income distribution and other children. Subject to caveats that they discuss, these imply benefit-to-cost ratios generally well above 1, in the range of 14.3 to 17.6 for a 3% discount rate and in the range of 6.4 to 7.8 for a 6% discount rate. These are suggestive of significant potential, but are fairly far removed from the estimates for specific ECD interventions in specific contexts in developing countries that would be valuable for better policy guidance.

There are a few benefit-cost estimates for specific interventions in developed countries: 4.10 for the Abecedarian Project (Masse & Barnett, 2002), 5.70 for the Nurse Family Partnership (Karoly et al., 2005), and 2.2–31.5 for the Perry Preschool program (Barnett, 1996 Heckman et al., 2010;). These are substantially above 1, indicating significant gains from these programs (although there is some question of whether these estimates truly measure real resource costs rather than just public-sector budgetary costs). But, as for the impacts discussed in the previous subsection, these results cannot be transferred directly to developing countries due to the substantial differences in contexts, although they are suggestive of possibilities that should be investigated in developing countries. In fact, recent evidence showing substantial benefit-cost estimates in Turkey (between 3.7 and 5.8) confirms the potential impact of interventions in developing economies (Yilmaz & Yazihan, 2010). Behrman et al. (2004) provides another example of sizeable benefit-cost estimates. These authors document the positive effects of Bolivia's day care program *Proyecto Integral de Desarrollo Infantil* (PIDI).[11]

Finance and Management

As noted in the previous section, an important distinction exists between finances and real resources. Real resource costs are what are important in assessing benefit-cost ratios to prioritize among various interventions. But finances are important operationally, with financing coming from various mixtures of public, private, and nongovernmental (NGO) sources and, within governments, often from multiple ministries. Usually closely related to financing sources are questions of management and advocacy. Within governments, ECD programs at times are financed and managed across ministries or located within a ministry in which there may not be very high priority for ECD programs versus long-standing activities with long-standing and often powerful vested interests. For example, Ministries of Education tend to be dominated by long-standing commitments to formal schooling that may limit the possibilities for considering the expansion of preschool programs on an equal footing.

From the point of view of efficient use of resources, the point is not that ECD programs should be given special consideration regarding financing and management, but that they should be given equal consideration as alternatives, in which case the limited but growing evidence suggests that their probable benefits relative to costs should result in allocating increased resources to them. Therefore, one very important reason for undertaking estimates of benefit-to-cost ratios of ECD interventions in developing countries is to assure that appropriate attention and resources are given to such interventions.

Another important point is that finances, as noted, are likely potentially to come from multiple sources, not just governments. Indeed, a basic concern of public policy should be to attempt to increase efficiency, in the sense defined above, by interventions that reduce gaps between social and private rates of return, but not replace or "crowd-out" too much private or NGO resources. If, say, social rates of return to ECD interventions are higher than private rates of return (a topic on which systematic evidence would be very useful and currently is lacking), an argument exists for using public resources for providers of the ECD-related services to the extent necessary to increase the private to the social rate of return. Note that this argument holds independent of the ownership of the ECD service provider. It holds whether the service provider is public, private, or an NGO. Indeed, making such subsidies dependent on who owns the service provider by, for example, giving them only to public providers, is likely to increase inefficiency by creating different incentives for different types of providers. In fact, when it comes to increasing the efficiency of ECD interventions, private providers and NGOs should be considered important players: They do not have to deal with the bureaucracy of public institutions, they typically have high-quality human and physical capital, they can rapidly adjust to new developments in the field (such as new curricula or technology), and they share with the public providers a genuine interest for improving children's well-being. Consequently, public policies (including financing) should not discriminate against nonpublic providers.

These are important general points about financing and managing ECD programs. But to investigate them in particular contexts requires much more data and analyses than currently are available.

Gaps in the Literature and Moving Forward

In this chapter, we have tried to present an economic perspective on ECD in developing countries and summarize the limited empirical evidence that currently is available to inform the benefits and costs of ECD interventions, the policies that should be followed in various contexts, and how interventions should be financed and managed. Some systematic evidence suggests that ECD programs in developing countries may have substantial positive effects in some contexts, reinforced by aggregate estimates and estimates from developed economies that are suggestive of possibly high benefit-to-cost ratios. But, from undertaking this review, we are struck with how much we do not know as compared with what we do know. There are large gaps in the literature regarding the benefits of ECD and ECD programs in developing countries, with respect to incorporating the full range of possible impacts over the life cycle, and variations in the quality of ECD service-related providers, the importance of timing and of family background, and the role of different types of providers and their responsiveness to various incentives schemes (e.g., financing). Even greater gaps exist in measuring real resource costs and in understanding alternative financing and management possibilities and related appropriate policies.

Given the suggestions of substantial impacts, there is a high priority for collecting more and new information and undertaking much more systematic analyses of ECD in developing countries. These are critical issues that must be considered when designing, implementing, and developing ECD policies. The new types of data should include longitudinal information on treated groups and comparable control groups, as well as integrated information on various characteristics of ECD service providers that might affect not only child development, but also the responsiveness of these providers to various incentives and the costs of ECD service provision. It should also include experimental evidence through more randomized controlled trials that will illuminate the effectiveness of various policy strategies, including providing incentives and not simply trying to change inputs directly. With such data, more systematic methods could be used to estimate impacts and costs with less risk of biases caused by behavioral responses, measurement error, and unobserved variables—and structural models could be developed to investigate counterfactual policies and the longer-run impacts of such policies.

In summary, the economic analysis of ECD in developing countries is itself in its infancy but already shows some substantial possible benefits from expansion of ECD programs, and it has considerable potential for healthy growth in informing questions regarding what types of ECD programs and other interventions are most promising in various developing country contexts.

Conclusion

In this chapter, we present an economic perspective on ECD in developing countries and summarize the limited empirical evidence. We conclude that the economic analysis of ECD in developing countries is itself in its infancy. Some systematic evidence suggests that ECD programs in developing countries may have substantial effects in some contexts, probably more so for children from poorer families. However, there are large gaps in the literature regarding the benefits of ECD and ECD programs in these countries and how the benefits are distributed among children from different types of families. There are even greater gaps in measuring real resource costs and in understanding alternative financing and management possibilities and related appropriate policies.

A high priority exists for collecting more information and undertaking much more systematic analyses of ECD in developing countries. Certain dimensions of data are critical: longitudinal information on treated groups and comparable control groups, household-based sampling strategies to avoid the selectivity associated with ECD center-based sampling, integrated information on various characteristics of ECD service providers that might affect various dimensions of child development and the costs of ECD service provision, and experimental evidence through more randomized controlled trials that illuminate the effectiveness of various policy strategies. With such data, more systematic methods could be used to estimate benefits and costs with less risk of biases due to behavioral responses (self-selection into programs), measurement error, and unobserved variables—and structural models could be developed to investigate counterfactual policies and the longer-run impacts of such policies. The potential of what can be learned through better data and better analyses is substantial.

Acknowledgments

We thank Patrice Engle, Pia Britto, and other participants in the project workshop in Bellagio, Italy, for useful comments.

Notes

1. Presumably, this argument for investing more in early life is based on perceptions that the marginal rates of returns to investing in early life, versus the alternative of investing in later life-cycle stages, are relatively high. But it does not mean that more and more resources should be shifted from later-life to early-life investments. If enough resources are shifted from later-life to early-life investments, presumably the marginal rates of return to early-life investments will decline and those to later-life investments will increase until the two are equated—at which point any further shifts in investments from later-life to early-life investments are not warranted from a productivity point of view.

2. More specifically, governmental expenditure may include transfers designed to redistribute purchasing power in the society, which may be linked to ECD programs but are not inputs into those programs.

3. Such endowments have been found to be important determinants of adult outcomes in developing and developed economies (e.g., Alderman & Behrman, 2006; Behrman & Rosenzweig, 1999, 2002, 2004; Behrman, Rosenzweig, & Taubman, 1994; Heckman, Stixrud, & Urzúa, 2006; Urzúa, 2008).

4. These methods include difference-in-difference estimates that compare the changes in children exposed to a treatment with those not exposed; instrumental variable estimates that purge the observed ECD indicators of the components that are correlated with the unobserved variables; propensity score matching estimators that compare children who received a treatment with children who did not receive the treatment but who, in terms of the probability of receiving the treatment based on observed characteristics, are comparable; and regression discontinuity estimators that compare children right below with those right above some eligibility threshold for treatment.

5. A counterfactual policy is defined as a policy that has not happened but could, would, or might occur under a set of specific conditions.

6. Additional illustrations of estimating the benefits from improved early life nutrition are given in Alderman and Behrman (2006) and Behrman, Alderman, and Hoddinott (2005).

7. Private benefits are what individuals actually receive as the result of their actions. It does not include the benefits of the actions that might spill over to the other members of the community. These external benefits (also known as externalities) are captured in the social benefits.

8. Estimates of the impacts of some early-life nutritional interventions without psychosocial program components find that the impacts are considerable (e.g., Behrman, Alderman, & Hoddinott, 2004; Victora et al., 2008; and, in some cases, there is evidence of long-run effects three to four decades later in adulthood or in the next generation (e.g., Hoddinott et al., 2008; Behrman et al., 2009; Maluccio et al., 2009).

9. For no other outcome measure is there as many as five studies with effect sizes. The estimates for comprehensive programs in Engle et al. (2007) are included with the early childhood learning centers in this summary.

10. For the other measures used, some of the median effect sizes are of the same general magnitude as for cognitive skills (e.g., for parenting, 0.28 for motor skills in one study and 0.35 for socioemotional skills for three studies) but not all of them (e.g., for parenting, 0.17 for the HOME measure for three studies).

11. The PIDI program provides full-time day care and nutritional and educational services to children between the ages of 6 and 72 months in the homes of mothers living in low-income areas.

References

Ahnert, L., & Lamb, M. (2003). Shared care: Establishing a balance between home and child care settings. *Child Development, 74*(4), 1044–1049.

Alderman, H., & Behrman, J. R. (2006). Reducing the incidence of low birth weight in low-income countries has substantial economic benefits. *World Bank Research Observer*, *21*(1), 25–48.

Armecin, G., Behrman, J. R., Duazo, P., Ghuman, S., Gultiano, S., King, E. M., et al. (2006). *Early childhood development through integrated programs: Evidence from the Philippines, Cebu City*. New York/Philadelphia/Washington, DC: Universities of Pennsylvania and San Carlos (Office of Population Studies), Population Council and World Bank.

Barnett, W. S. (1996). *Lives in the balance: Age-27 benefit-cost analysis of the HighScope Perry Preschool Program* (Monographs of the HighScope Educational Research Foundation, 11). Ypsilanti, MI: HighScope Press.

Bartick, M., & Reinhold, R. (2010). The burden of suboptimal breastfeeding in the United States: A pediatric cost analysis. *Pediatrics*, *25*(5), 1048–1058.

Baydar, N., & Brooks-Gunn, J. (1991). Effects of maternal employment and child-care arrangements on preschoolers' cognitive and behavioral outcomes: Evidence from the children of the National Longitudinal Survey of Youth. *Developmental Psychology*, *27*(6), 932–945.

Behrman, J. R., Alderman, H., & Hoddinott, J. (2004). Hunger and malnutrition. In B. Lomborg (Ed.), *Global crises, global solutions* (pp. 363–420). Cambridge, UK: Cambridge University Press.

Behrman, J. R., Calderon, M. C., Preston, S., Hoddinott, J., Mortorell, R., & Stein, A. D. (2009). Nutritional supplementation of girls influences the growth of their children: Prospective study in Guatemala. *American Journal of Clinical Nutrition*, *90*, 1371–1379.

Behrman, J. R., Cheng, Y., & Todd, P. (2004). Evaluating preschool programs when length of exposure to the program varies: A nonparametric approach. *Review of Economics and Statistics*, *86*(1), 108–132.

Behrman, J. R., Engle, P., & Fernald, L. (In press). Preschool programs in developing countries. In P. Glewwe (Ed.), *Education policy in developing countries: What do we know and what should we do to understand what we don't know?* Minneapolis, MN: University of Minnesota.

Behrman, J. R., & Rosenzweig, M. R. (1999). Ability biases in schooling returns and twins: A test and new estimates. *Economics of Education Review*, *18*(2), 159–167.

Behrman, J. R., & Rosenzweig, M. R. (2002). Does increasing women's schooling raise the schooling of the next generation? *American Economic Review*, *92*(1), 323–334.

Behrman, J. R., & Rosenzweig, M. R. (2004). Returns to birth weight. *Review of Economics and Statistics*, *86*(2), 586–601.

Behrman, J. R., Rosenzweig, M. R., & Taubman, P. (1994). Endowments and the allocation of schooling in the family and in the marriage market: The twins experiment. *Journal of Political Economy*, *102*(6), 1131–1174.

Bernal, R., & Keane, M. P. (2010). Quasi-structural estimation of a model of childcare choices and child cognitive ability production. *Journal of Econometrics*, *156*(1), 164–189.

Bernal, R., & Keane, M. P. (2011). Child care choices and children's cognitive achievement: The case of single mothers. *Journal of Labor Economics*, *29*(3), 459–512.

Blau, D. (1999). The effect of child care characteristics on child development. *The Journal of Human Resources*, *34*(4), 786–822.

Blau, D., & Currie J. (2006). Preschool, daycare, and afterschool care: Who's minding the kids? In E. Hanushek & F. Welsh (Eds.), *Handbook of the economics of education* (Vol. 2, pp. 1164–1278). Amsterdam: North Holland.

Crockenberg, S. C. (2003). Rescuing the baby from the bathwater: How gender and temperament (may) influence how child care affects child development. *Child Development*, 74(4), 1034–1038.

Cunha, F, & Heckman, J. J. (2007). The technology of skill formation. *American Economic Review*, 97(2), 31–47.

Cunha, F., & Heckman, J. J. (2008). Formulating, identifying and estimating the technology of cognitive and noncognitive skill formation. *Journal of Human Resources*, 43(4), 738–782.

Cunha, F., Heckman, J. J., Lochner, L. J., & Masterov, D. V. (2006). Interpreting the evidence on life cycle skill formation. In E. Hanushek & F. Welch (Eds.), *Handbook of the economics of education* (pp. 697–812). Amsterdam: North Holland.

Currie, J., & Thomas, D. (1995). Does Head Start make a difference? *American Economic Review*, 85(3), 341–364.

Dmitrieva, J., Steinberg, L., & Belsky, J. (2007). Child-care history, classroom composition, and children's functioning in Kindergarten. *Psychological Science*, 18, 1032–1039.

Duncan, G. (2003). Modeling the impacts of child care quality on children's preschool cognitive development. *Child Development*, 74(4), 1454–1475.

Engle, P. L., Black, M. M., Behrman, J. R., Cabral de Mello, M., Gertler, P. J., Kapiriri, L., et al. (2007). International Child Development Steering Committee. Strategies to avoid the loss of potential among 240 million children in the developing world. *The Lancet*, 369, 229–242.

Engle, P. L., Fernald, L. C. H., Alderman, H., Behrman, J. R., O'Gara, C., Yousafzai, A., et al. (2011). Strategies for reducing inequalities and improving developmental outcomes for young children in low and middle income countries. *The Lancet*, 378(9799), 1339–1353.

Fabes, R. M., Hanish, L. D., & Martin, C. L. (2003). Children at play: The role of peers in understanding the effects of child care. *Child Development*, 74(4), 1039–1043.

Ghuman, S., Behrman, J. R., Borja, J. B., Gultiano, S., & King, E. M. (2005). Family background, service providers and early childhood development in the Philippines: Proxies and interactions. *Economic Development and Cultural Change*, 54(1), 129–164.

Grantham-McGregor, S., Cheung, Y. B., Cueto, S., Glewwe, P., Richter, L., & Strupp, B. (2007). Child development in developing countries 1: Developmental potential in the first five years for children in developing countries. *The Lancet (Series, Child Development in Developing Countries)*, 369, 60–70.

Greenspan, S. I. (2003). Child care research: A clinical perspective. *Child Development*, 74(4), 1064–1068.

Harberger, A. C. (1997). New frontiers in project evaluation: A comment on Devarajan, Squire and Suthiwart-Narueput. *World Bank Research Observer*, 12(1), 73–82.

Haveman, R., & Wolfe, B. L. (1994). *Succeeding generations: On the effects of investments in children*. New York: Russell Sage Foundation.

Heckman, J. J. (2006). Skill formation and the economics of investing in disadvantaged children. *Science*, 312, 1900–1902.

Heckman, J. J., Moon, S., Pinto, R., Savelyev, P., & Yavitz, A. (2010). The rate of return to the HighScope Perry Preschool Program. *Journal of Public Economics*, 94(1–2), 114–128.

Heckman, J. J., Stixrud, J., & Urzúa, S. (2006). The effect of cognitive and non-cognitive abilities on labor market outcomes and social behavior. *Journal of Labor Economics*, 24(3), 411–482.

Heckman, J. J., Urzúa S., & Vytlacil, E. J. (2006). Understanding instrumental variables in models with essential heterogeneity. *Review of Economics and Statistics, 88*(3), 389–432.

Hoddinott, J., Maluccio, J.A, Behrman, J. R., Flores, R., & Mortorell, R. (2008). The impact of nutrition during early childhood on income, hours worked, and wages of guatemalan adults. *The Lancet, 371,* 411–416.

Karoly, L. A., Kilburn, M. R., & Cannon, J. S. (2005). *Early childhood interventions: Proven results, future promise.* RAND Corporation Monograph Series Rand Corporation, Santa Monica, CA.

Knowles, J. C., & Behrman, J. R. (2004). *A practical guide to economic analysis of youth projects.* Philadelphia, PA: University of Pennsylvania and Bangkok, for World Bank, mimeo.

Knowles, J. C., & Behrman, J. R. (2005). Economic returns to investing in youth in developing countries: A review of the literature. In J. R. Behrman, B. Cohen, C. Lloyd, & N. Stromquist (Eds.), *The transition to adulthood in developing countries: Selected studies* (pp. 424–490). Washington, DC: National Academy of Science-National Research Council.

Lamb, M. (1996). Effects of non-parental child care on child development: An update. *The Canadian Journal of Psychiatry, 41,* 330–342.

Love, J. (2003). Child care quality matters: How conclusions may vary with context. *Child Development, 74*(4), 1021–1033.

Maccoby, E., & Lewis, C. (2003). Less day care or different day care? *Child Development, 74*(4), 1069–1075.

Maluccio, J. A, Hoddinott, J., Behrman, J. R., Quisumbing, A., Martorell, R., & Stein, A. D. (2009). The impact of nutrition during early childhood on education among Guatemalan Adults. *Economic Journal, 199*(537), 734–763.

Masse, L. N., & Barnett, W. S. (2002). *A benefit-cost analysis of the Abecedarian Early Childhood Intervention.* New Brunswick, NJ.: National Institute for Early Education Research.

Network (N.E.C.C.R.). (2003). Does amount of time in child care predict socioemotional adjustment during the transition to Kindergarten? *Child Development, 74*(4), 976–1005.

Noboa, H. G., & Urzúa, S. (2012). The effects of participation in public childcare centers: Evidence from Chile. *Journal of Human Capital, 6*(1), 1–34.

Paxson, C., & Schady, N. (2007). Cognitive development among young children in Ecuador: The role of health, wealth and parenting. *Journal of Human Resources, 42*(1), 49–84.

Robinson, L. A. (2007). Policy monitor: How U.S. government agencies value mortality risk reductions. *Review of Environmental Economics and Policy, 1,* 283–299.

Sammons, P., Sylva, K., Melhuish, E., Siraj-Blatchford, I., Taggart, B., Barreau, S., et al. (2007). *Influences on children's development and progress in key stage 2: Social/behavioral outcomes in year 5.* London: Institute of Education, University of London.

Schady, N., Behrman, J., Araujo, M. C., Azuero, R., Bernal, R., Bravo, D., et al. (2011). *Wealth gradients in early childhood cognitive development in five Latin American countries.* Washington, DC: Inter-American Development Bank.

Schweinhart, L. J., Montie, J., Xiang, Z., Barnett, W. S., Belfield, C. R., & Nores, M. (2005). Lifetime effects: The HighScope Perry Preschool Study through age 40. *Monographs of the HighScope Educational Research Foundation, 14.* Ypsilanti, MI: HighScope Press.

Shonkoff, J. P., & Phillips, D. (2000). *Neurons to neighborhoods: The science of early child development.* Washington, DC: National Academy Press.

Summers, L. H. (1992). Investing in all the people. *Pakistan Development Review, 31*(4), 367–406.

UNESCO. (2010). *Institute for statistics.* Paris, France: UNESCO.

Urzúa, S. (2008). Racial labor market gaps: The role of abilities and schooling choices. *Journal of Human Resources, 43*(4), 919–971.

Urzúa, S., & Veramendi, G. (2010). *The impact of out-of-home childcare centers on early childhood development.* Evanston, IL: Northwestern University, for IDB Research Network on Early Childhood Development.

Victora, C. G., Adair, L., Fall, C., Hallal, P. C., Martorell, R., Richter, L., et al. (2008). On behalf of the maternal and child undernutrition study group. Undernutrition 2: Maternal and child undernutrition: Consequences for adult health and human capital. *The Lancet, 371*(9609), 340–357.

Viscusi, W. K. (1993). The value of risks to life and health. *Journal of Economic Literature, 31*, 1912–1946.

Viscusi, W. K. (2008). How to value a life. *Journal of Economics and Finance, 32*, 311–323.

Viscusi, W. K., & Aldy, J. E. (2003). The value of a statistical life: A critical review of market estimates throughout the world. *Journal of Risk and Uncertainty, 27*(1), 5–76.

Woodhead, M. , & Streuli, N. (2013). Early education for all: Is there a role for the private sector? In P. R. Britto, P. L. Engle, & C. M. Super (Eds.), *Handbook of early childhood development research and its impact on global policy* (Chapter 16). New York: Oxford University Press.

Yilman, H., & Yazihan, N. (2010). *Early childhood development: Cost benefit analysis of ECD policies and fiscal space on combating child poverty in Turkey.* UNICEF Annual Report for Turkey.

7

Culture and Early Childhood Development

IMPLICATIONS FOR POLICY AND PROGRAMS

Sara Harkness, Charles M. Super,
Caroline Johnston Mavridis, Oumar Barry,
and Marian Zeitlin

Beneath the trappings of costume and custom, young children in different cultures around the world are surprisingly similar. No longer babies but not yet established in middle childhood, young children are creatures in rapid developmental transition, who often surprise their parents with their newfound competencies while also showing just how determined they can be to follow the dictates of their own interests. The unevenness of young children's development—competence in some areas paired with delays in others—has perplexed both parents and researchers, giving rise to concepts such as Piaget's "horizontal *décalage*," itself a description more than an explanation (Piaget, 1977). Some of this unevenness may be the natural result of the sheer scope and complexity of the developmental tasks of early childhood. Edwards and Liu (2002) suggest that these tasks include achieving increased autonomy and independence, the emergence of a sense of self, the beginnings of self-control, and the ability to empathize with others, to learn moral rules, and to identify oneself in relation to gender. Any one of these developmental tasks (in addition to growth, acquisition of language, problem solving, and a host of other physical, motor, linguistic, and cognitive skills) presents a challenge of the sort that might well seem daunting to an older person. Fortunately, however, young children generally seem eager to launch themselves forward in relation to all of them.

The developmental agendas of early childhood are recognized across cultures and thus tend to be incorporated into local concepts of stages and of developmental expectations or "timetables" for these stages. In carrying out research in a Mayan village in the Yucatan, Mexico, for example, Suzanne Gaskins (1996) noted that infants and young children were conventionally described in terms that referred to both motor milestones and cognitive development, such as "scooter babies" for babies who could sit and "scoot" around the floor; "talking babies," who were beginning to produce words; or "beginning-to-start-understanding children," who could follow simple instructions to do a task. Interestingly, this last category marked the change of nomenclature from "baby" to "child."

There is cross-cultural consistency in considering the first 2 years of life as a physically vulnerable period, roughly corresponding to infancy. Nevertheless, developmental expectations and thus caretaking practices for this age group vary widely, from the traditional belief found among mothers in a Kipsigis community of Kenya that there was no point in talking to babies (other than "because you love them") since they would not understand (Harkness, 1977) to, at the other extreme, a New England mother who, in an interview about her baby, assured us that "of course we read to her since before she was born."

Likewise, cross-cultural research has found evidence for a universally recognized developmental shift that occurs around ages 5–7 years, which is marked across cultures by changes in expectations for more mature thinking and behavior (Rogoff, Sellers, Pirrotta, Fox, & White, 1975; Super, 2005). Again, however, culturally shared expectations about what one can reasonably expect of a child in this age period vary tremendously. In much of Sub-Saharan Africa, for example, children (especially girls) as young as 5 years of age are routinely expected to help their mothers take care of younger siblings—much to the amazement of Western observers. The task of sibling caretaker, in fact, is seen locally as a developmentally important experience that will help the caretaker assume socially responsible roles later in life. In contrast, last-born children are seen as being different: Lacking the early experience of caring for a younger sibling, according to local perceptions in the Kipsigis community where Harkness and Super did field research in the 1970s, such individuals may turn out as adults to be egocentric and "spoiled."

The core challenge of early childhood development (ECD) programs and policies is to integrate the goals of an intervention (for example, improved health or school readiness) with the developmental agendas of young children and the cultural agendas that shape their daily lives. In this chapter, we present a theoretical framework, the *developmental niche*, as it may help to clarify the issues involved in ECD across various cultural contexts, particularly in economically developing societies. First, however, it is worth considering what is meant by the term "culture," particularly as it applies to children and families. We then provide a description of the developmental niche as a framework for informing policy planning and improving program effectiveness. The final section of this chapter illustrates the relevance of the developmental niche for ECD policy, using examples from several cultural regions.

Culture: What Is It (and What Is It Not)

Forces of globalization and increasing ethnic diversity within societies have made it impossible to ignore the cultural dimensions of ideas and practices that underlie all behavior—including behavior that is usually taken for granted as normal within the cultural communities to which many researchers belong. Ideas about what "culture" *is* vary widely, however, with a sharp differentiation between theoretical frameworks in psychology and anthropology.

PSYCHOLOGICAL FRAMEWORKS

A framework frequently used by psychologists for the study of cross-cultural differences in parenting and child development is the *individualism/collectivism dichotomy* (or relatedly, *independence/interdependence*), even though researchers frequently report that the framework does not comfortably fit their data. In response, modifications have been proposed, such as the idea that individualism and collectivism can coexist in both cultures and individuals (Tamis-LeMonda et al., 2007). In another variant, Keller (2007) suggests that there are two basic prototypes of communities and respective psychologies: the traditional village in an economically developing society, and middle-class communities in Western postindustrial societies. The first type of community (represented by the Nso village in Cameroon that Keller and her colleagues have studied extensively) fosters the development of the "interdependent self," who defines him- or herself "as part of a social system (primarily the family), seeks harmonious relationships, accepts hierarchy (mainly age and gender based), values cooperation and conformity, and is identified with his or role in the social environment" (p. 32). In contrast, the individual who grows up in the second kind of cultural context (typified by middle-class communities in Germany) develops an "independent self," one that is "self-contained, competitive, separate, unique, and self-reliant; has an inner sense of owning opinions; and is assertive" (p. 32), as well as having "personal qualities supporting self-enhancement, self-expression, and self-maximization" (p. 33). Similarly, Greenfield's (2009) theory of social change focuses on the global socioeconomic transition from small, rural, subsistence-based communities to large, complex cities where wealth is accumulated, with resulting changes in children's learning environments.

Kağitçibaşi's (2007) model, in which "independence" is separated into two distinct dimensions representing relatedness versus separateness, and agency (autonomy) versus lack of control (heteronomy), offers a more differentiated framework for the study of cross-cultural differences in family structure and the individual psychological orientations that accompany them. This framework is particularly useful for analyzing changes in the context of large-scale social transitions ("modernization"). In this context, the "autonomous relational" family (and individual) emerges as a synthesis of the traditional closeness among family members, but without the hierarchical, authoritarian distribution of power that characterizes many traditional societies. As Kağitçibaşi notes, this model of family relationships also avoids the sense of isolation that many individuals in modern society experience.

Yet a fourth approach evident in the psychological literature on children and families across cultures is to apply Baumrind's (Baumrind & Black, 1967) categories of parenting styles (authoritative, authoritarian, and permissive), which were developed to study individual differences among middle-class Euro-American parents. Although this typology does capture some group differences, researchers have grappled with the poorness of fit between the model and differences observed at the cultural level in parents' beliefs about their children's social and emotional development. For example, the "authoritarian" parenting style in the U.S. context is expected to include a punitive, rejecting attitude. In contrast, Chao (1994) has described a "training" approach widely shared within Chinese populations, in which authoritarianism is seen as a positive element in responsible socialization practices and is, therefore, not related to punitiveness. Research by Lee and colleagues (Lee, Super, & Harkness, 2003) showed that strict parental discipline was actually associated with *higher* self-perceived competence and well-being in a sample of Korean students. These examples point to the importance of disentangling the constituent elements of cultural constellations: Beliefs and practices that may appear necessarily related within one cultural context may not "work" the same way in other contexts.

Approaches such as these, which have been mainly developed and used by researchers in psychological sciences, are ambitious as they attempt to explain many different aspects of variability under the rubric of a single construct. Although they can be helpful as a general orientation, this very feature can limit their applicability to specific settings. The individualism/collectivism contrast, for example, can be helpful as a first step toward understanding cultures other than that of the Western-educated researcher, but it does not differentiate among the many societies that are categorized as "collectivistic," or indeed among American and European cultures. To improve the effectiveness of ECD interventions, we must look more closely at culture.

ANTHROPOLOGICAL PERSPECTIVES ON CULTURE

Anthropologists who study child development—more typically in one or a small number of societies—are in general agreement on eight features of culture:

1. *Culture is shared among members of a community.* In LeVine's (1984, p. 68) words, "culture represents a consensus on a wide variety of meanings among members of an interacting community."
2. *Culture organizes meanings and actions across widely diverse domains.*
3. *Cultural beliefs exist in a variety of forms*, from those that are encoded in law or ceremony to those that are implicit, taken-for-granted ideas about the right and natural way to do something.
4. *All cultures are unique, but none is totally different from all others.* Rather, cultural communities tend to share some characteristics with other

communities, including geographic neighbors, due in part to common historical roots and the diffusion of ideas and technologies, and with communities that are similar in terms of their socioeconomic "mainte-nance systems" (Whiting, 1977).

5. *Cultural constellations of beliefs and values are resilient in the face of his-torical and ecological change.* Studies of immigrant families generally find strong continuity in beliefs and practices from the culture of origin, in addition to a variety of accommodations to the new, surrounding culture (Moscardino, Nwobu, & Axia, 2006; Raghavan, Harkness, & Super, 2010; Rice, 2000).

6. *Culture exists both as external environment and as something "inside the head" of members of a cultural community* (Handwerker, 2002). This apparent paradox can be understood with reference to language and the speech community: In both cases, a constant process of communication and transaction occurs between the individual participant and the social environment.

7. *Culture is* not *a larger version of personality.* Although members of a cultural community share a common set of (often implicit) rules about things such as the nature of the child, the proper way to interact with other family members, and perceptions of the self, every cultural community necessarily includes a wide variety of individually differing people.

8. *Understanding any particular cultural group necessarily involves a more complex, up-close and multi-method involvement than does social behavioral research* in which culture is not considered (Weisner, 1996).

Each of these aspects of culture plays an important role in the organization and maintenance of the developmental niche in early childhood. Understanding the systematic nature of the child's developmental niche in a particular cultural con-text, in turn, provides a basis for assessing the relevance of various psychological constructs to ECD policies and programs.

The Developmental Niche

The developmental niche is a theoretical framework for the integration of concepts and findings from multiple disciplines concerned with the development of chil-dren in cultural context (Harkness & Super, 1992a; Super & Harkness, 1986). Two overarching principles reflect its origins in cultural anthropology and develop-mental psychology: First, that a child's environment is organized in a nonarbitrary manner as part of a cultural system; and second, that the child's own disposition, including a particular constellation of attributes, temperament, skills, and poten-tials, affect the process of development. In this approach, one takes the perspective of the child, looking outward to the environment of daily experience as it is shaped by features of the larger sociocultural setting. The child's developmental niche consists of three components or subsystems: the physical and social settings of daily life, the customs and practices of care, and parental ethotheories.

Physical and Social Settings of Daily Life

Children's environments are organized in terms of where, with whom, and in what activities children usually spend their days. From the perspective of ECD, systematic observation of these settings can provide insight into what kinds of opportunities for learning they naturally offer. At the same time, a global perspective on ECD can also make us more aware of what opportunities are *not* available, either due to a lack of resources or, at least in part, because they are not seen as central to the cultural agenda for child development in that particular place.

Customs and Practices of Care

Customs and practices of care for children, the second subsystem of the niche, include the caretakers' repertoire of normative strategies for child-rearing. Insofar as these are part of shared patterns, they are comfortable and familiar methods that do not call for careful analysis or justification—they seem "natural" and obvious to all members of the cultural community. For the same reason, failure to carry out such customs of care is easily perceived as poor parenting (or poor educational practice). Customs and practices, from an outside perspective, are often the focus of interventions as they may seem to offer a clear opportunity for the improvement of child health and development. Nevertheless, unless the cultural meanings embedded in such practices are taken into account, interventions are unlikely to succeed.

For example, Harwood and her colleagues, who have carried out several studies of Puerto Rican mothers and infants both on the island and in the mainland United States (Harwood, Miller, & Irizarry, 1995; Harwood, Schölmerich, Ventura-Cook, & Schulze, 1996), have identified related themes of responsibility and good manners, which they refer to as a concern with inculcating "proper demeanor" (including being cooperative, showing respect toward others, and fulfilling role obligations), in contrast to the focus on "self-maximization" (e.g., being self-confident, developing one's personal potential, and becoming psychologically independent) found more typically among Euro-American mothers. These culturally structured goals are expressed, in turn, through a variety of parenting practices related to feeding, sleeping, and toilet training, such that the Puerto Rican mothers in their studies favored more mother-directed strategies (Schulze, Harwood, Schölmerich, & Leyendecker, 2002) than did the Euro-American comparison group. Knowing these goals would be important for any U.S.-based intervention during the first 2 years of life: In essence, today's standard pediatric advice about all these areas would probably be in conflict with Puerto Rican mothers' established customs and beliefs.

The Psychology of the Caretakers: Parental Ethnotheories

The psychology of the caretakers forms the third component of the child's developmental niche. Of particular relevance to ECD are parents' cultural belief systems or *parental ethnotheories*. These culturally constructed ideas about children's behavior and development, about the family, and about parenting are influenced by the larger environments that families occupy, and they are important in parents' decision making about children's settings of daily life, as well as about customs of care (Harkness & Super, 1996). Although parental ethnotheories are often not explicit or developed into a coherent and internally consistent set of beliefs, when parents confront choices about how to care for their children, the culturally influenced assumptions that give meaning to the available options may be talked about more explicitly.

For example, the concept of socially responsible intelligence, widely recognized as a core cultural model across many African societies, functions as a parental ethnotheory that directly influences practices of care and parents' decision making regarding their own children's individual developmental competences. This cultural model of intelligence, called *n'glouélé* by Baoulé of the Ivory Coast (Dasen et al., 1985), *nzelu* by the Chewa of Zambia (Serpell, 1993), and *ng'om* by the Kipsigis of western Kenya (Harkness & Super, 1992b), has a cognitive component, but the African terms add a social dimension that includes both awareness of the social surround and a readiness to act. "Social cognition translates into responsible intelligence, not in abstraction," according to Nsamenang (2006, p. 296), "but primarily as it enhances the attainment of social ends." The word has a distinct utility for parents who make daily decisions about whether a child is sufficiently mature, or "socially intelligent," to carry a message across the village, to care for a 1-year-old for part of the day, or to negotiate prices in the market. As Weisner (1989, p. 86) comments, among the Abaluyia of rural Kenya, "mothers use evidence that a child has the ability to give and receive social support, and assist others, as markers of a child's more general developmental level, in the same way as an American parent might use literacy skills ... or verbal facility" to indicate maturity. Among Kipsigis mothers in Kenya, a child's ability to carry out an errand unsupervised was closely matched with their perception of whether the child's personality had emerged (Harkness, Super, Barry, Zeitlin, & Long, 2009). Similar reports come from the Kpelle of Liberia (Lancy, 1996) and the Yoruba of Nigeria (Zeitlin, 1996). More broadly, the agenda for social intelligence is part of a larger orientation characterized by Nsamenang (2006) as "sociogenic," an understanding that emotional, social, and cognitive development are as much the result of becoming part of the social group as they are of internal growth.

The larger cultural contexts of these ideas and practices are traditionally small, rural communities, although, like other ethnotheories, they may travel with families who migrate to cities. Thus, the instantiation of practices and customs of care becomes part of the regular routines of daily life that constitute the physical and social settings of the child's developmental niche. This is a particularly important aspect to understand in a region where parenting programs are being promoted as a primary model for ECD programs (Garcia, Pence & Evans, 2008).

Parental ethnotheories form a hierarchy of beliefs that are linked indirectly, although powerfully, to behavior (Harkness et al., 2007). At the top of the hierarchy are the most general, implicit ideas about the nature of the child, parenting, and the family. Below this triad are ideas about specific domains, such as feeding, sleep, social development, and cognitive growth. These ideas are closely tied to ideas about appropriate practices (such as breast-feeding, provision of toys, assignment to chores) and further to imagined child or family outcomes. Before these ideas are translated into behavior, however, a number of mediating factors come into play, including specific characteristics of the child (such as gender and temperament), situational and logistical variables, and competing cultural models and their related practices. The final results can be seen in actual parental practices or behaviors, and, ultimately, in actual child and family outcomes.

THREE COROLLARIES

The three subsystems of the developmental niche—settings, customs, and caretaker psychology or ethnotheories—define the child's developmental experience within the larger culture.

1. *The three components of the developmental niche operate together as a system.* The settings, customs, and parental psychology all influence each other, with a press toward consistency. Thus, in a stable cultural environment, customs of care reflect parental ethnotheories about the child, and they are further supported by the physical and social settings of daily life that parents organize for their children. Consider, for example, the custom of sibling caretaking (Heymann, 2006; Weisner & Gallimore, 1977). In much of Africa and some other regions of the world, rural families customarily use older daughters—6 to 10 years old—to manage infants and toddlers during periods of the day when mothers are busy with agricultural work or food preparation. These long-standing practices are facilitated by the physical settings of farm life (e.g., outdoors and visible from a distance) and by traditional social settings of large families and young girls at home (rather than in school). They are also consistent with parental and community ideas about the needs of infants for safety and social interaction, and needs of the older siblings for experience in domestic tasks, often supervised by an "executive mother" (Whiting & Edwards, 1988). In short, the three subsystems of the niche—settings, customs, and cultural beliefs—are operating in harmony.

2. *Each subsystem is influenced by forces in the larger ecology.* The developmental niche is an open system, such that its functioning may be influenced by outside forces. Each of the three subsystems of the niche is intricately connected to aspects of the larger culture and economy. As the larger culture and economy change over time, they exert pressure for change on some element(s) of the developmental niche. To continue the example of research with Puerto Rican mothers, the observed cultural differences in ethnotheories were moderated by social class and mother's education: More educated Puerto Rican mothers expressed greater concern with the development of their child's own capacities and emotional independence, although still less than their Euro-American counterparts (Harwood, Schölmerich, & Schulze, 2000; Miller & Harwood, 2002). Research with Mexican families in both Mexico and the United States has found a similar emphasis on good moral values, obedience and responsibility, and respect for elders (Arcia & Johnson, 1998), as captured in the term *bien educado* (literally, "well educated," but meaning something more like "well brought up"). Delgado-Gaitan (1994) found, in a study of Mexican immigrants residing in California, that regardless of whether they were first- or second-generation immigrants (that is, recent immigrants or the children of immigrants), parents expressed high expectations for respect from their children. Second-generation immigrants, however, allowed their children more autonomy in relation to routine situations like watching TV, and they encouraged more critical thinking, whereas the concept of respect became construed more narrowly.

3. *Elements of the developmental niche are continually involved in a process of mutual adaptation with the individual child.* The age, gender, temperament, interests, and abilities of the individual child influence parents and others in the niche, modulating cultural expectations and opportunities for the child at any given time. Options for schooling, domestic responsibilities, play, and supervision rest on parental judgments about the individual child. For example, a 6-year-old child in rural Kenya who does not show qualities of being sufficiently mature and intelligent is less likely to be asked to take a message to a neighbor or go to a local store to make a small purchase (Harkness et al., 2009)—an adjustment of parental thinking and of settings. The fact that the determining features often are parents' perceptions and judgments concerning their child's individual qualities indicates that they are an aspect of parental ethnotheories in their own right. For example, mothers in Kokwet explained to us that all babies are alike, and individual differences can be seen only when the child becomes old enough to be given responsibilities (Super & Harkness, 1994). The American

parents in our studies, in contrast, felt that they could judge their child's personality from the first moment after birth (Harkness et al., 2009). Thus, some differences in the developmental niche reflect culturally regulated adaptations to the child.

CULTURAL THEMES

The developmental niche framework makes evident the kind of systematic regularity that culture provides—environmental organization that emphasizes repeatedly or with singular salience the culture's core "messages." It is through such cultural thematicity that the environment works its most profound influences on development. This quality of the developmental niche is important for the acquisition of skills and competencies as it offers multiple opportunities for learning the same thing, whether that "thing" is reading, sibling caretaking, or the communication of emotions (Super & Harkness, 1999). Similarly, the elaboration of cultural themes over the course of developmental time reinforces lessons learned earlier and recasts them in a more adequate format for meeting the challenges of increasing maturity. As an organizer of the environment, thus, culture assures that key meaning systems are elaborated in appropriate ways at different stages of development, and that the learning occurs across behavioral domains and various scales of time (Super & Harkness, 2002).

For example, parents across the Asian continent are consistently described by researchers (both Asian and non-Asian) in terms of a few central themes. Primary among them is emotional interdependence, especially between a mother and her children, and relatedly, harmony within the social group. These parental ethnotheories are expressed in customs and practices of care. According to Lebra (1994), Japanese parents believe that such qualities can be encouraged by treating the young child with indulgence and by modeling the sensitivity they expect the child to display later in broader social contexts (Osterweil & Nagano-Nakamura, 1992). Once this basic empathy is established in the child, mothers can begin to discipline, and compliance is achieved by getting the child to empathize with her wishes (Lebra, 1994). In the meantime, aggressive behavior is regarded as offering "teachable moments" for guiding the child to work on needed social skills. Teachers, as well as parents, stress the importance of fostering empathic, harmonious relationships. As found by Hayashi, Karasawa, and Tobin (2009), preschool teachers in Kyoto seek to foster a feeling of *omoiyari* in children, which can be translated as the urge to respond to others' displays of emotional need or *amae*. In one instance, these authors observed a teacher urging the children to eat their carrots so that the carrots would not be "sad" over not having been eaten like all the other vegetables! In these examples, thus, the ethnotheories and related practices are shared among teachers as well as parents across two major physical and social settings.

The Developmental Niche and Interventions
for Early Childhood Development

Policies and programs are cultural products (Harkness & Super, 2010). They are generated using concepts shared by members of a cultural group and implemented through culturally based institutions, and their effects play out in the natural laboratory of everyday life in a particular cultural place. The relationship between culture and policy in ECD is therefore intimate, complex, and multifaceted. Understanding the ways in which culture and policy reflect and influence each other should be part of the theoretical toolkit of educators, health care providers, and policymakers; but, in fact, culture and policy are rarely considered in the same context. Examining the cultural context of policy is of particular importance in the current era of rapid culture change and globalization.

The most general issue arising from the intersection of ECD research and policy concerns how the actions that follow from a particular policy fit into and shape—or fail to shape—family decision making and the daily lives of affected children in particular cultural contexts. The developmental niche framework can be helpful for understanding the challenges that face the creation of successful ECD programs, as illustrated in the following examples.

ADAPTATION OF A PRESCHOOL CURRICULUM
FOR FAMILIES IN TURKEY

The Home Intervention Program for Preschool Youngsters (HIPPY) was originally developed in Israel for improving the school readiness of children from low-income families (Westheimer 2003). In adapting this model for an early intervention program in Turkey, Kağitçibaşi (2007) added to the relatively structured cognitive curriculum a "mother enrichment" component that reinforced traditional Turkish values of "relatedness" and also introduced a focus on "autonomy," believed to be essential for success in the rapidly changing modern environment. After 4 years, the child results replicated advances noted in Israel, and the mothers increased their competence and confidence. It is noteworthy that this intervention drew from Kağitçibaşi's theory of family relationships mentioned earlier. Although the theory is sweeping in scope, it seems likely that the design of the Turkish project was further informed by the author's own personal familiarity with the culture. On the other hand, a Dutch implementation of the program designed for low-income mothers from Turkey, Morocco, and the Caribbean (as well as ethnic Dutch mothers), in which the home visitors made every effort to remain faithful to the original protocol, had no overall effects on children and mothers (Eldering & Vedder, 1999)—an outcome that was attributed in part to a high drop-out rate. One possible explanation for this is that the home visitors were not able to access the parental ethnotheories and goals for children's development that were most meaningful to these populations.

INCORPORATING A PRESCHOOL CURRICULUM IN A NUTRITIONAL
SUPPLEMENTATION PROJECT IN COLOMBIA

The cross-cultural application of a related preschool program in Colombia involved inclusion of the High/Scope Perry curriculum (Schweinhart, n.d.) in a 3-year study of the effects of a nutritional supplementation program to improve both child physical growth and cognitive development (Super, Herrera, & Mora, 1990). The Colombian adaptation of the original cognitive curriculum (delivered by home visitors) was effective in improving children's performance on measures of cognitive development. Unexpectedly, the cognitive intervention was also found to be nearly as powerful as nutritional supplementation over the same period in reducing long-term growth stunting. Post hoc analysis of this effect points to aspects of the developmental niche that mediated the physical growth result. Specifically, the researchers suggested that mothers, through their participation in the cognitive development curriculum, came to see their young children in a different light and therefore provided a more favorable environment for development, including better nutrition. Some support for this interpretation comes from the finding that more protein was "channeled" to these children within the family. Additionally, fathers of the cognitive intervention group were more likely to be directly involved in the follow-up evaluation encounters. If these interpretations are correct, it would appear that the intervention led to positive change across the three subsystems of the developmental niche, starting with a shift in the parents' beliefs about their child's development.

INTEGRATING DEVELOPMENTAL AND CULTURAL AGENDAS
IN A SCHOOL READINESS PROJECT IN SENEGAL

A major challenge facing ECD programs, particularly in non-Western cultural settings, is to disentangle the implicit cultural agenda of an imported intervention from its more general developmental goals. The didactic language that middle-class European and American parents often use with their young children—for example, teaching them colors and numbers, asking them questions—is a good match for the demands of school, with its abstract learning and language-based curriculum (LeVine, LeVine, & Schnell, 2001). Standardized developmental tests, such as the Bayley Scales of Infant and Toddler Development (Bayley, 1969), track the emergence of these culturally salient skills against the background of a presumed, generalized Euro-American middle-class environment. Because of the similarity between items for 3-year-olds on the Bayley test (e.g., naming colors) and the content of school curricula, poor performance on the former bodes poorly for success in the latter. Rural African children tend to score poorly on tests such as the Bayley after the first 12 or 18 months of life, as the tests become increasingly based on expressive language and on specific cognitive skills emphasized in the originating, Euro-American population, and this lag is evident as they encounter the demands of school.

The Louga District of Senegal presents an illustrative case study (Harkness et al., 2009; Super, Harkness, Barry, & Zeitlin, 2011; Zeitlin & Barry, 2004, 2008). Result of a culturally adapted version of the Bayley test found that 3-year-olds in Louga, reared in traditional ways, performed poorly on the Cognitive scale (average score = 87.6, or nearly 1 standard deviation from the international norm of 100). Maternal interviews, however, revealed that local ethnotheories included ideas about a variety of teaching activities for young children. The traditional cultural agenda for infancy and early childhood focused on motor skills and the exercise of responsible obedience. It taught the social skills and understanding of seniority in social relations needed to advance appropriately with age. Responding to a series of picture cards used as interview prompts, the mothers were lively and full of ideas with regard to motor development. Virtually all of the mothers also reported that they taught their young children "good behaviors" such as respectful greetings, as well as household tasks. These ethnotheories were put into practice in teaching vocabulary for concrete objects and actions in the context of early training for chores. A 6-month-old would have an object placed in his hand and be taught "take" and "give." With advancing age, the child would be instructed to deliver an object to another person in the room, and, later, to carry out more substantial errands. This agenda for development integrated young children into the fabric of daily life; it also enabled them to contribute to family maintenance tasks (e.g., food preparation) by the age of 3 years and to the family's income production by age 6 (usually through assisting with cash crop agriculture).

Based on understanding of local ethnotheories and practices that shaped young children's developmental niches in Louga District, the researchers developed a program for "curricular change" that built on traditional ideas about teaching and learning in infancy and early childhood, adapting them through group discussion to the existing educational demands on these children when they reached school age. The program incorporated already culturally accepted tenets of positive development, such as encouraging early motor development and the inculcation of traditional values, with the addition of culturally novel ideas about promoting early language development and cognitive skills. They found that whereas lessons about motor development were easily received and in fact considered self-evident, lessons about teaching language were more problematic. One mother of a 10-day-old baby described how other members of her family made fun of her efforts to talk to her newborn. It appeared that the importance of talking to babies needed to be explained very carefully, as mothers questioned the rationale of talking to a baby before the baby could respond verbally. In the process of introducing the intervention, however, the project personnel's experiences brought to light the importance of errands for the child's acquisition of vocabulary. In fact, the project staff found it impossible to persuade mothers to name objects for the baby without putting them into the context of an errand. The ingenuity with which the most highly motivated parents invented errands with the sole intention of teaching their children new words was impressive.

In this project, thus, the researchers' incorporation of the local, culturally constituted developmental agenda into an ECD agenda added to its credibility and thus increased the ease with which it could be implemented within the culturally normative developmental niche of young children.

Incorporating Culturally Based Competence into Early Childhood Development Programs and Assessments

Given the rich diversity of culturally constructed competencies, it seems unfortunate that assessments tend to be restricted to a relatively small repertoire of skills and abilities. For the most part, competencies emphasized in non-Western cultures have not been assessed comparatively; but when they have, the results have been instructive. Super (1976), for example, assessed motor development in infants from several different ethnic groups in Kenya, finding that motor milestones related to sitting and walking were early by comparison with a Euro-American sample, whereas crawling was not. Both trends were consistent with cultural emphases on teaching babies to sit and walk early, but not to crawl on the dirt floors of the huts. Similarly, Keller and her associates (Keller, 2007) found that children in a rural Nso community of Cameroon developed earlier competence in carrying out errands of the sort described above in Nigeria and Senegal, compared to toddlers in San José, Costa Rica, and Athens, Greece. Comparisons across Western countries have generally not included competencies beyond standard school-related skills of the sort that can be tested in a traditional paper-and-pencil format. We know little, therefore, about the long-term developmental significance of the differences in mothers' cultural models and practices, already evident even in early infancy (Harkness et al., 2007; Super & Harkness, 2009). East-West comparisons have received a great deal of attention in the research community due to the generally superior performance of Asian students in the United States, especially in math and science (Fuligni, 1997; Stevenson & Lee, 1990). Even here, though, the assessments are generally limited to traditional school curriculum-based tests.

Traditional beliefs and practices related to ECD and care can make a positive contribution to Western educational settings, as demonstrated by Huijbregts and colleagues' research on culturally diverse day care centers in the Netherlands (Huibregts, Tavecchio, Leseman, & Hoffenaar, 2009). Particularly in the larger cities, such as Amsterdam, where the research was carried out, both the staff and the children come from a variety of cultural backgrounds, with large representations of the country's main immigrant groups: Turkish, Moroccan, and Surinamese. The researchers found that the ethnic Dutch caregivers emphasized during interviews the "individualistic" socialization goal of independence, whereas the immigrant caregivers gave more importance to "collectivistic" goals of social development, group processes, and rules—even though they had all undergone the same professional training in the Netherlands. An examination of caregiver practices in these same settings found that Caribbean-Dutch caregivers, as contrasted to their ethnic Dutch colleagues, more actively encouraged collaborative group processes among the children; this in turn was related to greater cognitive complexity in the children's play and activities (van Schaik, Leseman, & Huibregts, 2011). Both of these studies concluded with the recommendation that collaboration and the encouragement of group processes should be included in the assessment of quality in early childhood care and education.

To broaden the competencies promoted and assessed in ECD programs in the context of globalization, it will be important to gain a fuller understanding of the ways that competence is understood and encouraged in various cultures. The framework of the developmental niche can be a helpful guide for this process. First, documenting children's settings of daily life—where they are, with whom, and engaged in what activities—can provide basic information about the cultural curriculum for the child's development, including opportunities for learning that are not even consciously provided by parents. The "literacy environment" of the home (presence, accessibility, and use of written materials) has often been cited as an important way that parents can help prepare their children for school; likewise, opportunities to observe and participate in important household maintenance activities such as weaving or cooking offer the young child practice in a variety of social, cognitive, and motor skills. Second, it can be noted that customs of care often highlight activities that parents consider the most important for young children's development. In this regard, the salience of the "errand" for training young children in West African societies becomes evident as a positive strategy, not just a way for busy mothers to pass off some of their work to others (and as any parent of a 2-year-old knows, "help" from the child is not the quickest way to get something done). Finally, understanding parental ethnotheories about children's behavior and development can help integrate these observations into settings and practices, thereby providing greater insight into their meaning and developmental consequences. In the process of taking such a structured inventory of the child's developmental niche, its characteristic "contemporary redundancy"—the way the same developmental themes are expressed across multiple domains, through settings, customs, and ethnotheories—becomes apparent (Super & Harkness, 2002). Children in all cultures are best at skills and competencies learned over and over in a variety of contexts, and the elaboration of the same themes over the course of development greatly adds to their power.

Conclusion

Bridging the gap between cultural agendas and policy agendas for ECD will require that we assess children and their environments for the competencies that are valued in their own cultures, not just those that outside funders and managers

judge *a priori* to be important. A fuller understanding of both agendas will facilitate devising ECD curricula that "make sense" to parents and can therefore be
accepted and integrated into family life. By learning more about how competence
is conceptualized and encouraged in a variety of cultural contexts, we will be better prepared to think of new and more globally relevant ways of assessing it. This
knowledge, in turn, has the potential to enrich ECD policy and programs around
the world, including not only in developing countries to which they are exported
but also in their postindustrial cultures of origin.

References

Arcia, E., & Johnson, A. (1998). When respect means to obey: Immigrant Mexican mothers'
values for their children. *Journal of Child and Family Studies, 7*, 79–95.

Baumrind, D., & Black, A. E. (1967). Socialization practices associated with dimensions of
competence in preschool boys and girls. *Child Development, 38*(2), 291–327.

Bayley, N. (1969). *Bayley scales of infant development.* New York: Psychological Corporation.

Chao, R. K. (1994). Beyond parental control and authoritarian parenting style: Understanding Chinese parenting through the cultural notion of training. *Child Development, 65*(4),
1111–1119.

Dasen, P. R., Barthelemy, D., Kan, E., Kouame, K., Daouda, K., Adjei, K. K., et al. (1985).
N'glouélé, l'intelligence chez les Baoulé [N'glouélé, intelligence among the Baoulé].
Archives de Psychologie, 53, 295–324.

Delgado-Gaitan, C. (1994). Socializing young children in Mexican-American families: An
intergenerational perspective. In P. M. Greenfield & R. R. Cocking (Eds.), *Cross-cultural
roots of minority child development* (pp. 55–86). Hillsdale, NJ: Erlbaum.

Edwards, C. P., & Liu, W.-L. (2002). Parenting toddlers. In M. H. Bornstein (Ed.), *Handbook
of parenting* (2nd ed., Vol. 1, pp. 45–72). Mahwah, NJ: Erlbaum.

Eldering, L., & Vedder, P. (1999). The Dutch experience with the Home Intervention Program for Preschool Youngsters (HIPPY). In L. Eldering & P. P. M. Leseman (Eds.), *Effective early education: Cross-cultural perspectives* (pp. 259–287). New York: Falmer Press.

Fuligni, A. J. (1997). The academic achievement of adolescents from immigrant families: The
roles of family background, attitudes, and behavior. *Child Development, 68*(2), 351–363.

Garcia, M., Pence, A., & Evans, J. L. (2008). *Africa's future: Africa's challenge: Early childhood
care and development in Sub-Saharan Africa.* Washington, D.C.: World Bank.

Gaskins, S. (1996). How Mayan parental theories come into play. In S. Harkness &
C. M. Super (Eds.), *Parents' cultural belief systems: Their origins, expressions, and consequences.* (pp. 345–363). New York: Guilford Press.

Greenfield, P. M. (2009). Linking social change and developmental change: Shifting pathways of human development. *Developmental Psychology, 45*(2), 401–418.

Handwerker, W. P. (2002). The construct validity of cultures: Cultural diversity, culture theory, and a method for ethnography. *American Anthropologist, 104*(1), 106–122.

Harkness, S. (1977). Aspects of social environment and first language acquisition in rural
Africa. In C. E. Snow & C. A. Ferguson (Eds.), *Talking to children: Language input and
acquisition* (pp. 309–356). New York: Cambridge University Press.

Harkness, S., & Super, C. M. (1992a). The developmental niche: A theoretical framework for analyzing the household production of health. *Social Science and Medicine, 38*(2), 217–226.

Harkness, S., & Super, C. M. (1992b). Parental ethnotheories in action. In I. Sigel, A. V. McGillicuddy-DeLisi, & J. Goodnow (Eds.), *Parental belief systems: The psychological consequences for children* (2nd ed., pp. 373–392). Hillsdale, NJ: Erlbaum.

Harkness, S., & Super, C. M. (Eds.). (1996). *Parents' cultural belief systems: Their origins, expressions, and consequences.* New York: Guilford.

Harkness, S., & Super, C. M. (2010). *Culture and policy in early childhood development.* Retrieved from http://www.child- encyclopedia.com/documents/Harkness-SuperANGxp.pdf

Harkness, S., Super, C. M., Barry, O., Zeitlin, M., & Long, J. (2009). Assessing the environment of children's learning: The developmental niche in Africa. In E. Grigorenko (Ed.), *Multicultural psychoeducational assessment* (pp. 133–155). New York: Springer.

Harkness, S., Super, C. M., Moscardino, U., Rha, J. -H., Blom, M. J. M., Huitrón, B., et al. (2007). Cultural models and developmental agendas: Implications for arousal and self-regulation in early infancy. *Journal of Developmental Processes, 1*(2), 5–39.

Harwood, R. L., Miller, J. G., & Irizarry, N. L. (1995). *Culture and attachment: Perceptions of the child in context.* New York: Guilford.

Harwood, R. L., Schölmerich, A., & Schulze, P. A. (2000). Homogeneity and heterogeneity in cultural belief systems. In S. Harkness, C. Raeff, & C. M. Super (Eds.), *Variability in the social construction of the child* (pp. 41–57). San Francisco, CA: Jossey-Bass.

Harwood, R. L., Schölmerich, A., Ventura-Cook, E., & Schulze, P. A. (1996). Culture and class influences on Anglo and Puerto Rican mothers' beliefs regarding long-term socialization goals and child behavior. *Child Development, 67*(5), 2446–2461.

Hayashi, A., Karasawa, M., & Tobin, J. (2009). The Japanese preschool's pedagogy of feeling: Cultural strategies for supporting young children's emotional development. *Ethos, 37,* 32–49.

Heymann, J. (2006). *Forgotten families: Ending the growing crisis confronting children and working parents in the global economy.* New York: Oxford.

Huibregts, S. K., Tavecchio, L., Leseman, P. P. M., & Hoffenaar, P. (2009). Child rearing in a group setting: Beliefs of Dutch, Caribbean Dutch, and Mediterranean Dutch caregivers in center-based child care. *Journal of Cross-Cultural Psychology, 40,* 797–815.

Kağitçibaşi, Ç. (2007). *Family, self, and human development across cultures: Theory and Applications* (2nd ed.). Mahwah, NJ: Erlbaum.

Keller, H. (2007). *Cultures of infancy.* Mahwah, NJ: Lawrence Erlbaum.

Lancy, D. F. (1996). *Playing on the mother ground: Cultural routines for children's development.* New York: Guilford.

Lebra, T. S. (1994). Mother and child in Japanese socialization: A Japan-US. comparison. In P. M. Greenfield & R. R. Cocking (Eds.), *Cross-cultural roots of minority child development* (pp. 259–274). Hillsdale, NJ: Erlbaum.

Lee, J., Super, C. M., & Harkness, S. (2003). Self-perception of competence in Korean children: Age, sex, and home influences. *Asian Journal of Social Psychology, 6,* 133–147.

LeVine, R. A. (1984). Properties of culture. In R. A. Shweder & R. L. LeVine (Eds.), *Culture theory: Essays on mind, self, and emotion* (pp. 67–87). New York: Cambridge University Press.

LeVine, R. A., LeVine, S. E., & Schnell, B. (2001). "Improve the women": Mass schooling, female literacy, and worldwide social change. *Harvard Educational Review, 71*(1), 1–50.

Miller, A. M., & Harwood, R. L. (2002). The cultural organization of parenting: Change and stability of behavior patterns during feeding and social play across the first year of life. *Parenting: Science and Practice*, 2(3), 241–272.

Moscardino, U., Nwobu, O., & Axia, G. (2006). Cultural beliefs and practices related to infant health and development among Nigerian immigrant mothers in Italy. *Journal of Reproductive and Infant Psychology*, 24(3), 241–255.

Nsamenang, A. B. (2006). Human ontogenesis: An indigenous African view on development and intelligence. *International Journal of Psychology*, 41(4), 293–297.

Osterweil, Z., & Nagano-Nakamura, K. (1992). Maternal views on aggression: Japan and Israel. *Aggressive Behavior*, 18, 263–270.

Piaget, J. (1977). *The development of thought: Equilibration of cognitive structures*. New York: Viking.

Raghavan, C. S., Harkness, S., & Super, C. M. (2010). Parental ethnotheories in the context of immigration: Asian Indian immigrant and Euro-American mothers and daughters in an American town. *Journal of Cross-Cultural Psychology*, 41(4), 617–632.

Rice, P. L. (2000). Baby, souls, name and health: Traditional customs for a newborn infant among the Hmong in Melbourne. *Early Human Development*, 57(3), 189–203.

Rogoff, B., Sellers, M. J., Pirrotta, S., Fox, N., & White, S. H. (1975). Age of assignment of roles and responsibilities to children: A cross-cultural survey. *Human Development*, 18, 353–369.

Schulze, P. A., Harwood, R. L., Schömerich, A., & Leyendecker, B. (2002). The cultural structuring of parenting and universal developmental tasks. *Parenting: Science and Practice*, 2(2), 151–178.

Serpell, R. (1993). *The significance of schooling: Life-journeys in an African society*. Cambridge: Cambridge University Press.

Stevenson, H. W., & Lee, S. Y. (1990). Contexts of achievement: A study of American, Japanese, and Chinese children. *Monographs of the Society for Research in Child Development*, 55(Serial No. 221).

Super, C. M. (1976). Environmental effects on motor development: The case of African infant precocity. *Developmental Medicine and Child Neurology*, 18, 561–567.

Super, C. M. (2005). The globalization of developmental psychology. In D. Pillemer & S. H. White (Eds.), *Developmental psychology and social change: Research, history, and policy* (pp. 11–33). Cambridge: Cambridge University Press.

Super, C. M., & Harkness, S. (1986). The developmental niche: A conceptualization at the interface of child and culture. *International Journal of Behavioral Development*, 9, 545–569.

Super, C. M., & Harkness, S. (1994). The cultural regulation of temperament-environment interactions. *Researching Early Childhood*, 2(1), 59–84.

Super, C. M., & Harkness, S. (1999). The environment as culture in developmental research. In T. Wachs & S. Friedman (Eds.), *Measurement of the environment in developmental research* (pp. 279–323). Washington, DC: American Psychological Association.

Super, C. M., & Harkness, S. (2002). Culture structures the environment for development. *Human Development*, 45(4), 270–274.

Super, C. M., & Harkness, S. (2009). The developmental niche of the newborn in rural Kenya. In J. K. Nugent, B. Petrauskas, & T. B. Brazelton (Eds.), *The newborn as a person: Enabling healthy infant development worldwide* (pp. 85–97). New York: Wiley.

Super, C. M., Harkness, S., Barry, O., & Zeitlin, M. (2011). Think locally, act globally: Contributions of African research to child development. *Child Development Perspectives*, 5(2), 119–125.

Super, C. M., Herrera, M. G., & Mora, J. O. (1990). Long-term effects of food supplementation and psychosocial intervention on the physical growth of Colombian infants at risk of malnutrition. *Child Development, 61,* 29–49.

Tamis-LeMonda, C. S., Way, N., Hughes, D., Yoshikawa, H., Kalman, R. K., & Niva, E. Y. (2007). Parents' goals for children: The dynamic coexistence of individualism and collectivisim in cultures and individuals. *Social Development, 17*(1), 183–209.

van Schaik, S. D. M., Leseman, P. P. M., & Huibregts, S. K. (2011). *Cultural diversity in center-based early childhood care in the Netherlands: Challenge or resource?* Paper presented at Biennual Meetings of the Society for Research in Child Development. Montreal, Quebec.

Weisner, T. S. (1989). Cultural and universal aspects of social support for children: Evidence from the Abaluyia of Kenya. In D. Belle (Ed.), *Children's social networks and social supports* (pp. 70–90). New York: Wiley.

Weisner, T. S. (1996). Why ethnography should be the most important method in the study of human development. In A. Colby, R. Jessor & R. Shweder (Eds.), *Ethnography and human development: Context and meaning in social inquiry* (pp. 305–324). Chicago: University of Chicago Press.

Weisner, T. S., & Gallimore, R. (1977). My brother's keeper: Child and sibling caretaking. *Current Anthropology, 18*(2), 169–190.

Westheimer, M. (Ed.). (2003). *Parents making a difference: International research on the Home Instruction for Parents of Preschool Youngsters (HIPPY) program.* Clinton, CT: Connelly-3-Publishing.

Whiting, B. B., & Edwards, C. P. (1988). *Children of different worlds: The formation of social behavior.* Cambridge, MA: Harvard University Press.

Whiting, J. W. M. (1977). A model for psychocultural research. In P. H. Leiderman, S. R. Tulkin, & A. Rosenfeld (Eds.), *Culture and infancy: Variations in the human experience* (pp. 29–48). New York: Academic Press.

Zeitlin, M. F. (1996). My child is my crown: Yoruba parental theories and practices in early childhood. In S. Harkness & C. M. Super (Eds.), *Parents' cultural belief systems: Their origins, expressions, and consequences* (pp. 407–427). New York: Guilford.

Zeitlin, M. F., & Barry, O. (2004). *Rapport intermédiaire du projet sur l'intégration des activités d'éveil et de stimulation psychosociale des jeunes enfants dans l'approche de la déviance positive mise en œvre dans le Département de Velingara. Deuxième partie: Les essais pratiques d'éveil améliorées à Yoff-Dakar et à Vélingara.* Dakar: Centre de Ressources pour l'Émergence Social Participative.

Zeitlin, M. F., & Barry, O. (2008). *Results of operational research by CRESP for Plan International, Dakar, on the adaptation and administration of the Bayley III infant development test in Louga.* Dakar, Senegal.

{ 8 }

Voices Less Heard

THE IMPORTANCE OF CRITICAL
AND "INDIGENOUS" PERSPECTIVES

Alan Pence

The ideal of a single civilization for everyone implicit in the cult of
progress and technique impoverishes and mutilates us. . . . Every view
of the world that becomes extinct, every culture that disappears,
diminishes a possibility of life.

—OCTAVIO PAZ, NOBEL PRIZE FOR LITERATURE, 1990,
QUOTED IN *PESCOSOLIDO & AMINZADE*, 1999, P. 221

The last two decades have witnessed unparalleled interest from international
organizations regarding the development of policies and programs for young
children. Although young children's well-being has concerned parents, families,
and societies since earliest times, the force and focus of international development organizations' current engagement with the topic is unique. This chapter will
explore that engagement by placing the contemporary discourse into historical and
sociophilosophical contexts that have shaped it. Doing so raises critical questions.
For example, although the current discourse is impressive in many respects, its narrow base in Western concepts and literature fails to adequately capture or promote
the diversity of humankind's understandings of children. As such, the discourse
advances a standardizing agenda based on Western orientations and precepts. It is
critical that a literature that seeks to be relevant and useful for populations globally
promotes understanding of the full scope of childhood. As Bornstein (2010) notes,
such is not the case for developmental science at present.

This chapter approaches this discord between diversity and normalizing standards not as an either/or dynamic, but as a potentially useful tension, each focus
reflecting certain histories, philosophies, and sociopolitical objectives that have
shaped the contemporary world, and each containing valuable perspectives for the
future of early childhood education, care, and development. These historical and
philosophical contexts, although presented only briefly in the first section, provide

a background for considering the contemporary early childhood development (ECD) international development discourse, key weaknesses it must address, and alternative perspectives that open up to a greater diversity of understandings. The section "Origins and Limitations of a Child Science" provides a brief history of the emergence of child psychology in the late 19th century, identifying a universalist perspective that was still dominant when international development interest highlighted young children circa 1989/1990. The conflation of this universalized understanding of child development with powerful and similarly narrow sociopolitical and development agendas produced an influential but problematic discourse regarding the role of ECD policies and programs as a key component of international development. Certain strengths and limitations of this discourse are discussed in the section "Children on the Development Agenda." The final section, "Hearing the Unheard Voices," considers policies, programs, research, and training approaches that have opened up to alternative perspectives, including local participation and decision making and an enhanced role for families and communities in program planning and delivery. Such means of opening to other views and becoming more truly global in nature are considered essential for the future of ECD in international development.

Images of Childhood: Historical and Cultural

It is axiomatic to note that childhoods, no less than children, come with diverse shapes and characteristics. That said, it is also axiomatic that the range of childhoods experienced has been greatly reduced over the past two centuries. One key contributor to this reduction has been the loss or endangerment of over half of the world's 6,700 languages (UNESCO, 2009a). With every language lost, we lose a way of understanding the world—and a unique experience of childhood as well (UNESCO, 2009b).

Language loss is not the only danger that childhood diversity faces. Diversity has also been reduced by efforts to "normalize" the "other," reshaping them in the image of those more powerful (Burman, 2008; Cannella & Viruru, 2004; Nsamenang, 2008; Swadener & Mutua, 2008). Introducing systems and institutions into others' environments has been a potent means to effect such change (Rahnema & Bawtree, 1997; Whiteford & Manderson, 2000). These interventions are typically reported as "progress" by their proponents, but institutions and instruments are not neutral. Like other exogenous introductions, they can have both positive and negative socioecological impacts, some not fully appreciated for generations (Davis, 2009; Lincoln & Denzin, 2008; Scott, 1998).

To take one example that is both powerful and germane to this volume, childhood in most countries has not been the same since the introduction of schools. International and country-level discourses—certainly those dominant in the 20th century—typically argued that schools are a good thing: How can children succeed in contemporary societies without schooling? However, the structure those schools imposed, their origins outside majority ("developing") world contexts, the content they deemed important, and their positions regarding traditional learning have all disrupted or destroyed long-established ways of learning and of becoming a useful adult in a given society. Nsamenang and Tchombe (2011) note, "We have learned that no people entirely dislodged from their ancestral roots have ever made collective progress with development and that the era of outsiders deciding and 'supplying' what Africans need has not yielded hoped-for outcomes" (p. xxvii).

Nsamenang and Tchombe call for a "generative approach" (Pence, Kuehne, Greenwood, & Opekokew, 1993) for African education that is based on including multiple knowledges and contexts as one means to address Dasen and Akkari's (2008) contention that "school education has not brought economic growth and social development in Africa, contrary to what was predicted by human capital theory" (p. 8).

Until recently, early childhood largely escaped the normalizing impacts that schools have had around the world. Although one can, with reasonable accuracy, imagine the schooling environment for a 9-year-old in mountainous Laos, in a Kenyan village, or in countless indigenous communities across North America, the environments experienced by children younger than school age in most parts of the world are less clear and far more diverse.

The eminent Policy Action Group on Learning (PAG-L) note in their recommendations regarding the Education for All (EFA) initiative:

> What is most noteworthy here is that [educational interventions] have been generated mostly by development institutions in search of specific "solutions" to "problems".... What is ignored is that context... determines the effectiveness of any given intervention. Context is complex; understanding it requires detailed and nuanced local knowledge. (Ndouye, Sack, & Cappon, 2010, p. 40)

This is the central message of this chapter: Much that has been done in the names of development, progress, and improvement has not only helped, but harmed. Initiatives tend to be driven by Western imperatives, understandings, and power; too seldom have local contexts and understandings been a key consideration in defining and designing progress. In moving ECD forward, arguably the most important sources of new knowledge are better understandings of the lives of the 90% of the world's population that have not, to date, informed the Western discipline of child psychology upon which many international ECD policies and programs are founded (LeVine & New, 2008). As Arnett (2008) reminds us, "research on the whole of humanity is necessary for a science that truly represents the whole of humanity" (p. 602).

Not only does the field of child psychology fail to include the vast majority of the world's children, its roots in, and continuing echoes from, social darwinism deserve attention too, as part of a background to the dominant contemporary discourse on ECD and international development.

Origins and Limitations of a Child Science

The intellectual environment that gave rise to psychology and a science of child development was steeped in darwinian and social darwinian thought (Morss, 1990). Ernst Haeckel, influential German scholar, connected darwinian themes with both individual and social evolution: "To understand correctly the highly differentiated, delicate mental life of civilized man, we must, therefore, observe not only its gradual awakening in the child, but also its step-by-step development in lower, primitive peoples" (1879, quoted in Morss, 1990, p. 18).

Sully, in his influential *Babies and Science* (1881), continued the theme, firmly embedding the origins of child development theory in rationales for colonization:

> The modern psychologist, sharing in the spirit of positive science, feels that he must... study mind in its simplest forms.... [He] carries his eye far afield to the phenomena of savage life, with its simple ideas, crude sentiments and naive habits. (1881, quoted in Riley, 1983, p. 47)

From its earliest formulations, one sees in the science of child development a Western "civilizing" imperative based on an image of deficiency.

General psychology has long been criticized for its failure to incorporate culture (from Berry, Poortinga, Segall, & Dasen [1992] and Shweder [1990], to Burman [2008] and Gielen [2004]). With its underpinning in positivism and its belief in an objective and knowable truth, the experimental method dominated psychology throughout much of the 20th century (Kessen, 1981). It is noteworthy that, while psychology continued throughout the 1950s, '60s, and '70s to strengthen its positivist orientation toward child development, the physical sciences, which psychology had sought to emulate, were engaged in processes of poststructural and postmodern critique and deconstruction, questioning the very possibility of separating the seer from the seen, the subjective from the objective. That the physical sciences could engage in such critical reflection while psychology, as a social science, could ignore its own social fabric is as astonishing as its long-standing marginalization of culture.

Despite such obvious problems and limitations, psychology's hold on the field of child development remained strong throughout the last half of the 20th century, partly because disciplines such as sociology and anthropology largely lacked a child focus. Both disciplines, however, were engaged with children by the 1990s, advancing a position of childhood as a social construction rather than a universal (for early influential work in sociology, see James and Prout [1990] and Qvortrup et al. [1994]; for renewed engagement by anthropology, see Bluebond-Langner and Korbin [2007], Lancy [2008], LeVine and New [2008], and Montgomery [2009]). Despite the value of such scholarly perspectives for an enhanced understanding of ECD and international development, these literatures, among others, are often absent in the contemporary dominant discourse.

Children on the Development Agenda: A Convergence of Forces 1989/1990–Present

The years 1989/1990 were a critical point in the evolution of international ECD. The persistence of a monolithic science of child development that was largely divorced from cultural context (Cole, 1996; Kessen, 1981) coincided with two key events: the 1989 passage of the United Nations Convention on the Rights of the Child (CRC; United Nations, 1989) and the 1990 approval of a global education agenda at Jomtien, Thailand (UNESCO, 1990, 1995). Through recognition that "learning begins at birth" (UNESCO, 1990) and that children's rights are innate, the young child was more firmly ensconced on the international development agenda than ever before.

These events were soon followed by an influential analysis of advances in child survival rates that sought to expand the focus on "third world" children from survival only to healthy development and well-being. Two decades after it was written, Robert Myers' foundational volume *The Twelve Who Survive* (1992) remains a key guide for ECD work in the majority world. In writing it, Myers focused on majority world examples, signaling a strong concern of that time with promoting a contextualized ECD development literature. In contrast, the overwhelming bulk of work that is currently contributing to the international ECD literature comes from the minority world and from minority world authors. This is a matter of grave concern—not for what the literature includes, but for the voices that are missing from it.

At its best, the literature presents a strong case for the need for and the value of ECD programs. Various strands of the literature highlight key rationales for investing in ECD. The following subsections consider the strengths inherent in a number of these rationales but also highlight a number of weaknesses, key among them the degree to which Western perspectives and understandings, particularly those of a positivist and universalist nature, continue to dominate our understandings of children and childhood. The overall purpose of this discussion is not only to issue a call for more research and scholarly production, particularly from those "voices less heard," but to place that action at the top of the international ECD agenda.

Human Development

Key references in the ECD discourse rightly highlight the dangers posed to children's health and development by maternal and child malnutrition, and underline the need for continuing concern with child survival and with programs focused on health and nutrition: If children's basic needs for nourishment, shelter, and sanitation are not met, children cannot thrive within any culture's vision for childhood or human life. In addition to valuable publications like the United Nations Children's Fund (UNICEF)'s annual *State of the World's Children* (see for example, UNICEF, 2009, special edition on the CRC) and EFA annual reports (of particular interest is the early childhood care and education report, UNESCO, 2007), a series in *The Lancet* (Engle et al., 2007; Grantham-McGregor et al., 2007; Walker et al., 2007) summarizes compelling evidence of the developmental risks faced by more than 200 million children in the majority world. The *Lancet* series is laudable for renewing the focus on effective majority world programs that extend and update earlier studies (see, for example, Bernard van Leer Foundation, 1999, 2001, 2002; Cohen, 2004; Myers, 1992). That said, in the 20 studies considered appropriate for inclusion in Engle et al., none was led by African scholars, despite the fact that approximately 20% of the world's children live in Africa.[1] The lack of opportunities for African and other majority world researchers to contribute to what should be a global discussion gnaws at the dominant discourse (Marfo, Pence, Levine, & Levine, 2011; Pence, 2011).

A recent addition to the human development argument comes from the neurosciences. Neuroscientific research is frequently cited to demonstrate the critical importance of the first 3 years of life in the development of the neural pathways necessary for physical, mental, and emotional development (Gopnik 1999; McCain & Mustard, 1999; Shonkoff & Phillips, 2000; Shore, 1997). As is often the case with streams of the international development ECD discourse, the neuroscientific arguments first appeared in the United States (Chugani, 1997; Chugani, Phelps, & Mazziota, 1987; Shore, 1997) and were refined there (Gopnik, 1999; Knudsen, Heckman, Cameron, & Shonkoff, 2006; National Scientific Council on the Developing Child, 2007; Nelson & Bloom, 1997; Shonkoff & Phillips, 2000) before key individuals and institutions brought them into the international literature (Mustard, 2007). Should this Western dominance be considered problematic? Given the neuroscientific evidence, coupled with genomic advances, why should it be important that child development is studied around the globe? To this question, Van IJzendoorn (2010) has a ready response: "Simply put, because gene by environment interactions can change, even be totally reversed, when the ecological niche is taken into account" (p. 2).

Although it is appropriate to use scientific evidence to highlight the importance and potential of the early years, it is also important to recognize that our understandings of neurodevelopment are still in their early stages, particularly in regards to diverse contexts. As Shonkoff (2010) notes, "scientific investigation of the impact of different childrearing beliefs and practices on early brain development is nonexistent" (p. 363).

SOCIAL JUSTICE AND THE (MIS)MEASURE OF CHILDREN

Although it is important to recognize and take advantage of the power of ECD programs to support children, it is equally important to acknowledge that the instruments and concepts typically used to measure and establish norms in child development may themselves confer disadvantage, further stigmatizing already disadvantaged groups. As early as 1984, a report published by the Bernard van Leer Foundation noted: "The normative approach [is] a strategy which itself brings disadvantage to children whose lifestyle, language, cultural heritage and social patterns do not conform to supposed...norms" (p. 8). "For such children standard educational 'processing' often devalues what they are, damages their self image of themselves, their families and communities...The dominant culture, and its expression through normatively based educational systems, becomes thus an instrument of repression" (p. 9).[2]

Measurement, in general, is strongly supported at present by various UN and international organizations, premised on arguments of "no data = no problem" and "numbers count." Such initiatives fail to appreciate the reductionist power of numbers and of predefined outcome priorities to elevate a few issues above all others, disabling a holistic view of the child, undermining local perspectives on what matters, and favoring exogenous and top-down priorities. Such faith in numbers is often misplaced, as expressed in the following truism often attributed to Albert Einstein: *Not everything that can be counted counts, and not everything that counts can be counted.*

Rose (1998) expands the concern: "We have entered, it appears, the age of the calculable person whose individuality is no longer ineffable, unique, and beyond knowledge, but can be known, mapped, calibrated, evaluated, quantified, predicted and managed" (p. 88).

With such cautions in mind, minority world researchers need to be receptive to majority world understandings of child development and support non-Western researchers in playing a key role in addressing international ECD policies and programs. If this does not occur, it is likely that many, if not most, majority world children will continue to be defined as disadvantaged or deficient. And, as Nsamenang (2008) notes, the labels are too often applied to the indigenous knowledge base as well:

> Whenever Euro-American ECD programs are applied as the gold standards by which to measure forms of Africa's ECD, they forcibly deny equity to and recognition of Africa's ways of provisioning for its young, thereby depriving the continent a niche in global ECD knowledge. (p. 196)

POVERTY ALLEVIATION

Running throughout contemporary arguments in support of ECD as a keystone of development is the issue of poverty. Indeed, poverty is the holy grail of development and the single greatest worldwide influence on children's development. It is important to appreciate, however, that studies based on poverty issues in the United States and other parts of the minority world are profoundly problematic for lived realities in the majority world. Cost–benefit analyses, common in the ECD literature, have historically been anchored by U.S.-based studies, where the issues of poverty, poverty alleviation, poverty impacts, and virtually all facets of a poverty discourse bear limited resemblance to poverty in the majority world.

It is concerning that one of the key rationales found in poverty and family/child-related work, "breaking the cycle of poverty," with its strong association with the 1960s' War on Poverty in the United States, is used as a call for action in dramatically different contexts in the contemporary world. (A quick internet search produced a plethora of URLs for virtually all parts of the majority world.) The cycle-of-poverty construct, as used in the United States, is profoundly individualistic and puritanistic, placing the onus on the individual to break out of her or his condition through meritorious activity (as defined by those not in that condition). The economic landscapes of poverty in the United States and in other parts of the minority world are dramatically different from those found in other parts of the world. And, here again, we find a relative paucity of appropriate and contextually informed child-related literature from the majority world.

Such a literature must include the local, seeking to understand poverty through the eyes of those who experience it—and who may not identify themselves as living in a state of poverty. Rather, they live their lives in the place they know, perhaps even unaware that others have given it the name poverty. One is reminded of Gustava Esteva's[3] comment regarding President Harry Truman's introduction of the term "underdevelopment" into the international discourse on development:

> On that day [January 20, 1949], two billion people became "underdeveloped."
> In a real sense, from that time on, they ceased being what they were, in all their
> diversity, and were transmogrified into an inverted mirror of other's reality:
> a mirror that belittles them...a mirror that defines their identity, which is
> really that of a heterogeneous and diverse majority [into a homogeneous]
> and narrow minority. (in Knutsson, 1997, p. 109)

In a very real sense, our own ECD literature has transmogrified the child and the diverse contexts of children. We see children not as they may see themselves or as those close to them may understand them, but as our literature has led us to see and understand them. An ECD and poverty literature that sought to hear from the local, and that used local realities and understandings as starting points, could inform the literature in ways not possible with preconceived or externally driven understandings. Early childhood development is, fortunately, in a position to benefit from some child and poverty research; one useful example is the Young Lives project, a four-country longitudinal study of child poverty (http://www.young-lives.org.uk/). In one of numerous papers, the project considered the issue of children's well-being in contexts of poverty (Camfield, Streuli, & Woodhead, 2008). The paper usefully makes the topic more complex, providing an appreciation of the contested nature of the concept, considering the strengths and weaknesses of diverse methodological approaches, and highlighting the importance of "children's views in the context of their communities" (p. 1). Community and context are recurring themes in this chapter and are considered in greater detail below.

LOCAL LEADERSHIP AND LOCAL KNOWLEDGE

The importance of local leadership is often referenced in the international ECD literature, but the call seems tokenistic when the great flow of information and dollars are from the top down. Critiques of these dynamics are common, but solid examples of ensuring local actors in the driver's seat are not.

Local leadership has more than face validity, and not only has it been demonstrated and called for by the broader development community (Chambers, 1997, 2002), it has a long-standing history in ECD international development as well. Myers, in his 1995 afterword to the paperback release of *The Twelve Who Survive*, concluded: "Our approach must stimulate and support local initiatives that will establish enduring processes and allow continuous learning from experience" (p. 463).

Myers' call from the early 1990s resonates with more recent publications that center children and children's programs in new initiatives for local democracy: "Early childhood institutions can be understood as *public forums situated in civil society in which children and adults participate together in projects of social, cultural, political and economic significance*" (Dahlberg, Moss, & Pence, 2007, p. 73, original emphasis, and see Moss, 2009).

Additional examples of local leadership are explored in the section "Hearing the Unheard Voices," but such "experiments" (no longer experimental, but established) stand in contrast to outside-in, top-down, and centralized approaches that have a long history of failure once the props or funds have been removed (Bebbington, Hickey, & Mitlin, 2008; Moyo, 2009; Quarles-van Ufford, & Giri, 2003).

That history of failure reinforces the importance of "local initiatives that will establish enduring processes" (Myers, 1995, p. 493), and it should not be lost on those at the highest levels of ECD-relevant international organizations. A critique of the EFA by the PAG-L notes:

> We have seen the extent to which "solutions" and approaches aimed at promoting EFA have been top-down.... This dissonance between the lack of ownership upstream, where policies are submitted to FTI, and full ownership downstream cannot be healthy.... What we can take away from this analysis is the extent to which context matters and will determine the fate of any educational plan. (Ndouye et al., 2010, pp. 43–44)

Context matters. Local leadership matters. But the world of international development—the "high-level committees" referred to by some UN organizations—represent a world disconnected from the local. The products of social engineering that emerge from those heights have little hope of fitting into the myriad contexts of humankind, and their use of terms such as the singular construction of "best practice" suggests no intent to do so.

One facet of addressing such imbalances and biases is to make locally conceived and led research a top priority within international ECD. As Shiva (2000) notes,

> [W]hen knowledge plurality mutated into knowledge hierarchy, the horizontal ordering of diverse but equally valid systems was converted into a *vertical* ordering of *unequal* systems, and the epistemological foundations

of Western knowledge were imposed on non-Western knowledge systems with the result that the latter were invalidated. (2000, p. vii)

Such subjugation of others' knowledge has taken various forms over the years, but a disturbing manifestation at present are the very few locally initiated studies that would pass "high-level" evidence-based screening, creating the illusion of a void where useful activity and hard-acquired knowledge do exist. As Shonkoff notes, "the question is not whether decisions...should be informed by evidence, but whether the current definition of evidence that guides early childhood investments may be too narrow" (2010, p. 362). This aspect of the field must be examined closely, considering both its enabling and disabling properties.

Such an examination is critical for the success of a key imperative—the opening of the ECD international development discourse to those less heard, to scholars steeped in their own contexts, with questions that may not appear on the dominant agenda nor be conceivable by its agents. As but one example of vast and largely untapped sources of knowledge, the absence of a robust literature on child and sibling caregiving within the international ECD literature bespeaks the presence of a cultural filter that impedes the study of a key practice common throughout much of the majority world—a point raised over 30 years ago by Weisner and Gallimore (1977).

Through support for majority world efforts to foster researchers and scholars committed to making a difference in their own contexts by employing their own ways of knowing, all of humankind will benefit. It is not only the "draining of brains" but the "framing of brains" that must be addressed to develop a truly global knowledge base. We can no longer behave as though 10% of the world is a suitable proxy, a generalizable base, for the 90% unheard. The next section explores approaches that bring such voices into discussions of policies, programs, research, and education.

HEARING THE UNHEARD VOICES

The preceding section has presented current arguments in support of ECD as a key component in advancing international development and suggested that a weakness throughout the literature is a failure to appreciate the presence and importance of multiple "knowledges"—including the local. The oversight is common—Robert Chambers, a development agronomist, was profoundly disturbed by what the "best and the brightest" in his field (himself included) had wrought in the majority world in the name of science and progress by overlooking local knowledge. In *Challenging the Professions* (1993), Chambers

questions the dominant approaches of professions, disciplines and bureaucracies concerned with...development. The theme is that "we," who call ourselves professionals, are much of the problem, and to do better requires reversals of much that we regard as normal. (p. ix)

Much that Chambers says applies to the largely acritical field of international ECD. The title of another book by Chambers, *Whose Reality Counts?* (1997), poses a fundamentally important question for all who work in international development, while the subtitle of a third, *Putting the Last First* (1983), suggests a way forward for ECD more broadly. A source of appeal for "putting the last first" is that the principle serves to connect some of the most interesting, unusual, and exciting policy, programming, research, and training work under way in ECD internationally. Examples taken from both minority and majority world contexts are considered below.

Government policies, almost by definition, are restrictive statements—they identify a particular course of action and, in doing so, typically restrict other possibilities (Scott, 1998). It was surprising, then, in the late 1980s, to read *Education to Be More* (Early Childhood Care and Education Working Group, 1988). This New Zealand government-commissioned report on the regulation of early childhood services recommended the devolution of authority for addressing issues of quality and program characteristics to the individual program level—the level of families and neighborhoods. The government's response to the report, *Before Five* (Lange, 1988), created a system that provided a contract between the Ministry of Education and the individual center drawn up through consultation with parents and the community (see Smith & Farquhar, 1994). The Meade Report, as *Education to Be More* came to be known, acknowledged the importance of research-based criteria, such as staff training, group size, and other elements common in Western research literature, but it also included a section titled "The Value Base of the Working Group" that recognized the importance of culture, traditions, and related social equity issues. Although full implementation of the policy proved challenging for various reasons, the principle of respecting diversity (as opposed to enforcing conformity) paved the way for significant Maori contributions a few years later to the creation of a national early childhood curriculum, *Te Whariki* (Carr & May, 1993).

In Maori language, *Te Whariki* refers to a "woven mat that all can stand on" (Ministry of Education, 1996). The consultants' aim was to create a "mat" that was sufficiently inclusive and flexible that it could indeed become a place on which diversity could stand. *Te Whariki* evolved through a broadly based consultative process that purposefully and deeply engaged diverse cultural groups in Aotearoa/New Zealand—very significantly, Indigenous Maori peoples, but other groups, including Pasifika peoples, as well. Such policy approaches support diversity and invite families, *whanau* (extended families), and communities to become active stakeholders, rather than passive consumers, in planning and implementing programs for their children.

Both the *Te Whariki* curriculum document and the Meade Report were influenced by an earlier movement led by Maori peoples fearful of losing their language, tradition, and values under the press of "progress" and globalization (see G. H. Smith, 1997; L. T. Smith, 1999). Following community discussions, Maori

Elders and community leaders established *Te Kohanga Reo* (see www.kohanga. ac.nz; Te Kohanga National Trust, 2012), language nest programs that were conducted in Maori and that promote traditional values and worldviews while remaining cognizant of Western approaches. *Te Kohanga Reo* programs grew rapidly throughout Aotearoa, and parents subsequently lobbied successfully for Maori-medium elementary schools (*Kura Kaupapa Maori*) and, as their children grew older, secondary schools (*Wharekura*; Bishop, 2008). By the early 2000s, Maori colleges (*Waananga Maori*) were the fastest growing tertiary education sector in the country. In 2002, a program was initiated to create 500 Maori Ph.D.s in 5 years (Ngā Pae o te Māramatanga, n.d.), dramatically stimulating research development as well. It is from such locally conceived and nurtured seeds that new possibilities and new knowledge can emerge to benefit all.

The experiences of Aotearoa/New Zealand in opening up policies, programs, and research to "voices less heard" and in "putting the last first" are reminiscent of approaches taken by the preschool programs of Reggio Emilia, Italy, which have long been noted as the "best early childhood programs in the world" (Wingert & Kantrowitz, 1991). Indeed, in conversations held with provincial authorities of the Emilia Romagna region (personal communication, 1998), Reggio Emilia was identified as only one of many outstanding civic program sites in the northern regions of Italy (see Bloomer and Cohen [2008] regarding an exceptional infant care program in the Tuscan region). One common element in these programs is their openness to local initiative and inspiration. A special quality of "listening deeply" is the hallmark of these programs, which follow and attempt to learn *from the lead and interests of the children*. Rather than mechanically following narrow, prescribed curricula targets (for example, school readiness, as defined by literacy and numeracy norms), the programs of Reggio Emilia and others in northern Italy attempt to address the "hundred languages of children" as identified by Loris Malaguzzi, founder of the Reggio Emilia preschools (Edwards, Gandini, & Forman, 1993). Such environments are not about children simply doing what they want, and chaos in no way reigns. Instead, one finds children deeply engaged in *their own* questions and quests, with teachers playing facilitative rather than narrowly directive roles. The opportunities for expansion and for connected learning are ever present, moving far beyond the possibilities of preestablished endpoints.

The uncommon threads that lace through the Reggio Emilia programs, *Te Whariki*, Maori preprimary through tertiary institutions, and the policy proposals in *Education to Be More* can also be found in education and training programs that move beyond knowledge transfer to an exploration of and engagement with diverse knowledges. One such approach is the "generative curriculum" advanced by Pence et al. (1993), which is designed to provide a space for the generation of new ideas within the context of mainstream literature, specific Indigenous knowledges, and other sources—respecting all and privileging none. The generative curriculum, initiated by a partnership with an indigenous community and described in numerous publications (see, for example, Pence & Ball, 1999) was recognized by UNESCO in 2002 as one of 20 "best [good] practices" across disciplines from around the world that incorporate Indigenous knowledge (Ball & Pence, 2002). The generative curriculum stepped beyond predetermined outcomes characteristic of most tertiary education to embrace an indeterminate outcome influenced by Western, non-Western, local, and individual influences. The approach taken has not only produced exceptional completion rates for individuals, but has had a lasting impact on the communities that co-delivered the program (Ball & Pence, 2006). The generative approach has been successfully adapted for graduate-level ECD programs through the Early Childhood Development Virtual University (ECDVU), which enrolls country-identified leaders in Africa and the Middle East and has produced completion rates in excess of 95%, with brain drain of less than 1% over 10 years of deliveries in Africa.

The examples noted above share certain similarities: They frame diversity as positive and desirable; they provide processes and procedures that encourage the emergence of local and individual engagement and creativity; they do not reject mainstream perspectives and literatures, but see them only as sources of knowledge among many that are useful; they avoid formulaic and prescriptive approaches; and they attempt to hear and put forward voices not typically heard and to learn from placing the last first. These examples have reconceived the role of professionals and sought to unleash the possibilities of local knowledge. They are powerful models relevant at family, neighborhood, community, regional, national, and international levels. Typically, the outcomes of such open and inclusionary processes exceed those achieved by more predetermined, standardized, and externally driven approaches, allowing space for local engagement, creativity, and ownership—key ingredients for achieving sustainability, particularly in diverse cultural contexts (Ball & Pence, 2006; Pence, Habtom, & Chalamanda, 2008). But perhaps most important, such processes allow perspectives beyond a given society's concept structure to arise and new possibilities to emerge. Such creative processes are important, not only for specific children, families, and communities, but for all peoples to learn from in a challenging and changing world.

The indeterminate approaches to policies, programs, practices, research, and training highlighted above are important in considering future possibilities for ECD and international development. Other activities, some long-standing, should also be included in a discussion of exemplary approaches. From its inception, the Bernard van Leer Foundation has emphasized the importance of culture, context, and listening to local voices. As stated in *Building on People's Strengths* (Bernard van Leer Foundation, 1994), "the Foundation believes that in order to improve opportunities for young children it is necessary to work with the people who surround them and who can have an influence on their lives" (Afterword). With this perspective in mind, the Foundation has supported a cluster of globally diverse initiatives, some of which have proven to be unusually sustainable and effective (Smale, 2002; Zimmermann, 2004).

Another set of long-standing and well-recognized ECD programs in the majority world are the Aga Khan Development Network's early childhood Madrasa centers, first established in the early 1980s in Mombasa, Kenya, but later expanded to Uganda and Tanzania/Zanzibar as well (Aga Khan Foundation, 2008). Unlike the Bernard van Leer Foundation programs, local leaders of the Madrasa centers initially adopted an approach rooted in the program philosophy developed by the High/Scope Foundation. However, the adoption quickly turned into adaptation, and a unique and innovative vision emerged (Mwaura & Mohamed, 2008). Such examples remind us that sharing ideas and approaches across diverse contexts can be constructive and creative, but they also underline the importance of multidirectional sharing (Evans & Bartlett, 2008).

In examining these enduring and respected programs, one can better appreciate the need for programs and policies to grow out of local contexts, concerns, and creativity. It is also clear that, over the past 50 years of international ECD, diverse currents of thought have dominated at various times. The work undertaken through the Bernard van Leer funding in the 1960s and 1970s and continuing through the founding of the Consultative Group in the early 1980s and in Myers' work on *The Twelve Who Survive*, emphasized the importance of local engagement and inspiration. By comparison, the early 21st century has been dominated by international conventions, declarations, and communiqués, and by disciplines and professions often removed from local dynamics. Although the framers of such initiatives would argue that each document recognizes the importance of the local, power is clearly lodged at the highest levels, in a handful of international organizations, within which a remarkably small number of individuals are shaping the future of children globally. We have experience with where "the best and the brightest" might lead, and we have also been advised to "put the last first." It is only through hearing multiple voices and appreciating the importance of diversity and social equity that a multitude of suitable ways forward will be found.

Conclusion

This chapter has employed a broad set of lenses to consider the current state of ECD policies, programs, research, and practices within international development. Such breadth is required if ECD is to be maximally useful and relevant in promoting the well-being and interests of children and societies globally. At present, the ECD international development discourse, although growing rapidly and richly in certain ways, is dramatically constrained by its roots and current sources in Western, modernist traditions and structures. The arguments and positions advanced are largely ahistorical, aphilosophical, and uncontested, and they situate the movement as recent, linear, progressive, and of unalloyed benefit. Calls for evidence-based policies and programs—reasonable and prudent on the face of it—serve to reinforce inherent privilege and obscure the power dynamics at work, cloaking dominating values in scientific rationales. Such structures threaten to continue a tradition of hegemonic privilege that fails to open up to the diverse realities of human societies and of children's possibilities within those societies. A lens of Western-based universalism, in place from the earliest formulations of child psychology, continues with inordinate power and privilege in the contemporary discourse of ECD and international development. It is only by addressing issues of power and privilege, by dramatically elevating the importance of diversity in such discourse; and by more fully supporting local voices in practice, programs, policies, and scholarly research, that the field will become capable of addressing its great mission—promoting the well-being of children globally.

Notes

1. The September 23, 2011, *Lancet* (Engle et al., 2011) has a follow-up article, similarly rich in majority world studies, but also very limited in research led by African scholars.
2. See Cleghorn and Prochner (2010) for a recent restatement.
3. Minister for Planning in Mexico in the 1970s.

References

Aga Khan Foundation. (2008). *The Madrasa early childhood programme: 25 years of experience*. Geneva: Aga Khan Development Network.

Arnett, J. J. (2008). The neglected 95%: Why American psychology needs to become less American. *American Psychologist, 63*(7), 602–614.

Ball, J., & Pence, A. (2002). The generative curriculum model. In K. Boven & J. Morohashi (Eds.), *Best practices using indigenous knowledge* (pp. 98–118). Paris: UNESCO-MOST.

Ball, J., & Pence. A. (2006). *Supporting Indigenous children's development: Community-university partnerships*. Vancouver, BC: UBC Press.

Bebbington, A., Hickey, S., & Mitlin, D. (Eds.). (2008). *Can NGOs make a difference? The challenge of development alternatives*. London, UK: Zed Books.

Bernard van Leer Foundation. (1984). *Multi-cultural societies: Early childhood education and care. Summary report and conclusions from international seminar*. The Hague: Author.

Bernard van Leer Foundation. (1994). *Building on people's strengths: Early childhood in Africa*. The Hague: Author.

Bernard van Leer Foundation. (1999, October). Special issue. The Effectiveness Initiative. *Early Childhood Matters, 23*.

Bernard van Leer Foundation. (2001, October). Special issue. The Effectiveness Initiative: First fruits. *Early Childhood Matters, 99*.

Bernard van Leer Foundation. (2002, December). Special issue. Following footsteps: ECD tracer studies. *Early Childhood Matters, 100*.

Bernard van Leer Foundation. (2004). Introducing tracer studies. Retrieved from http://www.bernardvanleer.org/

Berry, J. W., Poortinga, Y. H., Segall, M. H., & Dasen, P. R. (1992). *Cross-cultural psychology: Research and applications*. Cambridge, UK: Cambridge University Press.

Bishop, R. (2008). Te kotahitanga: Kaupapa Maori in mainstream classrooms. In N. K. Denzin, Y. S. Lincoln, & L. T. Smith (Eds.), *Handbook of critical and indigenous methodologies* (pp. 285–307). Thousand Oaks, CA: Sage.

Bloomer, K., & Cohen, B. (2008). *Young children in charge: A small Italian community with big ideas for children*. Edinburgh: Children in Scotland.

Bluebond-Langner, M., & Korbin. J. E. (2007). Challenges and opportunities in the anthropology of childhoods: An introduction to 'children, childhoods, and childhood studies.' *American Anthropologist, 109*(2), 241–246.

Bornstein, M. (Ed.). (2010). *Handbook of cultural developmental psychology*. New York: Psychology Press.

Burman, E. (2008). *Developments: Child, image, nation*. London, UK: Routledge.

Camfield, L., Streuli, N., & Woodhead, M. (2008). Children's well-being in contexts of poverty: Approaches to research, monitoring and participation. *Young Lives Technical Note 12*. Retrieved from http://ora.ouls.ox.ac.uk/

Cannella, G. S., & Viruru, R. (2004). *Childhood and postcolonization*. New York: Routledge Falmer.

Carr, M., & May, H. (1993). Choosing a model: Reflecting on the development process of Te Whāriki, National Early Childhood Curriculum Guidelines in New Zealand. *International Journal of Early Years Education, 1*(3), 7–22.

Chambers, R. (1983). *Rural development: Putting the last first*. Harlow, UK: Longman.

Chambers, R. (1993). *Challenging the professions. Frontiers for rural development*. London, UK: Intermediate Technology.

Chambers, R. (1997). *Whose reality counts?* London, UK: Intermediate Technology.

Chambers, R. (2002). Power, knowledge, and policy influence: Reflections on experience. In K. Brock & R. McGee (Eds.), *Knowing poverty: Critical reflections on participatory research and policy* (pp. 135–165). London, UK: Earthscan.

Chugani, H. (1997). Neuroimaging of developmental non-linearity and developmental pathologies. In R. Thatcher, G. Lyons, J. Rumsey, & N. Krasnegor (Eds.), *Developmental neuroimaging: Mapping the development of brain and behavior* (pp. 187–195). San Diego, CA: Academic Press.

Chugani, H., Phelps, M., & Mazziota, J. (1987). Positron emission tomography study of human brain function development. *Annals of Neurology, 22*, 487–497.

Cleghorn, A., & Prochner, L. (2010). *Shades of globalization in three early childhood settings: Views from India, South Africa, and Canada*. Rotterdam, NL: Sense Publishers.

Cohen, R. (2004). *Introducing tracer studies: Guidelines for implementing tracer studies in early childhood programs*. The Hague: Bernard van Leer Foundation.

Cole, M. (1996). *Cultural psychology: A once and future discipline*. Cambridge, MA: Belknap Press of Harvard University Press.

Dahlberg, G., Moss, P., & Pence, A. R. (2007). *Beyond quality in early childhood education and care* (2nd ed.). London, UK: Routledge.

Dasen, P. R., & Akkari, A. (2008). Introduction: Ethnocentrism in education and how to overcome it. In P. R. Dasen & A. Akkari (Eds.), *Educational theories and practices from the majority world* (pp. 7–48). New Delhi: Sage.

Davis, W. (2009). *The wayfinders: Why ancient wisdom matters in the modern world.* Toronto, ON: Anansi.

Early Childhood Care and Education Working Group. (1988). *Education to be more.* Wellington, NZ: Government Printer.

Edwards, C., Gandini, L., & Forman, G. (Eds.). (1993). *The hundred languages of children.* Norwood, NJ: Ablex.

Engle, P., Black, M., Behrman, J., de Mello, M., Gertler, P., Kapiriri, L., et al. (2007). Strategies to avoid the loss of developmental potential in more than 200 million children in the developing world. *The Lancet, 369,* 229–242.

Engle, P., Fernald, L., Alderman, H., Behrman, J., O'Gara, C., Yousafzai, A., et al. (2011). Strategies for reducing inequalities and improving developmental outcomes for young children in low-income and middle-income countries. *The Lancet, 378,* 1339–1353.

Evans, J., & Bartlett, K. (2008). *The Madrasa early childhood programme: 25 years of experience.* Brussels: Rosseels.

Gielen, U. P. (2004). The cross-cultural study of human development. In U. P. Gielen & J. L. Roopnarine (Eds.), *Childhood and adolescence: Cross-cultural perspectives and applications* (pp. 3–45). Westport, CT: Praeger.

Gopnik, A. (1999). *The scientist in the crib: Minds, brains and how children learn.* New York: William Morrow.

Grantham-McGregor, S., Cheung, Y. B., Cueto, S., Glewwe, P., Richter, L., Strupp, B., et al. (2007). Developmental potential in the first five years for children in developing countries. *The Lancet, 369,* 60–70.

Haeckel, E. (1879). *The evolution of man.* London, UK: Kegan Paul. (Original work published 1874).

James, A., & Prout, A. (Eds.). (1990). *Constructing and reconstructing childhood.* Basingstoke, UK: Falmer.

Kessen, W. (1981). The child and other cultural inventions. In F. S. Kessel & A.W. Siegel (Eds.), *The child and other cultural inventions* (pp. 26–39). New York: Praeger.

Knudsen, E., Heckman, J., Cameron, J., & Shonkoff, J. (2006). Economic, neurobiological, and behavioral perspectives on building America's future workforce. *Proceedings of the National Academy of Sciences of the United States of America, 103*(27), 10155–10162. Retrieved from http://www.pnas.org/

Knutsson, K. E. (1997). *Children: Noble causes or worthy citizens?* Florence, IT: UNICEF.

Lancy, D. (2008). *The anthropology of childhood: Cherubs, chattel, changelings.* Cambridge, UK: Cambridge University Press.

Lange, D. (1988). *Before five: Early childhood education and care in New Zealand.* Wellington, NZ: Government Printer.

LeVine, R. A., & New, R. S. (2008). *Child development: A cross-cultural reader.* Malden, MA: Blackwell.

Lincoln, Y. S., & Denzin, N. K. (2008). The lions speak. In N. K. Denzin, Y. S. Lincoln, L. T. Smith (Eds.), *Handbook of critical and indigenous methodologies* (pp. 563–571). Los Angeles: Sage.

Marfo, K., Pence, A., Levine, R., & Levine, S. (2011). Strengthening Africa's contributions to child development research: Overview and ways forward. *Child Development Perspectives, 5*(2), 104–111.

McCain, M., & J. F. Mustard. (1999). *The early years study.* Toronto, ON: Publications Ontario.

Ministry of Education. (1996). *Te whariki. He whariki matauranga mo nga mokopuna o Aotearoa/Early childhood curriculum.* Wellington, NZ: Learning Media.

Montgomery, H. (2009). *An introduction to childhood: Anthropological perspectives on children's lives.* London, UK: Wiley-Blackwell.

Morss, J. R. (1990). *The biologising of childhood: Developmental psychology and the Darwinian myth.* London, UK: Lawrence Erlbaum.

Moss, P. (2009). *There are alternatives! Markets and democratic experimentalism in early childhood education and care.* Working Paper No. 53. The Hague: Bernard van Leer Foundation and Bertelsmann Stiftung.

Moyo, D. (2009). *Dead aid.* New York: Farrar, Straus and Giroux.

Mustard, J. F. (2007). Experience-based brain development: Scientific underpinnings of the importance of early child development in a global world. In M. E. Young (Ed.), *Early child development from measurement to action: A priority for growth and equity* (pp. 35–63). Washington, DC: World Bank.

Mwaura, N., & Mohamed, B. (2008). Madrasa early childhood development program: Making a difference. In M. Garcia, A. Pence, & J. Evans (Eds.), *Africa's future, Africa's challenge. Early childhood care and development in Sub-Saharan Africa* (pp. 389–406). Washington, DC: World Bank.

Myers, R. (1992). *The twelve who survive: Strengthening programmes of early childhood development in the Third World.* London, UK: Routledge.

Myers, R. (1995). *The twelve who survive: Strengthening programmes of early childhood development in the Third World* (2nd ed.). Ypsilanti, MI: High/Scope Press.

National Scientific Council on the Developing Child. (2007). *The timing and quality of early experiences combine to shape brain architecture* (Working Paper No. 5). Retrieved from http://www.developingchild.harvard.edu/

Ndouye, M., Sack, R., & Cappon, P. (2010). *Education for all: What would it take to become a success?* Draft discussion paper. Paris, France: PAG-L. Retrieved from http://www.paglearning.org/

Nelson, C. A., & Bloom, F. E. (1997). Child development and neuroscience. *Child Development, 68,* 970–987.

Nsamenang, A. B. (2008). (Mis)understanding ECD in Africa: The force of local and imposed motives. In M. Garcia, A. Pence, & J. Evans (Eds.), *Africa's children, Africa's challenge: Early childhood care and development in Sub-Saharan Africa* (pp. 135–249). Washington, DC: World Bank.

Nsamenang, A. B., & Tchombe, T. M. S. (2011). *African educational theories and practices: A generative teacher education handbook.* Paris: l'Harmattan.

Pence, A. R. (2011). Strengthening Africa's contributions to early childhood care and development research: Historical, conceptual, and structural challenges. *Child Development Perspectives, 5*(2), 112–118.

Pence, A. R., & Ball, J. (1999). Two sides of an eagle feather: Co-constructing ECCD training curricula in university partnerships with Canadian First Nations communities. In H. Penn (Ed.), *Theory, policy, and practice in early childhood services* (pp. 36–47). Buckingham, UK: Open University Press.

Pence, A. R., Habtom, A., & Chalamanda, F. (2008). A tri-part approach to promoting ECD capacity in Africa: ECD seminars, international conferences, and ECDVU. In M. Garcia, A. Pence, & J. Evans (Eds.), *Africa's future, Africa's challenge: Early childhood care and development in Sub-Saharan Africa* (pp. 487–01). Washington, DC: World Bank.

Pence, A. R., Kuehne, V., Greenwood, M., & Opekokew, M. R. (1993). Generative curriculum: A model of university and First Nations cooperative, post-secondary education. *International Journal of Educational Development, 13*(4), 339–49.

Pescosolido, B. A., & Aminzade, R. (1999). *The social worlds of higher education: Handbook for teaching in a new century.* Thousand Oaks, CA: Pine Forge Press.

Quarles-van Ufford, P., & Giri, A. (Eds.). (2003). *A moral critique of development: In search of global responsibilities.* London: Routledge.

Qvortrup, J., Bardy, M., Sgritta, G., & Wintersberger, H. (Eds.). (1994). *Childhood matters: Social theory, practice and politics.* Aldershot, UK: Avebury.

Rahnema, M., & Bawtree, V. (Eds.). (1997). *The post-development reader.* London, UK: Zed Books.

Riley, D. (1983). *War in the nursery.* London: Virago.

Rose, N. (1998). *Inventing ourselves: Psychology, power and personhood.* Cambridge, UK: Cambridge University Press.

Scott, J. (1998). *Seeing like a state: How certain schemes to improve the human condition have failed.* New Haven, CT: Yale University Press.

Shiva, V. (2000). Foreword. In G. J. Sefa Dei, B. Hall, & D. G. Rosenberg (Eds.), *Indigenous knowledges in global contexts.* Toronto, ON: University of Toronto Press.

Shonkoff, J. P. (2010). Building a new biodevelopmental framework to guide the future of early childhood policy. *Child Development, 81*(1), 357–367.

Shonkoff, J. P., & Phillips, D. A. (Eds.). (2000). *From neurons to neighborhoods: The science of early child development.* Washington, DC: National Academy Press. Retrieved from http://www.nap.edu/

Shore, R. (1997). *Rethinking the brain: New insights into early development.* New York: Families and Work Institute.

Shweder, R. A. (1990). Cultural psychology: What is it? In J. S. Stigler, R. A. Shweder, & G. Herdt (Eds.), *Cultural psychology: Essays on comparative human development* (pp. 1–43). New York: Cambridge University Press.

Smale, J. (Ed.). (2002). Following footsteps: ECD tracer studies. Special Issue: *Early childhood matters.* The Hague: Bernard van Leer Foundation.

Smith, A., & Farquhar, S. -E. (1994). The New Zealand experience of charter development in early childhood services. In P. Moss & A. Pence (Eds.), *Valuing quality in early childhood services* (pp. 123–141). London: Paul Chapman.

Smith, G. H. (1997). *Kaupapa Maori as transformative praxis.* Unpublished doctoral dissertation, University of Auckland, New Zealand.

Smith, L. T. (1999). *Decolonizing methodologies: Research and indigenous peoples.* London: Zed Books.

Sully, J. (1881). Babies and science. *The Cornhill Magazine, 43,* 539–554.

Swadener, B. B., & Mutua, K. (2008). Decolonizing performances: Deconstructing the global postcolonial. In N. K. Denzin, Y. S. Lincoln, & L. T. Smith (Eds.), *Handbook of critical and indigenous methodologies* (pp. 31–43). Thousand Oaks, CA: Sage.

Te Kohanga Reo National Trust. (2012). History. Retrieved January 15, 2012, from www.kohanga.ac.nz.

UNESCO. (1990). *World declaration on education for all.* Retrieved from http://www.unesco.org/

UNESCO. (1995). *About education for all.* Retrieved from http://www.unesco.org/

UNESCO. (2007). *EFA global monitoring report. Strong foundations: Early childhood care and education.* Retrieved from http://www.unesco.org/

UNESCO. (2009a). *Atlas of the world's languages in danger.* Retrieved from http://www. unesco.org/

UNESCO. (2009b). Endangered languages, endangered thought. *The UNESCO Courier, 2, 3.*

UNICEF. (2009). *The state of the world's children.* Special edition: Celebrating 20 years of the CRC. New York: Author.

United Nations. (1989). *Convention on the rights of the child.* New York: Author.

Van IJzendoorn, M. H. (2010). SRCD international committee report. *Developments, 53*(3), 1–2.

Walker, S., Wachs, T., Gardner, J., Lozoff, B., Wasserman, G., Pollitt, E., et al. (2007). Child development: Risk factors for adverse outcomes in developing countries. *The Lancet, 369,* 145–157.

Weisner, T., & Gallimore, R. (1977). My brother's keeper: Child and sibling caretaking. *Current Anthropology, 18*(2), 169–190.

Whiteford, L., & Manderson, I. (Eds.). (2000). *Global health policy, local realities: The fallacy of the level playing field.* London: Lynne Reinner.

Wingert, P., & Kantrowitz, B. (1991, December 2). The best schools in the world. *Newsweek.* Retrieved from http://www.newsweek.com/

Zimmermann, R. (Ed.). (2004). *Stories we have lived, stories we have learned. About early childhood development programmes.* The Hague: Bernard van Leer Foundation.

Programmatic Approaches to Early Childhood Development

9

The Role of the Health Sector in Early Childhood Development

Patrice L. Engle, Mary E. Young, and Giorgio Tamburlini

Rationale for a Role of the Health Sector in Promoting and Protecting Child Development

THE WORLD HEALTH ORGANIZATION'S DEFINITION OF HEALTH AS WELL-BEING

A basic rationale for health sector involvement in early childhood development (ECD) is the concept of health as a state of well-being, first articulated in 1978 by the World Health Organization (WHO). A child's well-being depends, as much research has shown, on conditions from conception through the first few years of a child's life, the period of greatest risk and greatest opportunity for making a difference for children. Poverty, poor maternal and child health, undernutrition, and lack of early stimulation undermine children's development early in life, when the architecture of the brain is most sensitive to the influences of the external environment.

Despite the WHO's definition of health, the major focus of the health sector in low- and middle-income (LAMI) countries has, for years, been child survival alone. Awareness that children were surviving but not thriving (e.g., Myers, 1992), that many of the survivors were developing far below their potential (Grantham-McGregor et al., 2007), has recently led to the emergence of a broader view of child development in the health sector. In part, this shift is due to the success of the child survival efforts in some countries. In addition, however, the economic benefits of improving child development are being recognized (e.g., Heckman, 2006). The new focus on children's well-being responds to these current insights.

INCLUSION OF EARLY CHILDHOOD DEVELOPMENT
IN GLOBAL GOALS

A second, very direct rationale for health sector involvement in ECD has been ECD's inclusion in global declarations for health. In 2000, 189 nations agreed on the United Nations' (UN) eight Millennium Development Goals (MDGs) to improve health, nutrition, education, gender equity, and economic and environmental conditions in developing countries (Global Health Council, 2010). The MDGs have stimulated bilateral and multilateral organizations to intensify and implement interventions for child survival and national policies focused on improving child survival. Beyond that, however, the goal of improving children's development, as well as survival, was not a specific focus.

In 2005, the Global Health Council convened an international meeting in Bellagio, Italy, to identify priority actions in child health. Seeking to maximize investments in children ages 0–5 years, the expert panel recommended four principles to guide future work (www.globalhealth.org), one of which was to promote and stimulate children's cognitive development, thus broadening the approach to child health to include children's development, as well as their survival.

Subsequently, these principles were reinforced in the final report of the WHO's Commission on Social Determinants of Health, *Closing the Gap in a Generation: Health Equity Through Action on Social Determinants of Health* (Marmot & Wilkinson, 2006; World Health Organization [WHO], 2008). The report was specific in its endorsement of a broad approach to child health and recommended that nations "[c]ommit to and implement a comprehensive approach to early life, building on existing child survival programs and extending interventions in early life to include social/emotional and language/cognitive development." The report also emphasized that health inequities cannot be reduced by health services alone and that social and economic factors play a major role. The two key messages for the health sector were (1) to start at the beginning, to integrate child development, stimulation, and parenting tools into prenatal, early health, and education services and (2) to get "ready for success," that is, to ensure children's access to community services before they enter school, and begin with children who are most vulnerable and disadvantaged. The excerpt in Box 9.1 captures the integrated and comprehensive nature of the report.

ACCESS TO HEALTH SERVICES AS AN ENTRY POINT

A third rationale for incorporating early child development into the health sector is that health services have the greatest access to families and children during the critical first few years. In many parts of the world, this is the only service to reach children prenatally and under 3, during the critical window for

BOX 9.1. Equity from the Start: Early Childhood Development

A comprehensive approach to the early years in life requires policy coherence, commitment, and leadership at the international and national level. It also requires a comprehensive package of ECD and education programmes and services for all children worldwide.

Experiences in early childhood (defined as prenatal development to eight years of age), and in early and later education, lay critical foundations for the entire life course. The science of ECD shows that brain development is highly sensitive to external influences in early childhood, with lifelong effects.

Good nutrition is crucial and begins *in utero* with adequately nourished mothers. Mothers and children need a continuum of care from pre-pregnancy, through pregnancy and childbirth, to the early days and years of life. Children need safe, healthy, supporting, nurturing, caring, and responsive living environments.

Preschool educational programmes and schools, as part of the wider environment that contributes to the development of children, can have a vital role in building children's capabilities.

Early child development (ECD) – including the physical, social/emotional, and language/cognitive domains – has a determining influence on subsequent life chances and health through skills development, education, and occupational opportunities because what children experience during the early years sets a critical foundation for their entire life course.

Source: WHO Commission on the Social Determinants of Health 2008.

child development. Health workers are often seen as reliable and trustworthy sources of information, and therefore have great value as communicators of ECD messages.

INTERVENTIONS TO IMPROVE A CHILD'S DEVELOPMENT CONTRIBUTE TO ACHIEVING OTHER HEALTH GOALS

Finally, health, even by the most narrow definition, is promoted by parents' attachment to their children and the capacity of parents and caregivers to provide ongoing attentive care—exactly the kinds of strengths that ECD programs can provide. Improved caregiving practices, including feeding, hygiene, home health care, and consultation-seeking, all benefit children's health. Interventions can make parents and family members aware of developmental changes that can lead to injuries and death. They can reduce chances of abuse and neglect, inadequate upbringing, and maternal depression or mental illness. Further, identification of children exposed to negative circumstances and early intervention for children with disabilities or at risk of developmental delay can be incorporated into primary health services.

Models for Integrating Early Childhood Development into Health Systems

TYPES OF HEALTH CARE FOR EARLY CHILDHOOD DEVELOPMENT

Table 9.1 outlines a number of interventions for child development, including those that strengthen the caregiving environment, described in terms of level of care (promotive, preventative, and curative) and by child age (Engle, 2011a).

Promotive Care

The health sector has a unique role to play in supporting all young children's growth and development, labeled here as *promotive care*. The actions are primarily taken by families, but the guidance and encouragement comes through the health worker. Health care providers can give critical guidance, such as how to communicate with infants and children; stimulate children's development; handle common developmental problems such as sleep, feeding, and discipline; and reduce injuries through alerting families to rapid changes in development that result in periods of increased susceptibility for accidents (e.g., climbing).

Preventive Care

The health sector's role in preventative care includes identifying children in need of increased interventions (e.g., who are at risk of delay, deviance, or disability, or families at risk due to extreme poverty or distress) through the execution of well-planned child-centered interventions. These services could be facility-, home-, or community-based.

Curative Care

Finally, the health sector's role in curative care for ECD involves early detection of children with delays or disabilities, and overseeing and coordinating early interventions for children identified as developmentally delayed or with special needs. The health sector should work with families to help them help their children. The health sector may also deal with child mental health, behavioral disturbances, or child abuse and neglect. The health sector's role is also in developing and coordinating multisectoral linkages with social welfare, nutrition workers, and preschool program workers, and in increasing access to primary health care for those children and their families who require multiple, ongoing, and multidisciplinary interventions.

AGE-SPECIFIC STRATEGIES FOR INCORPORATING CHILD DEVELOPMENT INTO EXISTING PROGRAMS

Evidence-based interventions to support children's development can be categorized according to period of development (prenatal, intrapartum, newborn (birth to 1 month); 1 month to 3 years; and 3 to 5 years) and by purpose of the intervention. These are summarized in Table 9.1.

TABLE 9.1. Interventions for Early Childhood Development to complement health and nutrition and other primary health care interventions (items with * are in Care for Child Development Module)

Period	Promotive Care	Preventive Care	Curative Care
Prenatal	–Social and emotional support from male partner –Information on child development for new mothers*	–Social–emotional support for mothers evidencing depression or stress	–Special care for women at risk for mental illnesses.
Intra-partum and birth	–Encourage bonding of mother/infant by skin to skin contact, allowing infant to find the breast, immediate breast–feeding; –Father presence at birth	–Increased family and health worker support during childbirth in high risk cases	–Counselling and support for families with high risk birth and/or babies
Newborn to 1 month	–Age–appropriate recommendations for child play and communication to families and problem–solving for attachment difficulties, discipline, other care practices* –Show parents how newborns respond to stimuli and support traditional practices such as gentle massage	–Kangaroo care with skin to skin contact for premature or LBW infants	–For hospitalized or very low birth weight infants promote mother, newborn and family bonding
1 month to 36 months	–Age–appropriate recommendations to families for reading aloud, child play and problem–solving for attachment difficulties, discipline, other care practices* –Guided practice for families in these recommendations (hold group sessions with both parent and child present), –Increase early access to books and learning materials –Anticipatory guidance of risks of accidents associated with developmental changes (e.g., walking)	The previous column and: –Consultation and assessment *with* parents regarding concerns if a risk of disability or delay; –For LBW/ premature children gradually increase responsive stimulation from family –Encourage responsiveness in feeding particularly for malnutrition or over– nutrition* –Provide women at risk of maternal depression social support –Early recognition of children undergoing neglect, abuse, violence, or other high risk environments –Identify community resources for supporting family and child	The previous column and: –Early intervention with family for children at risk of disability, delay, or learning and behavioral difficulties –Monitoring of women with maternal depression to be sure that they are accessing treatment –Early intervention with families and communities for children experiencing neglect, abuse, violence, or mental health problems
37 months to 60 months	–Communicate the importance of family support for learning –Advice on family care and discipline –Encourage play with other children, participation in early child development programs	The previous column and: –Continued routine checks for child malnutrition, vision, speech and hearing, learning and behavioral problems, and developmental delays –Awareness of problems in interaction between family and child	The previous column and: –Early intervention for children at risk of disability or delay– interventions coordinated by health sector –Linkages with preschool workers for early inclusion / rehabilitation in available educational settings within the community

*These recommendations are in the WHO/UNICEF Care for Child Development and Care for Feeding Modules.

Prenatal

For a child's development, the most critical prenatal interventions relate to reduction in developmental risks related to nutritional deficiencies and to exposure to toxicants, such as smoking, excessive amounts of alcohol, or drugs such as cocaine, all of which have been found to have significant effects on children's brain development. Stress during pregnancy resulting in high cortisol levels has been linked with increased children's difficult temperament, a risk factor for later psychological disorders (Field & Diego, 2008). Maternal depression and anxiety during pregnancy and postnatally have been linked with poor child growth and development (Barker, Jaffee, Uher, & Maughan, 2011; Rahman, Iqbal, & Harrington, 2003; Wachs, Black, & Engle, 2009). Low birth weight due to intrauterine growth retardation has been associated with poorer development unless appropriate interventions are introduced (Rosato et al., 2008; Walker et al., 2011).

- *Promotive care.* Interventions should include a family-based approach, encouraging male partners to support the pregnant woman emotionally.
- *Preventive care.* Strategies include interventions with pregnant women who are abusing drugs, alcohol, or tobacco and social support for women who show symptoms of depression or excessive stress.
- *Curative care.* Conditions such as maternal diabetes, adolescent pregnancies, drug or alcohol abuse, or multiple pregnancies may have negative implications for child development and require special medical interventions and psychosocial support.

Intrapartum Care and Newborns

- *Promotive and preventative care.* Research supports the importance of mother–child bonding and skin-to-skin contact in the first hour after birth for breast-feeding and quality of attachment. Although this intervention appears to be important for all, it is particularly effective for high-risk mothers, such as very young mothers, those who may not have wanted the child, or who are at socioeconomic risk (Field & Diego, 2008). Parental attachment and investment in newborns increase if parents are more aware of their child's capacities early on. One strategy is to show families that children can see and hear from birth, as this knowledge may improve patterns of interaction in the first days of life (Ertem et al., 2007). A simple demonstration of these abilities has resulted in improved interaction and subsequent breast-feeding behavior (Hart, Field, & Nearing, 1998; Widmeyer & Field, 1981). Gentle massage, in some cultures, has been shown to increase weight gain and development for preterm infants as well (Field, Diego, Hernandez-Reif, Deeds, & Figuereido, 2006; Hernandez-Rief, Diego & Field, 2007).

- *Preventive care.* Strategies could include routine neonatal screening and surveillance of high-risk newborns (e.g., low birth weight, premature) and infants from high-risk pregnancies or births.
- *Curative care.* Congenital anomalies evident at birth or a very premature birth may interfere with the development of an adequate mother–child bond, resulting in a long-term risk for the child. Counseling with the family (not just the mother) and an honest discussion of the risks and possibilities is recommended. Strategies to keep the mother and father in as close contact as possible with a very-low-birth weight baby are helpful.

1 Month Through 36 Months

Promotive care strategies to improve ECD for all children through health promotion include advice and guidance by health workers during visits, providing additional tools such as books for children, or "baby passports" with information.

CARE FOR CHILD DEVELOPMENT

The *Care for Child Development Module*, published by the UN Children's Fund (UNICEF) and the WHO, was developed originally in 1999 as part of the WHO's Integrated Management of Childhood Illnesses (IMCI). It provides health workers with age-specific guidance for families on ways to improve children's development through play and communication, and gives health workers a series of possible problems that parents might face, plus recommendations when these problems arise. The module is linked with a module to improve parent–child interactions during feeding (Care for Feeding) in addition to other feeding recommendations. The modules encourage a positive view of the child and support for parents. Both modules were revised and updated in 2009, renamed Care for Child Development, and published in 2012 (WHO and UNICEF, 2012). Field experiments (Chopra, 2001; dos Santos et al., 1999), efficacy trials in Turkey (Ertem et al., 2006) and China (Jin et al., 2007) and an evaluation of programs in three Central Asian countries (Engle, 2011b) showed that the intervention took between 5 and 10 minutes per session and resulted in significant changes in either caregiver behavior or child outcomes.

POSITIVE DISCIPLINE

From 24 through 36 months, activity levels are higher than at any other period of time, and children have not yet developed a system of internal control or regulation of their behavior (Nagin & Tremblay, 2001). Discipline can be challenging, particularly if families expect a high degree of obedience and for those children with aggressive behavior. Families should be given anticipatory guidance to use positive discipline and avoid harsh discipline. One of the outcomes of the Healthy Steps program of parent counseling through health centers in the United States was improved parent discipline strategies (Caughy et al., 2003).

READING ALOUD TO CHILDREN

A strategy that encourages health workers to provide books for young children of 6–8 months of age and give advice to parents to read to their children has been shown to produce changes in parenting reading behavior and have significant impact on the development of child language and school readiness in the United States and other countries, with increased impact among minority and disadvantaged families (Byington et al., 2008; Fergusson et al., 2006, Theriot et al., 2003; Toffol, Melloni, & Cagnin, 2011; Weitzman, Roy, Walls, & Tomlin, 2004; Zuckerman, 2009).

BABY PASSPORTS

In Indonesia, the KKA program was an early leader in incorporating information about children's development on their health cards, and the *Posyandu* system incorporated group sessions for caregivers and young children on child development, along with nutrition interventions. Initial results were encouraging (Coletta, Satoto, Sockaling-Ham, & Zeitlan, 1993).

Birth to 36 Months

PREVENTIVE AND PROMOTIVE CARE

Children who are known to be at high risk for impaired development, such as those born prematurely or at low birth weight, have achieved normal levels of development with supportive interventions (McCormick et al., 2006; Meeks-Gardner, Walker, & Grantham-McGregor, 2003; Nair et al., 2009).

A review of health promotion actions in both high-income and LAMI countries found that home visiting was among the most effective models (Engle, 2011b). In the United States, the Nurse Partnership program with high-risk families found increases in school readiness, reduction in days hospitalized with injuries, reduced use of food stamps, and eventually greater economic productivity (Eckenrode et al., 2010; Olds et al., 2002, 2004). The authors estimate a benefit–cost ratio of 5.7:1 for the program of home visiting (Olds, Sadler, & Kitzman, 2007).

In high-income countries, success factors included a frequency of three to four visits per month, offering coaching for parents, and the parents' perception of vulnerability for the child. Programs with higher intensity and longer duration have greater impact (Minkovitz et al., 2007; Palfrey et al., 2005). These same factors have been found to be effective in LAMI countries (Engle et al., 2011a, Walker, 2011). When group sessions with parents provided them with opportunities for practice, feedback, and emotional support, they were more likely to show impacts (Engle et al., 2011b).

Maternal depression is increasingly recognized as a risk for young children; depression can be reduced through social support, although effects on infants may be modest (Rahman, Bunn, Lovel, & Creed, 2007). Loss of family members, or illness of family members, particularly with AIDS, is associated with poorer cognitive performance (Van Rie, Mupuala, & Dow, 2008), but Potterton and colleagues (2010) found significant differences between a group of HIV-positive infants in a home stimulation program who were additionally receiving antiretroviral medications and a comparison group receiving only the anti-retroviral medications and regular health visits. It is less clear how to reduce the effects of other risks, such as exposure to violence, conflicts, disasters, and excessive (or toxic) stress.

Curative Care for Children from Birth to 36 Months

CURATIVE CARE

This period of birth to 36 months is critical for interventions for children with developmental delays, disabilities, or mental health issues. The health sector has a role to play in coordinating services and providing health support. Although there is evidence that these interventions are effective in high-income countries, only a few studies test their effectiveness in LAMI countries (Engle et al., 2011b). One experimental study in Bangladesh reported that rural children with disabilities whose caregivers received a parent training package progressed better on adaptive skills and the mothers had significant improvement in supporting their children, compared with a minimal intervention group (McConachie et al., 2000). Community-based rehabilitation (CBR) is a WHO-advocated strategy for responding to children and adults with disabilities. However, few evaluations exist; of 128 studies published on CBR in 24 years, most were theoretical or descriptive articles (Finkenflugel, Wolffers, & Huijsman, 2005).

Incorporation of Early Childhood Development into the Health Sector: Policy and Program Considerations

Evidence for the effectiveness of interventions provided through the health sector to improve early child development, despite its persuasiveness, is not sufficient for putting these programs into practice and moving them to scale. This requires a number of policy and program actions, outlined below.

GOVERNMENT ACTION

In all countries, the health sector is the lead government sector for children's health before they enter school. In response to global goals such as the MDGs and WHO goals, the health sector needs to expand its scope beyond its traditional curative and preventive roles.

The healthy development of children depends on having a range of well-organized and coordinated programs that promote healthy pregnancies, births, infants, and young children. In the field of early child development, success often comes from a combination of actions. Doryan, Gautam, and Foege (2001) highlight six effective steps for government action:

1. Create a political constituency for children.
2. Earmark public resources to protect investments.

3. Provide incentives for community support of ECD initiatives.
4. Create demanding consumers.
5. Develop and disseminate information about ECD to the public and ECD professionals.
6. Create new providers.

A major decision for government is whether to promote ECD policies and programs universally (for a nation's entire population of young children) or to target programs to high-risk and otherwise disadvantaged young children and communities. This decision does not have to be an either/or decision, since the types and range of programs and providers will differ depending on context, and governments have to recognize these differences and accommodate them in program designs and strategies. In any case, all countries can benefit from a combined approach—universal and targeted—that utilizes available resources, both public and private, to the best advantage.

TRAINING AND CAPACITY DEVELOPMENT

Training and capacity development are major ingredients in the success of ECD programs. Success depends on having qualified, trained, and experienced providers. Although paraprofessionals are the most common providers of home visits (Drummond, Weir, & Kysela, 2002), in general they require more training and supervision than do professionals (Bilukha et al., 2005). Effectiveness is linked to having a specified curriculum and adequate training for those who administer the program (Norr et al., 2003), although a variety of factors influence effectiveness (Sweet & Appelbaum, 2004).

SECTOR LINKAGES

Often, in government, no one sector covers all of young children's health, nutrition, child development, and protection rights. Various sectors claim responsibility for young children's health and well-being. In all countries, the health sector assumes primary responsibility for the health and well-being of very young children, starting from prenatal care to children's health services. Education and social protection sectors are often responsible for these two domains of older children's development and well-being. Comprehensive, integrated early child development crosses at least these three sectors, and ECD policies and programs must do likewise.

It is not as important to identify which specific sector or agency is responsible for what domain as it is to integrate all aspects of ECD programs so that they focus on the child specifically and embrace inputs from all related ministries. For example, nine Organization for Economic Cooperation and Development (OECD) countries combine early education and child care systems for young children under one government department (e.g., ministries of education). In Jamaica, services for young children are coordinated from the Ministry of Health, and, in Brazil, the *Primeira Infância Melhor* program is led from health sector as well.

NATIONAL–LOCAL COLLABORATION

Good public policy requires collaboration between national and local levels of government. Strong national institutions can generate technical capacity in health, nutrition, and child development and provide the rigorous supervision needed to ensure the quality of programs. Local governmental structures, for their part, can team with communities to tailor programs and services to heterogeneous populations and to meet local needs and conditions. In summary national institutions complement local capacity and commitment; they do not, and cannot, substitute for it, in either developing or industrialized countries. National–local collaboration is as necessary to the U.S. Head Start program, for example, as it is to Colombia's *Hogares Communitarios* program or the *Hogares Bienestar Infantil* (HBI) homes for children's well-being.

MONITORING, EVALUATION, AND RESEARCH

Over the past four decades, more effort has been given to developing and evaluating specific program models than to monitoring and following outcomes of programs at scale. Consequently, knowledge about what works under what circumstances, and why particular programs are difficult to take to scale, is only beginning to emerge.

Monitoring is needed at local, regional, and national levels to provide feedback to policymakers and program planners on how well children are doing and whether ECD interventions are making a difference in children's outcomes.

The capability to measure how well young children are doing at various stages of their development exists. In ECD a few tools to measure cognitive or behavioral development are being developed. For example, the Early Development Instrument (EDI) is a teacher rating of child behavior, useful for children aged 3–5 years, observed in a center. Developed in 2000 by researchers at McMaster University in Canada, the EDI has been adapted and tested in several countries, both developing and industrialized. The World Bank and other nongovernmental organizations have supported countries' adaptation and piloting of a short version of the EDI (50 items) in numerous countries (Brazil, China, Chile, Jamaica, Jordan, Mexico, Moldova, Mozambique, and Peru).

UNICEF has adapted items from the EDI to create a parent report measure of 10 items included in its Multiple Indicator Cluster Survey (MICS) version 4 onward. Other efforts to develop regionally appropriate direct tests of child development are under way. A number of tests, primarily developed in Western countries, have been used for research purposes (see Fernald, Kariger, Engle, & Raikes, 2009).

This issue is discussed in Chapter 18 of this volume (Bornstein & Landsford, 2013), on assessment.

Taking effective small programs to scale (i.e., dramatically expanding their reach) presents even greater challenges. When scaling up programs, their design and implementation need to be standardized to reflect which types of programs work best and for whom the programs are most beneficial. Standardization will provide the data needed for future meta-analyses from which to draw conclusions (i.e., evidence) about which practices work best for specific populations and outcomes.

For example, Carroll and colleagues (2007) underscore the importance of home visiting programs remaining loyal to a specific framework and established guidelines. Lack of consistency in the implementation of these programs may hamper their impact when they are taken to scale. The ECD literature emphasizes that having consistent parameters across programs is key. Zercher and Spiker (2004) noted that standardization of implementation could help program planners and managers decide which types of programs to offer to whom when scaling up, although there is a critical need to adapt the program to the context.

Even as programs move to scale, it is critical to continue to provide new models if older ones do not work, and to evaluate what makes the implementation successful (implementation research). Many successful programs point to an ongoing research and monitoring program to provide the feedback for continued improvement and for advocacy for the program.

Large-Scale Early Childhood Development Programs in the Health Sector: Three Examples

Three large-scale programs are briefly described here to highlight the challenges and opportunities inherent in ECD programs provided through the health sector: a government-supported program in Brazil and two funded by the World Bank with collaboration of the national governments in Jamaica and China.

The state government of Rio Grande do Sul, Brazil, established the *Primeira Infância Melhor—PIM* (The Better Early Childhood Development Program) in 2003. With the passing of State Law 12544 in 2006, PIM officially became part of the State Policy for the Promotion and Development of Early Childhood in

Rio Grande do Sul. Through home visiting, PIM offers guidance to low-income families (those with a monthly per capita income of less than half the national minimum wage) to enable them to promote their children's holistic development beginning from a mother's pregnancy until a child is 6 years old. Emphasis is given to the first 3 years of a child's life.

The PIM program supports two modalities of care within a community-based approach: individual care and group care. The individual care modality is designed for families with children aged 0 to 2 years, 11 months, and to pregnant women. In home visits of approximately 1 hour, children are seen once a week and pregnant women are seen once every 2 weeks. The group care modality is designed for families with children aged 3–5 years and/or pregnant women (Schneider & Ramires, 2007).

The PIM program has been implemented in 361 towns in Rio Grande do Sul. The program has assisted 59,125 families, which includes 88,740 children and 7,095 pregnant mothers (PIM Database, July 2011, www.pim.saude.rs.gov.br). A randomized evaluation of PIM is under way.

JAMAICA

The Jamaica Early Child Development Project, which is supported by the World Bank, focuses primarily on children aged 0–3 years. The intent is to address the very low coverage of ECD services and the lack of a recognized national ECD model for this age group and the lack of a system for timely identification of children at risk for poor development. Parenting education is included, as Jamaica's parenting education programs have low coverage and involve many unregulated, small-scale initiatives of varying quality. The Jamaican project also seeks to improve services for children aged 3–5 years.

The three objectives of the project are: (1) to increase the access to quality ECD services for children aged 0–3 years and, specifically, at-risk children; (2) to improve the quality of ECD services for children aged 3–5 years; and (3) to improve the access of parents of children aged 0–8 years to quality parenting education services. The health system's focus on children aged 0–3 years includes the introduction of a Child Health and Development Passport, for parents' record keeping and surveillance of their children's development, and the establishment of well-child clinics to target and provide early stimulation services to children at risk.

The Jamaica Early Child Development Project promotes strengthening of the country's Early Childhood Commission (established as an executive agency in 2004). It also supports public organizations in the building of skills and capacity to develop ECD policies, regulatory frameworks, and financing mechanisms, and to integrate monitoring and evaluation efforts into a national system of ECD monitoring and evaluation. A key challenge has been the limited skills and capacity of ECD professionals and practitioners for working in a multisectoral environment, as most have previously worked in relatively isolated sectors (e.g., health and education).

CHINA

China's Maternal and Child Health (referred to as the Health Nine [IX] Project, 1999–2008) is supported by the World Bank and has introduced and strengthened health workers' skills in the integrated management of childhood illnesses (IMCI). Significantly, the project included a parenting education component in early child development. Inclusion of this component marked the first time, among any of China's health projects, that families and communities were included as equal partners with health workers to assure the healthy development of mothers and children.

The Health Nine project was implemented across 107 counties in five nationally designated poverty provinces. It utilized a participatory method to gather information from families and communities on the causes of disease, patterns of health behavior, adequacy of existing maternal and child health services, and obstacles to health care.

The parenting education component is focused on improving parents' skills in early child development through health education materials promoting good parenting practices to foster children's social and emotional development. The design effort included revision and adaptation of health education methods for rural users, production and adaptation of information on child development and maternal health, and tailoring of education communications to ethnic minority groups. It also included development of materials based on a "Learning through Play" concept for children from birth to age 3 years and the production of booklets and posters for mothers and for display at health centers in villages and townships.

An evaluation of the project (World Bank, 2008) found an increased expansion of coverage for IMCI. Appropriate techniques for IMCI, as recommended by WHO, had been introduced into the project areas, resulting in the control of childhood illnesses such as pneumonia, diarrhea, and malnutrition. In 2007, the coverage rate for IMCI reached 83.8%, and the nutritional surveillance rate for children under 5 reached 52.6%.

The evaluation also documented the promotion of early children development. In 2007, the number of villages that implemented ECD activities reached 21,369, or 83% of the number planned. By the end of 2006, the rate of breast-feeding for children who were 4 months old or younger reached 92.5%, which exceeded the target rate of 80%. Importantly, parents' demand for ECD materials exceeded the resources available. The overriding feature important to the success of the project was the national government's commitment, complemented by provincial and local-level collaboration.

As part of national poverty reduction efforts, the China Development Research Foundation, since 2009, has piloted in two counties an integrated infant nutrition (6–24 months) and prenatal vitamin and micronutrient nutrition supplementation program, parent education, and a mobile outreach ECD program. Originally carried out in western poverty areas through the existing three-tier maternal child health infrastructure (China Development Research Foundation, 2011), the program has now expanded province-wide in Qinghai and has been launched in Guizhou.

Conclusion

A number of strategies have been shown to be effective in promoting ECD through the mechanisms of the health sector. These include:

- *Promotive care.* The integration of ECD into well-child or ill-child visits (e.g., Care for Child Development), group sessions for parents in primary health care settings, baby passports and books for children, and home visiting or group sessions for all parents
- *Preventative care.* Services with a special focus on children at risk, either from family risk factors or child characteristics, including early and effective assessment, home visiting, treatment for maternal depression, and support for parent–child attachment when there is a risk of poor attachment or harsh discipline
- *Curative care.* Interventions with families and communities to help children with disabilities, developmental delay, or behavioral and mental problems, or who have experienced abuse and neglect

These strategies will be best utilized if the health sector ensures that:

- ECD is incorporated in primary health care training curricula and tasks.
- ECD components are fully reflected in performance indicators for primary health care centers and staff.
- Appropriate specific supervision is ensured.
- Financing is adequate to support the programs at scale.
- Local and national coordination is in place.
- Policies and mechanisms to guide the intersectoral work are effective.

References

Barker, E. D., Jaffee, S. R., Uher, R., & Maughan, B. (2011, August). The contribution of pre-natal and postnatal maternal anxiety and depression to child maladjustment. *Depression and Anxiety, 28*(8), 696–702. doi: 10.1002/da.20856. Epub ahead of print retrieved July 18, 2011.

Bilukha, O., Hahn, R., Crosby, A., Fullilove, M., Liberman, A., Moscicki, E., et al. (2005). The effectiveness of early childhood home visitation in preventing violence. A systematic review. *American Journal of Preventive Medicine, 28*(2S1), 11–39.

Bornstein, M. H., & Lansford, J. E. (2013). Assessing early child development. In P. R. Britto, P. L. Engle, & C. M. Super (Eds.), *Handbook of early childhood development research and its impact on global policy* (Chapter 18). New York: Oxford University Press.

Byington, C. L., Hobson, W. L., Olson, L, Torres-Nielsen, G., Winter, K., Oritz, K. A., et al. (2008). The good habit of reading (El buen habito de la lectura): Parental reactions to an enhanced Reach Out and Read Program in a clinic for the underserved. *Journal of Health Care for the Poor and Underserved, 19*(2), 363–368.

Carroll, D., Patterson, M., Wood, S., Booth, A., Rick, J., & Balain, S. (2007). A conceptual framework for implementing fidelity. *Implementation Science, 2*(40). Retrieved from http://www.implementationscience.com/content/2/1/40

Caughy, M. O. B., Miller, T. L., Genevrob, J. L., Huangc, K. Y., & Nautiyalb, C. (2003). The effects of Healthy Steps on discipline strategies of parents of young children. *Applied Developmental Psychology, 24*, 517–534.

China Development Research Foundation (CDRF). (2011). *CDRF Program on early child development: Qinghai pilot interim report.* Report prepared for the 2011 International Conference on Early Childhood Development, Beijing.

Chopra, M. (2001). *Assessment of participants on the Care for Development IMCI Training Course.* Unpublished report To WHO South Africa.

Coletta, N., Satoto, Sockaling-Ham, S, & Zeitlan, M. (1993). The child development milestone chart: An approach to low cost programming in Indonesia. *Early Child Development and Care, 96*, 161–171.

Doryan, E., Gautam, K., & Foege, W. (2001). The political challenge: Commitment and cooperation. In M. E. Young (Ed.), *From early child development to human development* (pp. 20–35). Washington, DC: World Bank.

dos Santos, I. (1999). *Pilot test of the child development section of the IMCI "Counsel the Mother" module: Study results and comments.* Pelotas, Brazil: Report to WHO.

Drummond, J., Weir, A. E., & Kysela, G. M. (2002). Home visitation practice: Models, documentation, and evaluation. *Public Health Nursing, 19*(1), 21–29.

Eckenrode, J., Campa, M., Luckey, D. W., Henderson, C. R., Jr., Cole, R., Kitzman, H., et al. (2010). Long-term effects of prenatal and infancy nurse home visitation on the life course of youths: 19-Year follow-up of a randomized trial. *Archives of Pediatric and Adolescent Medicine, 164*(1), 9–15.

Engle, P. L. (2011a). *Care for Development in Three Central Asian Countries.* Geneva: UNICEF.

Engle, P. L. (2011b). *Promoting early childhood development through the health system: A review of the evidence.* Paper prepared for WHO, September, 2011.

Engle, P. L., Fernald, L. C. H., Alderman, H., Behrman, J., O'Gara, C., Yousafzai, A., et al. (2011). Strategies for reducing inequalities and improving developmental outcomes for young children in low and middle income countries. *The Lancet, 378*(9799), 1339–1353.

Ertem, I. O., Gulsum, A., Bingoler, B. E., Dogan, D. G., Bayhan, A., & Sarica, D. (2006). Promoting child development at sick child visits: A controlled trial to test the effect of the intervention on the home environment of young children. *Pediatrics, 118*(1), e124–e131.

Ertem, I. O., Atay, G., Dogan, D. G., Bayhan, A., Bingoler, B. E., Gok, C. G., et al. (2007). Mothers' knowledge of young child development in a developing country. *Child: Care, Health and Development, 33*(6), 728–737.

Fernald, L., Kariger, P., Engle, P., & Raikes, A. (2009). *Examining early child development in low-income countries: A toolkit for the assessment of children in the first five years of life.* Washington, DC: World Bank.

Field, T., & Diego, M. (2008). Cortisol: The culprit prenatal stress variable. *International Journal of Neuroscience, 118*(8), 1181–1205.

Field, T., Diego, M. A., Hernandez-Reif, M., Deeds, O., & Figuereido, B. (2006). Moderate versus light pressure massage therapy leads to greater weight gain in preterm infants. *Infant Behavior and Development, 29*(4), 574–578.

Finkenflugel, H., Wolffers, I., & Huijsman, R. (2005). The evidence base for community-based rehabilitation: A literature review. *International Journal of Rehabilitation Research, 28*(3), 187–201.

Global Health Council (2010). www.un.org/en/mdg/summit2010/www.globalhealth.org

Grantham-McGregor, S., Cheung, Y. B., Cueto, S., Glewwe, P., Richter, L., Strupp, B., et al. (2007). Developmental potential in the first 5 years for children in developing countries. *Lancet, 369*(9555), 60–70.

Hart, S., Field, T., & Nearing, G. (1998). Depressed mothers' neonates improve following the MABI and a Brazelton demonstration. *Journal of Pediatric Psychology, 23*(6), 351–356.

Heckman, J. J. (2006). Skill formation and the economics of investing in disadvantaged children. *Science, 312,* 1900–1902.

Hernandez-Reif, M., Diego, M., & Field, T. (2007). Preterm infants show reduced stress behaviors and activity after 5 days of massage therapy. *Infant Behavior & Development, 30*(4), 557–561.

Jin, X., Sun, Y., Jiang, F., Ma, J., Morgan, C., & Shen, X. (2007). Care for development intervention in rural China: A prospective follow-up study. *Journal of Developmental and Behavioral Pediatrics, 28,* 213–218.

Marmot, M., & Wilkinson, R. (2006). Social determinants of health. *International Journal of Epidemiology, 35*(4), 1111–1112. doi: 10.1093/ije/dyl121

McConachie, H., Huq, S., Munir, S., Ferdous, S., Zaman, S., & Khan, N. Z. (2000). A randomized controlled trial of alternative modes of service provision to young children with cerebral palsy in Bangladesh. *The Journal of Pediatrics, 137*(6), 769–776.

McCormick, M., Brooks-Gunn, J., Buka, S. L., Goldman, J., Yu, J., Salganik, M., et al. (2006). Early intervention in low birth weight premature infants: Results at 18 years of age for the Infant Health and Development Program. *Pediatrics, 117*(3), 771–780.

Meeks-Gardner, J., Walker, S. P., & Grantham-McGregor, S. M. (2003). A randomized controlled trial of the effects of a home visiting intervention on the cognition and behavior of term low birth weight Jamaican infants. *Journal of Pediatrics, 143,* 634–639.

Minkovitz, C. S., Strobino, D., Mistry, K. B., Scharfstein, D. O., Grason, H., Hou, W., et al. (2007). Healthy steps for young children: Sustained results at 5.5 years. *Pediatrics, 120*(3), 658–668.

Myers, R. G. (1992). *The twelve who survive.* London & New York: Routledge.

Nagin, D. S., & Tremblay, R. E. (2001). Parental and early childhood predictors of persistent physical aggression in boys from kindergarten to high school. *Archives of General Psychiatry, 58*(4), 389–394.

Nair, M., George, B., Padmamohan, J., Sunitha, R. M., Resmi, V. R., Prasanna,G. L., et al. (2009). Developmental delay and disability among under—5 children in a rural ICDS block. *Indian Pediatrics, 46*(Supplementary), S75–S78.

Norr, K. F., Crittenden, K., Lehrer, E., Reyes, O., Boyd, C.B., Nacion, K. W., et al. (2003). Maternal and infant outcomes at one year for a nurse-health advocate home visiting program serving African Americans and Mexican Americans. *Public Health Nursing,* *20* (3), 190–203.

Olds, D. L., Robinson, J., O'Brien, R., Luckey, D.W., Pettitt, L. M., Henderson, C. R., Jr., et al. (2002). Home visiting by paraprofessionals and by nurses: A randomized, controlled trial. *Pediatrics, 110*(3), 486–496.

Olds, D. L., Robinson, J., Pettitt, L., Luckey, D. W., Holmberg, J., Ng, R. K., et al. (2004). Effects of home visits by paraprofessionals and by nurses: Age 4 follow-up results of a randomized trial. *Pediatrics, 114,* 1560–1568.

Olds, D. L., Sadler, L., & Kitzman, H. (2007). Programs for parents of infants and toddlers: Recent evidence from randomized trials. *Journal of Child Psychology & Psychiatry, 8,* 355–391.

Palfrey, J. S., Hauser-Cram, P., Bronson, M. B., Warfield, M. E., Sirin, S., & Chan, E. (2005). Family-centered early health and development intervention, The Brookline Early Education Project: A 25-year follow-up study of a family-centered early health and development intervention. *Pediatrics, 116,* 144–152.

Potterton, J., Stewart, A., Cooper, P., & Becker, P. (2010). The effect of a basic home stimulation program on the development of young children infected with HIV. *Developmental Medicine and Child Neurology, 52*(6), 547–551.

Rahman, A., Bunn, J., Lovel, H., & Creed, F. (2007). Maternal depression increases infant risk of diarrhoeal illness: A cohort study. *Archives of Disease in Childhood, 92,* 24–28.

Rahman, A., Iqbal, Z., & Harrington, R. (2003). Life events, social support and depression in childbirth: Perspectives from a rural community in the developing world. *Psychological Medicine, 33,* 1161–1167.

Rosato, M., Laverack, G., Grabman, L. H., Tripathy, P., Nair, N., Mwansamba, C., Azad, K., et al. (2008). Alma-Ata: Rebirth and revision 5: Community participation: Lessons for maternal, newborn, and child health. *The Lancet, 372,* 962–971.

Schneider, A., & Ramires, V. R. (2007). *Primeira infância melhor: Uma inovação em politica publica Brazeila.* Rio Grande do Sul, BR: UNESCO, Secretaria de Saude do Estado do Rio Grande do Sul.

Sweet, M. A., & Appelbaum, M. I. (2004). Is home visiting an effective strategy? A meta-analytic review of home visiting programs for families with young children. *Child Development, 75*(5), 1435–1456.

Theriot, J. A., Franco, S. M., Sisson, B. A., Metcalfe, S. C., Kennedy, M. A., & Bada, H. (2003). The impact of early literacy guidance on language skills of 3 year olds. *Journal of Clinical Pediatrics, 42,* 165–172.

Toffol, G., Melloni, M., & Cagnin, R. (2011). Effectiveness study of the project "Nati per Leggere". *Quaderni ACP, 5,* 195–201.

Van Rie, A., Mupuala, A., & Dow, A. (2008). Impact of the HIV/AIDS epidemic on the neurodevelopment of preschool-aged children in Kinshasa, Democratic Republic of the Congo. *Pediatrics, 122,* 123–128.

Wachs, T. D., Black, M. M., & Engle, P. L. (2009). Maternal depression: A global threat to children's health, development and behavior and to human rights. *Child Development Perspectives, 3*(1), 51–60.

Walker, S. P., Wachs, T. D., Grantham-McGregor, S., Black, M. M., Nelson, C. A., Huffman, S. I., et al. (2011). Inequality in early childhood: Risk and protective factors for early child development. *Lancet , 378*(9799), 1325–1338.

Walker, S. (2011). Promoting equity through early child development interventions for children from birth through three years of age. In H. Alderman (Ed.), *No small matter* (pp. 115–154). Washington, DC: World Bank.

Weitzman, C. C., Roy, L, Walls, T., & Tomlin, R. (2004). More evidence for Reach Out and Read: A home based study. *Pediatrics, 113,* 1248–1253.

Widmeyer, S. M., & Field, T. (1981). Effects of Brazelton demonstrations for mothers on the development of preterm infants. *Pediatrics, 67*(5), 711–714.

World Bank. (2008, May). *Final evaluation report of MCH Component of Health Nine Project, supported by WB.* Prepared by the Ministry of Health, Maternal and Child Health Department, Government of the People's Republic of China.

World Health Organization (WHO). (2008). *Final report of the Commission on Social Determinants of Health, closing the gap in a generation: Health equity through action on social determinants of health.* Geneva: WHO.

World Health Organization (WHO) and UNICEF. (2012). *Care for child development.* Geneva: WHO and UNICEF New York. Retrieved from / http://www.who.int/maternal_child_adolescent/documents/care_child_development/en/index.html

Zercher, C., & Spiker. D. (2004). Home visiting programs and their impact on young children. In R. E. Tremblay, R. G. Barr, & R. DeV. Peters (Eds.), *Encyclopedia on early childhood development [online].* Montreal: Centre of Excellence for Early Childhood Development 2004:1–8. Retrieved July 15, 2011 from http://www.child-encyclopedia.com/documents/Zercher-SpikerANGxp.pdf

Zuckerman, B. (2009). Promoting early literacy in pediatric practice: Twenty years of reach out and read. *Pediatrics, 124*(6), 1660–1665.

10

Nutrition-Based Approaches to Early Childhood Development

Aisha K. Yousafzai, Mohammad Y. Yakoob,
and Zulfiqar A. Bhutta

Early childhood undernutrition is prevalent in low- and middle-income (LAMI) countries, with serious consequences for both early survival and development. Stunting, severe wasting, and intrauterine growth restriction-low birth weight (IUGR-LBW) account for 2.2 million deaths in children less than 5 years of age annually. A further 1.4 million child deaths are attributed to suboptimal breast-feeding practices. As a result of co-exposure to multiple nutritional risks, it is estimated that undernutrition accounts for 35% of all child deaths (Black, Allen, Bhutta, Caulfied, de Onis, Ezzati, & Rivera, 2008). For every child who survives, persistent malnutrition compromises her or his healthy development. Of the four key risk factors associated with underdevelopment in the under-5 population, three are directly related to nutrition: stunting, iron deficiency, and iodine deficiency (Walker, Wachs, Gardner, Lozoff, Wasserman, Pollitt et al., 2007). Early childhood undernutrition has long-term repercussions that result in lower human capital (Victora, Adair, Fall, Hallal, Martorell, Richter & Sachdev., 2008). The numbers are significant and the consequences for children, families, communities and, nations devastating. Nutrition interventions must be recognized as an urgent priority in LAMI countries because they will benefit both the present and future generations. Global evidence firmly positions the nutrition approach as one that bridges survival and child development agendas.

The reasons for undernutrition are complex. Adequate dietary intake for an infant and young child is influenced by many factors, ranging from the immediate caregiving environment to the broader social, economic, and political context (Figure 10.1). Therefore, multisectoral involvement is necessary when planning local, regional, and global nutrition strategies. Current evidence also underscores the importance of not only examining food availability for the child at household level, but also the process by which the child is fed and the caregiving capacity of the mother and family (Black & Aboud, 2011; Pelto, Dickin, & Engle, 1999; Richter, 2004). For example, responsive feeding practices, a healthy household environment, and health status mediate a child's nutritional well-being. Synergies between different interventions suggest that an approach in which nutrition is integrated with a broader package of family-based services will be effective for improving survival, growth, and child development (Bryce, Coitinho, Darnton-Hill, Pelletier, & Pinstrup-Anderson, 2008; Engle, Black, Behrman, Cabra de Mello, Gertler, Kapiri et al., 2007).

Timing of nutrition intervention is critical. The period from preconception to the first 2 years of life is an important window of opportunity for preventing irreversible effects of malnutrition on growth and development (Barker, Bergmann, & Ogra, 2008). Research using animal models shows that early brain development can be affected by undernutrition. Poor maternal nutrition status can affect the delivery of nutrients to the fetus, leading to intrauterine growth retardation (IUGR), low birth weight (LBW), and preterm birth, all of which result in increased risks for impairments even in the absence of obvious neurological problems. In developing countries, not only is this a period of rapid brain development, but also a period of peak incidence for stunting, micronutrient deficiencies, and infectious illnesses that could have adverse effects on survival and development (Dewey & Adu-Afarwuh, 2008, Grantham-McGregor, Cheung, Cueto, Glewwe, Richter, & Strupp, 2007; Innis, 2003; Shonkoff & Phillps, 2000; Victora, Adair, Fall, Hallal, Martorell, Richter, & Sachdev., 2008).

In this chapter, we will summarize the major nutritional risks for healthy development during pregnancy, infancy, and early childhood. The interventions that are available to mitigate these risks will be described, drawing attention to partnerships and approaches that work together to improve survival, growth, and development outcome.

Summary of Evidence for Nutrition Approach to Guide Programs and Policies in Early Childhood Development

MAJOR NUTRITION RISKS FOR EARLY CHILDHOOD DEVELOPMENT

Nutrition Risks During Pregnancy

Maternal undernutrition (defined as a body mass index of less than 18.5 kg/m^2) ranges from 10% to 19% in most parts of the world; however, the problem is far more serious in Sub-Saharan Africa and parts of Asia. In India, Bangladesh, and Eritrea, the prevalence is as high as 40% (Black, Allen, Bhutta, Caulfied, de Onis, Ezzati, & Rivera., 2008). Maternal undernutrition can result in IUGR, defined as slow fetal growth based on two ultrasounds, or a small for gestational age (SGA) baby; these terms are frequently used interchangeably to reflect intrauterine growth and status at birth. An improvement in birth weight and a reduction in percentage of SGA infants as a result of balanced energy and protein supplementation during pregnancy have been observed in several studies (Bhutta, Ahmed, Black, Coussens, Dewey, Giugliani et al., 2008).

There is also evidence to suggest effects of maternal undernutrition on motor, cognitive, and behavioral development of infants (Black, Allen, Bhutta, Caulfied, de Onis, Ezzati, & Rivera, 2008; Hamadani, Grantham-McGregor, Tofail, Nermell, Fängström, Huda et al., 2010). A few studies have also assessed development outcomes in infants of mothers who received food supplementation during pregnancy. In Bangladesh, benefits were seen in motor, cognitive, and behavioral development at 7 months of age in infants whose mothers received food and micronutrient supplementation in early pregnancy, but the effects of intervention were not observed at 18 months (Hamadani, Grantham-McGregor, Tofail, Nermell, Fängström, Huda et al., 2010; Tofail, Persson, El Arifeen, Hamadani, Mehrin, Ridout et al., 2008). An earlier study of Colombian infants of mothers who received food supplementation during the last trimester of pregnancy showed no benefits in child development outcomes (Waber, Vuori-Christiansen, Ortiz, Clement, Christiansen, Mora et al., 1981). Therefore, we can conclude that supplementation to address undernutrition during pregnancy will reduce the risk for SGA infants. However, more research is needed to understand the most effective timing for maternal supplementation and the extent of benefits for infant development over time.

Micronutrient deficiency during pregnancy is also prevalent in LAMI countries. Iron deficiency anemia (IDA) is one of the most prevalent yet neglected nutritional deficiencies in the world. According to the World Health Organization (WHO), 42% of pregnant women are anemic, and this is mainly due to iron deficiency (Black, Allen, Bhutta, Caulfied, de Onis, Ezzati, & Rivera, 2008). Iron deficiency is primarily caused by low consumption of iron-rich foods. In pregnant women, iron status is further compromised due to the high demand for iron during pregnancy, even in women with adequate iron status at the start of pregnancy. Iron supplementation can improve iron status during pregnancy and postpartum (Black, Allen, Bhutta, Caulfied, de Onis, Ezzati, & Rivera, 2008). Risks associated with IDA include preterm deliveries, LBW, and poor neonatal health (Black, Allen, Bhutta, Caulfied, de Onis, Ezzati, & Rivera, 2008). More recent evidence indicates that maternal IDA is associated with poorer mother–child interaction and infant cognitive development (Frith, Naved, Ekstrom, Rasmussen, & Frongillo, 2009; Murray-Kolb & Beard, 2009). Although the risks for maternal mortality and morbidity need to be understood further, the weight of evidence suggests that iron supplementation during pregnancy is valuable.

Folate deficiency during pregnancy is a risk factor for a number of adverse outcomes, including neural tube defects. Folate supplementation during pregnancy and longer term development outcomes of infants has been extensively studied. A large retrospective study based on the 1981 National Maternal Infant Health Survey and the 1991 follow- up in the United States found that early folate use in pregnancy was associated with significant reduction of risk for child gross motor functioning (Wehby & Murray, 2008). In another study from a high-income setting, a significantly higher risk of behavioral problems in infants at 18 months of age was identified when mothers had not used folate in the first trimester of pregnancy (Roza, van Batenburg-Eddes, Steegers, Jaddoe, Mackenbach, Hofman et al.,2010). Therefore, folate supplementation during early pregnancy is beneficial for early child development outcomes.

Other micronutrient deficiencies, such as iodine, vitamin A, and zinc, are also associated with maternal and early child survival and development risks. Severe iodine deficiency is associated with risks of impaired infant cognitive development, as well as IUGR and miscarriage (Zimmermann, 2009). In parts of the world where iodine deficiency remains a major risk, prevention efforts must be intensified. The benefits of supplementation with zinc and vitamin A during pregnancy for survival, growth, and development needs further investigation (Bhutta, Ahmed, Black, Cousens, Dewey, Giugliani et al., 2008; Black, Allen, Bhutta, Caulfied, de Onis, Ezzati, & Rivera, 2008).

For many women in developing countries, co-exposure of multiple micronutrient deficiencies is likely. Therefore, there has been growing interest in multiple micronutrient supplementation (MMS). There is emerging evidence to show that MMS (defined as three or more micronutrients) during pregnancy is associated with a 39% reduction in maternal anemia compared with supplementation using two or fewer micronutrients (Bhutta et al., 2008). Benefits to birth weight (Bhutta, Ahmed, Black, Cousens, Dewey, Giugliani et al., 2008), child growth status (Huy, Le Hop, Shrimpton, & Hoa, 2009; Vaidya, Saville, Shrestha, Costello, Manandhar, & Osrin, 2008), infant motor development (McGrath, Bellinger, Robins, Msamanga, Tronik, & Fawzi., 2006; Tofail, Persson, El Arifeen, Hamadani, Mehrin, Ridout et al., 2008), and cognitive development (Li, Yan, Zeng, Cheng, Liang, Dang et al., 2009) have been found following MMS during pregnancy in studies from LAMI countries. Therefore, in contexts in which pregnant women are likely to be co-exposed to multiple micronutrient deficiencies, there are benefits to receiving MMS during pregnancy, with positive outcomes for mother and child.

Intrauterine Growth Restriction and Low Birth Weight

Low birth weight (of less than 2500 g) remains a significant public health problem in many parts of the world and is associated with a range of both short- and long-term adverse consequences. Although about one-half of all LBW infants in industrialized countries are born preterm (less than 37 weeks of gestation), most LBW infants in developing countries are born at term and are affected by IUGR that may begin early in pregnancy, leading to fetal nutrition deprivation during a sensitive period of early brain development Villar & Belizan (1982). The latest regional estimates of LBW range from 25% in south Asia to 10% and 12% in Sub-Saharan Africa and Latin America, respectively (UNICEF, 2010). Many LBW infants are not reported in LAMI countries because deliveries often occur in homes or small health clinics, which may result in an underestimation of LBW prevalence (UNICEF, 2010).

Walker and colleagues identified IUGR-LBW as one of the nine key developmental risk factors with sufficient evidence to recommend intervention (Walker, Wachs, Gardner, Lozoff, Wasserman, Pollitt et al., 2007). Evidence from a number of countries, including Guatemala, Jamaica, and Brazil, show an association of LBW with developmental deficits in the first 3 years of life (Walker, Wachs, Gardner, Lozoff, Wasserman, Pollitt et al., 2007). More recent studies from LAMI countries have investigated development outcomes in children aged 5 years and older with mixed results. No significant association with LBW and later cognitive and behavioral development in Jamaica, South Africa, and Brazil was seen (Emond, Lira, Lima, Grantham-McGregor, & Ashworth, 2006; Sabet, Richter, Ramchandani, Stein, Quigley, & Norrisl, 2009; Walker, Chang, Younger, & Grantham-McGregor, 2010). However, there is some evidence on LBW and subsequent academic achievement (Martorell, Horta, Adair, et al., 2010; Wang, Sung, Lu, Kuo, & Li, 2008). More studies are needed to investigate longer term consequences on development and academic achievement in LBW cohorts, taking in to account the many confounders.

Continued investment in strategies to improve maternal nutritional status is necessary to reduce the prevalence of LBW. Successful strategies must consider the many underlying causes of poor maternal nutrition status, including social determinants of health, such as the status of women, especially in south Asia where poor maternal nutritional status has remained worryingly high for several generations. Although LBW is associated with impaired development, more studies from LAMI countries are needed to understand the nature and extent of developmental deficit and academic achievement at older ages in children born LBW. These data are needed to develop appropriate ameliorative strategies, particularly as survival rates of infants with LBW and very LBW begin to improve in LAMI countries (Khan, Muslima, Parveen, Bhattacharyam Begum, Chowdhury et al., 2006).

Poor Breast-Feeding Practices

Inappropriate infant and young child feeding practices are a major cause of early childhood malnutrition. It is recommended that infants be exclusively breast-fed for the first 6 months of life, with continued supplemental breast-feeding until 24 months of life. In many parts of the world, breast-feeding prevalence is high, but exclusive breast-feeding (EBF) is not. For example, in Bangladesh, the majority of mothers will breast-feed their children over the first 2 years of life, but the median duration for EBF is 1.8 months, and national surveys indicate a rapid decline of EBF from the first month of life (64%) to the first 4–5 months of life (30%) (Faruque, Shamsir, Tahmeed, Islam, Hossain, Roy et al., 2008). This trend is observed across LAMI countries (Black, Allen, Bhutta, Caulfied, de Onis, Ezzati, & Rivera, 2008).

Several studies have reported benefits in infant and young child cognitive development as a result of breast-feeding. Motor development benefits have been observed in infants who were EBF for a longer duration, whereas early introduction of supplementary bottle feeding was shown to be associated with poor motor and cognitive functioning (Walker, Wachs, Gardner, Lozoff, Wasserman, Pollitt et al., 2007). More recent data have shown that appropriate EBF practices can also benefit older children. Follow-up of children aged 6.5 years who had been exposed to the Baby Friendly Hospital Initiative (BFHI), compared with unexposed children, had significantly higher IQ scores and significantly higher teacher-rated reading and writing scores (Kramer, Aboud, Mironova, Vanilovich, Platt, Matush et al., 2008a; Kramer, Fombonne, Igumnov, Vanilovich, Matush, Mironova et al., 2008b). Therefore, improving breast-feeding practices is an essential nutrition strategy for child development.

Poor Responsive Feeding Practices

The importance of caregiving practices as an underlying cause of undernutrition and poor growth has been recognized for a long time (Figure 10.1).

Responsive care is the capacity of the caregiver to recognize the child's signals and respond promptly, contingent on the signals being presented in a manner that is developmentally appropriate (Eshel, Daelmans, Cabral de Mello, & Martines, 2006; Richter, 2004). This caregiving skill promotes quality interactions between the parent and child, thereby promoting healthy development. When applied to feeding, responsive care can positively influence early feeding experiences that shape dietary behaviors. Figure 10.2 illustrates the steps required to promote responsive feeding patterns. Responsive feeding may be constrained due to a number of factors, such as cultural feeding styles that discourage responsive feeding, time constraints of the mother, and maternal stress. However, if successfully applied, it can improve quality of feeding and a successful transition to independent feeding.

Studies from a number of countries, including India, have used responsive feeding counseling to deliver nutrition education to families (Bhandari, Bahl, Nayer, Khokhar, Rohde, Bhan et al., 2001; Bhandari, Mazumder, Bahl, Martines, Black, Bhan, 2004). More recent data from Bangladesh showed that a responsive feeding strategy could significantly improve maternal responsive behaviors and nutrition knowledge, as well as independent feeding skills in infants aged 8–20 months, compared with a nonintervened group (Aboud, Shafique, & Akhter, 2009). A recent review of responsive feeding studies concluded that there was promising evidence showing that caregiver verbal communication during feeding increases the child's acceptance of food. However, the authors also point out that more research is needed to understand the effects of responsive feeding on undernutrition, thereby highlighting the limited attention given to the parent–child relationship and its influence on feeding in nutrition research (Bentley, Wasser, & Creed-Kanashirol, 2011).

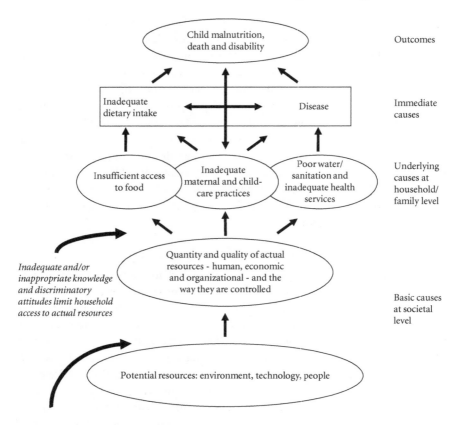

FIGURE *10.1 United Nations Children's Fund (UNICEF) framework for child undernutrition*
Source: Framework from UNICEF. (1998). State of the World's Children Report.

Stunting and Inadequate Stimulation

The prevalence of under-5 stunting (a height-for-age Z score of less than -2) is 32% in developing countries, with the majority of these children residing in south-central Asia (Black, Allen, Bhutta, Caulfied, de Onis, Ezzati, & Rivera, 2008). Stunting in early childhood is caused by poor nutrition and infection. Growth faltering can begin in utero and usually is pronounced by 24 months. Some growth catch-up may occur, but most children who are stunted will remain stunted through to adulthood (Grantham-McGregor, Cheung, Cueto, Glewwe, Richter, & Strupp, 2007).

There is well-established evidence to show the close association of stunting and developmental deficits. Stunted children are more likely to have poorer cognitive functioning, lower academic achievement, lower rates of school enrolment,

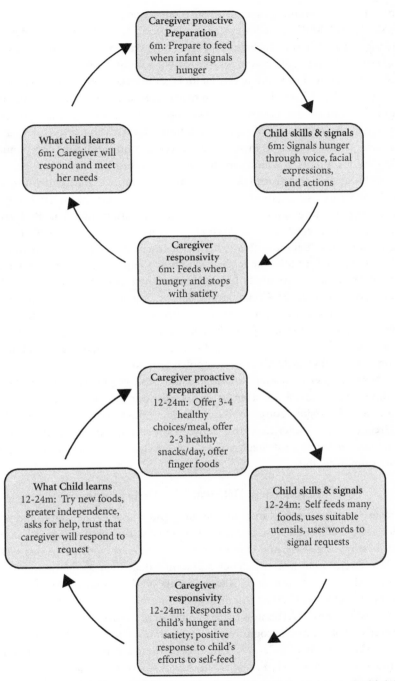

FIGURE 10.2 *Responsive feeding processes: Examples for a 6- and 12- to 24-month-old child*

Adapted from Black, M. M., & Aboud, F. E. (2011). Responsive feeding is embedded in a theoretical framework of responsive parenting. The Journal of Nutrition, 141, 490–494.

later enrolment in school, more drop out from school, poorer executive functioning skills, and subsequent lower economic productivity (Grantham-McGregor,
Cheung, Cueto, Glewwe, Richter, & Strupp, 2007; Walker, Wachs, Gardner, Lozoff,
Wasserman, Pollitt et al., 2007). A child growing up in a disadvantaged setting is
likely to be exposed to multiple risk factors that impact growth and development;
for example, a child at risk for stunting may also be exposed to inadequate stimulation. Early supplementation for at-risk populations is an important prevention
strategy, but a combination of supplementation and early stimulation interventions
can yield greater reduction in stunting, as well as mitigate future developmental
risks even for infants in whom growth faltering has begun.

Landmark research from Jamaica on growth-retarded children who received
supplementation, stimulation, or both showed each intervention had independent benefits to development at age 2. Supplementation also benefited growth
(Grantham-McGregor, Powell, Walker, & Himes, 1991). Studies from other
LAMI countries, including Bangladesh and Brazil, have also demonstrated the
independent and additive benefits of combined supplementation and stimulation interventions, particularly for undernourished children (Hamadani, Huda,
Khatun, & Grantham-McGregor, 2006; Santos, 2008a; Thuc-Duc, 2009; Walker,
2011). The Jamaica study provides strong evidence of the sustained benefits of
intervention over time: at 7 years, benefits were observed on cognitive development from each intervention; at 11 and 17 years, stimulation had an effect on cognition and reading ability, whereas supplementation no longer had any effects;
at 22 years, higher education attainment and positive behaviors were observed
in adults who received the stimulation intervention (Walker, Chang, Powell, &
Grantham-McGregor, 2005; Walker, Chang, Vera-Hernández, & Grantham-
McGregor, 2011). The critical link between nutrition and stimulation must be
recognized in nutrition strategies, not only to mitigate risks but also to promote
future human capital.

Micronutrient Deficiencies in Early Childhood

Exposure to deficiencies of iron, iodine, zinc, and vitamin A in infants and young
children have all been investigated, and supplementation may reduce risk of mortality, burden of disease, and deficits in growth and development. In this section,
we draw attention to iron deficiency and iodine deficiency as the two significant
micronutrient risk factors for poor early childhood development (ECD).

Globally, anemia affects 47% of preschool children and 25% of school-aged children, mostly due to IDA (Benton, 2010). A number of studies on iron deficiency have
reported deficits in motor, cognitive, socioemotional, and neurophysiologic development (Lozoff, 2007; McCann & Ames, 2007; Monga, Walia, Gandhi, Chandra, &
Sharma, 2010; Santos et al., 2008b; Shafir, Angulo-Barroso, Su, Jacobson, & Lozoff,
2009; Thomas, Grant, & Aubuchon-Endsley, 2009). Recent data from Costa Rica
reported long-term adverse consequences; adults who experienced chronic iron
deficiency in infancy had poorer recognition memory (Lukowski, Koss, Burdem,

Jonides, Nelson, Kaciroti et al., 2010). Supplementation trials suggest benefits to motor and socioemotional development during infancy and cognitive benefits for preschool-aged children (Walker, Wachs, Gardner, Lozoff, Wasserman, Pollitt et al., 2007). Early iron supplementation may improve micronutrient status for at-risk populations, and is recommended in non–malaria-endemic populations (Bhutta, Ahmed, Black, Cousens, Dewey, Giugliani et al., 2008; Walker, Wachs, Gardner, Lozoff, Wasserman, Pollitt et al., 2007).

Iodine deficiency is the single most important cause of preventable brain damage and mental retardation (Benton, 2010). Recent evidence from New Zealand and Albania on iodine supplementation of secondary school children with mild deficiency shows that supplementation significantly improves overall cognitive performance (Gordon, Rose, Skeaff, Gray, Morgan, & Ruffmann, 2009; Zimmermann, Connolly, Bozo, Bridson, Rohner, & Grimci, 2006). These data may be promising for young school-aged children with risk of mild iodine deficiencies.

By reducing the risks of undernutrition, it is likely that child survival and development outcomes will also be improved. Child nutrition approaches interlinked with other interventions in health and development will yield not only additive, but also synergistic benefits for healthy growth and development. The challenge is to identify synergies between different approaches and translate this from policy to point of intervention delivery.

NUTRITION APPROACHES THAT WORK TO MITIGATE RISKS AND IMPROVE EARLY SURVIVAL, GROWTH, AND DEVELOPMENT

Strategies to Prevent Undernutrition in Pregnancy: A Life-Cycle Approach

The nutritional health of the mother will influence her own survival, health, and productivity, as well as the survival, growth, and development of her child. There is evidence to recommend that balanced energy and protein supplementation during pregnancy can reduce the risk of a SGA baby by 32%. There is also favorable evidence to support MMS, iron, and folate supplementation of pregnant women in order to improve maternal health status and reduce risks of impaired infant development (Bhutta, Ahmed, Black, Cousens, Dewey, Giugliani et al., 2008).

In applying a life-cycle perspective to understanding nutrition approaches, an important strategy is to promote healthy nutritional status of women prior to pregnancy (Figure 10.3). For example, the Linkages Project recommends "birth spacing" as one of the five key strategies for improving maternal nutrition. Extended birth spacing provides women with the time to replenish their energy and micronutrient stores; therefore, counseling on safer sex, contraceptive use, and the promotion of breast-feeding practices (because of its fertility-inhibiting effects) should all be considered as a means to address maternal undernutrition (Linkages Project, 2001).

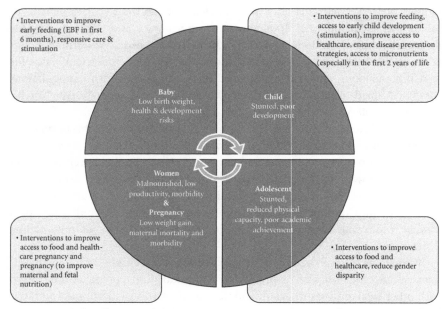

FIGURE 10.3 *Life cycle approach in nutrition: important opportunities for interventions that impact child development.*

Strategies to improve women's nutritional status must take into account the social determinants of health for women, as advocated in the WHO report on "Social Determinants of Health": the status of women in society, her access to and control over resources, her educational status, and her autonomy over her own health and nutritional well-being will vary from context to context. The improvement of women's nutritional status at a national level is closely linked with strategies to improve the empowerment of women in society. In some countries, gender disparities in nutritional status can start early but are often pronounced by adolescence (Oumachigui, 2002). The World Food Programme's (WFP) promotion of school feeding programs has had successful experiences worldwide in reaching out to vulnerable populations, and in Pakistan, the program was also seen as a possible pathway to address gender disparities (WFP, 2009). Such strategies need further evaluation to understand their impact not only on school enrollment, but also on the nutritional status of adolescent girls.

The life-cycle approach to tackling maternal undernutrition is a longer term strategy with a strong theoretical basis for addressing the healthy development of future generations and one that should consider local community partnerships and contexts for successful planning and implementation.

Promoting Breast-Feeding

Exclusive breast-feeding has been described as the safest and one of the most powerful and cost-effective interventions for reducing infant mortality and morbidity

(León-Cava, Lutter, Ross, & Martin, 2008). In their analysis of EBF promotional strategies, the Maternal and Child Undernutrition Study Group reported that universal promotion of EBF would increase the likelihood of EBF in the first month of life by 4, and in the first 6 months of life by 3.5. It is important to note that current data also support EBF for HIV-exposed infants, although more research is being undertaken on effects of early cessation of breast-feeding (Bhutta, Ahmed, Black, Cousens, Dewey, Giugliani et al., 2008).

Over the last 30 years, a number of global initiatives have been implemented to improve the rates of EBF; for example, the International Code of WHO for Marketing of Breast Milk Substitutes and the BFHI. Although these strategies have raised awareness on the importance of EBF, the impact at the community level—where most deliveries take place—can still be improved (Talukder, 2000).Further, such initiatives may be useful in encouraging the initiation of breast-feeding, but mothers may require support in maintaining EBF practices, as data tend to show the numbers reducing after the initial 1–2 months (Black, Allen, Bhutta, Caulfied, de Onis, Ezzati, & Rivera., 2008).

Although individual counseling for EBF has proven to be effective, there has been growing attention toward peer counseling strategies that, if successfully implemented, are potentially more cost effective. Peer counseling also provides the opportunity to engage other family members, such as mothers-in-law or fathers, which can prove beneficial in contexts in which the extended family plays an influential role in decisions about the child's health care (Faruque, Shamsir, Tahmeed, Islam, Hossain, Roy et al., 2008). More recently, in Pakistan, a research group has applied a counseling approach using the principles of cognitive-behavioral therapy (CBT) using community health workers, with promising results. This approach encourages a dialogue between the health worker and mother to examine the barriers she faces for EBF and how these can be overcome (Atif Rahman, personal communication). Successful community-based strategies need to understand local cultural and social norms and bring together all the family members who can support EBF practices.

Promoting Integrated Child Nutrition and Stimulation Approaches

Programs that integrate responsive care, responsive feeding, and stimulation with a nutrition strategy can be effective in improving overall child well-being (Bentley, Vazir, Engle, Balakrishna, Johnson, Creed-Kanashiro et al., 2010). An advantage, from a programmatic perspective, is that parents readily engage with approaches that address issues of concerns (e.g., "my child does not eat well") and also empower the caregiver by placing value on his or her role in supporting the child to eat well and develop healthily (Engle & Pelto, 2011).

Although such an approach would promote the growth and development of all children, benefits have also been observed in children with severe malnutrition. In Bangladesh, a time-lagged control study showed that children with severe malnutrition admitted to a nutrition rehabilitation unit who additionally received a simulation intervention showed significant improvement in development and weight gain compared with those who only received the nutrition intervention (Nahar, Hamadani, Ahmed, Tofail, Rahman, Huda, & Grantham-McGregor, 2009). Favorable results have also been observed for children who received combined interventions in an emergency context in northern Uganda (Jones, Morris, Berrino, Crow, Jordans, & Okema., 2011). Countries are gradually adopting integrated approaches, and, to meet this demand, the WHO/UNICEF "Care for Child Development" intervention package was developed that contains both recommendations for promoting stimulation and a "Care for Feeding" intervention package, which contains recommendations on responsive feeding. Both modules target the 0–3 years age group and are designed to be integrated within existing nutrition and health services. Some countries have adopted these guidelines as part of the integrated management of childhood illness. However, evaluations are limited, and more information is needed to help program planners implement such strategies effectively. Box 10.1 lists the lessons learned about what works for each of these interventions, and this information should be considered by program planners.

Another entry point for ECD promotion, in addition to nutrition education, is the inclusion of development milestones and advice in growth monitoring cards/ child health cards. India is one example of a country that has included development milestones and advice in child heath cards. Such strategies need careful implementation to ensure intervention is given for children who are identified as failing to thrive, and further evaluation is required to understand the impact of the combined strategy (Engle, Black, Behrman, Cabral de Mello, Gertler, Kapiriri et al., 2007).

Strategies to Prevent Micronutrient Deficiencies

Strategies to improve micronutrient intake of young children can occur at different levels. Food fortification strategies (e.g., iodization of salt and iron fortification of staple foods) can occur at the national level. Dietary diversity can be promoted at the community level using strategies such as community gardens or the fortification of foods at home, and micronutrient supplementation can be done through health services. These strategies highlight the importance of partnerships in nutrition with the private sector, the local community, and with health services as vehicles for reducing micronutrient deficiencies.

Food fortification strategies are associated with an improvement in the micronutrient status of infants and young children, as well as with a reduction in the incidence of some common illnesses (Bhutta, Ahmed, Black, Cousens, Dewey, Giugliani et al., 2008). Successful implementation requires political will for quality assurance and to ensure that the product reaches the at-risk population. Food fortification is also an example of emerging successful partnerships with the private sector; for example, national fortification alliances and international business alliances (SCN, 2009).

The cyclical relationship between nutrition and infection status is well recognized; therefore, strategies to reduce micronutrient deficiencies must be an integral component of health services (Khan & Bhutta, 2010; Yakoob, Pervez, & Bhutta,

BOX 10.1. Guidance for Implementing Integrated Early Childhood Development and Nutrition Approaches

RESPONSIVE PARENTING AND STIMULATION

- Structure curriculum to include opportunities for mothers to try activities with their children and experience successful interactions with their children.
- Content should reflect local resources and place value on nonharmful traditional practices.
- Structure training and supportive supervision to include opportunities for observation followed by feedback and guidance.
- Provide sufficient intensity (two visits per month are ideal) with adequate time during each visit to observe mother and child, counsel, and provide opportunities for mother to try an activity with her child and for her to receive feedback.

RESPONSIVE FEEDING

- Materials developed should reflect local conditions and messages that appeal to families.
- Key messages (examples from WHO/UNICEF "Care for Feeding"; responsive messages are in italics):
  - 0–6 months: Breast-feed day and night, *as often as baby wants.*
  - 6–9 months: Breast-feed as often as child wants; gradually introduce foods; provide 2–3 meals per day, offer 1–2 snacks per day *when child signals she is hungry.*
  - 9–12 months: Breast-feed as often as child wants, provide 3–4 meals per day, offer 1–2 snacks per day, *and let child choose to eat or not. Provide finger foods and encourage child to pick up food, with assistance if needed.*
  - 12–24 months: Breast-feed as often as child wants, provide 3–4 meals per day, offer 1–2 snacks per day; *feed slowly and encourage child to eat, but do not force child to eat.*
  - 24 months and older: Provide 3–4 meals per day, offer 1–2 snacks per day, *encourage child to eat, keep eye contact, and talk to child during meal times.*

SUPPLEMENTATION

- Ensure appropriate quality and quantity.
- Ensure appropriate delivery strategy and targeting.

SUCCESSFUL INTEGRATION

- Encourage ownership of programs through participatory planning and action with community and program staff.
- Evaluate existing systems to identify appropriate strategy to accommodate new interventions effectively.
- Evaluate combined intervention strategies and share lessons learned to improve quality and effectiveness of delivery for moving to scale.

2010). Disease prevention strategies, including those promoting a safe and clean environment, are necessary to prevent nutrient depletion through repeated infections. Strategies that we know work to improve nutrient and health status include universal vitamin A supplementation, MMS for at-risk populations, iodized salt for at-risk populations, iron/folate supplementation to treat anemia, therapeutic doses of zinc to treat diarrheal disease, and regular deworming to reduce the depletion of micronutrients (SCN, 2009).

Strategies for Vulnerable Children: Social Safety Nets

In food insecure populations, additional safety nets must be considered to reduce the vulnerability of infants and young children to malnutrition. Conditional cash transfers (CCTs) are an example of an intervention that can potentially support the nutritional well-being of infants and young children. The Families in Action program in Colombia showed a positive impact on nutritional status for children under 2 years and an increase of 0.58 kg in newborn weight in urban areas of treatment. However, no impact was seen on nutritional status of children over 24 months of age or on newborn weight in rural areas (Attanasio, Gómez, Heredi, &Vera-Hernandez, 2005). The Nicaraguan program reduced the magnitude of stunting and underweight in children aged 0–5 years, with no impact on wasting (Maluccio & Flores, 2004). Mexico's CCT program, Oportunidades, was started to improve the lives of poor families through interventions in health, nutrition, and education. A longitudinal follow-up of the Mexican program compared children whose families had participated in the program early with those who entered the program later. Data showed that an additional 18 months exposure to the program before age 3 for children whose mothers had no education resulted in a significant improvement in child growth by 1.5 cm, as well as in reduced behavioral problems (Fernald, Gertler, & Neufeld, 2009). Overall, CCTs are an important social safety net, and more programs are being evaluated worldwide.

In summary, we have described a number of nutrition approaches that work to improve survival rates, growth, and development. In all of these approaches, strategic partnerships are required for their successful implementation and going to scale. These partnerships must occur at both community and policy level; they are multisectoral, with partnerships in health, education, and water and sanitation; and they embrace civil society and private cooperation.

NEXT STEPS FOR NUTRITION-BASED APPROACHES TO EARLY CHILDHOOD DEVELOPMENT

Over the last decade, evidence for the critical link between nutrition and early child development has been strengthened, but a number of questions remain to be addressed, in order to advance our early childhood programs and policies. Table 10.1 shows the key risks, evidence for what we know works in nutrition, strategic partnerships, and areas where further research is needed.

TABLE 10.1 Summary of nutrition risks, interventions, strategic partnerships, and research questions to improve survival and development

Nutrition Risk	Nutrition Interventions to Reduce Risks for Poor Survival and Development	Potential Benefits	Strategic Partnerships to Enhance Survival and Development	Further Research
Maternal Undernutrition	Balanced energy protein supplements and nutrition counseling.	Improved weight gain in pregnancy. Reduced risk of intrauterine growth restriction.	*Birth spacing and family planning* strategies to reduce risk of nutrition depletion from pregnancies at close intervals.	What are the long-term outcomes on growth and development following maternal supplementation?
	Iron folate supplements in pregnancy.	Reduction in maternal anemia and risk of mortality related to postpartum hemorrhage.	*Life-cycle approach* with partnerships to reduce gender disparities and improve women's access to and control over health, nutrition, and education (including during adolescence) for healthier women across the life cycle. Possible civil society partnerships.	What is the most effective timing for balanced energy protein supplementation during pregnancy that will benefit mother and infant outcomes?
		Early folate supplementation leads to significantly reduced risks of poor gross motor function.		What are the mid- and long-term development and academic deficits for LBW infants, and what strategies can effectively support these children in the school years?
		Evidence for benefits to early infant development and emerging evidence for benefits to mother–child interaction.		
	Multiple micronutrient supplementation.	Reduced risk of intrauterine growth restriction.	*Early entry point for early child development strategies; parenting programs* to provide key information on attachment and bonding, exclusive breast-feeding, and newborn care.	
		Benefits to early infant growth, motor, and cognitive development.		
Inadequate Infant and Young Child Feeding Practices	Early initiation of breast-feeding and promotion of exclusive breast-feeding for 6 months through counseling approaches and responsive feeding advice.	Significantly improved infant and child growth and reduced morbidity.	*Entry point for early child development strategies: stimulation, responsive feeding and parenting programs* with additive and independent benefits to improve mother–child interaction, growth, development gains (short and long term), improved caregiving capacity.	More research at scale on combined nutrition and early child development interventions.
	Integrated nutrition and stimulation/parenting programs.	Improved maternal and infant bonding and evidence of improved developmental quotients and academic achievement.		

(continued)

TABLE 10.1 (Continued)

Nutrition Risk	Nutrition Interventions to Reduce Risks for Poor Survival and Development	Potential Benefits	Strategic Partnerships to Enhance Survival and Development	Further Research
	Appropriate complimentary feeding (6–24 months) with responsive feeding advice. Integrated nutrition and stimulation/parenting programs, especially from birth–3 years.	Reduced stunting and improved growth, lower risks of morbidity and mortality, improved development and academic achievement, as well as long term adult productivity.	*Growth and development monitoring and promotion* for counseling parents on early development and early intervention. *Strategies to improve maternal mental health* to reduce maternal morbidity, enhance caregiving capacity, improve mother–child interaction. *Social safety nets* to support vulnerable children, such as conditional cash transfers, food supplementation.	Evaluation of impact with growth and development milestones. Research on strategies to improve maternal mental health and outcomes for child growth and development. Evaluations of responsive parenting programs at scale for impact on growth and development. Research on the effect of responsive feeding in undernutrition through randomized controlled trials. Evaluation of most useful measures of responsive feeding.
Micronutrient Deficiencies Infants and Young Children	Vitamin A supplementation in newborns and children. Iron and folate supplementation. Iodine supplementation (iodized salt). Improved diarrhea management with zinc/ORS.	Improve survival. Improve micronutrient status and development outcomes. Improve survival and development. Improve survival and health.	*Food fortification strategies at community and national level* (e.g., iodization of salt): possible private sector collaboration. *Partnerships with water and sanitation strategies* to prevent disease and subsequent nutrition depletion. *Partnerships with health programs* to prevent disease and reduce micronutrient depletion such as deworming campaigns (also associated with improved classroom performance).	Evaluations of micronutrient supplementation and stimulation interventions (especially multiple micronutrient supplementation).

| Prevention and Treatment of Severe-Acute Malnutrition in Young Children | Therapeutic feeding (community therapeutic feeding, ready to use foods) and stimulation. | *Entry point for early child development strategies: stimulation, responsive feeding and parenting programs* with additive and independent benefits to improve mother–child interaction, growth, development gains (short and long term), improved caregiving capacity.

Safety nets for at-risk populations such as preschool or school feeding programs in partnership with education programs. | Evaluations of combined supplementation and stimulation programs for vulnerable children (e.g., SAM, in emergency settings). |

LBW, low birth weight; ORS, oral rehydration solution; SAM, severe acute malnutrition.

There are three important general comments to underscore here for researchers, program planners, and policymakers:

1. Although poor nutrition is a recognized risk factor for poor development, many nutrition studies miss the opportunity to collect data on development outcomes, in addition to collecting data on nutrition status and growth. Such data will help further elucidate the interactions that mediate health, growth, and development.
2. Traditional nutrition programs may benefit from the application of a child development perspective. Responsive parenting and feeding theories encourage a deeper examination of the parent–child relationship that influences feeding behaviors. Using behavioral change theories that allow health and nutrition workers to effectively deliver nutrition advice that supports families in implementing feeding recommendations, rather than didactic message-giving, is essential.
3. Nutritional adequacy alone is not sufficient to improve human capital. A strong evidence base supports the short- and long-term benefits of a combined nutrition and stimulation approach, but few large-scale nutrition and health programs have been persuaded to include stimulation. Partnerships to advocate this approach are essential.

An integrated package of nutrition, health, and development interventions has several advantages. First, from an economics perspective, it is likely to generate the most benefits per dollar than any individual approach (Kilburn & Karoly, 2008; Nores & Barnett, 2009). Second, integration through existing services will help target interventions during the critical early period (0–3 years) and also enable reach to at-risk populations. The challenge for program planners and policymakers is to identify synergies between these different approaches and translate this from policy to point of intervention delivery. Box 10.2 highlights some key policy

BOX 10.2. Policy Questions

- How can sectors that have a role to play in delivering integrated nutrition, health, and development strategies be effectively coordinated?
- How can adequate financing and accountability be ensured for multisectoral programs that are responsible for delivering integrated nutrition, health, and development strategies?
- How can ownership be created among stakeholders for new interventions when creating an integrated nutrition, health, and development strategy?
- How can programs be effectively monitored and evaluated to ensure:
  - Consistency of messages across programs, with a common goal for healthy growth and development of young children?
  - Effective delivery of all components of an integrated nutrition, health, and development strategy?

---

questions. The next generation of operational questions must focus on how to develop combined packages that work, are cost-effective, and can be scaled up. The nutrition community comprises international agencies, civil society, the private sector, and academia—these partners share a common goal and have the potential to effectively leverage resources to meet the challenge of enabling children to realize their full potential.

References

Aboud, F. E., Shafique, S., & Akhter, S. (2009). A responsive feeding intervention increases children's self-feeding and maternal responsiveness but not weight gain. *Journal of Nutrition, 139*(9), 1738–1743.

Attanasio, O., Gómez, L. C., Heredi, P., & Vera-Hernandez, M. (2005). *The short-term impact of a conditional cash subsidy on child health and nutrition in Colombia*. London: The Institute of Fiscal Studies.

Barker, D. J. P., Bergmann, R.L., & Ogra, P. L. (2008). *The window of opportunity: Pre pregnancy to 24months of age: Vol. 61. Nestle Nutrition Workshop Series: Pediatric Program*. Vevey, CH: Nestle Nutrition Institute.

Bentley, M. E., Vazir, S., Engle, P. L., Balakrishna, N., Johson, S., Creed-Kanashir, H., et al. (2010). A home-based educational intervention to caregivers in South India to improve complementary feeding and responsive feeding, and psychosocial stimulation increases dietary intake, growth and development of infants. *Journal of the Federation of the American Societies for Experimental Biology, 24,* 564.14.

Bentley, M. E., Wasser, H. M., & Creed-Kanashiro, H. (2011). Responsive feeding and child under nutrition in low- and middle-income countries. *Journal of Nutrition, 141,* 502–507.

Benton, D. (2010). The influence of dietary status on the cognitive performance of children. *Molecular Nutrition and Food Research, 54*(4), 457–470.

Bhandari, N., Bahl, R., Nayyar, B., Khokhar, P., Rohde, J. E., & Bhan, M. K. (2001). Food supplementation with encouragement to feed it to infants from 4–12 months of age has a small impact on weight gain. *Journal of Nutrition, 131,* 1946–1951.

Bhandari, N., Mazumder, S., Bahl, R., Martines, J., Black, R. E., & Bhan, M. K. (2004). An educational intervention to promote appropriate complimentary feeding practices and physical growth in infants and young children in Haryana, India. *Journal of Nutrition, 134,* 2342–2348.

Bhutta, Z. A., Ahmed, T., Black, R. E., Cousens, S., Dewey, K., Giugliani, E., et al. (2008). What works? Interventions for maternal and child under nutrition and survival. *Lancet, 371*(9610), 417–440.

Black, M. M., & Aboud, F. E. (2011). Responsive feeding is embedded in a theoretical framework of responsive parenting. *The Journal of Nutrition, 141,* 490–494.

Black, R. E., Allen, L. H., Bhutta, Z. A., Caulfield, L. E., de Onis, M., Ezzati, M., & Rivera, J. (2008). Global and regional exposures and health consequences. *The Lancet, 371,* 243–260.

Bryce, J., Coitinho, D., Darnton-Hill, I., Pelletier, D., & Pinstrup-Anderson, P. (2008). Maternal and child under nutrition: Effective action at national level. *The Lancet, 371,* 510–526.

Dewey, K. G., & Adu-Afarwuah, S. (2008). Systematic review of the efficacy and effectiveness of complementary feeding interventions in developing countries. *Maternal and Child Nutrition, 4*(Suppl. 1), 24–85.

Engle, P. L., Black, M. M., Behrman, J. R., Cabral de Mello, M., Gertler, P. J., Kapiriri, L., et al. (2007). Strategies to avoid the loss of developmental potential in more than 200 million children in the developing world. *The Lancet, 369,* 229–242.

Engle, P. L., & Pelto, G. H. (2011). Responsive feeding: Implications for policy and program implementation. *The Journal of Nutrition, 141,* 508–511.

Emond, A. M., Lira, P. I., Lima, M. C., Grantham-McGregor, S. M., & Ashworth, A. (2006). Development and behavior of low-birthweight term infants at 8 years in Northeast Brazil: A longitudinal study. *Acta Paediatrica, 95,* 1249–1257.

Eshel, N., Daelmans, D., Cabral de Mello, M., & Martines, J. (2006). Responsive parenting: Interventions and outcomes. *Bulletin of the World Health Organization, 84,* 992–999.

Faruque, A. S. G., Shamsir, A. M., Tahmeed, A., Islam, M. M., Hossain, M. I., Roy, S. K., et al. (2008). Nutrition: Basis for healthy children and mothers in Bangladesh. *Journal of Health Population and Nutrition, 26*(3), 325–339.

Fernald, L. C., Gertler, P. J., & Neufeld, L.M. (2009). A 10-year effect of *Oportunidades,* Mexico's conditional cash transfer programme, on child growth, cognition, language, and behavior: A longitudinal follow-up study. *Lancet, 374*(9706), 1997–2005.

Frith, A. L., Naved, R. T., Ekstrom, E. C., Rasmussen, K. M., & Frongillo, E. A. (2009). Micronutrient supplementation affects maternal-infant feeding interactions and maternal distress in Bangladesh. *American Journal of Clinical Nutrition, 90*(1), 141–148.

Gordon, R. C., Rose, M. C., Skeaff, S. A., Gray, A. R., Morgan, K. M., & Ruffman, T. (2009). Iodine supplementation improves cognition in mildly iodine-deficient children. *American Journal of Clinical Nutrition, 90*(5), 1264–1271.

Grantham-McGregor, S., Cheung, Y. B., Cueto, S., Glewwe, P., Richter, L., & Strupp, B. (2007). Developmental potential in the first 5 years for children in developing countries. *The Lancet, 369*(9555), 60–70.

Grantham-McGregor, S. M., Powell, C. A., Walker, S. P., & Himes, J. (1991). Nutritional supplementation, psychosocial stimulation and mental development of stunted children: The Jamaican Study. *The Lancet, 338,* 1–5.

Hamadani, J. D., Huda, S. N., Khatun, F., & Grantham-McGregor, S. M. (2006). Psychosocial stimulation improves the development of undernourished children in rural Bangladesh. *The Journal of Nutrition, 136,* 2645–2652.

Hamadani, J. D., Grantham-McGregor, S. M., Tofail, F., Nermell, B., Fängström, B., Huda, S. N., et al. (2010). Pre- and postnatal arsenic exposure and child development at 18 months of age: A cohort study in rural Bangladesh. *International Journal of Epidemiology, 39*(5), 1206–1216.

Huy, N. D., Le Hop, T., Shrimpton, R., & Hoa, C. V. (2009). An effectiveness trial of multiple micronutrient supplementation during pregnancy in Vietnam: Impact on birth weight and on stunting in children at around 2 years of age. *Food and Nutrition Bulletin, 30*(4 Suppl.), S506–S516.

Innis, S. M. (2003). *Nutrition and its impact on psychosocial child development: Preterm infants.* Vancouver: University of British Columbia. Retrieved from http://www.child-encyclopedia.com/documents/InnisANGxp.pdf

Jones, L., Morris, J., Berrino, A., Crow, C., Jordans, M., & Okema, L. (2011). *Does combining infant stimulation with emergency feeding improve psychosocial outcomes for displaced mothers and babies? A controlled evaluation from Northern Uganda.* A Draft Report on Infant Stimulation and Emergency Feeding in Uganda.

Khan, N. Z., Muslima, H., Parveen, M., Bhattacharya, M., Begum, N., Chowdhury, S., et al. (2006). Neurodevelopmental outcomes of preterm infants in Bangladesh. *Pediatrics, 118,* 280–289.

Khan, Y., & Bhutta, Z. A. (2010). Nutritional deficiencies in the developing world: Current status and opportunities for interventions. *Pediatric Clinics of North America, 57*(6), 1409–1441.

Kilburn, M. R., & Karoly, L. A. (2008). *The economics of early childhood policy: What the dismal science has to say about investing in children.* Rand Corporation occasional paper series. Santa Monica, CA: RAND Cooperation.

Kramer, M. S., Aboud, F., Mironova, E., Vanilovich, I., Platt, R.W., Matush, L., et al. (2008). (A): Breastfeeding and child cognitive development: New evidence from a large randomized trial. *Archives of General Psychiatry, 65*(5), 578–584.

Kramer, M. S., Fombonne, E., Igumnov, S., Vanilovich, I., Matush, L., Mironova, E., et al. (2008). (B): Effects of prolonged and exclusive breastfeeding on child behavior and maternal adjustment: Evidence from a large, randomized trial. *Pediatrics, 121*(3), e435–e440.

León-Cava, N., Lutter, C., Ross, J., & Martin, L. (2002). *Quantifying the benefits of breastfeeding: A summary of the evidence.* Washington DC: Pan American Health organization (PAHO).

Li, Q., Yan, H., Zeng, L., Cheng, Y., Liang, W., Dang, S., et al. (2009). Effects of maternal multimicronutrient supplementation on the mental development of infants in rural western China: Follow-up evaluation of a double-blind, randomized, controlled trial. *Pediatrics, 123*(4), e685–e692.

Linkages Project. (2001). *Essential health sector actions to improve maternal nutrition in Africa.* The Linkages Project. Retrieved from http://www.linkagesproject.org/media/publications/Technical%20Reports/EHSAbrief.pdf

Lozoff, B. (2007). Iron deficiency and child development. *Food and Nutrition Bulletin, 28*(4 Suppl.), S560–S571.

Lukowski, A. F., Koss, M., Burden, M. J., Jonides, J., Nelson, C. A., Kaciroti, N., et al. (2010). Iron deficiency in infancy and neurocognitive functioning at 19 years: Evidence of long-term deficits in executive function and recognition memory. *Nutritional Neuroscience, 13,* 54–70.

Maluccio, J., & Flores, R. (2004). *Impact evaluation of a conditional cash transfer program: The Nicaraguan Red de Proteccion Social.* FCND Discussion paper No. 184. Washington, DC: IFPRI.

Martorell, R., Horta, B. L., Adair, L. S., et al. (2010). Weight gain in the first two years of life is an important predictor of schooling outcomes in pooled analyses from five birth cohorts from low- and middle-income countries. *Journal of Nutrition, 140,* 348–354.

McCann, J. C., & Ames, B. N. (2007). An overview of evidence for a causal relation between iron deficiency during development and deficits in cognitive or behavioral function. *American Journal of Clinical Nutrition, 85*(4), 931–945.

McGrath, N., Bellinger, D., Robins, J., Msamanga, G. I., Tronick, E., & Fawzi, W. W. (2006). Effect of maternal multivitamin supplementation on the mental and psychomotor development of children who are born to HIV-1-infected mothers in Tanzania. *Pediatrics*, *117*(2), e216–e225.

Monga, M., Walia, V., Gandhi, A., Chandra, J., & Sharma, S. (2010). Effect of iron deficiency anemia on visual evoked potential of growing children. *Brain Development*, *32*(3), 213–216.

Murray-Kolb, L. E., & Beard, J. L. (2009). Iron deficiency and child and maternal health. *American Journal of Clinical Nutrition*, *89*, 946S–950S.

Nahar, B., Hamadani, J. D., Ahmed, T., Tofail, F., Rahman, A., Huda, S. N., & Grantham-McGregor, S. M. (2009). Effects of psychosocial stimulation on growth and development of severely malnourished children in a nutrition unit in Bangladesh. *European Journal of Clinical Nutrition*, *63*, 725–731.

Nores, M., & Barnett, W. S. (2009). Benefits of early childhood interventions across the world: (Under) Investing in the very young. *Economics of Education Review*, *29*, 271–282.

Oumachigui, A. (2002). Prepregnancy and pregnancy nutrition and its impact on women's health. *Nutrition Reviews*, *60*(5), ss64–ss67.

Pelto, G., Dickin, K., & Engle, P. (1999). *A critical link: Interventions for physical growth and psychological development—a review*. Geneva: Department of Child and Adolescent Health and Development, WHO.

Richter, L. (2004). *The importance of caregiver-child interactions for the survival and health development of young children—A review*. Geneva: Department of Child and Adolescent Health and Development, WHO.

Roza, S. J., van Batenburg-Eddes, T., Steegers, E. A., Jaddoe, V. W., Mackenbach, J. P., Hofman, A., et al. (2010). Maternal folic acid supplement use in early pregnancy and child behavioral problems: The Generation R study. *British Journal of Nutrition*, *103*(3), 445–452.

Sabet, F., Richter, L. M., Ramchandani, P. G., Stein, A., Quigley, M. A., & Norris, S. A. (2009). Low birth weight and subsequent emotional and behavioral outcomes in 12-year-old children in Soweto, South Africa: Findings from birth to twenty. *International Journal of Epidemiology*, *38*, 944–954.

Santos, D. N., Assis, A. M., Bastos, A. C., et al. (2008). (A). Determinants of cognitive function in childhood: A cohort study in a middle income context. *BMC Public Health*, *8*, 202.

Santos, J. N., Lemos, S. M., Rates, S. P., & Lamounier, J. A. (2008). (B): Hearing abilities and language development in anemic children of a public daycare center. *Pro Fono*, *20*(4), 255–260.

SCN. (2009). *Scaling up nutrition—A framework for action*. United Nations Sub Committee for Nutrition, 2009. Geneva: United Nations Standing Committee on Nutrition.

Shafir, T., Angulo-Barroso, R., Su, J., Jacobson, S. W., & Lozoff, B. (2009). Iron deficiency anemia in infancy and reach and grasp development. *Infant Behavior and Development*, *32*(4), 366–375.

Shonkoff, J. P., & Phillips, D. A. (Eds.). (2000). *From neurons to neighborhoods: The science of early childhood*. Development Committee on Integrating the Science of Early Childhood Development. Washington, DC: National Academy Press.

Talukder, M. Q. (2000). The importance of breast feeding and strategies to sustain high breast feeding rates. In A. Costello & D. Manandar (Eds.), *Improving new-born health in developing countries* (pp. 309–342). London: Imperial College Press.

Thomas, D. G., Grant, S. L., & Aubuchon-Endsley, N. L. (2009). The role of iron in neurocognitive development. *Developmental Neuropsychology, 34*(2), 196–222.

Thuc-Duc, L. (2009). *The effect of early age stunting on cognitive achievement among children in Vietnam* (Vol. 45, pp. 1–28). Working paper/ Young Lives (Project). Oxford, UK: Young Lives.

Tofail, F., Persson, L. A., El Arifeen, S., Hamadani, J. D., Mehrin, F., Ridout, D., et al. (2008). Effects of prenatal food and micronutrient supplementation on infant development: A randomized trial from the Maternal and Infant Nutrition Interventions, Matlab (MINIMat) Study. *American Journal of Clinical Nutrition, 87*(3), 704–711.

UNICEF (1998). *The state of the world's children: Focus on nutrition.* New York: Author.

UNICEF. (2010). *The state of the world's children 2010, special edition: Celebrating 20 years of the Convention on the Rights of the Child.* New York: Author.

Vaidya, A., Saville, N., Shrestha, B. P., Costello, A. M., Manandhar, D. S., & Osrin, D. (2008). Effects of antenatal multiple micronutrient supplementation on children's weight and size at 2 years of age in Nepal: Follow-up of a double-blind randomised controlled trial. *The Lancet, 371*(9611), 492–499.

Victora, C. G., Adair, L., Fall, C., Hallal, P. C., Martorell, R., Richter, L., & Sachdev, H. S. (2008). Maternal and child under nutrition: Consequences for adult health and human capital. *The Lancet, 371,* 340–357.

Villar, J., & Belizan, J. M. (1982). The relative contribution of prematurity and fetal growth retardation to low birth weight in developing and developed societies. *American Journal of Obstetrics and Gynecology, 143,* 793–798.

Waber, D. P., Vuori-Christiansen, L., Ortiz, N., Clement, R., Chritiansen, N. E, Mora, J. O., et al. (1981). Nutritional supplementation, maternal education, and cognitive development of infants at risk of malnutrition. *American Journal of Clinical Nutrition, 34*(Suppl. 4), 807–813.

Walker, S. (2011). Promoting equity through early child development interventions for children from birth through three years of age. In H. Aldrerman (Ed.), *No small matter* (pp. 115–154). Washington, DC: World Bank.

Walker, S. P., Chang, S. M., Powell, C. A., & Grantham-McGregor, S. M. (2005). Effects of early childhood psychosocial stimulation and nutritional supplementation on cognition and education in growth-stunted Jamaican children: Prospective cohort study. *The Lancet, 366*(9499), 1804–1807.

Walker, S. P., Chang, S. M., Vera-Hernández, M., & Grantham-McGregor, S. M. (2011). Early child stimulation benefits adult competence and reduces violent behavior. *Pediatrics, 127,* 849–857.

Walker, S. P., Chang, S. M., Younger, N., & Grantham-McGregor, S. M. (2010). The effect of psychosocial stimulation on cognition and behavior at 6 years in a cohort of term, low-birth weight Jamaican children. *Developmental Medicine and Child Neurology, 52,* e148–e154.

Walker, S. P., Wachs, T. D., Gardner, J. M., Lozoff, B., Wasserman, G. A., Pollitt, E., & et al. (2007). Child development: Risk factors for adverse outcomes in developing countries. *The Lancet, 369,* 145–157.

Wang, W. L., Sung, Y. T., Sung, F. C., Lu, T. H., Kuo, S. C., & Li, C. Y. (2008). Low birth weight, prematurity, and paternal social status: Impact on the basic competence test in Taiwanese adolescents. *Journal of Pediatrics, 153,* 333–338.

Wehby, G. L., & Murray, J. C. (2008). The effects of prenatal use of folic acid and other dietary supplements on early child development. *Maternal and Child Health Journal*, 12(2), 180–187.

World Food Programme. (2009). *Learning from experience: Good practices from 45 years of school feeding*. Rome: Author

Yakoob, M. Y., Pervez, Y., & Bhutta, Z. A. (2010). Maternal mineral and vitamin supplementation in pregnancy. *Expert Reviews in Obstetrics and Gynecology*, 5, 241–256.

Zimmermann, M. B. (2009). Iodine deficiency in pregnancy and the effects of maternal iodine supplementation on the offspring: A review. *American Journal of Clinical Nutrition*, 89(Suppl.), 668S–672S.

Zimmermann, M. B., Connolly, K., Bozo, M., Bridson, J., Rohner, F., & Grimci, L. (2006). Iodine supplementation improves cognition in iodine-deficient schoolchildren in Albania: A randomized, controlled, double-blind study. *American Journal of Clinical Nutrition*, 83(1), 108–114.

11

Education-Based Approaches to Early Childhood Development

Chloe O'Gara

A child born today must master skills and knowledge that were needed only by elites a century ago. Population growth, changing and fluid household structures, new gender roles, urbanization, conflict, disasters, and poverty have transformed the landscapes of childhood, while 20th-century technologies and transportation shrank the globe and thrust many people into a global market economy. The requirements for cognitive development now range from functional literacy, to higher order thinking for problem solving and wealth creation.

Concurrently, many factors have challenged the capacity of households and families to help children realize their potential, thus exacerbating equity gaps. Among marginalized populations in low-income areas, most parents know that their children need new skills and knowledge to succeed in the larger world, and they turn to schools to impart the skills and knowledge they want for their children.

The response of most governments to the need for a literate and skilled population has been rapid expansion of education systems. Education is a sound investment for national economic development goals that donors and businesses applaud, and that directly impacts and is impacted by early childhood development (ECD). The expansion of basic education is a politically popular step for most leaders that responds to international pressures and incentives for governments to assume the role of duty bearer for education as a universal human right.

Education pays off for children, directly and indirectly impacting multiple domains of development. More than half of the reduction in child mortality achieved from 1990 to 2007 can be attributed to the increase in female education (Gakidou, Cowling, Lozano, & Murray, 2010). Educated mothers have fewer, healthier, better nourished children, and those children go to school and succeed in school at much higher rates than do children of uneducated mothers.

The effects of education on ECD are intergenerational. Poverty compromises human development, and good-quality education appears to be a necessary if not sufficient condition for countries to achieve economic growth and for populations to move out of poverty. Figure 11.1 illustrates the average percent annual growth in gross domestic product from 1960 to 2000 as a function of the average years of schooling, for a variety of nations. Recent analyses of international test scores have revealed, in addition, that "It is not simply going to school but only actual learning that counts for economic growth" (Hanushek & Woessman, 2009).

Learning failure makes education an inefficient and ineffective investment. Education inefficiency matters to governments and donors because education is the largest national budget line for almost every developing country. Learning does not begin the day a child enters school, and developing country educators today are interested in ECD to help children succeed in early primary school. Education could take ECD programming to scale because primary schools are ubiquitous, have resources, and have access to young children and their families.

This chapter will use an ECD lens to examine the state of preprimary and early primary (grades 1 and 2) education today, and discuss the effects, implications, and potential for education to improve the development of children 4–8 years old. Reynolds and Temple (2008), in their review of ECD, state the rationale clearly:

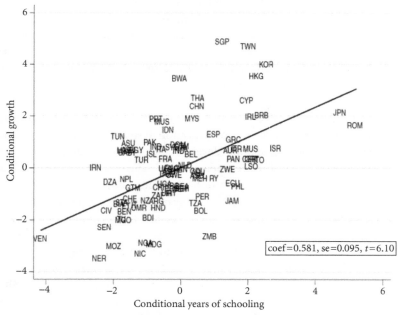

FIGURE 11.1 *Educational base and economic growth.* Adapted from Hanushek, E. A. & Woessmann, L. (2009). *The high cost of low educational performance: The long-run economic impact of improving Pisa outcomes.* Paris: OECD.

"Greater interest in kindergarten and early school-age services reflects the importance of policies and practices that enhance the continuity of development. The comparative or added effect of kindergarten programming and early school age programs and services is of major interest (to ECD)."

Early Childhood Development in Education Today

EDUCATION FOR ALL

Education for All (EFA), launched in 1990, in Jomtien, committed the world to education that was inclusive and equitable. The EFA program's first goal was to "Expand and improve early childhood care and education." Its second goal was to "Provide free and compulsory universal primary education by 2015" (UNESCO, 2007). The EFA compact transformed the historic purpose of schooling in many low-income countries, which was to weed out the less able and to groom elite individuals for leadership and management. EFA committed the global community to educate all its members equitably, to include and elevate all learners.

The EFA declaration emphasizes learning, notes that learning begins at birth, and declares that the first step of basic education is early childhood education. However, in operationalizing EFA, the challenge of inclusion and access to school was tackled before the challenge of helping children learn. Early childhood education was ignored as school systems cranked up to do more of what they already did—primary education. With rapid expansion, the quality of primary education plummeted, and children's learning plummeted too, especially in the early grades. The primacy of primary schooling was enshrined in the second Millennium Development Goal (MDG), which, in 2000, committed 189 world leaders to: "Achieve universal primary education—Ensure that, by 2015, children everywhere, boys and girls alike, will be able to complete a full course of primary schooling" (UNESCO 2010b).

LEARNING FOR SOME

EFA was a policy revolution, but the devil has been in the details. Children who could not have dreamed of going to school one decade earlier poured into schools, particularly in South Asia and in Sub-Saharan Africa, where 82 million children were in primary school in 1999; by 2007, that number soared to 124 million.

The net of this brave and laudable education revolution has been great success in getting children enrolled in school, and a sad failure in delivering the promise of lifelong learning (Figure 11.2). School failure starts very early, when children do not master the fundamentals of literacy that are the core tasks of grades 1 and 2 (Gove & Cvelich, 2010). The concentration of failure in the first years of school highlights the two facets of EFA: Schools must be ready for children, and children must be ready for school.

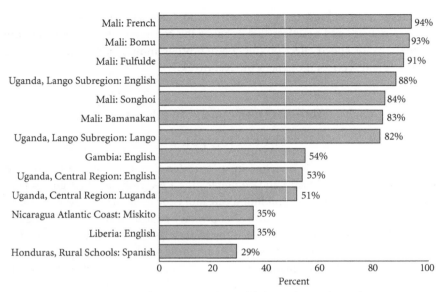

FIGURE 11.2 *Percentage of grade 2 students who could not read a single word, 2008–2009*
Reprinted with permission from Gove & Ovelich, 2010.

CHILDREN READY FOR SCHOOL: PREPRIMARY EDUCATION

Increasing numbers of governments are adding preprimary classrooms to schools
to meet community demand for more and better schooling, to prepare children for
school success, to ease the burden of underage children in primary school classrooms, and to comply with EFA. The weight of evidence confirms that children
who attend preschool perform better in school: They enroll at higher rates, they
pass to second grade at higher rates, they learn more (Engle et al., 2011; OECD,
2011). In recognition of these benefits, middle- and upper-class neighborhoods
around the world boast private preschools of many stripes. Increasing numbers
of today's better preprimary programs provide education for parents and communities about children's development, link families with parenting networks, and
monitor or directly support children's nutrition, health, and psychosocial well-being (Lugo-Gil, Sattar, Ross, Boller, & Tout, 2011). Many preschools emphasize
academic readiness, which is the most prevalent demand from parents, although
there is a strong tradition of "whole child" programming among many preschool
educators and some parents. Programs designed around a model of holistic child
development typically integrate or link health, nutrition, physical, and psychosocial components, whereas more academic preschools emphasize cognition,
addressing other domains as needed to support school readiness.

Private preschools are run by a great variety of proprietors, ranging from entrepreneurs seeking profits, to churches, to nongovernmental organizations (NGOs),
to cooperatives, to corporations sponsoring enriched child care. Licensing and

certification programs in developing countries are scarce; in many countries, preschools are under the rubric of social welfare, gender, or children and youth ministries that have little expertise in education. Curricula and models of private preschools are notable for their diversity of philosophies and approaches, ranging from play-based, to structured literacy and numeracy, to rote learning of religious texts. Research in industrialized and in developing countries has failed to confirm the superiority of any specific model, but there is growing consensus on the essential features of high-quality learning environments for young children. For example, the widely used Early Childhood Environment Rating Scale (2011) which has been adapted for use in a number of developing country contexts, examines language-reasoning, activities, interactions, program structure, personal care routines, and space and furnishings. Research evidence confirms that quality of learning environments is typically associated with improved cognitive outcomes for children who participate, and the preschool experience is generally predictive of improved school performance in developing countries, at least for the first year or so of primary school (Aboud, Hossein, & O'Gara, 2008; Engle et al., 2011). The cost of early childhood classrooms that meet quality standards of industrialized countries has been one of the impediments to government investments in ECD for low-income children.

Government-sponsored preschool programs are typically sited in or near primary schools and offer 1 year or, less frequently, 2 years of preprimary education. A notable exception is the Integrated Child Development System in India (World Bank, 2007), which boasts national multiyear ECD programming, but whose preschool component is very weak. Many developing country schools charge fees for preprimary education, although primary education is free. Preprimary teachers in public systems are seldom ECD specialists, and many do not have training or certification. Some preprimary curricula are little more than "dumbed down" versions of grade 1 curricula, using the same objectives, learning materials, and pedagogical methods but at a slower pace.

EQUITY?

"Preschool" gained momentum in high- and low-income countries throughout the 20th century. From early kindergartens in Germany, to Maria Montessori's pioneering work demonstrating that poor children particularly benefit from structured learning experiences in their early years, preschools have gained traction because they enhance, supplement, or replace what families and communities offered by way of preparation for academic success. As the social and neurological sciences of early development have confirmed the importance of the early years, preschool enrollment in higher income countries and families has risen. Access has also increased in lower income countries, see Table 11.1, but unevenly—Sub-Saharan Africa, for example, has reached only 14% enrollment, up from 9% (UNESCO 2010).

TABLE 11.1 Changes in preprimary gross
enrollment rates between 1999 and 2007, by
region

Region	Gross enrollment ratios		
Year	1999	2007	% change
World	33	41	26
Developing countries	27	36	32
Countries in transition	45	63	36
Developed countries	73	80	9

Adapted from UNESCO. Education for All Global
Monitoring Report 2010. Table 3B, page 330.

An inverse relationship exists between need for early childhood education and participation: disadvantaged children, who benefit most from preschool, are least likely to be in preschool. The EFA Global Monitoring Report (UNESCO, 2010a) shows that, in Egypt, where preprimary gross enrollment jumped from 11% to 17% from 1999 to 2007, "children from the richest families are more than 25 times more likely than those from the poorest families to participate in early childhood programs" p. 52. The "Young Lives" studies report similar inequities. Even where governments support system-based preprimary schooling, classrooms generally host a small enrollment compared with grade 1 classrooms in the same school. In addition to the barrier of fees and other costs, the logistics of getting small children to and from a program favor young children whose homes are close to the school, whose siblings can bring them and take them home, and whose families can pay for transport, fees, and food.

POLICY FRAMEWORKS

Government preprimary policies vary greatly, as Table 11.2 illustrates. The evidence base for the effects of policies on program quality and access for children is still very spotty, but access appears to increase over time in countries with preprimary policies. The World Bank's Systems Approach for Better Education Results (SABER) project will enrich the current evidence base on preprimary policies.

The cost–benefit analyses for provision of preschool to disadvantaged children are compelling. Increasing preschool enrolment to 25% or 50% in each low- and middle-income country would result in a benefit-to-cost ratio ranging from 6.4 to 17.6, depending on preschool enrollment rate and discount rate (Engle et al., 2011), see Table 11.3.

Recent work by Berlinski et al. (2009) examining preschool and school performance, as well as other analyses in developing countries, suggest that the returns on investment in a single year of preprimary education are especially high, so that, from a cost effectiveness perspective, the tendency of governments to endorse 1 year of preprimary education with wide coverage may yield the

TABLE 11.2 Preschool and education policies in four Young Lives countries

Country	Compulsory school age	Preschool	Programs for 0–3	Policy initiative goal
Ethiopia	7+	Not Compulsory. Enrollment: 52% Urban, 4% Rural	None	Universal primary access by 2015
Peru	6+	At least one year of preschool (ages 3–5) is free and compulsory. Enrollment: 89% Urban, 71% Rural	Programs targeting children under 6 exist	National Plan of Action for Children introduced in 2002
India— Andhra Pradesh	6+	3-stage preschool covers ages 1.5 to 5.5. Enrollment: 86% (with urban rural discrepancies)	Comprehensive policy targeting early childhood since mid '70s	Implement National Program for Nutritional support to Education
Vietnam	6+	Education law (1999/ 2005): Early childhood education (3 months to 6 years). Part of formal education system. Enrollment: 89%	89% nursery (attendance 77% for ethnic minorities)	On the way to reach education goals MDG

Reprinted with permission from Jordan, L. (2010). *Ensuring inclusion and protection in the ECCE system. Reducing child poverty through early childhood care and education.* Paris: UNESCO. Retrieved from http://www.unesco.org/education/WCECCE/presentations/LisaJordan.pdf; with permission of the Bernard van Leer Foundation.

greatest benefit for the greatest number of children. If policymakers are serious about achieving learning for all—not just schooling—investment in early childhood education for vulnerable children makes financial as well as humanitarian sense. Perhaps if the significance of social and behavioral learning is confirmed and compellingly communicated to educators, it could be the basis for shifting the academic skill and knowledge focus of preprimary programs toward more holistic programming.

TRANSITIONS

Preprimary programs improve children's transitions from home to school, but only a small percentage of children in developing countries are in preschool, and not all preschools help children and families navigate the transition to school. Preprimary transition activities, designed to smooth children's transitions from home to formal school, are increasingly popular for rising first graders. One element of almost all transition programs, whether based in communities or preschools, is a series of activities implemented by the receiving school, typically by the first-grade teacher(s). These include visiting days for preschool-aged children to go to their future school, meet teachers, sit in desks, look at the learning materials, use the play area and the latrines, and the like; parents are invited to meet other

TABLE 11.3   Analysis of benefits and costs of increasing preschool enrollments to
25%, 35%, and 50%

	Baseline	At least 25% preschool enrollment	At least 35% preschool enrollment	At least 50% preschool enrollment
Mean preprimary enrollment, 8–12 years prior (%)	17.6	30.6	38.3	51.1
Total number of 5 year olds enrolled, 8–12 years prior (millions)	11.4	19.8	24.8	33.1
Mean estimated average gap of schooling (grades)	1.9	1.7	1.5	1.2
BENEFITS (2008 US$) DUE TO INCREASING PRESCHOOL ENROLLMENT TO:				
Present discounted value (PDV) of lifetime earnings (3% discount rate) for one cohort (billions)		10.64	18.73	33.72
PDV of lifetime earnings (6% discount rate) for one cohort (billions)		4.73	8.32	14.97
COSTS (2008 US$) DUE TO INCREASING PRESCHOOL ENROLLMENT TO:				
Total cost (billions)		0.74	1.18	1.92
BENEFIT–COST RATIOS				
3% discount rate		14.3	15.8	17.6
6% discount rate		6.4	7.0	7.8

Reprinted from Engle, P., Fernald, L., Alderman, H., Behrman, J., O'Gara, C., Yousafzai, A., Cabral de
Mello, M., Hidrobo, M., Ulkuer, N., Ertem, I., Iltus, S., and the Global Child Development Steering
Group et al. (2011). Strategies for reducing inequalities and improving developmental outcomes
for young children in low-income and middle-income countries. *The Lancet, 378*(9799), 1339–1353,
doi:10.1016/S0140–6736(11)60889–1, with permission from Elsevier.

parents and staff, and to become oriented to the school and its opportunities and
expectations.

Some educators see an opportunity to meet the transition needs of those young
students who are not in preschool by opening the school during school vacations
when classrooms are vacant and teachers are without work. Vacation programs are
typically short, 1–6 weeks, but if well designed and implemented, intensive transition programs are far less expensive than full-year preprimary programs. Children
learn the basics in transition programs: when to speak, when to move, when to
play, how to hold a pencil, how to orient a printed page, a few rhymes and songs,
exposure to letters and numbers, and evidence suggests that these activities help
children transition successfully from home to school (Arnold, Bartlett, Gowani, &
Shallwani, 2007). More research is needed to sort out long-term effects.

EARLY PRIMARY: GRADES 1 AND 2

The great majority of children 6–8 years old today will enroll in primary school
unless they live in a very remote or conflict-affected community; the majority of

TABLE 11.4 Percent of enrolled young children repeating or dropping out by grade and sex, 2007: Developing countries

	Grade 1			Grade 2		
	Total	Boys	Girls	Total	Boys	Girls
Repetition	5.5	5.9	5.0	5.6	5.7	5.6
Dropout	4.4	4.5	4.3	2.1	3.2	1.0

Adapted from UNESCO. *(2010a). EFA global monitoring report: Reaching the marginalized.* Paris: Author. Retrieved from http://unesdoc.unesco.org/images/0018/001866/186606e.pdf ; Table 6, p. 354; and Table 7, p. 362.

them will enter grade 1 in a government-supported school setting when they are between the ages of 5 and 7 years. Few will experience developmentally appropriate instruction; many will be in overcrowded classrooms, with few teaching or learning materials. Despite many countries' automatic promotion policies in early grades, the highest primary school failure rates are in grades 1 and 2; that is, among young children (Table 11.4).

From a developmental perspective, two features of these data are notable: First, more than one in five young children enrolled in primary school experiences early failure (i.e., repetition or drop out); and, second, more boys than girls fail. Age at first grade entry has dropped in some areas to as young as 5 years, and boys tend to lag girls in developmental readiness for school. In many low-income countries, the majority of children who attend school never achieve functional literacy. Parents request early access, some put underage children in school to solve child care problems, others seek to improve their children's learning and school performance by starting early. It is no longer a matter of debate that millions of children go to school but do not get a sound basic education and that the failure of basic education begins at first grade—and earlier. The disillusionment creeping across the education establishment is beginning to focus on the earliest years of school and the lack of ECD programs to prepare children.

Good learning outcomes typically result from strong school leadership, hands-on classroom-based training and supervision, developmentally appropriate learning materials shared by no more than two students, and adequate time on task for young students. Child-centered, active learning is widely championed for many good reasons, and it shares many features with holistic ECD approaches to learning. However, the evidence linking improved learning outcomes to active learning approaches is less than compelling; perhaps most teachers (as well as their supervisors) have not experienced active learning themselves, many of the approaches urged upon them are difficult in overcrowded underresourced classrooms, and, thus, in reality, active learning approaches are not implemented by most early-grade teachers. Holistic models of education with strong linguistic, psychosocial, and physical development components remain the exception in public- and government-supported systems. Encouragingly, group work and some student participation other than call and response or "chalk and talk" are increasingly prevalent in systems around the world.

One policy response to the problem of poor learning outcomes and crowded classrooms has been automatic grade promotion through primary school, without regard to student achievement. Automatic promotion obscures the need for investing in preparing children for school and in developmentally appropriate and effective learning environments for 6- to 8-year-olds in grade 1, or in the supplementary or remedial help that some children need to catch up. In many schools, the classrooms for the final year of primary school have reasonable teacher-to-pupil ratios, high because children who do not learn drop out or stop attending later grades despite automatic promotion. By contrast the first-grade classrooms are desperately overcrowded, with high teacher-to-pupil ratios. Compounding the problems of crowded classrooms and inadequate teaching and learning materials, the least effective teachers are typically assigned to teach the youngest children because the early grades are the bottom of the teaching status ladder.

INVESTING IN EARLY PRIMARY

One reason that learning is dismal in early primary school is that per capita investment is too low. Average per primary pupil expense in the developed world is more than $5,000, whereas more than a dozen Sub-Saharan African countries report annual expenditures well under $100 per year per pupil. Within those numbers, expenditure is not equal for all students; investment in upper primary students is magnitudes higher than investments in first and second graders. The discrepancy at the school level is magnified at the system level, as Figure 11.3 shows.

Low-income countries invest heavily in education, often at national, district, community, and household levels; government investment is sharply skewed away from young learners and toward learners in the higher levels of the education

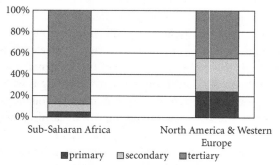

FIGURE 11.3 *Public expenditure per student as a percent of gross domestic product (GDP) per capita.*

From Makish, A., & O'Gara, C. (2009). *Public expenditure per student as a percentage of GDP per capita.* Westport, CT: Save the Children.

system, and especially toward males and elites in Sub-Saharan Africa and South Asia (Figure 11.3). Of the 14% of education resources that reach primary school, only a small proportion reaches early learners in grades 1 and 2—the foundation years for all that is to come. Schools and systems do not disaggregate budgets by grade; school and system budget tracking by grade would be an invaluable tool for improving the education of young children.

COMPLEMENTARY EDUCATION

Several additional approaches to education for young children show promise. Most build on mass media or technology, using either communications or interactive learning approaches to structure children's interactions, activities, skill building, or information acquisition. Some, like the Sesame Workshop family of television programming, are intended to supplement school-based curricula and programs; others, like interactive radio instruction, are designed to improve delivery and effectiveness of school or preschool curricula by diverse actors, in various circumstances from mainstream classrooms to hard-to-reach circumstances. Interactive radio produces significant improvements in early grade and second-language learning, and is now being used to improve preschools (Ho & Thukral, 2009). Changes in young children's social attitudes, as well as preliteracy and premath skills, have been linked with television programming, particularly when mediated by adults. Technology paired with human interaction leads to stronger learning results.

HIDDEN CURRICULA IN PRESCHOOLS AND SCHOOLS

Preschools and schools are complex and complete environments during the hours that children occupy them; as such, they have powerful psychosocial effects on children, often referred to in education circles as the "hidden curriculum," which generally refers to "the norms, values and social expectations indirectly conveyed to students by the styles of teaching, unarticulated assumptions in teaching materials and the organizational characteristics of educational institutions" (ICAAP, 2011).

Regardless of whether their curriculum acknowledges the socialization features of a preprimary or primary school, schools socialize young children to a wider world that is not defined or controlled by parents or other family member. Pre- and primary schools operate according to norms that are different from the norms of home; the holders of power are different people, may speak a different language, and their modes of operating can be a shock to young children. In particular, ethnic, class, and gender roles may be stretched, challenged, or reinforced. Cultural, national, and ethnic identity may be reinforced, valued, and empowered, or denigrated. Notions of gender identity and family hierarchy change when young children leave the orbit of their mother, home, and close relatives (both male and female) and encounter new authority figures.

LANGUAGE IN EARLY EDUCATION

Language is arguably the greatest challenge to inclusion and the promise of equity that pre- and early primary schooling ostensibly offer. Many children who are not familiar with the language of school will fail. Failure is a profound experience for any child, but linguistic dismissal has additional ramifications. Besides its central role in learning and cognition, language is a critical feature of psychosocial and cultural identity. Use of children's mother tongues is discouraged in many schools and classrooms, and in some is actively disparaged.

Some preschools embrace mother tongue instruction, so that children can learn school basics with understanding and confidence. Other preschools emphasize transition and prepare children for a new language environment, at least to the degree that sounds are familiar and mutual respect is the established norm for both languages. Preprimary classrooms attached to schools are typically conducted with the same language norms as the early grades of primary school (i.e., either mother tongue or an official language).

The right of every child to her or his linguistic and cultural heritage is enshrined in the Convention on the Rights of the Child, but the field of education has yet to determine how best to protect and promote that right in today's highly mobile, multilingual world. Approaches that value multilingualism, like child-centered, active learning, can be difficult for adults who themselves are monolingual and may have little patience or use for rich linguistic diversity in a classroom. Systematic design and testing of instructional strategies—with an eye on psychosocial as well as strictly linguistic outcomes—should be a high priority for this decade.

CHILD CARE

In most countries, there is a distinction between preprimary–preschool education, which has limited hours and a school readiness or holistic development goal, and child care or ECD programming, which has broader goals of keeping children safe, ensuring their physical well-being, and improving their cognitive and psychosocial development.

Education ministries in many countries oversee preprimary education, whereas other ministries such as welfare, women, work, gender, youth, and sport, and the like oversee child care or ECD programming. These institutional identities and boundaries mitigate against integrated programming in government-supported pre- and primary schools and against acknowledging the child care needs of families.

Preschools—and the early grades of primary schools—provide de facto child care. In addition to the compelling evidence of neuroscience about early learning, the child care feature of preprimary drives its expansion. It is difficult for schools to turn children away based on age, particularly children who are approaching school age and who do not have birth certificates. One argument for government-sponsored preprimary is the need to get younger children out of first- and second-grade classrooms. Underage children may be sent to preschool so that their older siblings can attend school (rather than take care of the little ones) or their mothers can work. Some are sent by ambitious parents who assume that more and earlier school attendance will give their child a good start on academic success. Whatever the causes in a given setting, the enormous enrollments in grade 1 are a formidable barrier to effective teaching and learning, and the addition of preschool spaces for younger children is one option to ease this.

Good child care complements good education. Finland, whose students excel in international tests, has an extensive child care/child development service network that supports children and families through age 6. Children enter school at age 7, well prepared by years of holistic ECD experiences. Examples like Finland are a proof-of-concept for sustaining ECD approaches and holding off on academics until most children are developmentally ready to learn to read. But, in the developing world, the child care crisis is just beginning. According to the World Bank, total fertility (births per woman) is 6.3 in countries as diverse as Afghanistan and Mali. Afghanistan reported .7% preschool enrollment in 2004, the year it last reported data; Mali reported coverage of 3.2% in 2010.

Conclusion

The near universal enrollment of young children in grade 1, the significant resources at play in the education sector, and the growth of public and private preprimary classes argue for more concerted efforts by ECD specialists to improve young children's schools. School can interfere with, rather than enhance children's developmental progress if school systems offer preprimary classes without quality standards and treat the early primary grades as the least significant period of formal education. If "do no harm" is a first principle for the ECD community, greater attention to young children's experiences in early primary school should be a high priority.

More children in developing countries will repeat or drop out of first or second grade this year than will go to preschool; many more young children will stay in school, enduring unnecessary failure. Millions of young children in preprimary, first, and second grades need ECD standards of practice in their classrooms. Too many schools deny young children opportunities for verbal interaction, for exploration, for play, for engagement with peers, or for building skills with manipulables and print materials. The low learning levels that result should be no surprise.

Most necessary changes could made by reallocating existing resources in education systems, if there were accurate recognition of the consequences of early grade failure. If per capita investments in early-grade students approximated per capita investments in junior secondary/middle school students, the impacts could be transformative: Schools could meet the needs of young children.

References

Aboud, F., Hossein, K., & O'Gara, C. (2008). The Succeed Project: Challenging early school failure in Bangladesh. *Research in Comparative and International Education*, *3*(3), 295–307.

Arnold, C., Bartlett, K., Gowani, S., & Shallwani, S. (2007). Transition to school: Reflections on readiness. Prepared for EFA Global Monitoring Report 2007. Retrieved from http://www.psych.utah.edu/people/people/fogel/jdp/journals/5/journal05-04.pdf

Berlinski, S., Galiani, S., & Gertler, P. (2009). The effect of pre-primary education on primary school performance. *Journal of Public Economics*, *93*, 219–34.

Early Childhood Environment Rating Scale. (2011). Retrieved from http://ers.fpg.unc.edu/early-childhood-environment-rating-scale-ecers-r.

Engle, P., Fernald, L., Alderman, H., Behrman, J., O'Gara, C., Yousafzai, A., et al. (2011). Strategies for reducing inequalities and improving developmental outcomes for young children in low-income and middle-income countries. *The Lancet*, *378*(9799), 1339–1353. doi:10.1016/S0140-6736(11)60889-1

Gakidou, E., Cowling, K., Lozano, R., & Murray, C. J. L. (2010). Increased educational attainment and its effect on child mortality in 175 countries between 1970 and 2009: A systematic analysis. *The Lancet*, *376*, 959–974.

Gove, A., & P. Cvelich. (2010). *Early reading: Igniting education for all*. A Report by the Early Grade Learning Community of Practice. Research Triangle Park, NC: Research Triangle Institute.

Hanushek, E. A., & Woessmann, L. (2009). *The high cost of low educational performance: The long-run economic impact of improving Pisa outcomes*. Paris: OECD.

Ho, J. & Thukral, H. (2009). Tuned in to student success: Assessing the impact of interactive radio instruction for the hardest-to-reach. *Journal of Education for International Development*, *4*(2), 34–51.

Jordan, L. (2010). *Ensuring inclusion and protection in the ECCE system. Reducing child poverty through early childhood care and education*. Paris: UNESCO. Retrieved from http://www.unesco.org/education/WCECCE/presentations/LisaJordan.pdf

Lugo-Gil, J., Sattar, S., Ross, C., Boller, K., & Tout, K. (2011). *The quality rating improvement system evaluation toolkit*. OPRE Report 20011–31. Washington, DC: US Department of Health and Human Services, Office of Children and Families, Office of Planning, Research, and Evaluation.

Makish, A., & O'Gara, C. (2009). *Public expenditure per student as a percentage of GDP per capita*. Westport, CT: Save the Children.

OECD. (2011). Does participation in pre-primary education translate into better learning outcomes at school? Paris: PISA in Focus. Retrieved from http://www.oecd.org/dataoecd/37/0/47034256.pdf

Online Dictionary of the Social Sciences, (2011). Retrieved from http://bitbucket.icaap.org/dict

Reynolds, A. J., & Temple J. A. (2008). Cost-effective early childhood development programs from preschool to third grade. *Annual Review of Clinical Psychology*, *4*, 109–139.

UNESCO. Strong Foundations: EFA Global Monitoring Report (2007). Retrieved from http://portal.unesco.org/en/ev.php-URL_ID=35377&URL_DO=DO_TOPIC&URL_SECTION=201.html

UNESCO. (2010a). EFA global monitoring report: Reaching the marginalized. Paris: Author. Retrieved from http://unesdoc.unesco.org/images/0018/001866/186606e.pdf

UNESCO. (2010b). Millennium development goals report. Paris: Author. Retrieved from http://www.uis.unesco.org/Library/Documents/MDGR_2010_En.pdf

World Bank. (2007). India—Fourth ICDS project. Washington, DC: Author. Retrieved from http://www- wds.worldbank.org/external/default/main?pagePK=64193027&piPK =64187937&theSitePK=523679&menuPK=64187510&searchMenuPK=64187283&theSit ePK=523679&entityID=000104615_20070313122153&searchMenuPK=64187283&theSite PK=523679

World Bank. World Development Indicators. (2011). Retrieved from http://datatopics. worldbank.org/gender/country/afghanistan and http://datatopics.worldbank.org/gen- der/country/mali Young Lives. (2010). Early childhood care and education as a strategy for poverty reduction: Evidence from Young Lives. Oxford, UK: Author. Retrieved from http://www.younglives.org.uk/files/policy-papers.

12

Preventing Violence Against Young Children

Cassie Landers, Clarice Da Silva e Paula, and Theresa Kilbane

A child's most essential protection is supposed to be secured by family and representatives of social institutions, such as teachers, law enforcement officers, and other civil authorities. Yet, the most egregious violations against children come from these same sources: parents and other family members, employed caretakers, teachers, employers, law enforcement authorities, and other state actors. Sadly, their acts of violence, exploitation, and abuse are rarely reported and investigated; few perpetrators are held accountable. Emerging, however, are nascent efforts to improve reporting and the protection of young children. This chapter addresses the magnitude of the problem and provides examples of efforts to counteract it. The first section of this chapter provides a conceptual framework for understanding the situation of violence against children and also for understanding child protection programs. The second section of the chapter is focused on evidence in three domains: the situation of child abuse and neglect, the impact of abuse on the developing child, and risk factors linked with child maltreatment. The third section of this chapter provides an overview of programs that are currently being implemented to improve child protection within the framework provided in the first section. The chapter concludes with recommendations for practice, policy, and research based on the gaps in current knowledge and effective programs.

Global Child Protection Framework

The child's right to be protected from violence, exploitation, and abuse is not simply a worthy goal but rather an obligation under international law. The child protection framework draws on several international conventions and documents, which are overviewed briefly here.

Children's rights have been for some time guaranteed by various international human rights treaties that were developed from the 1948 Universal Declaration of

Human Rights. These include the rights set out in several conventions, for example, the International Covenants on Economic, Social, and Cultural Rights and on Civil and Political Rights; the Convention on the Elimination of All Forms of Discrimination Against Women (which are fully applicable to girls under 18 years of age); the Convention on Rights of Persons with Disabilities; and the Convention Against Torture and other Forms of Cruel, Inhuman, and Degrading Treatment or Punishment. However, recognizing the need to provide specific rights for the protection of children, the General Assembly adopted, in 1989, the Convention on the Rights of the Child[1] (CRC; also covered in Hertzman, Vaghri, & Arkadas-Thibert [2013], Chapter 19, this volume)—a comprehensive and legally binding document that includes specific provisions on the promotion of protection, prevention, and response to all forms of violence (Pinheiro, 2006).

Article 19[2] of the CRC asserts children equal rights to full respect for their dignity and physical personal integrity (UNICEF, 2007). The Article calls for states party to "take all appropriate legislative, administrative, social and educational measures to protect the child from all forms of physical or mental violence, injury or abuse, neglect or negligent treatment, maltreatment or exploitation, including sexual abuse, while in the care of parent(s), legal guardian(s) or any other person who has the care of the child." The second part of the provision calls for the establishment of programs to provide support to the child and to caregivers and for measures to prevent and to respond to cases of violence that can be found in various articles of the CRC.[3]

A second set of documents that provide the foundation for the framework are international agency reports. In 2002, the World Health Organization (WHO) defined violence in the *World Report on Violence and Health* as "the intentional use of physical force or power, threatened or actual, against a child, by an individual or group, that either results in or has a high likelihood of resulting in actual or potential harm to the child's health, survival, development or dignity" (World Health Organization [WHO], 2002). The latter, combined with the definition provided by the CRC, was adopted by the 2006 United Nations Secretary-General Study on Violence Against Children, a landmark study that, for the first time, aimed to demonstrate the nature, extent, and causes of violence against children (Pinheiro, 2006).

The child protection framework, emanating from these critical documents, is part of the United Nations Children's Fund (UNICEF)'s overall mandate "to advocate for the protection of children's rights, to help meet their basic needs and to expand their opportunities to reach their full potential," as is the organization's commitment to protect children from all forms of violence, abuse, and exploitation.[4] The child protection framework is a rights-based strategy that calls for the development of a protective environment in which children are free from harm. This approach is supported by two main pillars: (1) promoting and strengthening child protection systems, and (2) supporting positive social change. The first pillar consists of supporting legal reform, policy development, and the establishment of government structures, programs, and services to reduce vulnerabilities and to prevent violence, as well as to respond to victims. The second pillar relates to addressing societal factors and social norms that, on one hand, perpetuate violence and, on the other, promote positive social change (UNICEF, 2008).

Although the child protection framework does not specifically refer to a life-cycle approach, starting at birth with an emphasis on continuity through life, child protection programs bear in mind that younger children are more vulnerable to violence in certain settings[5]; therefore, preventing and responding to abuse and neglect in early childhood is an integral part of UNICEF's child protection work.

GLOBAL ASSESSMENT OF THE SITUATION

The exact prevalence of child maltreatment is unknown. Physical abuse, neglect, domestic violence involving young children, and relatedly, early childhood trauma in the home are to a large extent invisible to the public eye. The available data do little to help us understand the scale and scope of the problem because complex definitional and measurement issues prevent both absolute assessment, as well as comparison within and between countries (Pereda, Guilera, Forns, & Gomex-Benito, 2009). Nevertheless, existing evidence suggests that violence against children is both highly prevalent and has severe developmental and physical consequences (Mikton, 2011). The WHO calculates that 20% of women and 8% of men worldwide have been sexually abused as children; well over 25% of children report being physically abused (WHO, 2010). Tragically, only a small proportion of maltreated children—less than 10% even in high-income countries—ever come into contact with child protection authorities (Gilbert et al., 2009).

The first year is the single most dangerous period in a child's life with respect to the risks to survival, not only from infectious disease, but also due to abuse and neglect. It is estimated that approximately 2% of deaths annually in the United States are associated with victimization and abuse (U.S. Department of Health and Human Services, 2002). Accidental death and injury remain high for at least the first 5 years of life (U.S. Department Health Human Services, 2002). In addition to violence directed toward children, witnessing violence in the home also harms young children (Brown & Bzostek, 2003). Global estimates indicate that domestic violence is more frequent in families with younger (compared to older) children (WHO, 2002). The two measures are not independent, however. A review of 35 published studies in the United States found a co-occurrence rate ranging from 30% to 60% of the cases (Appel & Holden, 1998). One-half to three-quarters of children exposed to domestic violence are also victims of physical abuse; conversely, about 40% of physically abused children are also exposed to domestic violence (Margolin, 1998). This association has been confirmed in low- and middle-income (LAMI) countries, with supporting studies from a range of countries including China, South Africa, Colombia, India, Egypt, the Philippines, and Mexico (WHO,

2002). Thus, for many of these children, victimization is more of a condition than a single event.

In understanding the prevalence of violence against children, it is important to recognize the substantial shortfall between the occurrence of maltreatment and reports of it to child protection agencies. Official maltreatment statistics, based on legal reports, dramatically underestimate its prevalence when compared to self-reports, obtained through community surveys (Gilbert et al., 2009). This discrepancy results in part from several factors that are linked to the potential risks and benefits, to all parties, at every step in the recognition, reporting, and investigation process. Official findings require a high level of certainty and legal justification; they may also informally take into account the availability (or not) of adequate child protection services.

In addition, variation in social and cultural norms can protect against violence, but can also hide it, or even, at times, support it as "necessary." Although often unrecognized, social and cultural norms, or expectations of behavior within a specific group, exert a powerful impact on both the existence and underreporting of violence against children (WHO, 2009). Often unspoken, these norms offer social standards of appropriate and inappropriate behaviors. Social tolerance of violent behavior is learned in early childhood through the use of or witnessing violence in the family, communities, and the media. In some communities, violence is accepted, either as a normal method of resolving conflict or as a usual part of child rearing. For example, there is a commonly held belief in many societies that if a child is not properly disciplined, including physical discipline, he or she will grow up to be disrespectful, lazy, and undisciplined. There is often a belief that using corporal punishment against children is a pattern of behavior that the larger community expects of good parents. This acceptance is a risk for all types of interpersonal violence and often prevents those affected from speaking out and gaining support. In many societies, victims of sexual violence also feel stigmatized, which inhibits reporting (UNICEF, 2010a).

Violence in the home is not limited by geography, ethnicity, or status; it is a global phenomenon. For too many children, home is far from a safe haven. Every year, hundreds of millions of children are exposed to and are victims of domestic violence, and this has a powerful and profound impact on their lives and hopes for the future. Violence in the home is one of the most pervasive human rights challenges of our time. It remains a largely hidden problem that few countries, communities, or families openly confront (UNICEF, 2006a). Although the evidence that violence is highly prevalent is compelling, more staggering is the degree of underreporting; as low as 1 in 10 for high-income countries and much lower in resource-poor settings (Gilbert et al., 2009). Although primary prevention is far more effective, the data gaps and glaring lack of evidence is a severe obstacle to progress. The invisibility of violence toward children, perpetuated by deeply held social norms and the perception that reporting might do more harm than good, is one of the most pervasive human rights challenges of our time (Feigelson, 2011).

SCIENTIFIC FINDINGS

The commonly held belief that children younger than 5 years of age do not remember acts of violence or other traumatic stressors, that they are too young to understand their significance, or that they recover readily from traumatic exposure due to inherent resilience is invalid and incorrect (National Scientific Council on the Developing Child, 2010). An extensive and growing body of literature documents that the impact of trauma on the biological, emotional, social, and cognitive function of young children is much like the effects on older children. Unlike older children, however, very young children cannot express in words whether they feel afraid, overwhelmed, or helpless. Nevertheless, their behaviors provide us with important clues about how they are affected (Lieberman & Van Horn, 2008).

Young children are less able to anticipate danger or to know how to keep themselves safe, and so are particularly vulnerable to the effects of exposure to trauma. Lacking an accurate understanding of the relationship between cause and effect, young children may believe that their thoughts, wishes, and fears have the power to become real and can make things happen. A 2-year-old who witnesses a traumatic event, such as his mother being battered, may interpret it quite differently compared to an 11-year-old because they are at different stages of cognitive development and understanding of their context. Children may blame themselves or their parents for not preventing a frightening event or for not being able to change its outcome. These misconceptions of reality compound the negative impact of traumatic effects on children's development (Fox & Shonkoff, 2011).

Young children's feeling of safety is linked with the physical and emotional availability of attachment figures, monitoring the environment for signs of danger and seeking proximity and contact of security when faced with threats. The quality of this attachment, then (Bowlby, 1969) is an important factor in young children's capacity to process and resolve traumatic experiences. Chu and Lieberman (2010) posit that, during traumatic events, when the child experiences overwhelming negative stimulation, the expectation that the attachment figure can comfort and protect is shattered. For children growing up with chronic and multiple traumas, this failing of expectation becomes the norm, thereby both stunting the ability to form relationships and facilitating a continued renewal of the negative emotions that were part of the first event. Conversely, an attachment figure who is available to the child under condition of stress can buffer the child's response. In traumatic situations in which the child witnesses violence and threats to the attachment figure, the young child may perceive those as threats to himself also. The degree to which the caregiver is able to read the child's cues and respond effectively may reduce the adverse effect of the traumatic event. As Chu and Lieberman (2010) assert, traumatic events may damage the quality of existing attachments by introducing unmanageable stress into the parent–child relationship, particularly when the parent has also been affected by the trauma.

Young children who experience trauma are at particular risk because their rapidly developing brains are very vulnerable. Chronic activation of the body's stress response systems has been shown to disrupt the efficiency of brain circuitry and lead to other immediate and long-term problems in learning, behavior, and both physical and mental health. This is especially true when stress-system overload occurs during sensitive periods of early brain development (Fox & Shonkoff, 2011). Chronic, unrelenting stress in early childhood caused by repeated abuse and anxiety can be toxic to the developing brain. Whereas positive stress (moderate, short-lived physiological responses to uncomfortable experiences) is an important and necessary aspect of healthy development, toxic stress damages developing brain architecture. In the absence of the buffering protection of adult support, toxic stress becomes built into the body through processes that shape the architecture of the developing brain. Toxic stress in early childhood can lead to a lifetime of greater susceptibility to physical illness, as well as mental health problems including depression, anxiety disorder, and substance abuse (National Scientific Council on the Developing Child, 2007).

In summary, the evidence clearly states that whereas young children recognize threat in their environment, unlike older children and adults, they do not have the cognitive or language skills to express their feelings, reduce the threat, or physically remove themselves from the fear-inducing situation. If young children are exposed to persistent fear and excessive threat during sensitive periods, healthy patterns of the stress response system are disrupted, and these are not easily corrected by removing the child from danger. The fear remains embedded within a child's memory, and the brain retains the learned links (National Scientific Council on the Developing Child, 2010).

Factors Contributing to Violence Against Children

Child abuse and neglect is regrettably a universal phenomenon that occurs across socioeconomic, religious, cultural, racial, and ethnic groups. Although there are no specific definitive causes that lead a parent or caregiver to abuse or neglect, research has identified a number of risk factors or attributes that have been associated with maltreatment (Goldman, Salus, & Wolcott, 2003). We provide a brief overview of these factors, as they are important for the design of child protection interventions. Although much of this evidence has been culled from studies conducted in high-income countries, it is recognized that there is no single cause of child maltreatment, and the cultural context needs to be considered in the interpretation of adverse and risk factors. We focus on two risk factors in the most proximal and influential context for early child development: parent or caregiver factors, and family factors. With respect to protective factors, or those that buffer the impact of negative life events, we focus on a series of five factors identified in the literature and linked with the child's context.

RISK FACTORS IN THE PROXIMAL ENVIRONMENT
ASSOCIATED WITH CHILD ABUSE

Parent or Caregiver Factors

Parent or caregiver factors include personality characteristics and psychological well-being, history of maltreatment, substance abuse, attitudes and knowledge, and age (Chalk & King, 1998). Characteristics associated with whether parents/caregivers are physically abusive or neglectful include low self-esteem, belief that events are determined by chance or outside forces, poor impulse control, depression, anxiety, and antisocial behavior. The maltreatment literature commonly supports the finding that some maltreating parents were victims of abuse and neglect themselves, giving rise to an intergenerational cycle of abuse (Belsky, 1993). Parental substance abuse is known to be a contributing factor to reported cases of abuse. But, the number and complexity of co-occurring family problems often makes it difficult to understand the full impact of substance abuse on child violence. Negative attitudes toward children, and unmet and unrealistic expectations of child capacities, can culminate in inappropriate punishment and violence. Research on maltreating parents found that they were more likely to use harsh discipline strategies and verbal aggression and less likely to use positive parenting strategies.

Family Factors

Family factors, such as marital conflict, domestic violence, single parenthood, unemployment, financial stress, and social isolation, have all be shown to increase the likelihood of negative patterns of family function. According to a review of research findings, child maltreatment was found in 30%–60% of families in which spouse abuse had also been reported (Appel & Holden, 1998). Children in violent homes may witness parental violence, may be victims of physical abuse themselves, and may be neglected by parents focused on their partners and therefore unresponsive to their children. Other known risk factors, not covered in this chapter, include child characteristics such as age and physical development, and cognitive, emotional, and social disabilities. Another category of factors include contextual and environmental conditions, such as poverty and unemployment, social isolation, and communities characterized by high levels of violence (Chu & Lieberman, 2010).

Protective Factors Associated with Reduced Child Abuse

Research has identified a set of factors that can help mitigate the impact of violence. Protective factors are conditions in families and communities that, when present, increase the health and well-being of children and families. These attributes serve as buffers, helping parents to find resources, supports, or coping strategies that allow them to parent effectively, even under stress. The following five protective factors have been linked to a lower incidence of child abuse and neglect: stable caring relationships, knowledge of parenting and of child development, parental resilience, social connections, and concrete supports for parents (Administration for Children and Families, 2011; Center for the Study of Social Policy, 2003; Kotch et al., 1995; National Scientific Council on the Developing Child, 2007; Pollard, Hawkins, & Arthur, 1999).

Stable Caring Relationships

A child's early experience of being nurtured and developing close attachment to a caring adult affects all aspects of behavior and development. Studies show that young children who have secure, trusting relationships with parents or nonparental caregivers experience minimal stress hormone activation when frightened by a strange event. Children who have insecure relationships experience a significant activation of the stress response system. Providing supportive, responsive relationships as early in life as possible can prevent or reverse the damaging effects of toxic stress.

Knowledge of Parenting and of Child Development

Effective discipline practices—setting limits and encouraging appropriate behaviors based on the child's age and developmental level—are critical parenting skills. Violence, neglect, and abuse against children is often associated with a lack of understanding of basic child development and the skills to put knowledge into practice.

Parental Resilience

Resilience is the ability to manage the stress of daily life and recover from crises. Families who are emotionally resilient have the skills to solve problems and address challenges, and are less likely to direct anger and frustration toward their children.

Social Connections

Research has highlighted the link between social isolation and the perceived lack of support to increased incidence of child neglect and abuse. Strong social networks provide emotional support and assistance to families confronting short- or long-term stress. Supportive adults within extended families and communities can model alternative parenting styles and serve as resources for parents and caregivers when needed.

Concrete Supports for Parents

Families need basic resources such as food, clothing, housing, and access to essential services to ensure the optimal health, development, and safety of their children. Some families may require assistance in identifying and accessing a variety of services including health care, early intervention, financial support, skills training, employment opportunities, and mental health services. Providing and/or connecting families to services helps them to cope with and prevent situations in which violence and maltreatment is likely to occur.

Successful interventions are those that both reduce risk factors as well as promote protective factors. Focusing on promoting protective factors is a more productive approach than reducing risk factors alone; protective factors are attributes that strengthen all families and help them build on existing strengths and support within families and communities. Building on the insights generated from both basic research and program evaluations, agencies such as the United Nations Children's Fund (UNICEF) are committed to a range of programs to prevent violence toward young children within the context of an overall child protection system. The next section of the chapter highlights selected country initiatives to strengthen families' capacities to care for young children, as well as more intensive interventions for at-risk families and children.

UNICEF Child Protection Programs: Linkages to Early Childhood Development

This section addresses UNICEF's interventions and initiatives to improve child protection. In general, UNICEF supports government ministries and civil society partners to prevent violence and protect children's rights through the strengthening of social welfare, justice, and local development systems. In most cases, this support includes technical assistance for legal reform and policy development, but it may also include capacity building efforts directed to government and civil society staff in the area of child protection, technical and direct supply support to strengthen child protection systems, and advocacy/communication strategies to raise awareness and prevent the violation of children's rights.

In the past, the majority of interventions have focused on school-aged children and adolescents (e.g., child labor laws) and violence prevention programs in schools and communities. Interventions for younger children have been limited. However, the importance of early intervention services combined with strengthened child welfare systems has increased recognition. In addition, UNICEF child protection interventions for young children include birth registration and support to children with disabilities and children living in institutions.[6]

For the purpose of this chapter, early childhood development (ECD) interventions aimed at improving the protection and care of young children within the home/family unit are reviewed. The data for this review were gathered through the annual reports submitted by UNICEF country offices in 2010. A relatively small number of country offices ($N = 24$) included a specific child protection component within their ECD programs ($N = 108$ countries with ECD programs). This low prevalence (less than a quarter of the countries) is a valid indicator of national and global attention to the issue of child protection in the early years.

We then reviewed the individual country-level programs and examined their key intervention strategies. Two primary areas of child protection interventions emerged: prevention programs that aim to improve parent/caregiver capacities and raise awareness; and the integration of child protection into existing programs and policies. We illustrate both these areas with examples from the country programs. It should be noted that country reports present more descriptive information and very little impact or analytical data. Therefore, the review of these programs is primarily descriptive and, again, a valid indicator of the limited state of knowledge of ECD child protection interventions.

Parenting Programs to Raise Awareness and Prevent Violence Against Children

Program evaluation research has demonstrated that parenting programs are a key intervention for reducing violence against children (WHO & IPSCAN, 2006). Corporal punishment is a common practice in many countries. Across the programs reviewed, the most common entry point for child protection in ECD programs was through parenting programs designed to improve parent/caregiver awareness of positive parenting practices and to discourage excessive or harmful child discipline. Parenting programs often included a module or series of modules on child discipline, effective bonding/communication techniques, and gender differences in parenting and expectations of childhood behavior. The parenting programs are implemented through a variety of modalities—peer to peer, community-based programs, formal training of caregivers, and large-scale radio and television information campaigns, as well as the development and distribution of written materials to parents and caregivers.

The review indicated that UNICEF program efforts to address harmful child discipline practices generally combine legal and policy initiatives with communication campaigns at the national level and feature parenting programs or community-based interventions designed to enhance parent's knowledge on positive parenting practices, link caregivers to other social services (if necessary) to improve child development outcomes (including health, education attainment, and cognitive development).

Two vivid illustrations of this model are presented from Jordan and Moldova. In Jordan, in response to harmful child-rearing practices (an estimated 50% of children are physically abused by parents/legal guardians, school teachers and administrators, and siblings), the *Better Parenting Program* (BPP) was started as a pilot in 1996. Ten years later, the BPP had reached more than 70,000 parents across all governorates, a total of 8% of the population (UNICEF, 2006d). Results of the impact evaluation demonstrate trend level improvements in reduction of harmful

disciplinary practices and increased awareness in parents of alternative disciplinary practices as compared to the control group (Al-Hassan & Lansford, 2010).

In Moldova, based on a national survey of family knowledge, attitude, and
practices on ECD, it was noted that 16.4% of parents beat their children who
were under 1 year of age and, by the age of 6–7 years, more than half of children
(57%) experience beating as a form of discipline (UNICEF, 2010b). In response,
an advocacy kit was developed and distributed to all relevant sectors, including
health, education, and social welfare. Nurses and doctors received training in "care
for development." Parents received information on positive parenting, nutrition,
health, and early stimulation. A parent's handbook and brochures were developed by a local nongovernmental organization, the International Step by Step
Association. The effectiveness of this intervention is yet to be evaluated.

Protection Integrated with Existing Early Childhood Development Programs and Policies

Although parenting programs emerged as the most common type to prevent abuse
and neglect in early childhood, other models of ECD protection programs were
also noted. One such approach is the inclusion of child protection services through
existing services and policies. New programs are not created; rather, existing programs are supplemented with issues linked with reducing child maltreatment.
Examples from Chile and Ghana highlight this approach.

Chile has adopted the Integrated Protection System for Early Childhood (*Chile
Crece Contigo*), which covers children from birth to school entry. Its goal is to
reduce socioeconomic, cultural, geographic, educational, and other inequality gaps
for children and families by giving them opportunities for their optimal development. Through *Chile Crece Contigo*, the health sector has provided technical
guidelines on home visiting to enhance the integral biopsychosocial development
of the child in early development as an important component of the prevention of
child maltreatment and gender-based violence. In 2009, health teams of 13 services, and in 2010, health teams of 16 services were trained to strengthen their home
visiting skills by including a violence prevention component, adding to a total of
1,089 health staff. An evaluation of this program is currently under way, in partnership with the Ministry of Health and UNICEF. The advantage of this program
was its ability to draw on the existing model of home-based services to include
modules linked with reducing child abuse.[7]

In 2007, the Ugandan government developed a holistic National Early Childhood
Development Policy to support the development of healthy and productive children between the ages of 0 and 8 through intersectorial collaborations (Uganda
Ministry of Education and Sports, 2007). Specifically in the area of child protection, the policy outlines the parents' or guardians' role to provide a safe home
environment and ensure discipline for the improvement of the child's behavior.

To support implementation of the policy, a communication strategy was developed by the Ministry of Education and UNICEF. The strategy emphasizes that children have the right and need to be protected from physical and psychological abuse. The strategy promotes the protective role of parents, caregivers, teachers, and communities to ensure that children are not abused and that all cases of violence should be reported to the authorities.

Conclusion

Research on the biology of stress powerfully illustrates how strong, frequent, or prolonged adverse experiences—such as living in violent and abusive environments—can weaken developing brain architecture and permanently set the body's stress response system on high alert. Significant fear-eliciting experiences have a cumulative toll on an individual's physical health, learning, memory, and social and emotional behavior. Children living in violent homes or communities exhibit more behavior problems, show greater evidence of posttraumatic physical symptoms, have a lower capacity for empathy, and experience feelings of low self-esteem. Research also demonstrates that early intervention can prevent the consequences of early adversity by providing stable and supportive responsive relationships as early as possible. Later interventions are less effective and more costly.

Yet, in spite of this knowledge, a gap remains in both policies and programs to address the needs of young children who have experienced violence, abuse, and neglect. The limited availability of protection programs is striking. We have a much clearer sense of what needs to be done. UNICEF, along with its partners, is committed to increasing both access to and availability of preventive and protective services. In moving toward this goal, several program recommendations have emerged from this review. These include (a) promote integration through existing entry points; (b) improve program quality and professional capacity; (c) design effective tracking, monitoring, and evaluation systems; and (d) develop supportive legal and policy frameworks.

PROMOTE INTEGRATION THROUGH EXISTING ENTRY POINTS

The protection of young children from violence, abuse, and neglect should be mainstreamed in all ECD interventions and national strategies. The example from Chile highlights the benefits of integrating child protection interventions into health and education services to ensure that young children grow and develop in safe, healthy, and enabling environments. Programs must also address the underlying causes of violence, including social norms and cultural practices, as was undertaken in Jordan. Promoting parent education and positive parenting is critical to ensuring that the child is raised in an environment free of violence. Positive discipline programs/messages can be delivered through home visiting programs, in health facilities through nurses and doctors, or in specialized community-based support centers for families and children. Although it is important to prevent violence, it is also equally important to ensure that children and families have access to support services in the case of violence. Parents should be aware of existing services in their communities, and professionals should have the capacity to detect and deal with cases of violence, thus protecting the interests and rights of the child.

Equally important is to ensure that ECD communication strategies include a component on the prevention of abuse and neglect in early childhood and that specific messages are delivered to communities, families, and children, as well as to policy- and decision-makers.

Although successful child protection programs begin with prevention, responding to violence and providing assistance to victims is also critical. Early childhood development programs should ensure that services are in place to respond to cases of abuse and neglect and to provide child victims with specialized services. This includes having social welfare, health, and education professionals with the capacity to identify signs of abuse and neglect and health, social welfare, and legal services available to the child and family.

IMPROVE PROGRAM QUALITY AND PROFESSIONAL CAPACITY

In general, policies that focus on the delivery of evidence-based services for the most vulnerable young children will achieve greater financial return than will services for children at a lesser degree of risk. In this perspective, issues of quality and cost must be viewed in light of a program's expectations. Programs for families coping with severe depression, substance abuse, or violence must be staffed by skilled providers. When program resources match the needs of the children and families they are designed to serve, they can be effective. When services are expected to address complex needs that are beyond their capacity, they are likely to have limited impact. Program effectiveness could be significantly enhanced by targeting interventions to explicitly address the developmental needs of young children beginning in the prenatal period, and targeting parents, caregivers, and professionals in direct contact with children. Greater attention should be directed toward maternal factors that place the health and development of children at high risk, including substance abuse, domestic violence, isolation, and maternal depression. The prevention of developmental impairments due to these complex factors requires proper identification, diagnosis, and treatment of both caregivers and children.

Training of physicians and health care personnel to manage these cases, as well the development of a cadre of skilled social services providers, is critical. Also, government structures need to be in place with trained staff to implement programs and deliver specialized services for those in need. For example, social workers should have the capacity to identify families and children at risk, and to conduct home visits to provide direct support or refer them to services to meet their needs. Health professionals should also be equipped to provide young mothers and pregnant women with information about care and parenting. This is particularly relevant in the case of child abandonment, where maternity ward staff play a key role in prevention.

DESIGN EFFECTIVE TRACKING, MONITORING, AND EVALUATION SYSTEMS

Data gaps and a glaring lack of evidence are severe obstacles to progress. The invisibility of violence toward children is perpetuated by deeply held social norms and the perception that reporting might do more harm than good. Although we must continue to increase our understanding of the scale and scope of violence, its causes and consequences, we must place greater attention on understanding the components of successful interventions at multiple levels (e.g., home, family, and community). Greater effort needs to be applied to establishing baseline data and systems for monitoring and evaluating program quality and outcomes.

DEVELOP SUPPORTIVE LEGAL AND POLICY FRAMEWORKS

Legislative efforts that prohibit corporal punishment of children will also contribute to greater protection of children from violence and abuse. To date, 31 countries have passed laws with full prohibition of corporal punishment, and many others have some degree of legislation that protects children. Efforts to revise laws and seek formal sanctions against parents and caregivers are essential and provide a legal framework. However, as in the case of many commonly held beliefs and practices, the passage of laws alone is not sufficient. Legislation or attempts to shift legal norms require similar and parallel efforts in the realm of social norms. Policies with a broad mandate to reduce poverty and community violence would likely have greater long-term impacts if they also included explicit and focused attention on the prevention of fear, anxiety, and the impact of toxic stress in young children. Early childhood development child protection programs are most effective when developed and implemented through a systems approach that links the prevention work with program interventions when children are at risk or victims of child abuse. This includes ensuring that ECD laws and policies are comprehensive, so that child protection issues are adequately integrated, particularly regarding the protection against abuse and neglect. Policies can promote caregivers to earn an income while children attend ECD centers, particularly in the case of single parents. Centers are also particularly important to families with children with disabilities since the latter are able to receive specialized care, and families are better equipped to care for their children. It reduces the risk of placing children in residential care, which has been proven to be significantly harmful to the child's development in the early years. Social protection and cash transfers can also alleviate the economic burden of vulnerable families with young children.

In closing, for too many children, home is far from a safe haven. Flagrant violation of young children often comes from the very social structures and institutions designed to care and protect them. Sadly, these acts of violence, exploitation, and abuse are rarely reported and investigated; few perpetrators are held accountable. Violence toward children is not limited by geography, ethnicity, or status; it is a global phenomenon, and one of the most pervasive human rights challenges of our time. As illustrated within this brief review, the lack of systematic program attention is a disheartening, yet valid, indicator of staggeringly limited national and global attention. Armed with increasing scientific and program evidence, and building on its country presence and program experience, UNICEF and its partners must now forge forward with greater systematic attention and commitment to this silent cry for help.

Acknowledgments

The authors would like to thank UNICEF colleagues from the field for the valuable inputs provided from their work in the area of child protection and early childhood development.

Notes

1. United Nations Convention on the Rights of the Child, adopted and opened for signature, ratification and accession on by the General Assembly Resolution on 44/25 of November 20, 1989.
2. In February 2011, the United Nations Committee on the Rights of the Child adopted General Comment 13 on Article 19—the right of the child to freedom from all forms of violence. General Comment 13 aims to provide guidance to states in understanding and complying with their obligations under Article 19 in a manner that is holistic, coordinated, and accelerated.
3. See http://www2.ohchr.org/english/law/crc.htm
4. See http://www.unicef.org/about/who/index_mission.html.
5. The UN Study on Violence against Children noted that infants under 1 year of age face around three times the risk of homicide than do children aged 1–4 and twice the risk of those aged 5–14.
6. For younger children aged 0–8, specific interventions are less common although increasing, as the links between early intervention to prevent and protect children from violence are becoming clearer and child welfare systems are strengthened, thus making them better able to respond and identify children at risk. For example, in this age group, the improvement of birth registration is supported as a critical and key activity. This is a fundamental and basic human right and is often seen as the foundation for accessing other rights and services. UNICEF supports birth registration within the context of an overall child protection system, and as part of civil registration. UNICEF's strategic actions are geared toward strengthening systems in order to reduce the obstacles to the

registration of every child. In 2010, UNICEF carried out birth registration programming activities in approximately 70 countries, with the majority in West and Central Africa (WCARO), Eastern Southern Africa (ESARO), and in the Latin America and Caribbean region (TACRO).

7. Information provided from the UNICEF Chile County Office.

References

Administration for Children and Families. (2011). *Strengthening families and communities: 2011 resource guide.* Washington, DC: Author.

Al-Hassan, S.M., & Lansdown, J. E (2010). *Evaluation of the Better Parenting Initiative in Jordan.* New York: UNICEF.

Appel, A. E., & Holden, G. (1998). The co-occurrence of spousal and physical child abuse. A review and appraisal. *Journal of Family Psychology, 12*(4), 578–599.

Belsky, J. (1993). Etiology of child maltreatment: A developmental-ecological analysis. *Psychological Bulletin, 114,* 413–434.

Bowlby, J. (1969). *Attachment and loss: Volume I: Attachment.* New York: Basic Books.

Brown, B., & Bzostek, S. (2003). *Violence in the lives of children. Cross currents issue I.* New York: Child Trends.

Center for the Study of Social Policy. (2003). *Protective factors literature review: Early care and education programs and the prevention of child abuse and neglect.* Washington, DC: Author.

Chalk, R., & King, R. A. (1998). Family violence and family violence interventions. In *Violence in families: Assessing prevention and treatment programs* (pp. 31–58). Washington, DC: National Academy Press; National Research Council.

Chu, A., & Lieberman, A. (2010). Clinical implications of traumatic stress from birth to age five. *Annual Review of Clinical Psychology, 6,* 469–494.

Feigelson, M. (2011). Preventing violence in young children's lives: A priority for our Foundation. Editorial in *Early childhood matters* (pp. 1–7). The Hague: Bernard van Leer Foundation.

Fox, N. A., & Shonkoff, J. (2011). How persistent fear and anxiety can affect young children's learning, behavior, and health. In *Early childhood matters (pp. 8–14). The Hague: Bernard van Leer Foundation.*

Gilbert, R., Kemp, A., Thoburn, J., Sidebotham, P., Radford, L., & Glaser, D. (2009). Child maltreatment 2: Recognizing and responding to child maltreatment. *The Lancet, 373* (9658), 167–180.

Goldman, J., Salus, M., & Wolcott, D. (2003). *A coordinated response to child abuse and neglect. The foundation for practice.* Washington DC: Office of Child Abuse and Neglect (HHS).

Hertzman, C., Vaghri, Z., & Arkadas-Thibert, A. (2013). Monitoring progress toward the fulfillment of rights in early childhood under the Convention on the Rights of the Child to improve outcomes for children and families. In P. R. Britto, P. L. Engle, & C. M. Super (Eds.), *Handbook of early childhood development research and its impact on global policy* (Chapter 19). New York: Oxford University Press.

Kotch, J. B., Browne, D. C., Ringwalt, C. L., Stewart, P. W., Ruina, E., Holt, K., et al. (1995). Risk of child abuse or neglect in a cohort of low-income children. *Child Abuse and Neglect, 19*(9), 1115–1130.

Lieberman, A., & Van Horn, P. (2008). Coping with danger: The stress-trauma continuum. In A. Lieberman & P. Van Horn (Eds.), *Psychotherapy with infants and young children: Repairing the effects of stress and trauma on early attachment* (pp. 35–63). New York: Guilford Press.

Margolin, G. (1998). Effects of witnessing violence on children. In P. Trickett & C. Schellenbach (Eds.), *Violence against children in the family and the community* (pp. 57–101). Washington, DC: American Psychological Association.

Mikton, C. (2011). Doing children more good than harm. *Early childhood matters* (pp. 15–22*)*. The Hague: Bernard van Leer Foundation.

National Scientific Council on the Developing Child. (2007). *The science of early childhood development.* Cambridge, MA: Center on the Developing Child, Harvard University. Retrieved from developingchild.net/pubs/persp/pdf/Science_Early_Childhood_Development.pdf

National Scientific Council on the Developing Child. (2010). *Persistent fear and anxiety can effect young children's learning and development.* Working Paper No. 9. Cambridge, MA: Center on the Developing Child, Harvard University. Retrieved from www.developingchild.net

Pereda, N., Guilera, G., Forns, S., & Gomex-Benito, J. (2009). The international epidemiology of child sexual abuse: A continuation of Finkelhor (1994). *Child Abuse and Neglect, 33,* 331–342.

Pinheiro, P. S. (2006). *World report on violence against children: United Nations Secretary General's study on violence against children.* New York: United Nations.

Pollard, J., Hawkins, J., & Arthur, M. (1999). Risk and protection: Are both necessary to understand diverse behavioral outcomes in adolescence? *Social Work Research, 23*(3), 145–158.

Uganda Ministry of Education and Sports. (2007). *The Early Childhood Development (ECD) Policy.* Kampala: Department of the Pre-primary and Primary Education.

UNICEF. (2005a). *Innocenti insight: Involving capacities of the child.* Florence: UNICEF Innocenti Research Center.

UNICEF. (2005b). *UN human rights standards and mechanisms to combat violence against children: A contribution to the UN Study Secretary-General's Study on Violence against Children.* Florence: UNICEF Innocenti Research Center.

UNICEF. (2006a). *Behind closed doors: The impact of domestic violence on children.* New York: UNICEF, Child Protection.

UNICEF. (2006b). *Programming experiences in early child development.* New York: UNICEF, Program Division.

UNICEF. (2006c). *Evaluation report: Evaluation of the Family Support and Foster Care Project (FS&FC) and Prevention of Infant Abandonment and Deinstitutionalization Project (PIAD)—Georgia.* Tbilisi, Georgia: UNICEF, Regional Office for CEE/CIS.

UNICEF. (2006d). Better parenting program. In *Early childhood matters.* The Hague: Bernard van Leer Foundation.

UNICEF. (2007). *Implementation handbook for the Convention on the Rights of the Child.* Geneva: UNICEF.

UNICEF. (2008). *Child protection strategy.* E/ICEF/2008/5/Rev.1

UNICEF. (2010a). *Child disciplinary practices at home. Evidence from a range of low and middle income countries.* New York: UNICEF, Division of Policy and Practice.

UNICEF. (2010b). *National survey on early childhood care and development: Family knowledge, attitudes and practice.* Chisinau, Moldova: UNICEF.

U.S. Department of Health and Human Services. (2002). *Child maltreatment: 2000.* Washington, DC: Administration on Children, Youth, and Families.

U.S. Department of Health and Human Services. (2007). *Administration for children youth and families.* Washington, DC: Author. Retrieved from acf.hhs.gov/programs/cb/pubs/cm07/cm07.pdf

WHO & IPSCAN. (2006). *Prevention child maltreatment: A guide to taking action and generating evidence.* Geneva: WHO

World Health Organization (WHO). (2002). *World report on violence and health.* Geneva: World Health Organization.

World Health Organization (WHO). (2009). Violence prevention the evidence: Changing cultural and social norms that support violence. *Violence Prevention Briefings,* 1–15.

World Health Organization (WHO). (2010). *Child maltreatment. Fact sheet: 150.* Geneva: WHO.

13

Social Protection and Welfare Systems

IMPLICATIONS FOR EARLY CHILDHOOD DEVELOPMENT

Lawrence Aber, Linda Biersteker, Andrew Dawes, and Laura Rawlings

Destitution, low and unpredictable household income, and vulnerability to external shocks like economic crises, famines, natural disasters, and chronic illness have serious negative effects on parents' and caretakers' abilities to promote children's health and overall development. These challenges are concentrated in low-income countries (and in low-income regions of middle- and high-income countries) and are most threatening in the early childhood phase of life, during which rapid development of neurobiological, cognitive/language, and social/emotional domains are especially open to the influence of experiences and environments, both positive and negative.

Efforts to address early childhood development (ECD) issues through policies and programs have largely been undertaken as part of overall efforts in health and education systems, although often at their margins. There has been comparatively little thinking about how to build effective early childhood policies and practices in the sphere most directly responsible for addressing issues of destitution, poverty, and risk management—the social protection and welfare system. The resulting situation is that an undesirable (and unnecessary) gap exists between traditional policies in social protection, health, and education and the need to make specific provision for early childhood.

To help close this gap and enhance the interest and ability of social protection systems to effectively address serious constraints on ECD caused by long-term poverty, income instability, and adverse shocks, this chapter has three goals: (1) to describe the recent history and multiple functions of social protection and explain their importance to ECD, (2) to identify critical challenges to and promising practices in closing the gap between social protection and early childhood development, and (3) to analyze and discuss a few key issues requiring new research initiatives (research agenda) and/or immediate cross-system collaboration (policy agenda) in order to advance the capacity of social protection systems to protect and promote ECD.

Social Protection and Its Importance to Early Childhood Development

Social protection systems have a long history and vary considerably in their focus, design, and operation, both across countries and regions of the world and across different policy eras (Midgley, 1997). For example, in most high-income countries, a rich array of policy approaches had been developed by the second half of the 20th century, including cash assistance to the poor, social insurance for the recently unemployed and elderly, and various social service and labor force strategies. By contrast, in most low-income countries, a much narrower range of approaches were in place during that same era. For instance, subsidizing retail food prices to ensure that all citizens (including the very poorest) could avoid starvation was the dominant strategy in Africa in the 1960s and 1970s (Ellis, Devereaux, & White, 2009). It was not until the 1980s and 1990s that a much broader set of strategies began to emerge, driven by a deeper understanding of economic vulnerability, both its causes and its consequences (Chambers, 1989; Sen, 1981). What all these strategies share across time and country is a common objective: to reduce economic and social vulnerability, particularly of the poor and marginalized.

To better understand differences among various social protection systems, it is useful to distinguish among three primary functions: (1) to *protect* minimally acceptable levels of consumption, especially of necessities like food and shelter; (2) to *prevent* people already vulnerable to adverse events and shocks from becoming even more vulnerable; and (3) to *promote* people's ability to become less vulnerable in the future (Guhan, 1994). Each of these functions of social protection systems has special relevance to ECD.

Protection

Research in high-income countries and also in middle- and low-income countries document the clear negative influence of poverty and low household consumption on health and development in early childhood (Aber, Bennett, Li, & Conley, 1997; Taylor, Dearing, & McCartney, 2004; Walker et al., 2007). In addition, a gap in health and development among low-, middle-, and high-income children emerges in the first 3 years of life and continues to grow throughout childhood (Naudeau, Martinez, Premand, & Filmer, 2011). Therefore, protecting households with young children from poverty, hunger, food insecurity, and the stress associated with poverty and insecurity is vital to promoting health and development, especially in the earliest years of life, and is among the most promising and cost-effective investments that can be made in human development (Heckman, 2006; Heckman & Masterov, 2007).

Prevention

Children in lower income households not only fall behind very early in life in their physical health and cognitive, social, and emotional development, they and their families are also more vulnerable to adverse events (like loss of a job, chronic illness, or death of a parent) and to external shocks (like famines, epidemics, natural disasters, armed conflict, and economic recessions) (Friedman & Sturdy, 2011; De Walque, 2011). In both the developing and developed world, very poor families are forced to consume limited assets vital to the future (e.g., seed corn, next month's rent) in order to cope with the emergency of an adverse event or external shock. This process (which can take many forms in different economies and cultures) increases the household's vulnerability in the future. By providing households with the means to cope with adverse events (such as parental illness that results in job loss) and external shocks (such as a severe recession or natural disaster) that do not require them to exhaust their vital assets for the future and allow them to smooth consumption over time, social protection systems can serve an important function in preventing both present poverty and future vulnerability. A growing body of evidence in the developing (and developed) world clearly shows that strategies that prevent household vulnerability to adverse events and external shocks have especially positive impacts on children's health (e.g., stunting) and development (e.g., cognitive development), especially in the earliest years when they and their families are most vulnerable (Friedman & Sturdy, 2011; De Walque, 2011).

Promotion

Historically, social protection systems focus first on the protection and prevention functions and appear to arrive at the promotion function later in their histories. Indeed, a major focus over the last two decades of welfare reform (in high-income countries) and the reform of social protection systems (in middle- and low-income countries) has been to design programs and systems that advance human capital development, asset accumulation, and skills as key aspects to promoting productivity, as well as protection and prevention (Aber & Rawlings, 2011). A growing number of social protection schemes are designed to link cash assistance for poor adults (including for parents of very young children) to job training and/or work requirements (U.S. and U.K.) and/or to documented parent investments in children's human capital development (as in holistic conditional cash transfer [CCT] strategies, especially in Latin America, but increasingly in South Asia and Africa as well). These changes appear to be driven both by the goal of enabling poor parents (with training and work requirements) and poor children (with investments in health, nutrition, and education) to become less vulnerable to chronic poverty, adverse events, and external shocks and by an ethos of co-responsibility of both the poor and the state. Research to date suggests that such human capital promotion strategies can have positive effects, but depend on how the strategy is designed and implemented (Fiszbein & Schady, 2009). Recent studies conducted in the Latin American region have indicated the promise of CCTs in improving young children's cognitive, emotional, language, and fine motor development (Naudeau et al., 2011).

Transformation

A fourth function of social protection has emerged over the last few decades among some scholars (Devereux & Sabates-Wheeler, 2004); governments (e.g., South Africa); and advocates (e.g., Oxfam). This *transformative function* advances social justice through building the rights and empowerment of the poor and vulnerable. The relevance of the transformative function of social protection to child development is most apparent in the passage and implementation of the United Nations (UN) Convention on the Rights of the Child (CRC). The signatories of the CRC (currently, all countries in the world except the United States and Somalia) are obligated to advance the best interests of the child (Article 3) and to "ensure to the maximum extent possible the survival and development of the child" (Article 6).

Other articles of the CRC also have implications for nations' social protection systems and their impact on early childhood development. Article 26 instructs state parties to "recognize for every child the right to benefit from social security . . . ." Article 27 commits state parties to "recognize the right of every child to a standard of living adequate for the child's physical, mental, spiritual, moral and social development." Further, "State Parties, in accordance with national conditions and within their means, shall take appropriate measures to assist parents and others responsible for the child to implement this right and shall in the case of need provide material assistance and support programs, particularly with regard to nutrition, clothing and housing." At a minimum, these four articles appear to establish children's rights to basic necessities required for their survival and their physical and mental development. Another article of the CRC critical to social protection is Article 4, in which state parties are obligated to "undertake all appropriate legislative, administrative and other measures for the implementation of the rights recognized in the present Convention. With regard to economic, social and cultural rights, State Parties shall undertake such measures to the maximum extent of their available resources and, where needed, within the framework of international cooperation." Together, Articles 3, 4, 6, 26, and 27 provide a strong basis for implementing an adequate social protection system, especially for early childhood, when threats to survival and development are most acute.

Philosophical Bases for Strongly Focusing Social Protection on Early Childhood

These four functions of social protection systems are rooted in part in different philosophical bases for action. The protection and prevention functions are both rights- and needs-based; the promotion function is both rights- and capabilities-based; and the transformational function is rights-based. There is considerable debate both within and across the countries of the world about which philosophical bases and values should motivate and direct policy and social action on behalf of poor households, including those households with young children.

In the context of this chapter, what is most compelling is not these differences in philosophy, as important as they are. Rather, we wish to emphasize that all four perspectives offer a basis for strongly focusing social protection on early childhood, which provides the opportunity to enhance the survival, health, and development of young children. More generally, children in the first 5 years of life have the greatest needs that they can't meet on their own. Prevention strategies have the greatest effect when focused on early childhood. Promotion strategies focused on early childhood show the greatest returns on investment in human capital development. And the most fundamental human right, the right to survival (Article 6 of the CRC), is at highest risk in early childhood. (See extensive literatures on infant and under-5 mortality in Rajaratnam et al. [2010].) Although all four philosophical bases for social protection would prioritize early childhood, a giant gap persists between rationale and concrete action. Social protection systems are not designed with special emphasis on early childhood. Fortunately, there is a growing realization of this problem in many places. Although aligning social protection and early childhood programs and policies entails many challenges, it also presents many opportunities.

Aligning Social Protection and Early Childhood Programs and Policies: The South Africa Case

Up to this point, we've argued quite generally and abstractly about the various functions of social protection systems and their special relevance to early childhood health and development. We've also suggested that country-specific patterns of emphasis across the four functions of social protection are rooted in different histories of and philosophical bases for action on behalf of the poor and vulnerable. But these various patterns are also rooted in widely varying country contexts concerning conditions of children, social compacts regarding the enhancement of children's rights and social welfare policy, and economic conditions and financial resources. To realize the benefits of focusing the social protection system on ECD requires country-specific strategies to bring social protection and early childhood systems into optimal alignment (see Box 13.1).

In this section, we present one country as a case illustration to highlight critical challenges to and promising practices in closing the gap between social protection and early childhood systems. We focus on South Africa, a middle-income country that is one the most economically unequal in the world. South Africa commits

BOX 13.1 Country-Specific Strategies to Bring the Social Protection and Early Childhood Systems into Optimal Alignment Depend on Country-Specific:

1. Conditions of children and families;
2. Economic conditions and resources;
3. Relative emphasis on protection, prevention, promotion, transformation;
4. Orientation to the enhancement of children's rights; and
5. Politics of social welfare policy

more public funds to social protection than any country in Sub-Saharan Africa. And it anchors its commitment to the social protection of children via incorporation of the CRC into its national constitution. South Africa faces a unique set of challenges and opportunities to more effectively align social protection and early childhood programs and policies.

In South Africa, the Bill of Rights establishes the right of *all* (regardless of age) to "a) health care, including reproductive health care; b) sufficient food and water; and c) social security, including if they are unable to support themselves and their dependents, appropriate social assistance."

The Role of Cash Transfers

The Bill specifically protects children's rights to nutrition, shelter, basic health care, and social services. It is on this basis that, since 1998, the unconditional cash transfer, the *Child Support Grant* (CSG), has been provided to means-tested[1] caregivers (not necessarily the biological parent). Recognizing the importance of social protection in early childhood, the grant initially targeted caregivers with children under 7 years of age (Hall, 2009; Lund, 2008; Lund, Noble, Barnes, & Wright, 2009). The age of eligibility has increased as the social protection system has expanded, and, in 2011, all children are now eligible for the CSG (R270 per child per month, about US$38). Recent data (April, 2011) indicate that 64% of children under age 5 and the same proportion of those under 9 years are in receipt of the grant (data provided by the South African Social Security Agency in June 2011). It is estimated that about 64% of South Africa's children live in households that are in the poorest 40% of the income distribution. However, the relative poverty line is not identical to the means-tested income level for eligibility. Using 2007 data, it is estimated that only 71% of children who were eligible were accessing the grant. (http://www.childrencount.ci.org.za/indicator.php?id=2&indicator=10).   More recent analyses are not available.

Studies of the impact of the CSG are limited, but there are indications of its positive contribution to the well-being of young children (Budlender & Woolard, 2006; Case, Hosegood, & Lund, 2005). Specifically, Delany et al. (2008) report that access to the grant improves growth status in early childhood, and that crèche or preschool attendance among beneficiaries is higher than among nonbeneficiaries assessed in the same areas. However, further research (Agüero, Carter, & Woolard, 2009) indicates that the CSG only has a positive impact on growth status if the child receives the benefit for *at least 50%* of the first 36 months of life (when neurological development is particularly likely to be compromised by undernutrition). This evidence suggests that the timing and duration of grant access is crucial for maximizing its benefits for growth and neurological development in early childhood.

Although there are many successes in South Africa's unconditional cash transfer policy (the most important being a degree of poverty alleviation), Lund et al. (2009) point to significant administrative and bureaucratic challenges that have hampered equitable access. Like many other countries, South Africa is striving to find ways for its social protection system to serve not only protection and prevention functions, but also promotion functions. Hence, the call by some in the country to consider additional cash assistance to poor households with children (over and above the CSG) but conditioned on family investments in children's health and education. Regarding the advisability of implementing CCTs in South Africa, Lund and colleagues (2009) point to significant supply-side challenges that would hamper recipients' abilities to comply with conditionalities. Conditioning upon access to preschool programs would not be possible because these programs levy fees,[2] thereby excluding the poorest children. A mere 30% of children under 5 have access to out of home care of any kind (Statistics South Africa, 2009). Where formal ECD center for under-5s and public school access exist for under-5s, quality is often poor, making it less likely that the positive educational outcomes expected by children and parents alike will be achieved (Centre for Education Policy Development, 2008; Western Cape Department of Social Development, 2010).

More broadly, CCTs that are designed to promote the health, development, and well-being of young children and tied to the use of ECD services are not likely to function effectively in settings in which supply-side factors place obstacles in the way of parents who are attempting to comply with the conditions, or where the services that are conditioned are of such poor quality that the child receives limited benefit from attendance.

The Role of Other Benefits, Services, and Support

Cash transfers alone, whether unconditional or conditional, will not be sufficient to reduce the impact of poverty conditions on young children. Universal free access to health care is a strategy that is increasingly applied (UNESCO, 2010), and one that is simpler to administer than exemptions for targeted groups (Mkandiwire, 2005). Furthermore, even if health facilities are free and are sufficiently staffed and equipped, access can be a challenge if transport is inaccessible or too costly. Such initiatives in South Africa targeted on early childhood include access to free health care for pregnant women and children under 6 years and school nutrition programs for 5-year-olds in the public schooling system. A poverty-targeted subsidy for children under 5 years of age is provided to nonprofit ECD centers. The subsidy is largely intended to cover feeding, but is also used in some facilities to contribute to operational costs. A recent study indicates that the subsidy does not contribute to the quality of the learning program (Western Cape Department of Social Development, 2010).

Measures that aim to improve household well-being, although not specifically targeting young children, may also reduce risks and support the well-being of this age group. For example, availability of potable water reduces the risk of illnesses such as diarrhea in young children (Saloojee & Bamford, 2006). Unsafe energy sources, such as paraffin, wood, and coal, used by large numbers of households are associated with an increased risk of acute respiratory infections and burns (Barnes, Mathee, Thomas, & Bruce, 2009; Sanders, et al., 2007) and paraffin poisoning (Van der Merwe & Dawes, 2007). South Africa provides *all* households with a basic quota of subsidized electricity and potable water in areas where these services are in place. Where a household uses more than the quota, fees are levied.

It is, of course, necessary that families have the information to access the available services and assistance, and community workers can play an important role in this regard (Budlender, 2008). Early childhood development community outreach workers in South Africa, some of whom are subsidized by government, play an important role as "weavers of safety nets" for families with young children by providing information on social security and other child services, as well as by offering psychosocial support to vulnerable caregivers (Biersteker, 2007; Ndingi, Biersteker, & Schaffer, 2008). Box 13.2 summarizes lessons learned from South Africa's efforts to align social protection and ECD programs.

BOX 13.2 Lessons Learned from South African Case

1. Cash assistance to poor families of young children can improve their health and development and increase their use of preschool and school.
2. It is possible to first target cash assistance on families of a nation's youngest children and then expand over time to include assistance to older children (via progressive realization).
3. Although it is possible to scale up cash transfer programs targeted on early childhood quite rapidly, it is also necessary to continue to reduce the administrative and other obstacles that many families face in accessing grants.
4. Cash transfers alone, whether unconditional or conditional, are not sufficient to reduce the impact of poverty on young children. Other benefits, services, and supports are essential.
5. Poor families benefit from clear, simple information about accessing cash transfer grants and other benefits and services. Outreach workers can play a critical role in effectively linking cash assistance with other health, education, and social services.

Developing Usable Knowledge About Social Protection and Early Childhood Development: Toward an Action Research Agenda

Over the last two decades, the knowledge base on how adverse events and external shocks affect children's health and development has grown rapidly (Alderman, 2011; Shonkoff, 2010). So, too, has our knowledge of effective early childhood interventions, both in the developed and developing worlds (Anderson et al., 2003; Karoly, Kilburn, & Cannon, 2005; Engle et al., 2007). But the knowledge base on (a) specific social protection policies effective at promoting ECD among poor and vulnerable families and (b) the optimal alignment among social protection and other programs and policies have grown at a slower pace. Two large and pressing questions should be at the center of a research agenda on social protection and early child development over the next decade.

Priority 1: Building Cost-Effective, Scalable Social Protection Approaches to Early Childhood Development

Which social protection programs, policies and strategies are most effective in promoting early childhood health and development? And, among those effective strategies, which are most scalable in the countries and regions of the world with the greatest need?

Fortunately, questions of intervention effectiveness are increasingly the focus of rigorous experimental and quasi-experimental research by both major international organizations (e.g., the World Bank's work on Conditional Cash Transfers [Fiszbein & Schady, 2009] and their ECD impact evaluation program) and university-based researchers (for example, Engle et al. 2007). Stage 1 efficacy trials are valuable starting points; but to address the scope of the global challenge, it is critical to move to effectiveness studies that focus on questions of scalability and sustainability. Until the issue of how to adapt effective social protection programs, especially cash transfer programs, to new countries and contexts is addressed, these programs cannot be scaled at population and policy levels.

A host of important specific questions should be addressed within this priority. How large must cash transfers be to have the optimal positive impacts on ECD, but without inducing untoward effects (e.g., reduced labor force effort)? What mechanisms are the best delivery systems for cash transfers in low-income countries? What impact do cash transfers have on other domains of development besides health and early learning (e.g., child abuse/neglect)?

Priority 2: Aligning Multisectoral Approaches to Early Childhood Development

How should social protection programs, policies, and strategies (especially cash transfers) be aligned with other health, education, and social welfare programs, policies, and strategies to achieve optimal benefit for young children? As the South African case example illustrated, alignment is a critical issue. But, as noted at the start of this chapter, the social protection system and other systems (notably health, education, and social welfare services) are rarely coordinated to optimal effect. When institutional coordination (for example between a local health and welfare service) does not work well, it is essential to find ways of linking children and their families to the services they require, in order to address the risks associated with early childhood. Otherwise, these risks will conspire to keep an estimated 200 million children in the developing world from reach their development potential through stunting, iron deficiency, iodine deficiency, and lack of cognitive and social-emotional stimulation (Grantham-McGregor et al., 2007).

A better understanding of the relationship between the social protection system (especially cash transfers) and the social welfare service system has been the focus of policy attention and research recently (Department for International Development, United Kingdom, 2009; Greenberg, 2009; Richter, 2009). It has generated a useful research agenda (see Giese, Greenberg, & Scherr, 2009). Similar agendas on the relationship of social protection to health and education are also needed. Specific foci of new research should include the role of community/outreach workers in linking access to cash transfers with critical health, education, and social grants and services; the impact of cash transfers on other domains of early childhood besides health (e.g., abuse/neglect); whether and how improving the supply (both quantity and quality) of health, education, and social services increases the effectiveness of cash transfers in improving ECD; and how to combine services to reach optimal combinations of needed early childhood interventions (Sherr et al., 2009).

Finally, mounting a robust action research agenda on social protection and ECD will require the cooperation of a large and complex global network of researchers, policymakers, and practitioners. Best practices in facilitating exchange across the research, policy, and program sectors must be identified and implemented for this ambitious research agenda to succeed.

Transforming Social Protection Systems to Promote Early Childhood Development: Toward a Policy Agenda

This chapter has presented a case for including ECD as a social protection priority, provided one country case example of how this is being done operationally, and argued for a strong research agenda. However, a prerequisite for implementing any part of this agenda is to position ECD as a policy priority—and this is a particularly challenging task. (See Box 13.3.)

Early childhood development policy can be thought of as a societal "tragedy of the commons," rooted in a market failure that has been persistently difficult to address, perhaps due to children's lack of voice and agency. There is a clear rationale for engaging the state in helping families and societies address gaps in ECD, given the returns to early childhood investments and the philosophical bases for action. The challenge, from a policy perspective, is that traditional actors in public

BOX 13.3 Priorities for Research and Policy Agendas for Social Protection and Early Childhood Development

RESEARCH PRIORITIES

- Moving from efficacy trials to effectiveness, scalability, and sustainability trials of innovative cash transfers (and other social protection) strategies to enhance early childhood health and development
- Identifying the optimal alignment of social protection strategies with health, education, and social services strategies to advance early childhood development

POLICY PRIORITIES

- Knowledge sharing and informed action
- Strong public-sector champions for prioritizing early childhood development within social protection
- Introduce and strengthen early childhood interventions in social protection, health, and education

policy (health ministries, education ministries, and social protection programs) who would be best positioned to address the market failure often do not consider ECD work as part of their mandate. The main challenge is therefore not only to find which programs will be effective and scalable (the research agenda outlined above), but to find the proper policy mandate and institutional home for these programs. The solutions to these policy challenges will vary across countries, but there are nonetheless some areas that can be useful to consider in moving the policy agenda forward.

A first area of action concerns knowledge sharing and informed advocacy, highlighting to policymakers (particularly among those in the treasury departments) and citizens the need for ECD approaches to be considered as part of an effective approach to social and economic policy broadly, and social protection specifically, with respect to each of its core functions of prevention, protection, and promotion, drawing from the evidence and appealing to rights. Second, although ECD encompasses a multisectoral agenda, it is essential that there be strong political will to both budget for and implement ECD policy. It can very useful to have a strong public sector champion with a well-developed institutional home, which can serve as a point of entry for prioritizing ECD. A third area of action is to introduce and strengthen early childhood interventions in larger programs, be they traditional social protection and welfare programs or health and education programs. This can be both practical, by building on existing institutional capacity, as well as efficient, given the contributions that ECD has with respect to human development outcomes. Early childhood interventions in health and nutrition programs increase children's health outcomes and chances of survival. Interventions in early stimulation and formal education programs prepare children for school, enhance the likelihood of good progress, and ultimately improve their life chances.

This analysis and its recommendations come together in a clarion call for building effective ECD systems and for ensuring that these systems are strongly focused on children at risk. A strong case exists for prioritizing access among vulnerable young children precisely because this is where lack of access is concentrated and the consequences of poverty and vulnerability on early childhood outcomes are most impactful.

Authors' Note

The findings, interpretations, and conclusions are those of the authors and do not necessarily reflect the views of the institutions with which they are affiliated.

Notes

1. The 2011 monthly income for a single parent is less than R2,500 (about US$360) per month; for a couple, it is less than R5,000 per month.
2. The South African state does not provide preschool programs. These are run as private businesses or nonprofit organizations. Both charge fees (Biersteker & Dawes, 2008).

References

Aber, J. L., Bennett, N. G., Li, J., & Conley, D. C. (1997). The effects of poverty on child health and development. *Annual Review of Public Health, 18,* 463–438.

Aber, J. L., & Rawlings, L. B. (2011). *North-south knowledge sharing on incentive-based conditional cash transfer programs.* SP discussion paper No. 1101. Washington, DC: World Bank.

Agüero, J. M., Carter, M. R., & Woolard, I. (2009). The impact of unconditional cash transfers on nutrition: The South African Child Support Grant.

Alderman, H. (Ed.). (2011). *No small matter: The impact of poverty, shocks, and human capital investments in early childhood development.* Washington, DC: World Bank.

Anderson, L., Shinn, C., Fullilove, M., Scrimshaw, S., Fielding, J., Normand, J., et al. (2003). The effectiveness of early childhood development programs: A systematic review. *American Journal of Preventive Medicine, 24*(3), 32–46.

Barnes, B., Mathee, A., Thomas, E., & Bruce, N. (2009). Household energy, indoor air pollution and child respiratory health in South Africa. *Journal of Energy in Southern Africa, 20*(1), 4–13.

Biersteker, L. (2007). *Rapid assessment and analysis of innovative community and home-based childminding and ECD programs in support of poor and vulnerable babies and young children in South Africa.* Pretoria: UNICEF South Africa.

Biersteker, L., & Dawes, A. (2008). Early childhood development. In A. Kraak & K. Press (Eds.), *Human resources development review 2008. Education, employment and skills in South Africa* (pp. 185–205). Cape Town: HSRC Press.

Budlender, D. (2008). *Feasibility and appropriateness of attaching behavioural conditions to a social support grant for children aged 15-17 years.* Report prepared for Department of Social Development. Johannesburg: Community Agency for Social Enquiry.

Budlender, D., & Woolard, I. (2006). *The impact of the South African child support and old age grants on children's' schooling and work.* International Program on the Elimination of Child Labour. Geneva: International Labour Office.

Case, A., Hosegood, V., & Lund, F. (2005). The reach and impact of the Child Support Grant in South Africa: Evidence from KwaZulu-Natal. *Development Southern Africa, 22*(4), 467–482.

Centre for Education Policy Development. (2008). *Technical assistance unit ECD grade r diagnostic project.* Inception Report, August 15, 2008. Pretoria: National Treasury Republic of South Africa.

Chambers, R. (1989). Editorial introduction: Vulnerability, coping and policy. *IDS Bulletin, 20*(2), 1–7.

Delany, A., Ismail, Z., Graham, L., & Ramkissoon, Y. (2008). *Review of the Child Support Grant: Uses, implementation and obstacles.* Johannesburg: Community Agency for Social Enquiry.

Department for International Development, United Kingdom, et al. (2009). *Advancing child-sensitive social protection: A joint statement.* London: Author. Retrieved from http://www.unicef.org/socialpolicy

Devereux, S., & Sabates-Wheeler, R. (2004). *Transformative social protection.* IDS working paper No. 232. Brighton, UK: Institute of Development Studies.

De Walque, D. (2011). Conflicts, epidemics and orphanhood: The impact of extreme events on the health and educational achievements of children. In H. Alderman (Ed.), *No small matter: The impact of shocks and human capital investments in early childhood development* (pp. 85–114). Washington, DC: World Bank.

Ellis, F., Devereaux, S., & White, P. (2009). *Social protection in Africa.* Cheltenham, UK.: Edward Elgar Publishing.

Engle, P. L., Black, M. M., Behrman, J. R., de Mello, M. C., Gertler, P. J., Kapiriri, L., et al. (2007). Strategies to avoid the loss of potential among 240 million children in the developing world. *The Lancet, 369*(January), 229–242.

Fiszbein, A., & Schady, N. (2009). *Conditional cash transfers: Reducing present and future poverty.* Washington, DC: World Bank Publications.

Friedman, J., & Sturdy, J. (2011). The influence of economic crisis on early childhood development: A review of pathways and measured impact. In H. Alderman (Ed.). *No small matter: The impact of shocks and human capital investments in early childhood development* (pp. 51–84). Washington, DC: World Bank.

Giese, S., Greenberg, A., & Sherr, L. (2009). Editorial: Spotlighting the relationship between social welfare services and cash transfers within social projection for children. *Vulnerable Children and Youth Studies: An International Interdisciplinary Journal for Research, Policy and Care, 4*(S1), 1–5.

Grantham-McGregor, S. M., Cheung, Y. B., Cueto, S., Glewwe, P., Richter, L.M., & Strupp, B.J. (2007). Over two hundred million children fail to reach their developmental potential in the first five years in developing countries. *The Lancet, 369*(January), 60–70.

Greenberg, A. (2009). Strengthening the social welfare sector: Expanding the reach and effectiveness of cash transfers. *Vulnerable Children and Youth Studies: An International Interdisciplinary Journal for Research, Policy and Care, 4*(S1), 81–85.

Guhan, S. (1994). Social security options for developing countries. *International Labor Review, 133*(1), 35–53.

Hall, K. (2009). Children's access to social assistance. In S. Pendlebury, L. Lake, & C. Smith (Eds.), *South African child gauge 2008/2009* (pp. 79–81). Cape Town: University of Cape Town Children's Institute.

Heckman, J. (2006). Skill formation and the economics of investing in disadvantaged children. *Science, 312*(5782), 1900–1902.

Heckman, J., & Masterov, D. (2007). The productivity argument for investing in young children. *Applied Economics Perspectives and Policy, 29*(3), 446–493.

Karoly, L. A., Kilburn, M. R., & Cannon, J. S. (2005). *Early childhood interventions: Proven results, future promise.* Santa Monica, CA: Rand Corporation.

Lund, F. (2008). *Changing social policy—The child support grant in South Africa.* Cape Town: HSRC Press.

Lund, F., Noble, M., Barnes, H., & Wright, G. (2009). Is there a rationale for conditional cash transfers for children in South Africa? *Transformation: Critical Perspectives on Southern Africa, 70,* 70–91.

Midgley, J. (1997). *Social welfare in a global context.* London: Sage.

Mkandiwire, T. (2005). *Targeting verses universalism in poverty reduction.* Social policy and development program paper No. 23. Geneva: UNRISD.

Naudeau, S., Martinez, S., Premand, P., & Filmer, D. (2011). Cognitive development in young children in low-income countries. In H. Alderman (Ed.), *No small matter: The impact of shocks and human capital investments in early childhood development* (pp. 9–50). Washington, DC: World Bank.

Ndingi, S., Biersteker, L., & Schaffer, A. (2008). *Scaling up early childhood development services (0–4 years): Illustrative cases of on the ground delivery models for holistic ECD services—formal, community and household.* Pretoria: Human Sciences Research Council.

Rajaratnam, J. K., Markus, J. R., Flaxman, A. D., Wang, H., Levin-Rector, A., et al. (2010). Neonatal, postneonatal, childhood and under-5 mortality for 187 countries, 1970–2010: A systematic analysis of progress towards Millennium Development Goal 4. *The Lancet, 375,* 1988–2008.

Richter, L. (2009). Can and should transfers be linked to social welfare? *Vulnerable Children and Youth Studies: An International Interdisciplinary Journal for Research, Policy and Care, 4*(S1), 72–76.

Saloojee, H., & Bamford, L. (2006). Key child health promotion and disease prevention programs. In P. Ijumba & A. Padarath (Eds.), *South African health review 2006* (pp. 181–202). Durban, SA: Health Systems Trust.

Sanders, D., Reynolds, L., Eley, B., Kroon, M., Zar, H., Davies, M. A., et al. (2007). *Western Cape burden of disease reduction project.* Final report Vol. 7. Decreasing the burden of childhood disease. Cape Town: Provincial Government of the Western Cape.

Sen, A. K. (1981). *Poverty and famines: An essay on entitlement and deprivation.* Oxford, UK: Clarendon Press; New York: Oxford University Press.

Sherr, L., Rodgers, A., Varrall, R., Mueller, J., & Adato, M. (2009). Examining ways in which contact opportunities associated with transfers might help identify vulnerable households and link them with social welfare services: A systematic review of the literature. *Vulnerable Children and Youth Studies: An International Interdisciplinary Journal for Research, Policy and Care, 4*(S1), 10–40.

Shonkoff, J. P. (2010). Building a new biodevelopmental framework to guide the future of early childhood policy. *Child Development, 81*(1), 357–367.

Statistics South Africa. (2009). *General household survey: Statistical release P0318*. Pretoria: Author.

Taylor, B., Dearing, E., & McCartney, K. (2004). Incomes and outcomes in early childhood. *Journal of Human Resources, 39*(4), 980–1007.

UNESCO. (2010). *Education for All monitoring report 2010: Reaching the marginalized*: Paris: Author.

Van der Merwe, A., & Dawes, A. (2007). Monitoring child unintentional and violence-related injury morbidity and mortality. In A. Dawes, R. Bray, & A. Van der Merwe (Eds.), *Monitoring child well-being. A South African rights-based approach* (pp. 129–146). Cape Town: HSRC Press.

Walker, S. P., Wachs, T. D., Gardner, J. M., Lozoff, B., Pollitt, E., & Carter, J. A. (2007). Child development: Risk factors for adverse outcomes in developing countries. *The Lancet, 369*(9556), 135–157.

Western Cape Department of Social Development. (2010). *Western Cape Department of Social Development 2009 audit of early childhood development facility quality*. Cape Town: Author. Retrieved December 10, 2010 from http://www.capegateway.gov.za/Text/2010/6/hsrc-qualitativeassessment-ecd-final_report-22-02-10.pdf

14

Community-Based Approaches to Early Childhood Development

A MATTER OF DEGREE

Jacqueline Hayden and Sithu Wai

Despite a significant increase in the number of early childhood development (ECD) national policies, the plans and delivery systems that operationalize ECD are not well developed in many majority world nations. There is a sound reason for this: National operational systems need to be supported by infrastructure, such as a legalized system for ensuring standards of delivery, qualified staff, monitoring mechanisms, appropriate settings, and other costly supports. Most governments in underresourced areas have difficulties prioritizing these expenditures.

In recent decades, nongovernmental organizations (NGOs) have been filling the gaps in provision and access to ECD. NGOs encompass a wide variety of sectors and organizations, including the independent sector, third sector, volunteer sector, civic society, grassroots organizations, private voluntary organizations, not-for-profit sector, transnational social movement organizations, grassroots social change organizations, and non-state actors (Hoffman & Zhao, 2008; Yanacopulos, 2008).

Programs that operate under the auspices of NGOs (such as philanthropic or religious organizations) rather than through a government department, are referred to as *community-based programs* (CBPs). Direct delivery of CBPs is often provided through *community-based organizations* (CBOs). "Community" is usually defined as a group of people with diverse characteristics who are linked by social ties, share common perspectives, and engage in joint action in geographical locations or settings (MacQueen et al., 2001). However, there are no clearly defined parameters for CBPs and CBOs. The literature suggests that programs in which providers and decision makers are from the same cultural, ethnic, geographical, and/or socioeconomic population as the users of the program are likely to fall under the rubric of "community-based." In some cases, CBPs are affiliated with governments through a designated role. Local committees and forums for women and children are examples of this structure. These groups define local goals and may oversee local programs, with some devolved government funds and concomitant reporting responsibilities. However, despite the government ties, these groups generally have relative autonomy over program development and delivery, and thus could be classified as CBPs.

Many benefits are associated with CBPs. Over and beyond augmenting provision and access, CBPs and CBOs are associated with increased participation by the target group in the development, management, and delivery of services. Participation is related to empowerment and enhanced efficacy of individuals and communities—and, concomitantly, to mobilization and influence on public and social policy making (Craig, 2002). However, some of the attributed benefits of CBPs could be negated through the mechanisms by which CBOs are developed and operate (Toomey, 2011).

This chapter discusses the issues related to community-based services and describes the interconnection between CBPs and effective early childhood service delivery.

The Rise of Community-Based Organizations: From Rescuing to Community Participation

In past decades, the concepts of aid and development were associated with the notion of *rescue*. The flow of assistance was seen to move in one direction— from richer nations to poorer nations. Implicit within assistance packages was the notion that the rescuers identified priorities and promoted those programs that they deemed to be in the best interest of the target populations and communities. Underresourced populations and contexts were seen to be monolithic and needy in similar ways. Thus, similar tactics could be applied universally (Toomey, 2011).

With all good intentions, rescuers in the form of aid agencies tended to reflect a hierarchical concept of development—whereby the helpers inflict their own ideas and approaches and devolve aid packages without much attention to context specifications (Daskon & Binns, 2010). Some analysts argue that aid, when distributed without an understanding of the experiences of the target population and context, facilitates inequities. Issues such as an urban–rural divide, the disempowerment of women, the exclusion of indigenous groups from service provision, and the tendency to cast segments of the population into narrow roles— such as victims and perpetrators—have been seen to be caused by early aid and development processes (Briggs, 2005). Further, the importation of goods, services, and technical "expertise" reduced the efficacy of communities and weakened local economies (Buxton, 2009; Yanacopulos, 2008).

Toomey provides an example of food security assistance to demonstrate some of the consequences of a rescuing approach to development:

By "rescuing" a hungry nation with imported food aid (where the threat of famine is not extreme), the Rescuer can decrease demand for food produced in the region with detrimental impacts to local and national farmers. Where demand decreases, local supply will follow, as returns on production become too low to justify farmers' investment in terms of time or resources. Thus, when the next famine occurs, there will be even fewer local supplies to abate the crisis, and starving people will be in even greater need of a *Rescuer* (Toomey, 2011, p. 184).

A similar story can be told for ECD or other services. Providing "foreign" goods (such as foreign materials, resources, and philosophical approaches to child care and education) can do much to undermine local confidence, capacity, and initiative (see Pence, 2013, Chapter 8, this volume).

By the mid-1970s, it was becoming apparent that well-meaning processes and activities developed by foreign governments, international NGOs, and other rescuers were failing to produce the desired effects of sustainability and efficacy. Indeed, it was feared that aid interventions might actually be working toward an opposing end, the *creation of dependency*. Analysts and donors recognized that even the best designed intervention could not succeed in a cultural vacuum and that the target population's ways of knowing and doing (including indigenous knowledge and practice) need to be incorporated if there is any chance for sustainable, meaningful community development (Daskon & Binns, 2010; Easterly, 2007; Kreuter, Lezin, & Young, 2000).

NONGOVERNMENTAL ORGANIZATIONS EMBRACE COMMUNITY-BASED PROGRAMS

In recent years, NGOs have changed their strategy from top-down assistance programs to CBPs that encourage participation in all aspects of development and delivery (Mansuri & Rao, 2004). NGOs are major players in introducing CBPs to developing countries and are credited with the importation of new ideas, techniques, and theories (Yanacopulos, 2008).

Participation is the hallmark of CBPs. Participation implies that the community (through representatives) has been involved in defining its own problems and needs. Indeed, the process of community problem identification is seen to be an outcome in itself. It is widely held that community agents who take part in exercises aimed at awareness raising and local problem identification simultaneously tend to develop enhanced capacity for solving those problems (Botchway, 2001; Kreuter et al., 2000).

However, problem awareness and solution identification can be complex. Communities may have insufficient awareness about potentialities and thus be unable to envision that a program gap exists. This is especially likely for programs that are unfamiliar or new, such as ECD interventions. Even when a program gap is identified, communities may not be sufficiently aware of options for filling the gap and/or may not be mobilized to initiate program development(s). For this reason, NGOs who are committed to community-based activity will step in to form committees, self-help groups, or local CBOs. These CBOs then become the vehicle for community representation and participation. It is common practice for NGOs to take it upon themselves to organize groups that become the CBO with whom they partner (Dongier et al., 2001).

Community-Based Early Childhood Development Programs

Officially, community-based ECD includes a range of holistic programs that respond to children's multiple developmental needs, build on and enhance traditional rearing practices, and empower community duty bearers, such as parents, health workers, and teachers, in ways that promote their ownership of ECD decisions, processes, and resources. Due to the holistic nature of ECD programs, they often overlap with health, nutrition, child rights, child protection, and similar services. Common community-based ECD programs address the needs of children from birth to school entry age, and target caregivers' support and awareness for enhancing the health, well-being, and development of young children, along with providing direct services to young children.

Because CBPs do not rely on government authorization, the range of services does not need to adhere to the limitations of ministerial and bureaucratic divisions such as health, education, and social welfare. Thus, community-based ECD programs are seen to be more likely to respond to direction from local needs. Although the specifics of community-based ECD programs vary between contexts, the goals and delivery options have similar characteristics. Some of the most common community-based ECD programs include caregiver education, support and awareness programs, home visiting, playgroups, child minding, preschools, and child-to-child programs. These are described below.

Caregiver Education, Support and Awareness Programs

Caregiver education programs provide an avenue through which information about children's development, including practical (context-specific) suggestions for caregivers on how to encourage growth and learning, are given. Programs are generally offered by trainers to small groups of caregivers and/or through the mass media, such as newspapers, magazines, radio, and television broadcasts. Health and hygiene messages are often included. Programs are frequently offered through health services or other community settings, such as schools.

Home Visiting Programs

Home visiting programs incorporate regularly scheduled visits by a support person to the home of one or a gathering of caregivers. The home visits follow a program and address specific goals, but also build in time for dealing with issues raised by the caregivers themselves.

Playgroups

Playgroup programs refer to informal gatherings for caregivers and children, often developed and run by a local organizer who has received some training on child development and other relevant topics. Usually, participants play active roles in determining the operations of the playgroup and in meeting its identified needs, such as providing a communal meal for attending children. Trained facilitators and/or health personnel visit the playgroups on a regular basis and may provide feeding supplements and/or other forms of support and advice.

Child Minding Programs

Formalized child minding programs involve an overarching agent or agency that provides training, monitoring, and support to caregivers who care for small groups of village children in their homes.

Preschools

Preschools are generally formal programs for children over the age of 3. Officially, preschools have a curriculum designed to enhance the readiness of children to transition into school settings. Thus, children in preschools are exposed to preliteracy and prenumeracy experiences, are taught communication and other skills for working in groups, and have opportunities to engage with school materials such as paper, pencils, books, and other items. Preschool programs are usually held in a setting that can house equipment, such as tables and chairs, toys, books, and outside play areas.

Child-to-Child Programs

Child-to-child programs provide training and support to older children who undertake action research projects related to local community issues. The older children engage in information dissemination and similar activities to enhance the health and well-being of younger children and peers within their communities.

Assessing Effectiveness of Community-Based Programs

Effectiveness studies are more prevalent in the area of public health, whereby community-based interventions are compared to a centralized clinical approach. The CBPs are found to be significantly more effective on several levels. Mbonye et al., for example, showed that community-based intermittent preventive treatment (IPT) of malaria in pregnancy was more effective and efficient in reducing preventable diseases than similar clinic-based programs. Besides significantly higher participation rates, the study also claimed that the community based approach induced peer influence, which made the program more acceptable to users and thus more sustainable (Mbonye, Bygbjerg, & Magnussen, 2008). Other comparative studies have shown the superiority of community-based IPTs over outreach services in terms of cure rate, reduced mortality, and general efficiency (Schiffman, Darmstadt, Agarwal, & Baqui, 2010; Zvavamwe & Ehlers, 2009).

However, beyond comparisons with clinical delivery services, few studies have evaluated the outcome of community-based interventions versus non–community-based interventions in the early childhood sector. Shiffman et al. suggest that community-based interventions face an evaluation barrier because community development outcomes emanate over a long period, whereas programs are accountable and need to show results within shorter timeframes (Schiffman et al., 2010). Similarly, the benefit of ECD programs for children, families, and communities can take years, decades, or generations to become apparent.

Despite a lack of comparative evidence about CBPs in the early childhood sector, there are well-documented studies from which implications about the strengths and weaknesses of CBPs can be drawn. These implications are described below.

COMMUNITY-BASED PROGRAM APPROACHES: THE STRENGTHS

It is generally acknowledged that interventions and programs that are initiated through community leadership have higher success rates than do government or other top-down programs (Botchway, 2001; Simpson, 2008). Compared to governmental bodies, CBOs are less bound by bureaucratic constraints and thus can be more fluid, flexible, and responsive to local changing issues. Institutionally, CBOs are more open to experimentation, without being bound by national political decision making (Yanacopulos, 2008). CBOs are deemed to be closer to the grassroots sector and thus more likely to incorporate local values and traditions into service provision than are centralized systems (Datta, 2007; Reimann, 2005).

Perhaps the most commonly reported benefit of CBPs and CBOs is the implicit participation of the program recipients. Multiple positive outcomes are associated with meaningful participation and control of programs by the population and the communities these programs and organizations serve.

Although the situation and context of health services differs from ECD goals and program features, the overarching conclusions from health research are that the participatory nature of community approaches enhances satisfaction, confidence, and self-control, and encourages personnel to commit themselves to high production goals (Schmid, Dolev, & Szabo-Lael, 2010).

Studies report that participation by the target population serves to increase feelings of moral attachment and ownership, which are associated with program sustainability (Amazigo et al., 2007; Gruen et al., 2008; Labonne & Chase, 2009). Other benefits of participation include the likelihood of enhanced inclusion;

effectiveness and efficiency; support for volunteerism, which underlies community cohesion and social capital; strengthened governance; and increased sustainability (Dongier et al., 2001). Further, participatory mechanisms of CBPs are seen to build community capacity and result in improved targeting (Fritzen, 2007), performance, accountability, and transparent monitoring mechanisms (Barrs, 2005; Fritzen, 2007).

Another benefit of CBPs is their widespread use of volunteers, not commonly found in government-run programs. Volunteers tend to come from the same population as the service users. They generally have good networking capacities and an understanding of and sensitivity to the community. Moreover, volunteers are not likely to move on; thus, they contribute continuity to programs. For these reasons, volunteers have been shown to make significant contributions to the effectiveness, efficiency, and sustainability of CBPs. Perhaps most importantly, volunteers enhance the cost effectiveness of CBPs although, in some cases, cost savings are related to low levels of training and other quality issues (Rao & Pearson, 2007).

COMMUNITY-BASED PROGRAMS: THE WEAKNESSES

A number of analysts are concerned that, beyond the positive goals of community-based approaches, programs can be mismanaged in ways that actually cause harm. Some attributes of CBPs that seem beneficial could, in fact, weaken community capacity and functioning and/or be damaging in other ways. These concerns are outlined below.

Participation May Not Be Representative

Participation is a right and a fundamental component of service delivery. Many scholars associate participation with empowerment as follows:

> Participation is about power and particularly about an increase in the power of the disadvantaged. It requires a capacity to identify those who are weaker and disenfranchised within a community and to empower them through shared knowledge and experience. (Rivera & Thomas-Slayter, 2009)

However, participation through representation is fraught with difficulties, especially when that participation is solicited by an external agent or agency. The participation of locals in development and decision making could be tokenistic, could unwittingly enhance exclusion of some groups, could undermine local systems and/or reinforce neglect by the state, and could reduce the efficacy of communities that become reliant on external resource allocations. For example, although volunteerism has been cited as a benefit associated with community-based service delivery, in reality, the use of community volunteers may bias participation toward a relatively elite population. Volunteer committees who advise and/or direct CBOs are often made up of local participants who have time for this endeavor, whereas the most burdened citizens are unlikely to spare potential wage earnings to engage in these and related activities. Meanwhile, it is not uncommon for different NGOs to be working in the same region or project area—and seeking committee members from the same pool. In these cases, a few key people from the community end up sitting on different committees and informing and participating in projects as varied as health, water and sanitation, food security, education, and children's services. This tendency to incorporate one segment of the population is known as *elite capture*. It refers to a situation whereby elites manipulate the decision-making arena and agenda and obtain most of the benefits of community-based services (Fritzen, 2007; Platteau, 2004; Wong, 2010).

In some cases, diverse representation does occur, but selected representatives are outnumbered by more highly educated or articulate members (frequently speaking in a language that is not well known). In these cases, there is a risk that voices and ideas from minority representation will not be heard—especially when the ideas differ from the majority of the participants.

In other cases, while forming a representative group and/or a CBO, NGOs may unwittingly disregard existing power relationships or may redistribute power in ways that privilege some groups—and thus undermine social and cultural systems. The significance of indigenous, traditional culture can be neglected or negated by this type of development strategy (Daskon & Binns, 2010).

Briggs reports that even when explicit attempts are made to incorporate indigenous knowledge systems, this is full of risks because of "problems emanating from a focus on the (arte)factual; binary tensions between western science and indigenous knowledge systems; the problem of differentiation and power relations; the romanticisation of indigenous knowledge; and the all too frequent decontextualisation of indigenous knowledge" (Briggs, 2005).

Conversely, some programs misunderstand the social processes of participation and consequently label some groups as socially excluded when they are not. Shortall relates the experience of farm families who opted not to participate in rural development programs: They do not see the point, and see them as competing with the farming industry. However, this does not mean they are excluded (Shortall, 2008). Similarly, Hayden et al. found that Aboriginal families had several reasons for not participating in accessible early childhood programs. Their nonparticipation was more a feature of their empowerment than their exclusion. Despite some pressure, they chose not to take part in programs that were seen as foreign to their notions of child care and rearing (Hayden, De Gioia, & Dundas, 2005).

Being aware of potential pitfalls, international NGOs commonly employ participatory techniques, such as participatory action research projects and/or social mapping. Participatory assessment methods (also known as participatory rural appraisal, participatory learning and action, participatory community assessment) are designed to help communities identify their own problems and to facilitate awareness and active involvement during the investigative process. This is seen to enhance the likelihood of participation or community ownership of the program (Kasaija & Nsabagasani, 2007; Pepall, Earnest, & James, 2007). However, proper conduct of participatory assessments can be challenged by financial and time limitations, limitations in project scope, and/or lack of experience and technical knowledge within the community (Botchway, 2001; Mansuri & Rao, 2004). Indeed, some participatory assessments run by external facilitators who are unfamiliar with local customs and key players have been accused of becoming short-cut legitimation exercises that, in fact, reinforce existing relations of power/ knowledge through "facipulation" exercises (Cornwall & Pratt, 2011).

Thus, the participation of communities within CBOs or other structures that appear to be community based could be illusionary at best, destructive at worst.

Limited Ability to Respond to Community Realities

Although the notion of "community-based" implies enhanced sensitivity to contextual issues and realities, NGOs, international NGOs, and other agents that work through local CBOs can be bound by strict protocols, time frames, budget forecasts, and other factors that limit their ability to respond to community realities and adapt to changing contexts. NGOs are under pressure to develop project plans with set targets and objectives, including identifying project areas long before they start engaging with CBOs. Thus, NGOs are caught in a dilemma between responsiveness to their target group and demands of boards and/or their donor agency. Donor agencies, however, need to be accountable for donations and adherence to policy and philosophical principles (Johansson, Elgström, Kimanzu, Nylund, & Persson, 2010).

Meanwhile, most NGOs and donor agencies are confined in terms of focus and indicators to one sector such as nutrition, health, education, child protection, water and sanitation, microfinance, or others. The CBO's scope of work becomes shaped by these sectorally based needs for accountability. This is especially problematic for ECD programs that, by their nature, call for an integrated approach to the care, education, and development of young children.

Capacity Is Not Built: Technical Assistance Takes Over

The stated goal associated for community-based development programs is to equip communities with the required knowledge and skills for self-reliance (building capacity). Thus, it is widely held that both technical and managerial or organizational capacity building are required to empower communities for effective and sustainable program development and management. However, it is not uncommon for external agents to assume that those community organizations do not have the capacity to manage an assistance program. Thus, "technical assistance" (TA) is provided. TA was initially associated with the importation of programs, tools, and technologies into development situations. More recently, TA represents attempts to empower local communities and citizens through training and other knowledge that is collaboratively generated. Walker et al., however, claim that TA "remains susceptible to neoliberal styles of development that have proceeded apace with withdrawal of state institutions in the funding and operation of social and economic development programs, and with the concomitant rise of NGOs" (Walker, Roberts, Jones, & Fröhling, 2008). This misapprehension, the authors claim, can lead to top-down program management from partner NGOs, with limited decision-making power by communities.

Community-Based Approach May Be Reductionist

It is increasingly recognized that community-based approaches involve more than enhancing the participation and ownership of representatives in the development and delivery of services, responding to community realities, and being sensitive to local knowledge bases. Rather, there are ecological (multilayered) influences on community-based programming (Mansuri & Rao, 2004). Dongier et al. have argued that community-based approaches incorporate a complex system of capacity development with at least four components: (1) the facilitation of strengthened and inclusive community groups; (2) the facilitation of financial support and accountability; (3) the facilitation of community access to information through a variety of media, including information technology; and (4) the facilitation of an enabling environment through appropriate policy and institutional reform. This latter mechanism includes decentralization reform, promotion of a conducive legal and regulatory framework, development of sound sector policies, and fostering of responsive sector institutions and private service providers (Dongier et al., 2001). Thus, program outcomes, including ECD outcomes, will be significantly influenced by the social, political, and economic context(s) that reside outside of the realm of CBPs and NGOs.

Devolution to Community Enables State Roll Back

Community-based programs and CBOs can undermine the need for government commitment by providing services that would otherwise be taken up by the state (Yanacopulos, 2008).

Roll back is a prevalent issue regarding ECD. The very success of community programs that bypass government support mechanisms detracts from the vision of ECD as a state responsibility. This is problematic because state responsibility for early childhood service delivery incorporates benefits that are less likely to be associated with CBPs. These include (1) the potential for a systematic and integrated approach that is inclusive of all groups and geographical regions; (2) a unified approach to learning that coincides with the public system of schooling; (3) a universal approach to access, with particular attention paid to children in need of special support; (4) adequate and consistent support, funding, and infrastructure; (5) quality assurance, including teacher training standards and appropriate working conditions for staff; (6) ability to undertake systemic data collection and monitoring; and (7) a long-term agenda for research and evaluation (OECD, 2006).

Indeed, some analysts believe that state systems of care and education of young children is the only strategy for ensuring equity and inclusive service delivery of early childhood services within any given context (Bennett, 2006).

From Community Participation to Community Centeredness: Policy Questions

Fowler (2007) suggests that as long as the resources (including knowledge, skills, and material resources) that are needed to implement a program or system emanate externally, the level of community input will always be one of relativity. Thus, rather than labeling a program as community based or not community based, it is most practical to look at the degree to which principles that underlie community-based approaches are actually in play.

The principles that underlie community efficacy in terms of ECD programs include (1) programs are flexible enough to reflect community issues; (2) decision makers and others with power over program development and delivery have knowledge of ECD principles and issues; (3) decision making about ECD reflects all factions of the community (is inclusive of all groups); (4) trust and solidarity exists between the community and the agents under whom the program will be funded, developed, and/or delivered; (5) ongoing monitoring and support are available, both horizontally and vertically; (6) there are trusted agents who can provide positive feedback and define program success; and, finally (7), if programs take place in multilinguistic contexts, the community has control over language choices (adapted from Fowler, 2007).

By focusing on the principles rather than the auspices, program developers may be able to advocate for and promote the positive aspects of government intervention in ECD, in order to overcome some of the pitfalls of community-based interventions and to focus upon those items that are most likely to produce effective results in terms of child-centered and community-centered outcomes.

Conclusion

Over past decades, NGOs have changed their strategy from top-down assistance programs to CBPs that encourage participatory programming. These community-based/community-driven programs have become the most popular mechanism for development assistance (Mansuri & Rao, 2004).

In light of the difficulties in developing national systems of ECD for many majority world nations, CBPs have become a prevalent program strategy. Community-based programs imply development and delivery by communities themselves. Sometimes, external agents will initiate community assessments and then facilitate program developments according to identified needs, even going so far as to create CBOs. Programs are still deemed to be community based and can have high levels of meaningful community participation through these and other CBOs who partner with external agents or NGOs. Indeed, there is a common belief that enhanced participation, effectiveness, efficiency, accountability, and sustainability of programs prevail under CBO auspices, regardless of how the CBO was developed and operated.

However, beyond the philosophical benefits of CBPs and CBOs, it is now recognized that community-based strategies are profoundly affected by how they are operationalized and by the sociopolitical and economic context. It cannot be assumed that CBPs and CBOs are always representative, that they incorporate traditional culture and indigenous knowledge, or that they are inclusive of all community groups. Differentiation and power relations are not necessarily addressed through the use of CBOs. Moreover, there is concern that, to the extent that CBOs effectively operate ECD and other programs, states have less cause to become involved and to ensure universal access, provision, and consistency in quality delivery.

In light of these complexities, we suggest that it is community centeredness or empowerment that defines effective outcomes, rather than the auspice under which programs operate. Following Fowler's suggestion that a series of investigating questions may be applied to measure the extent to which any CBP is authentic, we have adapted his questions for application to an assessment of the degree of community-centeredness of an ECD program, regardless of the auspice or system under which it operates. The questions can assist communities and agents to capture the positive aspects of community-based approaches while minimizing the potential pitfalls for CBP programs and services.

Measuring the Degree of the Community-Based Orientation in ECD Programs

1. To what degree can the application of an ECD system or program incorporate adaptations that reflect community issues and context?
2. What forms of power are in play in terms of the development, delivery, and accessibility of the ECD program? Where (in whom) is the power located? What capabilities, in terms of knowledge and understanding of ECD principles, lie with the agents of power?
3. How cohesive is the community in terms of ECD program development and delivery decision making?
4. What is the degree of trust and "solidarities" between the community and other stakeholders, such as trainers, funders, relevant policymakers who will be involved in ECD program development and delivery?
5. What (horizontal and vertical) connections, transmission mechanisms, and networks for ongoing support and monitoring of ECD are in play?
6. Who can provide positive feedback and define ECD program success?

7. What is the degree of language control exerted by the community (for multilinguistic contexts)?

Effectiveness studies of community-based interventions are difficult. As an alternative, this chapter has reviewed the strengths and the potential pitfalls of community-based service development and delivery, including ECD community-based service development and delivery in majority world contexts.

Recommendations

Community-based programs need to be situated within national structures and viewed in terms of state issues. Development efforts, in ECD or elsewhere, need to target systemic barriers, as well as program deficiencies at the grassroots level. Thus, we recommend that:

- ECD and related programs be assessed according to principles that transcend governing structure, auspice, and/or label; and
- The investigating questions (listed above) be applied to guide the assessment process.

References

Amazigo, U., Okeibunor, J., Matovu, V., Zouré, H., Bump, J., & Seketeli, A. (2007). Performance of predictors: Evaluating sustainability in community-directed treatment projects of the African programme for onchocerciasis control. *Social Science & Medicine, 64*(10), 2070–2082.

Barrs, J. (2005). Factors contributed by community organizations to the motivation of teachers in rural Punjab, Pakistan, and implications for the quality of teaching. *International Journal of Educational Development, 25*(3), 333–348. doi: 10.1016/j.ijedudev.2004.11.023

Bennett, J. (2006). *Starting strong II: Early childhood education and care.* Paris: OEDC.

Botchway, K. (2001). Paradox of empowerment: Reflections on a case study from Northern Ghana. *World Development, 29*(1), 135–153.

Briggs, J. (2005). The use of indigenous knowledge in development: Problems and challenges. *Progress in Development Studies, 5*(2), 99–114.

Buxton, C. (2009). NGO networks in Central Asia and global civil society: Potentials and limitations. *Central Asian Survey, 28*(1), 43–58.

Cornwall, A., & Pratt, G. (2011). The use and abuse of participatory rural appraisal: Reflections from practice. *Agriculture and Human Values, 28* (2), 263–272. doi: 10.1007/s10460-010-9262-1

Craig, G. (2002). Towards the measurement of empowerment: the evaluation of community development. *Journal of the Community Development Society, 33*(1), 124–146.

Daskon, C., & Binns, T. (2010). Culture, tradition and sustainable rural livelihoods: Exploring the culture–development interface in Kandy, Sri Lanka. *Community Development Journal, 45*(4), 494–517.

Datta, D. (2007). Sustainability of community-based organizations of the rural poor: Learning from Concern's rural development projects, Bangladesh. *Community Development
Journal, 42*(1), 47–62.

Dongier, P., Domelen, J. V., Ostrom, E., Rizvi, A., Wakeman, W., Bebbington, A.,
et al. (2001). Community-Driven Development. In *Poverty reduction strategy paper
sourcebook* (Vol. 1). Washington, DC: The World Bank.

Easterly, W. (2007). Was development assistance a mistake? *The American Economic Review,
97*(2), 328–332.

Fowler, A. (2007). *Civic driven change and international development.* Contextuals No. 7.
Utrecht: Context International Cooperation.

Fritzen, S. A. (2007). Can the design of community-driven development reduce the risk of
elite capture? Evidence from Indonesia. *World Development, 35*(8), 1359–1375.

Gruen, R. L., Elliott, J. H., Nolan, M. L., Lawton, P. D., Parkhill, A., McLaren, C. J.,
et al. (2008). Sustainability science: An integrated approach for health-programme planning. *The Lancet, 372*(9649), 1579–1589.

Hayden, J., De Gioia, K., & Dundas, R. (2005). *Meeting the needs of Aboriginal and Torres
Strait islander families entering preschool and school systems: Case studies from rural
Australia.* Paper presented at the Proceedings from the Our Children the Future 4 Early
Childhood Conference, Adelaide.

Hoffman, D. M., & Zhao, G. (2008). Global convergence and divergence in childhood
ideologies and the marginalization of children. In J. Zajda, K. Biraimah, & W. Gaudelli
(Eds.), *Education and social inequality in the global culture* (Vol. 1, pp. 1–16). Dordrecht,
The Netherlands: Springer.

Johansson, K. -E., Elgström, O., Kimanzu, N., Nylund, J. -E., & Persson, R. (2010). Trends in
development aid, negotiation processes and NGO policy change. *Voluntas: International
Journal of Voluntary & Nonprofit Organizations, 21*(3), 371–392.

Kasaija, J., & Nsabagasani, X. (2007). A handbook on participatory needs assessment.
Kampala: JSI Research & Training Institute, Inc.

Kreuter, M. W., Lezin, N. A., & Young, L. A. (2000). Evaluating community-based collaborative mechanisms: Implications for practitioners. *Health Promotion Practice, 1*(1),
49–63.

Labonne, J., & Chase, R. S. (2009). Who is at the wheel when communities drive development? Evidence from the Philippines. *World Development, 37*(1), 219–231.

MacQueen, K. M., McLellan, E., Metzger, D. S., Kegeles, S., Strauss, R. P., Scotti, R.,
et al. (2001). What is community? An evidence-based definition for participatory public
health. *American Journal of Public Health, 91*(12), 1929–1938.

Mansuri, G., & Rao, V. (2004). Community-based and -driven development: A critical
review. *The World Bank Research Observer, 19*(1), 1–39.

Mbonye, A. K., Bygbjerg, I., & Magnussen, P. (2008). Intermittent preventive treatment of
malaria in pregnancy: A community-based delivery system and its effect on parasitemia,
anemia and low birth weight in Uganda. *International Journal of Infectious Diseases,
12*(1), 22–29.

OECD. (2006). *Starting Strong II: Early childhood education and care* (Complete Edition
Ed.). Paris: Organization for Economic Co-operation and Development (OECD).

Pence, A. (2013). Voices less heard: The importance of critical and "indigenous" perspectives. In P. R. Britto, P. L. Engle, & C. M. Super (Eds.), *Handbook of early childhood*

development research and its impact on global policy (Chapter 8). New York: Oxford University Press.

Pepall, E., Earnest, J., & James, R. (2007). Understanding community perceptions of health and social needs in a rural Balinese village: Results of a rapid participatory appraisal. *Health Promotion International, 22*(1), 44–52.

Platteau, J. P. (2004). Monitoring elite capture in community-driven development. *Development and Change, 35*(2), 223–246.

Rao, N., & Pearson, E. (2007). *An evaluation of early childhood care and education programmes in Cambodia.* Cambodia: UNICEF.

Reimann, K. D. (2005). Up to no good? Recent critics and critiques of NGOs. In O. Richmond & H. Carey (Eds.), *Subcontracting peace: The challenges of NGO peacebuilding* (pp. 37–54): Political Science Faculty Publications.

Rivera, J., & Thomas-Slayter, B. (2009). Participatory approaches to community change: Building cooperation through dialogue and negotiation using participatory rural appraisal. In *Handbook on building cultures of peace* (pp. 333–348). New York: Springer.

Schiffman, J., Darmstadt, G. L., Agarwal, S., & Baqui, A. H. (2010). Community-based intervention packages for improving perinatal health in developing countries: A review of the evidence. *Seminars in Perinatology, 34*(6), 462–476.

Schmid, H., Dolev, T., & Szabo-Lael, R. (2010). Community-based programs for children at risk: The case of budget flexibility in Departments of Social Services in Israel. *Children and Youth Services Review, 32*(2), 178–184.

Shortall, S. (2008). Are rural development programmes socially inclusive? Social inclusion, civic engagement, participation, and social capital: Exploring the differences. *Journal of Rural Studies, 24*(4), 450–457.

Simpson, S. N. Y. (2008). Non-Governmental Organizations (NGOs) boards and corporate governance: The Ghanaian experience. *Corporate Ownership & Control, 6*(2), 89–98.

Toomey, A. H. (2011). Empowerment and disempowerment in community development practice: Eight roles practitioners play. Community Development Journal, 46(2), 181–195. doi: 10.1093/cdj/bsp060

Walker, M., Roberts, S. M., Jones, J. P., III, & Fröhling, O. (2008). Neoliberal development through technical assistance: Constructing communities of entrepreneurial subjects in Oaxaca, Mexico. *Geoforum, 39*(1), 527–542.

Wong, S., (2010). Elite capture or capture elites? Lessons from the 'Counter-elite' and 'Co-opt-elite' approaches in Bangladesh and Ghana, Working Papers, World Institute for Development Economic Research (UNU-WIDER).

Yanacopulos, H. (2008). NGOs (Nongovernmental Organizations). In H. Kris (Ed.), *International encyclopedia of public health* (pp. 536–542). Oxford, UK: Academic Press.

Zvavamwe, Z., & Ehlers, V. J. (2009). Experiences of a community-based tuberculosis treatment programme in Namibia: A comparative cohort study. *International Journal of Nursing Studies, 46*(3), 302–309.

15

Parents and Communities

THE KEY TO UNDERSTANDING "FAITH-BASED" EARLY CHILDHOOD SERVICES AND PROGRAMS

Kathy Bartlett, Paul Stephenson, and Louie Cadaing

Provision of services in early childhood that incorporate aspects of faith or spirituality or is supported by faith-based organizations (or both) is a complex and even a sensitive issue. There are different examples of such programs across contexts and countries, although these are not well understood in terms of scale, purpose, or impact. Given the increasing global efforts by governments, civil society actors, and international donor agencies to promote and expand early childhood development (ECD) services, there are important questions and issues that require reflection when considering the faiths of families and communities, faith-based organizations, and the promotion, development, and sustainability of ECD services.

This chapter aims to begin that process of reflection through a review of the literature on faith-based programs and two case studies presented as illustrations of this approach to ECD. The editors and those involved in the conceptualization of this volume believed it to be important to look at a variety of delivery platforms for ECD services across communities, including those supported by faith-based organizations. Yet, not all ECD services that have elements of faith and spirituality are driven by faith-based institutions, and not all faith-based organizations promote solely their particular faith. Rather, many ECD services emerge as a response to local parent and community demands and needs. Some international agencies see faith-based provision and support for ECD services as one potentially important avenue to reach more young children and their families, whereas others worry that it also can have negative repercussions. Thus, it could be said, what differentiates faith-based from other ECD approaches is a lack of clarity in the meaning of this approach across contexts and the recognition that it contains within it a world of diverse views and beliefs. Additionally, the use of this term within the U.S. domestic and international aid arena has created a range of views and contentious debate. The lack of available data has made reaching a resolution even more difficult. Nonetheless, in different national ECD contexts, faith-based

organizations are a key stakeholder in promoting and expanding ECD services—
sometimes reaching communities that otherwise are not reached by government
or other ECD efforts.

The term "faith-based" is used quite broadly in this chapter to cover various
dimensions. We explore faith-based provision as a modality of ECD services that
could be instituted to promote specific religious and spiritual values or a broader
sentiment of general respect and tolerance of one's own as well as others' different views/religious beliefs, or simply the sponsorship of the physical location and
mechanism for service delivery, with no implications on moral, spiritual, or religious development of the child, but, instead, a response to local needs. In this
chapter, we do not seek to detail enduring traditional belief systems or organized
faith groups (Buddhists, Muslims, Christians, Jewish, Hindus). Moreover, we are
not writing about religious views on ECD or, for that matter, other views that fall
outside of the "mainstream." Although we primarily focus on those ECD services
that fall within education, the issues, achievements, and challenges are likely to
be the same across health, protection, or social services that are faith-based or
supported by faith institutions.

Historically, the association between faith-based services and ECD may find
part of its roots in colonization and early exploration from Western Europe to
Latin America, Africa, and Asia. The history of colonization almost always
had as one function the process of converting indigenous peoples to the dominant faith of the colonizers (Pence, 2004). Much before this, and continuing
over time, the upbringing and education of children through informal and
more formal processes have been central to how cultures have passed on their
beliefs, values, and ways of being, including any spiritual or religious beliefs.
Such roots of ECD and faith-based approaches can be found in the indigenous
religions and cultures of civilizations and countries where children learned
their faith from birth (e.g., Hindu texts, called *Vedas* provide details on early
childhood spiritual development).

Over time, as education (and other social services) came to be seen as a vital public good, national governments became more involved. Nonetheless, faith-based
organizations have continued, in some places as a fairly significant provider of
social services. It should be noted that some organizations implement these services with subsidies from government. In some instances, these social services have
included ECD programs. These varying historical roots have differing implications for program philosophy and family uptake of faith-based services, which are
described below.

In the first section of this chapter, we explore the relationship between ECD and
faith-based programs through a multilevel conceptual framework of supply and
demand. Also discussed in this section are the current definitional and measurement challenges with respect to understanding program impact and policy effectiveness. In the second section of this chapter, we turn to the limited and nascent
evidence on faith-based ECD programs. We discuss two examples of approaches

to ECD provision that include faith/spirituality as part of their conceptual model for holistic ECD services. The first example is the East African Madrasa Early Childhood Program, which has nearly 30 years of experience across three countries (Uganda, Kenya, Zanzibar) in supporting communities to establish their own preschools. The program emerged as a result of a request to His Highness the Aga Khan from poor and marginalized Muslim communities and their leaders, who wanted to improve their children's access and success in formal schooling. The *Aga Khan Foundation* (AKF) responded to the request and worked closely with local leaders to create a preschool program that would prepare children for school and also ground them in their faith and local cultural traditions. The second example discusses findings from research on children's views of spiritual development conducted by *World Vision International*. The research, conducted in six countries with more than 500 children and their parents from Muslim, Buddhist, and Christian traditions, informed the development of resources to strengthen family care and nurturing in early childhood and through the life-cycle stages. Given that comprehensive and consistent data on this type of programming are scarce, we use case studies and other broader experience as the evidence to make programmatic and policy recommendations. These are presented in the third section, with our concluding comments.

The Relationship Between Faith-Based Provision and Early Childhood Development

An understanding of ECD programming requires a detailed examination of the supply and demand sides of the equation. Supply is typically associated with the provision of programs and services, and demand is defined as the families' take-up of the services and their perceived need and acceptance of them. In the first part of this section, we explore the relationship between faith-based approaches and ECD, using a supply-and-demand dynamics at policy and program levels as they address children, families, and communities. The second part of this section addresses the gaps in our knowledge due to the definitional, assessment, and monitoring challenges in this field.

At the policy level, the relationship between faith-based organizations and ECD can be seen in two facets: in the process of policy development and the stakeholders involved and in the policy provisions and the monitoring of the policies. Each of these facets is briefly described.

The first point to make is that policy development for ECD across virtually all regions of the world has received increasing attention over the last decade. As noted in the authoritative guidance for ECD policy development in Africa (Vargas-Barón, 2005), faith-based organizations are one of the key stakeholders in countries that are involved in the development, implementation, and monitoring of ECD policies and services. Marshall and Keough (2004) also address this at a global and multisectoral level with respect to poverty alleviation, also highlighting the role of faith-based stakeholders.

Faith-based provisions are noted also in the content of ECD policies in several countries that emphasize spiritual and moral development. For example, the Kenyan ECD policy framework (2006) outlines the roles and responsibilities of communities and parents, on the one hand, in providing important support and guidance to young children in religious, cultural, and moral areas. On the other hand, it suggests how faith-based organizations can contribute to improving access, quality, and sustainability of ECD services through, for example, sponsoring or directly providing ECD services, providing moral and spiritual guidance, supporting capacity building efforts for ECD programs, or advocating for broad support for ECD, among others.

With respect to programmatic directions within policies, we also see the inclusion of faith-based provisions. In New Zealand (chapter 8, this volume), an emphasis is seen in the ECD program curriculum on holistic development, including spiritual dimensions within the context of a diverse society. The 2006 Organization for Economic Cooperation and Development (OECD), *Starting Strong II: Early Childhood Education and Care*, highlights that a number of the OECD countries also provide for spiritual, religious, and moral aspects of education within each specific country curricula framework for ECD. For example, the Norwegian curriculum framework (Norwegian Ministry of Children and Family Affairs, 1996) formulates objectives for ECD that include basic competencies in five broad learning areas: society, religion, and ethics, aesthetic subjects; language, text, and communication; nature, environment, and technology; and physical activity and health. The OECD report also recognizes that migration patterns across countries necessitate attention to increasing diversity—including religious diversity—and that such shifts will require further reflection on the improvement of access and equity to ECD programs for different children and families.

The second level of supply is ECD programs themselves. With respect to the relationship between faith-based approaches and ECD, multiple facets are noteworthy, including program content and sponsorship of the services.

Muslim communities in the Gambia, Indonesia, Kenya, Morocco, Tunisia, Uganda, and the United Republic of Tanzania have created preschools in recent years to ensure that children learn the national curriculum within a context that also supports Islamic faith, values, and practices. Elsewhere, religious providers contribute to the availability of early childhood care and education (ECCE), including in the Caribbean, where there is significant Christian faith-based provision (e-mail communication with Sian Williams, May 3, 2011). In Indonesia, a variety of programs, ranging from secular to religious kindergartens, are run by faith-based women's organizations. In addition, the free National Strategies for Holistic-Integrated Early Childhood Development is a religious program followed by millions of Indonesian children of various ages, and is often followed in combination with other programs or with school (van Ravens, 2010). These examples highlight that, at both program and policy levels, understudied associations exist between faith-based programs and ECD.

Next, we explore the demand side of ECD programs with respect to child and family motivation to enroll and take up services. Here, we examine the underlying motivations for faith-based ECD provision. Parents in many places are keen to instill a sense of spiritual values, understanding, and positive attitudes toward their faith of choice. The majority of agencies, nongovernmental organizations (NGOs), and government staff working with parents and communities to establish ECD services, almost without exception, highlight the importance of promoting "locally and culturally relevant" practices and services for young children and their families. As a result, ECD program development is often preceded by different types of local needs assessments and studies on local child-rearing practices to inform the design and content of proposed interventions. Such participatory processes allow for parents and community leaders to express their views and perspectives on the overall proposed work, as well as on specific areas of particular interest to them. These may include aspects such as faith, spirituality, and the development of moral values within ECD efforts. Nonetheless, effective and sustained demand for any ECD service is influenced by many other factors, including distance of ECD services from households; overall costs (fees, uniforms, other in-kind or material contributions expected, etc.); and perceived quality and relevance of the ECD service (e.g., sufficient safety/hygiene measures in place, easier entry to grade 1, improved success in primary school). Faith-related aspects of ECD programs may fall within parents' overall assessment of quality and relevance, as has been found in the Bokamoso Early Childhood Program in Botswana, founded by the Dutch Reformed Church in 1988. The Bokamoso program provides training for rural preschool teachers serving marginalized groups. An increased understanding of the importance of ECD, coupled with a desire to instill religious values and moral development from early childhood, shaped demand and action (Nguluka, 2011).

Definitional and measurement challenges in understanding faith-based approaches to ECD globally, and assessing the actual scale of faith-based ECD provision is seriously hampered by the lack of definitional clarity and also an absence of systematic data at country level. The United Nation's Educational, Scientific, and Cultural Organization (UNESCO)'s Global Monitoring Reports, which provide information on enrollment of children across early childhood care and education services, disaggregate only between public and "private" provision. The latter includes everything from private, for-profit to private not-for-profit to community-based provision of services (Aga Khan Foundation, 2007). Faith-based can be a subcategory of either public or private ECD provision. Therefore, this lack of clear data makes it difficult to estimate the prevalence of ECD faith-based programs.

Early childhood development services categorized as "faith-based" are themselves diverse in terms of intent (mission), who they reach, and how they are financed and sustained. In the United States and the Caribbean, many churches financially support, offer, or even rent out space in their premises for early childhood care and preschool services. In Latin America, the *Fe y Alegria* network targets very poor and marginalized neighborhoods, offering a range of education services beginning with preschool education (Marshall & Keough, 2004). There are also networks for Jewish ECD services across the United States, such as the Jewish Early Childhood Education Initiative (www. JECEI.org). Although some of these programs might be open to any interested parent choosing to enroll and pay for ECD services, others draw from particular faith communities.

Understanding the various dimensions (ownership, curriculum content, financing) within and across countries and faith contexts is also a serious challenge. Data may exist at national levels or even within religious institutions and faith-based organizations that support ECD services. However, locating and synthesizing such data was not possible for this paper. Further, although exceptions exist, little specific research and only a few published articles and reports have been undertaken in either developed or developing country contexts related specifically to the nature, quality, scale, or impacts and benefits of this diverse form of ECD provision (Bouzoubaâ, 1998; Feinberg, Saracho, & Spodek, 1990; Malmberg et al., 2010; Marshall & Keough, 2004; Mwaura, Sylva, & Malmberg, 2008; Wagner & Spratt, 1987; Zero to Three, 2008). Given the lack of data, we use two case study examples to further explain faith-based ECD program modalities, implementation, and impact.

Case Study: The Aga Khan Foundation's East African Madrasa Early Childhood Program

The Madrasa Early Childhood Program has operated for nearly 30 years on the Coast of Kenya, in the islands of Zanzibar (part of Tanzania), and in central Uganda. Originally, the Madrasa Early Childhood Program began as a small pilot initiative on the coast of Kenya in the mid-1980s, after Muslim community leaders requested support from His Highness, the Aga Khan, to assist them in addressing their children's access to and success in school. Discussions across communities, needs assessments, and studies led to an agreement to focus on early childhood education as the critical starting point.

Three local NGOs—Madrasa Resource Centres (MRCs)—established by AKF in the late 1980s and early 1990s—serve as the institutional base in each country. More than 200 communities have established their preschools, benefitting over 80,000 children directly. Thousands of other children, teachers, communities, and government staff have been reached through additional training and support activities provided by the MRCs.

It should be noted that AKF projects like the Madrasa Early Childhood Development Program are integrated into the wider activities of the Aga Khan

Development Network (AKDN). The AKDN, a group of private, international, and nondenominational agencies working for people of all faiths and origins, draw together social, economic, and cultural projects in ways that creates a critical mass of development activity. Among its methods is the view that long-term engagement is critical to enabling sustainable change over time. A community-based and participatory approach that strengthens civil society and builds on local culture also permeates all interventions. Its work in early childhood programming—an area that is a growing priority for the AKF and the AKDN—reflects similar principles and aims. The Madrasa programme has created unity and self-respect within communities (interview with a MRC National Board Chairman, p. 20, in Mwaura, 2001):

> Many early childhood programmes are initiated without the understanding of the communities' actual needs or consideration of culture, religious beliefs or traditional values. As a result many communities do not participate in the programmes as fully as expected. Bi Swafiya Said, First Trainer, Director and Co-Developer of the Madrasa Program (Evans & Bartlett, 2008, p. 6)

At the time, the program was being developed, preschools sponsored by Christian churches, as well as the longer standing and numerous traditional *madrassahs* (or Qur'anic) schools,[1] already existed. Moreover, Kenya's Ministry of Education was promoting culturally relevant preschool education using the *harambee*—or self-help—tradition across the country. The Ministry encouraged adaptation of ECD services in order to fit local culture, language, strengths, and needs, and it developed specific guidelines for an "integrated approach" for Muslim communities around the same time.

The Madrasa Early Childhood Program was conceived as a community-owned and -led preschool program that was embedded within—and drew from—local cultural traditions and values (including faith). It also put a high value on using and strengthening available resources (human and material) and creating local institutions (preschools, MRCs) to help build sustainability. Over the years, evaluations have identified key lessons and facets of the program evolution that contributed to its eventual success and the growth in demand (Brown, Brown, & Suleman, 1999; Morgan & Muigai, 2000). These speak to both the supply and demand aspects noted earlier.

USE OF LOCAL, KNOWN SPACES

The initial needs assessment identified underutilized spaces available in the community that could be used for the preschool classes, located within the local traditional *madrassahs*, which are present in virtually all the target communities. In East Africa, *madrassahs* were used mainly in the afternoons and evenings and therefore were empty in the mornings. Using these known spaces was critical to beginning conversations and building confidence with communities, even though later communities increasingly established their ECD centers nearby but separate from the mosque and/or *madrassah*.

IDENTIFYING AND NURTURING LEADERS AND TEACHERS

Identifying and nurturing leaders and teachers occurs at two levels—the community level and at the level of the MRC institution. The AKF began by hiring a local, well-respected Muslim woman, Bi Swafiya Said, who, trained as a primary teacher, took up the post as the first director cum trainer cum curriculum developer cum community organizer. Over time, and with increasing demand, the first MRC in Kenya was established; others in Zanzibar and then in Uganda followed. The heart of the work for Bi Swaifya, and for the trainers who came after her, was to provide training and mentoring support, and to problem-solve with the local teachers and communities as they established and built up their preschool operations. A small group of community and religious leaders was appointed to work with Bi Swafiya to help mobilize parents and shape the first curriculum as it was developed and piloted. (The MRCs now have formal national boards.) At the community level, leaders and parents not only identified those women to be trained as preschool teachers but also elected members to their local preschool management committee to help oversee, manage, and support the preschools.

The MRCs approach to the professional development of preschool teachers and preschool committee members has played a clear role in ensuring quality and coherence across communities. The in-service training and mentoring provided to teachers, particularly in the first 2 years as they learn and practice a range of skills and strategies in the context of their ECD settings, but also when they occasionally gather with other nearby preschool teachers to share and reflect on what is working or not, is seen as the heart of their work. Although the technical supports diminish considerably over time, the MRCs understand that in poor and marginalized communities, ongoing support can make a huge difference to sustainability and quality. The initial training and follow-up that the preschool committee members receive from the MRC staff includes building skills, knowledge, and understanding in community organization; accounting; management; quality oversight; and fundraising for their preschools.

CONTINUOUS DEVELOPMENT AND IMPROVEMENT
OF AN INTEGRATED CURRICULUM

The first integrated preschool curriculum was co-developed by Bi Swafiya and a group of local religious leaders, with additional inputs by AKF's ECD expert. They wove together the values, practices, and beliefs of the Swahili Muslim communities relevant for young children with well-known early childhood development knowledge and practices—in this case, the High/Scope preschool approach.

From the parents' perspective, the integrated curriculum was, in a sense, visible proof that the program was serious about building on and respecting their local beliefs and values. The curriculum purposefully did not prescribe to any specific interpretation of Islam, but rather drew upon broader agreed-upon principles and traditions—which was critical, given the diversity of Muslim communities in the three countries.[2] Further, as national policies and curricula for ECD evolved over time, efforts were made to align later revised versions of the MRC integrated curriculum with these policies. The MRC teams have updated and strengthened their integrated curriculum continuously over the last 30 years by incorporating new elements, knowledge, and understanding related to child development, health, nutrition, and care.

MANAGING EXPANSION AND INCREASING DIVERSITY

By 1995, the MRCs began to be more widely known in their respective countries and the region. Interest in preschool education also was increasing from communities, as well as from some governments and donor agencies. The MRCs responded by expanding their efforts to new geographic areas. An unanticipated result of the subsequent expansion was that these communities were more diverse in terms of their faith than in the original areas of intervention. This was especially true in Uganda and Kenya. (The Zanzibar Islands are more than 95% Muslim.) As a consequence, the MRCs began to consider how to respond to these changes—a consideration that is reflected in current responses to present circumstances. For example, when non-Muslim parents have been asked what their motivation for enrolling their children in the MRC-supported preschools is, their answers generally focus on the quality of the *madrasa* preschools, their affordability, or the lack of other nearby provision.

Additionally, the three MRCs began to receive increasing requests from a wide range of individuals (non-Muslim, NGO staff, government teachers) to offer more general preschool training courses. This "outreach" work by the MRCs focused on sharing their strategies and approach to community ECD programming and tended to address only the "secular" aspects of their ECD approach. In many cases, however, they were asked to explain how they arrived at their integrated approach and to share the lessons of embedding faith-related aspects within the curriculum and practices for others interested in doing the same for their own faiths. The MRCs have also engaged in advocacy and policy influencing by contributing to national ECD policy development and providing technical assistance to their respective governments and other interested organizations as these entities set up and expand their own ECD offerings. Across all outreach work is an understanding and belief in the importance of respecting and building on local cultures (including faith), ideas, and values in ECD. In many respects, their outreach work with others has, in a very real sense, "closed a circle" and brought them back to the origins of a culturally relevant program that began with a request from one faith community concerned about the future of its young children.

Impact and other external evaluation studies on the MRC program (Brown et al., 1999; Malmberg et al., 2010; Morgan & Muigai, 2000; Mwaura et al., 2008; Shallwani, 2010) provide program- and child-level outcomes. The results of program quality, as measured by an adapted version of two early childhood environmental rating scales (Harms et al., 1998; Sylva et al., 1999), showed significantly higher scores for *madrasa* preschools than for non-*madrasa* preschools across all three countries (Mwaura et al., 2008). Significant differences were also found in children's cognitive and social development, with those participating in MRC-supported preschools scoring higher than their peers in other similar preschools (Malmberg et al., 2010; Mwaura et al., 2008). Additional analysis (Malmberg et al., 2010) linked the child outcomes (e.g., improved school readiness) with program quality—most particularly highlighting the MRCs' approach to the training and mentoring of *madrasa* preschool teachers. This last finding is important, given that the majority of the *madrasa* preschool teachers had about a grade 10 education, and it showed that they could still provide a quality learning environment when given adequate supports.

The MRC program is not without its challenges, despite the high levels of community trust and family demand. Retaining trained teachers is not always easy, and a number have been hired away by the growing numbers of private providers. Financial sustainability of community ECD services, especially in the poorest areas, is perhaps one of the most important issues. More thinking, innovative piloting and research is needed if these programs are to reach the poorest communities, especially those in remote rural and slum areas. No one answer will fit all contexts.

LESSONS FROM THE *MADRASA* PROGRAM

The implementation of the MRC program is a valuable source of information on understanding effective ECD programs—faith-based or otherwise. The following is a summary of some of the key lessons (for a more detailed review, see Evans & Bartlett, 2008; Mwaura & Seif, 2008):

Time to Understand, Adapt, and Nurture

Taking time to understand and plan for appropriate ways to draw upon and strengthen available human, material, and cultural resources, and allowing for program evolution and change over time (e.g., introducing health and nutrition aspects and piloting parenting components) created the necessary foundation for a healthy and vibrant program. The other aspect of *time* is the variation in pace with which communities, as well as teachers, can incorporate new ideas, therefore accommodating individual pace.

Valuing Professional Development

Valuing relevant professional development and mentoring of teachers has been critical. This begins with the initial in-service training but goes beyond this to gather clusters of teachers together to share and learn from each other. The attention to mentoring teachers—especially new ones—in their own classroom settings has clearly linked theory and practice with local realities.

Engagement and Accountability at Local Level

Creating a system of mutual accountability, together with a commitment toward quality among all levels strengthened further local interest, investment, and demand. Demand was furthered by engaging local leaders and parents and building trust, including through involving parents and school committees in the monitoring of the quality of the learning experience for the children (Brown et al., 1999).

In conclusion, the *madrasa* program works continuously to identify and test mechanisms to improve quality and support the community preschool's ability to sustain itself by working with communities to identify local resources, manage their preschools locally, and create and nurture multiple stakeholders to provide supports to the teacher and the preschool. The AKF has worked with the MRCs to identify and test ways to enhance sustainability, including through the development of mini-endowments and local community resource teams and through encouraging them to link to other available resources and programs, such as micro-finance or income-generation activities (Evans & Bartlett, 2008).

Case Study: World Vision International's Early Childhood Development Program

The second case study focuses on ECD programming sponsored by another major global civil society actor, World Vision International. In this case study, we present the process of developing a faith-based ECD program as a critical step in ensuring its effectiveness. Provided is a brief description of the agency, its perspective on ECD, and its process for developing the curriculum of their ECD programs.

World Vision is a Christian, nongovernmental relief and development organization that works in more than 90 countries with the goal of sustaining the well-being of children within their families and communities, especially the most vulnerable. The agency takes a child-focused approach to its community development work, which is rights-based, ecological, and holistic, working through integrated sector interventions. World Vision's interventions for children's survival, development, and growth include Maternal Child Health, a parenting curriculum for children 0–5 years old; community-managed early childhood learning centers; and home-based care and support for preschool improvement.

World Vision recently set out to strengthen its ECD work by focusing on one area of children's development that rarely receives attention in traditional early childhood programming—spiritual development. An emerging body of research on adolescent spiritual development emphasizes the importance of integrating spiritual development into policies, programs, and practices (Benson & Roehlkepartain, 2008; Yust et al., 2006). However, less is known about how younger children and their parents perceive and understand spiritual development. So, the agency, in an effort to determine both the importance of this dimension for children's overall well-being and its relevant characteristics, conducted extensive focus group discussions with more than 400 children from 5 to 18 years of age and their parents. The participants came primarily from rural communities in six countries and from different religious backgrounds. Research conducted by the SEARCH Institute with adolescents from different faith groups (King, Clardy, & Ramos, 2010; Roehlkepartain 2012) informed World Vision's definition of spiritual development:

> [A]n inward and outward journey of discovery for children as they grow in awareness of a sense of meaning and purpose in life; connect, empathize with and are influenced by others, especially parents and peers; begin to explore their understanding of God, and live out their spiritual beliefs and commitments in daily life according to their maturity and evolving capacities. (*Policy Principles on the Spiritual Nurture of Children*, World Vision International, 2009)

In addition to seeking a basic understanding of the definition and role of spiritual development for overall holistic well-being, the agency also wanted to understand how best to integrate spiritual development into their work in a way that nurtured the whole child in a nonsectarian way, with sensitivity to all contexts and faith backgrounds. One of the goals of this project was to learn of ways to provide ECD programs that supported parents and partners within the communities to create opportunities for children to pursue their spiritual development in a holistic way.

Participative methodologies were used to engage children and adults. This included the use of drawing, story telling, and other participatory learning and action tools. The data were collected and analyzed using a grounded theory approach. Emergent themes from the focus groups informed World Vision's understanding of spiritual development from the children's perspective, and of issues that children and adults identified as being critical to nurturing spirituality and holistic development.

The results of the children's focus group discussions indicated that the foundation of spiritual development of children is a safe and caring environment that allows them to explore, make sense of their life experiences, and attribute this to a bigger purpose in life. Furthermore, children identified three primary stimuli from their early childhoods that led them to pursue their spiritual development and an awareness of it: awe and amazement at creation, acts of love and kindness, and miracles.

The first, awe and amazement at creation, was referenced in the following quote from a 10-year-old boy from Uganda: "I know there is a God because of the rain. Because who can fetch so much water, go up the sky, and pour it on us? Only God can do that." The second, acts of love and kindness from people around them, was captured in the following quote from a young boy from South Africa: "When I was young I fell from a tree and broke my arm. My father took me to a clinic. While waiting for the doctor, a nurse came by and saw me. She said 'Do not worry, God loves you, He will heal you,' and then she left. I was very happy and felt not afraid anymore. I never saw her again." The third, miracles, was understood as events that children attribute to a higher being:

> When I was eight years old, I had a skin disease. It itched very much. My parents brought me to different doctors but I did not get well. One day, a lady prayed for me and I got healed. Look, until today I am clean. The God of the Christian lady healed me. (12-year-old girl from Cambodia; Focus Group with Children on Spirituality Documentation Report, World Vision International, 2009)

The results from the parents' focus groups indicated that parents believed that care, protection, love, wonder, and opportunity to ask questions about life and faith are ways to nurture spiritual development in children. It should be noted that although both parent and child focus groups discussions did talk about love, affection, and care, several of the child focus group discussions mentioned harmful practices and abuse and their impact on their well-being and spiritual development.

Informed by the results of the focus groups, World Vision developed a curriculum focusing on children and parents/caregivers as families. The curriculum, Celebrating Families, is aimed at building safe, caring, and loving homes for children so that they may live in an environment that enables them to thrive. The objectives of the curriculum, drawn from the focus group results, emphasize the role of families in the pursuit of children's spiritual nurturing and well-being; seek to broaden the understanding of the realities and context of families; work to understand the framework, processes, and tools that can support families; and seek to identify practical ways to equip, support, and affirm families.

The curriculum is facilitated either by World Vision staff or by their faith-based partners. Celebrating Families is used as part of an integrated approach to ECD that takes into account health, early stimulation, and protection issues. Initial field testing with Christian, Muslim, and Buddhist communities and religious leaders has been positive. Early results indicate that communities are open to exploring and transforming attitudes and behaviors with regard to the care and nurture of their children, when linked to an understanding of how this can positively impact children's spiritual and physical development.

Celebrating Families uses a dialogical approach that combines personal experience and local knowledge with information about holistic child development.

It complements World Vision's ECD parenting resources, which use transformative learning theory (Mezirow, 1997) to critically examine child-rearing practices, child development, and gender relations. Both resources were generated together with children and local caregivers, and are designed to be easily adapted to multiple contexts and faith groups. They not only help families and faith leaders to become more aware of and better equipped to address children's spiritual and developmental needs, but also catalyze dialogue within communities (and also between faiths) about how to support children's well-being and rights. This includes addressing sensitive issues of gender-based violence and child protection and safety.

Conclusion

Faith-based ECD programing is clearly present in many countries; however, information and knowledge about it is missing from the ECD literature. In this chapter, we have attempted to define this approach to programming in its very complex manifestations and delineate the challenges in understanding its impact on young children's well-being. The two case studies demonstrate the very tenet of this approach—that although there is great diversity in programs, they are very much rooted in the context of the community.

SUMMARY OF MAIN INSIGHTS

We conclude this chapter where we started—with the understanding that this is a complex, sometimes sensitive area in which the lack of clear and systematic global data hampers understanding. There are no systematic data on the scale, contours, and effectiveness of faith-based provision at a global level. Although we did review examples from the Caribbean, Indonesia, and parts of Africa, there are undoubtedly diverse examples of faith-based organizations supporting ECD service provision, and clearly we only accessed a small handful. Our brief review suggests that numerous ECD national policies look to faith-based entities as one source of support for services on the ground, as well as include elements of faith and spirituality within their specific understanding of holistic child development. This further heightens the need to obtain clearer and more systematic information on faith-based programs. Available documentation also suggests that parents make choices in terms of their children's participation in ECD services based on a variety of factors including the well-being/safety of their young children, costs, quality and relevance of the service, and the trustworthiness of the provider. For some parents, the inclusion of faith or spiritual elements is part of this equation when making a choice for their children. These findings are important for improving access and enrollment in ECD. Further, most other approaches focus on the supply of programs, whereas the faith-based approach provides insight into how demand for ECD services can be increased. Finally, there are different examples of faith-based institutions, working in partnership with parents, local communities, and government. These can help to bridge the gap in access by advocating for more ECD provision at all levels; supporting local, culturally relevant ECD services; and ensuring that the poorest and most marginalized participate.

Although the definition of what is considered faith-based ECD is complex, the two case examples highlight important commonalities. Both AKF's *madrasa*-based early childhood program and World Vision's work sought to understand and draw upon their communities' values and beliefs. Further, they let these values and beliefs inform the development of the curriculum and looked to make full use of local resources. Third, they both have purposefully and regularly checked in with the communities to make sure the preschool provision is meeting their needs and instilling the values and beliefs that community members want for their children. These indeed are arguably similar to other "culturally/locally relevant" non–faith-based ECD programs. Finally, there is a common thread of embedding core ECD principles within a faith-based program. Stated differently, the important principles with regards to good teaching, parental involvement, and teacher training within a quality ECD program applies also to a faith-based program, but the common objective/need is to have the program grounded in the set of beliefs/ values that are shared by the faith-based community or organization.

A more cautionary note is that attention and monitoring of faith-based provisions is also important, keeping in mind the realities of changing diversity and the dynamics of communities across most countries and regions. Early childhood development services can bring communities together to work toward the common goal of improved opportunities for their children (Myers 1995) but must also seek to nurture inclusiveness, tolerance, and respect for a diversity of views and beliefs.

RESEARCH QUESTIONS AND POLICY RECOMMENDATIONS

With the growing recognition of the critical importance of ECD to broader human development and the expansion of different ECD policies and services across many more cultural contexts and geographic areas than has previously been seen, it is important to place more attention on understanding what is happening on the ground, how these efforts are evolving and why, and what their impacts are for children, their families, and society more broadly in the future. More specifically, we urge researchers to work toward improved understanding with regards to the scale, quality, impact, and sustainability of existing faith-based organizations and networks supporting ECD service provision, and also with regards to how the same are involved in ECD policy development and advocacy at broader levels in countries.

Given that diversity is increasing across most national and subnational levels, questions that need to be addressed include: What are the issues and questions at play for faith-based provision? How can such provision be used to bring communities together, rather than be seen as enabling division? Another potential area for research is that of understanding the contributions of existing faith-based ECD services within a broader framework of culturally appropriate, holistic, and demand-driven ECD services. Ultimately, we hope that a clearer definition of faith-based ECD initiatives—or even a better terminology—can emerge from the above research initiatives. This might be assisted with the development of a conceptual continuum for faith-based ECD provision to enable more transparent and improved understanding of the scale, scope, and main stakeholders and funders. Such a continuum could be done by country or region to help to clarify the cultural, socioeconomic, and political factors influencing the role and stature of faith-based or religiously funded preschools. For example, the continuum might, at one end, have ECD services with a religious focus as the central purpose of program, and then, at the other end of the continuum, the use of religiously affiliated spaces (churches, mosques, temples, etc.) for ECD programs without any particular religious influence. Greater clarification is also needed to address how a comprehensive ECD definition would be incorporated into any continuum.

Notes

1. See AKF Madrasa Publication (2007) as well. *Madrassahs* are referred to by various names across the countries in which they exist (*madrassah, madaris, Qur'anic* schools, etc). Some focus solely on the teaching and memorization of the Koran, whereas others may also teach other subjects such as maths, science, and the like. For the purposes of this chapter, *madrassah* is used when related to this traditional system and *madrasa* is used when referring to the AKF-supported *madrasa* early childhood program described in this chapter.
2. Within the Muslim faith, there are two main strands—Sunni and Shi'a—and within each of these are various subgroups that have evolved historically.

References

Aga Khan Foundation. (2007). Non-state providers and public-private-community partnerships in education – contributions towards achieving EFA: A critical review of challenges, opportunities and issues. Background paper for the *EFA Global Monitoring Report 2008, Education for All by 2015: Will we make it?*

AKF/Madrasa Regional Programme monitoring system, data compiled by the Madrasa Regional Office 2011 and sent by e-mail.

Benson, P. L., & Roehlkepartain, E. C. (2008). Spiritual development: A missing priority in youth development. In P. L. Benson, E. C. Roehlkepartain, & K. L. Hong (Eds.), *New directions for youth development: Spiritual development* No. 118 (pp. 13–28). San Francisco: Jossey-Bass: Wiley Periodicals, Inc.

Brown, G., Brown, J., & Suleman, S. (June, 1999). *The East African Madrasa Programme: The Madrasa Resource Centres and their community-based pre-school programme*. Evaluation Report for the Aga Khan Foundation, Geneva.

Bouzoubaâ, K. (1998). *An innovation in Morocco's Koranic pre-schools*. Working papers in early childhood development. The Hague: Bernard van Leer Foundation.

Evans, J., & Bartlett, K. (2008). *The Madrasa Early Childhood Program: 25 years of experience*. A project of the Aga Khan Foundation, an Aga Khan Development Network Series publication. Geneva: AKDN.

Feinberg, M., Saracho, O., & Spodek, B. (1990). Identifying sectarian content for Jewish early childhood educational programs. *International Journal of Early Childhood, 22*(2), 23–38.

Harms, T., Clifford, R. M., & Cryer, D. (1998). The Early Childhood Environment Rating *Scale: Revised edition*. New York, NY: Teachers College Press.

Kenya ECD Policy Framework. (June 2006). *Ministry of Education, Government of Kenya*, Nairobi, Kenya: Author.

King, P. E., Clardy, C. E., & Ramos, J. S. (2010). *Spiritual exemplars from around the work: An exploratory study of spiritual development in adolescents*. Paper presented at the Biennial Meeting of the Society for Research on Adolescence, Philadelphia, PA.

Malmberg, K., & Keough, L. (2004). *Mind, heart and soul in the fight against poverty*. Washington, DC: World Bank.

Malmberg, L. -E., Mwaura, P., & Sylva, K. (2010). Effects of a preschool intervention on cognitive development among East-African preschool children: A flexibly time-coded growth model. *Early Childhood Research Quarterly, 26*(2011), 124–133. doi:10.1016/j.ecresq.2010.04.003

Mezirow, J. (1997). Transformative learning: From theory to practice. In S. B. Merriam (Ed.), *New directions for adult and continuing education* (pp.5–12). San Francisco: Jossey-Bass.

Morgan, P., & Muigai, S. (2000). *CIDA programme evaluation: The work of the Aga Khan Foundation in the education sector in East Africa*. Report submitted to the Canadian International Development Agency Partnership Branch, Ottawa.

Mwaura, P. A. M. (2001). *Propositions on the "what and why" of program effectiveness: A case of Madrasa Resource Centre, East Africa*. Draft report. Mombasa, Kenya: Madrasa Regional Research Programme.

Mwaura, P., & Seif B. T. (2008). Madrasa Early Childhood Development Program: Making a difference. In M. Garcia, A. Pence, & J. Evans (Eds.), *Africa's future, Africa's challenge: Early childhood care and development in sub Saharan Africa* (pp. 389–405). Washington, DC: the World Bank.

Mwaura, P., Sylva, K., & Malmberg, L. -E. (2008). Evaluating the Madrasa pre-school programme in East Africa: A quasi-experimental study. *International Journal of Pre-School Education, 16*, 237–255.

Myers, R. (1995). *The twelve who survive: Strengthening programs for early childhood in the developing world* (2nd ed.). London: Rutledge.

Norwegian Ministry of Children and Family Affairs (1996), Framework Plan for Day Care Institutions, Oslo.

Nguluka, S. (2001). *Brief description of Bokamoso early childhood program*. Ghanzi, Botswana: Bokamoso Trust.

OECD. (2006). *Starting Strong II: Early childhood education and care*. Paris: OECD Publications.

Pence, A. (2004). *ECD policy development and implementation in Africa*. UNESCO Early Childhood and Family Policy Series n°9, November, 2004, UNESCO, Paris.

Roehlkepartain, E. C. (2012). "It's the way you look at things": How young people around the world understand and experience spiritual development. In K. E. Larson (Ed.), *Understanding children's spirituality: Theology, research, and practice* (pp. 152–172). Eugene, OR: Cascade Books.

Shallwani, S. (2010). *Madrasa preschool sustainability study*. Geneva: Aga Khan Foundation.

Sylva, K., Siraj-Blatchford, I., Taggart, B., & Coleman, P. (1999). *The Early Childhood Environment Rating Scale Extension (ECERS-E): Four Curricular Subscales (draft)*. London : Institute of Education.

van Ravens, J. (2010). *Holistic ECD for All in Indonesia: Supporting communities to close the gap*. Commissioned by: UNICEF Office in Jakarta. Draft version as of February 15, 2010.

Vargas-Barón, E. (2005). *Planning policies for early childhood development: Guidelines for action*. Sponsored by ADEA Working Group for ECCD, World Bank, UNICEF and United Nations Educational, Scientific and Cultural Organization (UNESCO).

Wagner, D. A., & Spratt, J. E. (1987). Cognitive consequences of contrasting pedagogies: The effects of Quranic preschooling in Morocco. *Child Development, 58*, 1207–1219, Society for Researcher in Child Development, Inc.

World Vision International. (2009). *Policy principles for the spiritual nurture of children*. Monrovia, CA: World Vision International.

Yust, K. M., Johnson, A. N., Sasso, S. E., & Roehlkepartain, E.C. (Eds.). (2006). *Nurturing child and adolescent spirituality: Perspectives from the world's religious traditions*. Lanham, MD: Rowan and Littlefield.

Zero to Three. (2008). *Faith-based services and very young children*, Vol. 28, No. 3. Washington, DC: National Center for Infants, Toddlers, and Families.

16

Early Education for All

IS THERE A ROLE FOR THE PRIVATE SECTOR?

Martin Woodhead and Natalia Streuli

Other chapters in this volume explore the contribution of governments, nongovernmental organizations (NGOs), and faith-based organizations in provision of early childhood services for young children and families. This chapter is focused on the potential of the private sector, which is receiving increasing national and international attention as part of the search for alternative models for financing early childhood care and education (ECCE) (e.g. Nadeau et al., 2011, section 4). One attractive possibility is establishing a global fund for ECCE, harnessing private philanthropies and corporate engagement into development initiatives, including education (Burnett & Bermingham, 2010). Although acknowledging these initiatives, our focus in this chapter is on a more localized aspect of the financing debate; namely, the role of the private sector as a service provider—especially the "private-for-profit" sector. Specifically, the chapter asks how far growth in private ECCE services that are often little (or lightly) regulated is compatible with ensuring equity in access and quality of ECCE.

Private-for-profit covers a very wide spectrum indeed, from single individuals running a small business that offers children a few hours care in their homes, through to large corporations running major chains of multipurpose nurseries. It also encompasses both highly committed, professional private providers as well as entrepreneurs whose main interest is to exploit a market opportunity. Private providers are long established on the ECCE scene in some of the richest economies, notably in the United States, especially in child care and especially for the youngest children (Lloyd & Penn, 2012; Myers, 2002). Private provision is also growing quickly in countries that have long traditions of public sector welfare and education services, as in the United Kingdom, Belgium, and the Netherlands (Moss, 2009; UNESCO, 2006). Most significantly for this chapter, the private sector is often filling an ECCE vacuum in developing and middle-income countries, especially in rapidly growing cities. These are "raw markets" for private sector providers (Penn, 2010), who are frequently neglected by governments and largely unaccounted for in official monitoring and statistics.

The de facto penetration of the private sector within many education systems throughout the world is justification enough for ECCE strategies to acknowledge their significance. For example, the World Bank 2020 Strategy now reframes the agenda as about Learning for All and makes clear that: "Learning opportunities include education services offered by the nonstate sector. This sector—which encompasses both for-profit and not-for-profit entities—functions as a provider, funder, and/or innovator in education" (World Bank 2011, p. 34).

For some commentators, private ECCE services are a positive expression of neo-liberal values, offering choice, quality, accountability, and value for money through competitive market processes. For others, private ECCE services—especially unregulated private services—are incompatible with equity goals, and with the goals of prevention, intervention, and social inclusion for the most disadvantaged, marginalized, and developmentally at-risk groups. This "public versus private" debate is fueled as much by ideology as by evidence. For example, quality is frequently identified as a weakness of some public (i.e., government run) early childhood systems that encourage parents to look toward the private sector. Yet, claims about high quality from the private sector may also be exaggerated; for example, with one U.S. study reporting private child care as more often employing less trained and poorly paid staff and receiving lower quality ratings (Sosinky et al., 2007).

This short chapter cannot do justice to the actual and potential ways in which the private sector contributes to global ECCE for children from 0–8 years of age. Our focus is on the role of the private sector in contributing toward Education for All (EFA) goal 1: "Expanding and improving comprehensive early childhood care and education (ECCE), especially for the most vulnerable and disadvantaged children" (World Education Forum, Dakar, April 26–28, 2000).

Most countries are far from achieving this goal. On the contrary, despite widespread agreement about the potential benefits of targeting disadvantaged groups, it is these groups that are currently least able to access ECCE across most regions of the world (Engle et al., 2011). So, key questions are:

1. Is growth in private sector ECCE serving to amplify these inequities?
2. What kinds of government financing and regulation would be required to harness private sector providers to contribute to EFA Goal 1?

Until recently, the role of private sector providers has been largely neglected in ECCE policy analyses. The conventional image of private ECCE has been about a fee-charging service largely affordable for a minority of privileged children from elite business and professional communities, and subject to little—if any—regulation. Some commentators, by contrast, look positively at the private sector as an alternative route for governments to deliver on core policy goals and obligations through various forms of public-private partnership (PPP) programs (Patrinos & Sosale, 2007). These PPPs can take many forms, but typically involve outsourcing the provision and management of services to private-for-profit (and/or not-for-profit community-based providers), with government funding provided either direct to providers or via voucher schemes (Patrinos, Barrera-Osorio, & Guáqueta, 2009). Public-private partnership programs can seem especially attractive in resource-poor countries where "going to scale" with public ECCE provision is unsustainable, despite high popular demand and/or arguments about the importance of harnessing education to early human capital formation. In these situations, PPPs can redistribute the burden of costs among stakeholders, with governments as providers, families as consumers, and national and international donors or charities (and, in some enterprising cases, corporate sectors) as social investors (UNICEF/ADB, 2011).

The role of the private sector in achieving (or impeding) the goals of the EFA and the United Nations Millennium Development Goals (MDGs) has been much more extensively evaluated in respect to primary education than for ECCE. For example, in India, the private sector has grown at a phenomenal rate, as poor parents seek out what they consider to be better quality school for their children (Walford & Srivastava, 2007). This trend has been proposed as contributing to the achievement of EFA goals (Tooley, 2009; Tooley & Dixon, 2005; Tooley, Dixon, & Gomathi, 2007) but has also been subject to critical review showing evidence of incompatibility with the equity principles that are central to EFA (Harma, 2009, 2011; Lewin, 2007; Rose, 2010; Woodhead, Frost, & James, 2013).

Private sector engagement in primary education is instructive for two reasons. First, many of the models proposed for PPP in primary education are also relevant to ECCE, and a much more extensive research literature is available sharing many of the same underlying debates. Second, ECCE does not function in isolation. The presence of a large, private primary sector impacts down into the early years, as entrepreneurs set up kindergarten classes to capture their market early in the education cycle, and as parents are keen to ensure their young child is well prepared to progress through their chosen education trajectory (Streuli, Vennam, & Woodhead, 2011).

In the next section, we argue that a simplistic "public" versus "private" distinction is inadequate as a basis for capturing the complexity of finance, governance, and function of ECCE services. We offer a conceptual framework that highlights some major ways that the private sector is currently functioning in global ECCE. The rest of the chapter illustrates these functions through a series of short country case studies (drawing on *Young Lives* longitudinal research in Ethiopia, India, and Peru; see www.younglives.org.uk). Finally, we offer some examples of PPP initiatives before returning to the core debate surrounding public versus private, and we conclude with a set of key questions for policy development in this area.

Defining the Private Sector

Definitions of public and private ECCE are an essential starting point:

1. The public sector is typically funded, managed, and regulated by national/ and or local governments; paid for by government (from taxation revenues

or via donors); and made available to all, universally or according to need, as a "public good" and in the public interest.

2. The private sector, by contrast, is typically owned and managed by individuals, businesses, and, in some countries, large corporations. The private sector is relatively autonomous of government and run according to a business model of service delivery financed by fees, paid for wholly or mainly by parents. As a market-driven service, the consumers of private provision gain access according to their ability to pay, rather than according to their need or entitlements.

3. It is important to distinguish "for-profit" from "not-for-profit," in order to recognize the role of many faith-based, NGO-managed, and community-based ECCE programs (Aga Khan Foundation Team, 2007). Chapters 14 and 15 have reviewed "not-for-profit" sectors. This chapter is mostly concerned with the private-for-profit sector as it relates to government/public sector services.

In recent decades, there has been a trend for government withdrawal from direct provision of services, including among affluent democracies with long traditions of national public services, through various forms of service "marketization" and also through PPPs. This "third way" between public and private encourages the creation of markets within public services, with the goal of reducing public expenditure (Giddens, 1998). It is often combined with ideologies of increased choice, accountability, and empowerment to parents, which is claimed to drive up quality, along with significant decentralization of control and shifts from supply-side funding to consumer subsidy funding, notably via voucher systems (Bennett 2008). These public–private distinctions can appear even more blurred from the parents' perspective. Paying for and organizing the daily routines that support children's development are the "private" responsibility of family and community, with ECCE services supporting and complementing parents, to greater or lesser to degree. Even where public services are offered as "no fee," parents are often required to cover the costs of uniforms, meals, transport, learning materials, and more. And, many publicly funded ECCE services also request (or demand) a parental contribution, which may be means-tested according to families' ability to pay. At the same time, private services may be advertised as giving parents greater opportunity to shape their children's learning by offering choices and management structures that are responsive to consumer demand. Yet, claims about "increasing choices" may appear hollow to families who lack the resources to make choices for their children, or who live in remote areas where no such choices are available. For poor families, more significant choices are often about which of their children will attend a government or a private ECCE setting, and/or about which of their children will be encouraged to complete school or drop-out early (Streuli, Vennam, & Woodhead, 2011; Woodhead, Frost, & James, 2013). It is also important to recognize that families may use a range of public and private services for individual children, even at the same time. For example, in some countries, it is common for children to attend government school by day and then receive private tuition out of school, sometimes even offered by the same teacher (Foondun, 2002).

In short, polarizing "public" versus "private" is not helpful as a basis for moving forward in policy terms. It is useful to recognize ECCE services as varying on three major dimensions (following Bangay, 2007): finance, management, goals and client group.

Finance

Early childhood care and education services are currently funded via multiple sources, including supply-side funding from national and local governments and/or demand-driven funding via fees charged to parents' fees and contributions (Myers, 2000). In many low-resource countries, national and international charities and donors play a major role, along with corporate contributions or social investments. Although some provision may be predominantly funded either by governments or via fees to parents, "third-way" models often assume a mixture of public subsidy and fees or voucher systems that can be redeemed in either public or private settings. The increased marketization of ECCE has been a feature of Organization for Economic Cooperation and Development (OECD) countries in recent years (OECD, 2006), notably in England and the Netherlands (Moss, 2009; Penn, 2007) and seems likely to be offered as an attractive, low-cost route for resource-poor countries, especially given the inevitable transience of international aid and philanthropy that currently supports many ECCE initiatives (van Ravens & Aggio, 2008).

Management

Early childhood care and education services may be publicly or privately owned, or owned by independent trusts or charities. They may be highly centralized as national systems or decentralized to local municipalities and communities. One of the biggest risks of current trends occurs when governments neglect to carry out their responsibilities to regulate private sector services, based on the false premise that "if it is private then it isn't the responsibility of government." On the contrary, systems for legal registration are essential, and governments have a responsibility to ensure compliance with basic health and safety standards for buildings and equipment, appropriate staff–child ratios, training, qualifications and working conditions, curriculum and assessment systems, and child protection procedures, all of which will be subject to monitoring and inspection.

Goals and Client Group

Early childhood care and education has a long history of being targeted toward disadvantaged children and families, serving goals of human development, social intervention, and community development, notably through breaking cycles of poverty and deprivation and reducing social exclusion. These goals appear, on the face of it, incompatible with the "for-profit" goals of the private sector and its traditional focus on serving affluent elite groups. This is another oversimplification. Although public services may be more or less standardized according to national or regional statutes and guidelines on teacher qualifications, ratios, curricula, and the like, private ECCE is usually less constrained and able to tailor provision to meet the aspirations (and the purse-size!) of parents as well as the perceived needs of children. Although promoting high academic achievement for elite and high-ability pupils is a traditional goal of private education, the private (especially not-for-profit) sector also serves specific interest groups by offering a distinctive (seen by some as "alternative") philosophy and approach to learning, cultural ethos, or language medium.

Functions for the Private Sector

Taking these three dimensions into account, Table 16.1 offers a taxonomy of some major functions of the private-for-profit sector in current ECCE. This taxonomy can serve as a starting point for a series of brief country case studies, focusing especially on countries within Young Lives longitudinal child poverty research. Reducing the private sector to four functions is inevitably an oversimplification, especially when applied to specific countries, which often have complex histories of ECCE and that provide a significant role for not-for-profit as well as for-profit providers. But they do convey the range of starting points for policy development in this area.

To obtain more detailed insights into the role and potential of public and private ECCE, the rest of this chapter builds on evidence collected as part of the Young Lives longitudinal study of 12,000 children growing up in Ethiopia, India (in state of Andhra Pradesh), Peru, and Vietnam (Woodhead, 2011) (see www.younglives.org.uk).[1]

FUNCTION A: PUBLIC FOR THE MAJORITY—PRIVATE FOR THE MINORITY IN PERU

Amongst the three Young Lives countries discussed in this chapter, Peru has the highest preschool coverage for 3- to 5-year-olds, and a well-established, mainly publicly funded preschool system that has been a priority for the government since 1972. In 2003, preschool became part of basic education, making it free and compulsory for children from 3 years of age (Government of Peru, 2003). Gross enrollment rates in preschool education more than doubled from 30% in 1991 to 66% in 2009 (INEI, 2009). Peru also pioneered the WawaWasi program for children from 6 months to 4 years old. In these ways, public ECCE has been a major resource for child development among families in Peru, and it is the foundational stage for an equally well-established primary school system, with a net enrollment

TABLE 16.1 Four functions of the private-for-profit sector in current early childhood care and education (ECCE)

Relationship to Public Sector	Major Features	Country Examples (elaborated below)
A. Well-established public sector for the majority, with private for more affluent minority	Well-developed national public programs, with independent private sector mainly for advantaged and elite groups. Minimal government engagement in licensing and quality of private sector.	Peru
B. Private sector growing in the absence of a public sector	Few public ECCE programs. Demand partially met by NGOs and community provision, plus private sector, mainly for advantaged and elite groups. Minimal government engagement in licensing and quality of private sector.	Ethiopia
C. Private sector competing with public to provide for relatively poor as well as more affluent families	Private sector offering alternative service to national public program, attractive to poorer aspiring families as well as to advantaged and elite groups. Increasing government engagement, including funding to ensure access to poor	India
D. Governments regulate and support private sector toward achieving public policy goals	Private sector is incorporated within public policies, licensed and regulated by government, and part funded via grants or voucher systems. Various forms of public-private partnerships	Singapore, Hong Kong, Chile, Colombia

ratio of 96% in 2005 (UNESCO, 2007). However, high enrollments have not been reflected in children's achievement levels, with Peru's students scoring lowest among the Latin American study countries in the Program for International Student Assessment (PISA), and about 20% behind the average for Argentina, Brazil, Chile, and Mexico (World Bank, 2007). Concern about children's earliest school experiences in Peru was first expressed during the 1990s, when the highest repetition rates were in first grade (24%). In 1995, in line with other Latin American countries, the Peruvian Ministry of Education banned repetition in the first grade and introduced automatic promotion. Repetition rates dropped to 5%, but concerns about quality continue (Ames, Rojas, & Portugal, 2010; Woodhead, Ames, Vennam, Abebe, & Streuli, 2009).

One complexity is that public preschool provision is split between two programs, resourced at different levels. Early education centers, known as *Centros de Educación Inicial* (CEIs), were especially established in growing urban areas. Later, government recognized the challenge of providing public ECCE more widely and rolled out a program of community-based programs known as PRONOEIs (*Programas no Escolarizados de Educación Inicial*), which account for much of the growth during the 1970s and '80s. PRONOEIs became a lower-cost alternative for the government to expand coverage and enrollment, and were a means of reaching remote and smaller communities and overcoming a shortage of teachers. Lately, they have become lower resourced versions of CEIs with less impact on students' overall achievement in first grade (Cueto & Díaz, 1999; Díaz, 2007). This two-tier public ECCE system in Peru is a cause for concern, since the lower resourced PRONOEIs are offered mainly to children living in economically and socially deprived areas (60% in rural areas), thus reinforcing inequalities of access to quality educational services (Ames, Rojas, & Portugal, 2009).

Most families in Peru have little choice but to accept the public education opportunities on offer at preschool and primary levels. However, there is a growing private sector, especially in urban areas, in which parents are more able to pay fees and make choices among a range of public and private centers available in areas of high population density. In 1998, the ratio of public to private provision of early education stood at 4:1; in 2008, this ratio decreased to 1.5:1. Indeed, the number of private early education centers increased by more than 57% from 1998 (5,200 centers) to 2008 (7,543 centers) (Woodhead et al., 2009). This evidence of increased demand and supply in private education can be seen, in part, as indication of the increased wealth among a growing minority of relatively affluent Peruvian families, especially in the cities. Accessing a good-quality private preschool is seen as an essential first step toward a successful trajectory through the private education sector. Between 1990 and 2005, private schools grew from 13% to 16% for primary aged children, and from 15% to 22% for the secondary level (Patrinos et al., 2009).

These trends are reinforced by data from Young Lives. When the 2,000 younger cohort children (born 2001/2002) were around 5 to 6 years old, their parents were asked about attendance at preschool since the age of three. Although participation rates across all types of provision were remarkably high (84%), with only a small gender difference (85% boys and 82% girls), other inequities were quite marked. Twenty-nine percent of 6-year-old children from the poorest households in the Young Lives sample had no experience of attending preschool, whereas only 4% of children from more advantaged households had not attended preschool at some point since they were 3 years old.[2] These differences are largely accounted for by the greater access to private preschool among the more affluent households. For example, in rural sites, around 60% of children attended a government preschool, across all household poverty levels. But an additional 30% of the children from the "least poor" households attended a private preschool, whereas only 1% of the poorest children accessed private sector education. In urban settings, the picture is more complex. Participation rates in government–run preschools are higher among households in the mid-range. Children living in the poorest households had less access to government preschools. At the other end of the scale, the least poor households also made less use of government preschools, but this is mainly because 34% of these children were attending a private preschool, which, in many cases, would be their stepping off point into a relatively privileged private education trajectory.

Although the private sector has, for the most part, served this traditional function for more affluent urban families, the government of Peru began looking toward greater involvement of the private sector through a framework law containing overall guidelines to enable PPPs in the provision of specific services, such as infrastructure and transportation (Government of Peru, 2008). In respect to education, the government has also set a favorable framework for PPPs through its *Proyecto Educativo Nacional* (CNE, 2006), but, to date, there is neither specific legislation nor guidelines for developing PPPs for core service delivery. Finally, a new government elected in 2011 has reaffirmed that early childhood should be a national priority, with new initiatives being plannednotably *Cuna Mas*. These developments reinforce the priority for strong governance of ECCE, which is the responsibility of several ministries, as well as a recognition of the state's role as a facilitator and coordinator as well as a provider of services (Cueto, 2011).

FUNCTION B: PRIVATE SECTOR IN THE ABSENCE OF A STRONG PUBLIC SECTOR IN ETHIOPIA

Ethiopia offers a contrasting case study to Peru. It shares a major challenge with other countries in the region to consolidate its basic service infrastructures, including ECCE as well primary education. It is estimated that less than 12% of Africa's 4- to 6-year-olds were enrolled in any form of ECCE, which in many countries is provided through a combination of NGO and church-based initiatives, plus a growing private sector, which has capitalized on the demand from relatively better-off parents keen to give their children the best start in education (UNESCO, 2010a,b).

The case of Ethiopia highlights the challenges for low-resource economies moving toward EFA goals. Ethiopia is currently the second most populous country in Africa and ranked 171st out of 181 countries on the United Nations (UN) Human Development Index of least-developed countries. Until recently, the priority for the government of Ethiopia has been to expand primary education very rapidly, in order to achieve EFA/MDG targets, and early childhood has been relatively neglected. The net enrollment ratio in primary education increased from 33% to 68% between 1999 and 2005, and gender equity has improved (38% of boys vs. 28% of girls in 1999 to 71% of boys vs. 66% of girls; UNESCO, 2007, p. 291). Despite such rapid progress in enrollment statistics, the quality challenges have been enormous, with large classes, few resources, poorly qualified teachers, and high student dropout. In the absence of universal birth registration, uncertainty about whether children have reached school age, combined with a large influx of children seeking admission to school for the first time, results in first-grade classes attended by children of very different ages and levels of maturity. These challenges are highlighted by evidence from the Young Lives sample, that 39% of the poorest quintile children were at least two grades behind the expected grade for their age, compared with 12% of children from the least poor quintile. These challenges are gradually being addressed, notably through a General Education Quality Improvement Program (GEQIP) launched in 2009 (Orkin et al., 2012).

Against this background of the rapid construction of a universal primary education system, the government of Ethiopia has until recently given little attention to provision of ECCE. For the vast majority of young children, their first experience of education has been primary school, although this is by no means universal, given that late enrolment (as well as early drop-out) is still very common. The early years vacuum has been filled by the private sector, including a tradition of church-linked preschools and, in Addis Ababa and other urban centers, a small but growing for-profit sector, exclusively available to those few families able to afford fees. Nearly 58% of the Young Lives sample in urban communities had attended preschool at some point since the age of 3. But only 5% went to a government-run program. In contrast, less than 4% of rural children had attended preschool of any kind (Orkin et al., 2012).

In 2010, the government of Ethiopia conducted a situation analysis with the support of the UN Children's Fund (UNICEF), revealing a number of weaknesses within the current system, including high fees, lack of teacher training, lack of standard curriculum, lack of culturally relevant story books, low teacher salaries, and high teacher turnover, among other things. The government has now developed an ambitious policy for ECCE, with four strands covering child health and parental education, kindergarten classes attached to primary schools, and a child-to-child program, through which grade 6 children, trained by grade 1 and grade 6 teachers, act as young facilitators in a program of play designed to improve children's school readiness (Government of Ethiopia, 2010). Under this new policy framework, the government is given increased responsibility for training teachers, further developing a curriculum, and providing play and teaching materials, supervision, and quality guidance.

Although the new policy framework is a step forward for ECCE in Ethiopia, it may also put strain on an already overstretched primary education system, and on children and families as well (see Orkin et al., 2012). Unless donor resources are mobilized or responsible PPPs for ECCE are developed, the new policy may compromise the quality of education provided and/or the extent of service development, especially into "hard to reach" communities and districts. Given the financial constraints and lack of skilled personnel, one option would be for the Ethiopian government to focus on community- and home-based early childhood programs, instead of setting up new ECCE centers (Okengo, 2010). Lesotho, Kenya, Namibia, and South Africa, among others, have already done so and have managed to increase preprimary gross enrollment rates by more than 7% over 2 years (UNESCO, 2010b).

FUNCTION C: PRIVATE COMPETING WITH PUBLIC IN ANDHRA PRADESH, INDIA

Young Lives research in the state of Andhra Pradesh, India, offers a very distinctive example of the issues raised in this chapter. A long-established public early childhood program, the Integrated Child Development Services (ICDS), is being increasingly displaced by private kindergartens, especially in urban areas, but increasingly in rural communities too, and including for significant numbers of relatively poor families. The consequence is that children follow a range of pathways through public and private preschools and primary schools, in some cases switching between sectors at several points in their school career. The growth of private early childhood services is part of a wider trend of families choosing private primary schools in preference to government schools, in the belief that this will lead to higher achievement and increased opportunities for their children (Woodhead, Frost, & James, 2013).

One of the major attractions of the private sector is that English is offered as the medium of instruction, beginning in kindergarten. By contrast, the language of instruction in government primary schools is traditionally Telugu, the regional language in Andhra Pradesh, which is not spoken in other parts of India. The impact of choice on equity is crucial, with concerns that traditional social stratification is reinforced and some evidence that private school choices are shaped by traditional gendered expectations, especially in poorest families, as parents anticipate a higher return from investing limited resources in sons than in daughters (Streuli et al., 2011).

As noted above, the growth of private preschools in India is taking place despite the existence of a public early childhood care system based on *anganwadi* centers (literally "courtyard shelter" in Hindi), under the umbrella of India's ICDS. Claimed to be one of the world's largest and longest established public early childhood programs, ICDS originated in 1974, with a comprehensive vision, including immunization, growth monitoring, and health and referral services, as well as preschool education. But ICDS depends largely on individual states for implementation through the establishment of a network of *anganwadi* (preschool) centers in both urban and rural areas. The quality of provision is highly variable, with poorly trained and low-paid staff often working in inadequate buildings and with few learning resources in some states. The nutrition component and some basic child care are the major attractions for many poor parents, especially in rural areas (CIRCUS, 2006).

In rural communities of Andhra Pradesh, ICDS *anganwadis* dominate, and the majority of enrolments come from the poorest households. Parents report that they have no choice since the *anganwadi* is the only option available. It is only for more advantaged groups that private preschools are a significant option, accounting for 31% of the children in the least poor rural group in the Young Lives sample (see Figures 16.1 and 16.2). In urban Andhra Pradesh, by contrast, private preschools dominate. Poverty levels are strongly predictive of whether children attend private preschool, but a surprising 34% of the poorest households opted for a private preschool, compared to 46% attending government preschools. The strong trend toward private preschool is confirmed by 123 cases in the Young Lives sample in which caregivers reported that their children had attended more than one preschool since the age of 3. In 82% of these cases, the caregiver reported that the child had been moved from a government *anganwadi* preschool to a private kindergarten class.

Selective enrollment in private kindergartens is also linked to gender differentiation, with girls more likely to be educated within the government sector and expected to leave school earlier than their brothers. Attitude data reinforce evidence of gender differentiation, with 68% of 12-year-old boys anticipating university education compared to 54% of girls (and only 42% of girls' caregivers).

Figures 16.1 and 16.2 are based on Round 2 of Young Lives longitudinal survey in 2006/2007, when children were around 5–6 years old. These same children's pathways into primary school have since been followed up through household surveys in 2009, when they were around 8 years old, along with in-depth qualitative research (Streuli et al., 2011). Our most recent evidence confirms the ways in which early childhood opportunities to attend private versus government school (linked to location, poverty, and gender) are established during children's crucial school transition years (Woodhead, Frost, & James, 2013).

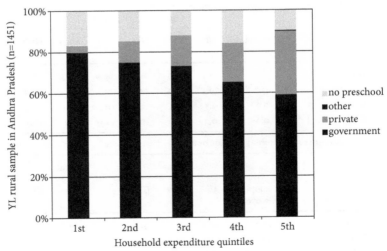

FIGURE *16.1 Attendance by preschool type and poverty levels: rural sample in Andhra Pradesh, India*

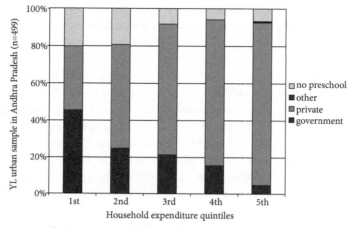

FIGURE 16.2 *Attendance by preschool type and poverty levels: urban sample in Andhra Pradesh, India*

Table 16.2 compares school attendance up to the age of 8 for the Young Lives "younger cohort" (born 2001/2002) (the same children as in Figures 16.1 and 16.2) with an older cohort of children who were born in 1994/1945. Although almost all children in both cohorts were in school by the age 8, a marked shift has taken place in a few years, with the proportion of 8-year-olds attending private schools

TABLE 16.2 Trends in primary school attendance among Young Lives 8-year-olds (comparing younger and older cohorts)

2009—YOUNGER COHORT AT THE AGE OF 8 (%)

	Full sample (*n* = 976)	Urban			Rural		
		All	*Boys*	*Girls*	*All*	*Boys*	*Girls*
Government	54.6	18.1	16.5	20.0	66.9	59.3	75.5
Private	43.7	79.3	81.3	76.8	31.7	39.2	23.2
Other	0.9	2.5	2.3	2.7	0.3	0.4	0.3
Out of school	0.9	0.2	0.0	0.5	1.1	1.2	1.0

2002/2003—OLDER COHORT AT THE AGE OF 8 (%)

	Full sample (*n* = 976)	Urban			Rural		
		All	*Boys*	*Girls*	*All*	*Boys*	*Girls*
Government	73.7	32.9	31.5	34.5	87.4	86.9	87.8
Private	23.7	63.8	64.6	63.0	10.1	11.1	9.3
Other	0.9	2.0	3.1	0.8	0.5	1.1	0.0
Out of school	1.7	1.2	0.8	1.7	1.9	0.9	2.9

Source: Woodhead, Ames, Vennam, Abebe , & Streuli (2009) Survey Data for Younger and Older Cohort

jumping from 23.7% to 43.7%. Young Lives evidence also suggests that gender differences have increased as private education has become more widespread among poorer families with fewer resources to pay fees for all their children (see Table 16.2). Nearly 50% of boys from the younger cohort were attending private primary schools, compared with only 36% of girls. Conversely, girls were overrepresented in government schools (62%) compared with 48% of boys. This gender difference was most marked among rural children, with a difference of around 16% in private school intake between boys and girls (39.2% vs. 23.2%) (Woodhead, Frost, & James, 2013).

In response to concerns about the inequities created by recent trends, the Right to Education Act (RTE) 2009 requires that 25% of places in private primary schools be reserved for disadvantaged children, with the fees being reimbursed by the government (Government of India, 2009; see Streuli et al., 2011). At the time of writing, this small step in the direction of "public-private partnership" is still being implemented, with many challenges from a highly decentralized education system. A first step is to ensure that the many "unrecognized" private schools are officially registered and can be monitored to ensure that they implement the 25% rule in ways that are fair and transparent (Srivastava, 2007).

FUNCTION D: HARNESSING THE PRIVATE SECTOR TOWARD PUBLIC GOALS IN SINGAPORE, HONG KONG, CHILE, AND COLOMBIA

Functions A–C (discussed above) highlight the importance of the private sector in three diverse contexts, but uncover the limited government engagement to harness private sector services toward achieving public ECCE goals, through Public Private Partnerships (PPPs). This contrasts with the attention given to the potential of the private sector in primary education (e.g., Patrinos & Sosale, 2007; Srivastava & Walford, 2007; and see special issue of *Development and Change*; Rose, 2010). In this final section, we offer a few brief examples of PPPs for early childhood from Singapore, Hong Kong, and Chile.

All preschools and child care centers in Singapore are entirely managed and operated by individuals, communities, NGOs, or enterprises. The government makes regular visits to the early childhood centers for supervision, licensing, health checks, and the like, and finances these nonpublic services but does not involve itself in delivery. The government, however, continues subsidies for all families by paying up to 30% of the fees, whereas for the poor, there is an additional financial assistance program (UNESCO, 2007b).

Another example of PPP comes from Hong Kong where, in 2007, the government introduced the Preschool Education Voucher Scheme that was designed to increase government investment in preschool education and to enhance its quality. This scheme was implemented from the 2007–2008 school year. These vouchers are given to parents and can be redeemed in kindergartens whose fees do not exceed

HK$24,000 per year (around US$3,080) for a half-day session or HK$48,000 per year for a full-day session. Schools receive HK$13,000 per year per child, and HK$3000 is to be used for teacher professional development. Li et al. (2010) argue that the voucher scheme promotes the accessibility, accountability, and affordability of preschool education in Hong Kong. As part of its regulative role, the government has linked voucher redemption to the quality of preschool education. To continue to be a "voucher" kindergarten, all teachers must have a Certificate in Early Childhood Education by the end of the 2011 academic year, and all newly appointed kindergarten principals must have a B.Ed. in early childhood education and 1 year of post-qualification experience. Further, from 2012–2013 vouchers can only be redeemed at kindergartens that have met government benchmarks for quality (Rao, 2010, p. 32).

Despite the interest in these examples, Singapore and Hong Kong are distinctive in being geographically condensed, urban populations with relatively strong infrastructures and thriving economies. Caution is needed in assuming that these models would generalize to large countries with diverse populations, weaker infrastructures and high levels of extreme poverty and inequalities. Chile offers some insight into the possibilities and challenges of such schemes.

Chile introduced a voucher system in the early 1980s, under which public and private subsidized schools receive a common direct subsidy from the government for each student admitted. Although this reform sparked a redistribution of students across private and public schools, it also created some controversy (Bellei, 2005). The most questionable characteristic in Chile's voucher system is that public schools are forced to accept all students, whereas private subsidized schools can select students in accordance with their education objectives. As a result, to minimize costs, private subsidized schools have incentives to select students who are less expensive to educate; that is, students with better skills, presenting fewer special needs, and possibly from higher socioeconomic groups (Contreras, Bustos, & Sepúlveda, 2010).

Another type of partnership comes through corporate engagement in ECCE funding. In Colombia, in 2000, the *Cajas de Compensación Familiar* (Family Benefit Fund, CAFAM), along with Bogota's Major Office and the *Instituto Colombiano de Bienestar Familiar* (ICBF, Colombian Institute for Family Welfare) created an alliance to increase ECCE coverage in the capital city. They created a network of early childhood services called *Red de Jardines Sociales* as a way of implementing the law that requires Family Benefit Funds to allocate a share of its members' contribution to ECCE programs. Both central and local governments fund set up and infrastructure costs, whereas CAFAM is responsible for operating and managing the ECCE programs. At the time of writing (2011), *Red de Jardines Sociales* reaches around 7,000 children from the most disadvantaged neighborhoods in Bogota (www.mineducacion.gov.co).

POLICY QUESTION: IS THE PRIVATE SECTOR
A CHALLENGE OR AN OPPORTUNITY?

Finally, we return to the core question: What is—and could be—the role of the private-for-profit sector in delivering on goals for ECCE in terms of management, resourcing, and reaching target groups? It seems appropriate to declare that our starting point has been one of skepticism about current trends, in two respects. First, growth of private preschools may benefit individual children when families can pay for a quality service, but it is hard to reconcile with EFA goal 1, which prioritizes disadvantaged, vulnerable, and excluded groups. To achieve this goal, much more active government engagement is essential, as set out in successive UNESCO GMR reports, notably in 2006 and 2009. The priority to develop positive, proactive, pro-equity agendas to achieve good outcomes for all young children is also the core message of UNCRC General Comment 7 (UN Committee, 2005), reinforced in the Secretary General's Report to the UN General Assembly, 2010 (A65/206). Second, the private sector contributes to the delivery of high-quality public services in many countries, through contracts for buildings and materials, outsourcing arrangements for delivery of professional training and inspection systems, and more. Some countries have also taken the more radical step of entering into PPPs that privatize all or part of service delivery. Although these schemes are worth exploring with the private-for-profit sector, this should not be at the expense of well-proven partnership arrangements with NGOs, community-based services, and other not-for-profit providers who are more likely to be working with disadvantaged, vulnerable, and excluded groups. For example, the Open Society Foundation's Step by Step program was initiated in 15 countries in 1994, and has grown into a network of 29 NGO partners (Klaus, 2011; Stasz, 2008).

Finally, we offer three conclusions:

Positive Early Childhood Policies Should Encompass the Actual or Potential Role of the Private Sector

A permissive or laissez-faire approach to the private sector is not a positive, proactive agenda, nor will this alone achieve EFA goals, especially in respect to equity and targeting of the most disadvantaged. Public services generally claim to offer equitable access or targeted services according to need and entitlement. But a highly decentralized, deregulated, and market-driven service offers no such promises. In so far as the provision of services is driven by parents' willingness and ability to pay the whole or part cost, and providers' ability to make a profit, then majority groups, the affluent, and urban areas will tend to benefit over minority groups, the poor, and rural areas. Although many individual children will benefit from private provision, this will be at the expense of equity and social justice. Marginalized groups and disabled children are especially at risk of exclusion within market-driven models, with the effect of reinforcing or even amplifying the very disparities that fuel cycles of intergenerational poverty and inequality. It follows that any comprehensive policy for ECCE will encompass all sectors and all providers, in order to progress toward pro-equity goals in respect to access and quality.

The Private Sector Is Not an Alternative to Quality Public Services

The inefficiencies and quality challenges of public services in many low-resource countries is a major factor driving the growth of an unregulated private sector in some countries. Parents in India are choosing to pay for private ECCE and primary schooling because they judge the government sector to be of poor quality or failing to meet their aspirations for their children (Harma, 2009, 2011; Woodhead et al., 2009). Improving quality in existing services and making sure they are accessible to all is an important priority for any government. Some would argue that it is healthy in liberal democracies that public and private programs co-exist and serve different markets. This enables government to prioritize scarce funding to at-risk groups. The benefits are investment in those most likely to gain, so it is depressing to note that minority groups and the disabled are also underrepresented in many publicly funded systems.

Public-Private Partnerships Require High Levels of Governance and Finance

It is important to emphasize that governments retain crucial responsibilities for licensing, regulating, and supporting all services to ensure children's rights are respected and their learning optimized. Public-private partnerships can appear an economical and efficient solution. However, they are not necessarily a low-cost solution, and risks are attached in terms of ensuring access to the most disadvantaged and vulnerable groups, which will require direct subsidies or a voucher system. Public-private partnerships can reduce the burden on government and public providers to set up, manage programs, and train staff. But they require very proactive government engagement. They may involve a complex funding system, in which capital costs are covered by government, corporates, charities, or international donors, but recurrent costs are also shared with users. Minimally, it is essential in any ECCE system that all provision is licensed and inspected in a rigorous and positive way (Fielden & LaRocque, 2008). In short:

> Although the financing of ECCE services may be shared by a range of different funding sources—public, private, business, parents and communities—it is clear that public investment by national regional and local government is necessary to support a sustainable system of quality, accessible services. If ECCE is to be treated as a vital public service—like primary schools—it cannot be funded largely by the parents who use it. (OECD, 2001, p. 130)

Notes

1. Young Lives is core-funded from 2001 to 2017 by U.K. aid from the U.K. Department for International Development (DFID) and co-funded by the Netherlands Ministry of Foreign Affairs from 2010 to 2014. The research reported in this chapter was supported by additional funding from the Bernard van Leer Foundation, Netherlands. We acknowledge the contribution of many Young Lives' colleagues in the preparation of this chapter. The views expressed are those of the authors. They are not necessarily those of or endorsed by Young Lives, the University of Oxford, DFID, or other funders. For more information, see www.younglives.org.uk

2. Twenty percent of families with the lowest per capita household expenditure within the sample are considered the poorest in the sample, whereas the 20% of families with the highest per capita household expenditure are the least poor.

References

Aga Khan Foundation Team. (2007). *Non-state providers and public-private-community partnerships in education* (Background paper to the EFA Global Monitoring Report 2008, Education for All by 2015: Will We Make It?) Paris: UNESCO.

Ames, P., Rojas, V., & Portugal, T. (2009). *Starting school: Who is prepared? Young Lives' research on children's transition to first grade in Peru* (Working Paper No. 47). Oxford, UK: Young Lives.

Ames, P., Rojas, V., & Portugal, T. (2010). *Continuity and respect for diversity: Strengthening early transitions in Peru* (Working Paper No. 56). The Hague: Bernard van Leer Foundation.

Bangay, C. (2007). Cinderella or ugly sister? What role for non-state education provision in developing countries? In P. Srivastava & G. Walford (Eds.), *Private schooling in less-economically developed countries: Asian and African perspective* (pp. 111–128). Abingdon, UK: Symposium Books.

Bellei, C. (2005, October). *The private-public school controversy: The case of Chile. Paper presented at the Mobilizing the Private Sector for Public Education Conference,* Cambridge, MA.

Bennett, J. (2008). *Early childhood services in the OECD countries: Review of the literature and current policy development in the early childhood field* (Working Paper). Florence: UNICEF, Innocenti Research Center.

Burnett, N., & Bermingham, D. (2010). *Innovative financing for education* (Working Paper No. 5). London: Open Society Institute, Education Support Program.

CIRCUS. (2006). *Focus on children under six.* New Delhi: Citizen's Initiative for the Rights of Children under Six.

CNE. (2006). *Proyecto educativo nacional al 2021: La educación que queremos para el Perú.* Lima: Consejo Nacional de Educación, CNE.

Contreras, D., Bustos S., & Sepúlveda, P. (2010). When schools are the ones that choose: The effects of screening in Chile. *Social Science Quarterly, 91*(5), 1349–1368.

Cueto, S. (2011). Early childhood educational policies and programs in Peru: Challenges and prospects. *Early Childhood Matters, 117* (pp. 117–120).

Cueto, S., & Díaz, J. J. (1999). Impacto de la educación inicial en el rendimiento en primer grado de primaria en escuelas públicas urbanas de Lima. *Revista de Psicología de la Pontificia Universidad Católica del Perú, 17*(1), 74–91.

Díaz, J. J. (2007). Educación inicial y rendimiento en la escuela. *Boletín Análisis y Propuestas*, *12*, 1–4.

Engle, P. E., Fernald, L. C. H., Alderman, H. A., Behrman, J., O'Gara, C., Yousafzai, A., et al. (2011), Strategies for reducing inequalities and improving developmental outcomes for young children in low-income and middle-income countries. *The Lancet*, *378*(9799), 1339–1353.

Fielden, J., & LaRocque, N. (2008). *The evolving regulatory context for private education in emerging economies (Discussion Paper)*. Washington, DC: The World Bank Group International Colloquium on Private Education.

Foondun, R. A. (2002). The issue of private tuition: An analysis of the practice in Mauritius and selected South-East Asian countries. *International Review of Education*, *48*(6), 485–515.

Giddens, A. (1998). *The third way: The renewal of social democracy*. Cambridge, UK: Policy Press.

Government of Ethiopia. (2010). *National policy framework for early childhood care and education*. Addis Ababa: Addis Ababa University.

Government of India. (2009). *The Right of Children to Free and Compulsory Education Act, 2009*. New Delhi: Ministry of Human Resource Development.

Government of Peru. (2003). *Ley general de educación, No. 28044*. Lima: Government of Peru.

Government of Peru. (2008). *Ley marco de asociaciones Público-privadas para la generación de empleo productivo* (Decreto Legislativo No. 1012). Lima: Government of Peru.

Harma, J. (2009). Can choice promote education for all? Evidence from growth in private primary schooling in India. *Compare: A Journal of International and Comparative Education*, *39*(2), 151–165.

Harma, J. (2011). Low cost private schooling in India: Is it pro poor and equitable? *International Journal of Educational Development*, *31*(4), 350–356.

INEI. (2009). *Encuesta nacional de hogares*. Lima: Instituto Nacional de Estadística e Informática. Retrieved from www.escale.minedu.gob.pe/indicadores-nacionales

Klaus, S. (2011). Stepping-up: Scaling up the Step by Step program. *Early Childhood Matters*, *117*, 56–61.

Lewin, K. (2007). *The limits to growth of non-government private schooling in Sub Saharan, Africa* (Create Pathways to Access Research Monograph No 5). Falmer, UK: Consortium for Research on Educational Access, Transitions and Equity (CREATE), University of Sussex.

Li, Wong, J., & Wang, C. (2010). Affordability, accessibility, and accountability: Perceived impacts of the pre-primary education vouchers in Hong Kong. *Early Childhood Research Quarterly*, *25*, 125–138.

Lloyd, E., & Penn, H. (Eds.). (2012). *Childcare markets: Can they deliver an equitable service?* London: Policy Press.

Moss, P. (2009). *There are alternatives! Markets and democratic experimentalism in early childhood education and care (Working Paper No. 53)*. The Hague: Bernard Van Leer Foundation.

Myers, R. (2000). Financing early childhood education and care services. *International Journal of Educational Research*, *33*, 74–49.

Myers, R. (2002). Role of the "private sector" in early childhood development. In M. Young (Ed.), *From early child development to human development. Investing in our children's future* (pp. 257–292). Washington, DC: The World Bank.

Nadeau, S., Kataoka, N., Valerio, A., Neuman, M., & Elder, L. (2011). *Investing in young children: An early childhood policy guide for policy dialogue and project preparation.* Washington, DC: World Bank.

OECD. (2001). *Starting Strong: Early childhood education and care.* Paris: Organization for Economic Co-operation and Development.

OECD. (2006). *Starting Strong II: Early childhood education and care.* Paris: Organization for Economic Co-operation and Development.

Okengo, L. (2010). *Overview of ECD in Southern Africa.* Nairobi, KE: Open Society Institute Southern Africa.

Orkin, K., Yadete, W., & Woodhead, M. (2012). *Delivering quality early learning in low resource settings: Progress and challenges in Ethiopia* (Working Paper 59). The Hague: Bernard van Leer Foundation.

Patrinos, H. A., Barrera-Osorio, F., & Guáqueta, J. (2009). *The role and impact of public private partnerships in education.* Washington DC: World Bank.

Patrinos, H. A., & Sosale, S. (Eds.). (2007). *Mobilizing the private sector for public education: A view from the trenches.* Washington, DC: World Bank.

Penn, H. (2007). Childcare market management: How the United Kingdom government has reshaped its role in developing early childhood education and care. *Contemporary Issues in Early Childhood, 8*(3), 192–207.

Penn, H. (2010). *Childcare markets.* Keynote lecture at UNESCO World Conference on ECCE, Moscow.

Rao, N. (2010). Educational policy, kindergarten curriculum guidelines and the quality of teaching and learning: Lessons from kindergartens in Hong Kong. *International Journal of Early Childhood Education, 16*(2), 27–39.

Rose, P. (2010). Achieving education for all through public-private partnerships? *Development in Practice, 20*(4&5), 473–483.

Sosinky, L., Lord, H., & Zigler, E. (2007). For-profit/non-profit differences in center-based child care quality: Results from the National Institute of Child Health and Human Development Study of Early Child Care and Youth Development. *Journal of Applied Developmental Psychology, 28*(5), 390–410.

Stasz, C., Krop, C., Rastegar, A., & Vuollo, M. (2008). *The Step by Step Early Childhood Education Program: Assessment of reach and sustainability.* Santa Monica, CA: RAND Corporation.

Streuli, N., Vennam, U., & Woodhead, M. (2011). *Increasing choice or inequality? Pathways through early education in Andhra Pradesh, India* (Working Paper No. 58). The Hague: Bernard van Leer Foundation.

Tooley, J. (2009). *The beautiful tree: A personal journey into how the world's poorest people are educating themselves.* New Delhi: Penguin; Washington, DC: Cato Institute.

Tooley, J., & Dixon, P. (2005). *Private education is good for the poor: A study of private schools serving the poor in low-income countries.* Washington, DC: Cato Institute.

Tooley, J., Dixon, P., & Gomathi, S. V. (2007). Private schools and the Millennium Development Goal of Universal Primary Education: A census and comparative survey in Hyderabad, India. *Oxford Review of Education, 33*(5), 539–560.

UN Committee. (2005). *Implementing child rights in early childhood* (General Comment No. 7). CRC/C/GC/7/Rev.1. Geneva: United Nations Committee on the Rights of the Child.

UNESCO. (2006). *Strong foundations: Early childhood education and care. Global monitoring report 2007.* Paris: Author.

UNESCO. (2007). *Education for All by 2015: Will we make it? Global Monitoring Report 2008.* Paris: Author.

UNESCO. (2007b). *Partnership with non-public actors: Singapore's early childhood policy* (Policy Brief on Early Childhood No. 36). Paris: Author.

UNESCO. (2010a). *Reaching the marginalized. EFA global monitoring report, 2010.* Oxford, UK: Oxford University Press; Paris: UNESCO.

UNESCO. (2010b). *Early childhood care and education regional report: Africa.* Dakar: Regional Bureau for Education in Africa.

UNICEF/ADB. (2011). *Non-state providers and public-private partnerships in education for the poor.* Bangkok: UNICEF East Asia and Pacific Regional Office and Asian Development Bank.

van Ravens, J., & Aggio, C. (2008). *Expanding early childhood care and education: How much does it cost? A proposal for a methodology to estimate the costs of early childhood care and education at macro-level, applied to the Arab States* (Working Papers in Early Childhood Development). The Hague: Bernard van Leer Foundation.

Walford, G., & Srivastava, P. (2007). Examining private schooling in less economically developed countries: Key issues and new evidence. In P. Srivastava & G. Walford (Eds.), *Private schooling in less-economically developed countries: Asian and African perspectives.* Abingdon, UK: Symposium Books.

Woodhead, M. (2006). Changing perspectives on early childhood: Theory, research and policy. *International Journal of Equity and Innovation in Early Childhood, 4*(2), 5–48. (Originally published as commissioned background paper to UNESCO GMR 2006)

Woodhead, M., Ames, P., Vennam, U., Abebe, W., & Streuli, N. (2009). *Equity and quality? Challenges for early childhood and primary education in Ethiopia, India and Peru* (Working Paper No. 55). The Hague: Bernard van Leer Foundation.

Woodhead, M., Frost, M., & James, Z. (2012). Does growth in private schooling contribute to Education for All? Evidence from a longitudinal, two cohort study in Andhra Pradesh, India. *International Journal of Educational Development, 33*(1), 65–73

World Bank. (2007). *Toward high-quality education in Peru. Standards, accountability and capacity building.* Washington, DC: The International Bank for Reconstruction and Development and the World Bank.

World Bank. (2011). *Learning for all: Investing in people's knowledge and skills to promote development.* Washington, DC: Author.

17

Media and Early Childhood Development

Dafna Lemish and Barbara Kolucki

In this chapter, we are specifically concerned with the role media can play in bettering the lives of young children globally. We focus on electronic media such as children's television, and print media, especially children's books. Our threefold aim is, first, to outline media issues related to ensuring child rights. Second, we review the evidence that media, and specifically communication for development,[1] can strengthen, be supportive to, and complement broader integrated early child development strategies and specific development goals in low- and middle-income (LAMI) countries, especially the most disadvantaged and vulnerable. Third, we provide guidance for action. We summarize key principles and guidelines for communication for, with, and about young children that can help them develop cognitively, socially, and emotionally, and we discuss pioneering efforts in communication to produce media that are appropriate to the developmental level and cultural context of the child, and effective strategies for making the maximum impact through collaborative efforts of all sectors together with specially trained local media.

The Media and Children's Rights

Four issues in young children's access to communication (for), participation in communication (with), and in information about young children for their caregivers (about) can be identified. To address these issues, this chapter will provide examples of communication efforts that are not only *about* children, but also aim to communicate *with* and *for* children, by addressing them directly in child-appropriate communication.

First, communication for, with, and about young children should support the young child's rights, but too often it does not. The rights of children, as delineated in the United Nations Convention on the Rights of the Child (1989), include a variety of communication rights: the right to be heard and to be taken seriously, to free speech and to information, to maintain privacy, to develop cultural identity, and to be proud of one's heritage and beliefs. Yet these rights are rarely realized. Whether girls and boys live in deprived, resource-poor societies or in overwhelmingly commercialized, profit-driven ones, few children's voices are heard or taken seriously, and this is even less frequent for children under 8. Even in cases when young children appear to be provided space to offer their "voice," as in making a decision about who to live with, the voice heard often reflects the adults' perspective. There are too few possibilities for them to express their needs and opinions. Even an infant can express needs, and parents and caregivers should respond appropriately.

Second, although there is a growing movement in many developing countries to produce media for children and youth, the specific needs of the children younger than 8 years of age are often neglected in these parts of the world. They are often exposed to communication designed for older children or adults, and often it is imported from the Western world, which does not reflect their own culture or lives. The purpose of many of the imported programs is profit rather than the education of young children. As a result, young children around the globe are exposed to a wide range of content and audiovisual stimulation that is frequently not age- or culturally appropriate, but rather is designed for adults and for profit rather than for healthy child development.

Third, we should relate to children as people in their own right, rather than thinking of them as "little people" who are in the process of becoming fully grown adults. According to this view, we need to allow children, at each stage of their development, to be fully recognized as having unique needs and skills, as well as a personal voice that deserves to be listened to and understood with respect and empathy. Furthermore, communication often does not support children's sense of pride or cultural identity, particularly for those from disadvantaged groups. We want to create conditions that empower even the youngest children to be active agents of social change in their own lives.

Fourth, inequality in access to media, and in being represented or shown in media, is still prevalent in many LAMI countries. Many young children never own or even hold a book or have it read to them, or have an opportunity to see age-appropriate educational media. Globally, children differ in their access to a variety of media such as books and magazines, radio, television, computers, the internet, music players, and mobile phones (e.g., Drotner & Livingstone, 2008; Pecora, Osei-Hwere, & Carlsson, 2008). In some war- and disaster-affected areas, children may have no access to any form of media whatsoever. The digital inequalities that characterize our world today present a wide variety of challenges: Although some young children live in media-rich environments, where many media converge into a screen culture that dominates their lives, other young children are deprived of the most basic forms of communication technology that characterize our global world.

Yet, as processes of technological and cultural globalization accelerate, we expect that access to various media will become more common, even in remote areas of the world. Indeed, several pilot projects are attempting to study socialization to the media by introducing children living in remote areas to communication technologies—such as solar-powered radios or computers, the internet, and mobile phones—on an experimental basis encompassing a variety of age groups (e.g., Bachan & Raftree, 2011; RISE Project, 2009). These innovations have been used in places as diverse as Rwanda and Afghanistan, and in emergencies like earthquakes and hurricanes in parts of the majority and minority world. At the same time, many children raised in the middle class of the majority world are already exposed to the same wide range of media as their counterparts in countries with vast media access (Drotner & Livingstone, 2008; Van Feilitzen, Carlssoh, & Bucht, 2011).

However, access alone is not enough to make a difference in children's lives. It is the kind of content available to them when they have access to the television and/ or the computer or books that will make a difference (Calvert & Wilson, 2008; Singer & Singer, 2010; Strasburger, Wilson, & Jordan, 2009). Similarly, having access to and ability to use a mobile phone or an internet connection are insufficient in and of themselves to realize children's potential for growth and development. Rather, children's use of these media and the kind of connections they foster are the educational opportunities that contribute in qualitative ways to their development. The issues of unequal access and inappropriate use of media challenges us to consider the following questions: How can we reach children (and their caregivers) and enrich their lives by using media wisely and responsibly for their well-being and healthy development? How can we use different means of communication to make a difference, most specifically to vulnerable and disadvantaged children, in ways that build their resiliency to survive and thrive and that set them off on a trajectory of a better life?

The Research Evidence: Effects of Media on Young Children

The vast and rapidly accumulating scholarly work on the role of media in children's lives suggests that media serve as one of the most powerful socializing agents; that is, they teach children behaviors, attitudes, and worldviews (see for example, Calvert & Wilson, 2008; Drotner & Livingstone, 2008; Kirsh, 2009; Lemish, 2007; Mazzarella, 2007; Pecora, Murray, & Wartella, 2007; Strasburger et al., 2009). These media are the central storytellers of our time. They provide an array of sources of information and entertainment for persons of all ages, in all cultures around the globe. However, the knowledge accumulated from years of studying children and media demonstrates that children are active users of media: They react to, think, feel, and create their own meanings. They bring to media encounters a host of predispositions, abilities, desires, and experiences. They watch television or listen to a story in diverse personal, social, and cultural circumstances that influence what they take from the experience. We can never assume that what we, as adults, acquire from a television program, a book, an oral story, a song, game, or a poster is what children take away from it (Lemish, 2007).

MEDIA CAN HAVE BOTH POSITIVE AND NEGATIVE INFLUENCES

Scholars and the public-at-large often view media in two different ways: On one hand, we think of them as very positive. We have grand hopes and expectations that the media will enrich children's lives, change unhealthy behaviors, stimulate their imagination and creativity, widen their education and knowledge, encourage inclusion and tolerance, narrow social gaps, and stimulate development and civil society. On the other hand, there is also great anxiety associated with electronic media's ability to numb the senses, inhibit imagination or free play, develop indifference to the pain of others, encourage destructive behaviors, desensitize children to violence, perpetuate stereotypes, lead to a deterioration of moral values, suppress local cultures, and contribute to social estrangement.

Our accumulated knowledge about the role of media in children's lives suggests that they can have both positive as well as negative effects on children, depending on the content they convey, the context in which they are consumed, the uses made of them, and individual children's age and other characteristics. However, media are not in and of themselves inherently good or bad. Rather, they are technologies that are used in multiple ways by various audiences. This is true for all media: Just as television is not necessarily good or bad, so too are books, as they too need to be scrutinized for their content and child-appropriateness, as well as for portrayals of stereotypic or violent messages.

POSITIVE INFLUENCES

Research conducted around the world suggests that good educational as well as other quality media products produced for children are effective in promoting a host of child development goals. For example, educational television can advance school preparedness among preschoolers, encourage early literacy, and teach specific school curricula effectively. The accumulated research on the ground-breaking preschool program *Sesame Street*, for example, provides strong evidence for such a potential (Fisch, 2004). This has also been found to be the case in evaluation studies of their co-productions around the world, such as in *RechovSumsum/ Shaar'aSimsim* aimed at reconciliation efforts between Israeli and Palestinian preschoolers (Brenick et al., 2007), as well as in *Sisimpur,* in Bangladesh, where family members assessed that there were positive influences based on the child's viewing of the series (Jain & Kibria, 2009).

Quality media products for the majority world (LAMI countries) are grounded in the field of development communication, which systematically applies processes and strategies of communication to promote individual and social development and change. Most of these efforts employ the media to transform resource-poor and underdeveloped societies into more socially and economically advanced and liberated societies in terms of social equity (Prasad, 2009).

Entertainment-education ("edutainment") interventions that integrate educational goals with the attractive features of entertainment are among the most promising strategies for advancing children's development through the media. These efforts bridge the arbitrary dichotomy between entertainment and education by combining their benefits and strengths. Thus, recruiting the appeal and popularity of entertainment genres aims to promote social change oriented to improving well-being on individual as well as social levels (Singhal, Cody, Rogers, & Sabido, 2004). Specific edutainment programs have addressed areas such as health (e.g., hygiene, HIV/AIDS prevention, immunization); environment (e.g., safety, pollution, resource preservation); and social issues (e.g., disability-tolerance, peace-building, aggression and violence, or abuse reduction).

Successful television interventions aimed at early childhood include projects like *First Steps Early Child Development* in Maldives (Acharya & Bhargava, 2004), *Sesame Street Panwapa Project* on global citizenship (Cole & Lee, 2009), and the Peace Initiative Institute (Pii) promoting tolerance and diversity among kindergarten children in Northern Ireland (Connolly, 2009; Connolly, Fitzpatrick, Gallagher, & Harris, 2006).

The accumulated literature suggests that age-appropriate and well-designed and executed educational media interventions for young children and caregivers can have the intended effects on cognitive, social, and emotional development. Evaluating the effectiveness of such interventions is a complicated endeavor as it depends to a large degree on the project's goals, as well as definitions of effectiveness. A project may aim to enable children to think about an issue from a different point of view, to be more predisposed to messages about it, to serve as a role model, or to change the framing through which the issue is being viewed (Prasad, 2009; Singhal et al., 2004). Others have argued for the need to apply a subaltern, non-Western perspective to such interventions around the world (Dutta, 2006).

There are also very valuable initiatives promoting literacy and reading with young children. The goal is to expose them to daily conversation, stories, songs, and books. Research suggests that these efforts strengthen bonding and communication between children and their caregivers, support children's confidence and learning, enhance language development and school readiness, and sustain literacy skills among older siblings and adults (e.g., Zuckerman & Khandekar, 2010).[2]

NEGATIVE INFLUENCES

At the same time, mounting evidence suggests that media can have very negative influences on young children. For example, routine exposure to violence on television, and in films and video games—common in much of the media content traveling around the globe—has been found to affect children in multiple negative ways: behaviorally, in increased aggressive behavior; mentally, in developing fear and anxiety toward the world they live in; and, socially, in desensitization to the suffering of fellow humans and the legitimization of violence as the sole way for resolving various forms of conflict. Even violence portrayed in order to transmit an antiviolence message, the presenting of social conflicts, or cases of the violation of children's rights can have such negative implications on viewers. Much of television animation aimed at young children is saturated with fantasy violence, which is glorified and presented with no apparent consequence to the aggressor or the victim. The blurring of fantasy and reality typical of this age group poses special challenges to the ability to critically view animated violence. Thus, violence presented in the media can affect children in different ways depending on their age, personalities, gender, the nature of their home and social environments, their life experiences, and the like. However, cumulatively, we can conclude that violence can be associated with many antisocial processes that are not conducive to children's well-being and healthy development (Kamalipour & Rampal, 2001; Lemish, 2007; Potter, 1999).

A second, extensively researched area of negative effects relates to short- and long-term influences of human stereotyping in media content. Stereotypic images of young boys transmit the message that they are violent, bullying, leaders of their group, who are primarily problem solvers who do not show emotions and physically active. The stereotypic characteristics of girls suggest they are concerned with their appearance and in pleasing others from a very young age, are often passive, submissive, emotional, vulnerable, and often treated unequally. Such stereotyping is prevalent in programs aimed at young children as well as older ones and influences the way boys and girls develop their gender identities and expectations from themselves and from the opposite sex, as well as their self-confidence, body image, and early romantic and sexual experiences (Durham, 2008; Lemish, 2010; Levin & Kilbourne, 2008).

Third, the absence of fair representations of diversity of race, ethnicity, class, religion, disability, geography, age, and so forth contribute to promoting a limited and discriminatory worldview among children that affects the way they perceive themselves and others (Asamen, Ellis, & Berry, 2008). Many of these attitudes are formed in the first 3 years of life.

Thus, the issue of inclusion in media products is of primary concern because the media reflect to children and adults who and what are valued in their society. In doing so, children gather answers in their media consumption to such important questions as: "Do I see myself represented regularly? If not, what does this say to me? When I do see myself, how am I reflected—especially if I am a girl (or boy), or if I am someone who is disadvantaged or disabled, from a minority group, or living in an extremely vulnerable situation?" Overall, we know that many children who live in a variety of difficult circumstances, rarely, if ever, see themselves reflected positively in the media. When they do see themselves, they are often represented as disempowered victims in need of saving by the developed world.

Finally, there is growing research evidence concerned with the implications of early and intensive exposure to screen culture during the first 2 years of life (Barr, 2008; Christakis, 2010; Kirkorian, Wartella, & Anderson, 2008). Although there is some evidence that babies and toddlers can learn words and concepts from television, there is also mounting concern that overstimulation can effect normal brain development and substitute for responsive, loving face-to-face relationships and interactions with family and caregivers, as well as physical exploration and manipulation of the environment, both necessary for healthy development at this stage of life. As access to all forms of media for this young age group grows in all parts of the world, it is imperative that careful selection of early media exposure and designing new productions aimed at them complement and support these vital aspects of early child development.

Principles and Guidelines for Creating Media and Examples from Low- and Middle-Income Countries

Based on these issues and the research evidence, we outline in this section those principles and guidelines for creating human rights–based quality communication for early childhood development and strategies for working within countries. These principles have one overarching goal: an obligation to shift to a new paradigm in communication for young children that values and actively reaches out to them using an integrated approach that is developmentally appropriate, culturally sensitive, and inclusive. These principles and guidelines are relevant to all forms of media: electronic, digital, and print, and the principles can be used in evaluating all types of media content. A leader in this area is the United Nations Children's Fund (UNICEF)'s Communication for Development (C4D) Unit (UNICEF, 2011), which contributes by promoting processes, strategies, and media that support personal and social transformation of both the youngest citizens and of the most marginalized groups. The examples and principles here are based on the authors' experiences with UNICEF, as well as the research literature.

UNICEF Headquarters and Country Offices have experimented with development communication in producing creative materials in many landmark projects. These efforts, aimed mostly at middle childhood audiences, included promoting gender equality in the *Meena* communication initiative in South Asia and the *Sarah* communication initiative, originally in Africa. For younger audiences below the age of 8, UNICEF supported local adaptations of *Sesame Street* in countries such as Mexico, Kosovo, and South Africa. It supported culturally specific programs, such as the animated preschool series *The Magic Journey* in Kyrgyzstan (Komerecki, 2010). Media products have been developed for both children and caregivers in the Maldives, Myanmar, Vietnam, Tanzania, Turkmenistan, Lesotho, and the Pacific Islands, among others (Kolucki, 2006, 2010). In many of these countries, these interventions have focused on specific priority needs, such as the impact of the tsunami or other emergency, HIV/AIDS, inclusion of children with disability, and supporting the psychosocial needs of orphans and vulnerable children, especially those under the age of 6 years.

In creating media in countries that will use them, a number of working strategies have been shown to be effective.

- All partners and stakeholders in the creation of the media should have a common goal of developing methods that communicate about and for the unique holistic developmental needs of the youngest children.
- Groups such as the government, agencies, parents, teachers, and creative media experts should work together in innovative communication policies, strategies, and programs.
- These groups should include a creative communication focus on the critical needs of young children and their caregivers who are living in especially difficult circumstances such as HIV/AIDS, emergencies, child protection, gender inequality, or other child rights issues.
- This communication should not only educate young children but also inspire them, build resilience, and help them heal in times of stress, trauma, and pain.
- Media should complement and support the nurturing, responsive care provided to young children by parenting caregivers, as well as care by front-line workers and the broader community. Communication can mobilize these workers and the community, building skills and instilling in them a sense of confidence in their ability to support the development of young children in all circumstances.

Principle 1: Communication for Young Children Should Be Age-Appropriate and Child-Friendly

Children need and have a right to be presented with clear, interesting, and child-centered media. Yet, media in low-resource countries often do not address preschool-aged children appropriately. Simply adding child characters or animation or comics does not necessarily result in "appropriate" media for young children. Age-appropriate media could include locally produced books on topics relevant to child survival, growth, protection, and development, and child-appropriate puppet shows, songs, and some electronic media. Children learn best through communication that is playful, creative, respectful, and interactive—the same child-friendly principles used in education.

USE CHILD-APPROPRIATE LANGUAGE, CHARACTERS, STORIES, MUSIC, AND HUMOR

Evidence demonstrates that children learn best when communication meets their specific developmental age, needs, and interests. Good-quality, effective communication begins with understanding the basic principles of child development and applying them in a manner that nurtures children's development and learning, such as using age-appropriate storylines, characters, and contents, and ensuring that materials are enjoyable and fun, that make children feel valued and loved, even when topics are sensitive (e.g., illness, fears, or emergencies).

ENCOURAGE AND MODEL INTERACTION

Interactive communication occurs when children are attracted to be attentive and to participate in the story or another medium, and it helps them be more fully engaged—cognitively, physically, and emotionally. Even with traditional media such as books, radio, and television, the audience can be "invited" to express themselves by using their bodies as well as minds, to think critically or extend learning after engaging with specific media.

USE SPECIAL EFFECTS JUDICIOUSLY AND WISELY

Learning and entertainment come from a good story and interesting characters. Special effects, such as a zoom photographic shot, were an ingenious invention that made something special out of the ordinary. However, the fast-paced, continuous changing of frames, pixilation, and dozens of visual and auditory effects that are the norm in today's "commercial TV culture" may overstimulate children and be so overwhelming as to lose their potential learning value.

Principle 2: Communication for Children Should Address the Child Holistically

Since survival, growth, and development are inextricably interlinked, communication needs to provide balance and complementary attention to children's physical, cognitive, social, and emotional development and needs. Experience suggests that producing communication on these topics together (e.g., health, hygiene, protection) as an integrated communication strategy is cost-effective and can complement the integrated early child development policy and planning occurring in a number of countries.

USE AN INTEGRATED APPROACH IN PRESENTING AN ISSUE OR MESSAGE

Communicators should design productions that address early child development holistically when presenting a single message. Children learn from incidental and unintended elements of a story (e.g., background information and behavior about girls/boys, how caregivers visually react to a child's fears or mistakes, etc.) as well as from the main message.

OFFER POSITIVE MODELS OF ADULT–CHILD RELATIONSHIPS

Communication for children should present positive models of caregiver and adult interactions with children, especially in situations in which children are living in difficult circumstances. Children may not have access to nurturing and attentive caregivers and/or there may be few positive media alternatives. Media can present models of caregivers who nurture development and resilience, and

BOX 17.1 The Potential of Books for Children

Developing and providing low-cost culturally appropriate books for children has been successfully used in several countries to support a wide range of early child development goals. The value of this approach is based on research (Klass, Needlman, & Zuckerman, 2003; Rosenkoetter & Barton, 2002; Zuckerman & Khandekar, 2010) illustrating the role of reading to children on emerging literacy. Books have been developed with dual audiences in mind: the child and the caregiver. Books for infants focus on the relationship, companionship, language, and exposure to nonstereotypic images and resilient children and families. Several UNICEF Country Offices and NGOs like Save the Children, the Aga Khan Foundation, or Soros Foundation, together with other partners, have successfully developed simple children's books that have been used as part of parenting education and school preparedness. These books (as well as complementary songs and short animated or live-action TV spots) model responsive care as part of a daily routine of disadvantaged caregivers. These books serve at least three purposes for adults. First, they model holistic nurturing and early learning. Second, they help build the confidence of caregivers who live in resource-poor and difficult circumstances. Third, they provide a local culture of literacy for both the young child and adult.

In countries as diverse as Myanmar, Vietnam, Bangladesh, Turkmenistan, Kyrgyzstan, Macedonia, Tanzania, Lesotho, and South Africa, "dual audience" (child and caregiver) books have, for example:

- Modeled a loving relationship between a baby and a mother who has one arm during routine activities like breast-feeding, bathing, massage, working in the field, or during a long wait in a health care clinic
- Told a story through rhyme of a toddler washing hands while counting and scrubbing each finger
- Taught about prevention of malaria through a tale of a young girl visiting her grandparents in a village
- Showed children affected by the death of a parent from AIDS and modeled acceptance of and support on a wide range of difficult emotions
- Supported early learning through playful actions using each sense modality and a range of relational concepts
- Nurtured resiliency in a child who has experienced a natural disaster or has learned to reach out to a trusted adult when abused
- Inspired gender progressive roles, using examples of children with disabilities helping others and celebrating differences in children from a range of ethnic, religious, or socioeconomic backgrounds

(continued)

BOX 17.1 (Continued)

One example of the potential reach of this project can be found in Myanmar, where, since 2005, over 80,000 sets of locally produced sets of books have been distributed to early childhood development programs around the country, benefiting 436,350 children under 5 years. UNICEF is also providing a "Box Library" for all grade 1 classes in the country. So far, more than 14,000 have been distributed. Initial monitoring shows that the books are being used by the children, and appreciated by parents and teachers. After Cyclone Nargis caused tremendous damage to the country in 2008, books were also widely distributed to affected children, and it was clear during monitoring visits that they were being fully used not only by young children but also in "one-room" schools. The books provided a space for these children to exercise their imagination and coping skills to deal with the great tragedy they faced.

Children's books can be an effective tool in supporting a range of sectoral programs and can also provide infants, young children, and families developmentally and culturally appropriate reading materials in their mother tongue and in the lingua franca.

---

who build skills in children that will help them cope with everyday crises, such as being bullied or exploited, living with illnesses like HIV/AIDS, or surviving disasters and emergencies.

CREATE "SAFE HAVENS" AS PART OF COMMUNICATION

Just as a *safe haven* can be a physical space where vulnerable children can go in a time of crisis, it can also be a mental or emotional space that opens up when children feel they are being listened to and others know how they feel. Children feel protected and safe from harm when this happens. They can begin to regain a sense of trust in the world and optimism about their life. Examples of safe haven communication include books and television spots modeling how a child can cope in healthy ways when frightened, how families and communities can support a grieving child, or how a child with a disability models resiliency when attending preschool for the first time.

Principle 3: Communication for Children Should be Positive and Strengths-Based

Strengths-based communication focuses on portraying and nurturing the strengths and potential in every child, rather than focusing on a child's "deficits" or problems. This type of communication both teaches and improves resiliency and the child's capacity to cope with large and small struggles in life, and it moves from presenting the problem to presenting action and solutions. This approach invites children to imagine being transported to another place, to see things they have not seen or experienced before, and to become excited about possibilities for today or the future.

BUILD SELF-CONFIDENCE AND COMPETENCE

Evidence suggests that a child's confidence is associated with increased learning capacity and curiosity. Media that can help young children not only learn skills but also to see and hear that they are valued and important can help build confidence, motivation for learning, and improve critical thinking.

USE POSITIVE MODELING

Much research shows that children and adults learn from models of behavior that they have observed repeatedly. Yet, some children's media present behaviors that that are not desirable, such as violent actions, stereotypical behavior, name-calling, and unsafe or unhealthy practices. They then end with an admonishment and brief message that tells children simply "don't do this." An alternative and more effective approach is to portray positive actions along with reinforcing messages about healthy behaviors, including generosity, fairness, honesty, caring, and responsibility.

INCLUDE YOUNG CHILDREN AS ACTIVE CITIZENS LEARNING
ABOUT AND MODELING SOCIAL JUSTICE AND MOBILIZATION

Even young children can show their strengths and contributions to family, peers, community, and the world through communication. Helping to develop their own communication materials can also model the positive involvement of children in community life.

DO NO HARM

There is a fine line between providing children with useful information and truthful depictions of reality and sharing information and visuals of events that may be too explicit or graphic and inadvertently harm or further traumatize them. It is better to err on the side of caution by presenting positive solutions, including seeking physical and emotional "protection," when presenting sensitive issues such as armed conflict, sexual or other abuse, emergencies, and the like.

Principle 4: Communication for Children Should Address the Needs and Abilities of All, Including Those Who Are Most Disadvantaged

Media portray *who* and *what* is valued in a particular society. Communication should allow all children to hear and see themselves reflected positively (as opposed to communication that employs marginalization as well as shame, or negative or patronizing portrayals). Children from different cultures and ethnic groups, all socioeconomic groups, children with a range of disabilities, those in need of special protection, and children who have or are experiencing trauma or grief, or are living through emergencies should be portrayed in all types of communication.

REFLECT THE DIGNITY OF EACH AND EVERY CHILD AND ADULT

In order to represent all children, the full range of children in a given community should be included. Conscious efforts are required to avoid reinforcing feelings of disparity or low self-esteem among vulnerable and disadvantaged children.

BE INCLUSIVE: CELEBRATE AND VALUE ALL TYPES OF DIVERSITY

Media contribute to awareness of differences between people by presenting people in negative or stereotypic ways, or by excluding particular groups. Explicit and implicit messages can address differences directly and indirectly by presenting a diverse world, including differences in the characters of stories, providing practical information, and answering questions honestly and accurately.

ENSURE COMMUNICATION IS FREE OF STEREOTYPES

From traditional stories to modern media, one can find class, ethnic, disability, age, religion, and gender stereotypes presented to children in nearly every country. Media should intervene to change such stereotypes, create good practice, and break out of stereotypical patterns, and to create respect for diversity.

REFLECT AND NURTURE THE POSITIVE ASPECTS OF INDIGENOUS CULTURES AND TRADITIONS

Media often employ a "master-narrative" that presents only the Western point of view. However, effective media will celebrate and promote the *positive* practices of all cultures and people, including indigenous groups. Stories from Africa, South American, Asia, the Arab world, and other regions celebrate local and global strengths.

BOX 17.2 Lesotho Case Study: Reaching the Most Marginalized Children and Families

In June 2010, a national workshop supported by UNICEF was held In Maseru, Lesotho, on "Innovative Communication for Early Child Development." The workshop included participants from all sectoral programs, people with a range of disabilities, people working directly with preschool children (especially those who were orphaned, abandoned, or disabled), and a range of creative local media talent (writers, producers, illustrators, photographers, musicians, etc.). The goal of the workshop was to produce a set of materials for children and their families, ensuring that they were representative of and meeting the needs of the most marginalized. These materials were designed to build the confidence as well as competence of children and caregivers and to present models of resilience, creativity, and strength in the most difficult circumstances.

The workshop participants produced children's books, posters for children and caregivers, and radio and TV spots for both children and adults. The group was tasked with ensuring that nontraditional, gender-progressive, and inclusive stories were told. Some of these included:

- A photo-based book about a mother who is deaf who is "The Best Mommy in the World." There have been examples of "Best mom/Best dad" stories in many countries as part of parenting programs. But here the aim was to ensure that real Lesotho parents living with a disability, who are often excluded, are also portrayed as "Best parents."

(continued)

BOX 17.2 (Continued)

- A pioneering book about a severely disabled girl and her friends who help, love, support, and play with each other. Often, a child with a mild disability is included in books or television programs. Here, the aim was to include a child with extreme disabilities as someone who can and who is included in diverse activities of young children.
- A poster about a child who is HIV-positive and models all of the fun, educational, and nondiscriminatory activities he does with his friends.
- A TV spot about a boy living in a "safe haven home" for children orphaned or abandoned who is saddened and confused—and supported in a gentle, loving way by a nurturing male caregiver.
- An animation spot (just in time for the World Cup) shows how a girl who is blind is a talented goalie when she uses a ball that has a bell attached to it.
- Radio spots sharing real stories of parents of children who are disabled and who give hope, practical suggestions, and support to other parents.

The prototype materials were pretested with children and adults and edited based on the feedback from this formative testing. In addition to attention, interest, and comprehension, a range of comments about caregiving were asked of the adults. Some of the positive feedback included:

- Adults liked the materials, especially those that showed men being good caregivers.
- Children loved the book about the mother who was deaf, many saying that "they wished their parents were just like this mommy."
- Several children stated that they would like to play with the children with disability.
- Caregivers liked how posters and other materials showed simple and educative ways to take care of children.

These materials have been finalized, published, and will be distributed and utilized as part of several ongoing sectoral programs. There are plans to monitor the impact of these media and a commitment to ensure that subsequent media continue to include, celebrate, and meet the needs of the most disadvantaged. There will also be continued monitoring on the utilization of the materials with the primary target audiences of children, parents/caregivers, and preschool teachers. Feedback thus far has been positive, with UNICEF staff indicating that they have generated positive interest in holistic care practices and innovative materials (especially books) for young children.

From Mantsopa Communications (2010). "ECCD Materials Development: Qualitative Research, Focus Group Discussions, Pretest Report," Mantsopa Communications, Lesotho, June 2010.

Conclusion

The accumulating research provides us with evidence of the media's potential—positive and negative—to make a difference in early childhood development in LAMI countries. Such differences may be behavioral (e.g., imitating sharing vs. imitating aggression); social (e.g., making friends on the internet vs. bullying classmates); cognitive (e.g., learning preparedness skills for school vs. developing attention deficit); and even physical (e.g., learning hygiene skills or how to protect oneself from sexually transmitted diseases and rape vs. developing bad eating habits and obesity). All these skills develop and require attention from early childhood.

Clearly, the possible influences of the media on early childhood development are not simply "good versus bad," as the examples above suggest. Rather, these influences work in a dynamic, intertwined fashion, leaving many gray areas open to multiple interpretations, depending upon audience members' cultural value systems and worldviews. As a result, many issues remain open. For example, is playing video games or exploring websites related to their favorite television programs dangerous, or does it widen a child's horizons? Is exposure to expressions of intimacy in the media healthy, traumatizing, or morally inappropriate for young children? Does watching American programs that dominate the global market expand cultural experiences or damage one's cultural identity and self-worth? Does addressing topics like trauma or death help children cope with difficult experiences, or does it traumatize them and make them even more fearful and distrustful of adults? Do productions documenting the abrogation of children's "rights" help improve their lives or do they present the worst rather than the best in families, communities, and societies relevant to one's own groups and to the wider world?

The answers to these and similar questions are not clear-cut, but depend on personal and social variables, and should be examined with the specific child and circumstances in mind.

Overall, as discussed above, there can be both positive and negative effects from media consumption. Research suggests that many positive effects of media have been identified: enriching children's lives, informing them about the world and other cultures, promoting peace-building and tolerance to diversity, teaching cognitive skills and preschool-relevant knowledge, modeling caregiving by adults, and bringing joy into the lives of both children and adults. The principles and guidelines above are aimed at maximizing the positive potential and mitigating the negative effects of media. Therefore, the recommendation from research to producers and users of media for early child development is that there is evidence for its potential in cognitive, social, emotional, and skill development, but we need more systematic formative and evaluative research to develop better strategies for communicating with children in ways that promote their well-being and achieve our other international development goals.

RECOMMENDATIONS FOR POLICY MAKERS AND PROGRAMMERS

Recommendation 1: If one has limited resources, begin with producing high-quality developmentally and culturally appropriate books for young children based on the suggested principles and guidelines. These books can eventually be adapted to other media technologies.

Recommendation 2: It is important to build local capacity to produce communication for children. An intersectoral approach, in which health, education, child protection, and child development experts and creative artists work and create together often works best.

Recommendation 3: Use the principles and guidelines as a basis for selecting or purchasing media content, as well as for producing indigenous communication for young children. Focus on meeting the holistic needs of children of different ages and their families, as opposed to using a single issue/sector approach.

Recommendation 4: Brainstorm and use innovative strategies to ensure that communication is utilized well and that families, communities, and individual sectors are mobilized in creative ways. For example, health workers could distribute books at well-child check-ups, quality videos can be screened in waiting areas, older children can set up reading corners for younger children in libraries or community centers, and the like.

Recommendation 5: More research on the impact of various media on the lives of children is needed. Research should include impact on a wide range of behaviors and attitudes, as well as on school preparedness.

Acknowledgments

This chapter is based on Kolucki, B. & Lemish, D. (2011). *Communicating with children: Principles and practices that nurture, inspire, excite, educate and heal.* New York: Communication for Development Unit UNICEF, available at http://www.unicef.org/cwc/index.html. We thank Rina Gill, Associate Director, Policy and Practice, for her support and substantial contribution to this project. See http://www.unicef.org/cwc.

Notes

1. UNICEF Strategic Framework on C4D, 2008—Communication for Development (C4D) in UNICEF is a systematic, planned, and evidence-informed strategic process to promote positive and measurable behavior and social change that is integral to development programs.

2. See for example projects such as *Reach out and Read* (http://www.reachoutandread.
   org); *Reading with Children,* Save the Children/Bangladesh (http://www.savethe-
   children.org/programs/education/?WT.mc_id=1109_sp_prog_Ed); and *Something to
   read, something to learn: Print media for and about young children. An example from the
   Kyrgyz Republic.* Regional Office CEE/CIS UNICEF.

References

Acharya, S., & Bhargava, V. (2004). *First steps … Maldives: A giant leap for mankind!
Evaluation of the ECCD multi-media campaign.* Maldives: UNICEF, Government of the
Maldives.

Asamen, J. K., Ellis, M. L., & Berry, G. L. (Eds.). (2008). *The Sage handbook of child development, multiculturalism, and media.* Los Angeles: Sage.

Bachan, K., & Raftree, L. (2011). *Integrating information and communication technologies
into communication for development strategies to support and empower marginalized
adolescent girls.* Paper presented at the XIIth UN Round Table on Communication for
Development, New Delhi.

Barr, R. (2008). Attention to and learning from media during infancy and early childhood.
In S. L. Calvert & B. J. Wilson (Eds.), *Blackwell handbook of child development and the
media* (pp. 143–165). Malden, MA: Blackwell.

Brenick, A., Lee-Kim, J., Killen, M., Fox, N., Raviv, A., & Leavitt, L. (2007). Social judgments in Israeli and Arabic children: Findings from media-based intervention projects.
In D. Lemish & M. Götz (Eds.), *Children and media in times of war and conflict*
(pp. 287–308). Cresskill, NJ: Hampton Press.

Calvert, S. L., & Wilson, B. J. (Eds.). (2008). *The handbook of children, media, and development.* Oxford, UK: Blackwell.

Christakis, D. A. (2010). Infant media viewing: First, do no harm. *Pediatric Annals, 39*(9),
578–582.

Cole, C., & Lee, J. (2009). Creating global citizens: The Panwapa project. *Communication
Research Trends, 28*(3), 25–30.

Connolly, P. (2009). *Developing programmes to promote ethnic diversity in early childhood:
Lessons from Northern Ireland* (Working paper No. 52). The Hague: Bernard van Leer
Foundation.

Connolly, P., Fitzpatrick, S., Gallagher, T., & Harris, P. (2006). Addressing diversity and
inclusion in the early years in conflict-affected societies: A case study of the Media Initiative for Children—Northern Ireland. *International Journal of Early Years Education,
14*(3), 263–278.

Drotner, K., & Livingstone, S. (Eds.). (2008). *The international handbook of children, media
and culture.* Los Angeles: Sage.

Durham, M. G. (2008). *The Lolita effect: The media sexualization of young girls and what we
can do about it.* New York: The Overlook Press.

Dutta, M. J. (2006). Theoretical approaches to entertainment education campaigns: A subaltern critique. *Health Communication, 20*(3), 221–231.

Fisch, S. (2004). *Children's learning from educational television: Sesame Street and beyond.*
Mahwah, NJ: Lawrence Erlbaum.

Jain, S., & Kibria, N. (2009). Sisimpur, Sesame Street in Bangladesh: Exploring the challenges in early childhood development. *Journal of Children and Media, 3*(1), 95–100.

Kamalipour, Y. R., & Rampal, K. R. (Eds.). (2001). *Media, sex, violence, and drugs in the global village*. Boston: Rowman & Littlefield.

Kirkorian, H. L., Wartella, E. A., & Anderson, D. R. (2008). Media and young children's learning. *Future of Children, 18*(1), 39–61.

Kirsh, S. J. (2009). *Media and youth: A developmental perspective*. West Sussex, UK: Wiley-Blackwell.

Klass, P. E., Needlman, R., & Zuckerman, B. (2003). The developing brain and early learning. *Archives of Disease in Childhood, 88*, 651–654.

Kolucki, B. (2006). *Programme communication for early child development*. New York: UNICEF: Early Child Development Unit.

Kolucki, B. (2010). Media for Pacific children. Retrieved from http://www.unicef.org/pacificislands/12599_14238.html

Komerecki, M. (2010). *Documenting capacity development: "Keremet Koch/The Magic Journey." A case study of UNICEF's approach and practice*. New York: UNICEF Division of Policy and Practice Working Paper series.

Lemish, D. (2007). *Children and television: A global perspective*. Oxford, UK: Blackwell.

Lemish, D. (2010). *Screening gender on children's television: The views of producers around the world*. NY: Routledge.

Levin, D. E., & Kilbourne, J. (2008). *So sexy so soon: The new sexualized childhood and what parents can do to protect their kids*. New York: Balantine Books.

Mantsopa Communications (2010). *ECCD Materials development: Qualitative research, focus group discussions, pretest report*. Lesotho:Author.

Mazzarella, S. R. (Ed.). (2007). *20 questions about youth and the media*. New York: Peter Lang.

Pecora, N., Murray, J. P., & Wartella, E. (Eds.). (2007). *Children and television: Fifty years of research*. Mahwah, NJ: Lawrence Erlbaum.

Pecora, N., Osei-Hwere, E., & Carlsson, U. (Eds.). (2008). *African media, African children*. University of Gothenburg, Sweden: The International Clearinghouse on Children, Youth and Media.

Potter, W. J. (1999). *On media violence*. Thousand Oaks, CA: Sage.

Prasad, K. (2009). *Communication for development: Reinventing theory and action*. New Delhi: B.R. World of Books.

RISE Project. (2009). *Radio instruction to strengthen education (RISE) in Zanzibar*. Education Development Center. Retrieved from www.edc.org

Rosenkoetter, S., & Barton, L. (2002, February/March). Bridges to literacy: Early routines that promote later school success. *Zero to Three*, 33–38.

Singer, D. G., & Singer, J. (Eds.). (2010). *Handbook of children and the media* (2nd ed.). Los Angeles: Sage.

Singhal, A., Cody, M., Rogers, E., & Sabido, M. (Eds.). (2004). *Entertainment-education and social change: History, research, and practice*. Mahwah, NJ: Lawrence Erlbaum.

Strasburger, V. C., Wilson, B. J., & Jordan, A. (2009). *Children, adolescents and the media* (2nd ed.). Thousand Oaks, CA: Sage.

UN General Assembly. (1989). *Convention on the rights of the child*. Retrieved from http://www2.ohchr.org/english/law/crc.htm

UNICEF. (2011). *Communication for development*. New York: Author. Retrieved from http://www.unicef.org/cwc/index.html

Von Feilitzen, C., Carlsson, U., & Bucht, C. (Eds.). (2011). *New questions, new insights, new approaches: Contributions to the research forum at the World Summit on Media for Children and Youth 2010*. University of Gothenburg, Sweden: The International Clearinghouse on Children, Youth and Media.

Zuckerman, B., & Khanderkar, A. (2010). Reach out and read: Evidence based approach to promoting early education development. *Current Opinion in Pediatrics, 22,* 539–544.

Measurement and Monitoring of Programs and Policies

18

Assessing Early Childhood Development

Marc H. Bornstein and Jennifer E. Lansford

The Goals of Assessing Early Childhood Development

Assessing early childhood development (ECD) is crucial for researchers and for policymakers and practitioners who work directly with children and their families around the world. Indicators such as infant and child mortality rates and incidence of disease within a child population are important in providing information about how children are faring in different parts of the world, but they reflect child survival rather than child development. Even in countries with high childhood mortality rates, most children survive but they may not achieve their full potential. To promote children's rights and their optimal development, it is imperative to develop ECD indicators that provide more comprehensive assessments of children's well-being and that are predictive of children's future academic achievement and social, emotional, and behavioral adjustment, as well as positive civic engagement into maturity. Measuring ECD should take a holistic approach to the child, including: (1) physical well-being and motor development, (2) social and emotional development, (3) approaches to learning, (4) language development, and (5) cognition and general knowledge (Goal One Technical Planning Group, 1991).

Measuring ECD serves to increase awareness of the significance of multiple aspects of child development in the general population, as well as among practitioners and policymakers. From a policy perspective, measuring ECD is essential because ECD measurement can form the basis of decisions to promote the survival and positive physical, cognitive, emotional, social, and educational development of children at national, regional, and local levels. Cross-national comparisons of ECD indicators can be used by policymakers to justify devoting more financial and human resources to ECD in nations where children develop more poorly than in other nations and to assess how well some nations fare compared to other nations in meeting international standards for the well-being of children. Within-country comparisons of ECD indicators across different regions, ethnic groups, genders, or socioeconomic classes can be used by policymakers to understand which groups are struggling or excelling, thus enabling the allocation of resources to enhance the developmental potential of those who are not thriving and build on the strengths of those who already are succeeding. If ECD indicators are assessed over time, they can be used to measure progress in meeting ECD standards. Policymakers tend to devote more funds to intervention programs when particular social groups are statistically demonstrated to have significantly poorer outcomes than other social groups (Fernald, Kariger, Engle, & Raikes, 2009). Thus, from a policy perspective, the main goals of ECD measurement are to be able to shape meaningful and effective policy at an aggregate level.

From the perspective of practitioners or interventionists, the aims of ECD measurement often include identifying specific children or families who are at-risk to be able to offer programs to prevent problems before they emerge or to mitigate problems after they have become manifest. Although aggregate-level measurement can be useful to identify communities that would benefit from interventions, individual-level measurement is also crucial as a screening tool to identify specific children in need of targeted interventions and to measure progress of individual children (Wesley & Buysse, 2003). Without rigorous evaluations of interventions by measuring ECD, it is impossible to know whether interventions have their intended effects, either at the group or individual level. Interventions that objectively demonstrate positive effects on child survival and development are more likely to be supported in the future than are interventions that lack demonstrated efficacy.

Comparisons across countries/cultures and between social groups within a country are facilitated by the use of indicators that are clearly defined and measured in consistent ways. For example, the ECD module of the United Nations Children's Fund (UNICEF)'s Multiple Indicator Cluster Survey is designed to enable countries to monitor child development over time, compare child development across regions, evaluate child development outcomes in one country vis-à-vis outcomes in other countries, and assess ECD interventions and programs (Bornstein et al., 2012). Using the same set of ECD indicators in different countries facilitates cross-national comparisons, such as those made in UNICEF's (2012) *Annual Report on the State of the World's Children*. However, country and cultural comparative research brings with it a host of unique issues and problems (translation, measurement equivalence), and risks associated with this research are increased when it is conducted without full awareness of and sensitivity to various issues associated with these comparisons.

Children's lives generally have improved the most over time in domains that can be assessed readily because such assessment enables countries/cultures to detect problems and monitor progress in working toward solutions. For example, standards for assessing children's nutritional status and immunization history are clearer and better established than are standards for assessing children's rights to protection and participation as set forth in the Convention on the

Rights of the Child (United Nations, 1989). There is some evidence that children's nutritional and immunization status has improved faster than less clearly operationalized indicators of adjustment, such as child neglect. Even so, associations between indicators and rates of change are complicated because simpler interventions might be sufficient to change indicators that are easy to operationalize (e.g., immunization), whereas more complex interventions might be needed to change indicators that are more difficult to operationalize (e.g., child neglect). When the measurement of ECD constructs is better operationalized, and when a consistent measure is agreed on, countries/cultures have an easier time working toward desirable outcomes that are clearly measurable. Achieving this goal requires acknowledging the value of ECD, that there is a relatively simple intervention that can be implemented to effect change, and a constituency that will work for it.

The availability of measures of ECD at national or international levels has several key implications for practice and policy. Such measures provide ways to gauge progress over time. For example, a reduction in the proportion of children categorized as "at risk" on a particular indicator would suggest an overall improvement in child well-being. Disparities between scores on indicators for different demographic groups within a country or culture could also have notable implications for interventions or policies to help children who are falling behind, and children categorized as "at risk" could be targeted for receiving services and resources.

Regardless of the method used, assessing ECD involves ethical responsibilities. International guidelines base research ethics on three general principles: *beneficence*, the obligation to maximize research benefits and minimize research harms; *respect*, the responsibility to ensure that research participation is informed, rational, and voluntary; and *justice*, the obligation to ensure the fair distribution of research benefits and burdens across populations (Fisher & Anushko, 2008). Before measures are used to assess children, the procedures and protocols employed to recruit the sample and administer the measures should be reviewed by in-country institutional review boards, ethics committees, or government agencies. These steps help to ensure that the rights of participants are protected and that risks are minimized. In any ECD evaluation that leads to conclusions about a child's abilities, there is a risk that this knowledge could be used to stigmatize or lead to labeling that will countervail child well-being, either at the individual or group level. If assessments are being used to identify children with developmental delays, there are risks in false negatives (i.e., the child is delayed but not labeled), because children then may not receive needed interventions or services, as well as in false positives (i.e., the child is not delayed but is so labeled), because such labeling may result in negative perceptions by others or unnecessary distress for parents. Consistent with the Convention on the Rights of the Child, ECD assessments should be nondiscriminatory, and results of ECD assessments should be used only in ways that are in the best interests of the child.

Overview of Early Childhood Development Assessment

The remainder of this chapter addresses issues related to research design, psychometrics, comparison, measurement equivalence, and other technical points germane to ECD assessment. We also provide illustrations to demonstrate these issues in the case of the development of specific ECD indicators. At the outset, we note that cultural differences and gender need to be considered in interpreting ECD indicators. Throughout, we define "indicators" as being measurement scales that reflect behavior, knowledge, or other attributes of children that are being assessed. Indicators sometimes have cut-points for the determination of risk status (e.g., an indicator of nutritional risk is a height for age z score 2 standard deviations below the mean; an indicator of developmental delay would be performance on a measure of cognitive functioning that is more than 2 standard deviations below the mean performance of same-age peers).

Decisions to Be Made in Selecting or Developing an Assessment of Early Childhood Development

Research to develop assessments of ECD is best determined by the questions the assessments are meant to address. What is the purpose of the assessment? For example, the purpose could be to evaluate the impact of a specific program, to design an intervention for a particular child, or to monitor the progress of all children at a national level. The purpose of each assessment has implications for all aspects of designing or selecting the instruments to be used, as well as the research methods to be employed in administering the instruments. Instrument design and research entail six considerations. Two concern content and include the ECD domain and the measure of interest; three are procedural and include the method, source, and context of ECD measurement; and one is temporal (i.e., the age of children when ECD is measured).

With respect to content, a first question is what aspect(s) of a child's development will be assessed? For example, if an intervention is expected to affect particular domains of child functioning, it is these domains that should be measured; if one is undertaking a national assessment, then which domains to assess may be guided by national goals for children. Take the domain of child language as an example. Language is composed of a combination of phonology (the sounds of language), lexicon (vocabulary), syntax (how words are correctly assembled), pragmatics (how language is used in everyday communication), and so forth, and individual measures typically target only one of these subcomponents of language. Therefore, when deciding which aspect of language to assess, one should consider which aspect(s) of language an intervention is designed to change. The ECD assessment then needs to identify specific measures that assess the particular aspect(s) of language that would be expected to change as a result of participation in the intervention (e.g., receptive vocabulary, mean length of utterance in child speech).

The three principal options to study ECD include assessing children directly by recording what children do or say in a natural situation, seeking out those people closest to children (like their parents, teachers, or other caregivers) to report about them, and interviewing or testing children directly. Each option proffers a unique and valid perspective on ECD, but each perspective has limitations and implications that can yield different ECD estimates. A brief discussion of each illustrates why. Again, the purpose of the ECD assessment will help guide decisions regarding which of these three main methods is preferable to measure ECD (Grigorenko & Sternberg, 1999; Snow & Van Hemel, 2008).

Observation of what children themselves naturally and spontaneously do or say has the undeniable appeal of ecological validity that is capturing how children behave in real-life situations, and is seemingly direct and objective. Child observations are usually conducted in naturalistic settings, such as homes and schools, as children engage in their everyday activities. They can also be conducted in more structured situations that are constructed to enable observers to watch a child's behavior in a specific context that may be more difficult to observe in the course of everyday life. Ainsworth's (1993) Strange Situation to measure how infants respond in the presence of a stranger and the extent to which they use their mothers as a source of security in this novel context is an illustration. Observations have the advantage of being valid indicators because they are based on children's actual behavior, and they can provide information about how the child behaves in a specific context. However, records of free behavior or speech can underestimate a child, and numerous decisions about recording and analysis (when to observe, how frequently, where, under what conditions, and with whom) necessarily frame the resulting picture of the child (Bornstein, Painter, & Park, 2002). Researchers can sample only a small fraction of a child's everyday life, and so ECD estimates based on naturalistic sampling may not capture the full range of a child's abilities or behaviors. Other limitations of observations are that they address performance (what a child does or says spontaneously) rather than competence (what a child can do or say). Other disadvantages of observations are that extensive training of observers usually is required to reach reliable standards for behavioral coding, and conducting observations is time-consuming and expensive.

An alternative approach to assessing ECD employs reporters, and much of the classic information about children since Darwin (1877) has derived from the reports of parents, teachers, or other caregivers. This method involves asking reporters to answer questions about the child based on what they know about the child from previous interactions. Diaries, interviews, and questionnaires (or checklists) can provide sources of information about the child's behaviors and abilities in contexts that purportedly reflect everyday life (Snow & Van Hemel, 2008; Squires, Potter, Bricker, & Lamorey, 1998). Parental reports offer valid and comprehensive information about children because they come from observers who know the child best and are with the child all the time (Thomas, Chess, Birch, Hertzog, & Korn, 1963). They have proved indispensable for accounts of rare occurrences, such as when children first meet key developmental milestones (Bowerman, 1985), when extensive contextual information is required (Gopnik & Meltzoff, 1986), and as comprehensive estimates of selected features of development as well as the basis for a rapid overall evaluation (Dale, Bates, Reznick, & Morisset, 1989). For example, if the goal of an ECD assessment is to understand the child's overall pattern of behavior across a wide variety of situations, contexts, and times, then parents are the most likely to be able to provide such a generalized rating. In some domains, using reports by adults knowledgeable about the child is the only practical way to obtain information, such as children's social competence in a variety of situations that would not be practical to observe or test directly. Checklists are efficient, economical, and presumably based on extensive sampling across a wide range of situations, and they do not require extensive training of interviewers.

Parent report has drawbacks, however. For example, asking parents to complete fixed-item checklists provides some information about children, but these are not exhaustive diaries, and so can never give a complete picture of a child. Moreover, reports tend to be unsystematic and are often retrospective, and they may include subjective as well as objective components reflective of extraneous characteristics of the reporter (e.g., employment status, achievement orientation, personality). The capacities of reporters in terms of literacy and cognitive functioning need to be considered as well. Reporters are not generally trained, they may have different interpretations of items in different cultural contexts, they may fail to notice subtle aspects or other features of the child (such as behaviors to which the parent is accustomed but that would be unusual in comparison to other children of the same age), and parents, teachers, or other caregivers alike may be motivated to have the child appear in a favorable light or their caregiving to be perceived as socially desirable, thus leading to biased responses. All of these factors can modify estimations of the child (Achenbach, McConaughy, & Howell, 1987; Bornstein, Gaughran, & Homel, 1986).

Tests are a third method to assess ECD in children. Tests typically include related items or tasks, and children receive scores based on the number of items they complete successfully (relative to other children the same age). The context is normally controlled, and assessing children in such a structured way is seemingly equal and fair. This method has the advantage of providing a relatively unbiased assessment of a child's abilities because the adult conducting the assessment is presumed to be an objective nonfamily observer, and therefore not subject to biases of social desirability (trying to make the child look "better" than he or she really is) or recall (remembering information from the past).

However, child test performance may reflect, in part at least, the testing method as well as the child's motivation and personality (Zigler, Abelson, & Seitz, 1973), and the child's performance is subject to internal factors, such as sleepiness or hunger, and external factors, such as distractions in the environment, which may detract from the child's ability to perform well on tests. Children can prove to be poor participants in formal assessments; they may be unfamiliar with the testing conditions, thus masking their true abilities and resulting in lower scores (Bracken, 2007). For these reasons, questions inevitably arise about the validity of standardized test results. Also, tests can show that some capacity or performance is possible, but they do not show whether the capacity or performance is typical. Measurement may tell more about children's ability to meet the demands of testing (e.g., interacting with a novel adult, understanding unfamiliar words) than their actual abilities (Snow & Van Hemel, 2008). Testing also requires highly trained personnel (Bradley-Johnson & Johnson, 2007).

The method of data collection selected will have implications for sampling, attrition (when children drop out of an assessment over time), and effect size (the magnitude of differences found between groups). A key aspect of research design is sampling (composition, size, and so forth of the participants). Representative sampling is indispensable for both researchers and policymakers who want a reasonable probability of finding statistically significant results and want to be able to generalize findings from the study sample to a larger population. How will the sample be selected, and what sample size will confer the statistical power to detect differences between groups, if this is desired (e.g., in an evaluation of a program)? Factors such as the age range of the children to be assessed have implications for sample selection because a narrower target age range means that a larger number of families will need to be located to find families with children of the specific target age. If the study design is longitudinal (i.e., following children over time), researchers will have to determine how to address attrition and its consequence: unplanned, missing scores.

If a comparison between groups is the goal, then sample sizes will affect the ability to find a difference if one exists. Statistical significance of a difference is directly proportional to sample size; the larger the sample, the easier it is to demonstrate statistical significance. However, statistical significance does not necessarily reflect practical standing in the real world; two or more group means may differ statistically from each other, but these differences may not reflect vital differences among individuals in those groups. Measures of effect size or the magnitude of the difference help to interpret the practical significance of findings. Generally, it is easier to obtain larger samples if adult ratings are used than if it is necessary to observe or directly test individual children.

In addition to the method and source of information, another procedural characteristic can be expected to affect the measurement of ECD: the cultural and socioeconomic contexts of assessments. To make a measure fair and valid for children, it is necessary to take into account factors such as their education and literacy; language used in the home; cultural relevance of the items; and familiarity with writing, numbers, and pictures that may be included in the test materials. Where assessments are made matters as well: For example, free play might elicit one set of skills from children, whereas structured interactions, such as at a meal or while learning, might elicit quite a different set (Bornstein, Haynes, Painter, & Genevro, 2000). The setting in which assessments are conducted needs to be considered, so that children will be comfortable and not distracted by external factors such as noise or poor lighting or many other children observing.

Child age is an additional central factor to consider. The domains of ECD that are salient, as well as how to assess them, depend, in part, on the child's age. For example, motor development is prominent in the first year of life, followed by the development of receptive and then productive language in the second year of life. Basic knowledge about developmental milestones that most children can be expected to attain across cultural contexts by a given age is crucial in planning developmentally appropriate ECD assessments. ECD characteristics may not be stable at a young age but stabilize at a later age; generally, people become increasingly consistent in relation to one another as they age (Roberts & DelVecchio, 2000), and correlations among assessments are higher.

Another methodological issue is whether one is measuring ECD at one point in time, or changes in the child's development over time. Most ECD study is cross-sectional, which means that children are assessed at one time only, but children of a variety of ages may be assessed to determine how children of different ages perform. Developmental science is concerned with two separate temporal issues. The first is group average performance across time, the so-called *developmental function*. The other is individual variation around that average (Bornstein & Bornstein, 2008; Hartmann, Pelzel, & Abbott, 2011; Wohlwill, 1973). In developmental study, group mean level consistency or inconsistency (continuity/discontinuity) is contrasted with individual order consistency or inconsistency (stability/instability); see Lerner, Leonard, Fay, and Issac (2011). Longitudinal developmental study is special for several reasons. One reason is that findings of stability or instability inform about the overall developmental course of a given ECD characteristic. Whether individuals maintain rank order on some characteristic through time informs not only about individual variation, but contributes to understanding the possible nature, future, and origins of the ECD characteristic as well (Appelbaum & McCall, 1983; McCall, 1981). Past performance in a given domain is often the best predictor of future performance in that domain. Looking at an individual's stability or instability over time helps to identify factors that could change it.

Several additional constraints need to be considered when deciding which methods and measures to use in assessing ECD (Fernald et al., 2009). First, budget is a consideration because some standardized tests and copyrighted measures may be too expensive to administer in large-scale studies, and training of interviewers and observers adds to costs associated with direct testing and conducting observations.

Second, the time needed to train researchers and to administer measures may constrain what is feasible to complete with allocated resources; as discussed earlier, for example, direct testing and observations generally are more time-consuming, both to train testers and to test or observe children one-on-one, than are obtaining reports provided by parents or other caregivers. Third, the amount of time and effort expected of children or other respondents needs to be considered to be sure that they do not overburden participants in ECD assessments.

In addition to measuring the child, the quality of learning opportunities and psychosocial support in the environment can also be measured. The primary reason to assess children's environments is that material resources in the home and interactions with caregivers are predictive of children's physical, social, emotional, and cognitive development (Bradley & Corwyn, 2005). These factors are potentially modifiable, and therefore they have special relevance for policy. The most widely used instrument for assessing the intellectual stimulation and emotional support that children receive in their families is the HOME Inventory (Bradley, 2010). The infant and early childhood versions of the HOME are designed to be used with children through the age of 6 years. For example, the early childhood version includes 55 items that comprise eight scales: (1) learning materials (e.g., Child has at least 10 children's books); (2) language stimulation (e.g., Parent talks to the child while doing housework); (3) physical environment (e.g., Child's play environment appears safe and free of hazards); (4) responsiveness (e.g., During the visit, the parent answers the child's questions verbally); (5) academic stimulation (e.g., Child has toys that teach colors, size, and shapes); (6) modeling of socially desirable behavior (e.g., Parent teaches the child simple manners); (7) variety of stimulation (e.g., Child has been taken on an outing by a family member at least every other week); and (8) acceptance (e.g., When speaking of or to the child, the parent's voice conveys positive feelings). During a home visit with the parent and child that lasts approximately 1 hour, a trained researcher rates each item as yes or no, based on direct observations or parents' responses to questions about aspects of the environment that cannot be directly observed. An abbreviated version of the HOME has been adapted for use in UNICEF's Multiple Indicator Cluster Survey (www.unicef.org/statistics), a large-scale data collection effort conducted every 3–5 years in more than 60 developing countries to monitor the situation of children.

In summary, different contents, procedures, and times used in measuring children contribute to ECD assessment; no one approach to ECD assessment is superior to all others under all situations. However, if used together, these different approaches might complement one another to bring into focus a more coherent assessment of the child. Thus, an approach that combines several domains, measures, methods, and sources for examining ECD emulates the advantages of the multitrait-multimethod perspective (Campbell & Fiske, 1959) in pursuit of comprehensive validity in ECD assessment.

Psychometric Adequacy of Child Developmental Tests

To judge the adequacy of a test, a number of standards of quality should be present in the test design. These include whether the measurement device captures individual variation within a population, whether it is applied in a standard fashion, and whether the resulting scores are replicable (reliable) and measure what they are supposed to measure (valid). Each criterion is discussed in turn.

INDIVIDUAL VARIATION

Within any group at every age, children vary dramatically among themselves on any given ECD characteristic. It is commonly understood that variation among individuals in diverse characteristics appears to be normally distributed in the population, which means that there is a range of scores, distributed around a mean. So, for example, at virtually every age, children vary in terms of individual differences in their language (Bornstein & Haynes, 1998; Fenson et al., 1993, 1994; Thal & Bates, 1990). Twenty-month-olds around the world have a range in their reported productive vocabulary from as few as 1 to as many as 487 spoken words (Bornstein et al., 2004). Thus, one consideration when evaluating the psychometric adequacy of a measure of ECD is whether it captures naturally occurring individual variation within a population. Such variation might not be captured if the items are too easy, too hard, or poorly constructed.

STANDARD FORMS OF ADMINISTRATION

Standard administration is intended to ensure that procedurally comparable ECD scores are obtained for all children assessed. Some tests do not define their questions adequately, the manner of administration of items, or the criteria for judging the correctness of responses. A standard administrative procedure requires clear instructions (e.g., timing and setting for observations); clearly specified criteria for coding, materials (such as pictures for tests or questionnaires); and methods of recording responses and of arriving at scores. Without standard systems of test administration, individual differences in ECD scores may plausibly be attributed to differences in the testing conditions or other external factors rather than to differences in children's actual development.

RELIABILITY

Reliability concerns the dependability, consistency, and generalizability of ECD scores. Reliability is fundamental because it indicates that scores are replicable rather than occurring merely by chance. Reliability has several variants. *Internal consistency* assesses uniformity of performance across an ECD measure's constituent items. Internal consistency generally is measured with Cronbach's alpha. *Interobserver reliability* assesses the extent to which observers/scorers obtain equivalent ECD scores when assessing the same individual. Interobserver reliability is measured with agreement statistics (e.g., percent agreement, correlation coefficient, kappa). *Parallel-form reliability* determines the degree to which alternate (parallel) forms of an ECD instrument provide equivalent scores. *Situational consistency* (generalizability) indexes the extent to which scores from an ECD instrument are consistent across settings, a form of reliability analogous to the concept of the external validity of investigations. *Temporal reliability* (stability) measures the degree to which an ECD instrument provides equivalent scores across time. A high degree of stability is prerequisite to establishing that a measure constitutes a suitable individual differences variable. It is generally assumed that, to be meaningful, a characteristic should show substantial consistency across time (Hartmann et al., 2011). Test–retest correlations are frequently used to assess stability over relatively short periods of time (e.g., less than a month). ECD indicators must demonstrate temporal reliability to provide confidence that scores on the indicator are replicable.

VALIDITY

Validity measures the meaning or fidelity of the assessment: Does the ECD instrument measure what it was intended to measure? The validity of ECD instruments can be judged in a variety of ways and is often assessed in relation to an ECD instrument's correspondence with other measures of a given construct and the degree to which the scores from an ECD assessment device are useful for predicting other criteria. Threats to validity occur when an ECD assessment instrument either underrepresents the intended ECD construct or includes surplus components. An ECD instrument should be rejected if it does not demonstrate validity because one could not have confidence in its ability to assess what it was intended to measure.

Early Childhood Development Comparisons Across Countries and Cultures

ECD assessments are often used to compare the results of children in a program with those not in a program, or to compare across countries, or cultural or socioeconomic groups. Because of the design of such comparisons, interpretation of differences must be careful. They are rarely true experiments that can allow statements of causality. True experiments require manipulation of an independent variable and control of extraneous variables by random assignment of participants to conditions. Much more common are quasi-experiments, in which groups are matched on relevant variables, but participants are not randomly assigned to conditions. In quasi-experiments, cause and effect cannot be specified as unambiguously, although some causal inferences are possible. Nonexperimental designs, such as comparing two groups that are not randomly assigned or matched, do not allow investigators to reach conclusions about causality, although statements can still be made about associations.

ECD comparisons usually involve quasi-experimental or nonexperimental designs in which samples are not randomly selected from a population or assigned to conditions. (Researchers cannot randomly assign an individual to a country/culture, socioeconomic status [SES], ethnic group, or the like.) Interpreting findings about ECD similarities and differences is much more difficult in such studies than in experiments that are based on random assignment of participants. The major questions that challenge comparative ECD assessments concern how to isolate the source of potential differences and how to identify the active country, culture, or other ingredients that produced differences. When researchers attribute the source of observed differences in a quasi-experimental design solely to country, culture, or other source and conclude that country or culture caused the observed differences, this mistaken inference has been termed the *cultural attribution fallacy* (Matsumoto & Yoo, 2006). Samples in different countries/cultures may differ on many demographic characteristics, and these demographics often confound observed ECD differences. Various procedures are available to untangle rival explanations for country/cultural comparisons, such as the inclusion of additional variables like measures of SES, maternal intelligence, education, or tendency to respond in a socially desirable fashion to confirm or disconfirm specific interpretations. Thus, it is possible to draw conclusions based on country or culture versus a demographic variable.

Nonexperimental, quasi-experimental, and true experimental designs meet, or fail to meet, two threats to validity. Threats to internal validity represent mistaken inferences about the causal connectedness between the independent variable and dependent variable in a particular investigation. Threats to external validity include ecological validity, generalizability, and representativeness. Before drawing conclusions about the implications of research results, it is critical to be cautious not to make causal inferences when the data can only suggest correlational associations between variables and to be sure that the ECD assessment measures what it was intended to measure and can be generalized beyond the specific research situation.

Methods for Assessing Equivalence of ECD Measurements Across Cultures: Adapting Instruments to Cultural and Linguistic Differences or Developing a New Instrument

Studies of more than one country or cultural group often require the collection of data in different languages. As such, issues concerning equivalence between the languages used must be overcome. Steps need to be taken to promote cross-linguistic appropriateness and validity of instruments to achieve at least "adapted equivalence" of instruments (Van de Vijver & Leung, 1997). Hambleton and Zenisky (2010) described 25 criteria with which to evaluate the adequacy of translations. To minimize language and cultural differences, ECD measures that have been translated should also be translated back into their original language and then scrutinized for items that are confusing or culturally inappropriate. Procedures of forward- and back-translation thus ensure linguistic and conceptual equivalence of measures across languages (Brislin, 1980, 1986; Erkut, 2010; Maxwell, 1996; Peña, 2007). In addition, researchers must note and correct (1) words in research instruments that do not translate well, are inappropriate for the different groups, or are culturally insensitive; (2) identify words that elicit several meanings in particular contexts; (3) suggest improvements of instruments if they identify problems; and (4) indicate reasons for altering the translated versions if discrepancies are identified and alterations are deemed necessary. These efforts are implemented to ensure that ECD measures are valid in all sites by focusing on linguistic equivalence, as well as on the cultural meanings that would be imparted by the measures. Beyond language per se, pictures of unfamiliar objects or stimuli (such as plastic toys) may be novel to children living in certain circumstances, and they might best be replaced with locally appropriate alternatives.

If extensive modifications to an ECD instrument are needed, it may be necessary to reconsider using the instrument. Rather than adapting an existing assessment for use in a new context, it is possible alternatively to develop assessments that are indigenous to the new contexts. An advantage of that approach is that the assessment can then be designed to match the needs of the specific context. A disadvantage is that such an approach makes it difficult to compare ECD in one context with ECD in other contexts, as the same measures and standards are not applied across contexts. Thus, if a goal of assessment is to make comparisons across countries or cultural groups, it is necessary to develop measures that are equivalent across groups.

With any test of between-group differences, there is a chance that the measures are not equivalent in the groups. To be able to make reasonable comparisons between groups, the measurement equivalence of the beliefs, responses, and items in the instruments should be tested. Vandenberg and Lance (2000) wrote a comprehensive article on the topic of (and statistical packages like AMOS have built-in procedures for testing) different levels of invariance. If investigators choose not to test measurement invariance, they must at least provide empirical or conceptual justification that the measures used in a comparative assessment have the same meaning in different groups.

Illustrations of Early Childhood Development Assessment

Following extensive background research and pilot testing, UNICEF created an Early Child Development Index, which was designed as a global indicator of ECD

(Zill & Ziv, 2007). Given the global relevance of this indicator and the utility of the process through which it was derived, we refer to it here to illustrate the process of constructing an ECD measure that can be used across a wide range of contexts. As UNICEF began the process of developing a global ECD indicator, the first question was which developmental domains should be included in the indicator. In an effort to describe child development holistically, the UNICEF team decided to assess children's abilities, skills, and behaviors in six domains: physical/motor, social, emotional, cognitive, language, and approaches to learning. A second key question was how to gather information about these different developmental domains. The UNICEF team decided to collect data using reports that could be provided by parent caregivers. One factor contributing to the decision not to use teachers' or nonparental caregivers' reports was that many children were expected not to have any nonparental caregiver who would be knowledgeable enough about their development to provide such a report. Another question was how the information should be combined across developmental domains into a composite indicator. The team agreed to assign equal weight to each developmental domain when summing across domains to create the final composite indicator (Zill & Ziv, 2007, provide details on the construction and scoring of the indicator). A constraint was that the index needed to be incorporated into a household survey that is already very long, and the possibility of administering a test seemed unlikely.

Through a process of pilot testing and winnowing of items (e.g., Janus, Brinkman, & Duku, 2008), benchmark accomplishments were identified in each of several developmental domains for children in the age range of 3–4 years. Each benchmark reflected an accomplishment that children of the specified age were expected to have achieved if they were developing typically. Benchmarks were not included if they were not relevant across all cultures. For example, after considerable discussion, benchmarks related to color identification were rejected because the number of words describing colors in some languages is limited (Bornstein, 2006, 2007). Likewise, there was extensive discussion regarding whether a benchmark that involved holding a pencil should be included as an indicator of fine motor skills, given that children in rural areas of developing countries often have little exposure to writing implements such as pencils, but writing with a different type of instrument was accepted. All of the benchmarks that were ultimately retained could be objectively and fairly easily assessed during a brief interview with the caregiver and were deemed to be globally appropriate and culturally relevant (Zill & Ziv, 2007). The final indicator provides a good starting point as a measure to be used globally to assess, compare, and monitor children's early development, but the items were also limited by the constraint that they needed to be incorporated into household surveys conducted in dozens of countries.

Numerous other examples of ECD assessment have had different goals, constraints, and opportunities than the UNICEF Early Child Development Index. For instance, the World Health Organization (WHO), in the 1980s and 1990s, examined the ages at which children achieved milestones in different domains of child development using more than 15,000 children ages 0–5 from India, China, and Thailand (Lansdown et al., 1995; Vazir, Naidu, Vidyasagar, Lansdown, & Reddy, 1992). Such information is valuable in providing benchmarks against which to compare milestones of at-risk populations in these contexts to determine whether interventions are working as intended, and it was designed to serve as a locally appropriate screening tool. The WHO took the approach of including milestones such as sitting and using a cup that were applicable across countries for cross-country comparisons, as well as milestones such as using chopsticks to pick up small pieces of food and carrying a block on one's head for at least five steps that were country-specific milestones that were germane in specific cultural contexts (Lansdown et al., 1995). In a second effort in the early 2000s, the WHO collected information on six motor milestones as part of their assessment of growth in well-nourished children in the United States, Norway, Oman, Ghana, and India. These norms were to be used as part of a global assessment (World Health Organization, 2006).

Fernald et al. (2009) provide an extensive review of ECD indicators that have been used with success in developing countries and a set of recommendations regarding different indictors that are appropriate in a wide variety of assessment situations. For example, the Bayley Scales of Infant Development (BSID) are the most widely used indicators of infant development around the world and are appropriate for children from birth through 42 months of age. Fernald et al. (2009) summarized 44 published studies using the BSID in countries other than the United States. This work establishes both the validity and reliability of the items, the possibility of translating the scales into many languages, and administering the assessment meaningfully in a diverse set of cultural contexts, all important considerations in deciding which measures to use to assess ECD. Currently, efforts are under way to create regionally appropriate measures in Latin America by the Inter-American Development Bank, and in East Asia based on countries' own standards for child development with support from UNICEF and the Open Society Institute.

What Is Not Known and Needs More Work

Despite increasing recognition of the needs to take a holistic approach to ECD and assess children's development in a variety of physical, cognitive, social, and emotional domains, ECD assessments that capture children's physical and cognitive development are better developed than are assessments that capture children's social or emotional development. Additional work is therefore needed to develop measures of children's social and emotional development that are meaningful in a wide range of cultural contexts. In addition, although there is agreement regarding the general principles needed to establish cross-cultural or cross-linguistic equivalence of measures, there is less understanding of the specific criteria by which to

BOX 18.1 Recommendations

Early childhood development assessments should be:

- Obtained ethically, with care taken to ensure the protection of children's rights and that results are used only in the best interests of children
- Appropriately linked to the purpose of the assessment (e.g., should measure what an intervention was intended to change or, in the absence of intervention, align with national goals for children or other desired outcomes)
- Valid and reliable
- Adapted from existing measures with careful attention to making the measures culturally appropriate or developed anew using principles of sound test construction
- Easy to obtain and use in low-resource settings

establish cut-points for deeming measures to be equivalent or not between two or more groups. Furthermore, additional work is needed to guide researchers in how to proceed when measurement equivalence cannot be established across groups. Additional attention to these measurement issues will provide more confidence in results obtained from ECD assessments.

Conclusion

Because policymakers and practitioners use assessments of ECD to make fundamental decisions regarding allocation of resources, interventions for children, and national policies, it is crucial to measure ECD in rigorous and methodologically sound ways. Measurement should be designed with the goals of the assessment in mind and should include considerations of questions related to which domains of ECD will be assessed, methods and sources of data collection, the psychometric adequacy of the measures, the equivalence of measures across economic and cultural contexts, and the ethics of the proposed data collection. The rigorous assessment of ECD that will result can benefit children by raising public awareness regarding the import of ECD, by encouraging policymakers to devote more resources to ECD for groups of children who are struggling, by enabling practitioners to target selected interventions toward children who are at risk, and by promoting efforts to improve the well-being of children worldwide.

Acknowledgments

We thank D. Breakstone. Supported by the Intramural Research Program of the NIH, NICHD, *Eunice Kennedy Shriver* National Institute of Child Health and Human Development grant RO1-HD054805, and Fogarty International Center grant RO3-TW008141. Correspondence to: Marc H. Bornstein, Child and Family Research, *Eunice Kennedy Shriver* National Institute of Child Health and Human Development, National Institutes of Health, Rockledge 1, Suite 8030, 6705 Rockledge Drive, MSC 7971, Bethesda MD 20892-7971, USA. Email: Marc_H_Bornstein@nih.gov.

References

Achenbach, T. M., McConaughy, S. H., & Howell, C. T. (1987). Child/adolescent behavioral and emotional problems: Implications of cross-informant correlations for situational specificity. *Psychological Bulletin, 101*, 213–232.

Ainsworth, M. (1993). Attachment as related to mother-infant interaction. *Advances in Infancy Research, 8*, 1–50.

Appelbaum, M. I., & McCall, R. B. (1983). Design and analysis in developmental psychology. In P. H. Mussen (Ed.), *Manual of child psychology: Vol. 1. History, theory, and methods* (pp. 415–476). New York: Wiley.

Bornstein, M. H. (2006). Hue categorization and color naming: Physics to sensation to perception. In N. J. Pitchford & C. P. Biggam (Eds.), *Progress in colour studies volume II. Psychological aspects* (pp. 35–68). Amsterdam/Philadelphia: John Benjamins.

Bornstein, M. H. (2007). Hue categorization and color naming: Cognition to language to culture. In R. E. MacLaury, G. V. Paramei, & D. Dedrick (Eds.), *Anthropology of color: Interdisciplinary multilevel modeling* (pp. 3–27). Amsterdam/Philadelphia: John Benjamins.

Bornstein, M. H., Britto, P. B., Nonoyama-Tarumi, Y., Ota, Y., Petrovic, O., & Putnick, D. L. (2012). Child development in developing countries: Introduction and methods. *Child Development, 83*, 16–31.

Bornstein, M. H., & Bornstein, L. (2008). Psychological stability. In W. A. Darity, Jr. (Ed.), *International encyclopedia of social sciences* (2nd ed., Vol. 8, pp. 74–75). Detroit, MI: Macmillan Reference USA.

Bornstein, M. H., Cote, L. R., Maital, S., Painter, K., Park, S. -Y., Pascual, L., et al. (2004). Cross-linguistic analysis of vocabulary in young children: Spanish, Dutch, French, Hebrew, Italian, Korean, and American English. *Child Development, 75*, 1115–1139.

Bornstein, M. H., Gaughran, J. M., & Homel, P. (1986). Infant temperament: Theory, tradition, critique and new assessments. In C. E. Izard & P. B. Read (Eds.), *Measuring emotions in infants and young children* (Vol. 2, pp. 172–202). Cambridge, UK: Cambridge University Press.

Bornstein, M. H., & Haynes, O. M. (1998). Vocabulary competence in early childhood: Measurement, latent construct, and predictive validity. *Child Development, 69*, 654–671.

Bornstein, M. H., Haynes, O. M., Painter, K. M., & Genevro, J. L. (2000). Child language with mother and with stranger at home and in the laboratory: A methodological study. *Journal of Child Language, 27*, 407–420.

Bornstein, M. H., Painter, K. P., & Park, J. (2002). Naturalistic language sampling in typically developing children. *Journal of Child Language, 29*, 687–699.

Bowerman, M. (1985). What shapes children's grammars? In D. Slobin (Ed.), *The crosslinguistic study of language acquisition* (pp. 1257–1319). Hillsdale, NJ: Erlbaum.

Bracken, B. A. (2007). Creating the optimal preschool testing situation. In B. A. Bracken & R. Nagle (Eds.), *Psychoeducational assessment of preschool children* (4th ed., pp. 137–154). Mahwah, NJ: Erlbaum.

Bradley, R. H. (2010). The HOME environment. In M. H. Bornstein (Ed.), *Handbook of cultural developmental sciences* (pp. 505–530). New York: Psychology Press.

Bradley, R. H., & Corwyn, R. F. (2005). Caring for children around the world: A view from HOME. *International Journal of Behavioral Development, 29*, 468–478.

Bradley-Johnson, S., & Johnson, C. M. (2007). Infant and toddler cognitive assessment. In B. A. Bracken & R. J. Nagle (Eds.), *Psychoeducational assessment of preschool children* (4th ed.). Mahwah, NJ: Erlbaum.

Brislin, R. W. (1980). Translation and content analysis of oral and written materials. In H. C. Triandis & J. W. Berry (Eds.), *Handbook of cross-cultural psychology: Vol. 2. Methodology* (pp. 137–164). Boston: Allyn and Bacon.

Brislin, R. W. (1986). The wording and translation of research instruments. In W. J. Lonner & J. W. Berry (Eds.), *Field methods in cross-cultural research* (pp. 137–164). Newbury Park, CA: Sage.

Campbell, D. T., & Fiske, D. W. (1959). Convergent and discriminant validation by the multitrait-multimethod matrix. *Psychological Bulletin, 56*, 81–105.

Dale, P. S., Bates, E., Reznick, J. S., & Morisset, C. (1989). The validity of a parent report instrument of child language at twenty months. *Journal of Child Language, 16*, 239–249.

Darwin, C. (1877). A biographical sketch of an infant. *Mind, 2*, 285–294.

Erkut, S. (2010). Developing multiple language versions of instruments for intercultural research. *Child Development Perspectives, 4*, 19–24.

Fenson, L., Dale, P. S., Reznick, J. S., Bates, E., Thal, D. J., & Pethick, S. J. (1994). Variability in early communicative development. *Monographs of the Society for Research in Child Development, 59*(5).

Fenson, L., Dale, P. S., Reznick, J. S., Thal, D., Bates, E., Hartung, J. P., et al. (1993). *The MacArthur Communicative Development Inventories: User's guide and technical manual.* San Diego: Singular Publishing Group.

Fernald, L. C. H., Kariger, P., Engle, P., & Raikes, A. (2009). *Examining early child development in low-income countries: A toolkit for the assessment of children in the first five years of life.* Washington, DC: World Bank.

Fisher, C. B., & Anushko, A. (2008). Research ethics in social science. In P. Alasuutari, L. Bickman, & J. Brannen (Eds.), *The Sage handbook of social research methods* (pp. 95–110). Thousand Oaks, CA: Sage.

Goal One Technical Planning Group. (1991). The Goal One Technical Planning Subgroup report on school readiness. In National Education Goals Panel (Ed.), *Potential strategies for long-term indicator development: Reports of the technical planning subgroups* (Report No. 91–0). Washington, DC: National Education Goals Panel.

Gopnik, A., & Meltzoff, A. N. (1986). Relations between semantic and cognitive development in the one-word stage: The specificity hypothesis. *Child Development, 57*, 1040–1053.

Grigorenko, E. L., & Sternberg, R. J. (1999). *Assessing cognitive development in early childhood.* Washington, DC: World Bank.

Hambleton, R. K., & Zenisky, A. L. (2010). Translating and adapting tests for cross-cultural assessments. In D. Matsumoto & F. J. R. van de Vijver (Eds.), *Cross-cultural research methods in psychology* (pp. 46–74). New York: Cambridge University Press.

Hartmann, D. P., Pelzel, K. E., & Abbott, C. B. (2011). Design, measurement, and analysis in developmental research. In M. H. Bornstein & M. E. Lamb (Eds.), *Developmental science: An advanced textbook* (6th ed., pp. 109–198). New York: Taylor and Francis.

Janus, M., Brinkman, S., & Duku, E. (2008). *Pilot test results: Child development outcome instruments to be included in UNICEF's MICS household survey.* New York: UNICEF.

Lansdown, R. G., Goldstein, H., Shah, P. M., Orley, J. H., Di, G., Kaul, K. K., et al. (1995). Culturally appropriate measures for monitoring child development at family and community level: A WHO collaborative study. *Bulletin of the World Health Organization, 74*(3), 283–290.

Lerner, R. M., Leonard, K., Fay, K., & Isaac, S. S. (2011). Continuity and discontinuity in development across the life span: A developmental systems perspective. In K. L. Fingerman, C. A. Berg, J. Smith, & T. C. Antonucci (Eds.), *Handbook of life-span development* (pp. 141–160). New York: Springer.

Matsumoto, D., & Yoo, S. H. (2006). Toward a new generation of cross-cultural research. *Perspectives on Psychological Science, 1*, 234–250.

Maxwell, B. (1996). Translation and cultural adaptation of the survey instruments. In M. O. Martin & D. L. Kelly (Eds.), *Third International Mathematics and Science Study (TIMSS) technical report, Volume I: Design and development.* Chestnut Hill, MA: Boston College.

McCall, R. B. (1981). Nature–nurture and the two realms of development: A proposed integration with respect to mental development. *Child Development, 52*, 1–12.

Peña, E. D. (2007). Lost in translation: Methodological considerations in cross-cultural research. *Child Development, 78*, 1255–1264.

Roberts, B. W., & DelVecchio, W. F. (2000). The rank-order consistency of personality from childhood to old age: A quantitative review of longitudinal studies. *Psychological Bulletin, 126*, 3–25.

Snow, C. E., & Van Hemel, S. B. (Eds.). (2008). *Early childhood assessment: Why, what, and how.* Washington, DC: National Academies Press.

Squires, J. K., Potter, L., Bricker, D. D., & Lamorey, S. (1998). Parent-completed developmental questionnaires: Effectiveness with low and middle income parents. *Early Childhood Research Quarterly, 13*, 345–354.

Thal, D., & Bates, E. (1990). Continuity and variation in early language development. In J. Fagen & J. Colombo (Eds.), *Individual differences in infancy: Reliability, stability, prediction* (pp. 359–386). Hillsdale, NJ: Erlbaum.

Thomas, A., Chess, S., Birch, H. G., Hertzog, M. E., & Korn, S. (1963). *Behavioral individuality in early childhood.* New York: New York University Press.

United Nations. (1989). *United Nations Convention on the Rights of the Child, Geneva.* Washington, DC: Office of the United Nations High Commissioner for Human Rights. Retrieved from www.unhchr.ch/html/menu3/b/k2crc.htm

UNICEF. (2012). *The state of the world's children 2012.* New York: UNICEF.

Van de Vijver, F. J. R. & Leung, K. (1997). *Methods and data analysis for cross-cultural research.* Newbury Park, CA: Sage.

Vandenberg, R. J., & Lance, C. E. (2000). A review and synthesis of the measurement invariance literature: Suggestions, practices, and recommendations for organizational research. *Organizational Research Methods, 3*, 4–70.

Vazir, S., Naidu, A. N., Vidyasagar, P., Lansdown, R. G., & Reddy, V. (1992). Screening test battery for assessment of psychological development. *Indian Pediatrics, 31*, 1465–1475.

Wesley, P. W., & Buysse, V. (2003). Making meaning of school readiness in schools and communities. *Early Childhood Research Quarterly, 18,* 351–375.

Wohlwill, J. F. (1973). *The study of behavioral development.* New York: Academic Press.

World Health Organization Multicentre Reference Study Group. (2006). WHO motor development study: Windows of achievement for six gross motor development milestones. *Acta Pædiatrica, S450,* 86–95.

Zigler, E., Abelson, W., & Seitz, V. (1973). Motivational factors in the performance of economically disadvantaged children on the Peabody Picture Vocabulary Test. *Child Development, 44,* 294–303.

Zill, N., & Ziv, Y. (2007). *Toward a global indicator of early child development: Final report.* New York: UNICEF.

19

Monitoring Progress Toward Fulfilling Rights in Early Childhood Under the Convention on the Rights of the Child to Improve Outcomes for Children and Families

Clyde Hertzman, Ziba Vaghri, and Adem
Arkadas-Thibert

The Problem

What happens to children in their earliest years is critical for their development throughout the life course. The years from birth to school age are foundational for brain and biological development. Attachment and face recognition, impulse control and regulation of physical aggression, executive function in the prefrontal cortex and focused attention, fine and gross motor functions and coordination, receptive and expressive language, and understandings of quantitative concepts are all established during this time and become embedded in the architecture and function of the brain. Brain and biological development are in turn expressed through three broad domains of development of the whole child: physical, social-emotional, and language-cognitive, which together form the basis of "developmental health." Developmental health influences many aspects of well-being, including obesity and stunting, mental health, heart disease, competence in literacy and numeracy, criminality, and economic participation throughout life. The problem explored in this chapter is: How can the United Nations (UN) Convention on the Rights of the Child (CRC) be used as a tool to support developmental health in the early years?

Children's human rights were made into legally binding international law with the CRC, through unanimous adoption by the UN General Assembly in 1989. The CRC is the human rights treaty that provides a firm legal basis for a comprehensive framework for early childhood, as well as international standards for fulfilment of children's rights in early years (See Chapter 4, this volume for a detailed description of the CRC). Its legal power is strengthened by the fact that it is the most widely agreed-upon international human rights treaty in the world, with 193 signatory countries. However, signatory countries, although aware of the importance of early childhood, often overlook their obligations in the early years largely because of the perceived invisibility of very young children. Moreover, improving early child development requires finding ways for social determinants and child rights approaches to work together in common purpose. To date, this has not occurred.

The Issues

Economic and population health approaches have tended to focus on society's collective interest in the future of the child; that is, on early childhood contributions to their capacities as adults. Developing in parallel, the philosophy of human rights, as enshrined in the CRC, has led to a different approach. Rather than viewing the young child as a passive recipient of "interventions" to aid them on the way to becoming healthy, economically productive adults, it emphasizes the young child as a being with inherent human rights, *in present time*. Human rights discourse maintains that young children are holders of rights and should be respected for their inherent value as human beings, as well as for their skills and competencies. General Comment 7 (GC7) was appended to the Convention in 2005. It focuses exclusively on children 0–8 years old; accordingly, that will be the age range considered in this chapter. It makes explicit young children's right to enjoy their childhood to the full; the right to have good health, to learn, and to play (UNCRC, 2005). Although the human rights approach might appear in conflict with economic and population health approaches, it is not. Birth cohort studies from around the world document experiences that violate children's rights in early childhood, showing how they damage developmental trajectories across the life course. Thus, if rights in early childhood are not respected, protected, and fulfilled *in present time*, children are unlikely to thrive and contribute socially and economically in future.

Despite the potential synergies, rights and population health cultures have generally been unaware of each other, appealing to different constituencies and missing opportunities for making common cause. Indeed, there have been tensions. For example, consider this statement about the Millennium Development Goals (MDGs), which are a paragon of the outcome orientation of population health, from a leading rights scholar "while an ideal version of the MDGs is certainly compatible [with human rights], a bare-bones version which is sometimes put forward might accord only a token role to civil and political rights and endorse a very limited portion of the overall economic, social and cultural rights agenda" (Alston, 2003). The central concern here is that rights holders be "active *claimants* of their rights, rather than passive beneficiaries of charitable works" (Levi, 2009). This active/passive distinction is important to acknowledge and transcend, because it is fair to claim that population health has, in fact, inadvertently conceived of the child in passive terms, emphasizing the role that societies should play in improving the intimate environments of stimulation, support, and nurturance *on behalf of* young children. Without a complementary human rights approach, emphasizing young children's right to active participation in their lives and legitimizing their de facto role in influencing the environments where they grow up, live, and learn, the population health approach amounts to reducing the child to a passive beneficiary of society's good works.

Placing the "rights environment," with its emphasis on active participation, on an equal footing with the population health approach, with its emphasis on environments of stimulation, support, and nurturance, transcends the active/passive dichotomy described above. The CRC and GC7 provide minimum legal standards for governments to observe in order to uphold the human dignity of young children but, also, these documents provide an impetus to act upon the fact that fulfilment of young children's rights requires special attention to their intimate, and broader socioeconomic, environments. In practice, this means that opportunities for survival, physical, and social-emotional and language-cognitive development for all young children are guaranteed in law, provided without discrimination, and implemented in ways that encourage young children to be active participants in their own lives.

INEQUITY FROM THE START AS A RIGHTS VIOLATION: THE EXAMPLE OF CANADA

In Canada, population-based assessments of early child development are conducted during the transition year to formal schooling, at age 5, using the Early Development Instrument (EDI). The EDI allows each child to be scored as "vulnerable" or "not vulnerable" in his or her development (Janus et al., 2007) and, by the end of the 2007/08 school year, EDIs had been done on approximately 80% of the age 5 Canadian population. These data revealed that 25%–30% of Canadian children were vulnerable in their development, ranging from a low of 4% in some communities to a high of 68% in others (Hertzman, 2009). Approximately half of this 17-fold range is explained, statistically, by socioeconomic conditions, whereas the rest relates to parenting styles, community governance, and neighborhood access to quality programs and services for young children. Most important here, by conservative estimates, more than 60% of the vulnerability measured on the EDI could have been avoided if the children had had better quality experiences in their first 5 years. According to the World Health Organization (WHO) Commission on the Social Determinants of Health, this state of affairs would violate the principle of "equity from the start." Moreover, under GC7, it is possible to construe such high levels of avoidable vulnerability and inequality in early child development as a human rights issue. Although it is true that social justice is not *just* a rights issue, and rights are not *just* a social justice issue, there are very good strategic reasons to emphasize the overlap. As evidence continues to emerge, globally, on modifiable vulnerabilities in early child development (Grantham-McGregor et al., 2007), there will be an impetus to build coalitions between those with an equity orientation and those with a rights perspective, in order to deal from a position of strength in the policy arena for the benefit of young children. A bridging of approaches means that "equity from the start" is seen as the fulfilment of social justice, as a sound investment in health and human development, and, also, as the fulfilment of a basic human right.

THE CASE FOR MONITORING THE IMPLEMENTATION OF CHILD RIGHTS IN EARLY CHILDHOOD

The CRC is the first comprehensive human rights legal instrument linking civil and political rights with economic, social, and cultural rights (ESCR). The right of a young child to develop, like the right to food, health, housing, family, education, and work, falls into the category of ESCR (Green, 2001), which are recognized, internationally, as "substantive" rights. Unlike "procedural" rights, such as the right to nondiscrimination, substantive rights are subject to the obligation of "progressive realization." What does this mean? Procedural rights always create an *immediate* duty on the state to be fulfilled at once, since they are amenable to direct control by responsible individuals. In contrast, substantive rights cannot be fulfilled overnight, because a wide range of societal conditions influence their fulfilment, and these conditions are not under the control of specific individuals who can be held directly responsible. International rights treaties recognize this by holding the state and other duty-bearers responsible for taking steps toward *gradually, but incrementally* achieving the realization of substantive rights over time (i.e., progressive realization). In other words, it is understood that the barriers to fulfilling the substantive rights in GC7 are deeply embedded in society, such that they will take considerable time and effort to remove (Green, 2001).

To achieve progressive realization of substantive rights, policies, programs, and practices must be consistent with the commitments governments have made to CRC, including general comments adopted under CRC article 45(d). Once governments make this commitment, they are held accountable by periodically reporting on progress to the UN Committee on the Rights of the Child (herein, the Committee) (Khattab & Arends, 2009). Reporting is essential in the case of commitments requiring progressive realization, since evidence of progress (or lack of it) may be diffuse, slow changing, and contested. In the case of rights in early childhood, progressive realization is largely bound up in the conditions of children's daily lives. Without active efforts at monitoring and reporting on these conditions, progressive realization would go unmonitored. Moreover, as things improve, what is expected of a state to fulfil its CRC obligations toward young children will increase over time. Accordingly, paragraph 39 of GC7 suggests that indicators and benchmarks should be used by "states parties" to monitor the realization of child rights in early childhood. The logic is straightforward: Child rights indicators for early childhood should derive from GC7, since it provides the normative framework for the indicators to monitor the implementation of CRC in early years, with a view to holding duty-bearers to account (Hunt, 2003).

In theory, indicators make it possible for people and organizations to identify important actors and hold them accountable for their actions; serve as tools for making better policies and monitoring progress; identifying unintended impacts of laws, policies, and practices; provide early warning of potential violations; enhance social consensus on difficult trade-offs that need to be made in the face of resource constraints; and identify when policy adjustments are required. (Hunt, 2003)

Already, there are many examples of indicators that have the capacity to monitor progress in early childhood care and development, such as the Early Development Instrument (Janus et al., 2007) and relevant modules of the Multiple Information Cluster Survey conducted in more than 40 countries by UNICEF (United Nations Department of Economic and Social Affairs [UN DESA], 2006) (although not yet on its companion, the Demographic Household Survey). This raises crucial questions. Do we need a new indicator framework based on young children's human rights? What is the added value of having rights-based indicators? In general, what is the relationship between population health/human development indicators in childhood, on the one hand, and child rights indicators, on the other? In answer to the last question, the former are oriented toward goals, usually defined in terms of survival and well-being, whereas the latter are usually a means of determining the extent to which a government is complying with its treaty obligations, whether or not they further human development goals (Green, 2001). Specifically, two main characteristics of child rights indicators are not typical of other childhood indicators:

1. *They are based on international binding legal documents* and measure not only the progress in the situation of children but also how governments, as duty-bearers, fare in fulfilling their legal obligations toward young children.

2. *They do not just look at the progress made, but they identify gaps and missing capacities* and ask further questions to understand discrepancies. Did the process leading to progress respect and protect young children's rights, including their right to be heard and to participate in the process in an equitable and non-discriminatory manner? Has the best interest of the young child been made the paramount consideration in the mechanisms? What measures have been taken to uphold the right to non-discrimination, including creating equality of opportunity and outcome?

Translating the diverse conditions of children's daily lives into measurable indicators requires an element of reductionism. Reductionism connotes loss of information, but there is a trade off with commensuration. Commensuration transforms qualities into quantities and difference into magnitude, and allows us to quickly grasp, represent, and compare differences. It offers a standardized way of constructing proxies for uncertain and elusive qualities and condenses and reduces the amount of information people have to process, thereby simplifying decision-making (Espeland & Stevens, 1998). The monitoring protocol for GC7, described below, is designed to strike a feasible balance between reductionism and commensuration.

A Theory of Change

The environments where children grow up, live, and learn influence the quality of their early experiences, which, in turn, shape long-term outcomes (Irwin, Siddiqi, & Hertzman, 2007). Environments and experiences that influence development range from the most intimate (i.e., moment-to-moment interactions in the family), to the societal (i.e., the influence on living conditions of the globalizing economy). The WHO's Commission on the Social Determinants of Health recognized these realities in its 2008 final report, "Closing the Gap in a Generation: Health Equity Through Action on the Social Determinants of Health" (Commission on Social Determinants of Health [CSDH], 2008). Chapter five of the report, called "Equity from the Start," was devoted to early child development from the perspective of population health. It called upon all 193 WHO member countries "commit to and implement a comprehensive approach to early life, building on existing child survival platforms and extending interventions in early life to include social/emotional and language/cognitive development."

The CRC provides a monitoring mechanism for all signatory countries, placing a legal obligation on countries to write periodic reports to the Committee on the Rights of the Child as the monitoring body of the CRC.[1] The committee, as a part of their mandate under CRC article 45(d), also issues "General Comments" to guide governments in better understanding, implementing, and monitoring the implementation of the CRC in their countries. One of these is GC7: Implementing Rights in Early Childhood. It was adopted in response to the observation by the Committee that children under the age of 8 years were often entirely overlooked in states parties' reporting of progress toward implementing CRC. GC7, adopted in 2005, reiterates that every child should enjoy a safe and nurturing childhood in which to develop and grow to his or her full potential, free from violence and want. Young children have the right to enjoy their childhood to the full, the right to have good health, to learn, and to play. Young children have the same rights and freedoms as all other children, but they are deemed to be particularly vulnerable due to their age and special developmental needs.

Because of the monitoring role of the committee, GC7 has also provided a timely opportunity for developing early childhood indicators based on human rights.

The theory of change, here, is that GC7 can be used as a tool for achieving equity from the start, if it is accompanied by a commitment to both corrective and distributive justice. Equity means reducing avoidable inequalities in early child development according to (for example) socioeconomic status, ethnicity, geography, and gender. These are aspects of distributive justice; that is, they are concerned with reducing the variance in the distribution of life chances facing young children (de Grieff, 2009). At the same time, concern with the distribution of life chances is not just about monitoring outcomes, but recognizing that children from different walks of life may face very different barriers to thriving, such that the correction of past inequities ultimately has an impact on future life chances. Thus, both corrective and distributive justice is necessary, and need to be made to support and reinforce one another. We believe that a human rights–based approach to early childhood development provides a legal basis for this to happen. For example, prohibition of discrimination is "customary law" (i.e., it is accepted by all countries as a norm, even if they are not a party to the specific human rights treaty at issue). Corrective and distributive justice is derived from well-established nondiscrimination and equality provisions in both domestic and international law. Accordingly, a human rights approach would assert that it is not enough to simply open the doors to a program or service that could assist in early development, such as quality child care, and say "everyone can come." Because children from different walks of life may experience very different de facto barriers of access (e.g., cost, transportation, language, social trust, stigmatization, etc.), attendance will differ, not necessarily according to who wants or could benefit from the service, but according to the range and intensity of barriers that stand between the child and the program. A rights-based approach dictates that these barriers must be addressed in order that children's rights not be violated (Kitching, 2005).

A MONITORING PROTOCOL FOR GC7

Support for the value of child rights indicators is provided by the startling fact that there is no consistent association between ratification of human-rights treaties and health or social outcomes (Palmer et al., 2009). Why aren't these treaties prepared with good intentions and a sound knowledge base conducive to improved rights status? One theory is that it is due to the lack of tools to monitor the progressive realization of social and economic rights, tools that are sensitive enough to detect and measure relevant change. Accordingly, development of such tools should be helpful in an environment of good faith. Where good faith fails, improved accountability mechanisms to monitor compliance of states with treaty obligations, and financial assistance to support the realization of the right, could be a part of the solution.

As one of the leading international nongovernmental organizations (NGOs) that helped develop GC7, the Bernard van Leer Foundation led a study to explore obstacles to its implementation, to evaluate how GC7 was being received by signatory countries, and to determine how the General Comments have been interpreted since 2005. One of the main components was a pilot study of GC7 in Jamaica, which attempted to evaluate, in situ, its value to experts and community members, and whether it allowed the voices of young children to be heard.[2]

Based upon this study and the work of the WHO Commission on the Social Determinants of Health in January 2006, the committee formally requested that an ad hoc group of researchers, WHO, UNICEF, and child rights advocates from several NGOs create a framework of indicators for GC7. The result was the Early Childhood Rights Indicators Group (hereinafter, the Group). The Group worked to create a framework of indicators that countries could use to assess their current rights environment, to monitor the implementation of rights in early childhood, and to facilitate reporting to the committee. This framework, completed in May 2008, specifically addressed the rights that are upheld in the CRC but elaborated in GC7. It also addressed the following underlying and cross-cutting themes: the need to recognize young children as rights holders and active social participants; countries' obligations to provide appropriate and adequate support for caregivers of young children; the need for integrated service provision in support of holistic approaches to child development; the need to support the evolving capacities of young children through positive education and health promotion, preschool, and play experiences; freedom from social exclusion by virtue of young age, gender, race, ethnicity, and disability; freedom from violence; and measures to increase understanding of the particular vulnerabilities of young children.

ORGANIZATIONAL FRAMEWORK OF THE INDICATORS

The framework includes 15 indicator sets that build on existing UNICEF and WHO indicators but proposes new configurations of administrative data to gauge the implementation and enjoyment of rights in early childhood. Indicators are arranged according to a hybrid model that combines elements of the structure of the CRC reporting guidelines (UNCRC, 2010), the format of UNICEF's Multiple Information Cluster Surveys, and the structure of the WHO's Right to Health framework.

To simultaneously promote rights in early childhood and pursue the goal of equity from the start, the Group had to finesse the distinction, made above, between human rights and population health approaches. As will be seen below, the Group's approach was to merge them, organizing indicators according to structure, process and, notably, outcome, congruent with the approach of the UN Office of High Commissioner for Human Rights (OHCHR, 2008).

The indicator sets proposed in the framework are organized according to the CRC Reporting Guidelines (UNCRC, 1991). Under each cluster heading, a rationale for the indicator sets provides appropriate references to relevant articles in the CRC and paragraphs of GC7. Next, an overarching question is presented that provides easy understanding of the purpose of each indicator. These are then unpacked into sets of questions that are divided into sections titled Structure, Process, and Outcome (Appendix I; Figure 19.1). *Structure*, as an indication of commitment, refers to the existence of institutions and policies aligned with the CRC to realize the particular right in question. *Process* refers to efforts made and actions taken to fulfil the commitment, and thus to specific activities, resources, and initiatives in pursuit of rights realization. *Outcome* refers to a resultant and measurable change either in the "rights environment" or directly in the status of young children's development. Within these tables, we also identify potential sources of information, specify the relevant duty bearers, and provide references to sections of the reporting guidelines (Vaghri et al., 2009).

The indicator framework is not only a tool for governments to fulfil their obligation for periodic reporting to the committee, it is also meant to be an efficient institutional self-assessment tool and an inventory check list to help governments become aware of what policies, programs, and outcome information are (or are not) already available across a wide range of ministries, Non-Governmental Organizations (NGOs), and localities. Each indicator set contains a flow chart (Appendix II) that is meant to be the focal point for evaluation. It walks the report writer(s) through a series of questions regarding existing policies and programs, then moves to explore outcomes. In cases where a country's answer to a given policy/program question is negative, the flow chart provides examples of model policies/programs from countries across the globe. A conscious attempt has been made to include as many examples from the resource-poor countries as possible, often followed by website addresses or additional information. Upon completion of the indicators, governments should have a clear idea about the existing gaps in their systems, thus giving them a head start in filling in these gaps.

The contextual relevance of indicators is a key consideration in their acceptability and use. Countries often differ in terms of their level of development and realization of human rights. As a result of these differences and the nature of institutions, the policies and the priorities of states may differ. Therefore, it is not always possible to create indicators for child rights that are strictly universal. The GC7 Indicators Group kept this in mind and left open the possibility that there might be a need to customize certain parts of the indicator sets. Moreover, in May 2008, upon presentation of the framework to the committee, although a strong letter of support was sent to the GC7 Indicators Group, the committee articulated that it:

> [W]elcomes the plans to finalize this project so that a set of broadly applicable indicators regarding the implementation of rights of young children becomes available. The next steps have to be pilot studies in order to test and revise the list of indicators if necessary. (Dr. Yanghee Lee, UNCRC)

Summary of Evidence

In accordance with this directive from Dr. Lee, pilot implementations have been taking place in selected countries. Starting in Tanzania, the piloting protocol unfolded in a planned sequence: feasibility assessment, gathering stakeholders in a roundtable setting, identifying the country taskforce, training the taskforce in workshop format, face-validation of the indicators, data collection, mid-term evaluation, data review upon completion, interpretation, and wrap-up feedback meeting with all stakeholders and participants. Each event was designed to help build a community of understanding among the GC7 Indicators' project team, the country taskforce, and the stakeholders. Data were summarized, tabulated, and interpreted by the project secretariat during the data review and analysis phase, allowing it to identify the areas of the implementation manual that needed improvement. It also provided a basis for summary feedback to Tanzania about its existing capacities and gaps within its policies and programs and its outcome information.

Piloting the GC7 Indicator Framework has been an essential step toward building an internationally credible child rights monitoring tool. In addition to helping identify areas of confusion and ambiguity in the manual and indicators, the pilot helped the Group identify practical problems, such as the need for an electronic system for responding to the indicators that would be feasible in low-, middle-, and high-income countries. This would not only reduce the time required to create countries' periodic reports, but could also improve the efficiency of reporting to the committee.

The Group also learned that, although quantification simplified reporting, the qualitative aspect remained indispensable. When an attempt is made to quantify and compare a country's capacities regarding a given right, the transformation of country-specific knowledge into numerical representations does, indeed, strip meaning and context from the phenomena. Without any information on outcomes, a scarcity of policies and programs might be interpreted as limited capacity in the country, whereas in reality it may be due to the efficiency and effectiveness of the limited number of existing policies and programs, which has eliminated need for anything further. For example, in Tanzania, birth registration is one of the least fulfilled among child rights, with a birth certification rate among the lowest in Sub-Saharan Africa at less than 8% (Cody, 2009). The limited number of policies and programs regarding this right (indicator 5) is, in this case, indicative of limited capacity. However, in the absence of outcome data, one could not reach such a conclusion. In contrast, the right to education is probably one of the best attended. Tanzania has one of the highest literacy rates in Africa, reaching 98% by the mid-1980s and with preprimary enrollment rates experiencing a steady increase throughout the 1990s (Sitta, 2007). The number of policies and programs reported for indicator 11 "the right for early education services" are also limited and comparable to the numbers reported for indicator 5, the right to birth registration. In the absence of outcome indicators, these two rights could be mistakenly put in the same category, the category of severely unfulfilled rights, whereas the outcome data tell a very different story.

Data collection is somewhat constrained everywhere. Although the most obvious reason for this is usually cost, Davis et al. (2010) have argued that sometimes the concerns about what data could reveal is the underlying reason for it being missing. For example, a UN study found that, in 2005, only 59 countries (or sub-national regions) had reported the total number of households, based on census sources, and only 42 disaggregated these figures by sex and age of the head of the household (UN DESA, 2006, pp. 13, 18–19). Information on the number of first marriages, according to the age of the bride and groom, was stated by only 85 countries (or regions), representing 27% of the world's population. None of the 50 least developed countries provided these data to the UN (UN DESA, 2006, pp. 11, 18–19). Although data collection capacity is likely one reason for this, an unwillingness to open a discussion on child marriage is undoubtedly another. In any case, the data deficit inhibits evaluating the extent of child marriage worldwide.

Irrespective of these obstacles, progressive realization of rights in early childhood demands better information flows. The components of an efficient system include regular data collection and a well-organized and transparent archiving system that facilitates data retrieval and minimizes redundancy. Such a system should facilitate data linkage, which itself can promote intersectoral and multilevel approaches. Data retrieval appeared to be one of the main challenges in our first pilot. Many government officials were certain about the existence of specific data but had considerable problems retrieving it. In Tanzania, the retrieval problem seemed to be due to two factors: a disorganized, paper-based system for managing written legislation, policies, and outcome reporting, and, also, the well-known tendency, common in governments across the world, of shelving and forgetting about things that are difficult to implement.

An ironic aspect of the Tanzanian pilot was that the justice system was virtually absent from the process. Since the core aspects of Rights in Early Childhood are substantive, rather than procedural, they fell under ministries of health, education, and community/gender, rather than justice. Yet, the lack of involvement of the putative "enforcing" ministry was notable. It will be important to see if this pattern plays out in other pilot countries.

Finally, the Group found virtually no familiarity with GC7 among the government officials of our first pilot country. Conducting the pilot not only introduced the indicators of GC7, but also GC7 itself. It is our belief that, paradoxically, a country's willingness to implement the indicators will serve as a method of consciousness-raising for the very existence of GC7.

The Tanzanian experience showed that there were two distinct aspects to piloting: the technical and the human. Whereas the technical aspect represented an opportunity for a thorough inventory of the country's capacities for implementing child rights, the human aspect created opportunities to improve inter- and intraministerial communication. It also engaged some vital players who traditionally went underrepresented in the process of preparing CRC reports. At this point, the Group is not in a position to state which of the challenges, noted above, are country specific and which are common to countries across the globe. The next pilot, in Chile, may help sort this out.

Conclusion

There are two overarching conclusions that emerge from this paper, which are also its leading policy implications.

1. There needs to be a commitment from the UN-CRC Monitoring Committee and key relevant international agencies (WHO, UNICEF) to a long-term program of monitoring compliance with GC7 *in conjunction with* monitoring of early child developmental outcomes, in all signatory countries, in order to ensure progressive realization of rights in early childhood and equity from the start.

2. Within states, the process of data collection must be part of a program of interministerial cooperation with government and intersectoral collaboration at the local level, thus raising the profile of the early years and increasing buy-in for taking action at all levels of society. Academic and civil society partners are indispensable for guaranteeing the integrity, validity, and transparency of this work as it spreads around the world and, also, over the long-term.

Implementing the monitoring protocol for rights in early childhood will only be worthwhile if, over time, it contributes to fulfilment of rights, improved quality of life, and enhanced developmental outcomes for young children. Thus, its ultimate value can only be evaluated over a time horizon measured in years. To this end, our strategy is to find ways to use the process and outputs of implementing the monitoring protocol as an anchor for a range of diffusion and social change processes. These include:

- Implementing the monitoring protocol, per se, is a tool to create new interministerial "policy coalition" among those who were brought together from different ministries to do the work. The unifying focus of this latent policy coalition is the range of duties that the state has to young children. If it gains influence over time, the policy research literature gives us reason to believe that evidence-based social change may result (Jenkins-Smith & Sabatier, 1994). In practice, this would take the form of using the indicators as a guide for making better policies; creating a willingness to identify negative impacts on young children of existing laws, policies and practices; and reducing the prospects that children will be on the short end of policy trade-offs that are made in the face of resource constraints. Our approach to country feedback recognizes this coalition-building process and gives it a boost toward sustainability.
- Although most of the world's legal systems are much more attentive to procedural than substantive rights, the monitoring protocol, if it is implemented conscientiously, will generate trend data over place and time and

among vulnerable population groups that will be usable to make claims, through legal as well as political channels, of violation of substantive rights. Already, in countries with children's commissioners, a process of legal claims making is emerging with respect to substantive rights.

- Since the items in the monitoring protocol are fixed and known in advance, they create a "level playing field" for community and civil society groups whose job it is to hold governments accountable for their duties to young children.

Domestically, there is a principle that "what gets counted, counts." In other words, the information flows per se should raise the profile of young children's issues, put evidence in the hands of those who work with young children, and improve the quality of public discussion about young children's issues. Internationally, the Committee on the Rights of the Child encourages civil society alternate reporting as part of its monitoring process. Working with a predictable set of indicators should make the job of alternate reporting much more effective than previously, when states parties were allowed to send the committee non–protocol-based, open-ended reports that concealed more than they revealed. Under those circumstances, alternate reporting was mostly about hunting for concealment in the official reports. With measured indicators, reported in a predictable way, alternate reporting has a better chance to focus on barriers to progress, which is where the focus ought to be.

RESEARCH AND POLICY QUESTIONS FOR THE FUTURE

- Can implementation of the monitoring protocol be shown to contribute to improvement in young children's outcomes over time? What are the differing methodological challenges to studying this question in low-, middle-, and high-income countries?
- Can policy coalitions based upon compliance with rights in early childhood be sustained over time? If the answer is "yes in some countries and no in others," then what are the country factors that matter?
- How do we measure the effectiveness of policy coalitions for young children?
- Can the bridge that we have built between population health and rights cultures be sustained at the international level, such that the efforts of these diverse groups can have a cumulative positive effect on young children over time?
- Can rights in early childhood be effectively brought to failed states through direct collaboration with local and regional actors?

Notes

1. Articles 43–45 of the UNCRC.
2. The final report of this work has never been published. Accordingly, the lessons learned from it came in the form of personal communications from Lothar Krappmann and Alan Kikuchi White, who were leaders of the study.

References

Alston, P. (2003). *A human rights perspective on the Millennium Development Goals.* Paper prepared for the Millennium Project Task Force on Poverty and Economic Development. New York: NYU Law School, Center for Human Rights and Global Justice.

Cody, C. (2009). *Count every child: The right to birth registration.* Woking, UK: Plan Ltd.

Commission on Social Determinants of Health (CSDH). (2008). *Closing the gap in a generation: Health equity through action on the social determinants of health.* Final Report of the Commission on Social Determinants of Health. Geneva: World Health Organization.

Davis, K. E., Kingsbury, B., & Merry, S. E. (2010). *Indicators as a technology of global governance* (NYU Law and Economics Research Paper No. 10–13). NYU School of Law, Public Law Research Paper No. 10–26. Retrieved from http://ssrn.com/abstract=1583431

de Greiff, P. (2009). Articulating the links between transitional justice and development: Justice and social integration. In P. de Grieff & R. Duthie (Eds.), *Transitional justice and development* (pp. 41–42). New York: Social Science Research Council.

Espeland W. N., & Stevens M. L. (1998). Commensuration as a social process. *Annual Review of Sociology, 24,* 313–343.

Grantham-McGregor, S., Cheung, Y. B., Cueto, S., Glewwe, P., Richter, L., Strupp, B., et al. (2007). Developmental potential in the first 5 years for children in developing countries. *The Lancet, 369*(9555), 60–70.

Green, M. (2001). What we talk about when we talk about indicators: Current approaches to human rights measurement. *Human Rights Quarterly, 23,* 1062–1097.

Hertzman, C. (2009). The state of child development in Canada: Are we moving towards, or away from, equity from the start? *Paediatric and Child Health, 14*(10), 673–676.

Hunt, P. (2003). *WHO workshop on indicators for the right to health.* UN Special Rapporteur on the right to health. Washington, DC: World Health Organization.

Irwin, L., Siddiqi, A., & Hertzman C. (2007). *Early child development: A powerful equalizer.* Report to the WHO International Commission on the Social Determinants of Health. Retrieved from http://www.earlylearning.ubc.ca/globalknowledgehub/documents/WHO_ECD_Final_Report.pdf

Janus, M., Brinkman, S., Duku, E., & Hertzman, C., Santos, R., Sayers, M., et al. (2007). *The early development instrument: A population-based measure for communities. A handbook on development, properties and use.* Hamilton, ON: Offord Centre for Child Studies, McMaster University. Retrieved from http://www.offordcentre.com/readiness/pubs/publications.html

Jenkins-Smith, C. H., & Sabatier, P. A. (1994). Evaluating the advocacy coalition framework. *Journal of Public Policy, 14,* 175–203.

Khattab, M., & Arends, D. (2009). *EGRI for children: Foundations for an Egypt Child Rights Index as instrument for evidence-based child-friendly public policies.* Egypt: UNICEF Egypt and National Council for Childhood and Motherhood.

Kitching, K. (Ed.). (2005). *Non-discrimination in international law: A handbook for practitioners.* London: The International Centre for the Legal Protection of Human Rights (INTERIGHTS).

Levi, R. (2009). *Memos to the Successful Societies program.* Toronto: Canadian Institute for Advanced Research.

Palmer, A., Tomkinson, J., Phung, C., Ford, N., Joffres, M., Fernandes, K., et al. (2009). Does ratification of human rights treaties have effects on population health? *The Lancet, 373*(6), 1987–1992.

Sitta, M. S. (2007). Towards universal primary education: The experience of Tanzania. *UN Chronicle,* New York: United Nations. Available at http://www.un.org/Pubs/chronicle/2007/issue4/0407p40.html

UNCRC. (2005). *Implementing child rights in early childhood* (General Comment No. 7). [Online]. Retrieved from http://www2.ohchr.org/english/bodies/crc/docs/AdvanceVersions/GeneralComment7Rev1.pdf [5 January 2010]

UNCRC. (2010). *CRC Treaty specific reporting guidelines, harmonized according to the common core document* (CRC/C/58/Rev.2). Retrieved from http://www2.ohchr.org/english/bodies/crc/docs/treaty_specific_guidelines_2010.doc

UNCRC. (1991). *General guidelines regarding the form and content of initial reports to be submitted by State Parties under article 44, paragraph 1(a) of the Convention.* New York: United Nations.

United Nations Department of Economic and Social Affairs (UN DESA). (2006). *The world's women 2005: Progress in statistics.* New York: United Nations.

United Nations Office of High Commissioner for Human Rights (OHCHR). (2008). *Report on indicators for promoting and monitoring the implementation of human rights.* Seventh Inter-Committee Meeting of the Human Rights Treaty Bodies.

Vaghri, Z., Arkadas, A., Hertzman, E., & Hertzman, C. (2009). Manual on implementing Early Childhood Rights Indicators Framework. Retrieved from http://content.yudu.com/Library/A1nitv/ChildRightsIndicator/

Appendices

Appendix I: Unpacking the Indicators

Indicator Set 12: Educational Provision for Vulnerable Young Children (CRC Articles 2, 28 and 29; General Comment 1: Aims of Education; General Comment 6: Treatment of Unaccompanied and Separated Children Outside Their Country of Origin; General Comment 9: The Rights of Children with Disabilities; General Comment 10: Children's Rights in Juvenile Justice)	
Structure	• What policy commitments exist in your country to ensure equitable access to appropriate quality early childhood education for vulnerable populations? • Does policy in your country include a commitment to research the underlying factors of vulnerability, address direct exclusion, provide redress, and challenge the root causes of such exclusion? • Does policy make sufficient provision to inform parents/caregivers and children in vulnerable groups about their rights with regards to educational opportunities for their young children?
Process	• Are there efforts in place to initiate or support programs and provisions that promote inclusive education and the participation of children from all vulnerable groups in mainstream education? • Are there efforts in place to introduce programs and/or initiatives that provide specific educational opportunities to vulnerable groups where mainstream service provision is lacking or unavailable? • Has the existing data on the provision of education been reviewed and disaggregated by school attendance and different criteria of vulnerability? • Are there awareness-raising initiatives that promote understanding of children who are excluded and initiatives that seek to address the root causes of the exclusion? • Have there been any government publications or distribution of other information resources provided to the State party on the educational rights of vulnerable children and families?
Outcome	• Has there been an increase in the number and/or proportion of young children from vulnerable groups who have been included in mainstream or appropriate specialist education systems, for the past five years? • Has there been an improved understanding of the specific circumstances of exclusion and its root causes and prevention that have been demonstrated through specific mechanism, such as, policy development, public awareness, judicial measures and proceedings?
Sources of Information	• Desk review of policy and measures to ensure inclusive mainstream access for vulnerable groups or specific measures targeted to vulnerable groups • School attendance ratios—general population vs. vulnerable groups • Populations/household surveys questions on pre-primary and primary school attendance; home-based provisions
Duty Bearers	• National and local government departments responsible for educational provision and also justice and equality • Civil society and private-sector providers of educational services for young children • Professional teaching associations and other relevant professional bodies • Social care service providers across all sectors: public, private and non-governmental • Parents, other caregivers and professional and/or lay bodies representing or supporting and/or informing these stakeholders
General Comment 7 (paragraphs)	Reporting Guidelines (sections)
3 : young child as rights holder 24 : monitor and evaluate access and use 36 : vulnerable groups	6b : programs 6c : resources 6d : statistical data 34a : education, training, guidance 34b : aims and quality of education 34c : rest, leisure, culture (play also) 35 : excluded groups 36 : organizational co-operation

FIGURE 19.1 *Indicator Set 12*

Source: Vaghri, Z., Arkadas, A., Hertzman, E., & Hertzman, C. (2009). Manual on implementing Early Childhood Rights Indicators Framework. Retrieved from http://content.yudu.com/Library/A1nitv/ChildRightsIndicator/

Appendix II: An Example Flow Chart

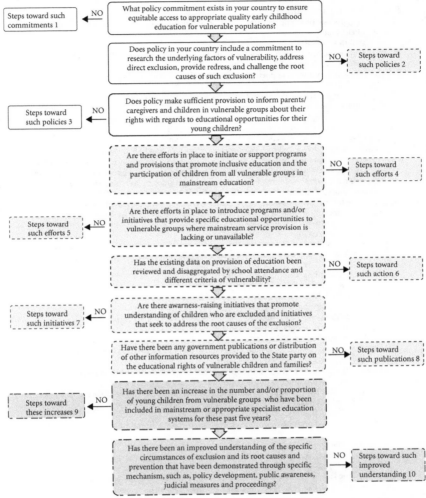

FIGURE 19.2 *Schematic presentation of some steps to take to verify the presence of structure (_____), process (_____), and outcome (_____) for indicator 12, Realization of Educational Services Provision for Vulnerable and Excluded Young Children.*

Source: Vaghri, Z., Arkadas, A., Hertzman, E., & Hertzman, C. (2009). Manual on implementing Early Childhood Rights Indicators Framework. Retrieved from http://content.yudu.com/Library/A1nitv/ChildRightsIndicator/

Suggestions for Indicator 12

1. Develop policies that support social inclusion and insure equitable access to education, such as policies that
    a. abolish school fees
    b. provide income support to poor and rural households to reduce reliance on child labour
    c. promote teaching in children's mother tongue
    d. promote educational opportunities for disabled children and children affected by HIV/AIDS
        For example, see the European Union National Strategy reports for social protection and social inclusion:
        http://ec.europa.eu/employment_social/spsi/strategy_reports_en.htm
2. Develop policies that support a commitment to research. The *Encyclopedia of Early Childhood Developme nt* website provides multiple examples of international research initiatives: http://www.child-encyclopedia.com/en-ca/recherche.html?q=research.
3. Expand on policies that make provisions to inform parents and children from vulnerable or excluded populations about their rights with regard to educational opportunity. For example, educational quotas for children from vulnerable or excluded populations, such as First Nation, Aborigine, Roma children in Europe, children living with disabilities, and so on.
4. Advocate for programs that encourage inclusive education and participation of children from all vulnerable groups in mainstream education. The National Inclusive Education Awareness ca mpaign in Canada website offer examples of multiple awareness -raising initiatives: http://www.inclusiveeducation.ca.
5. Encourage and implement programs that provide specific educational opportunities to vulnerable groups. For examples on educational programmes for vulnerable populations, see:
    UNICEF Educational Priority Areas project:
    http://www.unicef.org/romania/education_1617.html
    Aga Khan Foundation Madrasa Early Childhood Education Programme:
    http://partnershipsinaction.org/work/focus_education.php
    Public Health Agency of Canada's Aboriginal Head Start Program: http://www.phac-aspc.gc.ca/dca -dea/programs-mes/ahs_main-eng.php
6. Work with university -based researchers and data managers to improve data resources.
7. Create awareness -raising campaigns, for example the "Leave No Child Out" Campaign:
    http://www.unicef.org/ceecis/kids_6643.html .
8. Work with WHO and UNICEF offices in your country to develop publications, translate relevant information into suitable languages, as well as carry out research from within your country to publish information on educational rights for vulnerable children and families. Valuable readings include:
    A Human Rights Based Approach to Education for All:
    http://www.unicef.org/publications/files/A_Human_Rights_Based_Approach_to_Education_for_All.pdf
    Poverty Reduction Begins With Children:
    http://www.unicef.org/publications/files/pub_poverty_reduction_en.pdf
9. Create a monitoring and evaluation system based on existing int ernational studies.
10. Explore the lack of improvement through, evaluation of policies, judicial measures and proceedings, and also conduct focus groups or investigate by using questionnaires.

FIGURE 19.3 *Suggestions for Indicator 12*

20

Improving Policies and Programs for Educational Quality

AN EXAMPLE FROM THE USE OF LEARNING ASSESSMENTS

Daniel A. Wagner

Introduction

It is early morning in Kahalé village, about 45 kilometers from the capital city. It has been raining again, and the water has been flowing off the tin corrugated roof of the one-room schoolhouse at the center of the village. The rain makes it difficult for Monsieur Mamadou, a teacher, to get to his school on this Monday morning, as the rural taxi keeps getting stuck in the mud, forcing the six other passengers to help the driver get back on the road to the village. Once at school, Monsieur Mamadou waits for his school children to arrive. At 9 a.m., the room is only half-full, probably not a bad thing, as a full classroom would mean 65 children, and there are only benches enough to seat 50.

Now about 35 students have arrived. Those with proper sandals and clean shirts that button are in the first row or two; those with no sandals and not-so-clean shirts sit further back. The children, all in first grade, range in age from 6 to 10 years. Monsieur Mamadou speaks first in Wolof, welcoming the children, telling them to quiet down and pay attention. He then begins to write a text on the blackboard in French, taking his time to get everything just so. The accuracy of the written text is important since only a few children (all in the front row) have school primers in front of them. Mamadou's writing takes about 15 minutes, during which time the children are chatting, looking out the window, or have their heads bent down with eyes closed on their desks. Some are already tired and hungry as they have had nothing but a glass of hot tea and stale bread or mash in the morning. When Monsieur Mamadou finishes his writing, he turns around to address the class in French: "You are now to copy this text into your *carnets* (notebooks)." The children begin to work and Monsieur Mamadou steps outside to smoke a cigarette. It is April, and the rains have come, but he is tired—it has been a long year.

Aminata, 8-years-old, sits in row three. She has her pencil out, and begins to work in her *carnet*, carefully writing down each word written on the blackboard. She is thankful to make it to school that day, since her little baby sister was going to need Aminata to be a caretaker at home—except that her Auntie was visiting, so Aminata could go to school after all. Although going to school is better than staying home, Aminata has a sense that she is not making very good use of her time. She can copy the text, but doesn't understand what it says. Aminata can only read a few French words on the street signs and wall ads in her village. Thus, even as the only "school" child in her family, she is not much help to her mother, who wants to know what the writing on her prescription bottle of pills really says. Aminata feels bad about this, and wonders how it is that her classmates in the first row seem to already know some French. She also wonders why Monsieur Mamadou seems only to call on those pupils to come to the front of the class and work on the blackboard, and not her. She's heard that there is a school after primary school, but only the first-row kids seem to get to enroll there. What is the point of studying and staying in school, she wonders?

In the above story, there is nothing remarkable about Monsieur Mamadou or Aminata. The vignette tells an all too familiar tale that is repeated in countries around the world. Although dysfunctional classroom contexts exist in all nations, their consequences are exacerbated when resources for learning are so limited, as in the poorest countries in Africa. This vignette is about poverty, the cultural context of failing educational systems, and the communities that fail to notice what is wrong in their midst.

For many of us, it tells a story about non-learning, non-reading, and incipient school failure (for both children and the school). Most young children similar to Aminata will not be adequately assessed for learning before they drop out of school. Many children similar to Aminata do not even exist, when considered from a national statistical perspective. They will not make it to secondary school, will not go to university, and will not get a job in the global economy. This year or next will likely be Aminata's *last* in school. She will likely marry around puberty and begin a similar cycle of non-education for her own children. This is not true of all children, but it is true of most children in poor parts of poor countries. This sad and familiar story needs to be addressed and changed. Aminata's story is at the heart of the education problem in the low-income countries (LICs).

The above vignette is also a contextual "data point" (or really data *points*) that represent how to *collect* data, *interpret* the data, and *inform* policy making. It is also a story about how culture intersects with theories based on data collected in relatively affluent (Western) contexts quite different from those that may be the focus of improving the lives of children in poor contexts. The conceptual and practical responses to the above problems have been with us for many decades and

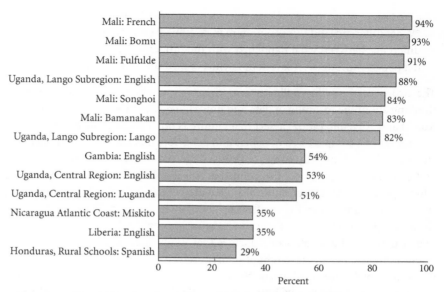

FIGURE 20.1 *Percentage of students who could not read a single word, 2008–2009.*
Reprinted with permission from Gove & Cvelich, 2010, p. 10. Children were at end of
grade 2 (about 7–9 years of age) from nationally representative samples; "language"
indicates which language was used in the reading assessment.

are not easy to resolve. Irrespective of various scientific perspectives (e.g., anthropological, neuroscientific, maturational) around what to do from a perspective of
improving child development, we do know this: lots of children are like Aminata,
and cannot read a single word after a year or more in school (Figure 20.1). As a first
step in thinking about Aminata's "problem" (that is, to Aminata herself, her family, her community, and national and international policymakers), we need first to
consider what data count.

Measurement and Change in Two Developments

We regard culture as a patterned configuration of routine, value-laden ways
of doing things that make some sense as they occur together in the somewhat
ordered flux of a community's ways of living. Cultural processes do not
function in isolation or in mechanical interaction among independently
definable entities. Research efforts that try to control for all but a few aspects
of community functioning—to be able to separately examine the effects of
stand-alone variables—overlook the meaning that is given to each aspect by
their integration. (Rogoff & Angelillo, 2002, p. 216)

Generating knowledge about whether a program achieved its basic aims
requires impact evaluation, which analyzes and documents the extent to
which changes in the well-being of the target population can be attributed to

a particular program or policy. Such evaluation tries to answer the question: "What difference did this program make?" Impact evaluation asks about the difference between what happened with the program and what would have happened without it . . . (Savedoff, Levine, & Birdsall, 2006, p. 12)

The two quotations above illustrate a dilemma, or rather two different ways of thinking about the meaning of data and how change can be measured. In the first, Rogoff and Angelillo (2002) assert that culture is not a single indicator, but rather is made up of a complex web of beliefs and behaviors that cannot be extracted and studied independently. By contrast, drawn from the field of economics, Savedoff and colleagues (2006) make the point that it is absolutely essential to determine which specific inputs (fiscal, cultural, policy, etc.) determine specific outcomes (i.e., impact evaluation) in trying to affect behavioral change. In the case of Aminata, the anthropologist would be focused on the various cultural, social, and cognitive (e.g., cannot read a single word) factors that might keep her in school now, or might influence her to leave school prematurely. An educational psychologist or economist might tinker, adjust, or change the type of textbook used in class or the incentives that might be put into play (e.g., conditional cash transfer; Behrman, Parker, & Todd, 2009) to persuade parents that schooling has value.

In the context of childhood development, the term "development" connotes what develops over *chronological time*—over the experiences that young people go through in their homes, schools, and societies (what is called *developmental science* in psychology). However, when employed by United Nations (UN) and donor agencies, the second meaning of "development" is generally thought of as representing international *economic* development. These two different connotations of development underscore another dilemma—namely, that change over individual chronological (lifespan) time, and that of societal change overlap—both take chronology seriously. But child development and international development have almost completely different conceptual and empirical bases. (For early explorations of the intersection of human development and international development, see Wagner [1983, 1986].)

One way to pursue this inquiry in the education field is to consider one of the core goals of all development agencies and ministries of education—namely, the production of children who can read.

Reading: A Globally Desirable Outcome and Developmental Challenge

The goal of reading—and a literate world—is at the top of UN Millennium Development Goals (MDGs) for education and economic development. Indeed, it is widely accepted that, despite its importance, literacy rates have not changed very much over several decades (Table 20.1), especially in LICs. If one were to engage in a substantive internet-based search of publications in the field of

TABLE 20.1 Estimates of adult illiterates and literacy rates (population aged 15+) by region, 1990 and 2000–2004

	Number of Illiterates (thousands)		Literacy Rates (%)		Change from 1990 to 2000–2004		
					Number of Illiterates		Literacy Rates
	1990	2000–2004	1990	2000–2004	thousands	(%)	(Percentage points)
World	871,750	771,129	75.4	81.9	−100,621	−12	6.4
Developing countries	855,127	759,199	67.0	76.4	−95,928	−11	9.4
Developed countries	14,864	10,498	98.0	98.7	−4,365	−29	0.7
Countries in transition	1,759	1,431	99.2	99.4	−328	−19	0.2
Sub-Saharan Africa	128,980	140,544	49.9	59.7	11,564	9	9.8
Arab States	63,023	65,128	50.0	62.7	2,105	3	12.6
Central Asia	572	404	98.7	99.2	−168	−29	0.5
East Asia and the Pacific	232,255	129,922	81.8	91.4	−102,333	−44	9.6
South and West Asia	382,353	381,116	47.5	58.6	−1,237	−0.3	11.2
Latin American and the Caribbean	41,742	37,901	85.0	89.7	−3,841	−9	4.7
Central and Eastern Europe	11,500	8,374	96.2	97.4	−3,126	27	1.2
North America and Eastern Europe	11,326	7,740	97.9	98.7	−3,585	−32	0.8

Note: Figures may not add to totals because of rounding.

Adapted from UNESCO, 2005, p. 63

Source: Statistical annex, Table 2A.

reading today, the outcome would surely show millions of articles, books, and chapters. Yet, the vast majority of these would be in only a handful of languages, largely contained within a dozen major languages of the world. This statistic would leave the remaining 2,000–3,000 languages most commonly used in the world with near-zero research as to how reading is acquired or utilized. As with other developmental phenomena, such as language, motor skills, and personality, one might (indeed should) ask the question of how much of a global sample of humanity is necessary before we can reach generalizable conclusions about a particular domain of behavior. Given a long-standing tendency in scientific psychology to look for universals, education and child development specialists have mainly not been very concerned (with some notable exceptions) about whether their conclusions might apply to peoples in far-away places, or even to ethnic groups much closer to home.

As one example of this universalistic trend, the study of reading acquisition remains heavily biased in favor of research undertaken in the industrialized world.[1] Further, much of this research is actually on the acquisition of cognitive skills, such as perception and memory, and reading subskills, such as decoding and comprehension (Kamil, Mosenthal, Pearson, & Barr, 2000). Most of this work has been carried out with school-aged children who are learning to read in English or in a handful of other languages, with relatively little research on reading acquisition undertaken in the large variety of the world's languages and scripts. The role of culture in theories of reading, although considered important, has often been marginalized in Western-dominated approaches to reading (however, see Street, 2001; Wagner, Venezky, & Street, 1999; Wagner, 2004).

In a more culture-sensitive model, a number of key learner characteristics need to be taken into account, most particularly what a child has learned at home before arriving at school and the cultural context of learning outside of the schooling process. The school provides, in addition, a set of inputs that includes time, teaching methods, teacher feedback, learning materials, and so forth. In the child, then, a set of outcomes would include cognitive skills learned (such as reading and writing), as well as social attitudes and values. This model points to the importance of measuring a variety of outcomes, but leaves out which outcomes depend on which intermediate contextual variables and how one might measure them. By understanding the factors that promote learning, a path toward improvement begins to come into focus. As one example, multiple studies have confirmed the role of a mother's education in the academic success of her children. Many claim that maternal education is one of the most powerful determinants of children's staying in school and learning achievement (Figure 20.2; UNESCO, 2005). Yet, how does a mother actually transmit skills, attitudes, and values to her children, especially if she herself is poorly educated? Recent evidence suggests that a key causal variable is how the mother communicates with her children (LeVine, LeVine, Schnell-Anzola, Rowe, & Dexter, 2012).

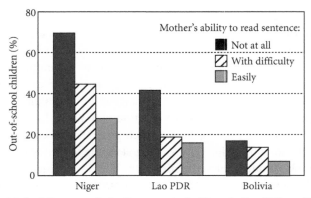

FIGURE 20.2 *Mother's literacy and schooling status in the Niger, the Lao PDR, and Bolivia, 2000.*
Adapted from UNESCO, 2005, p. 130.

In addition, we know that the presence of qualified teachers, well-prepared curricula and textbooks, supportive parents, and engaged communities are all factors that can and do affect children's learning. What is less than clear is how to determine what inputs and outputs need to be studied in which cultural contexts, and then to decide what implementation steps are needed to reinforce and expand policies that support them. Improved measurement tools necessarily will play an important part in this process.

Measurement of Learning Outcomes

Educational measurement intersects with the world of population variation in ways that are predictable, but also can be difficult to address. This is not only a matter of international or cross-cultural comparability. Rather, variation in populations is endemic in each and every context where children are raised. Even variation in what households contain, such as the availability of books, has been found to be highly related to reading outcomes in Sub-Saharan Africa (see Figure 20.3). Each household may also contain significant variation in the learning environments of children.

Reading test scores serve as a proxy for general educational quality. Therefore, the use of such indicators can provide solid information on how well the content in a school curriculum is being understood as *learned* cognitive skills, a formative measure of teaching and learning policies, and a benchmark for how well children

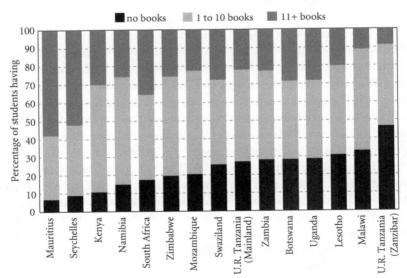

FIGURE 20.3 *Grade 6 student reports of quantity of books in their homes in 15 SACMEQ African education systems, 2000.*

Adapted from UNESCO, 2004. p. 208.

have done at the main exit points from the school system. This latter type of summative assessment may be used as a means of determining (and legitimizing) access to educational (and hence economic) advancement. The policy upside is that tests may help to ensure that the intended curriculum is taught and learned, whereas the downside is that they can provide ways for nonachieving students to be forced out the schooling system altogether if their learning is poor. Thus, one key goal of understanding how children learn to read is to determine better ways to intervene in the learning process and to remediate skills before dropout occurs.

Educational assessments come in a wide variety of styles, contents, and purposes. At the dawn of the 20th century, Alfred Binet (also known as one of the fathers of intelligence testing) was requested by the French government to develop an assessment instrument that could help predict which students would be most likely to succeed in public schools. This element of prediction—of success, or not, in schooling—was a watershed moment in the use of testing for policy making. Over the next century, educators and policymakers across the world have endeavored to make similar decisions based on examinations. As a consequence, even countries with relatively low incomes and poorly financed educational systems have begun to actively participate in such learning assessments. For the present purposes, with a focus on reading in LICs, we will consider only three principal types of assessments: international, regional, and hybrid.

International Assessments

International assessments (sometimes termed large-scale educational assessments or LSEAs) are designed to measure learning in multiple countries. Their aims include (a) cross-national comparisons that target a variety of educational policy issues, (b) provision of "league tables" that rank-order achievement scores by nation or region or other variables, and (c) within-country analyses that are then compared to how other countries operate at a subnational level. Such assessments gather data principally from learners, teachers, and educational systems—parameters that help to provide better ways of interpreting test results. These studies, many of which include reading tests, are planned and implemented by various international organizations and agencies, including the International Association for the Evaluation of Educational Achievement (IEA) that conducts the Progress in International Reading Literacy Study (PIRLS), and the Organization for Economic Cooperation and Development (OECD), which is responsible for the Program for International Student Achievement (PISA) studies. These assessments may also be characterized by their attention to high-quality instruments, rigorous fieldwork methodology, and sophisticated analyses of results. Each of these international reading assessments is now in use in dozens of countries and is expanding to LICs, well beyond the OECD country user base that formed the early core group of participation. International assessments often attract media attention and thus provide an opportunity for greater focus and debate on the education sector and national outcomes relative to other countries.

Regional Assessments

As part of an effort to extend the use of LSEAs into LICs, regional and international organizations have collaborated to create three major regional assessments: the Latin American Laboratory for Assessment of Quality in Education (LLECE), the Southern and Eastern African Consortium for the Monitoring of Education Quality (SACMEQ), and Program for the Analysis of Educational Systems of the CONFEMEN (Francophone Africa) countries (PASEC). These regional assessments have much in common with the international assessments, but there are several important differences, including the relatively greater proximity in content between test and curriculum, normative scales that may or may not be tied to local (normed) skill levels, and attention to local policy concerns (such as the role of the French language in PASEC countries). The overlap in expertise between the specialists working on the international and regional levels has generally meant that these regional tests are given substantial credibility, and they are largely used by specialists within national ministries of education.

Hybrid Assessments

In recent years, a new approach to assessment has sought to focus more directly on the needs of poor LIC assessment contexts. Initially, this approach was conceptualized under the acronym *smaller, quicker, cheaper* (SQC) methods of literacy assessment (Wagner, 2003; subsequently in Wagner, 2011). The idea was to see whether LSEA methodologies could be reshaped into hybrid methods that are just big enough, faster at capturing and analyzing data, and cheaper in terms of time and effort.[2] The resulting methodology would be flexible enough to be adaptable to local LIC contexts, and, in particular, be able to deal with key problems such as ethnolinguistic diversity in many of the world's poor countries. The Early Grade Reading Assessment (EGRA; Research Triangle Institute, 2009) contains a number of the above features and is probably the best-known current example of a hybrid assessment in reading acquisition. The EGRA was initially designed with three main assessment goals: early reading (grades 1–3), local context focus (rather than comparability across contexts), and local linguistic and orthographic variation. Hybrid assessments (such as those used to produce the data in Figure 20.1) can provide relatively simple outcome indicators that may be conducted on specific population samples.

What Is Compared in Assessments?

Comparability is at the heart of all assessment instruments. It is also a core function for ensuring early child development and to determining which children need more attention in order to achieve a benchmark of sufficient progress. It is possible to identify four key areas that allow assessments themselves to be compared with one another: credibility (in terms of validity and reliability), sampling, scaling, and

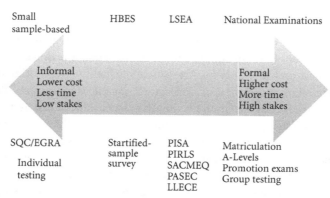

FIGURE 20.4 *Assessment continuum. Ranging from SQC hybrid assessments to LSEA and National Examinations.* Adapted from Kanjee, A. (2009, October). *Assessment overview.* Presentation at the First READ Global Conference, Moscow.

(Note: HBES refers to household-based educational surveys; see text for other acronyms.)

implementation. Each will be considered in turn; a schematic diagram of assessment types is shown in Figure 20.4.

Credibility

All assessments depend on the credibility through which well-trained scientists and experts can achieve consensus on the merits of a particular set of findings, even if they might disagree with the interpretation of such findings. The two most oft-cited components of assessment science are validity and reliability. The *validity* of an assessment instrument is the degree to which items on a test can be credibly linked to the conceptual rationale for the testing instrument. Thus, having read a paragraph in an assessment, does the child's answers to questions (on, say, a multiple-choice test) really relate to a child's ability to read, or to the ability to remember what he or she has read earlier? Validity can vary significantly by setting and by population, since a test that might be valid in London may have little validity in Lahore. A reading test used effectively for one language group of mother-tongue speakers may be quite inappropriate for children who are second-language speakers of the same language.

Reliability is typically measured in two ways. Generically, *reliability* refers to the degree to which an individual's score on a test is consistently related to additional times that the individual takes the same (or equivalent) test. High reliability usually means that the rank ordering of individuals taking a given test would, on a second occasion, produces a very similar rank ordering. In the psychometrics of assessment, it is not unusual to obtain relatively high test–retest reliability on LSEAs. This result stems in large part from the fact that assessments of human cognitive function (of many kinds) tend to be highly stable. A second way to measure reliability is in terms of the internal function of the test items: Do the items in each part of an assessment have a strong association with one another? This is inter-item reliability (measured by Cronbach's alpha statistic). And, if the test is administered by two different individuals, then the reliability of the instrument can also be judged by interrater reliability.

Overall, there are numerous ways of thinking about the credibility of any assessment. Within the measurement community, credibility is typically thought of as a combination of validity and reliability. Yet, in the non-statistical sense, credibility implies more than the particular statistical tools available to test designers. This is so largely due to the fact that many of the difficult decisions about credibility are made *before* statistical tests are employed. For example, is an assessment credible if many of the poorest children are excluded from participation? Is an assessment credible if the enumerator does not speak the child's language? Is an assessment credible if some children have taken many such tests before, while for others this is the first time? These are not merely choices that are internal to the test, but rather are related to the context in which the assessment is deployed, and who is the user of the assessment.[3]

Sampling of Skills and Populations

The majority of LSEAs tend to utilize standardized tests in a particular domain, such as reading, math, or science. The approach relative to a domain can vary widely across tests, even if the same domain is tested in multiple different assessments. The assessments mentioned earlier—PIRLS, PISA, LLECE, SACMEQ, and PASEC—are essentially based on the school programs of the countries concerned. These assessments generally try to evaluate the match between what should have been taught (and learned), and what the student has actually learned (as demonstrated by the assessment). All are administered in writing as group-administered tests in school settings, with a main focus on reading comprehension. By contrast, the EGRA contains a set of measures that are individually administered and are primarily based on a number of reading fluency skills developed originally for diagnostic purposes in beginning reading (see Wagner [2011] for a more in-depth analysis of these measures).

The representativeness of the sample population is a fundamental part of all assessments, and all the assessments mentioned above take seriously this aspect of measurement design.[4] Nonetheless, it is often the case that many of the populations of children most in need are systematically excluded from measurement in LSEAs. This seems to be both the result of, and indeed a cause of, exclusion from LSEAs of vulnerable and marginalized populations. The rationales vary from assessment to assessment, and from one national policy to another, and yet the result is the same—those least likely to succeed on tests, and those who are most disadvantaged, represent the groups most often excluded from the sample population for assessment. In particular, it is not unusual for children who speak "minority" languages to be excluded from assessments. This may be particularly accentuated in areas where civil conflict or economic distress leads to substantial cross-border migration, where immigrant groups (and their children) are treated as "transients,"

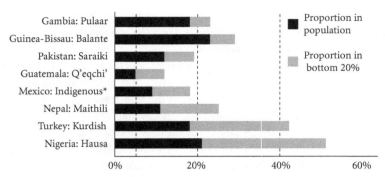

FIGURE 20.5 *Percent of selected language groups in the bottom 20% of the education distribution, selected countries.*
Note: *The indigenous language category in Mexico consists of those who speak indigenous languages only and do not speak Spanish
Adapted from UNESCO, 2010, p. 152.

and where groups may be provided with little or no schooling. This is particularly unfortunate since current evidence suggests that such ethnolinguistic minorities make up a disproportionate percentage of illiterates in LICs (Figure 20.5).

Further, each of the LSEAs described above selects children from those already enrolled in school, thus excluding out-of-school children, the group probably most in need of assistance. In addition, international and regional LSEAs contribute in other ways to exclusion, in singling out children already determined to be dyslexic or with mental or physical handicap (PISA), those who are enrolled in "small schools" (SACMEQ), those who have not sufficiently mastered the language of the assessment, and those too young to be tested in group format. The EGRA, with its focus and testing in local languages, individualized testing, and the propensity to sample among the most disadvantaged young children, has the least statistical need to make population exclusions.

Comparability Between and Within Countries

International statistical reports on education typically base their datasets on national reports, where data may have many different ways of being collected. In contrast (and as one of the attractions of LSEAs) is that nations may be rank-ordered in *league tables* (as in PISA and PIRLS). Naturally, there can be problems in applying a common skill sampling scale across widely differing populations. In the 2006 PIRLS study of reading achievement, the median score of South African grade 4 students was below the "0" percentile of the high-income OECD nations (Crouch, 2009). Also, EGRA scores used in English in rural Kenya are far lower than for same-age (or grade) English-speaking students in suburban Washington, D.C. (Research Triangle Institute, 2008). Such dramatic disparities raise considerable concern about the gap that will need to be closed for low-income countries to catch up to high-income countries.[5]

Can both comparability and context sensitivity be appropriately balanced in assessments? Should countries with low average scores be tested on the same scales with countries that have much higher average scores? If there are countries (or groups of students) at the "floor" of a scale, some would say that the solution is to lower the scale of difficulty. Others might say that the scale itself is flawed, and that there are different types of skills that could be better assessed, especially if the variation is strongly influenced by race, ethnicity, and language. Having different scales for different groups (or nations) seems to some specialists to be an unacceptable compromise of overall standards or international benchmarks.

To the extent that comparability can be achieved (and no assessment claims perfect comparability), the results allow policymakers to consider their own national (or regional) situation relative to others. This seems to have most merit when there are proximal (as opposed to distal) choices to make. For example, if a neighboring country in Africa has adopted a particular bilingual education program that appears to work better in primary school, and if the African minister believes that the case is similar enough to his or her own national situation, then comparing the results of, say, primary school reading outcomes makes good sense. A more distal comparison might be to observe that a certain kind of bilingual education program in Canada seems to be effective, but there may be more doubt about its application in a quite different context in Africa. But, proximity is not always the most pertinent feature: There are many cases (the United States and Japan, for example) where rivalries between educational outcomes and economic systems have been a matter of serious discussion and useful debate over the years.

The key issue here is the degree to which it is necessary to have full comparability, with all individuals and all groups on the same measurement scale. Or, if a choice is made to not "force" the compromises needed for a single unified scale, what are the gains and losses in terms of comparability? Alternatively, one might ask whether the assessments need to measure the same attributes: For example, the EGRA focuses mainly on cognitive prereading skills (such as phonemic awareness), whereas international LSEAs focus mainly on reading comprehension. Can international statistics be maintained as stable and reliable if localized approaches are chosen over international comparability? This question has led to situations in which some LICs, although tempted to participate in international assessments, nevertheless hesitate due to the possible appearance of very low results or the feeling that the expense of participation is not worth the value added to decision making at the national level. Others may participate because they do not want to be viewed as having "inferior" benchmarks to those used in OECD countries (Greaney & Kelleghan, 1996).

Implementation

School-based assessments are typically implemented with two key parameters in mind. First, there are "break points" at which a student will leave one level of education for another more advanced stage. Thus, there exist in many countries national examinations held at the end of primary, lower secondary, and upper secondary school, to determine who will be allowed into the next stage of the

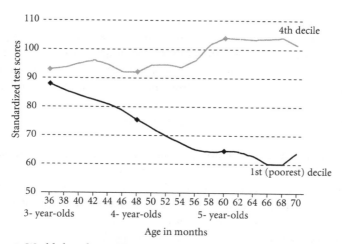

FIGURE 20.6 *Wealth-based gaps: Test scores across ages for the poorest and the fourth deciles in Ecuador, 2003–2004.*

Adapted from UNESCO, 2010, p. 50.

schooling system. Second, there are exams that view the level of competency as a more appropriate cognitive point in which students should be tested. As noted earlier, PIRLS tests children at the end of grade 4, which is the point at which (in OECD countries) it was determined that most children should have learned the basics of reading, writing, and math. Hybrid assessments like the EGRA focus mainly on the period from grades 1 to 3, which permits one to ascertain serious reading problems much earlier than do the other LSEAs. This aspect of early detection is made possible in part due to the one-on-one and largely oral assessments given to children. There is a very important policy rationale as well. In the field of early childhood education, there is growing consensus on the positive impact of early intervention (Heckman, 2006; see also Behrman & Urzúa, 2013, Chapter 6, this volume). Further, research in LIC contexts shows that wealth-based gaps in children's cognitive development grow over time (see Figure 20.6). Taken as a whole, it is widely accepted that the earlier one can detect and remedy educational problems, the more effective the intervention.

International and regional assessments are typically carried out on a 3-, 5-, or even 10-year cycle. If the goal is for a tighter relationship between findings and policies that can be implemented during the annual school cycle, or within the mandate of a typical minister of education, then greater frequency of assessment is required. Achieving this latter aim will likely necessitate instruments such as hybrid instruments whose turnaround time is usually less than 1 year and whose smaller sample size (and lower cost) will allow greater frequency of repetition (Wagner et al., 2011).

One of the most difficult implementation questions concerning LSEAs is how much data and of which kind to collect. The idea that one collects "just enough" data is easier said than done. What some term "right-sizing" data collection has been more recently called "evidence-centered design" (Braun & Kanjee, 2006). Each of the international and regional assessments utilizes a survey that is undertaken at the school level, with techniques that allow the use of extended passages, like a newspaper article, in the assessment of reading comprehension. But newspaper content can vary by language, topic, intent, and more. As has been pointed out by McCall (2009), comparing implementations of very similar interventions (such as assessments) can be remarkably problematic due to the varied contexts in which such activities are actually carried out in real-life settings.

Each of the three types of assessments reviewed above varies by sampling, scaling, and implementation parameters—with an overall impact on assessment credibility. Further, each assessment approach provides for a degree of comparison within and between population groups (or nations). The ultimate value of a given assessment will depend on the policy purpose to which it is put, such as international comparison or local validity. Finally, there is the key issue of who the end-users of such learning assessments are and how the information gathered impacts policy planning. This brings us to the matter of stakeholders, those persons who have an interest in the data collected.

Stakeholders, Learning Assessments, and Policy Outcomes as Public Goods

In most countries (and perhaps especially so in LICs), educational specialists and statisticians (composing a rather narrow group of individuals) are the primary guardians of learning assessment results. This restricted access to knowledge about learning achievement is likely due, at least in part, to the complexities of carrying out large-scale assessments and the difficulty of interpreting complex datasets. In addition, there may be reticence among policymakers who might worry about publicized assessment differences between the *internal* societal backgrounds of children (such as by ethnolinguistic groups, private and public schools, etc.) in national policy debates on education. Even *external* national comparisons (e.g., when Singapore or Finland clearly outdistances U.S. schoolchildren on various science and math tests) can be used to promote national policies by demonstrating that more investments are needed to "catch up" with top global educational winners. As has been studied in OECD countries, when parents and community groups become aware of the poor scores in their schools relative to others (perhaps through newspaper accounts), they, too, can become consumers of results and actors in social and political change.

In other words, the benefits of greater transparency in learning assessment outcomes are becoming more widely understood and sought after across the globe—and by a wider array of stakeholders. Whether due to improved accountability by governments, influences of international agencies, efforts of Non-Governmental Organizations (NGOs), or greater community activism, there is little doubt that interest in children's learning and educational success has become increasingly important. Parents the world over—rich and poor, in OECD or LIC contexts—increasingly recognize the importance of learning and learning assessment results in determining the future of their children in personal, social, and economic development. Collectively, parent and community involvement leads to empowerment, as outcomes have an impact on how policymakers collect data on learning and manage the results that come from assessments. In other words, educational outcomes, and the policies that derive from them, are rapidly becoming *public goods* that can empower community action in LIC contexts where centralized educational systems have held sway for decades.

Learning assessments, as part of educational impact measures, are playing an increasingly important role in the growth of policy transparency across the world. Although relatively recent in LICs, the utility of learning assessments will depend on the value of the information collected to specific groups of stakeholders—so that change is possible, negotiable, and expected. In this way, learning assessments will break new ground in educational, social, and (therefore) economic accountability. In order to achieve the educational priorities of the UN MDGs, it is critical to sustain a significant policy and assessment focus on poor and marginalized populations, and to enable parents and communities to be able to interpret the findings of this work. In other words, learning assessments can and should provide timely and understandable feedback to those who care about young girls like Aminata—and thereby enhance educational quality.

Acknowledgments

Parts of this paper are drawn from Wagner (2010, 2011). Thanks to Patrice Engle for her very helpful editing comments throughout. All remaining views are those of the author.

Notes

1. There is some ambiguity on whether it is universalistic scientific approaches that constrain inquiry to normative samples in industrialized countries or whether the limited research in other countries is simply due to historical limitations on human and fiscal support for such research. My own view is that both are likely to be responsible for our limited ability to bring adequate research to bear on educational problems, such as improving reading. This is, as noted below, beginning to change.

2. Another distinction is that hybrid measures, such as the EGRA, tend to be individually administered (made necessary in large part due to the younger age of children typically assessed—aged 6–8 usually), whereas the LSEAs tend to be group-administered tests made possible by the older age of the children involved.

3. There are many possible users (or stakeholders) in such assessments, from the parent to the teacher to the headmasters up to the minister of education. Each might define credibility in a somewhat different way.

4. The PIRLS uses a sample of at least 150 schools with students in grade 4, but the sample may be heterogeneous by age, especially in LICs, where late school enrollment and/ or grade repetition is frequent. The LLECE takes into account stratification criteria including type of geographical area and type of school (public or private); about 4,000 students are chosen, with half between the two grades tested (grade 3 and grade 4). The LLECE evaluates students in two adjacent grades (grade 3 and grade 4) as part of data collection. The SACMEQ evaluates students reading in grade 6, with a sampling technique similar to that of the PIRLS. The PASEC focuses on children enrolled in the grades 2 and 5. In the PISA, the main criterion for choosing students is their age (15 years). The EGRA assessments are done during grades 1, 2, and 3, with sample sizes typically ranging between 800 and 6,000 children.

5. In addition, floor and ceiling effects are much more likely when skill results vary significantly across population sampling, thus invalidating statistical comparisons.

References

Behrman, J., Parker, S., & Todd, P. (2009). Schooling impacts of conditional cash transfers on young children: Evidence from Mexico. *Economic Development and Cultural Change, 57*, 439–477.

Behrman, J. R., & Urzúa, S. S. (2013). Economic perspectives on some important dimensions of early childhood development in developing countries. In P. R. Britto, P. L. Engle, & C. M. Super (Eds.), *Handbook of early childhood development research and its impact on global policy* (Chapter 6). New York: Oxford University Press.

Braun, H., & Kanjee, A. (2006). Using assessment to improve education in developing nations. In J. E. Cohen, D. E. Bloom, & M. Malin. (Eds.), *Improving education through assessment, innovation, and evaluation* (pp. 1–46). Cambridge, MA: American Academy of Arts and Sciences.

Crouch, L. (2009). *Literacy, quality education, and socioeconomic development* (Powerpoint presentation). Washington, DC: USAID.

Gove, A., & Cvelich, P. (2010). *Early reading: Igniting Education for All.* A report by the Early Grade Learning Community of Practice. Washington, DC: RTI.

Greaney, V., & Kellaghan, T. (1996). *Monitoring the learning outcomes of education systems.* Washington, DC: World Bank.

Heckman, J. J. (2006). Skill formation and the economics of investing in disadvantaged children. *Science, 312*(5782), 1900–1902.

Kamil, M. L., Mosenthal, P. B., Pearson, P. D., & Barr, R. (Eds.). (2000). *Handbook of reading research: Volume III.* Mahwah, NJ: L. Erlbaum.

Kanjee, A. (2009, October). *Assessment overview.* Presentation at the First READ Global Conference, Moscow.

LeVine, R. A., LeVine, S. E., Schnell-Anzola, B., Rowe, M. L., & Dexter, E. (2012). *Literacy and mothering: How women's schooling changes the lives of the world's children.* New York: Oxford University Press.

McCall, R. B. (2009). Evidence-based programming in the context of practice and policy. *SRCD Social Policy Report, 23*(3), 3–20.

Research Triangle Institute (RTI). (2008). *Early grade reading Kenya baseline assessment analyses and implications for teaching interventions design* (Final Report). Washington, DC: Author.

Research Triangle Institute (RTI). (2009). *Early grade reading assessment toolkit.* Washington, DC: Author.

Rogoff, B., & Angelillo, C. (2002). Investigating the coordinated functioning of multifaceted cultural practices in human development. *Human Development, 45*, 211–225.

Savedoff, W. D., Levine, R., & Birdsall, N. (2006). *When will we ever learn? Improving lives through impact evaluation.* Washington, DC: Center for Global Development.

Street, B. V. (2001). *Literacy and development: Ethnographic perspectives.* London: Routledge.

UNESCO. (2004). *EFA global monitoring report 2005. The quality imperative.* Paris: Author.

UNESCO. (2005). *EFA global monitoring report 2006. Literacy for life.* Paris: Author.

UNESCO. (2010). *EFA global monitoring report 2010. Reaching the marginalized.* Paris: Author.

Wagner, D. A. (1983). (Ed.). *Child development and international development: Research-policy interfaces.* San Francisco: Jossey-Bass.

Wagner, D. A. (1986). Child development research and the Third World: A future of mutual interest? *American Psychologist, 41*, 298–301.

Wagner, D. A. (2003). Smaller, quicker, cheaper: Alternative strategies for literacy assessment in the UN Literacy Decade. *International Journal of Educational Research, 39*(3), 293–309.

Wagner, D. A. (2004). Literacy(ies), culture(s) and development(s): The ethnographic challenge. *Reading Research Quarterly, 39*(2), 234–241.

Wagner, D. A. (2010). Quality of education, comparability, and assessment choice in developing countries. *COMPARE: A Journal of Comparative and International Education, 40*(6), 741–760.

Wagner, D. A. (2011). *Smaller, quicker, cheaper: Improving learning assessments in developing countries.* Paris/Washington: UNESCO-IIEP and EFA-FTI.

Wagner, D. A., Babson, A., & Katie M. Murphy. (2011). How much is learning measurement worth? Assessment costs in low-income countries. *Current Issues in Comparative Education, 14*, 3–23.

Wagner, D. A., Venezky, R. L., & Street, B. V. (Eds.). 1999. *Literacy: An international handbook.* Boulder, CO: Westview Press.

Building and Strengthening the Early Childhood Development Programs

21

National Agency Systems

Maha B. Homsi and Lara A. Hussein

Early childhood care is the concern of many government sectors, especially health, education, and social development, and of many nongovernmental organizations (NGOs) and donors as well (Naudeau, Kataoka, & Valerio, 2010). However, in many settings, early childhood care and development policies are often fragmented, with services offered in isolation and reflecting the silos in which different ministries operate (Vargas-Barón, 2005). Because early childhood development (ECD) is a multifaceted concept that covers the early childhood period and consists of a set of intertwined processes for providing services to young children and families, the integration of these services is needed for holistic development (Britto, Yoshikawa, & Boller, 2011).

Holistic development is the result of good health, proper nutrition, early stimulation, positive social and emotional interactions with significant adult/caregiver, play as well as learning opportunities, and protection from violence. Coordination among the sectors that promote and support development in these areas, in policy development and implementation, is essential for ensuring both child holistic development and efficient use of national resources. Coordination issues include coherent regulation, funding; staffing schemes; and a common vision for all aspects of ECD care, and education (UNESCO, 2003).

Implicit in this definition of holistic ECD and the requirement for coordination is the need to establish a coordinating institution or organization (henceforth referred to as a *coordinating body*) of policy and program development and implementation. Regardless of the programmatic provisions, a coordinating body must adopt a comprehensive and integrated approach, embracing the concerns of all sectors and mobilizing the respective strengths and competencies of each sector. This coordinating body must master the art of balancing between leadership and partnership to help converge all of the sectors' efforts of reaching a common goal. For coordination to be effective, it needs to engage sectors at the national and local levels and public and private institutions.

Coordination among the primary sectors of ECD (e.g., health, education, and child protection) in policy development and service delivery is crucial if a country wishes to deliver integrated programs that provide children with the best start to life and enable them to reach their highest potential. Given that, the ultimate concern of any ECD program should be to implement a holistic approach encompassing health, nutrition, protection, development, learning, and overall well-being regardless of the institutional setting. One such model to achieve this goal is the establishment of a national agency as a coordinating body that will ensure that all programs maintain a unified approach that guarantees the continuity, and reliability of these programs and allows the smooth transition of children from one program or level to another, such as moving from kindergarten to the first year of schooling (Lombardi, 1992). By ensuring coordination, this national agency eliminates the overlap between similar programs albeit under different names targeting children of the same age.

Selecting the best approach to coordinate national efforts depends on many factors that vary according to ideological context and the country priorities. There is no one-size-fits-all formula for deciding on coordination modality for a country—a consultative and reflective process needs to take place to reach a consensus around this issue. Some countries integrate all ECD matters under one ministry, others divide the sectoral responsibilities by age groups, many have set up committees with narrow and specific mandates. Presented in this chapter is a successful model of a coordinating body through the establishment of a national agency to coordinate all ECD programs sponsored and supported by government agencies, NGOs, the private sector, and donors. The National Council for Family Affairs (NCFA) is Jordan's flagship coordination agency for ECD.

In this chapter's four sections, we present Jordan's national agency system as an illustrative model for coordination of policies and programs. The first section provides the context for such an agency by describing the sociopolitical and economic context of Jordan. As stated earlier, context plays an important role in determining the nature of the coordinating body and its effectiveness. The second section presents the national agency's governance and management, with a particular emphasis placed on its role in coordination of the country's ECD. The third section highlights the challenges of implementing such a system, and the fourth section presents policy implications and recommendations for future research, emanating from the lessons learned from Jordan's national agency model.

Jordan: The Context

A small, resource-starved, middle-income country in the midst of a volatile region, Jordan made enormous strides in achieving basic human development standards for its people (UNICEF & NCFA, 2007). Jordan's population is approximately 6 million, with a very young population—approximately one-quarter (25.3%) are under 9 years of age and fall under the early childhood stage as defined by the

Jordanian ECD Strategy (Hashemite Kingdom of Jordan, 2009). The Hashemite kingdom of Jordan is a constitutional monarchy. The shift toward democratization has been gradual and still continues with reform initiatives.

Although Jordan's national economy has improved significantly since the late 1990s, the country remains vulnerable due to insignificant successes in reducing poverty (standing at 13.3%) and the prevailing unsatisfactory job market (unemployment rate is 13%) (DoS, 2010).[1] Equity of income distribution has improved, as reflected by the decrease in the Gini coefficient between 2006 and 2008 from 0.399 to 0.393. However, income disparities still exist, in particular because of the influx of refugees from neighboring countries enmeshed in chronic conflict (Salehyan & Gleditsch, 2006).

National Council for Family Affairs: A Jordanian National Institution

In this section, we provide a description of the NCFA, with respect to its history, governance and management, mission and purpose, main functions, and work in the area of ECD.

HISTORICAL BACKGROUND: RATIONALE FOR THE NATIONAL COUNCIL FOR FAMILY AFFAIRS

As a follow-up to Jordan's ratification to the United Nations (UN) Convention on the Rights of the Child (CRC), the country established in 1995 the National Taskforce for Children (NTFC), headed by Her Majesty Queen Noor, wife of late King Hussein and Queen of Jordan. The NTFC was established as the coordinating agency of Jordan's national efforts to monitor and evaluate the condition and status of Jordan's children, in response to the Arab Charter on Child Rights (ACRC) of 1983 that called for the establishment of childhood committees in every Arab country.

The NTFC's mission was to improve the current levels of achievement on child-related issues and to accelerate the attainment of child survival, development, protection, and participation rights for Jordan's children.

To encourage and facilitate cooperation among often competing organizations, the NTFC established the National Coalition for Children in 1997, as a forum to coordinate and promote partnerships among public and private institutions and NGOs involved with children's affairs. The NTFC also established a national policy and research center, as well as Jordan's first online child information system, now known as the Information and Research Center (IRC).

Given the fact that Jordanian society is traditionally anchored around the family as the basic unit for securing and protecting child rights, the mandate of the NTFC was seen as too narrow to fulfil the aspirations of improving child well-being within the family context (Al-Hassan & Lansford, 2011). Thus, the NTFC ceased to exist as an organization but the IRC continued to operate under the auspices of the King Hussein Foundation.

MISSION AND PURPOSE OF THE NATIONAL COUNCIL FOR FAMILY AFFAIRS

The NCFA agency in Jordan operates by responding to the situation and needs of the country. Therefore, understanding the situation is important for a discussion of this coordinating agency model. Although Jordan enjoys a relatively strong base of social development, there are rising concerns about family income and disparities in living conditions among regions within the country. Among the disadvantaged population, economic pressures are disproportionately felt by children and their families (Jordan Ministry of Planning, 2000). Most efforts at supporting disadvantaged children and families have been initiated by governmental and nongovernmental institutions working in isolation from one another and, therefore, have had limited impact in tackling intractable problems such as broken families, abused children, street children. Addressing these problems required an institution that would relate with and coordinate different agencies involved in the same area of work, monitor and share information on the well-being of children and families, monitor and support the activities of the various agencies, and develop and advocate for policies linked with effective interventions.

Given these issues, and in recognition of the family as the natural and fundamental unit of society and the best environment in which to prepare generations for productive lives and responsible citizenship, the NCFA (also referred to as "the Council") was established in 2001. The NCFA's mission is to contribute to ensuring a better quality of life for Jordanian families through a national vision that supports the country's development policies and enables all Jordanian families to achieve their optimal aspirations.

GOVERNANCE AND MANAGEMENT OF NATIONAL COUNCIL FOR FAMILY AFFAIRS

Key responsibilities assigned to the NCFA are (a) to contribute to the formulation of policies for families and children based on research and innovative programs, (b) to coordinate the existing efforts of partner institutions, (c) to monitor the implementation of national strategies, and (d) to act in advocacy.

Of note is the NCFA's governance structure, which is represented by the line ministries or single-sector ministries (e.g., health, education), governmental and non-governmental institutions, and agencies that are concerned with family affairs and have interest and experience in this field. This structure provides the Council with the impetus required to work as an "umbrella" organization or a coordinating body for the relevant governmental and NGO agencies in the field of human and social development. Moreover, it enables the Council to build constructive relationships between service providers and the Council in order to ensure the provision of the appropriate legislative, socioeconomic, and cultural policy environment for families. This avoids duplication of efforts, ensures the credibility and transparency of the Council and its partners, and provides the latter with a sense of ownership of the results and products of the Council's work.

The paramount effect on the Council's strength and influence comes from the enthusiastic and committed patronage of its president, Queen Rania Al-Abdullah of Jordan. The board of the Council is composed of representatives from the main ministries or sectors directly linked with ECD. The composition of the board is crucial in that it enables the Council to work with a diverse set of partners to successfully coordinate policy responses to support early childhood services and programs (Sultana, 2009).

FUNCTIONS AND ACTIVITIES OF NATIONAL COUNCIL FOR FAMILY AFFAIRS

The functions of the Council are implemented through several technical groups, such as taskforce, advisory committees, and other consultative groups. Typically, these groups are composed of multidisciplinary national experts, practitioners, and decision makers. The result of the work of these groups is evidenced through the technically sound and practical national agenda that have been produced by the NCFA. One such technical recommendation is "to set national priorities concerning family affairs [...] in accordance with the needs of the Jordanian society" (Article 6 (b) of the Law). In light of this recommendation, the structure of the Council reflects an innovative approach, known as the multidisciplinary "participatory" approach, which the Council utilizes in all its activities.

Furthermore, in carrying out its mandate, the Council "follows up on the efforts pertaining to accomplishing the goals of international agreements and conventions concerning the family, women, children and youth, which have been ratified by Jordan" (Article 6(g) of the Law), such as the UN Millennium Development Goals (MDGs; UN General Assembly, 2000). The Council serves as the national policy "think tank," assigned to follow-up on the progress Jordan has made in this field, thereby "facilitating and monitoring regional and global interaction."

EARLY CHILDHOOD DEVELOPMENT AGENDA OF NATIONAL COUNCIL FOR FAMILY AFFAIRS

The NCFA's work in ECD can be understood within the framework of the five strategic directions that are legally mandated for the agency: policy formulation, research and data management, financial planning, advocacy and awareness raising, and coordination and monitoring of ECD programs and policies.

The first legal mandate is related to policy functions to facilitate the development and appropriate reform of policies, legislations, and guidelines. For example, the NCFA promoted and supported the implementation of the ECD Action Plan (2003–2007) and the National Plan of Action for Children NPA (2004–2013). A second major thrust of the NCFA is management of research and data resources. To that end, the NCFA was also able to provide scientific policy-oriented research on issues affecting children and their well-being, for example by conducting a study on disadvantaged children, the results of which held important implications for the National Plan of Action. A third function is financial planning. The NCFA's new initiative to analyze the national budget from a child-rights perspective to identify children's share in the national budget is another example of practical, scientific policy research. This child budget analysis will provide policy argument to increase children's allocation from national budgets. Fourth, the NCFA has also been active in mobilizing support and increasing awareness and support for programs and policies.

The fifth function of NCFA pertains directly to the coordination of ECD. Coordination to facilitate and monitor the development and implementation of policies and national initiatives have focused on ensuring an enhanced quality of life for all Jordanian families. With respect to ECD, the NCFA has been working with national stakeholders to improve the quality of the kindergarten programs by setting standards for kindergarten licensing, developing early childhood learning standards and indicators, and supporting the implementation of a comprehensive project to improve services provided for children in nurseries and child care centers. These vital coordination functions have been able to catalyze financial support for kindergartens, to achieve national-level policy support for holistic ECD, and to develop regulations to improve the quality of programs. By coordinating across the ministries, the NCFA was able to catalyze these developments.

NATIONAL COUNCIL FOR FAMILY AFFAIRS: ACHIEVEMENTS AND GAPS

We now turn to an analysis of the effectiveness of the NCFA for ECD as a means of generating recommendations for coordinating agencies. In this analysis, we examine the key factors that have contributed to or hindered the effectiveness of the NCFA. The factors reviewed are related to institutional structure, mandate, coordination mechanisms, their multiple roles, and resources, both financial and human.

Institutional Structure

To evaluate the strengths of the NCFA's intuitional structure, we present it in the context of other modalities that exist in the region. Four modalities for early childhood institutions have emerged in the Middle East and North Africa Region (MENA): childhood units within ministries, ministries of childhood, national councils for childhood, and national agencies for childhood (i.e., the Jordanian model).

CHILDHOOD UNIT WITHIN MINISTRIES

In the childhood unit within ministries model, individual ministries can elect to have a department or division focused on early childhood (e.g., the General Directorate of Social and Family Solidarity in Algeria). Although this model reflects the current thinking of establishing committees to coordinate ECD matters, it is also considered the least effective of the four models since it is dependent on the status of the unit within the ministry's hierarchy. Thus, the allocation of resources and decision-making powers given to it stem from the same hierarchical structure bestowed on it. It is usually headed by a minister, with representation of mid-managers from other relevant ministries and NGOs or experts.

MINISTRIES OF CHILDHOOD

Ministries of childhood, such as the Ministry of Social Development, Family, and Solidarity in Morocco, deal with children and adolescents as a separate social entity, with specific needs and requirements, rather than as simply a biological stage in the life cycle of a person. For example, these ministries address programs linked with children's development. Although this model does ensure the allocation of sufficient financial and human resources to the particular ministry, it accentuates the silo approach to ECD. As a result, ECD does not get the interministerial coordination that is required to ensure a coordinated and integrated approach to fulfilling children's needs.

NATIONAL COUNCILS FOR CHILDHOOD

National Councils for Childhood, lead by heads of a country (e.g., prime minister), is a third model that is prevalent in the MENA region. This modality is usually well resourced due to its linkages with the head of executive power. The membership in such councils is usually comprised of relevant ministers, in addition to prominent public figures and experts. This model is seen in Sudan, Yemen, and Palestine. Although this model does benefit from the support and endorsement of the highest powers in the country, it remains out of the purview of national legislative and executive bodies, such as line or sectoral ministries. Therefore, the extent of its influence is linked with the extent of the power of the head of state who supports it (Bulbul, 2010).

NATIONAL INSTITUTIONS FOR FAMILY AFFAIRS

National Institutions for Family Affairs, such as those in Jordan, Syria, and Qatar, take the role of coordination and convener for all stakeholders in relation to family. The Jordanian model has been described, in this chapter, however, Syria and Qatar have a similar framework. Several of these models are still experimenting with the hierarchical and administrative structures that reflect their vision and objectives. Some opted to establish departments for planning, research, monitoring and evaluation, advocacy, and administrative affairs. Others operate through specialized committees of representatives from the concerned ministries and entities, whereas many combine both structures. Across these models, although variations exist, a commonality is the crucial role of the technical secretariat, headed usually by a secretary general who liaises the work of the council with other entities working in the ECD sphere. Female representation and adolescent participation in these entities varies according to a country's gender and youth priorities, with Syria and Jordan women's representation reaching 50% and 40%, respectively.

For a national agency to influence the early childhood agenda, it needs to operate on two distinct tiers. The first tier focuses on leveraging support from high-level decision makers for legal reform, policy development, and plans and advocacy. The goal of this tier is to ensure political support and endorsement for all ECD-related programs and policies. The second tier works with interministerial bodies for coordination, management, and implementation of the plans at the national and community levels. This second tier ensures that that policies and programs endorsed by high-level decision makers are implemented intersectorally to achieve holistic development. The efficiency of such a council depends on the degree to which it can translate the needs and aspirations of diverse groups in the country, thus requiring the Council to be able to reach out to various ethnic or disadvantaged groups and different regions.

Mandate

The scope of the institution's mandate is an important determinant of its success or failure. The majority of ECD councils' or units' mandates focus on policy and advocacy work, development of national plans, coordination among various actors, and technical oversight and monitoring; a few agencies even combine program implementation with their mandate. It has been observed, however, that having too broad a mandate results in altering the work of the council to coordination and oversight roles only. In many instances where councils undertook an implementation role, NGOs and government came to believe that these agencies were competing with them for donor funding and their role in service provision.

For the NCFA, its mandate covers policy research; advocacy and policy development; coordination and institutional development for the promotion of women; and adolescent, child, and family well-being and rights. Due to this large mandate, the NCFA has primarily focused its efforts on coordination efforts for planning for ECD and oversight. Here, we describe a series of functions linked to the role of a national agency. For each of the roles, we describe the NCFA's achievements, challenges, and mode of operations.

National Council for Family Affairs as Coordinator

The NCFA has been effective as a coordinator and convener for ECD policies. For example, it promoted and coordinated an inclusive, participatory, and multisectoral approach to the development of three key ECD strategies: the first and second ECD Plans of Action and the Jordanian National Plan of Action. The process of coalition building in the development of these plans has been effective, with the

NCFA setting and aligning national priorities and fostering consensus around them. This is done through a series of workshops and consultation meetings, held to create a forum to exchange ideas and views around the national issues and hear the different perspectives shared by various stakeholders from the government and civil society organizations.

Although NCFA has set a strong precedent for coordination with stakeholders, similar efforts are required for building coalitions with program beneficiaries to ensure sustainability of pressure for action and services in light of the Jordanian reality of frequent ministerial changes. Special communication strategies need to be in place to inform the public of the importance of ECD and the plans and programs that are essential to ensure a healthy beginning for Jordan's children.

Furthermore, partners and collaborating institutions often view the NCFA as an umbrella agency. NGOs, in particular, would like to see the role of the NCFA expand beyond that of coordinator to ensure that sufficient resources are allocated to effectively implement the plans of action. Moreover, national agencies need to have a strong national monitoring and evaluation system to systematically collect data on the implementation of the plans supported by various stakeholders. At NCFA, this monitoring is implemented through regular meetings attended by partner organizations. The representative of these partners organizations are tasked with providing regular reports on the progress of the plans of action at the network meetings.

Certain realities of the Arab world create a unique set of challenges in terms of coordination, coalition building, monitoring of systems, and fund-raising strategies, all of which form the foundation for an effective coordination role. By having a high level of technical capacity and the proper mandate, councils are able to overcome different coordination problems, such as those faced in Tunis where it succeeded in achieving higher levels of coordination between public and private sectors and civil society organizations through having the private sector as partner in implementing ECD capacity building programs (Bulbul, 2010).

Numerous similar councils have been established in many countries in the MENA region, a region that embraces an abundance of comparable commonalities relating to culture, developmental profiles, and challenges. Taking coordination to a higher level, collaboration among such councils capitalizes on the knowledge and experience generated and contributes toward joint programs that can have a cross-border effect, such as developing indicators for the Arab child or having a strong, unified, culturally sensitive communication plan to counter violence against children.

National Council for Family Affairs as a Legislator

Legislation-related tasks are one of the robust aspects of the national agency's work. With respect to international human rights instruments, the council has been influential in achieving legislative amendments, in adherence to the CRC and the Convention on the Elimination of All Forms of Discrimination Against Women

(CEDAW) (UN Division for the Advancement of Women, 1979). The NCFA has drafted the Childhood Act in collaboration with Ministry of Social Development and the UN Children's Fund (UNICEF), and in consultation with wide array of partners from the government and civil society organizations. It has been instrumental in proposing a set of recommendations in relation to family protection and well-being through a systematic process of legislative review and analysis from a child and family perspective.

Beyond the endorsement of laws, however, there has been insufficient follow-up on the implementation of the laws after approval or the setting of mechanisms to guarantee the proper implementation of laws. It is a reality that, in many Arab countries, the implementation of child-related laws is faced with many unresolved challenges.

National Council for Family Affairs as a Research Agency

National agencies can position themselves as national research and knowledge base authorities around those issues pertaining to their mandate. In ECD, the NCFA, with the support of UNICEF, has been instrumental in establishing the Early Learning Development Standards (ELDS; Britto & Kagan, 2010), a milestone development in the Jordanian ECD landscape. The ELDS outline the expected outcomes for Jordanian children in the early years; by aiming to assess child progress, guide curriculum development, and evaluate programs, these standards set the platform and benchmarks for Jordanian children's development that all policies and programs should work toward. This key national-level achievement is acknowledged as a valuable contribution to the regional and global ECD knowledge base.

National agencies might play this role of a research "think tank" by linking with research organizations or national statistics bureaus to obtain and periodically update key indicators on child and family well-being. Crucial to an effective evidence-based policy decision-making process is being equipped with the fundamental data needed to prepare a strategic approach to policy changes and advocacy work. The NCFA has embarked on establishing a National Information System for Family Affairs and a violence-tracking system; this will serve as the reference for vital indicators and information on ECD and family issues. For this to happen, this database needs to be accessible to organizations and experts in the field.

Apart from conducting research, a challenge lies in transforming the findings of the research into sound policy and program interventions for the government to adopt. Informed policy making requires the capacity to analyze and interpret data specific to sector ministries, perform routine analysis of household survey and census data, and generate reliable social indicators for use in this analysis. Jordan needs to invest in building national capabilities to undertake social policy analysis, which is a component of good governance and also important for enhancing equity. Moreover, monitoring the situation of children would require setting up a focal point monitoring system into which various governmental organizations feed data. Cutting through the bureaucracy of government procedures to collect information on the status of children could prove a challenge. Furthermore, obtaining subnational data is critical for revealing disparities among regions and population groups, in order to translate these data into equitable services that cater to the specific needs of these groups. These councils have an obligation under the CRC to ensure that children enjoy the right to equality of opportunity in life. As evidence has demonstrated, early childhood is the most effective and cost-efficient time to intervene to address inequalities and to break the intergenerational cycle of poverty (Engle, 2011).

National Council for Family Affairs as an Advocate

The NCFA has gained extensive knowledge and data on family-related issues, especially ECD. Because of this, it has, to some extent, been the voice advocating for policy changes, especially with the Ministry of Education in the ECD domain. However, greater efforts are required to transfer this knowledge into policy documents and advocacy tools and to engage NGOs in advocacy planning and dissemination.

In general, national agencies, such as the NCFA, due to their affiliation with high-level decision makers, can be very effective in realizing tangible legislative and regulatory changes. Thus, the NCFA's concrete knowledge and expertise in ECD has enabled it to effect many regulatory changes within the Ministry of Education system. Having a strategic communication plan aimed at addressing specific topics, with key messages geared to decision makers, the public, and professionals is vital in amplifying public outreach to create a forum for national dialogue around key issues.

However, advocacy efforts need to be exerted with all relevant governmental agencies to advocate for the advancement of the children's agenda. This could be challenged by prevalent societal attitudes that sometimes hinder proper child development. Building strong advocates from NGOs and government goes a long way toward generating momentum for policy and behavioral change.

Inherent to the core of many councils' mandates is advocating global concerns and their relevance to a country's situation. One example is climate change, the effects of which are likely to impact the health status of millions of families. The NCFA needs to highlight the impact of climate change-related exposure on children, given Jordan's severe scarcity of water. The NCFA could support the development of child-sensitive policies for tackling climate change to mitigate its impact on child development and tap on international funding to support these policies.

Human Resources and Manpower

Advancing a mandate as ambitious as the NCFA's requires high-caliber staff that is able to set priorities and facilitate the development of plans for diverse sectors that are of importance to the Jordanian family. Staffing in these councils is always an issue of concern since it is difficult to attract highly qualified professionals due to budgetary constraints. Additionally, for current NCFA staff, the responsibilities are great since the NCFA holds two of the most important portfolios in the country: namely, ECD and child protection. Thus, current staff spread themselves too thinly in an attempt to live up to the expectations of their mandate.

The NCFA thrust has suffered a few setbacks due to the high turnover of its secretary general position; this is a key position that needs to provide leadership and insight for the work of the council. These setbacks have been accentuated by the loss of key staff at the NCFA, thus jeopardizing its institutional memory and its reservoir of knowledge around its mandate. High turnover poses an additional burden on staff as it tries to understand and accommodate the different agendas and modes of operation that emerge from newly appointed secretaries general. To overcome the problem of the frequent turnover in management, middle managers need to be empowered to develop their knowledge and skills and to possess some level of decision-making power to ensure the sustainability of the agency's work.

Council staff should be seen as a source of expertise that NGOs and the government can turn to for knowledge and technical assistance. Thus, capacity-building programs for council staff and counterparts is a crucial step in keeping abreast of all new developments in the ECD sphere, and sufficient resources should be secured for this purpose. Many councils across the region have invested heavily in recruiting highly qualified staff and advancing their training

Financial Resources

The Council has a set budget from the government for its core functions, and it fund raises to finance its other operations and for the implementation of programs. Given its status as the national agency for family affairs, it receives a favored approach from donors since its workplan is expected to reflect national priorities. Thus, the NCFA needs to nurture a long-term relationship with key donors to secure ongoing resources for the country's priorities. Intrinsically, the UN mandate interconnects with the mandate of the Council in providing ample opportunities for collaboration and funding prospects.

Including private sector representation on the Council's board of trustees is a first step in engaging the private sector as a financier and partner in development issues, especially with the growing culture of community social responsibilities in Jordan's private sector.

Stemming from the NFCA's role as leader in the development of the National Plan of Action for children (NPA) and its endorsement, some NGOs expect the NCFA to fund-raise on their behalf to support the unfunded part of the plan; the NCFA is strategically positioned to undertake this task.

Challenges

Coordination among the public sector, civil society organizations, and the private sector is a time-consuming endeavor that requires enormous efforts on the part of the Council. Organizations need to see the Council as an honest broker and neutral agency that represents their voice and concerns and, yet, at the same time, acknowledges their contributions and achievements.

Being the voice of the vulnerable and secluded requires the Council to have an effective mechanism for reaching those who are hard to reach, and this puts extra strain on both human and financial resources. One of the primary concerns and an obstacle for the effective functioning of such councils is insufficient budgetary allocation to the council and its workplan, and the intricacy of securing other sources of funding. The NCFA has been able to somewhat overcome this impediment through strategic partnerships with the Arab Gulf Program for Development (AGFUND) and UNICEF.

Based on this review, it can be concluded that for some councils, organization structure can contribute to failure and inefficiency. Bureaucracy and complex hierarchical regulation often plays a big role in incapacitating staff and hindering the implementation of programs.

Leadership is significant factor in determining the success or failure of a council in building coalitions and effectively coordinating and leading the work for early childhood. Directors of such organizations need to spread a culture that promotes cooperation with all organizations without overshadowing the uniqueness and specialization of each. This is a tough balancing act but one that is critical to the credibility of the councils.

One particular area of concern arises when high-level decision makers are requested to participate in a process that does not need their level of expertise and power. Consequently, these decision makers often delegate their authority to participate to more junior staff in their organization who lack decision-making powers to advance the ECD agenda. This problem, which occurs fairly frequently, hampers the effectiveness of the council.

Robust information databases and monitoring and evaluation systems are of paramount importance to allow the council to follow up on the implementation of plans and policies, and to measure their impact on the well-being of children and beneficiaries. This needs to be achieved either by building internal capacities or linking with national research machinery.

Finally, the context in which the councils operate influence their ability to work on specific topics, such as family protection from violence, especially when societal and familial attitudes and beliefs intervene to restrict the involvement of the council in the family sphere.

Research Agenda and Policy Questions

Although the Council has been in operation for a while, its impact is yet to be studied. Evaluating the Council's effectiveness over time and its impact on child outcome needs to be studied closely. In addition to evaluating the role of the Council in influencing policies and budget for ECD, we need to understand its impact on quality of services. To that end, we propose the following questions to further understand the role of such a council for ECD and to improve its effectiveness.

- How can the effectiveness of councils be translated across diverse country settings and contexts?
- In the council's advocacy work, how can it best deploy the arguments of children's rights, climate change, social justice, and human and economic arguments?
- How can an equity-focused approach be sustained while promoting the rights of all children?

Conclusion

PRINCIPLES FOR ACTION

In closing, the presence of a childhood councils is essential to the protection of children's rights and to safeguarding the well-being of children. These functions can only be effective when done through coordinated and consolidated national efforts in policy development, planning, management, implementation, and monitoring and evaluation. This is true particularly in early childhood, where a convergence of services ensures holistic child development, thus making the sum of whole larger than its parts. Broad stakeholder involvement from national and international agencies, communities, and parents is essential to ensure robust public support for the ECD agenda, a shared vision of ECD among all, and sustainable political will. Being the voice of children and families from all walks of life, encompassing their needs and concerns, is fundamental to securing an ECD agenda and national plans that reflect the people's aspirations and realities. Rigorous social policy analysis to improve the efficiency and effectiveness of social services and incorporate the results of this research and analysis in public policy making is required.

Acknowledgments

This report would not have been possible without the full support of UNICEF and its commitment to improving the ECD landscape in Jordan and the world. It is our hope that the findings of this report will pave the way for a thorough review and reappraisal of approaches to coordination in the ECD field, and herald the strengthening of the existing systems and services for the securing children's rights to development and growth in safe and stimulating environments.

A special thanks goes to Dr. Pia Rebello Britto, who has inspired and motivated us to take our ECD work to higher levels and has been instrumental in the development and editing of this chapter.

We would like to acknowledge the work that NCFA has done and is doing in advancing the ECD agenda in Jordan, inspired by Her Majesty Queen Rania Al-Abdullah's vision.

Note

1. Poverty Report for Jordan (using the Household Expenditure and Income Survey 2008), 2010.

References

Al-Hassan, S. M., & Lansford, J. E. (2011). Evaluation of the better parenting program in Jordan. *Early Child Development and Care, 181*(5), 587–598.

Britto, P. R., & Kagan, S. L. (2010). Global status of early learning and development standards. In P. Peterson , E. Baker, & B. McGraw (Eds.), *International encyclopedia of education* (Vol. 2, pp. 138–143). Oxford, UK: Elsevier.

Britto, P. R., Yoshikawa, H., & Boller, K. (2011). Quality of early childhood development programs in global contexts: Rationale for investment, conceptual framework and implications for equity. *Social Policy Report, 25*(2).

Bulbul, L. (2010). *An analytical study of childhood institutions in the Arab Region.* League of Arab States—Dept. of Childhood and Family.

Choi, S. H. (2003). *Cross-sectoral co-ordination in early childhood: Some lessons to learn* (UNESCO Policy Brief on Early Childhood, No. 9). Paris: UNESCO.

Department of Statistics (DoS). (2010). *Using the household expenditure and income survey 2008.* Poverty Report for Jordan. Amman: Author.

Engle, P. (2011). Child development in developing countries. *The Lancet, 378*(9799), 1339–1353.

Faour, B. (2010). *Mapping early childhood services and programs in Arab countries.* Paper presented to the Regional Consultative Workshop on Advancing ECCD Agenda in the Arab Region, Amman.

Hashemite Kingdom of Jordan. (2009). *Jordan population and family health survey 2009.* Amman: Jordan Department of Statistics.

Jordan Ministry of Planning. (2000). *Jordan human development report 2000.* Amman, UNDP, Retrieved from http://www.arab-hdr.org/publications/other/undp/hdr/2000/jordan-e.pdf

Lombardi, J. (1992). *Beyond transition: Ensuring continuity in early childhood services [EDO-PS-92–93].* Champaign, IL: ERIC Clearinghouse on Elementary and Early Childhood Education.

Naudeau, S., Kataoka, N., & Valerio, A. (2010). *Investing in young children: An early childhood development guide for policy dialogue and project preparation.* Washington, DC: World Bank.

Salehyan, I., & Gleditsch, K. S. (2006). Refugees and the spread of civil war. *International Organization, 60,* 335–366.

Sultana, R. (2009). *Making Jordan fit for its children.* Amman: UNICEF.

UN Division for the Advancement of Women. (1979). *Convention on the elimination of all forms of discrimination against women: Overview of the convention.* Retrieved from http://www.un.org/womenwatch/daw/cedaw/

UN General Assembly. (2000). *United Nations millennium declaration.* New York: United Nations.

UNESCO. (2003). *Cross-sectoral co-ordination in early childhood: Some lessons to learn* (Policy Brief on Early Childhood. No. 9). Paris: Author.

UNESCO. (2007). *Jordan's strategies for early childhood education in a lifelong learning framework* (Policy Brief on Early Childhood No. 39). Paris: Author.

UNESCO. (2007). *Good governance of early childhood care and education: Lessons from the 2007 EFA global monitoring report* (Policy Brief on Early Childhood. No. 40). Paris: Author.

UNICEF, NCFA. (2007). *Children in Jordan: Situation analysis (2006/2007).* Amman: Authors.

Vargas-Barón, E. (2005). *Planning policies for early childhood development: Guidelines for action.* Paris: Association for the Development of Education in Africa.

World Bank. (2005). *Education reform for the knowledge economy.* Loan No.7170-JO: Draft Aide Memoire.

Young, M. E., & van der Gaag, J. (2002). *Ready to learn: An assessment of needs and programs for children ages 4–6 in Jordan.* Washington, DC: World Bank.

22

Capacity Building for Early Childhood Development

Sara L. Hommel

The process of expanding and sustaining quality early childhood development (ECD) programs is a complex undertaking that depends on diverse elements such as political will, donor financing, physical infrastructure, and community engagement. At the core of all these elements, however, is the capacity of stakeholders—designers, planners, trainers, managers, practitioners, monitors and evaluators, and funders.

A critical mistake often made by engineers of strategies to expand and sustain ECD is to focus their considerations of capacity on training and implementation only (i.e., on trainers and practitioners), rather than the capacities of all stakeholders (e.g., policymakers, donors, and evaluators). As the underlying determinant of how and whether ECD projects or programs are implemented successfully and capable of successful scaling, the capacity of all stakeholders should be considered through two interlinked categories: capacity in practice and capacity in knowledge.

Capacity in Practice and Capacity in Knowledge

Successful ECD projects and programs depend specifically on the capacities of practitioners to provide services and interventions; of training institutions to produce competent practitioners; of policymakers to design, fund, manage, and/or monitor interventions (and the systems encompassing these interventions); and of local and international donors, program designers, and implementing organizations.

Discussions surrounding ECD capacity usually refer to technical capacity, or the capacity of service delivery professionals and the systems that train them. This category of capacity, which for the sake of this discussion will be referred to as "capacity in practice," is critical to the functionality of quality

ECD systems that are scalable and sustainable. But to truly understand the complexity of ECD capacity, we must look across the entire spectrum of ECD stakeholders and consider another category, that of "capacity in knowledge." This category encompasses nonpractitioner stakeholders relevant to ECD systems, not simply those related to service delivery and training. In order for necessary stakeholders to effectively engage in ECD, they must be convinced of the value of investing in early childhood and understand the specifics of their roles within a complex ECD system, and this is dependent on their ECD knowledge capacity.

CAPACITY IN PRACTICE

Capacity in practice includes stakeholders for whom practice capacity is critical to their ability to perform functions of ECD service delivery or the training of such individuals. They may be preschool teachers, child care providers, nutritionists, nurses, doctors, social workers, ECD trainers at local and international nongovernmental organizations (NGOs), and professors at universities and other training institutes.

Capacity in practice is critical to scaling up and sustaining quality ECD services, programs, or systems. Without capable service providers and quality training programs that produce capable providers with the necessary skills to perform well, the expansion of ECD programs cannot succeed. This may seem obvious when considering ECD scale-up, but capacity building processes often do not mirror scaling-up strategies, and this situation results in inadequate capacity among service providers to accommodate the expansion of programs.

CAPACITY IN KNOWLEDGE

Capacity in knowledge includes stakeholders for whom knowledge capacity is central to their ability to engage in supportive ECD roles. Such roles do not provide direct services or training. These stakeholders design policies, make funding decisions, coordinate stakeholder groups, or monitor and evaluate programs and services. They may be policymakers, donors, researchers, ECD professionals at local or international NGOs, and community leaders.

Although the dependence of a quality ECD service on capable professionals delivering the service and on quality training seems obvious, much less obvious and much more complicated to plan is the need to build capacity in knowledge of ECD among the broad array of stakeholders involved. If policymakers who are tasked with designing, funding, or managing ECD programs do not have the necessary knowledge to play their roles effectively, then effort must be made to build their capacity in knowledge of ECD. The same applies to donors, community leaders, and others involved in the design, management, funding, coordination, and maintenance of ECD services, programs, and systems.

Strategies for Capacity Building

The most commonly addressed capacity issue is that of capacity in practice. When ECD stakeholders discuss "capacity," it is most often the capacity of ECD practice to which they refer. Strategies for addressing the needs to build capacity in practice most commonly center on providing appropriate technical support and training to practitioners and the trainers of practitioners. The focus is on the individuals responsible for providing direct services and their trainers. But any ECD scale-up strategy must address the capacity needs of not only ECD practice but those of ECD knowledge. The two should be carefully planned as parallel components of a scaling-up strategy that focuses on both improving the practice capacity of relevant ECD practitioners and improving the knowledge capacity of all other relevant stakeholders responsible for designing, planning, managing, funding, monitoring and evaluating a given ECD program or system.

Strategies for building capacity in knowledge should be at the core of any plan to scale-up an ECD program, policy, or system. The first step is often a mapping of relevant stakeholders and an assessment of their experience and/or knowledge of ECD. Such a mapping can then serve as a framework from which to design a knowledge capacity building strategy that can appropriately address the needs of individual stakeholder groups—noting that the knowledge needs of donors or policymakers might be different from those of community leaders or parents, and strategies for building knowledge capacity should address the specific needs of each stakeholder group.

No one method for building such knowledge capacity is suitable everywhere. Key questions in devising a strategy to build knowledge capacity are:

1. How advanced is the stakeholder's knowledge of ECD?
2. What type of knowledge sharing activities might improve the stakeholder's knowledge?
3. Who will design, organize, and implement these knowledge sharing activities?
4. How will stakeholders who need improvement in knowledge capacity be included in knowledge sharing activities?
5. How will outcomes of their participation be monitored (i.e., how effective is the activity in improving their knowledge capacity)?

Knowledge sharing activities have to be customized to the needs of specific stakeholders and scaling-up scenarios. One model will not work for all stakeholders or every service, program, or system. As the strategies for expanding and sustaining ECD programs vary with each situation, so will the activities to improve stakeholder knowledge capacity. Those who design knowledge sharing activities need to identify the stakeholders in need and monitor the effectiveness of capacity building activities.

A scaling-up strategy should aim to create "capacity" among all relevant stakeholders, so that they are able to play an effective role in supporting the scaling process and sustaining an effective program/system at scale. Successful scaling strategies begin in various ways. Often, one specific stakeholder (or stakeholder group) has a specific project, program, or model in mind for scaling and convinces other relevant stakeholders to join the process. At other times, a group of stakeholders will collectively design a model and process for scaling from the start. In either situation, capacity building should be at the core of the scaling strategy. Practice capacity building usually takes the form of training of practitioners and/or training of trainers, and the strengthening of the institutions that support such processes. Knowledge capacity building is a more complex process of consultation and advocacy, often ranging from small discussions with policymakers and donors to large consultations/meetings with designers, planners, and managers of ECD programming.

In a scaling process where one specific stakeholder is leading, capacity building should be aimed at sharing the knowledge held by the initiating organization with other stakeholder groups and/or leveraging the expertise of others to complement that of the initiating organization. In the case of a collaborative ECD model design and scaling planning process, the participants must identify their individual roles and responsibilities in building knowledge capacity among those they need to "convert." This knowledge capacity building process can take many forms, including media campaigns targeting local communities, introductory consultations with various stakeholders followed by more technical meetings to share expertise around the specific program model, and process/coordination planning that determines necessary roles and responsibilities. Some stakeholders may need more convincing (or more knowledge support) than others, so forming strong partnerships among "the converted" from the start to collectively advocate to those in need of extra attention is important.

It is critical to note that during expansion planning, knowledge capacity building is not only about the importance of ECD and the methods of the proposed intervention model itself, but also about the process for how best to implement it (and the roles various stakeholder groups must play in implementing, managing, funding, and evaluating it). Also important is the continuation of the capacity building strategies throughout the scaling process and after scaling has been completed. Individual stakeholders come and go. Policymakers are voted out of office, managers within policy institutions are promoted to new positions, international managers at international NGOs and donor organizations transfer to other regions, and practitioner "turnover" is common. As a result, capacity building is a never-ending process that must continue both throughout the scaling process and long after scaling is completed to ensure quality sustainability at scale.

EXAMPLES FROM THE FIELD

International development organizations, local NGOs, and other capacity organizing institutions should plan capacity building strategies to address both practice-based and knowledge-based capacity needs. In addition to service provider training, such a plan may include informative events, discussions, training sessions, and other forums in which policymakers, donors, and other stakeholders are introduced to new ECD concepts and methods and are provided space and opportunity to interact with each other and with those who are transferring ECD knowledge. Important across all of these capacity building strategies is a need to set clear benchmarks for success and methods for monitoring the outcomes of capacity building processes.

If we look to examples from the field, we can identify numerous strategies to build both practice-based and knowledge-based capacity in ECD scaling strategies. Approaches range from technical training workshops for practitioners and/or their trainers to policy roundtables with high-level public officials to broad-based media campaigns that target local communities with messages on the importance of early childhood and the types of services available to meet the needs of young children and their families.

Methods to improve capacity in practice during ECD scaling, such as training of trainers and training of practitioners, is present in ECD scaling strategies organized by multiple stakeholders such as national governments and international development organizations. For example, as part of a national strategy to scale-up ECD, the South African Department of Education conducted an audit in 2000 that revealed that only 12% of the 48,561 early childhood teachers working in public early education programs were qualified (i.e., had a high school diploma and 3 years of training). Due to a dearth of training programs, the government engaged NGOs to complement state-provided training and take on the task of training more than 70,000 under-qualified preschool teachers and new preschools teachers during the national ECD expansion process (Biersteker, 2010).

During the scale-up of the national Educate Your Child program in Cuba, at the beginning of the scaling process, a 1-year training program was designed to train new practitioners for expansion of the program. A multidisciplinary group of experts (including university professors, family doctors, and day-care teachers) was recruited as training instructors, and training manuals, which had been designed during the pilot phase of the program, were updated for use in the ongoing training of practitioners. The result was a significant increase in practitioner capacity that provided a foundation for successful scaling (Tinajero, 2010).

International development organizations, such as Save the Children, often place practice-based capacity building at the center of their ECD scaling strategies. For Save the Children, partnerships between the organization and local communities lead to capacity building processes in which Save the Children trains and re-trains (with refresher trainings over the course of several years) local preschool teachers and school management committees. Save the Children also facilitates knowledge-based capacity building through the organization of monthly parenting meetings (open to the entire community) that build knowledge capacity amongst families and community members (Martinez, Naudeau, & Pereira, 2012).

Strategies to improve capacity in knowledge during ECD scaling can also be seen through the efforts of national governments working to expand ECD. During the Cuban scale-up of the Educate Your Child Program, an initial challenge for program expansion was a lack of public knowledge about early childhood and human development. Without a strong knowledge base at the local level, communities may underutilize services, and target populations may be underserved. In Cuba, it was imperative to develop community knowledge ahead of the implementation of new services to convince those most in need to participate. Therefore, a communications strategy was designed to support a National Action Plan aimed to coordinate all government programs supporting human development. In the communications strategy, two government programs (focused, respectively, on health and education) presented messages of human development through cartoons and dramatizations broadcast on prime-time national television (Tinajero, 2010).

The United Nations Children's Fund (UNICEF) tackles the challenge of knowledge capacity by supporting ECD coordinating committees and regional networks. It also provides training courses on ECD for policymakers and organizes meetings and conferences for multiple stakeholder groups such as donors, policymakers, and international development organizations. (UNICEF, 2011).

Although both practice capacity and knowledge capacity are important components of ongoing ECD work within global development organizations and specific countries attempting to scale ECD, much greater attention is needed to improve ECD capacities amongst the diverse stakeholders necessary for successful ECD scale-up. With limited financial resources allocated to ECD within the global development agenda, efforts are slow and conditions challenging. There is a long way to go to meet the ECD capacity needs of the developing world.

Conclusion

The success of quality ECD programming to be scaled and sustained depends critically on the capacity in practice and capacity in knowledge among all relevant stakeholders and across all stages of a project or program's process of scaling. It is also critical that such capacity building strategies remain in place after the completion of the scaling process to ensure quality sustainability at scale.

ECD capacity building must be addressed far beyond the capacity of practitioners to meet the needs of all stakeholders. The designers, planners, trainers, managers, implementers, evaluators, funders, and receivers of ECD services (parents, caregivers) all require specific ECD knowledge to effectively play their roles in the process of scaling quality ECD and sustaining such quality programming at scale.

Those responsible for creating scaling strategies for ECD should carefully plan for meeting the capacity building needs of both practice and knowledge, and such plans should be not only part of the scaling strategy but of the final program model at scale.

References

Biersteker, L. (2010). *Scaling-up early child development in South Africa.* Washington, DC: Wolfensohn Center for Development, the Brookings Institution.

Martinez, S., Naudeau, S., & Pereira, V. (2012). *The promise of preschools in Africa: A randomized impact evaluation of Early Childhood Development in rural Mozambique.* Washington, DC: The World Bank Group and Save the Children.

Tinajero, A. (2010). *Scaling-up early child development in Cuba.* Washington, DC: Wolfensohn Center for Development, the Brookings Institution.

UNICEF (Evaluation Office). (2011). *Evaluation of UNICEF's Early Childhood Development Program with focus on government of Netherlands funding (2008–2010).* New York: UNICEF.

23

Barriers to Service Provision

LESSONS LEARNED FROM DONOR-SUPPORTED EARLY CHILDHOOD DEVELOPMENT PROJECTS

Mary E. Young

Science tells us that experience in the early years of children's development affects their brain's architecture and neurochemistry. We have evidence of both the importance of early years and the high economic returns to investments made in these years, compared with those in other periods in life. Policymakers have responded to increasing pressure to include young children's care and early education as an integral part of public policy. The pressure comes from diverse stakeholders—mothers, who increasingly participate in the labor force and demand child care for children under age 3; educators, who are challenged to account for children's performance and learning outcomes; businesses that require skilled labor in a marketplace dependent on a high quality of human capital; and health sectors that are burdened with the heavy costs of treating disease and illness that could have been prevented at less cost by interventions in the early years.

So, what are the constraints and how might more be done? Why do countries not take ECD programs to scale? Why is it difficult to bring small ECD projects up to scale? What are the impediments to implementing ECD projects? To address these questions, we need to recognize that the infrastructure for ECD is complex and that, throughout the world, early childhood programs uniquely depend on a complex network of local, regional, and national institutions for their financial, management, and implementation support.

This chapter reviews some lessons learned from implementing external donor-supported ECD projects in developing countries, to identify key factors causing delays in implementation. The factors fall into three groups: complexity of project design and planning, weak project management and implementation, and insufficient monitoring and evaluation.

TABLE 23.1 World Bank-supported early childhood development (ECD) projects, 1990–2005

Country	Project Title
FREESTANDING ECD PROJECTS	
Bolivia	Integrated Child Development Project
Colombia	Community Child Care and Nutrition Project
India	Integrated Child Development Services I
India	Integrated Child Development Services II
India	Tamil Nadu Integrated Nutrition Project II
Indonesia	Early Childhood Development Project
Kenya	Early Childhood Development Project
Mexico	Initial Education Project
Philippines	Early Childhood Development Project
Uganda	Nutrition and Early Childhood Development Project
SOCIAL SECTOR PROJECTS WITH AN ECD COMPONENT	
Brazil	Innovations in Basic Education Project
Brazil	Municipal Development Project in the state of Paraná
Brazil	Municipal Development Project in the state of Rio Grande do Sul
Chile	Primary Education Improvement Project
El Salvador	Social Sector Rehabilitation Project
Guyana	SIMAP/Health, Nutrition, Water, and Sanitation Project
Venezuela	Social Development Project

Methodology

The methodology used here was to review ECD projects or other social sector projects containing an ECD component that were supported by the World Bank and its partners in developing countries during 1990–2005 (see Table 23.1). All of the projects are now closed. Project information and data were obtained from the World Bank's ImageBank database.

Background

Since 1990, the World Bank has financed a growing number of ECD projects that have successfully supported the healthy development of thousands of the poorest children in the world. Even with these successes, most ECD projects suffer from substantial delays in implementation, as evident from analysis of disbursement patterns. In general, projects having a 5- or 6-year time frame are unlikely to be implemented completely within the proposed time frame and, instead, pass the closing date by 2 to 3 years. These delays are comparable to those in other human development projects.

What are the barriers to timely, on-target delivery of ECD services? What can we learn from externally supported projects that can help countries design and conduct ECD services?

Lessons Learned

The lessons learned cross three stages: design and planning, management and implementation, and monitoring and evaluation.

DESIGN AND PLANNING

Project design forms the basis for subsequent implementation and outcomes. Experience indicates that several factors that have been shown to hamper timely progress were decided on during the design phase and could have been shaped differently. Issues such as the focus and complexity, size and scope, piloting and flexibility, and time frame of a project have considerable impact on future perform- ance. Implementation is affected not only by the content of a design, but also by its readiness when a project starts. Having a plan to build capacity among stakeholder groups is critical. The plan may include informative events, discussions, training sessions, and other forums in which policymakers, donors, and other stakehold- ers are introduced to new ECD concepts and methods and are provided space and opportunity to interact with those who are transferring knowledge of ECD. Possible approaches range from technical training workshops in ECD for policy advisors to policy roundtables with high-level public officials.

Some of the lessons learned follow.

Do Not Plan in Haste

Projects prepared in haste to respond to crises are at greater risk of subsequent delays. Haste in planning results in lack of specificity in the design of a project's components, particularly when organizational or managerial capacity are not developed sufficiently during the planning stage.

Keep the Strategy Simple

The design of a project includes a strategy to reach the objectives formulated. Keeping the strategy simple, focused, and coherent is key.

Devise a Simple, but Cooperative Structure

As with strategy, the structure of a project should not be complex. Very complex organization and management structures may do more harm than good during implementation. The choice of an executing agency for an ECD project strongly affects the complexity of the project. Integrated ECD projects usually involve three ministries, and a decision on the ministry implementing the project has to be made. Often, the executing agency is neither the ministry of education nor the ministry of health, but, rather, the ministry of social and family planning. The executing agency has the difficult task of stimulating cooperation among agencies, which is often problematic. The structure of the ECD project should be as simple as possible, while still allowing for sufficient cooperation. And, ideally, the executing agency will have sufficient experience in managing ECD projects. However, the agency may have other assets that are just as important, so the decision needs to be made carefully.

For example, in selecting an executing agency for the Early Childhood Development Project in Indonesia, the choice was made in favor of the directorate-general of community education, instead of primary education, although the latter had functional responsibility for kindergartens and the former did not have any experience with ECD programs. However, the directorate-general did have one great strength—it was used to working with communities, and community participation was an important aspect of this ECD project. In this case, the choice of executing agency was a trade-off between management capacity and community experience. Insofar as lack of capacity can be resolved through training and technical assistance, selection of the agency with community experience was the better choice.

Do Not Be Overly Ambitious in Scope and Size

The design stage includes deciding about the scope and size of a project. Covering a large area and a large population may be tempting, but an overly ambitious scope and size inevitably lead to problems during implementation. Experience shows that projects designed to cover too many districts at a time or to support too many innovative programs and studies suffer from serious delays in start-up and often do not reach objectives within the time frame specified. In addition, as a project continues, insufficient preparation of management and too much focus on quantity can lead to poor quality outcomes.

MANAGEMENT AND IMPLEMENTATION

Capacity is critical to implementation. A common problem is that scaling up commences without adequate capacity in place. Capacity is a critical precursor to scaling up ECD and should be the first stage of any implementation strategy. Practical capacities in institutional, infrastructural, and service delivery are at the core of successful implementation. Some of lessons learned in management and implementation follow.

Allow Sufficient Time Up Front to Build Institutional Capacity

The major issue in managing ECD projects is a lack of institutional capacity among implementing agencies. This situation leads to substantial initial delays in implementation. Integrated ECD projects typically are prone to suffer from subsequent delays in a country because they are mostly new concepts for the executing agency and are carried out in the poorest regions, with the weakest capacity. In external donor-supported ECD projects, lack of institutional capacity is often the cause of delays in implementation and the inability to meet timetables. Moreover, the ability of sectoral ministries to provide adequate guidelines and standards for implementation is limited.

More time is needed at the beginning of a project to train the executing agency's project officers and staff in development and enforcement of contracts for goods and services. Agencies that have little experience in implementing large-scale programs will encounter difficulties at different stages of implementation. The units in charge of execution should have at least basic skills in project planning, financial management (e.g., procurement, disbursement, accounting), and monitoring.

The time reserved for building institutional capacity often is underestimated or insufficient. Although 1–2 years are needed in many cases, this time is seldom allocated to projects prior to implementation. One example of the lack of local institutional capacity for project management that is typical among ECD projects occurred with the Nutrition and Early Childhood Development Project in Uganda. The design of this project allowed for capacity building in the first year, but this amount of time turned out to be insufficient. Thus, either the time frame for building capacity had to be adjusted to allow for a second year, or the scope of the project had to be scaled down. Sizing down capacity building should not be an option, because problems in management are likely to continue throughout a project and can severely affect outcomes.

Provide High-Quality Technical Assistance

An initial lack of management capacity can be mitigated with training and technical assistance. Using technical assistance wisely, government ministries can address a lack of expertise in selecting or preparing specifications for equipment and in infrastructure design. Technical assistance is available for establishing financial, administrative, and operational procedures, and for designing and executing impact evaluation studies. Such technical assistance has been provided for many ECD projects, including the Social Sector Rehabilitation Project in El Salvador and the Health, Nutrition, Water, and Sanitation Project in Guyana. Technical assistance and training should be of very high quality, and technical assistants should work closely with the ECD project's management team and support them in their management tasks until they have gained enough experience. In the two cases cited, the technical assistance provided resulted in significant strengthening of institutional capacities within the projects' first 2 years. This gain in capacity was accompanied by a reorganization of the functional structures of the ministerial departments implementing the projects, which included redefinition of job descriptions, adoption of a planning approach to management, and definition of operational procedures.

Fund Training as a Precondition to a Project

In the context of projects funded and supported by external donors, the lack of technical and management capacity can be addressed through training—as a precondition to the start of a project. Allocating sufficient funds to develop and finance training before implementing a project is in the interest of borrower countries, for it avoids their having to pay interest charges once a project is started and faces delays because of the need for training. The entire team for a project should know and understand the aim and objectives of the project, the strategies to be followed, and the requirements of their role and function. By the time a project starts, everyone on the team should know *what* to do and then can begin as a team to gain capacity in *how* to do it and ensure its effectiveness.

Often, borrower governments are reluctant to spend loan monies on mostly expensive (foreign) technical assistance even if it is needed and they have the money for it. Instead, they prefer having grants to support this part of the project. Partnerships and bilateral grants tied to ECD projects or specific ECD costs such as training and technical assistance offer one solution. One example is the Early Childhood Development Project in Indonesia, which used a grant from the Dutch government to support a technical assistant.

Avoid a High Turnover of Staff

Despite efforts to build capacity, staff turnover is an issue that needs to be addressed, as it may be detrimental to implementing an ECD project or program. Turnover of staff may lead to loss of management capacity, the need to train new people and refill vacancies, loss of continuity in the project, and a reduced commitment by the team. High turnover is common among ECD projects, and vacancies at important positions sometimes stay unfilled for long periods. Providing for competitive salaries could be a solution for a high turnover caused by a lack of adequate compensation.

Make a Commitment to Training and Supervision of ECD Workers

High-quality and timely training of ECD workers is a sine qua non in ensuring good-quality service delivery. In most developing countries, delivery of ECD services is poor, even for the most basic services, such as monitoring of children's growth and supplementary feeding (e.g., in India's Integrated Child Development Services [ICDS] projects). This poor delivery is associated with inadequate training of staff and village workers. Yet, in most ECD projects and programs, considerable time and money are devoted to training.

Experience shows that executing ECD training successfully is not easy. The key issues in most countries pertain to funding of training; type, level, and content of training; methods; and follow-up.

FUNDING

Although the importance of adequate training is recognized, the funding of training is often insufficient and is the reason service delivery is poor, largely because governments are unwilling to allocate loan funds for training. This situation was resolved in India's ICDS program, for example, by requiring subsequent projects to demonstrate a higher commitment to training as a condition for approval of the project loan, and by establishing new norms and political guidelines requiring training budgets to be at least 3 to 4 times higher than in previous ICDS projects, thus assuring the effectiveness of the loan. Alternative approaches might include, for example, engaging the private sector or nongovernmental organizations to participate in ECD training programs—as was done in Indonesia's Early Childhood Development Project, in which public universities bid for government monies to develop ECD training programs.

TYPE, LEVEL, AND CONTENT

One of government's roles in promoting ECD services is to specify the type, level, and content of training needed for ECD workers. The type of training supported may be specific and short term or longer term, leading to an ECD degree.

The level of training provided should be targeted and realistic. Experience shows that effective training targets the specific expertise needed, is not too broad, and does not embrace expectations that workers cannot achieve. Training that aims to integrate all aspects of ECD into one person is unrealistic. Initially, in the Philippines' Early Childhood Development Project, all four ECD workers (a midwife, day care provider/child development worker, grade 1 teacher, and health specialist) were fully trained in ECD—an effort that turned out to be too ambitious and overlapped with the Philippine Department of Health and Education's separate, specialized training programs. The training was subsequently changed so that all four workers were still trained in ECD, but only in their field of expertise, and the child development worker was fully trained in all aspects to function as the integrator across service networks. The same lesson was learned in India's ICDS projects, in which simultaneous training of one worker in nutrition, health, and preschool education proved almost impossible. Training that fosters close cooperation of workers who are meeting different needs results in a greater overall impact of ECD services.

The content of ECD training must emphasize communication skills. This lesson has been learned from projects in which sufficient or insufficient attention was paid to the interpersonal skills of ECD workers dealing with both children and parents. Children's outcomes in ECD programs strongly depend, in particular, on modifying the behavior of parents. In training ECD workers, priority must therefore be given to improving workers' interpersonal communications skills to foster the necessary home-based behavioral changes that will sustain children's outcomes (e.g., improved nutrition) over time. As demonstrated in Mexico's Initial Education Project, choosing the right communication methods can make a big difference.

METHOD

In community-based programs, a key element of success is training that avoids a lecture approach. Instead, emphasis should be given to participatory training that involves dynamic promoter–participant interactions and is complemented by small-group discussions and frequent reinforcement through weekly meetings. The aim is to develop skills in ECD trainers and village workers, rather than have them learn general principles.

SUPERVISION OR FOLLOW-UP

A last and very important aspect of training is subsequent supervision of village workers. Supervisors are in an excellent position to provide regular, local follow-up training, advise on issues that emerge, function as problem-solvers, and provide general support to ECD workers. However, they are not always employed in these roles. For supervisors to act as trainers and supporters, they need to be adequately trained, and the ratio of supervisors to workers must not be too high. At the start of a project, a ratio of 1:10 or 1:15 could be appropriate, and as supervisors gain more experience, they could increase the number of workers under supervision.

MONITORING AND EVALUATION

To scale up ECD projects, quality monitoring and evaluation mechanisms are needed to identify elements of success and failure and to feed this information back to the designers and coordinators of the scaling-up process. Feedback is critical to identifying inadequacies and creating solutions to overcome them. It is also critical to building supportive evidence of the impact of ECD to justify continued expansion of programs to stakeholders, particularly those who need convincing (e.g., new donors, policymakers).

Monitoring mechanisms track the progress made in a project or program's components—that is, the inputs and outputs achieved. If projects are not monitored, failures in implementation (e.g., delays in inputs, insufficient progress on outputs) can continue unnoticed. Evaluation mechanisms determine whether a project or program's objectives are reached, and they are essential for demonstrating a project's effectiveness. If projects are not evaluated, the impact of a program cannot be ascertained.

Some lessons learned in monitoring and evaluation follow.

Instill a Culture of Planning, Monitoring, and Evaluation Within Project Management

An important aspect of any monitoring and evaluation system is that the users of this system need to fully understand and appreciate the strengths and opportunities that the system offers. For example, in Guyana's Health, Nutrition, Water, and Sanitation Project, staff initially perceived the Management Information System (MIS), which incorporated monitoring and evaluation, only as a financial tool. Integrating systematic monitoring and evaluation into the daily work of managers and project officers took several years. Instilling a culture of planning, monitoring, and evaluation within project management may require additional efforts or a course on the uses of an MIS.

Emphasize Follow-Up and Feedback

After a strong monitoring and evaluation system has been established, and staff become skilled in using it, the project management team can use the results for program improvement—this result, after all, is as important as the MIS itself. Data that are gathered need to be compared with expectations, deviations need to be analyzed, and appropriate actions need to be initiated.

A quality impact evaluation system can be the foundation of a permanent system of future follow-up and longitudinal studies of child development and outcomes. Development of a quality evaluation system is not easy. Two often-mentioned shortcomings of evaluation surveys and systems relate to (a) the control group (e.g., it may be too small, not very well matched, or not available) and (b) the match between baseline and evaluation surveys (e.g., they may be conducted during different seasons). These limitations may impede analyses and understanding of a project's effects in comparison with similar programs or secular trends.

Select Indicators Carefully

The importance of having well-chosen indicators of success and failure cannot be overstated. The indicators also need to be selective, for an abundance of indicators clearly does not help in monitoring a project effectively. Indicators should consist not only of outcome variables, but also of costs in relation to outcomes. Unit costs can be accounted for regularly (e.g., annually) for specific products or outputs. This information should be used for decision making and for future cost-effective improvements in program design.

Conclusion

Assuring the full return that is possible on investments in ECD, whether they are for small-scale projects in specific geographic areas or for larger-scale programs in regions and countries, depends on building capacity in the design and planning of projects among all stakeholders (e.g., policymakers, funders, designers, planners), across all stages of a project. From the outset, during project design and before implementation, decisions have to be made about a project's strategy or focus and its structure, complexity, size, and scope. These decisions are critical to whether a project can actually take off. They are dependent on stakeholders having sufficient knowledge about ECD. Once a project is launched, management and implementation of the project cannot be effective unless the managers and implementers have sufficient professional knowledge and institutional support in ECD practice to perform well. Finally, monitoring and evaluation depend on how supervisors and evaluators work with practitioners to assess progress, identify problems, and create solutions.

RECOMMENDATIONS

One cannot emphasize enough that the lessons learned from the many ECD projects worldwide point to capacity development as the fundamental underpinning of the successful scaling up of ECD projects. Projects that are designed and carried out successfully rely heavily on capacity and technical expertise at each stage, from design and planning to management and implementation, and then monitoring and evaluation, to assure sustainability. Specific recommendations relative to developing this capacity during these three stages are set forth below. They include the lessons learned highlighted previously.

Design and Planning

- Choose project development objectives that are specific, measurable, appropriate, realistic, and time-bound. Plan deliberately, not in haste.
- Formulate a strategy that is simple, focused, and coherent. Project components should be limited in number, and all should strongly contribute to reaching the objectives. Avoid too much complexity in the structure of the project.
- Choose an executing agency that has experience and the necessary capacity to support coordination and cooperation among the various agencies involved.
- Set a sufficiently long time frame to ensure that adequate attention is given to building capacity early. Annual disbursements can be increased as the project is implemented after the initial capacity building phase.
- Decide the scope and size of the project in relation to the institutional capacity available and the time frame desired.
- Assure that good-quality manuals and guidelines for implementation, management, procurement, and disbursement are ready when the project takes effect.

Management and Implementation

- Dedicate sufficient time and money at the beginning of the project to build institutional capacity in the implementing units.
- Provide for high-quality technical assistance from the start to prevent future problems in management and implementation.
- Seek funds for training and make training a precondition for approval of the project.
- Emphasize retention of staff and discourage high turnover.
- Make a commitment to training and supervision of ECD workers, to ensure good-quality service delivery. Assure funds for training; select the type, level, and content of training (based on actual needs); adopt participatory training methods; and follow-up with subsequent supervision of trained ECD workers.

Monitoring and Evaluation

- Build monitoring and evaluation into the project design.

- Instill a culture of planning, monitoring, and evaluation within project management. Use a MIS to measure progress, analyze intermediate results, and provide the necessary feedback to improve implementation.
- Conduct a baseline survey at the start of a project from which to assess progress and evaluate outcomes.
- Emphasize follow-up and feedback. An MIS is of no use when data are not analyzed or used for adjustments and when there is no follow-up on recommended actions.
- Select indicators carefully that can be used to steer the project toward its objectives and to demonstrate its impact. Include output and input variables and costs in relation to outcomes.

24

Building and Strengthening National Systems for Early Childhood Development

Emily Vargas-Barón

Since the 1970s, early childhood development (ECD) systems have expanded rapidly throughout the world. These ECD systems are composed of national multisectoral and sectoral policies, strategic plans, and comprehensive services that are provided at all levels by public and nonpublic sectors of education, health, nutrition, sanitation, and protection. They include institutional, human, training, and financial resources, and monitoring and evaluation activities that interact to improve child and family development. However, most ECD systems do not yet meet national needs for child and family development, and few of them focus adequately on improving the status of vulnerable children.

To become sustainable, ECD programs at community, municipal, and district levels require an enabling and protective policy umbrella, formal legal status, public sector technical and financial support, policy advocacy, standards, guidelines, well-trained human resources, and supervision, combined with effective monitoring and in-service training.

Given decentralization, complex national ECD systems are increasingly planned, implemented, and coordinated at provincial and community levels, as well as at national levels. Annual ECD plans are increasingly being developed at all levels.

Some Challenges

Conducting activities for ECD policy planning and systems development overwhelm many planners and practitioners—and with good reason. The multisectoral approach to ECD requires considerable knowledge and experience in child development and in planning integrated and coordinated programs with the five ECD sectors of health, nutrition, sanitation, education, and protection. Early childhood development planners must have strong negotiation and consensus building skills and be adept at working at all country levels. They should understand how to develop culturally and linguistically appropriate services, and be able to design monitoring and evaluation (M&E) activities for ECD systems.

National politics, policies, and economic and cultural circumstances influence ECD systems, and, consequently, systems vary greatly from country to country. Service decisions are eminently national and cultural and should be made on the basis of evidenced-based recommendations, children's needs, and existing policies and resources. Common attributes across systems can be discerned, and some are described below.

Strengthening ECD policy planning, implementation, and systems constitutes a major challenge (O'Gara et al., 2008). Increasingly, countries are employing the terms "integrated" or "integrated approach" for activities related to multisectoral coordination and service integration with the goal of developing cost-effective and higher quality ECD services through consolidating administrative functions and ensuring services take a holistic approach to child development. However, multisectoral coordination sometimes functions poorly:

- "Institutional cultures" tend to be highly sectoral and do not reward personnel for engaging in multisectoral coordination or service integration.
- Ministerial leaders and personnel are rarely trained in ECD policy planning, participatory processes, negotiation, and consensus building skills.
- Coordination and joint communication strategies are needed to link ECD services of the public and nonpublic sectors.
- Sectoral competition for ministerial budgets is a barrier to multisectoral cooperation.

These challenges have been overcome in several countries, and lessons learned are presented in this chapter.

Objectives

The objectives of this chapter are to (a) present eight key elements required to build and strengthen national ECD systems, (b) provide evidenced-based guidance for ECD systems, and (c) cite relevant experiences and research findings. Research on ECD systems development is limited. Consequently, both field experiences and studies are included. Recommendations for building ECD systems are provided in the concluding section.

MAJOR SECTORS AND ACTORS

ECD systems usually include the five ECD sectors listed above. Increasingly, social protection and inclusion is becoming the "umbrella" for ECD in progressive countries, including several in Europe and Eastern Europe (Bennett, 2008; European

Commission, 2008; OECD, 2006). In Chile, for example, the Intersectoral Social Protection System includes integrated ECD, health, education, and protection services, focusing on vulnerable children (Ministerio de Planificación, 2007).

The main actors in ECD systems are line ministries and their agencies at all levels, institutes, tertiary education establishments, and various ministries such as finance, planning, justice, women's affairs or gender, rural development, and social service ministries. In most nations, civil society and private sector institutions play roles, either in concert with the public sector or separately, depending on institutional cultures and national leadership for ECD. To ensure ECD program and system sustainability and growth in Latin America, governmental structures lead service planning (Vargas-Barón, 2009a). This may prove to be the case in other world regions.

AGE RANGES

Age ranges for ECD systems vary from country to country. Increasingly, national ECD leaders are becoming aware of research results showing that preconception education is essential for improving birth outcomes (Atrash, Johnson, Adams, Cordero, & Howse, 2006; Boulet et al., 2006). However, most nations officially begin their ECD systems at pregnancy. A few nations begin ECD service systems at birth, especially when education is the lead ECD ministry. For some countries, primary school entry is the end period to avoid an overlap with primary education policies. Other countries include the transitional period up to 8 years of age. A few nations extend their ECD systems to age 10, to ensure that children progress well in school and to harmonize ECD with youth policies (e.g., Bosnia and Herzegovina, 2011). These are national decisions. The period from pregnancy to age 8 is generally advocated internationally (Consultative Group, 2009).

SERVICES INCLUDED IN COMPREHENSIVE EARLY CHILDHOOD DEVELOPMENT SYSTEMS

Comprehensive ECD systems include many services for children and parents, from preconception to primary school transition. Box 24.1 presents services often found in ECD systems.

This list is not exhaustive. Some services are designed to extend from preconception to early primary school years, as found in several European nations. Achieving service continuity is a major challenge, especially given vulnerable children's needs. Some ECD services are sectoral, whereas others are multisectoral in structure and/or content.

Each country builds its own ECD system using a variety of ECD programs, with priority given to certain services. Countries affected by conflict, natural dis-

BOX 24.1 Examples of Services in Comprehensive Early Childhood Development (ECD) Systems

---

Preconception to Neonatal
- Preconception education and counseling
- Prenatal education, linked to prenatal health and nutrition care, and preparation for delivery and parenting
- Delivery, neonatal care, health and nutrition activities, plus educational components through home visits and center-based activities

Neonatal to 36 Months
- Parent education and support (parenting services) with components to meet national needs, from health, nutrition, hygiene, safety/injury prevention, and first aid to child development and early education
- Well-child, preventive physical health, special health, and mental health services, including public/insurance schemes, immunizations, health and developmental screenings, and referrals for assessments, and conditional cash transfer services as available
- Intensive and individualized early childhood intervention services for children with developmental delays, malnutrition, HIV/AIDS, and disabilities
- Nutritional rehabilitation services with early childhood stimulation and parent education
- Home- and center-based early child care and development services
- Child and parental rights
- Child and social protection services, as needed
- Home and ECD center sanitation and hygiene services

37 Months to Primary School Entry (Children 3–6 Years)
- Formal preschool or preschool classes in a primary school
- Community center-based informal preschool services
- Home-based preschool activities and groups through continued age-appropriate parent education services
- Feeding programs for preschool-aged children
- Continued health and nutrition care for children 3–6 years of age
- Continued child and parental rights and protective services
- Home and center sanitation and hygiene services

Early Primary School (Children 6–8 or 10 Years)
- Transition services: from home or preschool to primary school
- Parent involvement in primary school activities
- Continued parent education and support

Special Services for Children and Parents Affected by Conflicts or Natural Disasters
- Environmental education and preparedness
- Peace education, conflict resolution, and reconciliation (values and behaviors)

asters, and climate change are developing special ECD services to meet the needs of children, parents, and communities.

Main Elements of Sustainable Early Childhood Development Systems

Figure 24.1 presents eight essential elements for building strong and sustainable national ECD systems. They are discussed below.

EQUITY AND RIGHTS

For an ECD system to be comprehensive and sustainable, ECD policies, strategic plans, legislation, and related sectoral and multisectoral policies should call for equitable ECD services for vulnerable children and parents (Naudeau, Kataoka, Valerio, Neuman, & Kennedy Elder, 2010). Vulnerabilities are often related to ethnicity, language, gender, socioeconomic status, conflicts, disabilities, HIV/AIDS

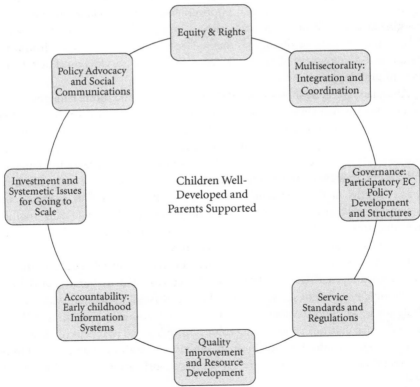

FIGURE 24.1 *Key elements for building strong and sustainable national early childhood development systems*

and other diseases, and a lack of child and parental rights. Early childhood development policies and plans should include strategies to achieve child and parental rights, as stipulated in the Convention on the Rights of the Child and General Comment 7: Implementing Child Rights in Early Childhood (United Nations, 1989, 2006). A recent review of child rights in early childhood emphasizes equity and serving vulnerable children (United Nations, 2010).

If international mandates are not observed, ECD programs mainly serve children of urban, well-to-do parents who can pay for early education and health services (UNESCO, 2006). Nutrition, sanitation, and protective services are also slow to reach disadvantaged children (United Nations, August 2010, Article 35).

The greatest gains in child development accrue to those living in poverty and from marginalized groups (UNESCO, 2006). Yet, these children usually receive far fewer services due to inequities in public investment, inability to pay for private sector services, and limited social policy reforms (MICS analyses in UNESCO, 2006). During the Eastern European transition, countries initially reinforced single sectors, with little regard to equity. This situation is changing as social protection and inclusion policies are developed. Most disadvantaged children in Central and Eastern Europe and the Commonwealth of Independent States (CEECIS) region live in remote rural areas, impoverished urban enclaves, or belong to marginalized ethnic or other underserved groups. Some have developmental delays, malnutrition, or disabilities due to stressors in their home environments (Grantham-McGregor et al, 2007). To serve them, ECD services must be targeted and culturally appropriate.

Abundant research shows that ECD services should be mother tongue–based (MTB). Jessica Ball states, "Research confirms that children learn best in their mother tongue as a prelude to and complement of bilingual and multilingual education" (Ball, 2010, p. 2). Children who learn to read and write in their mother tongue tend to achieve better in school than do those who try to learn in a language and cultural framework that is alien to their homes (Benson, 2002, 2009; Kosonen, 2005). Effective methods exist for developing educational materials, methods, and manuals in mother tongues, but they are not widely used in ECD. Few linguists and educators skilled in MTB education develop comprehensive ECD services, and few early educators are trained in linguistics.

Educational materials and methods must fit parents' cultural belief systems and ideals regarding childrearing (Harkness & Super, 1996; Vargas-Barón, 2010). Early childhood development services should be as consistent as possible with parents' ideals for good child development. Effective innovations in parenting skills are based on each culture's child rearing values, attitudes, and practices (Cole & Cole, 2000). Parents require help to eliminate practices scientifically determined to be dysfunctional or harmful (e.g., genital cutting of girls, suppression of nutritious foods, etc.).

Impoverished children and mothers in conflict- and disaster-prone countries are often negatively affected. During crises, children's basic rights are overlooked unless ECD policies and services are developed during and immediately after an emergency.

Low-birth-weight infants and young children affected by malnutrition and chronic diseases such as HIV/AIDS, malaria, or tuberculosis usually exhibit notable developmental delays (Walker et al., 2007). They require intensive, individualized early childhood intervention (ECI) services (Guralnik, 2011; Shonkoff & Meisels, 2006). Although essential, ECI services are rarely included in nutritional rehabilitation services. However, ECI services are beginning to be developed in low- and middle-income (LAMI) countries, where they are urgently needed.

Gender equity is best achieved during children's early years, including preschool and primary school transition. Equitable beginnings help achieve gender equity in schools (Irwin, Siddiqui, & Hertzman, 2007; Pressoir, 1999; UNICEF, 2007).

MULTISECTORALITY: INTEGRATION AND COORDINATION

Well-integrated and coordinated ECD services should be established to ensure children's holistic development. However, few studies exist regarding national ECD service coordination, and many planners and service practitioners do not understand well the distinctions between multisectoral coordination and service integration. It is generally agreed that a multisectoral approach should be used to develop ECD systems (Naudeau et al., 2010). It is also accepted that ECD policies and plans should contain guidance for multisectoral coordination, service integration, and evaluations to demonstrate that outcomes are being achieved.

Multisectoral Early Childhood Development Services

Multisectoral services include all ECD sectors in an ECD service system. Multisectorality occurs at central, provincial, and community levels. Sectoral and multisectoral services are the main types of ECD services in most countries.

Multisectoral services are not integrated; rather, they are separate sectoral services that are linked with other sectoral services through formal or informal agreements or networks. Each sectoral service has its own administrative center. The multisectoral service system, the *Zones de Convergence* of Cameroon, featured five sectoral "entrance doors" to community ECD services (Institut National de la Statistique and UNICEF, 2007; UNICEF, 2005; Vargas-Barón, 2007). See Figure 24.2.

Founded by Cameroon's Ministry of Planning in Adamaoua Province, the *Zones de Convergence* included public and nonpublic community ECD services. The *Zones de Convergence* were planned at the national level, guided at the provincial level, and flexibly adapted at the local level. This approach is useful when several agencies exist, and national and provincial leaders promote convergence.

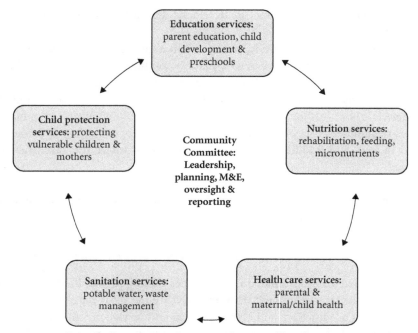

FIGURE 24.2 *Zones de Convergence, Cameroon; five entry "doors" and universal referrals*

Formal coordination includes written interagency agreements among sectors to plan, implement, monitor, and evaluate services. Formal coordination is preferable because when leadership changes, informal agreements may not be honored.

Ministries establish interagency agreements with explicit roles and responsibilities. Within ministries, incentives and support for multisectoral work should be established, including job descriptions stating that multisectoral activities are core responsibilities. Top-level ministerial leaders should model positive multisectoral behaviors and attitudes. Ministerial documents should emphasize the importance of multisectoral ECD coordination and integration. Performance reviews should include interagency work results, plus comments from colleagues in other agencies.

Integrated Early Childhood Development Services

Integrated services unite content, personnel, and resources from two or more ECD sectors in one administrative unit to create a synergy for providing holistic, child-centered, and family-focused services. Examples of integrated ECD services include:

- Personnel receive training in the contents and methods of several sectors, especially to serve impoverished communities (e.g., *Hogares Comunitarios* of the Colombian Institute of Family Welfare [ICBF]; *Madres Guías*, Honduras; *Educa a Tu Hijo*, Cuba).

- Several ministries unify their services, conduct cross-training, pool budgets, and provide "one-stop" services to improve access and service quality (e.g., Integrated ECD Centers, Central African Republic; ECD Center Models, Rwanda.
- Policies mandate that service networks collaborate to reduce costs and expand services (e.g., *Chile Crece Contigo*; ECI Centers in polyclinics and education centers, Belarus).
- A network of integrated service sites work as teams with one administration per site, and sign formal agreements with other local service providers (e.g., IECD Centers, Bosnia and Herzegovina; Any Baby Can and Ounce of Prevention's Educare Centers, United States; Child and Family Centers, Australia).

Figure 24.3 presents the Integrated ECD Centers of Bosnia and Herzegovina that combine services across all five ECD sectors and have systems for M&E, case management, tracking, and referrals.

COMMON CHALLENGES REGARDING MULTISECTORAL PLANNING AND SERVICES

Sectoral ECD planning and services still predominate in most countries, primarily due to national sectoral budgets and sectoral funding from international donors. In spite of this, multisectoral ECD coordination is increasing, and, increasingly, multisectoral and integrated services are going to scale in many countries.

The National Level

Exceptions to sectoral approaches occur, especially when planning and/or finance ministries assume ECD leadership. Chile's Ministry of Planning and Cooperation and the Executive Secretariat for Social Protection developed *Chile Crece Contigo's*

Preconception & Prenatal Education	Parent Education & Support	Early Childhood Intervention	Preschool Play Groups & Support to Preschools	Family Support & Case Management	Monitoring & Evaluation
Home & center-based	Home & center visits & toy & book libraries	Home visitis with center support services	Play groups with parents & children together	Center-based social work services & referrals	Monitoring & evaluation for all ECD services
Complements health services	Fills gaps in 0 to 3 services	Children from 0 to 3+ with delays, malnutrition disabilities	Fills gaps in preschool education	Ensures support for vulnerable children	Assesses inputs, outputs and outcomes

FIGURE 24.3 *Integrated early childhood development centers, Bosnia and Herzegovina*

ECD services and *Chile Solidario* to integrate, improve, and expand services, and break Chile's cycle of poverty. The planning ministries of Cameroon and the Central African Republic were mandated to lead ECD planning and coordination (Cameroon) and integration (Central African Republic). Planning and finance ministries have led consultative processes, convened line ministries for ECD policy planning, and conducted cross-service M&E.

Some assert that integrated approaches to ECD cannot be established at the national level due to competing budgets, differing ministerial guidelines, a lack of experience in integrated programming, and similar arguments. Upon closer examination, this is not universally the case. Several nations (i.e., the United States, Chile, Colombia, Russia, and Lesotho) have combined health and protection ministries, in which ECD is emphasized, resulting in coordinated and integrated services for health and child protection. Protection ministries often are mandated to coordinate services related to the United Nations (UN) Convention on the Rights of the Child (CRC) and other international instruments. In several nations, ECD is found in multisectoral ministries for gender, children/families, community development, national solidarity, and rural development. However, combined education and health ministries are rarely found. These ministries usually have large budgets and compete for funds.

The Provincial Level

Provincial ECD activities for planning, training, supervision, and M&E are usually sectoral unless policies mandate multisectorality. Sometimes, policies instruct provinces to establish multisectoral ECD committees, but many provinces only develop ECD infrastructures once they perceive potential financial and other benefits. Integrated provincial ECD activities are found mainly when communities have strong, integrated systems. If a country lacks a system for provincial ECD planning, coordination, and reporting, it either has a weak ECD system or has not developed a fully decentralized system. Large-scale ECD programs in Latin America were found to have established vertical and horizontal coordination systems (Vargas-Barón, 2009a). It may be posited that the provincial level develops best once community and central ECD systems have been well established and demand provincial support. It might be best for countries to focus first on developing central and community ECD systems, and then add provincial infrastructure.

The Community Level

Well-coordinated or integrated ECD programs that include two or more sectors are usually found at the community level. However, many integrated ECD services begun in communities lack attributes required for successful expansion, such as a legal basis, strong policy support, organizational leadership, effective educational materials, training manuals and systems, and internal M&E systems. They remain pilot programs, and most disappear after a few years (Vargas-Barón, 2009a). Some pilot models, such as *Promesa* in Colombia, developed innovative approaches that subsequently were adopted by larger-scale multisectoral programs (Arango & Nimnicht, 1984).

Some community ECD services are sponsored from either central or provincial levels, and these are more likely to have complete program development processes and other attributes required for growth and sustainability. However, they must have flexible systems that meet local needs and use local resources.

Annual community ECD plans increasingly are developed to access budgetary resources from all levels. Experience has shown that program reports are submitted regularly if they are linked to budgetary provision. Systems for consistent reporting, planning, and budgeting appear to help maintain coordinated and integrated ECD services.

Governance: Participatory ECD Policy Development and Structures

Early childhood development policies should be developed in a participatory manner, and structures and processes for effective policy implementation are required for countries to achieve their policy objectives. The 2010 CRC Report of the UN Secretary General asks nations to: "Establish a framework of laws, policies and programs ensuring that the rights of the child are implemented within a continuum of care (maternal, newborn, child health), education and protection throughout the early years of life . . . . " (United Nations, 2010, Article 61a.)

ECD POLICY DEVELOPMENT

Usually, a sine qua non for building and strengthening ECD systems is an effective policy structure with legal provisions for a sustainable system of services (Vargas-Barón, 2009b). Currently, more than 40 countries have adopted ECD policies, and more than 40 more are developing or close to adopting them (author's count, 2011). However, some industrialized countries have built ECD systems without establishing a multisectoral policy for young children. For example, Belarus has a web of sectoral policies, plans, legislation, and interagency agreements for multisectoral coordination rather than a single ECD policy (Vargas-Barón & Janson, 2009b). Concern has been expressed regarding the viability of this ECD system once the regime changes. The United States has some state-level "children's plans," but the country depends on sectoral legislation at all levels and the private sector to form a "safety-net" of ECD services. Lacking an equitable national ECD policy, many gaps exist that negatively impact the nation's most vulnerable children (Stebbins & Knitzer, 2007).

Guidance for conducting participatory ECD policy planning processes may be found in Vargas-Barón (2005b) and Britto and van Ravens (2009). For policy advocacy and some content options, Naudeau et al. prepared a useful guide (2010).

Countries that have forged strong multisectoral agreements have drafted and adopted ECD policies and plans in from 18 months to 3 years. Others drafted their policies but have been slow to adopt them. Ghana took 10 years to adopt its policy. Cameroon drafted its policy and plan 4 years ago, but, because highly participatory planning approaches were used, many designated services have been implemented even without policy adoption. Each country situation is different, but participatory policy-planning processes are well understood. If followed, most countries should be able to develop, adopt, and implement their ECD policies quite effectively.

In addition to ECD policies, most countries develop 3- to 5-year strategic plans, and they also prepare annual action plans. Some countries opt for brief "ECD policy statements." Usually, they hope to gain commitments for a simpler multisectoral policy as a basis for a more detailed ECD plan (i.e., Bosnia and Herzegovina and Cambodia). Some nations use restrictive policy formats that stipulate the preparation of brief policy statements. Policy adoption tends to be lengthy in contrast to easier approval for plans by councils of ministers or other officials.

Research is needed on the ECD policy implementation, but some cautious observations may be made. Early childhood development policies and plans should reinforce elements of other sectoral and multisectoral policies dealing with young children and parents. They should fill existing policy and service gaps with innovative ECD strategies and activities, and also propose improvements in existing ECD services. Evaluated and promising services can be proposed for expansion, in accordance with cost-effectiveness measures and projected service needs. Early childhood development policies and plans should call for harmonizing the elements of existing policies and services. They usually establish an organizational structure for policy implementation and provide guidance to ensure that each agency becomes fully operational. Central, provincial, and community structures should include membership criteria, terms of reference, operational guidelines, delegated planning and budgetary authority, responsibilities for vertical/horizontal coordination, M&E, and reporting linked to planning processes.

National-Level Structures

A multisectoral ECD council is often established that includes ECD ministers and directors of leading civil society and private sector agencies. Because these councils usually meet infrequently, a multisectoral ECD technical committee of leading professionals from each of the organizations on the council is often established and meets frequently. The technical committee reviews reports, plans, and proposals before they are sent to the council and works with the ECD operational agency.

To ensure ECD policies and plans are well implemented, a permanent operational "ECD motor" is needed, with an organizational structure, terms of reference, and annual core budget. Often, this is a department within the lead ECD ministry. Alternatively, this ECD motor may be a public sector "executive agency" or a semi-autonomous agency. Relatively few such agencies have been created to date. Colombia's semi-autonomous institute (ICBF) has been successful in meeting many of its goals, and it was able to function nationwide even during violent national events in that country. Its success is due principally to its permanent legal status, sustained funding from a 3% payroll tax, ability to meet community service demands, and enduring presidential support (Vargas-Barón, 2006).

The ECD motor functions as the "secretariat" of the multisectoral council and technical committee, prepares an annual plan and budget based on reports and plans from communities and provinces, and reports to the technical committee, which in turn reports to the council. The ECD motor implements the ECD policy, carries out council decisions, guides coordination at all levels, and prepares work plans for selected multisectoral or integrated activities. It ensures agencies in charge of ECD content prepare, field-test, revise, produce, and distribute educational and training materials for pre- and in-service training. It guides M&E, reporting, and program and financial planning in a continuous feedback loop, and it prepares annual plans for policy advocacy and social communications.

It appears that countries whose ECD policy or plan did not establish an operational unit have been unable to implement their policies effectively. Further, lacking a single point of contact for ECD, countries are unable report reliable ECD data to international agencies.

Lead Ministry for ECD

The lead ministry for ECD is often the education ministry. A few countries have designated the ministry of health, protection, planning/finance, or a multisectoral ministry for children and families as the lead. Ministries such as justice, sanitation, and rural affairs cooperate with ECD activities but are not selected as lead ministries.

If education is the lead agency, it must reach out to other ministries to ensure their full involvement, but this does not always happen. To improve learning outcomes and the internal efficiency of education systems, the education ministry should collaborate closely with health and protection ministries to improve preventive and basic maternal–child health care; nursery and preschool feeding, nutrition, and sanitation services; special health care; and women's and children's protective services. Parent educators, nursery and preschool teachers, and others need cross-training in health, nutrition, hygiene, and other topics.

Services for Children 0–3

Some education ministries lack mandates to serve children aged 0–3 years. However, due to neuroscience research (Shonkoff & Phillips, 2000) and demands for parent education, quality nursery care, and ECI services, they are increasingly focusing on "0–3 services."

In the absence of an education policy mandate for serving infants and toddlers, health ministries and nonpublic agencies have partially assumed this role. Occasionally, these services have been placed with protection ministries, along with services for abused children and orphanages. Except for ECI services in health ministries, child development services conducted by health or protection ministries rarely develop standards, regulations, educational curricula, materials, methods, pre- and in-service training, and M&E.

Provincial-Level Structures

Some countries have established provincial multisectoral ECD committees to conduct activities mandated at the national level and to respond to requests for support from communities. They often play roles for multisectoral coordination, plan multisectoral or integrated services, and provide community support. ECD policies should include roles, responsibilities, and guidance for provincial ECD structures.

Community-Level Structures

Community ECD committees frequently become subcommittees of municipal councils. Oversight by parents, ECD committees, the municipal council, traditional or religious leaders, and others was found in all successful community services in Latin America (Vargas-Barón, 2009a). Committee members are often dedicated because they work for community children, and they usually participate in ECD activities. Community ECD structures are greatly influenced by local social organization and leadership methods. If the communal organization is strong, then ECD committees tend to be effective. In scattered hamlets or communities affected by violence, it is challenging to develop community ECD committees, and they need considerable technical support and training.

Legislation, Standards, Regulations, and Agreements

In addition to helping with ECD policies and plans, parliamentarians work with ministries to establish ECD legislation, service standards, guidelines, regulations, and interinstitutional agreements to achieve system-wide quality assurance.

ECD policies and plans often list ECD legal documents that need to be developed. However, without policy mandates, strong technical leadership, and accountability mechanisms, these documents tend to be ineffective. Existing legal instruments should be reviewed, and activities to revise or replace them should be included in ECD policies or plans.

Some ECD specialists doubt the value of ECD service and personnel standards in LAMI countries. Others advocate the use of "minimum standards." However, ECD specialists invariably call for quality standards that are flexible and implemented progressively. Although these legal instruments are called for in ECD policies and plans, they are rarely included in them. An exception was Kenya's standards, which were appended to their ECD policy (Ministry of Education, Kenya, 2006a,b).

Formal interagency ECD agreements are usually called for in ECD policies, including partnerships for multisectoral planning, coordination, M&E, and reporting.

Quality Improvement and Resource Development

In addition to structural issues and key program outcomes as called for by the Organization for Economic Cooperation and Development (OECD, 2006), ECD systems and resource centers should improve the quality of the contents of ECD systems and their transmission through pre- and in-service training programs. Culturally and linguistically appropriate curricula, educational materials, training manuals, teaching methods, media, and M&E instruments are called for in ECD policies. Materials and instruments should be field tested, revised, produced, and distributed in sufficient quantities before training begins. Early childhood development policies also call for the development of pre- and in-service training systems that build on existing training resources and fill in gaps. Tertiary institutions are reinforced to provide training. Although international nongovernmental organizations and other partners often provide shorter term training of trainers, sustainable national in-service systems are essential and usually require improvement and expansion.

Distance learning is increasingly being used to improve ECD services. Evaluations of the ECD Virtual University show that the program is high in quality, and its graduates have positively impacted national ECD policy and services (Vargas-Barón, 2005a; Vargas-Barón & Joseph, 2011). Although distance learning can augment national training systems, it cannot replace them.

To reach vulnerable groups, it is necessary to train ECD professionals, paraprofessionals, and volunteers from ethnic groups, rural and marginalized groups, and persons with disabilities. Paraprofessionals and volunteers require frequent in-service training, monitoring, and supervision to ensure good program quality. In-service training is best provided through continuous systems from central, provincial, and community levels. To provide cost-effective services, field supervisors should be prepared to provide frequent in-service training sessions, combined with monitoring and supervision.

Accountability: ECD Management Information Systems

Accountability for quality improvement and equity is essential for building and strengthening ECD systems. However, comprehensive and unified national systems for ECD accountability are rarely developed. Such systems should include project-level M&E, unique codes for children and parents, privacy rights, case management from birth registration onward, and provisions for referrals, tracking, and interagency coordination.

The lack of national systems for accountability is especially due to the nature of multisectoral ECD services and a pervasive lack of funding for M&E. Given needs for national ECD databases and "single points of contact," countries should develop management information systems (MIS) and/or M&E systems for ECD. They would use selected indicators from existing education and health MIS systems, Demographic Health Surveys (DHS), and Multiple Indicator Cluster Surveys (MICS), plus add some indicators regarding ECD policy implementation processes, services, children, and parents. Although some international indicators exist for the five ECD sectors, few countries have developed child development indicators with age bands and other types of service outcomes.

Most ECD policies or strategic plans provide a wide variety of policy indicators, and a recent study assessed 283 discrete types of indicators found in 51 policy instruments of 39 countries (Vargas-Barón & Schipper, 2012). It was also discovered that accountability systems to measure ECD policy indicators have rarely been developed as expected. Through a broad coalition of agencies led by the UN Educational, Scientific, and Cultural Organization (UNESCO), an international index of core ECD indicators is currently under preparation, and this initiative may help promote more interest in the development of national ECD M&E systems and databases keyed to achieving national targets.

Investment and Systemic Issues for Going to Scale

ECD investments should be increased to expand coverage and ensure services are sustainable, high in quality, and cost-effective. Increasingly, studies are being conducted on ECD costs and finance, including in-kind support (Coordinators' Notebook, 2008; Hueston et al., 2007; Levin & Schwartz, 2006; Myers, 2008). Apart from routine preschool education budgets, comprehensive ECD budgeting tools are needed for all five ECD sectors, plus integrated services.

National ECD investment targets have been recommended regarding gross domestic product (GDP) and the proportion of ministerial budgets devoted to ECD (Coordinators' Notebook, 2008; GTZ, 2009). Each nation should establish investment targets and budgets in their ECD policy and plan.

Investment in system-wide expansion, improvement, and sustainability has critical dimensions (Tinajero, 2010; Vargas-Barón, 2009a). Studies demonstrate that investment is only one requirement for achieving scale. Legal status, policy support, coordination, and program development processes are just as important.

In addition to large-scale programs, another way to expand coverage is to create a mosaic of services with common standards, high-quality inputs, joint training, and M&E. If an ECD system depends upon pilot programs, it will not achieve adequate program coverage. Most pilots face barriers to expanding coverage equitably, and few are designed to go to scale. Elements for taking high-quality ECD services to scale are listed in Box 24.2 (Vargas-Barón, 2009a).

BOX 24.2 Essential Elements for Going to Scale

1. Secure and maintain strong leadership, legal, and policy support for early childhood development (ECD) programs.
2. Design programs to go to scale from the outset.
3. Prepare and implement well-targeted, comprehensive, culturally appropriate, and community-based ECD programs.
4. Include internal and external procedures for program coordination, monitoring, evaluation, accountability, reporting, and revision.
5. Prepare a sound and diversified investment plan.
6. Prepare to face typical barriers to achieving program expansion and quality by studying other programs' experiences.
7. Develop partnerships with pilot programs sponsored by civil society institutions and the private sector.

Policy Advocacy and Social Communications

Policy advocacy and ECD media campaigns are required for national leaders, parents, and communities. Policy advocacy is needed before, during, and after ECD policies and plans are developed. Policy briefs should be prepared for decision makers, presenting short-, medium-, and long-term reasons for investing in ECD, and policy advocacy meetings promote high-level dialogue. Advocacy workshops should be held at all levels because parent and women's groups have often secured increased support for ECD. In Colombia, unionized women workers were instrumental in securing the payroll tax for children's services (Vargas-Barón, 2006).

Policy implementation usually includes activities for advocacy. Early childhood development panels are held on radio and television, and Op-Ed pieces and articles are prepared. Kits are prepared to encourage parliamentarians and other decision makers to expand investments in ECD.

Annual ECD communication plans should include media campaigns through radio, television, print media, banners, posters, and national children's days. Culturally adapted and linguistically appropriate messages from parent education services are selected for reinforcement through national media.

Recommendations for Building Strong and Sustainable ECD Systems

All eight elements for building strong and sustainable ECD systems should be addressed during ECD policy planning processes and reviewed annually to assess implementation progress. Selected recommendations for each element are presented here.

EQUITY AND RIGHTS

- Ensure services are universal and equitable, paying special attention to meeting the needs of vulnerable children from ethnic and linguistic minorities; those living in poverty or with special health, nutritional, or developmental needs; and victims of domestic or community violence, natural disasters, or other major stressors.
- Provide culturally and linguistically appropriate ECD services for children of all ethnic groups in each country, and ensure mother tongue–based educational materials are used.
- Build strong linkages among ECD services and CRC implementation and reporting activities, while helping to ensure provisions of the CRC and General Comment 7 are fully implemented in each country.

MULTISECTORALITY: INTEGRATION AND COORDINATION

- Promote and achieve multisectoral coordination at all levels through ECD policies and strategic plans, with an emphasis placed on multisectoral planning and coordination at the national level, and service integration and coordination at the local level, to the extent advisable in each country.
- Prepare formal agreements for intersectoral and multisectoral ECD activities, and ensure roles and responsibilities are clearly defined and energetically pursued at each level.
- Create an "institutional culture" in ECD-related ministries that promotes and rewards multisectoral coordination and integrated activities, and partnerships and networks for planning and implementing well-coordinated and integrated services.

GOVERNANCE: PARTICIPATORY EARLY CHILDHOOD POLICY DEVELOPMENT AND STRUCTURES

- Develop and implement ECD policies accompanied by comprehensive and detailed strategic plans, annual action plans, and budgets, and establish an effective national multisectoral ECD council and/or an ECD technical committee in each country.
- Ensure a ministerial department or a semi-autonomous institute is officially established as an "ECD motor" in each country, with an organizational structure, terms of reference, and a core budget to implement the ECD policy and strategic plan, and to conduct continuous reporting and planning activities.
- Promote and enable decentralized and comprehensive municipal planning for ECD services through integrating some early childhood services, ensuring multisectoral coordination, providing municipalities with

continuous pre- and in-service training, offering timely and quality services, and conducting processes for internal program monitoring and evaluation, combined with effective community oversight.

SERVICE STANDARDS AND REGULATIONS

- Include provisions for developing ECD service and personnel standards, guidelines, and regulations in all ECD policies and strategic plans.
- Develop and implement jointly agreed upon service and personnel standards, guidelines, and regulations, including program policies and procedures for specific services, such as ECI.
- State time periods for instrument review and revision, to maintain flexibility and openness to improvement.

QUALITY IMPROVEMENT AND RESOURCE DEVELOPMENT

- Ensure the development of culturally and linguistically appropriate, high-quality curricula, educational materials, methods, and media for all ECD services, with sufficient time for field-testing, revision, production, and distribution.
- Improve human resources through developing a pre- and in-service ECD training system for professionals, paraprofessionals, and volunteers, with a special focus on cost-effective supervisors who train, monitor, and supervise local services.
- Evaluate program inputs, outputs, and outcomes, and use the results to improve program contents and training systems.

ACCOUNTABILITY: EARLY CHILDHOOD DEVELOPMENT MANAGEMENT INFORMATION SYSTEMS

- Develop ECD MIS and/or M&E systems with national ECD indicators and targets for ECD policies and strategic plans, in collaboration with other relevant national databases in each country.
- Design national ECD database systems with unique codes for children and parents, case management, referrals, tracking, and interagency coordination.
- Conduct impact evaluations of all leading ECD programs, with the goal of improving them over time.

INVESTMENT AND SYSTEMIC ISSUES FOR GOING TO SCALE

- Develop cost studies, projections, and simulations for program assessment, improvement, and expansion.

- Establish national ECD investment targets, including both amounts and deadlines.
- Take successful multisectoral and integrated ECD services to provincial or national scale, as needed.
- Use integrated and coordinated approaches to develop "mosaics of services and support activities" and to enable innovative, high-quality early childhood services to achieve scale.

POLICY ADVOCACY AND SOCIAL COMMUNICATIONS

- Conduct policy advocacy activities before, during, and after establishing an ECD policy and strategic plan, and prepare and implement an annual policy advocacy plan.
- Prepare an annual ECD communication plan for and with communities and parents, focusing on key parenting and child development messages.

Conclusion

To achieve a high level of innovation and ensure high service quality, research on ECD must be conducted continuously in each country. However, due to the paucity of research on ECD systems, coordination, and service integration, a global research initiative should be established with a website, policy briefs, and program exchange visits focused on ECD research and evaluation. Specific research areas could include:

- Assessment of cultural and mother tongue–based ECD services and their results
- Baseline and pre–post evaluations combined, where possible, with experimental or quasi-experimental designs to measure outcomes reliably
- Effectiveness of pre- and in-service national ECD training systems
- Analysis of "institutional cultures" of ministries and agencies that favor multisectoral coordination and/or integrated services
- Methods and effectiveness of vertical and horizontal coordination systems at all levels
- Effectiveness of alternative national approaches to home visits, group sessions, and center-based services
- Effectiveness of ECD team-building strategies for establishing integrated services
- Analysis of ECD costs and finance in relation to effectiveness and efficiency
- Effectiveness of ECD policies and strategic plans in achieving implementation objectives, and especially for improving birth, child, and parenting outcomes

In conclusion, decision makers in all nations should identify those ECD outcomes required to achieve national development goals. Fundamental decisions regarding roles of the state, civil society, and private sector should be made in order to provide essential ECD services and support parents as the best nurturers and teachers of their children.

To build ECD systems, nations are increasingly focusing on decentralized planning, service implementation, and oversight, as well as on central normative leadership, investment, and coordination. Quality assurance systems are required to ensure ECD services are high in quality, equitable, and effective. Above all, it is the dedication of inspired and hard-working ECD specialists, community paraprofessionals, and volunteers that make ECD services successful and ensure all children will achieve their potential.

Acknowledgments

Appreciation is expressed to Charles M. Super and other early childhood specialists who reviewed this chapter: Selena Bajraktarevic, Brigitte Izabiriza, Itana Kovacevic, Natalia Mufel, Michelle Neuman, Eveline Pressoir, Sheldon Shaeffer, and Alfredo Tinajero. Correspondence should be addressed to the author at vargasbaron@hotmail.com.

References

Arango, M. M., & Nimnicht, G. P. (1984). *Algunas reflexiones sobre el problema de la ampliación* de alternatives de atención a la niñez a nivel regional y nacional. Bogotá, CO: CINDE and Bernard van Leer Foundation.

Atrash, H. K., Johnson, K., Adams, M., Cordero, J. F. & Howse, J. (2006). Preconception care for improving perinatal outcomes: The time to act. *Maternal Child Health Journal, 10*, S3–S11.

Ball, J. (2010). *Enhancing learning of children from diverse language backgrounds: Mother tongue-based bilingual or multilingual education in the early years.* Paris: UNESCO.

Bennett, J. (2008). *Discussion Paper: Improving the well-being of young children in Europe: the role of early years' services.* Brussels, Belgium: Eurochild Secretariat.

Benson, C. (2002). Real and potential benefits of bilingual progammes in developing countries. *International Journal of Bilingual Education and Bilingualism, 5*(6), 303–317.

Benson, C. (2009). Designing effective schooling in multilingual contexts: The strengths and limitation of bilingual "models." In A. Mohanty, M. Panda, R. Phillipson, & T. Skutnabb-Kangas (Eds.), *Multilingual education for social justice: Globalising the local* (pp. 60–78). New Delhi: Orient Blackswan.

Bosnia and Herzegovina. (2011). *Policy for early childhood development in the Federation of Bosnia and Herzegovina.* Sarajevo, Bosnia and Herzegovina: Federation of Bosnia and Herzegovina.

Bosnia and Herzegovina. (2011). *Policy for improving early childhood development in Republika Srpska.* Banja Luka, Bosnia and Herzegovina: Republika Srpska.

Boulet, S., Parker, C., & Atrash, H. (2006). Preconception care in international settings. *Maternal Child Health Journal, 10,* S29–S35.

Britto, P. R., & van Ravens, J. (2009). *Sustainable national policies for ECD* (Concept Note). New Haven, CT: Yale University.

Cole, M., & Cole, S. R. (2000). *The development of children* (4th ed.). New York: Worth.

Consultative Group on Early Childhood Care and Development. (2009). *Four cornerstones.* Toronto: Consultative Group on Early Childhood Care and Development. Retrieved from http://www.ecdgroup.com/

Coordinators' Notebook. (2008). *Early childhood investment, finance and costs.* Toronto: Consultative Group on Early Childhood Care and Development.

Engle, P. L., Black, M. M., Behrman, J. R., DeMello, M. C., Gertler, P. J., Kapiriri, L., et al. (2007). Strategies to avoid the loss of developmental potential in more than 200 million children in the developing world. *The Lancet, 369,* 229–242.

European Commission. (2008, 2010). *Joint reports on social protection and social inclusion.* Brussels, BE: European Union.

Grantham-McGregor, S., Bun Cheung, Y., Cueto, S., Glewwe, P., Richer, L., Trupp, B., et al. (2007). Developmental potential in the first 5 years for children in developing countries. *The Lancet, 369,* 60–70.

GTZ. (2009). *Getting the basics right: Contribution of early childhood development to quality, equity and efficiency in education.* Eschborn, DE: GTZ.

Guralnik, M. J. (2011). Why early intervention works: A systems perspective. *Infants and Young Children, 2*(1), 6–28.

Harkness, S. , & Super, C. M. (Eds.). (1996). *Parents' cultural belief systems: Their origins, expressions, and consequences.* New York: Guilford Press.

Hueston, W. J., Quattlebaum, R. G., & Bentch, J. L. (2008). How much money can early prenatal care for teen pregnancies save: A cost-benefit analysis. *Journal of the American Board of Family Medicine, 21*(3), 184–190.

Institut National de la Statistique et UNICEF. (2007, March). Étude comparée des résultats des enquêtes EBA-ESA-MICS3: Suivi et *évaluation de la situation des enfants et des femmes dans l'Adamaoua-Zone de Convergence.* Yaoundé, CM: Direction Générale, Institut National de la Statistique et UNICEF.

Irwin, L. G., Siddiqui, A., & Hertzman, C. (2007). *Early child development: A powerful equalizer. Final report for the World Health Organization's Commission on the social determinants of health.* Vancouver, BC: Human Early Learning Partnership.

Kosonen, K. (2005). Education in local languages: Policy and practice in Southeast Asia. In *First languages first: Community-based literacy programs for minority language contexts in Asia (pp. 96–134).* Bangkok: UNESCO Bangkok.

Levin, H. M., & Schwartz, H. (2006). *Costs of early childhood care and education programs* (Background paper for the Education for All Global Monitoring Report). New York: National Center for the Study of Privatization in Education, Teachers College, Columbia University.

Ministerio de Planificación. (2007). *Chile Crece Contigo: Sistema de protección integral a la primera infancia.* Santiago, CL: Secretaría Ejecutiva de Protección Social.

Ministry of Education, Kenya. (2006a). *Early childhood development service standard guidelines.* Nairobi, KE: Republic of Kenya.

Ministry of Education, Kenya. (2006b). *National early childhood development policy.* Nairobi, KE: Republic of Kenya.

Myers, R. G. (2008). *Costing early childhood care and development programs* (Outline Outreach Paper No. 5). The Hague: Bernard van Leer Foundation.

Naudeau, S., Kataoka, N, Valerio, A., Neuman, M., & Kennedy Elder, L. (2010). *Investing in young children: An early childhood development guide for policy dialogue and project preparation.* Washington, DC: World Bank.

OECD. (2006). *Starting Strong II: Early childhood education and care.* Paris: Education Directorate of the Organisation for Economic Co-operation and Development.

O'Gara, C., Long, L, & Vargas-Barón, E. (2008). Policy options for early childhood development in developing nations. In W. K. Cummings & J. H. Williams (Eds.), *Policy-making for education reform in developing countries: Policy options and strategies* (pp. 27–64). Lanham, MD: Rowman and Littlefield Publishers, Inc.

Pressoir, E. (1999). *Promouvoir la perspective de genre dans les soins au jeune enfant pour sa survie, sa croissance et son développement* (Mainstreaming gender in early child care for survival, growth and development). Dakar, Senegal: UNICEF/WACARO.

Shonkoff, J. , & Meisels, S. (Eds.). (2006). *Handbook of early childhood intervention* (2nd ed.). New York: Cambridge University Press.

Shonkoff, J. P., & Phillips, D. A. (2000). *From neurons to neighborhoods: The science of early childhood development.* Washington, DC: National Academy Press.

Stebbins, H., & Knitzer, J. (2007). *State early childhood policies.* New York: National Center for Children in Poverty.

Tinajero, A. R. (2010). *Scaling-up early childhood development in Cuba. Cuba's Educate Your Child Program: Strategies and lessons learned from the expansion process* (Working Paper No. 16). Washington, DC: Wolfensohn Center for Development at The Brookings Institution.

United Nations. (1989). *Convention on the rights of the child.* New York: Author.

United Nations. (2006). *Implementing child rights in early childhood* (40th session, 2005) [UN General Comment No. 7]. New York: Author.

United Nations. (2010, August 2). *Status of the Convention on the Rights of the Child: Report of the Secretary General, Section 4: Implementing child rights in early childhood* (65th session, 2010, Item 65). New York: Author.

UNESCO. (2000). *Dakar framework for action, Education for All: Meeting our collective commitments.* World Education Forum, Dakar, Senegal. Paris: UNESCO.

UNESCO. (2006). *EFA global monitoring report: Strong foundations.* Paris, France: Author.

UNICEF. (2005). *Rapport d'évaluation externe de la stratégie de convergence: Document Intermédiaire.* Yaoundé, CR: Author.

UNICEF. (2007). *State of the world's children 2007: Women and children: The double dividend of gender equality.* New York: Author.

UNICEF. (2009). *The state of the world's children: Special edition celebrating 20 years of the Convention on the Rights of the Child.* New York: Author.

Vargas-Barón. E. (2005a). *Impact evaluation: Early childhood development virtual university in sub-Saharan Africa.* Washington, DC: World Bank.

Vargas-Barón, E. (2005b). *Planning policies for early childhood development: Guidelines for action.* Paris: UNESCO, UNICEF, ADEA, Red Primera Infancia. (English, French, Spanish and Russian.)

Vargas-Barón, E. (2006). *Payroll taxes for child development: Lessons from Colombia* (UNESCO Policy Brief on Early Childhood). Paris: UNESCO.

Vargas-Barón, E. (2007). Community evaluation of an integrated health access system in Cameroon. In *Global forum for health research: Helping correct the 10/90 gap*. Geneva: Global Forum for Health Research.

Vargas-Barón, E. (2009a). *Going to scale: Early childhood development in Latin America*. Washington, DC: The RISE Institute.

Vargas-Barón, E. (2010). *Future challenges of MTB-MLE for ECD: Research, evaluation and collaboration* (PowerPoint Presentation). Bangkok: The RISE Institute.

Vargas-Barón, E., & Janson, U. (2009b). *Early childhood intervention, Special education and inclusion: A focus on Belarus*. Geneva: UNICEF.

Vargas-Barón, E., & Joseph, L. (2011). *Participant outcomes: Early childhood development Virtual University*. Washington, DC: World Bank.

Vargas-Barón, E., & Schipper, J. (2012). *The Review of Policy and Planning Indicators in Early Childhood*. Paris: UNESCO.

Walker, S. P, Wachs, T. D., Meeks Gardiner, J., Lazoff, B., Wasserman, G. A., Pollitt, E., et al. (2007). Child development: Risk factors for adverse outcomes in developing countries. *The Lancet, 369*, 145–157.

25

Effective Financing
Alexandria Valerio and Marito H. Garcia

Early childhood development (ECD) is a fundamental building block in the formation of human capital (Heckman, Moon, Pinto, Savalyev, & Yavitz, 2009; Naudeau, 2009; UNESCO, 2006; Verdisco, 2008). A wide body of research demonstrates the economic and social returns of investing in ECD and identifies program inputs that are effective at promoting healthy and nurturing environments for children (Aos, Lieb, Mayfield, Miller, & Pennucci, 2004; Committee for Economic Development, 2006; Karoly & Bigelow, 2005; Masse & Barnett, 2002; Nores, Belfield, Barnett, & Schweinhart, 2005; Reynolds, Temple, Robertson, & Mann, 2001, World Bank et al., 2011). Although the benefits of investing in ECD, including significant long-term spillover effects, are well established, competing demands for funding often pit these investments against other social and economic priorities. As a result, countries can face critical ECD finance shortfalls, which ultimately impact the quality, comprehensiveness, and coverage of the ECD services.

Realizing the potential returns to investing in ECD requires a coherent financing strategy that sustains access to quality services. However, comparing ECD finance across countries to identify effective and sustainable finance practices is a challenge. First, ECD encompasses a range of different services that are targeted at diverse populations including parents, infants, and preschool-aged children (Britto, Yoshikawa, & Boller, 2011). Additionally, countries often draw upon a range of public and private resources to fund these services (Belfield, 2006). To address the challenge that this heterogeneity poses, this chapter presents a conceptual framework that provides a set of normative elements for effective ECD finance. The framework also identifies several contextual factors that may need to be taken into account when designing strategies to finance a set of ECD objectives.

The chapter begins with a brief description of the heterogeneity of ECD programs in order to place ECD investments in context. The chapter then describes commonly used revenue raising and revenue allocation mechanisms, and argues against finding a single "best" approach to financing ECD. Given that much of the data on ECD financing is more readily accessible from high-income countries, this section draws on that data, in addition to information available from low- and middle-income (LAMI) countries. The third section of the chapter presents the framework and identifies three elements to keep in mind when designing an ECD financing strategy; namely, sustainability, equity, and administrative simplicity. The framework also lays out two sets of contextual factors that can impact the effectiveness of a finance strategy. Finally, the chapter offers several recommendations to policymakers seeking to design or strengthen effective finance strategies for ECD programs.[1]

Putting Early Childhood Development Investments in Context

Distinctive features of ECD programs include the sheer heterogeneity of services falling under the umbrella of ECD interventions and the wide range of target groups covered under different programs (UNESCO, 2006). Vegas and Santibáñez (2010) provide a comprehensive picture of the services and policy interventions usually carried out under the umbrella of ECD. As Figure 25.1 shows, services draw upon a number of sectors from health to education to social protection and nutrition, and can differ substantially in the scope and intensity of service delivery. Moreover, providers typically offer services in different settings, including at home, in health clinics, community centers, day care facilities, preschools, or churches, and these often operate independently of one another. This heterogeneity in programs and variety of service delivery mechanisms makes direct comparisons of costs and finance strategies a challenge.

Amidst this heterogeneity, the bulk of comparative data on ECD cost structures and finance strategies center around preschool, a recognized educational level (ISCEDO) in the United Nations Educational, Scientific, and Cultural Organization

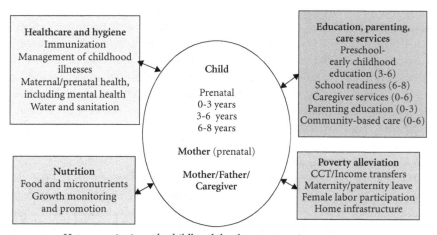

FIGURE 25.1 *Heterogeneity in early childhood development services*

Reprinted with permission from Vegas, E., & Santibáñez, L. (2010). *The promise of early childhood development in Latin America and the Caribbean.* Washington, DC: World Bank.

(UNESCO) international standard of classification (UNESCO, 2011); therefore, we focus a bit more specifically on this program modality, given the availability of data. It is important to note, however, that preschools target only one of the age cohorts and represent only one of the service types illustrated in Figure 25.1. Notwithstanding this limitation, a glance at the variations in the levels of funding for and enrollment in preschool can yield useful insights. For example, data from the Organization for Economic Cooperation and Development (OECD) demonstrates a broad acceptance of the importance of investing in preschool, albeit with great variation in the levels of investment across countries. On average, OECD member states' investments in preschool for children aged 3–6 represents 0.49% of gross domestic product (GDP), with public sources accounting for 0.435% of GDP (Tayler & Bennett, 2006).

UNESCO's Education for All (EFA) Global Monitoring Report 2007 also uses the preschool setting to provide a snapshot of ECD levels of investments in the developing world. EFA, which examines countries' ECD investments as a percentage of gross national product (GNP), finds that Central and Eastern Europe have the highest level of public expenditure on preschool—on average, 0.5% of GNP. Latin America and the Caribbean ranked second as a region, with an average of 0.2% of GNP, whereas countries in Sub-Saharan Africa have the lowest levels of public expenditure on preschool. There is also evidence of variation within the regions. Within Eastern Europe, public expenditures can range from a high of 1.0% of GNP in Belarus to a low of 0.3% in Estonia and Romania; in Latin America and the Caribbean, expenditures range from a high of 0.6% of GNP in Guyana to a low of 0.02% in Nicaragua; and in Sub-Saharan Africa intraregional variation is evident in the difference in spending among the Seychelles, Kenya, and Senegal, which spend 0.5%, 0.1%, and 0.01% of GNP, respectively.

Another trend that the EFA Global Monitoring Report reveals is that, across the world, preschool represents a relatively minor proportion of overall education expenditures. Public investment in preschool as a percentage of total education spending ranges from 10% to less than 1% of total spending. Developing countries with at least 10% of public education expenditure dedicated to preschool included Belarus, Bulgaria, Costa Rica, Croatia, the Czech Republic, Guyana, Hungary, Mexico, Mongolia, Moldova, the Slovak Republic, and Slovenia. Several countries have expenditure levels of less than 1% of the total public education budget, including the Republic of Congo, Nicaragua, South Africa, Senegal, and Jordan.

Last, the EFA Report illustrates the relationship between the level of investment in preschool and enrollment levels. Gross enrollment rates commonly follow regional public expenditure patterns, with rates being the highest in the developed world, on average 80%, and the lowest in the developing world, on average 36%. By subregion, gross enrollment rates are the highest in the Caribbean (82%) and the lowest in Sub-Saharan Africa (15%) and the Arab states (19%). This trend suggests a potential link between effective financing and ECD results. Policymakers can therefore recognize the centrality of developing an effective ECD financing strategy to realizing key ECD outcomes and, in turn, the potentially rich social and economic returns of investing in children.

Sources and Uses of Funds: A Primer

There is no universally appropriate approach to financing ECD. Drawing upon Belfield (2006), this section provides an overview of the various finance strategies being employed around the world to fund ECD interventions (see Table 25.1). This section also shows how different financing strategies can yield similar results in different countries, as well as how similar financing strategies can engender drastically different outcomes in different contexts. This suggests that the relative effectiveness of a financing strategy is contextual. The conceptual framework presented later in this chapter will attempt to unpack the contextual factors that can influence a finance strategy's relative effectiveness.

Belfield (2006) argues that the principal sources of funding for ECD programs can be broken into four categories: public, private, public-private partnerships (PPPs), and international agencies. In most countries, public funds are the predominant source of funding for ECD (Tayler & Bennett, 2006; UNESCO, 2006; Vargas-Barón, 2008). Public funds can originate at the federal, state, provincial, municipal, or district level and can be mobilized through taxes (income, sales, payroll, property), lotteries, and fees (toll roads, licensing, admission levies). The United States employs a multitude of approaches for mobilizing public funds (Witte & Trowbridge, 2005). Other countries also evidence this variation, such as Colombia, which utilizes a dedicated national payroll tax, as well as Jamaica, where ECD programs are funded through dedicated taxes on gaming (Vegas & Santibáñez, 2010).

Belfield (2006) also provides examples of the many ways private funds support ECD services. Private funds come predominantly from households in the form of user fees, levies, tuition, and co-payments (see Woodhead & Streuli, 2013, Chapter 16, this volume). This is the case in India, where public ECD services require a significant level of cost sharing. Private funds can also be generated from industry, foundations, community groups, and other nongovernmental organizations (NGOs). As an example, NGOs play a particularly important role in financing ECD services on the community level in several countries. Public-private partnerships can be formed between governments, private enterprises, foundations, and community groups or other NGOs in order to raise matching funds, especially for large-scale capital improvement initiatives. International agencies such as development banks, bilateral agencies, and international NGOs can finance the design or scaling up of ECD programs by providing loans or grants as a way to extend ECD services in countries where revenue generation is constrained.

In addition to mapping the sources of ECD funds, Belfield (2006) identifies the diversity of the ways that funds are channeled to ECD service providers and participants. Public funds purposed for ECD by federal, state, provincial, municipal, or district authorities can be allocated directly or indirectly to public or private ECD service providers or program participants. Direct modalities of public fund allocation include budget line allocations, block or earmarked grants, and matching funds, in which the government matches a predetermined level of investment while service providers or households finance the remainder. In the United States, the Head Start Program is a federal grant awarded to states that agree to meet prescribed matching requirements (Witte & Trowbridge, 2005). France (Neuman & Peer, 2002) and Sweden (Gunnarsson, Martin Korpi, & Nordenstam, 1999) also serve as examples of countries employing a mixed approach to public funding, relying on different levels of government to share responsibilities for ECD finance.

Funds can also be allocated directly through vouchers for service providers or program participants, as is the case in Chile, the United States, and Taiwan (UNESCO, 2006). They can additionally be allocated through subsidies for specific program elements (staffing salaries, physical plant development, curriculum, quality assurance systems) or via conditional cash transfers to families, as has been implemented in Colombia and Mexico (Tayler & Bennett, 2006). The indirect allocation of public funds can occur through various tax credits, rebates, or need-based sliding scale subsidies. A host of OECD countries, including Denmark, Germany, Poland, and Sweden, indirectly allocate funding to ECD by instituting parental leave policies (Kamerman, 2000).

Private ECD funds are allocated either directly or indirectly. The most prevalent form of direct allocation is direct payments to private and public service providers from households in the form of user fees, levies, tuition, or co-payments. Kenya and Indonesia are examples of countries that heavily rely upon private resources (Belfield, 2006). Some other direct forms of private allocation include matching funds schemes and workplace-based child care. For example, in Colombia, cooperatives of employers and employees fund a variety of ECD services (Vargas-Barón, 2008). Indirect methods for channeling private resources into ECD include vouchers or in-kind donations to faith-based and nonprofit organizations. A common way to allocate funds from PPPs is through matching funds. Funds from various international agencies are channeled in the form of loans or grants to public or private service providers, as well as to program participants.

Available evidence on ECD finance demonstrates how countries around the world simultaneously deploy a combination of these different sources and modalities to pursue their ECD objectives. For example, funding to support child care centers and preprimary education in Hungary comes primarily from the public sector. However, that funding originates at different levels, with the central government contributing about 25%–30% of costs, whereas municipal and local governments provide about 60%. The remaining 10%–15% comes from private resources. In Thailand, direct budget allocations are made to centralized entities

TABLE 25.1 Sources and modalities of early childhood development finance

Sources of Funds	Modalities for Allocating Funds
Public funds—General revenues from taxes (sales, income, property, payroll), lotteries, excise taxes (tobacco and alcohol) and fees (toll roads, licensing), admission levies that can be originated at the federal/central, state/provincial, municipal, district or local level	Direct—budget line allocations, block grants, matching or partial matching funds, vouchers, direct subsidy for program elements, conditional cash transfers Indirect—need-based sliding scale subsidies, parental and maternity leave policies
Private Funds—Private enterprises, foundations, community groups/NGOs, households (user fees, levies, tuition, co-payments)	Direct—workplace-based care, payments to providers, matching funds Indirect—vouchers, in-kind donations to faith-based and nonprofit organizations
Public-Private Partnerships—Government, private enterprises, foundations, community groups/NGOs	Matching funds for capital investment initiatives to expand ECD services
International Agencies—International financing agencies (loans and grants), bilateral agencies (grants), international NGOs (grants)	Funds for government approved programs: recipients can be public or private providers, or program participants

Source: Adapted from Belfield, C. (2006). *Financing early childhood care and education: An international review.* Paper commissioned for the Education for All Global Monitoring Report 2007: Strong Foundations: Early Childhood Care and Education. Paris: United Nations Educational, Scientific and Cultural Organization (UNESCO).

responsible for infrastructure, equipment, teacher and staff salaries, and basic operating expenses. However, funding is also raised from the private sector, NGOs, communities, external sources, and the parents themselves, as many child centers require monthly fees to cover excess operational expenses, such as meals and materials.

Different combinations of financing sources and modalities can yield similar results within different contexts. When comparing outcomes, it is helpful to look at the more standardized preschool setting as data are more readily available. For example, Finland relies on a decentralized finance strategy, with state and local authorities responsible for channeling public funds to public and private providers, and parents contributing 15% of the cost. Conversely, Colombia funds ECD through a national payroll tax, with the central government channeling the majority of ECD funding to public providers through budget line allocations. On paper, these countries' financing approaches are quite distinct, yet both yield comparatively high enrollment rates for preschool (73% and 86%, respectively). Similarly, the Czech Republic's decentralized approach of heavily relying on regional school authorities, municipalities, and user fees to fund different aspects of ECD programming differs from that of Mexico, where 80% of ECD funding comes from the federal government, yet both countries achieve similar enrollment levels (76%–95% and 81%, respectively).

Conversely, similar sources and methods of allocation can engender drastically different outcomes. Kenya serves as an example of a country that relies heavily on private resources for ECD finance, with households bearing 95% of the cost of child care and preschools, but achieves only a modest enrollment rate of 26%. Indonesia and Senegal also exhibit a similar reliance on private resources and poor enrollment rates (19% and 3%, respectively). However, the largest contributors to ECD finance in developed countries, such as the United States and the United Kingdom, are private families and yet they enjoy high enrollment rates (90% and full enrollment, respectively), underscoring that country specific factors (such as the existence of targeted public support for ECD in the United States and United Kingdom to complement private expenditure) influence the relationship between financing strategies and outcomes across different countries. These examples reinforce the point that it is impossible to examine the effectiveness of an ECD finance strategy without taking country context into account. The framework presented in the following section aims elaborate on the importance of these contextual factors and suggests that, in accounting for them, policymakers can develop an effective strategy for financing ECD.

Conceptual Framework

The first section of this chapter provided a picture of the heterogeneity of ECD services. The second introduced the various strategies that exist for financing ECD and demonstrated that different strategies can lead to similar outcomes, and similar strategies can yield different outcomes. One can therefore assert that the effectiveness of an ECD finance strategy might have less to do with what specific finance mechanisms are in place and more to do with how these mechanisms interact with local conditions. That said, this chapter suggests that high-performing ECD systems share certain characteristics. The conceptual framework presented in this section first proposes a series of characteristics that are shared by effective finance strategies: sustainability, equity, and simplicity. Next, the framework seeks to identify the contextual factors that can drive strategy's impact on these elements by proposing that context is shaped by the relative cost structure of an ECD policy and a country's capacity to mobilize resources to support ECD.

CHARACTERISTICS OF EFFECTIVE FINANCE

Drawing upon international scholarship on ECD (Belfield, 2006; Tayler & Bennett, 2006; UNESCO, 2006; Vargas-Barón, 2008; Vegas & Santibáñez, 2010; World Bank, 2011) and effective public finance (Le Blanc, 2005; Lee et al., 2008; Stiglitz, 2000; Tanzi & Zee, 2001), it is possible to identify three key characteristics of an effective finance strategy: sustainability, equity in access, and administrative simplicity. The framework proposes that these three characteristics are critical to the effective financing of ECD. Unsustainable financing strategies threaten the comprehensiveness, reach, and existence of ECD services; inequitable strategies undermine the foundations of expanded opportunity that ECD aims to provide; and administratively complex strategies can reduce the efficiency of service provision and levels of program participation.

For example, payroll taxes are vulnerable to economic downturns and periods of prolonged unemployment, which can jeopardize sustainability (Vegas & Santibáñez, 2010). ECD services funded through regressive sales taxes disproportionally impact low-income communities and individuals, and can negatively impact equity (Lee et al., 2008). ECD finance strategies that overly rely on fees from participants can have an adverse and potentially inequitable impact on participation (Belfield, 2006). ECD subsidies awarded through the tax code can be administratively complex and limit the number of individuals who take advantage of the benefit (Lee et al., 2008). Simplicity can also be important within the allocation of public funds, as certain decentralized ECD finance strategies, such as block grants to providers and voucher systems, require the engagement of many actors on the local level for effectiveness (Vargas-Barón, 2008).

The framework also suggests that these characteristics are interrelated; meaning that failure to adequately address one ultimately impacts the others. As an example, unsustainable funding strategies can lead to increases in provider fees, which impact participation and the equity dimension. Administratively complex tax subsidies that require extensive paperwork by parents with low literacy skills lowers participation, disadvantages their children, and adversely impacts the equity of the finance strategy. Therefore, when designing a strategy for financing, ECD policymakers should seek to achieve an effective balance among these three dimensions.

FACTORS INFLUENCING EFFECTIVE FINANCE

Evidence from the earlier sections demonstrates the variation in how ECD finance strategies impact preschool enrollment within different country contexts. We suggest that the centrality of context extends to a given finance strategy's relative impact on sustainability, equity, and simplicity. The framework seeks to identify what contextual factors might influence a finance strategy's impact on these key elements and, importantly, the extent to which policymakers can manipulate these factors to develop a finance strategy that can effectively support their unique ECD objectives. This conceptual framework posits that there are two principal factors influencing a finance strategy's sustainability, equity, and simplicity: the cost structure of ECD services, and the resource mobilization dynamics within a country (see Figure 25.2). These factors link two fundamental practices within public finance: adequate costing of the services provided and securing adequate resources to cover those costs. Although simple in theory, both undertakings can be complex within the context of ECD.

Early Childhood Development Service Cost Structure

Given the heterogeneity of ECD programming, the costs associated with delivering ECD services must take into account differences in program objectives, design, quality, and intensity (Charles & Williams, 2008; Levin & Schwartz, 2006; Mingat, 2006; van Ravens & Aggio, 2008). This framework proposes that, in addition to these program-specific factors, costing must also account for the existing ECD policy environment within a given country. Policymakers seeking to design an effective strategy for financing ECD need be aware of how the policy conditions they set for ECD influence the cost of ECD programs. We suggest that in setting

Context

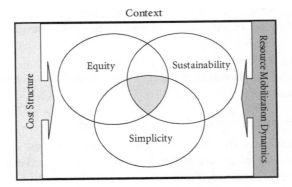

Example A-Sustainability Distortion

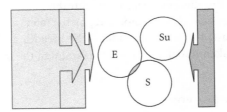

Example B - Simplicity Distortion   Example C - Equity Distortion

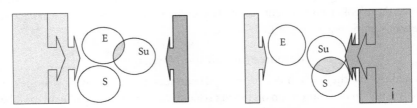

FIGURE 25.2 *Contextual factors influencing effective early childhood development finance.*

requirements for the strategic scope of ECD services, oversight mechanisms, and service delivery components, policymakers are effectively dictating the threshold of resources required to support ECD service provision. This, in turn, can influence the sustainability, equity, and simplicity of a finance strategy.

STRATEGIC SCOPE OF ECD SERVICES

Here, key determinations are made regarding the strategic comprehensiveness of ECD services. The scope of ECD services a country seeks to provide influences the level of financing that will be required to meet any particular intensity or coverage objectives. France's commitment to extensive coverage of preprimary education requires a finance strategy capable of generating significant resources and spreading them across a broad population (Neuman & Peer, 2002). Although supporting these policy objectives with an adequate level of resources appears sustainable, equitable, and simple within the French context, this may not be the case within another country.

ECD OVERSIGHT MECHANISMS AND ADMINISTRATION

Costs are associated with how authorities oversee the pursuit of their ECD objectives. The resources needed to fund quality assurance activities, as well as the capacity of providers to fulfill their role in oversight, influences the overall cost structure of delivering ECD services. For example, Charles and Williams (2008) introduce the potentially distinct oversight roles of the government within different ECD policy settings, from full-cost government provision to full private sector provision. Naturally, costs will vary with the nature of the government's oversight responsibilities. Furthermore, reporting and accreditation requirements could add costs to private providers. The breadth and form of oversight activities must be taken into account when examining the overall cost structure of ECD services.

SERVICE DELIVERY COMPONENTS

Standards set for service delivery dictate the costs of providing and accessing ECD services. For example, policies can require qualifications for ECD staff, facility certifications, or specify staff–student ratios in order to receive public funds (Behrman, Cheng, & Todd, 2004). As the level of standards will dictate program costs, these policy components ultimately influence a finance strategy's effectiveness in supporting a level of ECD services.

Resource Mobilization Dynamics

In addition to the costs of delivering ECD services, this framework also seeks to focus policymakers' attention on factors related to a country's capacity to mobilize resources to meet the costs of those ECD services. The framework suggests that the contextual factors related to ECD resource mobilization can influence the relative sustainability, equity, and simplicity of a finance strategy with a given national setting. Although we acknowledge that a variety of complex and dynamic factors can impact a country's capacity to mobilize resources, the three "levers" presented here directly relate to some key issues in ECD finance.

POLITICAL/LEGAL LEVERS

Political/legal levers refer to the ability of a country to mobilize public resources through political capital for "the cause" of ECD or through a codified legal framework. Vegas and Santibáñez (2010) discuss the how the formation of "a comprehensive ECD policy" can positively influence the sustainability of an ECD finance strategy. UNESCO (2006) also describes how legislation in several countries to make preprimary education compulsory can influence resource flows to ECD.

INSTITUTIONAL LEVERS

Institutional levers originate in the institutional setting within a country that enables it to mobilize public resources for ECD at different levels of governance and administration. The potential impact of a country's institutional setting on the effectiveness of ECD finance can be observed within the equity challenges many post-Soviet states experienced with the decentralization of ECD finance in the 1990s (Belfield, 2006; UNESCO, 2006). Policymakers therefore may want to consider the capacity of local institutions to mobilize resources for ECD should they pursue a decentralization agenda.

PRIVATE LEVERS

A country's capacity to draw upon domestic private resources to finance ECD is related to the country's relative wealth and the perceived value of ECD. These factors influence the sophistication of the market for ECD and the extent to which relying on certain finance strategies can effectively support ECD objectives. For example, private resources from households are the dominant components of both Indonesia's and Korea's ECD finance strategies, but the comparatively advanced private market for ECD in Korea leads to substantially higher levels of participation than in Indonesia (Belfield, 2006).

EVALUATING FINANCE STRATEGY EFFECTIVENESS

In the absence of a single, ideal, and replicable model for effective ECD finance, we set forth three characteristics to serve as a normative framework for evaluating the effectiveness of an ECD finance strategy: sustainability, equity, and administrative simplicity. The framework also suggests that two sets of contextual factors can shape a finance strategy's relative impact on these elements: the cost structure of ECD services and the capacity to mobilize resources for ECD in a given country. Policymakers may want to give attention to these contextual factors as they can be responsible for distortions in a finance strategy's overall sustainability, equity, or simplicity. In turn, we argue that policymakers can take steps to manipulate these contextual factors to effectively balance the sustainability, equity, and simplicity of their ECD finance strategy. However, evidence from around the world shows that, in many countries, this balance can be elusive.

Examples from Belfield (2006) reveal weaknesses along these elements in a number of countries. Brazil utilizes earmarked funding for basic education, raised from tax revenue at the state and municipal levels to support ECD services. However, these funds support all basic education. In the absence of a specific commitment to ECD, Brazil's financing strategy could be considered weak with regards to sustainability. South Africa funds ECD largely with private resources. This finance strategy experiences weakness in equity, as South Africa demonstrates significant differences in enrollment rates across ethnic groups. In Vietnam, the central government mandates that 10% of the national education budget be allocated to ECD. The provinces, however, experience constraints in meeting this threshold. The evident capacity issue between levels of government demonstrates a weakness in the administrative simplicity of Vietnam's ECD finance strategy, with provincial authorities facing apparent barriers to meeting the financing strategy's demands. Naturally, in this case, weakness in administrative simplicity is clearly related to the sustainability of funding. Furthermore, simplicity and sustainability deficiencies impact equity in that they compromise the government's ability to broaden access to ECD services. Vietnam clearly exhibits the interrelatedness of these elements, whereas Brazil and South Africa would also likely reveal interrelated weaknesses.

ENGINEERING EFFECTIVE ECD FINANCE

Achieving balance among sustainability, equity, and simplicity in a finance strategy is challenging. However, policymakers have the ability to engineer effective ECD financing strategies in light of particular weaknesses. Colombia funds ECD through a national payroll tax, but faces sustainability concerns given the economic and political vulnerabilities of this revenue source. Early childhood development financing and service delivery in Mexico is fragmented, which compromises administrative simplicity given the lack of coordination and leadership across ministries (Vegas & Santibáñez, 2010). Both countries sought to craft comprehensive national ECD policies to address their distinct strategic issues in ECD finance. Although their issues related to sustainability and simplicity are contextual, both examples exhibit the ability of countries to take action and influence the relative effectiveness of their ECD finance strategies and thus the returns on their ECD investments.

Engineering effectiveness in ECD financing, however, is a task best undertaken in conjunction with ECD program design. Although resource mobilization dynamics within a country are more or less fixed in the short term, the cost structures of ECD services within a country are malleable. By aligning the cost structure of ECD services from a strategic, oversight, and service delivery standpoint within a country's resource mobilization environment, policymakers can effectively manipulate the sustainability, equity, and simplicity of a finance strategy. It is therefore essential to design ECD policies and programs with the sustainability, equity, and simplicity of financing and, ultimately, the services they aim to expand and strengthen kept in mind from the outset.

TAKING THE LONG VIEW IN ECD FINANCE

By setting policies and standards for ECD services, countries are effectively determining the future costs of ECD programs and thus their sustainability, equity, and simplicity. Service delivery standards that, for example, dictate staff-to-infant ratios also dictate costs. Those costs subsequently dictate whether or not block grants to providers or subsidies to participants are sustainable over the long term. Should those block grants or subsidies fail to be sustainable sources of financing over the long term, this weakness will impact the equity of the overall finance strategy as providers raise fees to cover shortfalls.

Investing in ECD requires taking a long view. The well-established benefits of investing in broadening access to high-quality ECD services take time to materialize. Given the long-term orientation of the many robust returns on ECD investments, policymakers must apply a similar philosophy in the design of ECD financing strategies. Doing so will not only ensure that ECD interventions are adequately supported to meet their strategic scope, oversight, and service-delivery objectives, but also ensure that ECD investments are able to demonstrate their positive effects and thus rationalize the expansion of investment to strengthen and broaden the reach of ECD services.

Policymakers must therefore look at diverse issues, including how the policy landscape, service standards, points of delivery, and the intensity and reach of services dictate the level of financing that is required to provide and sustain ECD services. Decisions such as these will ultimately impact the kinds of services that can be reliably provided at what cost, and therefore, who will be able to access those services over the long term. If the prescribed level of services cannot be sustained by a given financing strategy, the quality and reach of ECD services can be jeopardized, along with the overall benefits that ECD investments have been demonstrated to yield.

Take, for example, a country seeking to expand access to ECD across socioeconomically diverse populations. To do so, the country sets up a system of subsidies for certified private providers serving disadvantaged populations, and, in turn, sets strong standards for certification to ensure a minimum level of quality in service provision. However, in setting up the funding for the subsidies, policymakers did not account for the impact of quality standards, program costs, or the complexity of channeling subsidies from the central government to individual providers. To cover the cost of gaining and maintaining certification, as well as the paperwork that is required to secure funding from the government, providers face an increase in operating costs. To cover these costs, providers raise fees, which, despite the subsidies, have an adverse impact on the equity dimensions of ECD services.

Although it is not desirable to compromise the quality of ECD services in order to make a financing strategy more sustainable, it is necessary to realistically align the design of a finance strategy with the cost structure of the ECD services being provided. In other words, the above example is not the story of an ECD investment that should have lowered quality standards, but instead a story in which policymakers should have sought better alignment between their financing strategy and their cost structure. To do so would have required policymakers, as the framework has sought to show, to consider sustainability, equity, and simplicity in the design of the program's strategic scope, oversight, and service delivery components. This consideration of ECD cost structure is fundamental to a country's ability to finance its ECD objectives.

Furthermore, alignment between cost structures and finance strategies is also important to a country's ability to expand ECD services in terms of both comprehensiveness and coverage. Strong monitoring and evaluation efforts that track the quality and effectiveness of ECD investments justify the expansion of successful services through the increased mobilization of public and private resources to reach more ambitious ECD goals. This means that the benefits of taking the long view and designing a sustainable ECD finance strategy accrue only with time.

Conclusion

The framework presented in this chapter puts forth three principal insights regarding effective ECD financing. The first relates to the importance of the relationship between ECD program design and the sustainability, equity, and simplicity of a financing strategy. Policymakers must ensure that financing mechanisms take into account the costs of delivering ECD services. This is best done at the outset, by designing the strategic scope, oversight, and service delivery components of ECD services in conjunction with shaping a financing strategy. Manipulating the alignment between ECD service cost structure and a financing strategy is a more challenging task after the implementation of a program or after a financing strategy proves inadequate.

Second, policymakers should take the long view in designing financing strategies. Strong monitoring and evaluation of the resources supporting ECD programming provides evidence of their effectiveness in meeting prescribed social and economic objectives. However, ECD investments often yield returns only after a lag. Countries must therefore actively monitor the ability of a financing strategy to adequately sustain a level of services. This evidence base enables countries to build upon the success of existent ECD programs and, ultimately, expand the breadth and depth of ECD services.

Last, the heterogeneity of ECD services means that, in most countries, the administration and financing of programs is spread across a number of ministries (education, health, nutrition) and authorities (national, state, municipality). Therefore, countries should seek to identify possible overlaps or duplication of efforts and harmonize programming to leverage their investments across various administrators. Harmonizing fragmented ECD programming has the potential to reduce costs and increase the impact on the shared objective of providing a sound foundation for expanding opportunity for all children.

Acknowledgments

The authors wish to highlight the contribution of Brent Parton, who provided extensive research and analytical support, and Ryan Flynn, who edited the entry.

Note

1. The information provided in this chapter substantially draws upon the authors' work presented in the ECD Program Costing (Note 4.1) and Financing ECD Programs (Note 4.2), within *Investing in Young Children: An Early Childhood Development Guide for Policy Dialogue and Project Preparation* (2011).

References

Aos, S., Lieb, R., Mayfield, J., Miller, M., & Pennucci, A. (2004). *Benefits and costs of prevention and early intervention programs for youth.* Olympia, WA: Washington State Institute for Public Policy.

Behrman, J., Cheng, Y., & Todd, P. (2004). Evaluating preschool programs when length of exposure to the program varies: A nonparametric approach. *Review of Economics and Statistics, 86*(1), 108–132.

Belfield, C. (2006). *Financing early childhood care and education: An international review.* Paper commissioned for the Education for All Global Monitoring Report 2007: Strong Foundations: Early Childhood Care and Education. Paris: United Nations Educational, Scientific and Cultural Organization (UNESCO).

Britto, P., Yoshikawa, H., & Boller, K. (2011). Quality of early childhood development programs: Rationale for investment, conceptual framework and implications for equity. *Social Policy Report, 25*(2), 1–31.

Charles, L., & Williams, S. (2008). A model to support ECD decision-making: Caribbean regional experiences with costs and simulations. In *Coordinators' notebook: An international resource for early childhood,* No. 30 (pp. 52–56). Toronto: The Consultative Group on Early Childhood Care and Development.

Committee for Economic Development. (2006). *The economic promise of investing in high quality preschool: Using early education to improve economic growth and the fiscal sustainability of states and the nation.* Washington, DC: Committee for Economic Development.

Gunnarsson, L., Martin Korpi, B., & Nordenstam, U. (1999). *Early childhood education and care policy in Sweden.* Stockholm: Ministry of Education and Science.

Heckman, J. J., Moon, S. H., Pinto, R., Savalyev, P. A., & Yavitz, A. (2009). *The rate of return to the High/Scope Perry Preschool Program* (Working Paper 200936). Dublin: Geary Institute, University College Dublin. Retrieved from http://www.ucd.ie/geary/static/publications/workingpapers/gearywp200936.pdf

Kamerman, S. (2000). Early childhood education and care: An overview of the developments in OECD countries. *International Journal of Education Research, 33,* 7–30.

Karoly, L. A., & Bigelow, J. H. (2005). *The economics of investing in universal preschool in California.* Santa Monica, CA: The Rand Corporation.

Le Blanc, D. (2005). *Economic evaluation of housing subsidy systems: A methodology with application to Morocco* (Policy Research Working Paper 3529). Washington, DC: World Bank.

Lee, R. D., Johnson, R. W., & Joyce, P. G. (2008). *Public budgeting systems.* Sudbury, MA: Jones and Bartlett.

Levin, H., & Schwartz, H. (2006). *Costs of early childhood care and education programs*. Paper commissioned for the Education for All Global Monitoring Report 2007: Strong Foundations: Early Childhood Care and Education. Paris: United Nations Educational, Scientific and Cultural Organization (UNESCO). New York: National Center for the Study of Privatization in Education, Teachers College, Columbia University.

Masse, L., & Barnett, W. S. (2002). *A benefit-cost analysis of the Abecedarian Early Childhood Intervention*. New Brunswick, NJ: National Institute for Early Education Research (NIEER).

Mingat, A. (2006, March). *Early childhood care and education in Africa: Towards expansion of coverage and targeting of efficient services*. Paper presented at the ADEA Biennale in Gabon. Paris: ADEA.

Naudeau, S. (2009). Supplementing nutrition in the early years: The role of early childhood stimulation to maximize nutritional inputs. *Child and Youth Development Notes, 3*(1), 1–4.

Neuman, M., & Peer, S. (2002). *Equal from the start: Promoting educational opportunity for all pre-school children. Learning from the French experience*. New York: Franco-American Foundation.

Nores, M., Belfield, C. R., Barnett, W. S., & Schweinhart, L. (2005). Updating the economic impacts of the High/Scope Perry Preschool Program. *Educational Evaluation and Policy Analysis, 27*(3), 245–261.

Reynolds, A. J., Temple, J. A., Robertson, D. L., & Mann, E. A. (2001). Long-term effects of an early childhood intervention on educational achievement and juvenile arrest: A 15-year follow-up of low-income children in public schools. *Journal of the American Medical Association, 285*, 2339–46.

Stiglitz, J. E. (2000). *Economics of the public sector*. New York: W. W. Norton.

Tanzi, V., & Zee, H. (2001). *Tax policy for developing countries* (Economic Issues No. 27). Washington, DC: International Monetary Fund.

Tayler, C., & Bennett, J. (2006). *Starting strong II: Early childhood education and care*. Paris: Education Directorate of the Organization for Economic Co-operation and Development.

United Nations Educational, Scientific and Cultural Organization (UNESCO). (2006). *Education for all global monitoring report 2007: Strong foundations: Early childhood care and education*. Paris: UNESCO.

United Nations Educational, Scientific and Cultural Organization (UNESCO). (2011). *Revision of the International Standard Classification of Education* (Document 36 C). Paris: UNESCO.

van Ravens, J., & C. Aggio. (2008). *Expanding early childhood care and education: How much does it cost? A proposal for a methodology to estimate the costs of early childhood care and education at macro-level, applied to the Arab States* (Working Paper No. 46). The Hague: Bernard Van Leer Foundation.

Vargas-Barón, E. (2008). Observations on the financing of early childhood development at the national level. In *Coordinators' notebook: An international resource for early childhood* No. 30 (pp. 11–14). Toronto: The Consultative Group on Early Childhood Care and Development.

Vegas, E., & Santibáñez, L. (2010). *The promise of early childhood development in Latin America and the Caribbean*. Washington, DC: World Bank.

Verdisco, A. (2008). Solving Latin America's most urgent problems: ECD and the Consulta de San José. In *Coordinators' Notebook: An international resource for early childhood*, No. 30 (pp. 22–23). Toronto: The Consultative Group on Early Childhood Care and Development.

Victora, C. G., Adair, L., Fall, C., Hallal, P. C., Martorell, R., Richter, L., et al. (2008). Maternal and child undernutrition: Consequences for adult health and human capital. *The Lancet, 371*(9609), 340–357.

Witte, A. D., & Trowbridge, M. (2005). The structure of early care and education in the United States: Historical evolution and international comparisons. *Tax Policy and the Economy, 19*, 1–37.

Woodhead, M., & Streuli, N. (2013). Early education for all: Is there a role for the private sector? In P. R. Britto, P. L. Engle, & C. M. Super (Eds.), *Handbook of early childhood development research and its impact on global policy* (Chapter 16). New York: Oxford University Press.

World Bank, Naudeau, S., Kataoka, N., Valerio, A., Neuman, M. J., & Elder, L. K. (2011). *Investing in young children: An early childhood development guide for policy dialogue and project preparation*. Washington, DC: World Bank.

Conclusions

26

Paradigm Shifts and New Directions in Research on Early Childhood Development Programs in Low- and Middle-Income Countries

Hirokazu Yoshikawa and Ana María Nieto

The last two decades have seen a revolution in the "mainstreaming" of early childhood development (ECD)—as reflected in prioritization in national policies—in many countries and regions. Forty nations, for example, have national early childhood policies at the time of this writing, many with concomitant action and implementation plans (Vargas-Barón, 2013, Chapter 24, this volume). ECD services have, in most of these and many other nations, expanded in domains of health, nutrition, feeding, parent support, and early educational services (UNESCO, 2011). Academic research and theoretical discussions across various disciplines sustain a view of young children both as present and future citizens—raising expectations for ECD and its lifespan benefits for health, learning, and behavior.

In the low- and middle-income (LAMI) countries, mounting evidence suggests that this expansion in ECD services can have positive impacts on young children's health, learning, and behavior. The *Lancet* series of syntheses has found that a large majority of the more rigorous evaluations of ECD programs—encompassing health education, parenting support, conditional cash transfers, and early childhood education—show positive impacts on children's development in at least one domain (Engle et al., 2007, 2011).

In this chapter, we identify emerging paradigm shifts for research that can address the next generation of practice and policy questions in ECD in LAMI countries. Drawing on the many rich lessons found in the chapters of this volume, we highlight how the field of ECD is changing and discuss several innovative directions in the integration of research, practice, and policy. These include new developments in approaches to considering equity, quality and its improvement, the multisectoral nature of ECD programs and policies, and research capacity. Here, we focus on paradigm shifts in research and its relationship to practice and policy; other chapters in this volume summarize developments in the policy and practice domains with less emphasis placed on research.

Beyond Impacts on Mean Level of Children's Development
to Impacts on Equity and Inequality

Educational and economic inequality are growing globally—both within and across countries. Engle, Rao, and Petrovic (2013), in Chapter 3 of this volume, rightly call for efforts to reduce disparities in health, learning, behavior, and long-term outcomes for children. Early childhood programs are a powerful lever for reducing inequality. For example, Engle and colleagues' second *Lancet* article (2011) on ECD programs shows compelling data on how increases in preprimary education enrollment can reduce inequities across the richest and poorest quintiles.

The call for attention to inequality includes a powerful lesson for researchers—that is, to examine not only the effects of ECD programs on average levels of child outcomes, as is most common, but also on the distribution of child outcomes, resources, human capital, and other factors in a particular population. It is not necessarily true that a program that increases the mean level of a positive developmental outcome reduces inequalities based on poverty, social exclusion, or marginalization. Specific approaches to ECD may exacerbate inequality by benefiting particular groups of children over others. For example, a quality improvement program for Early Childhood Care and Education (ECCE) in Mexico implemented a competitive process for accessing supplemental funds for quality enhancement. The largest and most resourced preschools were the most successful in receiving the improvement funds (Yoshikawa et al., 2007). Woodhead and Streuli (2013) pointed out, in Chapter 16 of this volume, that without proactive public coordination, the rapidly expanding private sectors in ECCE can potentially increase inequality according to class, urban/rural residence, minority status, and child disability. These authors also discuss how current private sector involvement in early childhood education in India may be expanding disparities in that nation between boys and girls, especially in poor, rural contexts. As Hayden and Wai (2013) argue in Chapter 14 of this volume, even community-based participatory approaches to ECD can exacerbate inequities if they give voice only to local elites, thereby reinforcing existing power/knowledge structures. Closely monitoring ECD indicators in different subpopulations and using information with a framework of corrective and distributive justice can be an effective tool against unintended effects of ECD programs in the direction of greater inequality or social exclusion (Bornstein & Lansford, 2013, Chapter 18, this volume; Hertzman, Vaghri, & Arkadas, 2013, Chapter 19, this volume).

Inequities are not limited to the provision of care, education, or health services. As pointed out by Lemish and Kolucki (2013) in Chapter 17, although technology and media advances may promote the healthy development of children, they may also reproduce social exclusion, marginalization, limited world views, and discrimination. Currently, there are access gaps between different regions and social groups and failures in the fair representation of diversity of race, ethnicity, class, religion, disability, geography, and age, as well as stereotypical representations of boys and girls. As argued by Harkness et al. (2013, Chapter 7, this volume) and Pence (2013, Chapter 8, this volume), there is also a lack of representation of diverse cultures and languages in ECD research.

Beyond Quality to Effectiveness Factors in ECD Settings, Networks, and Systems

The ECD field consistently calls for quality programs. Yet, quality often is undefined in these calls, leaving practitioners and policymakers with few guidelines for how to ensure that programs are achieving their intended goals to improve children's health, learning, or behavior. Far too often, the only benchmark used for progress in ECD policies and programs is enrollment. And when the concept of quality is defined, it is often restricted to only one or two kinds of settings—characteristics of centers for preschool education, or characteristics of caregiver's provision of care in more informal programs.

The concept of *effectiveness factors* reframes quality in a way that can more specifically meet practice and policy needs, as well as focus research on key dimensions of quality. Such factors have been defined as features of programs that are associated with larger positive effects on children's health, learning, and behavior (National Forum on Early Childhood Programs and Policies, 2007). We are at an exciting point in the development of the field where effectiveness factors—key dimensions of quality associated with more positive effects—are emerging from the ECD program evaluation literature in LAMI nations.

The recent *Lancet* reviews (Engle et al., 2007, 2011), as well as chapters in this volume, have begun to identify effectiveness factors for particular kinds of programs for parents and caregivers. For health and nutrition programs, for example, evaluation studies consistently show that those that integrate health, nutrition, and feeding information with an emphasis on supporting stimulating interactions and responsiveness between parents and their very young children have stronger effects than solely information-based programs (Engle et al., 2011; Yousafzai, Yakoob, & Bhutta, 2013, Chapter 10, this volume). More broadly, parenting support programs are more effective when they incorporate structured curricula, systematic training, and opportunities for parents to build skills, rather than simply absorb didactic information (Engle et al., 2011). And the powerful role of mutual support and empowerment among parents in home-based programs is highlighted among successful examples across several countries (Kagitcibasi, Sunar, Bekman, Baydar, & Cemilcinar, 2009; Rao, Sun, Pearson, Sun, Pearson, Costas, & Engle, 2012). In Chapter 10, Yousafzai, Yakoob, and Bhutta provide two examples of empowering nutrition interventions in LAMI countries. In Vietnam, the HEARTH/Positive Deviance model for nutritional rehabilitation and improvement brings participants together to learn successful practices from other caregivers in their own communities (Engle, Bentley, & Pelto, 2000). Bangladesh has developed peer counseling strategies that provide support among mothers in maintaining exclusive breast-feeding practices and that engage other family members, such as grandmothers and fathers, who also have an influential role in caregiving decisions (Faruque et al., 2008). Future evaluations of ECD home-based programs should include assessments not only of effects on caregivers' skills and parent–child interactions, but also on the functioning and supports of broader social networks of these families.

Evaluations in LAMI countries of center-based preschool, compared to no preschool, have consistently found positive effects on cognitive and achievement outcomes. Promising evidence of both short- and long-term impacts was found—however, only a small number of LAMI studies have examined long-term effects (Engle et al., 2011). Currently, no consensus on effectiveness factors seems to have been reached in the literature on LAMI countries—however, intentional curricula focused on particular domains or increasing teacher–child interactivity, if provided with adequate supports and training, were features of some of the more successful programs (Engle et al., 2011).

Research in the ECD field has only begun to identify broader features of ECD systems that are associated with more positive impacts on children. The characteristics of larger implementation systems—at the district, province or state, and national levels—that are associated with more effective implementation of programs at scale, for example, are only beginning to be studied. Hommel (2013), in Chapter 22 of this volume, summarizes the work of a Brookings Wolfensohn Center study on scale, an examination of the features of scaled-up systems of ECD services. Based on studies conducted in South Africa and Cuba by Biersteker (2010) and Tinajero (2010), Hommel indicates that the traditional focus of scale-up efforts is on training and professional development capacity for front-line service providers. Although acknowledging that this is a critical central feature of effective programs at scale, she points out that the capacity of other stakeholders in an ECD system—including policymakers, donors, researchers, nongovernmental organizations (NGOs), and community leaders—may be just as critical in successful ECD systems. Hommel identifies capacity in ECD knowledge and practice as the two key dimensions that distinguish the work of this broader set of stakeholders. Other chapter authors in this volume identify additional dimensions. Hayden and Wai (2013, Chapter 14, this volume), in discussing community-based approaches to ECD, suggest that trust among stakeholders is key in cohesive community-based ECD systems.

Governance and finance represent another set of features in ECD systems that have long been recognized by experts in the field as crucial factors in service delivery but are rarely systematically studied (Naudeau, Kataoka, Valerio, Neuman, & Elder, 2011; van Ravens & Aggio, 2008; Young, 1996). For example, work on governance in a variety of policy areas typically examines dimensions not only of effectiveness, but of reliability and legitimacy. Operational capacity, management structure, accounting systems, and performance assessments are typical indicators of NGO and government functioning. It is clear that these are not yet part of the literature in studies of ECD (Jordan, 2005). In finance, many governments and NGOs do not monitor unit costs for ECD comprehensively; such information therefore often does not inform budget planning or policy decisions concerning investments in expansion, access, or quality (van Ravens & Aggio, 2008). Challenges include the complex mix of user fees and NGO, public, and private funding, and the many kinds of services across health, education, social protection, and child protection that can make up an ECD system. The analysis of money flows to examine where leakage occurs is carried out in many policy areas, but is not often part of accountability in ECD systems (Jordan, 2005). Analysis of policy architecture—capturing both vertical dimensions such as supervision; budget flows across national, subnational, and community levels; and feedback loops up and down across these levels, and horizontal dimensions across sectors at each of these levels—are rarely carried out in ECD. Vargas-Barón (2013), in Chapter 24 of this volume, presents a useful analysis of this type. She emphasizes, for example, that coordination and/or integration across sectors should be considered at the national, provincial, and community levels. Three recent studies on governance and finance in ECD in low-income countries take this approach, examining vertical and horizontal dimensions of governance simultaneously (Britto, Dimaya, & Seder, 2011; van Ravens & Ponguta, 2011; Yoshikawa, Oh, & Seder, 2011).

Beyond "Does ECD Work?" to "How Can ECD Services and Systems Be Improved?"

The large majority of studies of ECD programs to date have compared program to no program. For example, most studies of preschool education have compared children who received preschool to those who did not. These studies answer the question of whether ECD programs work to improve children's outcomes.

The field of ECD in LAMI countries is now beginning to address a second-generation question that emerges once a basic level of ECD investments and program implementation has occurred: How can ECD services be improved? Some chapters in this volume show that such efforts can result in improved outcomes for children. The bar is higher in these studies, in that the comparison is not of a program to no program, but of a modified program to a program as it is currently implemented. Yet, promising evidence suggests that such improvements in programs—for example, curricula focused on particular domains, like language or preliteracy skills (Rolla San Francisco, Arias, Villers, & Snow, 2006), socioemotional skills (Baker-Henningham, Walker, Powell, & Gardener, 2009), or increased intensity in professional development (Bernal, 2010; Yoshikawa, Leyva, Snow, Treviño, Barata, & Weiland, 2011)—can show positive impacts on indicators of quality or their targeted child outcomes. In each of these cases, teacher/caregiver professional development or a structured curriculum was added to an existing ECD program. For example, evidence of the relatively low quality of the

Hogares Comunitarios multicomponent parent support program in Colombia (Bernal et al., 2009) led to the implementation of intensive professional development and training. This program consisted of a training curriculum of quite high intensity (20 hours a week for three semesters), although of relatively low cost (US$650 per *madre comunitaria*). The program, evaluated in comparison to a waiting-list control group, resulted in improvements in observed quality of care, as well as in improvements in parent-reported child health and socioemotional and cognitive development for 0- to 3-year-old children in the sample (but not 3- to 6-year-old children). One study in Jamaica found that training preschool teachers in effective behavior management and encouragement of prosocial behavior resulted in declines in behavior problems (Baker-Henneman et al., 2009). A 2-year professional development program for teachers in low-income Chilean preschools that focused on improving classroom practices related to language and health, did indeed improve observed classroom instructional quality and emotional climate after 1 year, in an experimental evaluation (Yoshikawa, Leyva et al., 2011).

Features of quality may be locally effective rather than "structural" and "process" features that may be assumed to be universal. As one example, native-born staff efforts to be responsive to the daily routines of immigrant families may be a very localized aspect of quality, one that differs depending on the particular linguistic, cultural, and immigrant backgrounds of families in an ECD program (Vandenbroeck, 2009).

Beyond Sectoral and Multisectoral to Community-Based and Participatory

Calls for multisectoral integration of ECD programs are well-justified. The examples of true cross-sectoral integration, such as in the Cuban *Educa tu hijo* program or *Chile Crece Contigo*, show the benefits of addressing health, education, social protection, and child protection in an integrated manner. Some sectors are overlooked in ECD. Chapter 12 (Landers, Da Silva e Paula, & Kilbane (2013, this volume), for example, demonstrates a disappointingly low rate of inclusion of child protection components into national ECD systems (24 out of 104 countries in a United Nations Children's Fund [UNICEF] analysis). This is of particular concern given the fact that studies from low-, middle-, and high-income nations alike find that children between the ages of birth to 5 years, particularly infants in the first year of life, are at the very highest risk of child maltreatment.

There are substantial challenges to coordination across sectors and systems in ECD. Several chapters in this volume call for combination programs to address multiple risks or protective factors in the lives of the vulnerable (e.g., Aber, Biersteker, Daws, & Rawlings, 2013, Chapter 13, this volume; Engle, Rao & Petrovic, 2013, Chapter 3, this volume). For example, the conditioning of cash transfers on take-up of other forms of ECD services that address parenting and nutrition, not just immunization and health, is an emerging program and policy direction (Aber et al., 2013, Chapter 13, this volume). Such an approach, now being implemented in several countries in ECD, requires substantial integration of monitoring and implementation efforts across social protection, health, and education sectors.

A central national ECD unit has been recommended by several authors in this volume as a promising mechanism to facilitate cross-sector coordination and integration. Some countries, for example, have created childhood units within ministries and established committees to coordinate ECD matters. However, as Homsi and Husein (2013, Chapter 21, this volume) point out, this model can have unpredictable results, as it depends on the status of the unit within the ministry's hierarchy and the allocation of resources and decision-making powers bestowed on it. A second alternative is to create ministries specifically devoted to children and adolescents, like the one in Morocco. As pointed out by Homsi and Hussein, although this structure may ensure the allocation of financial and human resources, it may also accentuate the "silo approach to early childhood" requiring interministerial coordination. Vargas-Barón (2013) cites the usefulness of a central, cross-ministry unit coordinating ECD services. Successful examples of these units include those in Jamaica, Jordan, Syria, and Qatar. Sudan, Yemen, and Palestine have created National Councils for Childhood headed by prime ministers or heads of the country and comprised of relevant ministers, prominent public figures, and experts (Homsi & Husein, 2013, Chapter 21, this volume).

Other chapters in this volume argue that certain ECD issues may best be handled by civil society structures and communities. Hayden and Wai (2013, Chapter 14, this volume), for example, note that community-based programs and organizations can more flexibly respond to community needs, particularly when they fall outside the traditional realms of the government, through ministries or offices of health, education, women and gender, sports, and the like. Community-based programs may be more likely to utilize certain theories of action, such as those involving peer-to-peer support, rather than solely social-service or professional change agents (Hayden & Wai, 2013, Chapter 14, this volume; Mbonye, Bygbjerg, & Magnussen, 2008). Programs based in community-based organizations, rather than instituted in a top-down manner through government, may be more likely to involve the participation of residents and local governance. Variations in local beliefs and values about children and families are often perceived as barriers to programmatic success. However, programs that integrate local cultural norms, such as that in the Louga district of Senegal described by Harkness et al. (2013, Chapter 7, this volume), show that local norms can be recruited to advance a new developmental goal. In that case, the program emphasized language development in the context of everyday errands and tasks, as was common in local households. On the other hand, as mentioned earlier, careful attention must be paid to concerns such as lack of representativeness in local governance or resource and time constraints. As Pence (2013, Chapter 8, this volume) notes, recent developments in ECCE research have been dominated by the economic perspective and by emphases on domains of development and approaches to enhancing them that are assumed to be universal. They may rather be impositions of North American and Western European world-views and practices on a huge range of global ECD programs and policies. Aid policies can fall into the trap of the "rescuer" providing unidirectional help to those perceived as only vulnerable (Hayden & Wai, 2013, Chapter 14, this volume). Community-based ECD programs and efforts can suffer as a result.

Participatory processes, particularly those involving mid-level staff as well as frontline caregivers, parents, and children themselves, are an important link between community-based input and policy development. Participation can occur at multiple levels, from the micro-events in a playgroup to interactions among parents and caregivers or teachers, to involvement of ECD stakeholders in local, subnational, or national health and education policies and governance. Notions of replication and scale, which can imply uniformity of intervention, may work at cross purposes with local participation in the content and structure of ECD interventions.

National-level efforts to coordinate multiple sectors of ECD services are thus important to integrate with community-based coordination and participation in future research on best practices and in evaluation. A key link in this regard is mid-level participatory processes and governance. Strategies that aim to increase participation at this level should go beyond representing the interests of government sectors, such social protection, health, education, and child protection, to also include the needs and perspectives of local communities. Mid-level (e.g., provincial-, district-, or state-level) structures, whether private or public, can integrate these perspectives. The challenge of including local voices requires investing sufficient time and resources to create structures that guarantee that mid-level participatory processes promote a genuine dialogue between local actors and national program designers and policymakers. Researchers trained in gathering and systematizing qualitative data have a fundamental role in this respect.

New Models for Developing Research Capacity to Inform the Future of ECD

Current investments in the development of programs and policies for young children call for equal attention to the knowledge production that will guide them. Although training and professional development of teachers, caregivers, and policymakers is crucial to ensure that the needs of children are met, there is also an increasing need to invest in the training and professional development of researchers who should be able to conduct policy-relevant developmental research and both process and impact evaluation studies. As argued by many authors in this volume, strengthening the current research capacity requires broader theoretical and methodological practices, new alliances, and greater inclusion of diverse actors in research ranging from the construction of standards and child assessments to program evaluation and funding of research.

ECD is a sector that, by definition, requires multidisciplinary collaboration. ECD services must, by necessity, address the setting and systems sources of health, cognitive, and socioemotional outcomes during a developmental period of extraordinarily rapid growth and increasing integration. Research on such services and their impact on children's growth and development therefore must transcend divisions in traditional research foci among the health and education professions, among the social sciences, and among perspectives on epistemology, data collection and analysis methods.

As ECD services expand in LAMI countries and as forces of globalization and migration increase population diversity within countries, research training on child development increasingly requires a strong understanding of the role of broader contexts in developmental trajectories. Traditionally, the risk and protective frame has emphasized the individual and parent, rather than broader ecological contexts. Engle et al. (2013, Chapter 3, this volume) usefully pose social exclusion as a broader concept than family income poverty—a construct that shifts our attention to more contextual and societal sources of risk than the family. As proposed by Harkness and colleagues (2013, Chapter 7, this volume), Behrman and Urzúa (2013, Chapter 6, this volume), and Wachs and Rahman (2013, Chapter 5, this volume), theoretical models should take into account the complex interaction of individual child characteristics and larger cultural, political, and economic contexts. This shift benefits from researchers who can closely study issues of culture and meaning-making privileged by qualitative and ethnographic methodologies, as well as assess these larger contexts across populations.

The rich traditions of research in culture and human development in culturally diverse contexts (LeVine et al., 1996; Nsamenang, 1992; Whiting & Whiting, 1975) provide a perspective that can be integrated into practice and policy in ECD. The principle of interrogating culture in daily practice is an example. As forces of globalization and migration render ECD programs increasingly diverse, challenges grow in professional development related to deep engagement with culture. Vandenbroeck (2009) has written about professional development approaches for the ECCE workforce that involve interrogating assumptions about culture in daily practice with diverse children and families.

Developing local capacity to build culturally and contextually specific research literatures in ECD continues to be an urgent need (Marfo, Pence, LeVine, & LeVine, 2011). Approaches to research capacity-building in LAMI nations includes the ECD Virtual University, an initiative that incorporates cross-sectoral teams of practitioners, policymakers, and researchers collaborating in Sub-Saharan African nations to share knowledge and develop more comprehensive and integrated ECD policies and programs (Pence, 2006). This initiative more recently includes senior–junior research partnerships, in order to provide explicit mentorship within research institutions in participating nations. Such a focus on mentorship is critical for the development of scholars who can cross disciplinary and methodological borders to advance ECD research.

Collaboration to improve knowledge production goes beyond alliances between researchers to include a more active role on the part of practitioners, families, and communities. In addition, since features of quality may be locally effective, quality of ECD can be considered as a culturally based construct. Implications for the process of developing culturally valid quality measures include involvement of multiple stakeholder groups; building constructs from localized practice knowledge rather than the international research literature; and testing measures against the diversity of regional, geographic, linguistic, and cultural backgrounds within a nation (Myers, 2006, 2010).

This same principle applies to the development of standards and indicators. In indicator research, advances are being made toward integrating direct child assessments as child indicators, rather than relying solely on parent or teacher report. Regional and national efforts are as important in this realm as global ones, in their ability to build in attention to local and cultural variation (Rao et al., 2011). As Harkness and colleagues argue (2013, Chapter 7, this volume), the construction of assessments should go beyond competencies judged to be important in Western research, to include skills and abilities that are valued and encouraged in local communities. Including the perspectives of caregivers and communities not only increases the validity of instruments but broadens our understanding of the diversity of culturally constructed competencies in children (Harkness et al., 2013, Chapter 7 this volume; Wagner, 2013, Chapter 20, this volume). The same can be said about the overwhelming task facing the ECD field of creating child assessments in literally hundreds of languages (Wagner, 2013, Chapter 20, this volume). The mixed-methods work of Theresa Betancourt in developing measures of mental health with indigenous communities in Sierra Leone and other African nations provides excellent examples of possibilities in this area (Betancourt, Brennan, Rubin-Smith, Fitzmaurice, & Gilman, 2010).

There is an urgent need to pair child and family indicators with contextual indicators of quality, whether in programs for parents/households or those for children. Doing so will allow government, service providers, and communities to determine the effectiveness of such programs. In addition, according to Wagner (2013, Chapter 20, this volume), child outcomes are rapidly becoming public goods—as families and communities increase their understanding of measurement instruments and indicators, transparency increases along with community action and empowerment, especially when such indicators yield widely different results between different populations.

Conclusion

The chapters in this volume signal important shifts in both the content and role of research in informing practice and policy in global ECD. Rapid expansions in some countries in ECD services occasion a shift from addressing questions of "do ECD services work?" to "how can ECD systems be improved?" Increased public and private investments in ECD necessitate new work to examine whether these investments are actually producing the desired results in improving communities, families, and children's development. The challenges of integrating services across multiple sectors are mirrored in the challenges of research that crosses borders of disciplines, methods, and epistemological perspectives. New approaches to examining patterns of equity, inclusion and exclusion, and cultural specificity are required. The promise of expanding both knowledge bases and programs and policies in ECD across the LAMI countries requires new collaborations among researchers, practitioners, caregivers, community members, and policymakers.

References

Aber, L., Biersteker, L., Dawes, A., & Rawlings, L. (2013). Social protection and welfare systems: Implications for early childhood development. In P. R. Britto, P. L. Engle, & C. M. Super (Eds.), *Handbook of early childhood development research and its impact on global policy* (Chapter 13). New York: Oxford University Press.

Baker-Henningham, H., Walker, S., Powell, C., & Gardner, J. M. (2009). A pilot study of the Incredible Years teacher training programme and curriculum unit on socio-emotional skills in community preschools in Jamaica. *Child Care, Health and Development, 35*, 624–631.

Behrman, J. R., & Urzúa, S. S. (2013). Economic perspectives on some important dimensions of early childhood development in developing countries. In P. R. Britto, P. L. Engle, & C. M. Super (Eds.), *Handbook of early childhood development research and its impact on global policy* (Chapter 6). New York: Oxford University Press.

Bernal, R. (2010). *The impact of a technical training program for child care providers on children's well-being* (Working Paper). Bogotá, CO: Universidad de los Andes.

Bernal, R., Fernández, C., Flórez, C. E., Gaviria, A., Ocampo, P., Samper, B., et al. (2009). *Evaluación del impacto del Programa de Madres Comunitarios de Bienestar del ICBF* (Working Paper). Bogota, CO: CEDE.

Betancourt, T. S., Brennan, R. T., Rubin-Smith, J., Fitzmaurice, G. M., & Gilman, S. E. (2010). Sierra Leone's former child soldiers: A longitudinal study of risk, protective factors, and mental health. *Journal of the American Academy of Child and Adolescent Psychiatry, 49*, 606–615.

Biersteker, L. (2010). *Scaling up early child development in South Africa.* Washington, DC: Brookings Institution, Wolfensohn Center.

Bornstein, M. H., & Lansford, J. E. (2013). Assessing early child development. In P. R. Britto, P. L. Engle, & C. M. Super (Eds.), *Handbook of early childhood development research and its impact on global policy* (Chapter 18). New York: Oxford University Press.

Britto, P., Dimaya, R., & Seder, R. C. (2011). *Governance and finance systems in early childhood in the People's Democratice Republic of Lao.* New Haven, CT: Yale University Zigler Center in Child Development and Social Policy.

Engle, P. L., Bentley, M., & Pelto, G. (2000). The role of care in nutrition programmes: Current research and a research agenda. *Proceedings of the Nutrition Society, 59*, 25–35.

Engle, P. L., Black, M. M., Behrman, J. R., DeMello, M. C., Gertler, P. J., Kapiriri, L., et al. (2007). Strategies to avoid the loss of developmental potential in more than 200 million children in the developing world. *The Lancet, 369(9557)*, 229–242.

Engle, P. L., Fernald L. C. H., Alderman, H., Behrman J., O'Gara, C., Yousafzai A., et al. (2011). Strategies for reducing inequalities and improving developmental outcomes for young children in low-income and middle-income countries. *The Lancet, 378(9799)*, 1339–1353.

Engle, P. L., Rao, N., & Petrovic, O. (2013). Situational analysis of young children in a changing world. In P. R. Britto, P. L. Engle, & C. M. Super (Eds.), *Handbook of early childhood development research and its impact on global policy* (Chapter 3). New York: Oxford University Press.

Faruque, A. S. G., Shamsir, A. M., Tahmeed, A., Islam, M. M., Hossain, M. I., Roy, S. K., et al. (2008). Nutrition: Basis for healthy children and mothers in Bangladesh. *Journal of Health Population and Nutrition, 26*, 325–339.

Harkness, S., Super, C. M., Johnston Mavridis, C., Barry, O., & Zeitlin, M. (2013). Culture and early childhood development: Implications for policy and programs. In P. R. Britto, P. L. Engle, & C. M. Super (Eds.), *Handbook of early childhood development research and its impact on global policy* (Chapter 7). New York: Oxford University Press.

Hayden, J., & Wai, S. (2013). Community-based approaches to early childhood development: A matter of degree. In P. R. Britto, P. L. Engle, & C. M. Super (Eds.), *Handbook of early childhood development research and its impact on global policy* (Chapter 14). New York: Oxford University Press.

Hertzman, C., Vaghri, Z., & Arkadas-Thibert, A. (2013). Monitoring progress toward the fulfillment of rights in early childhood under the Convention on the Rights of the Child to improve outcomes for children and families. In P. R. Britto, P. L. Engle, & C. M. Super (Eds.), *Handbook of early childhood development research and its impact on global policy* (Chapter 19). New York: Oxford University Press.

Hommel, S. L. (2013). Capacity building for early childhood development. In P. R. Britto, P. L. Engle, & C. M. Super (Eds.), *Handbook of early childhood development research and its impact on global policy* (Chapter 22). New York: Oxford University Press.

Homsi, M. B., & Hussein, L. A. (2013). National agency systems. In P. R. Britto, P. L. Engle, & C. M. Super (Eds.), *Handbook of early childhood development research and its impact on global policy* (Chapter 21). New York: Oxford University Press.

Jordan, L. (2005). *Mechanisms for NGO accountability* (Research Paper No. 3). Berlin: Global Public Policy Institute.

Kagitcibasi, C., Sunar, D., Bekman, S., Baydar, N., & Cemalcilar, Z. (2009). Continuing effects of early enrichment in adult life: The Turkish Early Enrichment Project 22 years later. *Journal of Applied Developmental Psychology, 30*, 764–779.

Landers, C., Da Silva e Paula, C., & Kilbane, T. (2013). Preventing violence against young children. In P. R. Britto, P. L. Engle, & C. M. Super (Eds.), *Handbook of early childhood development research and its impact on global policy* (Chapter 12). New York: Oxford University Press.

Lemish, D., & Kolucki, B. (2013). Media and early childhood development. In P. R. Britto, P. L. Engle, & C. M. Super (Eds.), *Handbook of early childhood development research and its impact on global policy* (Chapter 17). New York: Oxford University Press.

LeVine, R., Dixon, S., LeVine, S., Richman, A., Leiderman, P. H., Keefer, C. H., et al. (1996). *Child care and culture: Lessons from Africa*. New York: Cambridge University Press.

Marfo, K., Pence, A., LeVine, R., & LeVine, S. (2011). Strengthening Africa's contributions to child development research. *Child Development Perspectives, 5,* 104–111.

Mbonye, A. K., Bygbjerg, I., & Magnussen, P. (2008). Intermittent preventive treatment of malaria in pregnancy: A community-based delivery system and its effect on parasitemia, anemia and low birth weight in Uganda. *International Journal of Infectious Diseases, 12,* 22–29.

Myers, R. G. (2006). Quality in programs of early childhood care and education. *Education for All Global Monitoring Report 2007. Starting strong: Early childhood care and education* (Background Paper).

Myers, R. G. (2010). *In search of educational quality: A Mexican experience.* Paper presented at the Conference on Beyond Child Indicators: A Framework to Assess and Evaluate the Quality of Early Childhood Services and Programs in Global Contexts. NYU Abu Dhabi Institute, Abu Dhabi.

National Forum on Early Childhood Programs and Policies. (2007). *A science-based framework for early childhood policies.* Cambridge, MA: Harvard Center on the Developing Child.

Naudeau, S., Kataoka, N., Valerio, A., Neuman, M., & Elder, L. K. (2011). *Investing in young children: An early childhood development guide for policy.* Washington, DC: World Bank.

Nsamenang, A. B. (1992). *Human development in cultural context.* Paris: Lavoisier.

Pence, A. (2006). Indigenous knowledge and early childhood development in Africa: The Early Childhood Development Virtual University. *Journal for Education in International Development, 2*(3), 1–16.

Pence, A. (2013). Voices less heard: The importance of critical and "indigenous" perspectives. In P. R. Britto, P. L. Engle, & C. M. Super (Eds.), Handbook of early childhood development research and its impact on global policy (Chapter 8). New York: Oxford University Press.

Rao, N. & Sun, J. (2011). Scaling-up early childhood programs: Moving towards evidence-based decision making in Asia. Bulletin of the International Society of Behavioral Development, Special Section on Intersections between Research and Social Policy. 60(2), 23–27.

Rao, N., Sun, J., Pearson, V., Sun, J., Pearson, E., Liu, H., Costas, M.A., & Engle, P. L. (2012). Is something better than nothing? An evaluation of early childhood programs in Cambodia. *Child Development, 83*(3), 864–876.

Rolla San Francisco, A., Arias, M., Villers, R., & Snow, C. E. (2006). Evaluating the impact of different early literacy interventions on low-income Costa Rican kindergarteners. *International Journal of Education Research, 45,* 188–201.

Tinajero, A. R. (2010). *Scaling up early child development in Cuba.* Washington, DC: Brookings Institution, Wolfensohn Center.

UNESCO. (2011). *EFA global monitoring report: 2011.* Paris: Author.

Vandenbroeck, M. (2009). Immigrant mothers crossing borders: Nomadic identities and multiple belongings in early childhood education. *European Early Childhood Education Research Journal, 17,* 203–216.

van Ravens, J., & Aggio, C. (2008). *Expanding early childhood care and education: How much does it cost? A proposal for a methodology to estimate the costs of ECCE at macro-level, applied to the Arab States.* The Hague: Bernard van Leer Foundation.

van Ravens, J., & Ponguta, A. (2011). *Governance and finance systems in early childhood in Kenya.* New Haven, CT: Yale University Zigler Center in Child Development and Social Policy.

Vargas-Barón, E. (2013). Building and strengthening national systems for early childhood development. In P. R. Britto, P. L. Engle, & C. M. Super (Eds.), *Handbook of early childhood development research and its impact on global policy* (Chapter 24). New York: Oxford University Press.

Wachs, T. D., & Rahman, A. (2013). The nature and impact of risk and protective influences on children's development in low-income countries. In P. R. Britto, P. L. Engle, & C. M. Super (Eds.), *Handbook of early childhood development research and its impact on global policy* (Chapter 5). New York: Oxford University Press.

Wagner, D. (2013). Improving policies and programs for educational quality: An example from the use of learning assessments. In P. R. Britto, P. L. Engle, & C. M. Super (Eds.), *Handbook of early childhood development research and its impact on global policy* (Chapter 20). New York: Oxford University Press.

Whiting, B., & Whiting, J. W. (1975). *Children of six cultures: A psycho-cultural analysis.* Cambridge, MA: Harvard University Press.

Woodhead, M., & Streuli, N. (2013). Early education for all: Is there a role for the private sector? In P. R. Britto, P. L. Engle, & C. M. Super (Eds.), *Handbook of early childhood development research and its impact on global policy* (Chapter 16). New York: Oxford University Press.

Yoshikawa, H., Leyva, D., Snow, C. E., Treviño, E., Rolla, A.S.F., Barata, M. C., Weiland, C., & Arbour, M.C. (2011). *Un Buen Comienzo: Interim impacts on classroom quality of an initiative to improve the quality of preschool education in Chile.* Manuscript submitted for publication.

Yoshikawa, H., McCartney, K., Myers, R., Bub, K., Lugo-Gil, J., Knaul, F., et al. (2007). *Preschool education in Mexico: Expansion, quality improvement, and curricular reform* (Working Paper). Florence, IT: UNICEF Innocenti Research Centre. Retrieved from http://www.unicef-irc.org/publications/pdf/iwp_2007_03.pdf

Yoshikawa, H., Oh, S. S., & Seder, R. C. (2011). *Governance and finance systems in early childhood in Cambodia.* New Haven, CT: Yale University Zigler Center in Child Development and Social Policy.

Young, M. E. (1996). *Early child development: Investing in the future.* Washington, DC: World Bank.

Yousafzai, A. K., Yakoob, M. Y., & Bhutta, Z. A. (2013). Nutrition-based approaches to early childhood development. In P. R. Britto, P. L. Engle, & C. M. Super (Eds.), *Handbook of early childhood development research and its impact on global policy* (Chapter 10). New York: Oxford University Press.

27

Closing Commentary

IMPLICATIONS FOR DEVELOPMENT

Deepa Grover

The body of evidence has grown exponentially. It is compelling, and it comes from scientific research and analysis in a variety of fields—economics, health, psychology, neuroscience, and education. Positive environments that support young children's growth, development, and protection buffer them from the risks (Engle et al., 2011) that might ordinarily compromise their capacity "to survive, be physically healthy, mentally alert, emotionally secure, socially competent and able to learn" (UNICEF, 2002). The expert articles in this volume are a testament to this vision. An increasing number of countries have put into place policies and programs to address the rights and needs of young children. At last count, some 49 nations had officially adopted early childhood development (ECD) policies, and more than 40 other nations are currently developing such policies (Vargas-Barón, 2011). The policies are grounded in evidence, informed by human rights treaties, and reflect the aspirations and commitments of nations. But, as the Education for All Global Monitoring Report 2011 (UNESCO, 2011) confirms, progress in early childhood care and education is uneven, planning is fragmented, and resources are scarce. Many countries need the support of the international community to transform words into action and action into results for young children.

A number of international partners have prioritized ECD; these include United Nations (UN) agencies, such as the United Nations Children's Fund (UNICEF); the World Health Organization (WHO); the United Nations Educational, Scientific, and Cultural Organization (UNESCO); and the United Nations Development Programme (UNDP). Development banks, including the World Bank, Inter-American Development Bank, and Asian Development Bank, have, over the last several years, supported countries with funds and technical expertise to advance the early childhood agenda. Bilateral donors, such as the German Agency for International Cooperation (GIZ), the Canadian International Development Agency (CIDA), the U.K. Department for International Development (DfID), the Norwegian Agency for Development Cooperation (NORAD), the Swedish International Development Cooperation Agency (SIDA), the Japan International

Cooperation Agency (JICA), and the Dutch government have also provided backing for national policies and programs (Vargas-Barón, 2013, Chapter 24, this volume). Also engaged in ECD are prominent foundations such as the Bernard van Leer Foundation, the Aga Khan Foundation, and the Open Society Foundations; international nongovernmental organizations (NGOs), such as Save the Children, Plan International, Child Fund International, and World Vision; and networks like the Consultative Group on Early Childhood Care and Development and World Organization for Early Childhood Education, among others. In industrialized nations, the Organization for Economic Cooperation and Development (OECD) and the European Union (EU) have given attention to the importance of promoting good practice and quality services in early childhood education and care (European Commission, 2011; OECD, 2001, 2006, 2012).

In light of its renewed commitment to promoting equity, UNICEF has a particularly important role to play in working with national and international partners to improve the lives and secure the rights of young children, especially the most disadvantaged. In fact, the agency's raison d'être is children. Mandated by the UN General Assembly to advocate for the protection of children's rights, to help meet their basic needs, and to expand their opportunities to reach their full potential, UNICEF is present in 190 countries (UNICEF, 2011), at national and subnational levels, through country programs and national committees; UNICEF is engaged in both social development and humanitarian actions.

In the past, UNICEF, together with its partners, played a signal role in vigorous advocacy for the preparation and the almost universal ratification of the UN Convention on the Rights of the Child (1989). UNICEF, in concert with the Committee on the Rights of the Child and the Bernard van Leer Foundation, helped to articulate General Comment No. 7, Implementing Child Rights in Early Childhood (2005).

The chapters in this volume call upon the international community, both explicitly and implicitly, to accelerate its role in placing young children at the center of public policy. There is resounding agreement among the authors, who come from a diversity of disciplinary backgrounds, that the early years—the period from conception to age 8 or 9 years, when transition to primary school is complete—present the best and most effective window of opportunity for an individual's development. Later remediation is not impossible, but it is expensive in both financial and human terms. There is consensus also that the path from evidence to policy to practice to results can be challenging and that countries, including their governments and civil society, need a variety of supports to design and fund programs and services for young children. Instituting integrated perspectives on child well-being and development within the different sectors, building national capacity (including the skill sets of service providers and the conditions under which they work), strengthening systems (including governance and quality assurance), combining upstream advocacy with downstream activities, and involving a variety of actors (private-sector and faith-based organizations) are key strategies for sustainable programs and effective results.

Happily, the field of ECD is characterized by a willingness to share, coordinate, and collaborate; this augurs well for improving the lives of the world's youngest citizens and their families. International organizations continue to have a critical role to play in advocacy, mobilizing technical expertise, and managing knowledge, both its generation and dissemination. States, and stakeholders within them, need to be kept alert to their performance vis á vis their accountabilities for young children through mechanisms such as regular reporting on the implementation of the CRC. In order to leverage the development of ECD policies, international organizations need to fast track their activities of sharing with influential decision makers (as well as with the public at large) cutting-edge evidence, gleaned from scientific analysis and lessons learned—both successful and unsuccessful—in different country contexts. Messaging must necessarily be simple, clear, and realizable. Relevant national institutions, particularly in low- and middle-income (LAMI) countries, need to be supported and strengthened to collect, analyze, and disseminate data on the situation of young children, particularly those who come from the most disadvantaged, marginalized, and vulnerable backgrounds. There needs to be an enhanced appreciation among those who develop national and sectoral budgets of how fiscal space can be identified or created to mobilize resources for young children and their families. Where resource constraints are intense, the international community has the obligation to use evidence to raise funds and enable countries to invest in social spending for their youngest populations.

At the same time as international organizations support countries and communities to advance ECD, there is a critical need for them to look inward. Reflection is required not only to reassess their internal human and financial resource distribution but to examine also sectoral boundaries that not infrequently inhibit a truly comprehensive vision of ECD from being realized. Greater attention must be given to understanding the various vertical and horizontal continua that have an impact on ECD outcomes. First, ECD is a sequence of several distinguishable stages—the prenatal phase, infancy (birth to 1 year of age), toddlerhood (2–3 years of age), preschool (4–6/7 years of age), and transition to school (age 6/7–8/9 years). Second, convergent and simultaneous action must take place within and between the health, education, child protection, social protection, and communication sectors to address the complete gamut of the early years and development in all domains—physical, cognitive, language, and social-emotional. These domains are highly interdependent, as are the interconnecting circles of influence that ring the young child, from proximal micro-systems to the most distal macro-systems (Britto, Engle, & Super, 2012). The impact of actions that do not address all the age groups, all the domains of development, and all the ecological contexts that affect child development outcomes is likely to be limited.

Although there is a general recognition of ECD in its true and comprehensive sense, there is a tendency to privilege the preschool years and, in so doing, ECD becomes identified with preparation for school and the education sector. The role of the health sector during pregnancy, infancy, and toddlerhood is still generally restricted to ensuring survival and physical health. And yet, even in the poorest of contexts, every contact with a health care provider can potentially be an opportunity for furthering child well-being through the closely intertwined elements of health *and* development (Yousufzai, 2012), be it through addressing maternal depression, encouraging infant–caregiver interaction, or assisting a family to obtain additional necessary services for a disabled child. Similarly, child poverty analyses need to take account of the possible lifelong negative impact of deprivation in the early years; for this reason, social protection specialists need to pay particular attention to engendering support for poor families with young children. Early identification and intervention can ameliorate the developmental trajectory of disabled children and enable them to be included in the mainstream of society. In fact, ECD should be everybody's business, and international agencies need to communicate and model this for others.

The year 2015 is approaching, and the world is preparing for the "post-Millennium Development Goals era." Planning for the next generation of development frameworks is already on the anvil, and international organizations will play an important role in inventing the future. The global community would do well to utilize the abundant available evidence and to call for enhanced and multisectoral investments in ECD in order to promote not only the rights of the most rapidly developing age segment of the world's children, but also to secure the economic and social development of societies and nations. Two hundred million of the world's young children are not achieving their full potential (Engle et al., 2007; Grantham-McGregor et al., 2007). This is a violation of their rights. A few simple, relatively inexpensive, family friendly, and culturally sensitive interventions that minimize risks and maximize protective factors could help children to grow and develop well. Within larger contexts of progressive education, employment, and social protection policies, today's young children could be the engine rather than the cargo of tomorrow's social change and economic growth. For this reason, as the world's aspirations for peace and progress are concretized, the best evidence has to be brought to bear to inform international frameworks and goals. The chapters in this volume are a step in just that direction. International organizations need to continue to work in tandem to redouble their advocacy and communication efforts and to ensure that ECD becomes an inextricable part of global thinking on human progress.

References

Britto, P., Engle, P., & Super, C. (2012) *Introduction to the handbook of early child development research and its impact on global policy.* New York: SRCD.

Engle, P. L., Black, M. M., Behrman, J. R., De Mello, M. C., Gertler, P. J., Kapiriri, L., et al. (2007). Strategies to avoid the loss of developmental potential in more than 200 million children in the developing world. *The Lancet, 369,* 229–242.

Engle, P. L., Fernald, L. C. H., Alderman, H., Behrman, J., O' Gara, C., Yousafzai, A. K., et al. (2011). Strategies for reducing inequalities and improving developmental outcomes for young children in low-income and middle-income countries. *The Lancet.* DOI:10.1016/S0140-6736(11)60889-1

European Commission. (2011). *Early childhood education and care: Providing all our children with the best start for the world of tomorrow.* Brussels, COM(2011) 66 final

Grantham-McGregor, S., Cheung, Y. B., Cueto, S., Glewwe, P., Richter, L., Strupp, B., et al. (2007). Developmental potential in the first 5 years for children in developing countries. *The Lancet, 369,* 60–70.

OECD. (2001). *Starting strong: Early childhood education and care,* Paris: Author.

OECD. (2006). *Starting strong II: early childhood education and care.* Paris: Author.

OECD. (2012). *Starting strong III: A quality toolbox for early childhood education and care.* Paris: Author.

United Nations. (2006). *Convention on the Rights of the Child: Implementing child rights in early childhood* (General Comment No. 7) CRC/C/GC/7/Rev. 1. Geneva: Author.

UNESCO. (2011). *The hidden crisis: Armed conflict and education.* Education for All Global Monitoring Report 2011. Paris: Author.

UNICEF. (2011). *About UNICEF: Who we are.* Retrieved from http://www.unicef.org/about/who/index_introduction.html

UNICEF. (2002). *A world fit for children* (pp. 15–16). New York: Author.

United Nations General Assembly. (1989). *United Nations Convention on the Rights of the Child.* New York: Author.

Vargas-Barón, E. (2011). Parliamentary leadership for improving early childhood development. In *Early Childhood Development: What parliamentarians need to know and do* (pp. 47–77). Geneva: UNICEF.

Vargas-Barón, E. (2013). Building and strengthening national systems for early childhood development. In P. R. Britto, P. L. Engle, & C. M. Super (Eds.), *Handbook of early childhood development research and its impact on global policy* (Chapter 24). New York: Oxford University Press.

Yousufzai, A. K. (2012, February). *Pakistan Early Child Development Scale Up (PEDS) trial.* Power point presentation at the 2nd Global Consultation on the Early Childhood Development Research Agenda, organized by UNICEF, Florence.

28

Closing Commentary

IMPLICATIONS FOR CAPACITY

Aster Haregot

It is very clear that great strides have been made to advance the child's welfare across the world, with much impetus being provided by international agencies and nongovernmental organizations (NGOs). In many countries, it is this support that has made all the difference as governments struggle with a growing realization of the importance of the early years on one hand and limited resources and the need to address competing interests on the other. As development partners continue working with governments to support the scale-up of early childhood development (ECD) services, a number of factors need to be considered, chief among them being the need to strengthen national capacity for ECD programming.

Institutions of higher education or tertiary education institutions play a critical role in strengthening national capacity, including by:

- Providing relevant and critical education to existing and future ECD program planners
- Generating research to provide relevant solutions to current problems
- Providing an empirical base and demonstrating the viability of models and approaches that are useful to guide national programming

Although the role played by these institutions is clear, there is need to strengthen their capacity to play this role more effectively and to ensure a strengthened link between research policy and practice. The current weak linkage, which often is due to a limited capacity for conducting rigorous studies, limited capacity for scholarly writing, and a mismatch between the research and training priorities of universities and national ECD policies, provides development partners a great opportunity to strengthen partnerships and enhance effective, efficient, and relevant national ECD programming. The need for governments, NGOs, and international organizations to support both the capacity of tertiary institutions to play key supportive roles in the evolution of integrated and evidence-based ECD in the respective countries and contributions to the international ECD and child development literature cannot be overemphasized.

The implication of a research agenda to help advance a science of child development that opens up to other populations and to other ways of thinking about childhood and child development is great. Current realities in our field make it difficult for those perspectives and agendas contemplated outside the Western world or high-income countries to receive serious consideration. Often, marginalized, contextually significant issues and perspectives in low- and middle-income (LAMI) countries rarely find their way into leading dissemination outlets in our field. Given that a majority of the world's young disadvantaged children live in Africa, I use that as an example to illustrate my point. Because African and other LAMI countries' voices and the contributions driven by unique African conceptions and realities are woefully underrepresented in a global knowledge base dominated by Western conceptions of child development and developmental inquiry, LAMI countries are disadvantaged in knowledge production and dissemination. With limited, often delayed, access to current literature from other parts of the world, many scholars are rendered noncompetitive in publishing their work in major journals outside the continent. However, this is not simply an African problem; left unaddressed, the underrepresentation of perspectives from other cultures places profound limitations on claims about the existence of a global developmental science knowledge base.

The following recommendations for a research agenda will hopefully lead to:

1. Examination of indigenous approaches to child development, and the exploration of ways to promote them in an effort to develop an African child development field that is (a) appropriate to the needs/challenges of the continent and (b) contributes unique insights and perspectives on developmental inquiry/practice globally

2. Presentation of insights from major research initiatives, with particular attention paid to the ways in which they help to advance African contributions to a global child development field

3. Identification of concrete strategies for using our collective assessments and insights to make a practical difference—for example, by supporting networking/capacity building activities in collaboration with African institutions of higher education and other organizations addressing children's development and capacity building on the continent.

{ 29 }

Closing Commentary

THE FUTURE OF EARLY CHILDHOOD DEVELOPMENT
IN THE GLOBAL DEVELOPMENT AGENDA

Charles M. Super, Pia Rebello Britto, and Patrice L. Engle

A distinctive feature of the human species is our long period of utter dependence in infancy and early childhood, a characteristic that, among other things, is a platform for our remarkable adaptability. Humans have always tended to the development of their young—well enough in aggregate at least to reach a current global population of 7 billion and to devise sufficient technologies to ease our existence and save lives, as well as kill each other and the entire biosphere we inhabit. So what does early childhood development (ECD) have to do with it?

Simply put, it may prove to be a key formulation that, if appropriately advanced and incorporated into the global developmental agenda, will provide a major advance in human welfare—including a reduction in disparities—and will thereby improve our chances for managing the predicted doubling of our number in the next century (United Nations, 2004). This hopeful statement is based on two observations, regarding science and globalization.

Developmental Science

First, the scientific understanding of human development in the opening years of life has reached a kind of tipping point. Branches of inquiry that were long grown apart—psychology, child development, anthropology, biology, medicine—have come together in the last few decades, and have matured sufficiently in their understanding and evidence to construct a convincing picture of the lifelong importance of early experience. It is more than "As the twig is bent, the branch shall grow." It is about protein and micronutrients, family life, education, sanitation, physical experience, responsive interactions, brain growth, and love. How those work in the first years will set a path and impose lifelong limits on physical and mental health, on economic productivity, and on making the next generation. Although there is no detailed formula for what an ECD program should be in every circumstance, it can safely be said that science and field experience have provided us with considerable evidence for where and how to focus our investments, what approaches are likely to be effective, and what their benefits will be for children. That is one essential message of this volume.

Globalization

The accelerating pace of travel, communication, and interfacing of national interests is a second factor behind the current interest and investment in ECD. Consider, for example, the global knowledge base represented in this volume—data, ideas, and examples from scores of countries, from every continent and culture area. Globalization is a trend affecting virtually everything—commerce, art, law, entertainment, manufacturing, media, economics, politics, finance, fashion. Shifts to urban living are part of that process, along with the engagement of ideas and technologies from both near and far. As more countries strive to join the "knowledge economy," expectations rise for every cohort of children. As O'Gara (2013, Chapter 11, this volume) correctly notes, "A child born today must master skills and knowledge that were needed only by elites a century ago." A century before that, those skills and knowledge may not have existed at all, and aspects of family life and child rearing that have been familiar for generations may no longer suffice. Furthermore, the institutions that contribute to globalization, including governments and international agencies, are themselves subject to it, and so policy is no exception to the trend. The nearly routine exposure of policymakers to events and outcomes in places far away necessarily broadens their vision.

An Early Childhood Development Global Knowledge Society

These two trends—the growth of developmental science and of shrinking of the world—overlap in the nascent international community of scholars, planners, and practitioners devoted to ECD. As Fedoroff (2012) points out, science has long been used for military advantage, but its collaborative use for peaceful initiatives is relatively new. An important component of that new role, both contributor and product, is the emergence of a global knowledge society. Shared science and technology are needed, Fedoroff concludes, to address the array of interlocking problems regarding energy, water, biodiversity, ecosystems, and economic development, all growing challenges for the expanding global population. The authors contributing to the present volume represent the emerging "global knowledge society" concerned with the early development of each member of that global population.

A distinct feature of this ECD global knowledge society is that it includes both scientists and field-based practitioners. The academy, mostly in high-income countries, has generated the key evidence regarding early child development.

Correspondingly, it is nongovernmental organizations (NGOs), along with governmental agencies in a number of countries, that have generated the bulk of knowledge about implementation. Just as the scientists are now engaged with the challenge of adapting theories and principles to the different contexts of low- and middle-income (LAMI) countries, so, in turn, are the NGOs and government implementers beginning to take on their new role of documenting and sharing their practical knowledge of requirements for success in implementation, scaling up, financing, and building capacity for ECD. The complementarity of these two bodies of evidence, as presented in this volume, is essential to moving forward globally with effective, sustainable, evidence-based policy and practice.

The importance of applying the expanding scientific knowledge and policy experience to create particular ECD programs adapted to specific places is a second essential message of this volume. Even though the present work is only a marker on a long journey—more than a beginning, less than a destination—several implications for the role of ECD in the global agenda are evident.

New Paradigms in Global Development Policy

THE EVIDENCE BASE AND ITS ROLE IN POLICY

Applied social research has a long but somewhat thin history. It flourished in progressive arenas as the social sciences matured during first third of the 20th century, and it became more forceful and formalized in mid-century as new institutions, many of them (such as the World Bank and the United Nations Children's Fund [UNICEF]) specifically international in concept, increasingly focused on the systematic, empirical analysis of policy options. ECD in the holistic sense used here, was not a significant focus of this work. Relevant strands are evident by the 1970s—witness the salience of infant mortality in the Health for All declaration in 1978—but not until the last decade of the 20th century did a broad concept of early childhood enter into policy considerations.

Since then, the evidence base has grown dramatically. We have a much improved picture of the situation faced by the world's children (Engle, Rao, & Petrovic, 2013, Chapter 3, this volume; Wachs & Rahman, 2013, Chapter 5, this volume). Regarding health specifically, a large knowledge base on child mortality was established during the decades when "child survival" was leading in the agenda; links to the modern ECD agenda are now more evident (see contributions by Engle, Young, & Tamburlini, 2013, Chapter 9, this volume; Shonkoff & Richter, 2013, Chapter 2, this volume). Our understanding of developmental risk and protection factors during early childhood has matured greatly (Wachs & Rahman, 2013, Chapter 5, this volume). There is an emerging framework for what kinds of programs make a difference in child nutrition (Yousafzai, Yakoob, & Bhutta, 2013, Chapter 10, this volume), education (Wagner, 2013, Chapter 20, this volume), and health (Engle et al., 2013, Chapter 9, this volume); how various sectors and agencies can contribute (Aber, Biersteker, Dawes, & Rawlings, 2013, Chapter 13, this volume; Bartlett, Landers, & Stephenson, 2013, Chapter 15, this volume; Behrman & Urzúa, 2013, Chapter 6, this volume; Hayden & Wai, 2013, Chapter 14, this volume; Lemish & Kolucki, 2013, Chapter 17, this volume; Homsi & Hussein, 2013, Chapter 21, this volume; O'Gara, 2013, Chapter 11, this volume; Woodhead & Streuli, 2013, Chapter 16, this volume); how to monitor and evaluate new initiatives (Bornstein & Lansford, 2013, Chapter 18, this volume; Wagner, 2013, Chapter 20, this volume); and how to scale up successes to reach a greater variety of young children, including those most in need (Hommel, 2013, Chapter 22, this volume; Valerio & Garcia, 2013, Chapter 25, this volume; Vargas-Barón, 2013, Chapter 24, this volume; Young, 2013, Chapter 23, this volume).

Although this evidence base, drawn from academic science and field applications in LAMI countries, is by no means complete or fully adequate, it is sufficient at present to move policy in certain directions and to provide a useful list of questions to ask as policies are formed. The nature and utility of today's evidence is changing the standard for sound policy development.

RIGHTS AND RATIONALITY

The rationality of investing in children is not new, but two aspects are changing. First, the level of training and education required to participate fully in modern societies is unprecedented, making the foundation of the early years more critical. As the standard for joining the global society is raised higher, it becomes more and more difficult for those left behind at the beginning to catch up. Second, we have grown in our understanding of why an investment in the early years is so critical (see commentary by Shonkoff & Richter, 2013, Chapter 2, this volume).

Rights, however, are a relatively recent entry in the conversation about ECD, and it remains an evolving domain (Hertzman, Vaghri, & Arkadas-Thibert, 2013, Chapter 19, this volume). This is not to say that many in the past have not considered young children to have rights, but only in recent decades has there been such broad consideration of what, specifically, those rights might be (Britto, Ulkuer, Hodges, & McCarthy, 2013, Chapter 4, this volume). Furthermore, with the increasingly rapid pace of global change, the issue of disparities in health and education becomes as salient within many countries as it is between countries. The discussion of equity therefore becomes more complex at the same time it is becoming more focused.

Both ways of thinking about the value of early childhood have an important role to play in the formation of policies. In addition, as both rationales undergo continued elaboration, their interaction becomes more evident. Many in the field, for example, take the rights that have been enumerated to be aspirational; that is, they are a statement of an ideal or an end condition toward which we should be working; and the "instrumental" argument, in turn, is seen as a vehicle to attain those goals (Landers, Da Silva e Paula, & Kilbane, 2013, Chapter 12, this volume).

Policies and programs, in this regard, are blueprints for providing young children with the structures needed to attain their full potential, economic, personal, social, and spiritual. As governments and NGOs increasingly use global declarations and conventions to orient their policies and activities, and as consideration of post-2015 declarations gets under way (e.g., follow-up on the Millennium Development Goals [MDG] and Education for All [EFA]), we can look forward to seeing declarations aimed more explicitly toward an integration of rights and rational investment considerations.

INTEGRATION OF PLANNING, SERVICES, AND FAMILIES

As the knowledge community for ECD takes shape, it is increasingly obvious that as a child is the integrated recipient of all ECD services, an integrated planning process is essential for both effectiveness and efficiency. Access to that child, of course, is virtually always through the family; how this interface operates, between program and family, is critical to success. When parents' aspirations and resources are consonant with a program's goals and daily elements, their role in that success may seem natural and nearly invisible, but when they undermine or fail to connect with an otherwise laudable initiative, the price of a misfit is obvious in failure (see Weisner, 2011, for a detailed example). If program staff flout local custom, if program content seems irrelevant, or if the cost or logistics of accessing the services are awkward, families will not participate. Families are the ultimate but often unspoken decision makers in the success of program (Engle et al., 2013, Chapter 3 and 9, this volume; Yousafzai et al., 2013, Chapter 10, this volume). It follows that families and communities need to have a voice, or at least have their viewpoint represented, in the design and delivery of ECD programs (Woodhead et al., 2013, Chapter 16, this volume; Bartlett et al., 2013, Chapter 15, this volume). Given the variety of family structures, cultural backgrounds, and economic and educational circumstances and needs, this means that there should be many variations of successful ECD programs (Pence, 2013, Chapter 8, this volume; Harkness, Super, Mavridis, Barry, & Zeitlin, 2013, Chapter 7, this volume).

There are, in fact, many ways of reaching parents to improve children's development. Examples in this volume illustrate the variety of avenues and platforms that may be relevant, including those organized by the traditional government agencies (health, nutrition, education, and social welfare) and newer ones (such as child protection, social protection, and human rights), as well as by services organized by faith-based, media-based, and private agencies, and by NGOs. The growing number of actors in ECD is positive in that it increases the availability and range of choices for families and opens opportunities for intersectoral planning and collaboration. Conversely, it can also lead to a chaotic jumble of overlapping and competing services. Because families with more resources are more likely to have access to some kinds of services (e.g., from the private sector), there is also an increased risk of creating greater inequity with these programs. Further, increasing families' understanding of the benefits of various programs, thereby increasing and broadening the level of demand, is often not part of traditional efforts.

All these considerations highlight the importance of an integrated approach—a point emphasized in almost every chapter in this volume. In the end, all the programs and services are inputs to an array of individual children and families, and no single sector or agency is likely to deliver them all in a single package. Although a variety of program examples are presented here, there are still shortcomings in our knowledge of how to craft policies and programs that retain a focus on the child, rather than fracturing into agency-oriented slivers.

Challenges and the Future

At the beginning of this chapter, we predicated our optimism for ECD on its appropriate advance and incorporation into the global development agenda. At this conclusion, we can better indicate what that might look like and the challenges along the way.

With regard to advancement, it must first be noted that the evidence base for ECD has become stronger over time. We know that the early years are crucial, we have some understanding of why, we have many examples of how to promote sound child development through policies and programs, and we know some principles of implementing such policies and programs. All this is outlined in the chapters of this volume. On the other hand, this knowledge is still limited and incomplete. Like the shoreline of an expanding island of knowledge in a sea of ignorance, the more we know, the more we see how much ignorance remains. Beyond the "basic science," which is only a small part of ECD as we are discussing it, there is much more to be learned. Consider the four primary threats to ECD today: disease, poverty, violence, and ignorance due to the absence of appropriate early educational experience. Although we do know some ways to reduce the impact of these threats, we do not know nearly enough about how to eliminate them, or how to implement, fund, and sustain the solutions if we had them. Advancing the evidence of ECD, then, must continue as a collaborative project of applied science and knowledge-building from practice. As is obvious from the chapters of this volume, fields with a longer engagement with aspects of ECD, such as health, draw on a far greater body of evidence. In part, this advantage can be traced to the global survival agenda of past decades. If we are to advance our ability to address the other risk factors—poverty, violence, and ignorance—then we must develop an equally robust and more complete ECD agenda for generating useful evidence.

It is only in recent decades that ECD has been identified and incorporated into the highest level of the global development agenda. As we approach the next round of goal setting, with regard to both rights and instrumental outcomes, the global ECD knowledge community needs to speak clearly about the fundamental role of

ECD in reaching humanity's best definition of who we can be. More—and less—than lofty aspirations, what will be needed is consideration of goals and measurable outcomes that have direct connection to the processes and policies discussed in the chapters of this volume.

A critical challenge for programming lies at the point where "universal" principles of development and institutionalization, working "downward," meet, coming "upward," the efforts of programs in the field to meet the needs and values of local families. ECD programs of the future bear this complex task of matching aspirational policies with workable and acceptable services that can themselves grow over time in quality and reach. Understanding community belief systems and families' hopes for their children will be a central challenge for successful ECD programs in the next iteration.

Of particular importance to the future of all these considerations, regarding knowledge, policies, and programs, is the nagging question of who will actually be able to accomplish this translation from evidence to practical policy. Neither developmental scientists nor field practitioners alone have the full array of knowledge and skills to move effectively from established principles to specific plans for a specific context. An additional challenge, therefore, is to continue the development of institutions and the education of individuals in the global south who can advance this translational science into the field and into the developmental agenda. Realization of the goals we have laid out—the advance and incorporation of ECD into the global developmental agenda—may depend on creative progress in this arena. It is the hope of the editors and authors of this volume that our efforts will contribute to proving our optimism correct.

References

Aber, L., Biersteker, L., Dawes, A., & Rawlings, L. (2013). Social protection and welfare systems: Implications for early childhood development. In P. R. Britto, P. L. Engle, & C. M. Super (Eds.), Handbook of early childhood development research and its impact on global policy (Chapter 13). New York: Oxford University Press.

Bartlett, K., Stephenson, P., & Cadaing, L. (2013). Parents and communities: The key to understanding "faith-based" early childhood services and programs. In P. R. Britto, P. L. Engle, & C. M. Super (Eds.), Handbook of early childhood development research and its impact on global policy (Chapter 15). New York: Oxford University Press.

Behrman, J. R., & Urzúa, S. S. (2013). Economic perspectives on some important dimensions of early childhood development in developing countries. In P. R. Britto, P. L. Engle, & C. M. Super (Eds.), Handbook of early childhood development research and its impact on global policy (Chapter 6). New York: Oxford University Press.

Bornstein, M. H., & Lansford, J. E. (2013). Assessing early child development. In P. R. Britto, P. L. Engle, & C. M. Super (Eds.), Handbook of early childhood development research and its impact on global policy (Chapter 18). New York: Oxford University Press.

Britto, P. R., Ulkuer, N., Hodges, W., & McCarthy, M. F. (2013). Global policy landscape and early child development. In P. R. Britto, P. L. Engle, & C. M. Super (Eds.), *Handbook of early childhood development research and its impact on global policy* (Chapter 4). New York: Oxford University Press.

Engle, P. L., Rao, N., & Petrovic, O. (2013). Situational analysis of young children in a changing world. In P. R. Britto, P. L. Engle, & C. M. Super (Eds.), *Handbook of early childhood development research and its impact on global policy* (Chapter 3). New York: Oxford University Press.

Engle, P. L., Young, M. E., & Tamburlini, G. (2013). The role of the health sector in early childhood development. In P. R. Britto, P. L. Engle, & C. M. Super (Eds.), *Handbook of early childhood development research and its impact on global policy* (Chapter 9). New York: Oxford University Press.

Fedoroff, N. V. (2012). The global knowledge society. *Science, 335,* 503.

Harkness, S., Super, C. M., Johnston Mavridis, C., Barry, O., & Zeitlin, M. (2013). Culture and early childhood development: Implications for policy and programs. In P. R. Britto, P. L. Engle, & C. M. Super (Eds.), *Handbook of early childhood development research and its impact on global policy* (Chapter 7). New York: Oxford University Press.

Hayden, J., & Wai, S. (2013). Community-based approaches to early childhood development: A matter of degree. In P. R. Britto, P. L. Engle, & C. M. Super (Eds.), *Handbook of early childhood development research and its impact on global policy* (Chapter 14). New York: Oxford University Press.

Hertzman, C., Vaghri, Z., & Arkadas-Thibert, A. (2013). Monitoring progress toward the fulfillment of rights in early childhood under the Convention on the Rights of the Child to improve outcomes for children and families. In P. R. Britto, P. L. Engle, & C. M. Super (Eds.), *Handbook of early childhood development research and its impact on global policy* (Chapter 19). New York: Oxford University Press.

Hommel, S. L. (2013). Capacity building for early childhood development. In P. R. Britto, P. L. Engle, & C. M. Super (Eds.), *Handbook of early childhood development research and its impact on global policy* (Chapter 22). New York: Oxford University Press.

Homsi, M. B., & Hussein, L. A. (2013). National agency systems. In P. R. Britto, P. L. Engle, & C. M. Super (Eds.), *Handbook of early childhood development research and its impact on global policy* (Chapter 21). New York: Oxford University Press.

Landers, C., Da Silva e Paula, C., & Kilbane, T. (2013). Preventing violence against young children. In P. R. Britto, P. L. Engle, & C. M. Super (Eds.), *Handbook of early childhood development research and its impact on global policy* (Chapter 12). New York: Oxford University Press.

Lemish, D., & Kolucki, B. (2013). Media and early childhood development. In P. R. Britto, P. L. Engle, & C. M. Super (Eds.), *Handbook of early childhood development research and its impact on global policy* (Chapter 17). New York: Oxford University Press.

O'Gara, C. (2013). Education-based approaches to early childhood development. In P. R. Britto, P. L. Engle, & C. M. Super (Eds.), *Handbook of early childhood development research and its impact on global policy* (Chapter 11). New York: Oxford University Press.

Pence, A. (2013). Voices less heard: The importance of critical and "indigenous" perspectives. In P. R. Britto, P. L. Engle, & C. M. Super (Eds.), *Handbook of early childhood development research and its impact on global policy* (Chapter 8). New York: Oxford University Press.

Shonkoff, J. P., & Richter, L. (2013). Commentary—The powerful reach of early childhood development: A science-based foundation for sound investment. In P. R. Britto, P. L. Engle, & C. M. Super (Eds.), *Handbook of early childhood development research and its impact on global policy* (Chapter 2). New York: Oxford University Press.

United Nations. (2004). World population to 2300. New York: United Nations.

Valerio, A., & Garcia, M. H. (2013). Effective financing. In P. R. Britto, P. L. Engle, & C. M. Super (Eds.), *Handbook of early childhood development research and its impact on global policy* (Chapter 25). New York: Oxford University Press.

Vargas-Barón, E. (2013). Building and strengthening national systems for early childhood development. In P. R. Britto, P. L. Engle, & C. M. Super (Eds.), *Handbook of early childhood development research and its impact on global policy* (Chapter 24). New York: Oxford University Press.

Wachs, T. D., & Rahman, A. (2013). The nature and impact of risk and protective influences on children's development in low-income countries. In P. R. Britto, P. L. Engle, & C. M. Super (Eds.), *Handbook of early childhood development research and its impact on global policy* (Chapter 5). New York: Oxford University Press.

Wagner, D. (2013). Improving policies and programs for educational quality: An example from the use of learning assessments. In P. R. Britto, P. L. Engle, & C. M. Super (Eds.), *Handbook of early childhood development research and its impact on global policy* (Chapter 20). New York: Oxford University Press.

Weisner, T. S. (2011). If you work in this country you should not be poor, and your kids should be doing better: Bringing mixed methods and theory in psychological anthropology to improve research in policy and practice. *Ethos, 39*(4), 455–476.

Woodhead, M., & Streuli, N. (2013). Early education for all: Is there a role for the private sector? In P. R. Britto, P. L. Engle, & C. M. Super (Eds.), *Handbook of early childhood development research and its impact on global policy* (Chapter 16). New York: Oxford University Press.

Young, M. E. (2013). Barriers to service provision: Lessons learned from donor-supported early childhood development projects. In P. R. Britto, P. L. Engle, & C. M. Super (Eds.), *Handbook of early childhood development research and its impact on global policy* (Chapter 23). New York: Oxford University Press.

Yousafzai, A. K., Yakoob, M. Y., & Bhutta, Z. A. (2013). Nutrition-based approaches to early childhood development. In P. R. Britto, P. L. Engle, & C. M. Super (Eds.), *Handbook of early childhood development research and its impact on global policy* (Chapter 10). New York: Oxford University Press.

{ INDEX }